Restless Souls
Pilgrim Roots

The Turbulent History of Christianity in Nottinghamshire and Lincolnshire

Adrian Gray MA

Bookworm of Retford

First published 2020
Bookworm of Retford, Retford, Nottinghamshire.
email: sales@bookwormretford.co.uk, www.bookwormretford.co.uk

ISBN 9781916041530 *Restless Souls, Pilgrim Roots* – Adrian Gray

Cover design and typesetting by Burgess Design & Print, Retford

A catalogue record of this book is available from the British Library.

Contents

'There will be large numbers of fish, because this water flows there and makes the salt-water fresh; so where the river flows, everything will live. Fishermen will stand along the shore...'
Ezekiel, 47: 9-10.

In honour of the fishers, who gave their all for the fish.

Introduction

This book is the first part of an attempt to show how Christianity has developed and changed in one small region of England, the two adjoining counties of Nottinghamshire and Lincolnshire. From this small area, roughly ninety miles from north to south or east to west, have emerged numerous great Christian leaders and thinkers most especially in the period from 1500 until the English Civil War but also later with the Wesleys, William Booth and numerous missionaries. The *Book of Common Prayer*, which became so influential and yet so contentious, was largely written by a man who learned to speak English in the Nottinghamshire-Lincolnshire borderlands. That period began the pattern of exporting radical thinking from this homeland across the World, which continued and accelerated in the later 1700s.

The story here includes significant Fenland figures such as Guthlac of Crowland, great medieval bishops of Lincoln including Hugh and Robert Grosseteste, great reformers in Cranmer and Latimer, then the emergence of radical puritanism in firstly Nottinghamshire and later Lincolnshire; this was a movement that produced not only the 'Mayflower' congregation, John Cotton and the 'Great Migration' but also the first English Baptists and perhaps the region's greatest contribution to global developments – the working out of religious freedom by separating government and the law from any issues of faith and worship practice. This, perhaps the greatest single story in more than a thousand years of history, is the locally uncelebrated 'Big Idea' that was developed by men with local connections such as John Smyth, Thomas Helwys, John Murton, Roger Williams and Sir Henry Vane. Slowly, their ideas have been heard across the world though seemingly as pressing now as ever.

Bringing two counties together in this way, across a diocesan boundary, reflects the logic of the story. At the story's beginning, when the Lindisii tribe was baptised in the River Trent, the river itself was not a boundary and county names were unknown. Though the counties were placed in different dioceses and provinces of the Church, people and themes interacted: for example, Lincolnshire's rebellion against Henry VIII was critical in strengthening reforming interests in the Nottinghamshire gentry. Thomas Cranmer had interests in both counties. Pivotal towns like Gainsborough brought together people from both counties. The story ebbs and flows across this line due to the patterns of population and economy with Nottinghamshire a sparsely populated county until the 1600s, then accelerating its place in our story very rapidly.

The biggest challenge for a book of this scope is when to stop. It can never be 'finished' and not everything can be included. Your favourite village or minister may not have made it to my printed page whilst I have also included some details because they add a specific human dimension to the story. The focus is on the bigger picture of how the faith developed, so it has been impossible to conduct endless research into every small detail but perhaps having this overview will inspire others to dig further into those.

All this has come from a local project to promote interest in our wonderful and often neglected Christian heritage. This has been energetically tackled as the celebration of *Mayflower 400* has provided an impetus, whilst the issue of religious liberty has also been promoted through annual events. To help encourage awareness, a team of us organise events, speakers, trips and tours for local people and those from across the Globe. You can find out more using the following links:

https://pilgrimsandprophets.co.uk/
https://bassetlawchristianheritage.com/
https://www.facebook.com/PilgrimsAndProphets/
Contact: mail@pilgrimsandprophets.co.uk

Please note, the original spelling is often used in quotations. Also, there are many supportive footnotes, but if anyone has a need for further bibliographical details it may be possible to provide this through an enquiry by email.

CHAPTER ONE

The Age of Saints and Miracles
up to 1066

There were undoubtedly Christians in Roman Britain, but in the area that became Lincolnshire and Nottinghamshire the continuous survival of the faith through to the arrival of missionaries in 627 can only be conjectured. Over the next four hundred years, the faith struggled to survive through a turbulent period of local rivalries, pagan invasion and the destruction of its monasteries. But by the year 1000, it appeared more settled though churches remained few and far between.

Chronology:
616: Battle of River Idle brings Northumbrian control
c627-8: Paulinus baptises the people of Lindsey
633: Edwin killed in battle
647: Oswald killed in battle, buried at Bardney
656: Diocese of Mercia and Lindsey formed
669: Chad becomes Bishop of Mercia and Lindsey
677: First bishop of the separate diocese of Lindsey
715: Death of Guthlac
867: Danes capture York
870: Danes destroy Bardney Abbey
956: Southwell Minster endowed
1014: Danish king Sweyn Forkbeard dies at Gainsborough

First Light

Christianity had probably reached our region within two hundred years or so of Christ's ascension, but little is known about what the early Christian life was like.[1] Three bishops from Britain attended the Council of Arles in 314AD – from London, York and either Lincoln or Colchester.[2] Others have argued that Adelphius went as bishop of Lincoln and that the other bishops were perhaps from Lichfield and Gloucester.[3] A wooden church was

---

1   There is a popular story that St Simon was crucified at Caistor in Lincolnshire in 61AD,
       but many other versions have him being executed in Persia or elsewhere.
2   W Friend, *Roman Britain – A Failed Promise*, in Carver (ed), *The Cross Goes North*, p.80
3   T Green, *Britons and Anglo-Saxons: Lincolnshire 400-650*, Lincoln, 2012, p.62

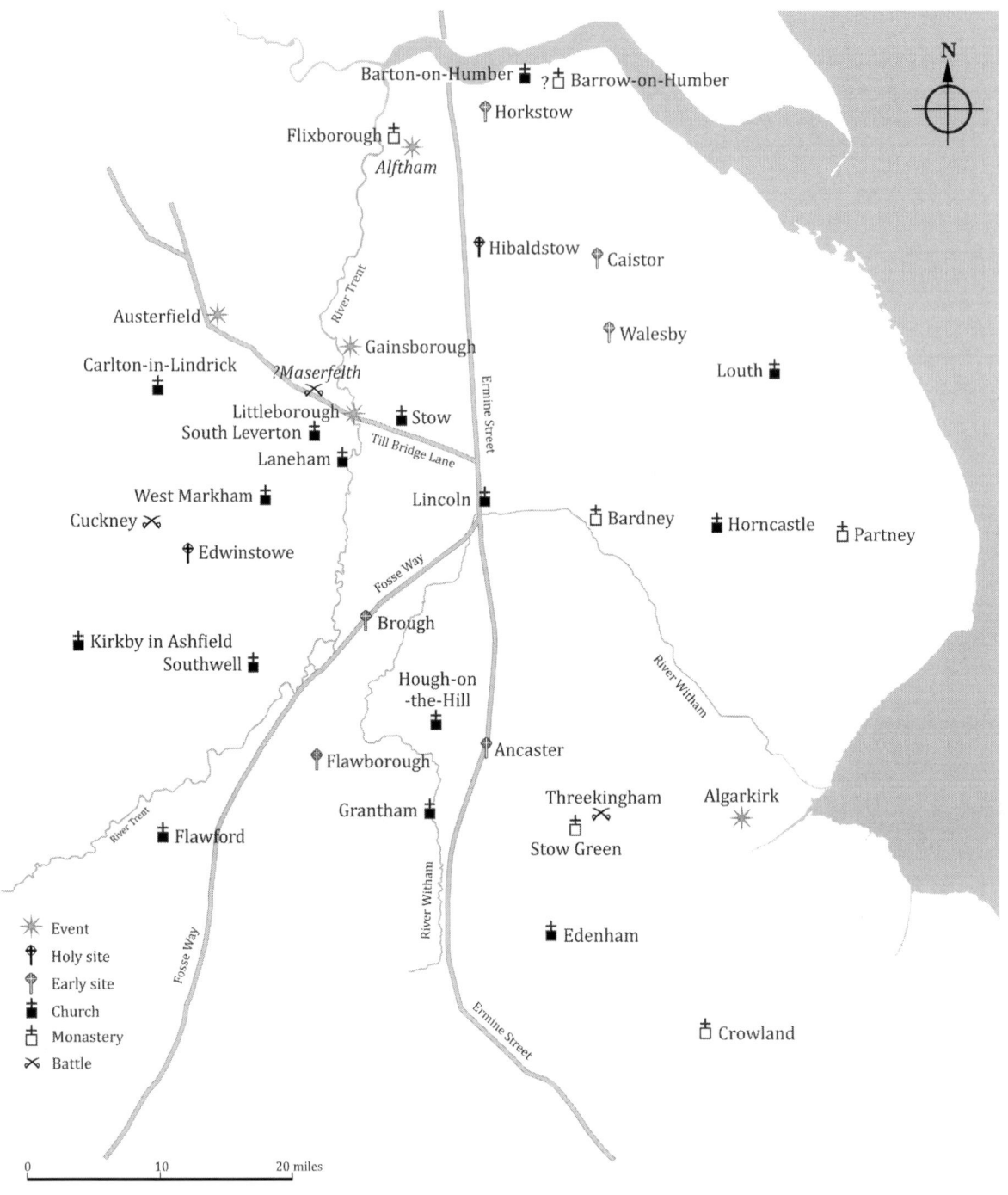

N

Barton-on-Humber ? Barrow-on-Humber
Horkstow
Flixborough
Alftham
Hibaldstow   Caistor
Austerfield
Walesby
Carlton-in-Lindrick   Louth
?*Maserfelth*
Gainsborough
Littleborough Stow
South Leverton
Laneham
Lincoln   Bardney   Horncastle   Partney
West Markham
Cuckney
Edwinstowe
Fosse Way
Kirkby in Ashfield
Southwell
Brough
Hough-on
-the-Hill
Flawborough   Ancaster
Grantham   Threekingham   Algarkirk
Flawford   Stow Green
Edenham

River Trent
Ermine Street
Till Bridge Lane
River Witham
Fosse Way
River Witham
Ermine Street

Event
Holy site
Early site
Church
Monastery
Battle

0   10   20 miles

Crowland

first built near St Paul's in Bailgate, Lincoln, in about 390AD,[4] and may have been the seat of a bishop. It continued in use, after being rebuilt on the same site,[5] into at least the 6th century with evidence of a cemetery from the 5th century underlining the continuity of this site[6] and therefore its significance in this story. There was possibly another church in the lower city at Flaxengate.

A 4th century Roman mosaic, which has arguably Christian elements to its design, was found at Horkstow in 1796. The mosaic was from a Roman villa and it has been suggested that this belonged to a former Roman soldier[7] – the church at Horkstow is dedicated to St Martin, a Roman soldier martyred for refusing to kill German Christians in 297AD. This village was also an early Anglo-Saxon site and its name indicates some holy status.

Christian symbols from the Roman era have also been found at Walesby, Bishop Norton and Caistor in Lincs and East Stoke,[8] Brough and Thorpe in Notts. The discovery of a lead baptistery tank at Walesby is one of the most important finds, though damaged by ploughing, and interesting not only for the fact that the figures decorating it appear to include a naked baptismal candidate.[9] A piece discovered by metal detector at Brough was first thought to be a coffin but later part of a tank with clearly Christian symbols. Another lead tank was found at Flawborough, Nottinghamshire, in 1998, partially decorated with the Chi-Rho symbol, whilst another fragment was found at Thorpe nearby.[10] Such artefacts suggest a well-established Christian culture. The Roman cemetery at Ancaster has attracted debate as to whether its burials are Christian[11] whilst there are also possible Christian cemeteries from this era at Brough, Margidunum and Lincoln.[12]

The discovery of a silver chalice at Water Newton, just north of Peterborough, confirms established Christian activity in the 4th century. After this came, perhaps, darkness. By the late 4th century this part of Britain was suffering attacks by the Saxons from the sea and raids from the Picts in the North. Christianity may have survived in Lincoln into the 5th century. The Church was still active in some form in 429AD but by 446AD Roman Britain was in its death throes and unable to resist invasion. Another reason why Christianity did not achieve binding roots appears to have been language.[13] Arguments have been put forward for the continuance of some form of Christianity based mainly on the Bailgate evidence which at least deserves serious consideration as an early Christian site.[14]

The St Paul in the Bail site is one of the most historic and debated Christian sites in the region. How long it has been a Christian site has been much debated. Recently it has been argued that a sequence of churches and graveyards has occupied the site from the

4   P Ottaway, *Archaeology in British Towns*, p.101; Alan Vince (ed), *Pre-Viking Lindsey*, Lincoln, 1993, p.25

5   Caitlin Green, *The British Kingdom of Lindsey*, Academia, 2012, pps17-19

6   D M Hadley, *Northern Danelaw*, London, 2000, p.250

7   www.churchtrails.com/barton-area/horkstow/; accessed 2 April 2014; Cookson, Neil. "The Christian Church in Roman Britain: A Synthesis of Archaeology." *World Archaeology* 18, no. 3 (1987): 426-33. http://www.jstor.org/stable/124595.

8   Known as Ad Pontem. C Thomas, *Christianity in Roman Britain*, Berkeley, 1981, p.

9   Thomas, p.221-4

10   J Fox, *People of Vision,* Nottingham, 2002, p.9

11   Thomas, p.236

12   Mark Patterson, *Roman Nottinghamshire*, p.340

13   Friend, p.89

14   Alan Vince, *Pre-Viking Lindsey*, Lincoln, 1993, p.25

late 4[15] century onwards and indeed the precise site shows continuity with the Roman era; aligned east-west, the church was sited within the old forum and appears to have been designed so that it was entered through the columns of the old building.[15] This first church was replaced by another probably in the late 5th or early 6th centuries, capable of holding 100 people, which was largely demolished by 600AD. The precise site matters greatly – this was a prominent building in the centre of the city. However, the second church was then demolished and largely replaced by a graveyard, perhaps reflecting the decline of Lincoln as much as that of Christianity. Whether it is the same site as St Paulinus's church, discussed later, is open to debate, and the continuity of Christianity from Roman times seems rather undermined by Bede's account of its revival.

From the 4th-century Saxon settlement developed in Lincolnshire with more than forty known pagan cemeteries in Lindsey and spreading into Nottinghamshire.[16]

By the time Augustine came to Kent in 597AD, there appeared to be no Christian communities with which he could connect although the *Anglo-Saxon Chronicle* commenting on 552AD reported that 'In this year Ethelbert, the son of Ermenric, was born, who on the two and thirtieth year of his reign received the rite of baptism, the first of all the kings in Britain'.

In the 5th and 6th centuries what is now Nottinghamshire was largely Anglo-Saxon, unpopulated and pagan in religion. Lincolnshire, and especially Lindsey, was more populated although the kingdom of Lindsey probably included parts of modern Nottinghamshire. Lindsey was a kingdom in its own right, while the region was very much 'border' territory between the powerful kingdoms of Mercia and Northumbria. There was a battle on the east bank of the River Idle[17] (some have suggested near Misson) in 616AD between the East Anglians and the Northumbrians following which Edwin became king of Northumbria and an influential figure in our region. We do not know where this occurred, but it is likely to have been on or near the course of the Roman road west of the Trent.

The first great influence on sustained Christian life in the region was Paulinus, an Italian sent as a missionary to England by Pope Gregory in 601AD, who first established himself in Kent where Augustine had had some success. He was described as 'tall of stature, stooping somewhat, his hair black, his visage thin, his nose slender and aquiline, his aspect both venerable and awe-inspiring'.[18] Paulinus agreed to accompany Æthelburh, the sister of King Eadbald of Kent and daughter of King Ethelberht, following her betrothal to the Northumbrian king Edwin. Before he moved north, probably in 625AD, Paulinus was made a bishop and probably already planned to set up a new see in York for which he was consecrated in 625 or 626AD.[19] Edwin remained a pagan after the marriage but he started

---

15 T Green, *Britons and Anglo-Saxons: Lincolnshire 400-650*, Lincoln, 2012, p.65-7. Green says that it is 'more than credible that we have a late 4th century or 5th century Romano-British church site up in a significant area of the city....'

16 Vince (1993), p.33

17 Several commentators have suggested a location where the Roman road met the river was most likely, hence around Bawtry and Clayworth. For example, David Rollason, *Northumbria, 500-1100: Creation and Destruction of a Kingdom*, Cambridge, 2003, p.35

18 Bede, chapter XVI

19 D P Kirby, *The Earliest English Kings*, p.65

to receive letters from Rome in 624AD, indicating the significance of the situation. In one story, Edwin had been in exile in East Anglia having been driven out by the Mercians when he saw a vision of a 'man of fair countenance, crowned with the cross of Christ' who promised him a happy life and to rule over his own people if he would but obey.[20]

Family links are one of the most recognised routes for Christianity to be established, but Paulinus was also aware of the risks to Æthelburh in marrying a pagan king. To marry her, Edwin had to promise to allow her and her retinue freedom of worship, but converting Edwin proved a complex task. This was finally accomplished through a series of visions and challenges to the king when Paulinus spoke to the Northumbria nobles and their own high priest condemned his pagan faith as worthless.

In 627AD (or possibly 628) King Edwin, his nobles, and large numbers of people were baptised at York by Paulinus. This conversion was hugely significant because there was, at the time, no Christian king in England outside of the Kent enclave.[21] In time Edwin persuaded Eorpwald, the king of the East Angles, to become a Christian too. According to a legend, in the same year Paulinus founded the church that was to become Southwell Minster but this has been much debated.[22]

After extensive missionary activity in the North, Paulinus came south as Edwin also held title to the kingdom of Lindsey. Lindsey, or the kingdom of the Lindissi, probably also included Axholme and the modern Nottinghamshire district of Bassetlaw which was a 'regio' of this little kingdom to be known as 'Hatfield' – a clearing in the forest.[23] The event that therefore marks the true start to Christianity in this region occurred near 'Tiovulfingacester'[24] which has been variously claimed to be Littleborough or, less probably, Torksey, close to the Roman ford across the Trent that was still then in use. If Bassetlaw was indeed in the same kingdom as Lindsey, then this was a convenient point – and we know the road was still an attraction since King Harold came this way in 1066. That day, in the presence of Edwin and the deacon James, thousands were said to have been baptised in the River Trent at noon – 'a great multitude', according to Bede's account.

Paulinus's first convert was the praefectus or reeve of Lincoln, a certain Blæcca, and in true New Testament tradition 'his whole house' was also converted according to Bede; Paulinus also led the building of the first stone church in the area 'of remarkable workmanship' – which has often been assumed (since the 20th century) to be at St Paul in the Bail.[25] This therefore, succeeded the probable earlier churches though it is impossible to know whether any believers had survived in the interim. Even though the roof of this church had collapsed by the time of Bede, he wrote that 'every year miraculous cures are

20   From the early biography of Pope Gregory, recounted in Matthew M Bodkin, *Celt and Saxon*, p.141
21   Kirby, p.65
22   This belief was recorded by William Camden, the antiquarian who also passed on local beliefs that the great baptisms took place near Southwell which seems unlikely given other topographical factors.
23   T Green (2002), p137. In 1992 it was suggested Hatfield covered parts of South Yorkshire and Notts down to Leverton. An ancient text known as the Tribal Hidage refers to the 'land of Lindesfarona with Hæpfeldlande', taken to mean Hatfield Chase. See also Vince (1993), p.129
24   Various spellings have been used, including Tiouulfingacaestir.
25   The chronology is unclear – Bede mentions the conversion of Blaecca and Paulinus preaching in Lin coln before the baptism on the Trent, but does not clearly indicate the sequence of events. See also *Medieval Archaeology*, vol.23, 1979, pps. 214-8.

wrought in that place, for the benefit of those who have faith to seek them'. A body in its dedication grave was removed in the 10th century, possibly to be reburied in a church then being constructed within what is now the castle area.[26] In 2013 a stone sarcophagus was discovered, built into a wall, causing speculation that the late Saxon cathedral was not built on the site of the present cathedral, which is Norman in origin. Bede reports on Paulinus preaching in Lincoln and that Honorius, another one of the missioners, was consecrated archbishop of Canterbury by him in Lincoln in 627. Some have suggested Paulinus also preached at Margidunum (East Bridgford).

The discovery of Anglo-Saxon stonework in the fabric of South Leverton church led to suggestions in 2007 that this might be recovered fragments of an earlier memorial associated with the baptisms in the River Trent.[27] This would be remarkable indeed and support the theory that Lindsey extended both sides of the Trent before the Norman Conquest.

The faith established some footholds across the area, such as the abbey at Partney, whose abbot later provided Bede with a description of Paulinus and the Trent baptisms. However, we know little about Partney other than the names of two abbots from the 7th century – Deda and Aldwine – who Bede mentioned.

The position of King Edwin was threatened by a new alliance of pagan Mercians and Welsh. On 12 October 633AD Edwin was defeated and killed in the Battle at 'Hæthfelth', normally referred to as Hatfield Chase. For long this was assumed to have been at Hatfield near Doncaster, but more recently there have been claims that this event was at a clearing in the forest – 'Hatfield' – near Cuckney in Nottinghamshire. The contention that the whole district was called Hatfield adds more substance to this view. This claim tends to be supported by the discovery in 1951 of three or four communal graves containing 200 bodies, laid with their feet to the east,[28] and the naming of 'Edwinstowe', meaning the sanctuary or burial place of Edwin, but a few miles from Cuckney and rather further from the other site. Legends relate that Edwin's body was brought to Edwinstowe after the battle[29] and some historians take the view that Edwin's body was buried at Edwinstowe whilst his head was taken to York; later the body was moved to Streanaeshalch (Whitby).[30]

The site of a chantry and hermitage dedicated to St Edwin was identified in 1911 by the Vicar of Edwinstowe and W. Stevenson. A cairn of some of the original building blocks was made in 1912 on the instructions of the Duke of Portland and surmounted by a metal cross. The earliest record of this is from 1201 when King John paid the hermit of Clipstone a stipend of 40 shillings for his services, and payments by succeeding kings are recorded to 1548. The chapel is shown on maps of 1610 and 1630 but little is known about

---

26 http://www.pasthorizonspr.com/index.php/archives/05/2013/early-church-and-burials-found-at-lincoln-castle. Accessed 1 January 2014.

27 *Transactions of the Thoroton Society*, 2007, p.41-3

28 This evidence is the source of much debate. The Heritage Gateway suggests that bodies are from the time of the Maudian revolt in the 12th century.

29 H Mutschmann, *The Place Names of Nottinghamshire, Their Origin and Development*, Cambridge, 1913, p.46

30 Martin Carver (ed), *The Cross Goes North: Processes of Conversion in Northern Europe*, 2006, p.322

its origins or whether, as has been conjectured, it marked the site of Edwin's resting place. How did the body get found and moved? According to one tradition from Lindsey recorded by a Whitby monk in *The Life of St Gregory*, the monk Trimma (possibly from Bardney[31]) had a dream in which a man appeared to him and told him to go to 'that district which is called Hatfield' and take the remains of Edwin to Whitby. He was directed to go to a settlement in Lindsey (of which he had forgotten the name) and to contact Teoful, who would tell him where to look. We can recognise this pattern as one based on Biblical principles. Trimma had this vision twice, and neither time took any action, but the third time the man appeared with a whip.[32] Trimma was able to achieve his mission, and the body was taken to Whitby and buried in the church.[33] As Thomas Green has argued, the search makes no sense if the district west of the Trent was not in Lindsey as no Lindsey villager would have been able to point out the site; 'the site was almost certainly Edwinstowe,' he concludes.[34] Trimma lived on at the burial site and often saw the spirits of four of the slain, it was said, who were 'certainly baptised persons who came in splendour to visit their bodies'.[35]

After Edwin's death, Paulinus and Æthelburh fled from Northumbria, and he became Bishop of Rochester in safely Christian Kent. In the North, and in the Nottinghamshire-Lincolnshire lands, Christianity struggled to survive although the deacon James clung on at York. James was 'a man of zeal and great fame in Christ and in the church'.[36]

In the end, Paulinus' work proved something of a false start. One biographer of Edwin has concluded that 'Paulinus's missionary journeys were made as part of the royal progress through the kingdoms, and there was insufficient manpower to follow up his preaching and mass baptisms by establishing permanent mission stations, as was done by monks from Iona in the next generation'.[37] With the regions of Lindsey and 'Hatfield' bordering onto pagan kingdoms, the Christian faith was not yet securely established.

The Affair of Oswald's Bones

The next significant King of Northumbria was Oswald, who reigned from 634 to 642AD. He had spent some formative years in the monastery at Iona, and stories of his faith were still fresh when Bede wrote of his 'constant habit of praying or giving thanks to the Lord' demonstrated as 'wherever he sat to hold his hands upturned on his knees'. Oswald reigned for nine years, during which time he re-established Christianity until he was killed in battle with the Mercians at 'Maserfelth', once believed to be Oswestry although some claims have now been made for Lindsey or 'Hatfield' (mainly north Nottinghamshire),

---

31 Although the 'Monk of Whitby' refers to an 'Anglian' monastery, rather than a Lindsey one specifically, although Teoful was in a Lindsey *vicus*.
32 M Bodkin, *Celt and Saxon*, p.125
33 This story appears in the *Life of St Gregory*, compiled by an anonymous Whitby monk.
34 Thomas Green, p.135
35 P Sawyer, *Anglo-Saxon Lincolnshire*, Lincoln, 1998, p.72
36 Bede, chapter XVI
37 Dictionary of National Biography: Edwin

in 642AD.[38] Oswaldbeck in 'Hatfield' at least has some claim on place-name evidence! Penda of the Mercians ordered that Oswald's head and arms should be cut off from his body and displayed on stakes, which is where they stayed for a year or so until Oswy (Oswiu) captured them and took them to Northumbria, burying the head at Lindisfarne and the arms at Bamburgh, according to Bede.

The trunk of the body was buried at the scene of the battle – at first. Bede reported that in this place healings of men and cattle continued until his own time. People began to take away the soil on which he died and mix it with water to be a drink and a medicine, so that a trench developed. One man collected up the dust in a cloth and hung it up in a house where he was staying; when the house caught fire, all but the dust and the post on which it was hanging burnt up.

Penda of Mercia went on to conquer much of Lindsey and the surrounding area, although he was himself killed by Oswy, Oswald's brother, in 655AD.

Osthryth,[39] queen of the Mercians, was Oswald's niece. She and her husband, Aethelred (Aedilred), had a great affection for the monastery at Bardney, in Lincolnshire, which they had probably founded and in about 679AD desired to lay Oswald's bones to rest there. The bones travelled down by water and were, according to legend, unloaded at Dunham-on-Trent presumably as the Fosse Dyke, a canal of the Roman era connecting Trent and Witham, was impassable.[40] They continued to Bardney by wagon where, as Bede explains, things did not go according to plan because, perhaps, Oswald was remembered as a hated Northumbrian who had conquered Lindsey – or the Lindsey monks disliked his Mercian relatives:

When the wagon in which those bones were carried arrived towards evening at the aforesaid monastery, they that were in it were unwilling to admit them, because, though they knew him to be a holy man, yet, as he was a native of another province, and had obtained the sovereignty over them, they retained their ancient aversion to him even after his death. Thus, it came to pass that the relics were left in the open air all that night, with only a large tent spread over the wagon which contained them. But it was revealed by a sign from Heaven with how much reverence they ought to be received by all the faithful; for all that night, a pillar of light, reaching from the wagon up to heaven, was visible in almost every part of the province of Lindsey. Hereupon, in the morning, the brethren of that monastery who had refused it the day before, began themselves earnestly to pray that those holy relics, beloved of God, might be laid among them. Accordingly, the bones, being washed, were put into a shrine which they had made for that purpose, and placed in the church, with due honour; and that there might be a perpetual memorial of the royal character of this holy man, they hung up over the monument his banner of gold and

---

38 See for example, https://www.heroicage.org/issues/9/clarkson.html. Tim Clarkson's argument here suggests a possible location in 'Hatfield Chase' but does not consider the place-name evidence of Oswald Beck. This is interesting, because Clarkson's criteria include being near the Trent and a Roman road – Oswald Beck at Sturton meets both criteria and is a name of medieval origin. South Wheatley church, only two miles away, is dedicated to St Oswald. Oswaldbeck became the name of the wapentake. Burnham on Axholme has also been suggested.

39 Also spelt as Osthyrda

40 The location of churches dedicated to St Oswald along or near the route is interesting. Examples include: Luddington, Crowle, Althorpe and Dunham. To this we can add the Oswald Beck between South Wheatley and Sturton-le-Steeple; this name was given to the Danish wapentake of Oswaldbeck covering the area.

purple. Then they poured out the water in which they had washed the bones, in a corner of the cemetery. From that time, the very earth which received that holy water had the power of saving grace in casting out devils from the bodies of persons possessed.

But this was not the end of the stories of miracles recounted by Bede, which included Partney: Lastly, when the aforesaid queen afterwards abode some time in that monastery, there came to visit her a certain venerable abbess, who is still living, called Æthelhild, the sister of the holy men, Æthelwin and Aldwin, the first of whom was bishop in the province of Lindsey,[41] the other abbot of the monastery of Peartaneu [Partney], not far from which was the monastery of Ethelhild.

When this lady was come, in a conversation between her and the queen, the discourse, among other things, turning upon Oswald, she said, that she also had that night seen the light over his relics reaching up to heaven. The queen thereupon added that the very dust of the pavement on which the water that washed the bones had been poured out, had already healed many sick persons. The abbess thereupon desired that some of that health-bringing dust might be given her, and, receiving it, she tied it up in a cloth, and, putting it into a casket, returned home. Sometime after, when she was in her monastery, there came to it a guest, who was wont often in the night to be on a sudden grievously tormented with an unclean spirit; he being hospitably entertained, when he had gone to bed after supper, was suddenly seized by the Devil, and began to cry out, to gnash his teeth, to foam at the mouth, and to writhe and distort his limbs. None being able to hold or bind him, the servant ran, and knocking at the door, told the abbess. She, opening the monastery door, went out herself with one of the nuns to the men's apartment, and calling a priest, desired that he would go with her to the sufferer.

Being come thither, and seeing many present, who had not been able, by their efforts, to hold the tormented person and restrain his convulsive movements, the priest used exorcisms, and did all that he could to assuage the madness of the unfortunate man, but, though he took much pains, he could not prevail. When no hope appeared of easing him in his ravings, the abbess bethought herself of the dust, and immediately bade her handmaiden go and fetch her the casket in which it was. As soon as she came with it, as she had been bidden, and was entering the hall of the house, in the inner part whereof the possessed person was writhing in torment, he suddenly became silent, and laid down his head, as if he had been falling asleep, stretching out all his limbs to rest. Silence fell upon all and intent they gazed, anxiously waiting to see the end of the matter. And after about the space of an hour the man that had been tormented sat up, and fetching a deep sigh, said, 'Now I am whole, for I am restored to my senses'. They earnestly inquired how that came to pass, and he answered, 'As soon as that maiden drew near the hall of this house, with the casket she brought, all the evil spirits that vexed me departed and left me, and were no more to be seen'. Then the abbess gave him a little of that dust, and the priest having prayed, he passed that night in great peace; nor was he, from that time forward, alarmed by night, or in any way troubled by his old enemy.

Bede also recounted a miracle when a little boy, badly affected by feverish fits, was advised to sit down by Oswald's tomb. Bede recounted the story as if the disease

---

41   Bishop from 680 to about 692AD.

were a demon: 'the disease durst not assail him as he sat by the saint's tomb, but fled in such fear that it did not dare to touch him, either the second or third day, or ever after'.[42] However, Oswald's remains were violated by his enemies, who had his corpse dismembered, which is how his head came first to be buried at Lindisfarne and then in the coffin of St Cuthbert.

Establishing Christianity

This was a time when there was much fighting between the Mercians and Northumbrians. King Oswy (Oswiu) of Northumbria – the brother of Oswald and his successor from 642AD – was instrumental in the conversion of the Mercians after the defeat of Penda in 655, and in 656AD Diuma became the first bishop of the Mercians and Lindsey. After him came Ceollach, who was Irish, whilst the third – Trumhere – was trained in Ireland but an Angle.

Northumbrian control south of the Humber was brief. The Mercians rebelled against Oswy in 658AD and set up Wulfhere, a son of Penda, as their own king including over Lindsey. Despite being Penda's son, Wulfhere was a Christian and praised God for his victory against Oswy, accepting Trumhere as the bishop of the whole of Mercia. King Wulfhere was known for his campaigns against idolatry and from this stage the future of Christianity in midlands England became more settled.

Wufhere approached Archbishop Theodore for a new bishop of the Mercians after Trumhere had retired and his successor, Jaruman, had died. Theodore decided in 669AD to select Ceadda (or Chad), who had been leading a monastic life at Lastingham in the lands of King Oswy, Wulfhere's Northumbrian rival until briefly elevated to the diocese of York in Wilfrid's lengthy absence. Ceadda was a humble man and was reluctant to ride around his diocese on a horse 'to accomplish the work of the Gospel'; Theodore told him to go by horse and, in Bede's version, lifted him bodily onto the beast. Ceadda's diocese included Mercians and the Lindsey people, a task he approached with 'great holiness'. Wulfhere gave him land at 'Ad Baruae' (assumed to be Barrow upon Humber, but now disputed) for a monastery[43] but he set up his cathedral at Lichfield rather than Repton which was the traditional site.

Ceadda/Chad was known as a great traveller and, as a bishop, would have been one of the prime baptisers of the people. By tradition, Ceadda was very active in Lindsey and the blow wells at Barton were reputed to have been used by him for baptisms – also the 'Shadwells' although the link of this name to that of Ceadda has been disputed. There appears to be no historical evidence for this, but they would have been an obvious venue for anyone intent on performing some baptisms.

Bede tells the story that a monk named Owini was with him, outside the oratory in which Ceadda was praying. The monk heard the sound of 'sweet and joyful singing' coming

---

42 Bede, chapter XII
43 Interpreted as Barrow on Humber in the past but more recently suggested to have been Barton. However, the ODNB notes that Barrow would have been 'a useful base'.

down from heaven. The sound came gradually closer, seemed to hover over the oratory and then came from within it where it stayed for half an hour. Then Ceadda threw open the window and commanded Owini to get seven brother monks, who he told he was shortly to die.[44] Only Owini had heard the heavenly singing and asked Ceadda about it. Ceadda smiled and told him that it was 'angelic spirits' who came to summon him to his reward in heaven. Then Ceadda was struck down by disease and died in a week. One witness later claimed to have seen angels and Ceadda's brother Cedd descend to earth to take his soul to heaven.

When Caedda died in 672AD, his successor was the abbot of Barrow, Wynfrith[45] who was bishop over both Mercia and Lindsey. Within a few years, Wynfrith fell out with archbishop Theodore and was deposed. He returned to his monastery at Barrow. The diocese of Mercia was now divided into five, with 'Sidnacester' covering Lindsey – though its actual location has not been proved Lindsey became a separate diocese from Lichfield in 677AD,[46] in which most of the future Nottinghamshire must have remained; Lindsey survived as a diocese until about 869 when it was joined with Dorchester.[47]

Æthelthryth (also 'Etheldreda' or 'Audrey') was an East Anglian princess who first married in 652AD despite having taken a vow of perpetual virginity. Her husband agreed to respect this vow but resolved the challenges by dying in 655AD. She retired to live as a nun on the Isle of Ely but in 660, for political reasons, was married off to Ecgfrith, King of Northumbria. At first, Ecgfrith also respected her vow and she was encouraged by Wilfrid, but in 672AD he changed his mind and attempted to take her from her nunnery by force. She escaped and made the long journey from Northumbria to Ely, crossing the Humber to Winteringham with her maids Sewenna and Sewara. She then stayed for several days at a village called 'Alftham',[48] surrounded by marshes, and constructed a church there.[49]

Wearing humble clothing, she avoided the Roman roads that would have taken her straight to Lincoln and south from there. Hot and weary, Æthelthryth (Etheldreda) prayed for a resting place and soon came across a pleasant flat meadow strewn with flowers where she and her companions fell asleep:

When, after a little while, she woke up from her sleep and rose to her feet, she found that her travelling staff, the end of which she had driven into the ground, dry and long-seasoned, was now clothed with green bark, and had sprouted and put forth leaves. Seeing this, she was stupefied with amazement and, along with her companions, she praised God and blessed him for this most extraordinary happening from her innermost heart.[50]

This place became known as 'Aedeldrethestowe' or 'Stow'; it was for long assumed to be Stow in Lindsey but is now thought to be Stow Green near Threekingham further south in Kesteven. Wherever the miraculous growth was perhaps symbolic of the planting of the Church. She then continued her journey, escaping capture due to the onrushing tides in the

---

44   This story comes from Bede, who spends longer on Chad's death than his life.
45   D P Kirby, *The Earliest English Kings*, p.95
46   Francis Hill, *Medieval Lincoln*, Cambridge, 1948, p21
47   Dorchester in the current Oxfordshire.
48   Assumed to be West Halton which has a church dedicated to the saint. Also suggested to be at or near Flixborough, see: http://www.roffe.co.uk/alftham.htm
49   J Fairweather (ed), *Liber Eliensis*, p.38
50   *Liber Eliensis*, p.39

fenland marshes. This gave rise to a popular image of Etheldreda, with representations to be found at Ely and on the west front at Lincoln.

Æthelthryth founded a nunnery at Stow Green, which became a holy site in the area and later attracted a medieval fair.[51] She also founded a double monastery at Ely and was buried there in 679AD. When her body was moved years later, it was found to be miraculously preserved. She became a popular saint from an early date in Lindsey, with two churches dedicated to her. Her three sisters also became saints. The Stow nunnery was also where Werburgh, another saint, died in about 700-707AD, as detailed below. Stow Fair, held annually on Æthelthryth's feast day from the 1200s, became an important Lincolnshire event and continued in one form or another until 1954.

The Mystery of Hygbald

Another saint from this era of whom we know little was Hygbald (or Hibald), a Northumbrian missionary, presumed to have given his name to the village of Hibaldstow and to have possibly been abbot of Bardney. He is also known for the survival of a penitential prayer in which he starts by describing himself as 'a miserable and unworthy homunculus' and then calls for forgiveness addressing the Father, the Son and the Spirit. It has been noted that 'he addresses the Son and the Spirit in the same way'.[52] His way of commenting on sins of thought, word and deed reflects Irish influence – Bede tells us that he went to Ireland to visit Ecgbehrt and had a prophetic vision of the death of Ceadda/Chad.

Hygbald was buried at 'Cecesey' or Hibaldstow in about 690AD and a shrine erected which became a place of pilgrimage. This survived until the Reformation when it was destroyed, and the saint's remains presumed lost. In the mid-1860s work began on rebuilding the church and a Saxon stone coffin containing the remains of a man and a crozier was discovered beneath the altar. He survived in church dedications at nearby Manton, Ashby de la Launde and Scawby as well as Hibaldstow itself. Possibly a monastery associated with him was close to the Ancholme and could even have been the later Gilbertine house.[53]

Despite having a notoriously pagan father, Wulfhere played a constructive role in spreading Christianity as he conquered lands to the south. One of his daughters, Werburgh[54] 'of Chester', became a saint, and her brothers Wulfade and Rufin died as martyrs.[55] After her father became committed to Christianity, she entered the abbey of Ely but left it when her father asked her to help supervise the religious houses of his kingdom. She is known for miracles that occurred while she was living at Weedon (Northamptonshire) and then

---

51 For a long period, the site at Stow Green was a mystery, with little to see and less known about its origins. Now something is understood about its archaeology, and its links to two saints of the period. Not to be confused with Stowe, a little further south.

52 P Sims-Williams, *Religion and Literature in Western England 600-800*, Cambridge, 1990, p.322-3. Hygbald's prayer, *Oratio sancti Hygbaldi abbatis*, survived in a royal prayer book.

53 Vince (1993), p.113

54 There are many alternative spellings, and two saints of this name or similar.

55 Butler, *Lives of the Saints*, vol 1, p.175

moved to a monastery at 'Triccengeham' – identified as Threekingham in Kesteven.[56] This is now known to be the Stow Green nunnery, founded by Ætheldreda, which was probably destroyed by the Danes in 870AD. She died in about 700AD and was buried at Hanbury, to which her body was moved despite some possible protests from Threekingham; indeed they tried to barricade it inside their church, but the people of Hanbury stole it away in the night after its guard fell asleep and the doors were opened by 'divine' means – a type of inverse of the story of Oswald and Bardney.[57] Nine years later her remains were found to have been miraculously preserved. Other miracles attributed to Werburgh include the rescue of Chester, where her remains had been moved, from fire in 1180.

By 677AD Eadhaed had been installed as the first bishop in Lindsey, as opposed to Mercia and Lindsey, after King Wulfhere had been driven out by Egfrid. Hill has suggested that the name of 'Biscop' Beding, king of Lindsey born in about 660, reflects a Christian background linked to bishops but others have disagreed.[58] Sexwulf had lost the Lindsey part of his diocese but continued as bishop of Mercia and the Middle Angles which we assume included much of the later Nottinghamshire. The site of Eadhaed's see was at 'Sidnacester'.[59] He was driven out in 678AD when Ethelred gained control of Lindsey. Thus we can see the Church was still entangled in the politics of kingdoms but in 679 Archbishop Theodore created a new system of five bishoprics across Mercia, sending Eadhaed to be bishop in Ripon. Next in Lindsey came Æthelwine,[60] until about 692, then Edgar and Cyneberht.

Æthelwine was 'a man…beloved by God' who studied in Ireland and returned to become bishop of Lindsey, where he 'long and nobly governed the Church'. He is regarded as a saint, though little is known of him. His brother was abbot of Partney and sister Æthelhild the abbess of a nearby nunnery. For the most part, though, we know frustratingly little of the lives of these early English Christians.

Cyneberht (d.732AD) probably abandoned the Lincoln church that had survived since the time of Paulinus and established a cathedral in lower Lincoln, perhaps St Peter at Pleas.[61] Another bishop of Lindsey we are aware of was Beorhtraed in 836-839AD who in his profession at the consecration referred to 'bishop of the people of Lindsey, together with *both* the congregations of the churches of those under vows…' This has been taken to assume some organisation made by his predecessor Eadwulf.

The Mercians regained control of the region from the Northumbrians when Wulfhere's brother, Æthelred – the husband of Osthryth, defeated Ecgfrith at the Battle of the Trent in 679AD. Queen Osthryth, who had moved Oswald's remains to Bardney, was murdered by her own Mercian nobles in 697AD. She was buried at Bardney, to which Æthelred retired to be abbot having given up his throne in 704AD. His visitors included Wilfrid, another

---

56 A Thacker, *Werburh*, in ODNB, accessed 2 January 2014. There appears to be some dispute about the location of her death, with Threekingham gaining preference over Trentham (Staffs).

57 This story is told in Bradshaw's *Life of St Werburgh*, written in the early 16th century.

58 Hill (1948), p.19; Vince (1993), p.133

59 D M Hadley, *Northern Danelaw*, London, 2000, p.249. The historian Camden thought it was near Gainsborough. In 803 Bishop Eadhulf signed himself as from 'Syddensis' but this location is also uncertain. Others have suggested it was Lincoln.

60 Aedelwin in Bede.

61 Sawyer (1998), p.79 and p. 229. The same author suggests that 'Syddensis' and 'Sidnacestensis' were both Lincoln. There is 'some evidence of a pre-Viking Christian site'.

leading figure in the church of the time also to become a saint, who had just returned from Rome. Soon he and his wife were both held to be saints[62] and this gave rise to the extraordinary situation in which Bardney hosted the venerated remains of *three* saints – including, of course, parts of Oswald.

Wulfhere's son Coenred succeeded Æthelread as king of Mercia but gave up this to go on pilgrimage to Rome. His cousin, Coelred, proved to be less spiritual – the chronicler Boniface records a monk's vision of Coelred being tormented by demons having raped and pillaged his way through various nunneries and monasteries; he died in 716, blaspheming to the last, but his wife Werburga 'of Mercia' became a nun and stayed 'in the temple of the Lord' for 65 years. She died at Bardney, probably in 783AD, from where her remains were later removed.[63]

Another saint of the period who had legendary if not actual links with the region was Botwulf, better known as Botolph. He lived, worked and died in East Anglia by about 670AD but later became associated with Thorney after some of his remains were moved there. However, the best-known link is with Boston, whose name is often taken as an abbreviation of 'Botolph's Town'. There are legends that Botolph founded the church there and battled nightly with Satan, who was keen to destroy it with the fenland winds, but there may have been two different people. The first known reference to St Botolph's is from 1091, with probable earlier settlement at Skirbeck.

Relatively little is known of Erkenwald or Earconwald/Eorconwald, who was possibly born in Lindsey[64] of royal stock and the brother of Æthelburg or Ethelburga. He had money to found religious houses at Chertsey and Barking in about 661, with his sister becoming abbess of the latter. In 675AD he was chosen to be Bishop of London and two years later is reputed to have converted King Sebba of the East Saxons to Christianity. He died in 693AD and was buried in St Paul's but is interesting to us as an early example of Christianity from Lindsey being taken to other regions. Æthelburg died at Barking, where a 9th-century source describes the vision of a nun who saw her abbess being taken up to heaven by golden chains.

A great event that occurred on the border of the region was the Synod of Austerfield ('Eostrefeld') held in 702 or 703AD. At this time there was an ongoing dispute between the northern, Celtic Church and the Rome-aligned southern Church over authority and the date of Easter in particular; Wilfrid, the bishop of York, had angered the Northumbrians in several ways and they had driven him out. King Aldfrith of Northumbria arranged the meeting with the archbishop of Canterbury presiding. Wilfrid had the support of the king of Mercia, but this was not enough to convince the Northumbrians. Wilfrid was forced to petition the Pope in Rome. Austerfield seems to have been a choice as it was convenient for the Mercians and the Northumbrians, who perhaps travelled part of the way by river.

62 Ann Williams, *Aethelred*, in ODNB, accessed 2 January 2014
63 Agnes Dunbar, *A Dictionary of Saintly Women, 1904*. This is different to Werburgh/Werburga, who was Coelred's cousin.
64 This has been disputed – see ODNB on this topic.

Saint Guthlac

Probably the most interesting saint of the period, at least in the account in his early biography (the first biography of an Englishman), was Guthlac (674-715AD). Although he lived for the key period on the very border of modern Lincolnshire at Crowland, this was still in Mercia and he came from a Mercian royal line that could be traced back to the infamous Penda. According to the early biography written about him, his birth was greeted with the miraculous sign of a hand descending from Heaven, holding a 'rood' and descending to the door behind which he was born. Born in about 674AD and spent some years in successful military career on Mercia's western border. At about the age of 24 he was struck by the futility of a 'heroic' military life and went to Repton (in modern Derbyshire) to become a monk. Only a few decades later, a Crowland monk recorded one of the earliest accounts of a spiritual conversion from England:

Guthlac 'was suddenly inspired with divine awe, and his heart within was filled with spiritual love; and when he awoke, he thought on the old kings who were of yore, who thinking on miserable death, and the wretched end of sinful life, forsook this world; and the great wealth which they once possessed, he saw all on a sudden vanish; and he saw his own life daily hasten and hurry to an end. Then he was suddenly so excited inwardly with godly fear that he vowed to God if he would spare him to the morrow, that he would be his servant'.[65]

Guthlac felt called to be a hermit and went by road to Cambridge, then by a skiff guided by a man named Tawtwine to Crowland – an island deep in the fens. This was such a lonely place that no man could live there 'on account of manifold horrors and fears, and the loneliness of the wide wilderness…everyone on this account had fled from it'.[66] It soon became clear that one of the reasons people fled was that evil spirits dwelt there too. Guthlac found an old burial mound that had been dug up by treasure seekers and chose a spot which formed a 'cistern' to build his cell. He decided not to wear soft cloths but only skins, and to live off barley-water and bread – fasting during the daylight hours. The Fens seem to have had an attraction to hermits then, for it has also been claimed there was a hermitage at Thorney in the 7th century.

Then Guthlac made a brief return to Repton, before going back to Crowland with two servants on St Bartholomew's Day. His first task was to battle the spirits, so 'endowed with heavenly grace' he 'took the shield of…faith' and 'clothed himself in the armour of heavenly hope'. Then 'he put on his head the helmet of chaste thoughts and used worship – 'the arrows of heavenly psalmody' – to fight 'the accursed spirits'.

One day Guthlac was attacked by 'the old enemy of mankind' with a 'poisoned arrow' in the form of spiritual depression. For three days he was cast down with despair until he cried a plea – 'My Lord, in my trouble I cry unto Thee, and hear Thou me, and support me in my tribulations'. Soon after this Guthlac had a vision of the saintly apostle Bartholomew who comforted and strengthened him.

---

65 C W Goodwin, *The Anglo-Saxon Version of the Life of St Guthlac*, Cambridge, 1848, p.15. A remarkable book, written at such an early date, and apparently informed by those who knew Guthlac including St Wilfrid.

66 *Life of St Guthlac*, p.21

On another occasion, two demons came to Guthlac and told him how impressed they were. Claiming to be expert on those who dwelt in the wilderness, they offered advice that the best way to wash yourself of sin was to fast and abstain – this was the best way to 'be exalted in God's eyes'. The demons advised him to fast for six days and to eat on the seventh, but Guthlac spotted this as deceit and immediately got up and ate a meal.

The demons were furious and soon returned with a whole host, pouring into Guthlac's house from all directions and filling it up:

They were in countenance horrible, and they had great heads, and a long neck, and lean visage; they were filthy and squalid in their beards, and they had rough ears, and a distorted face, and fierce eyes, and foul mouths, and their teeth were like horse's tusks, and their throats were filled with flame, and they were grating in their voice; they had crooked shanks, and knees big and great behind, and distorted toes, and shrieked hoarsely with their voices...[67]

The demons tied Guthlac up and dragged him out into the fens, throwing him into the black mud, pulling him through brambles and whipping him with irons. Then for good measure they took him up into the cold night air on their wings. Finally, they took him to the gates of Hell, and he saw the demons rush in and torment the souls within. The demons threatened to thrust Guthlac into Hell as well, but at this point, St Bartholomew arrived and told them to return him to his home with all gentleness – which they did.

Many stories are told about Guthlac, some more apocryphal than others. Higden's account mentioned that Guthlac had greater power over demons than other saintly builders, forcing them to do his building work for him and shutting one up in a boiling pot.[68]

A priest named Beccel came to Guthlac to learn about his ways, but was secretly tempted but he fame and honour that Guthlac was winning. Beccel wanted to be Guthlac's successor, and was tempted to achieve this by killing Guthlac while shaving him – he shaved every twenty days. But Guthlac had supernatural insight, and seeing the secrets of Beccel's heart, confronted him; Beccel fell weeping at Guthlac's feet, asking forgiveness, and was indeed forgiven. On another occasion, his island was assailed at night by demons in the shape of lions, vipers and wolves, but Guthlac commanded them to go away in the name of God.

Around 702AD Guthlac was visited by Headda, the bishop from the Mercian town of Lichfield, who consecrated his church, and the island on which it stood – and ordained him.

When Guthlac was visited by Wilfrid, two swallows came and sat on his shoulders. Guthlac told him that as a man withdrew from human contact, so he became more intimate with God's creatures, and angels approached nearer. 'He who frequently longeth for the converse of worldly men, cannot meet with angelic discourse'.[69] On another occasion men from East Anglia brought to Crowland a man who had for years been possessed by a destructive madness; Guthlac prayed for three days in his church, washed the man with

---

67   *Life*, 1848 edition, p.37
68   B Colgrave, *Felix's Life of St Guthlac*, Cambridge, 1956, p.22
69   *Life*, 1848 edition, p.53

holy water, blew on him, and he went away healed. Another man named Ecga, similarly tormented by an unclean spirit, was also healed. Guthlac was known to have a 'prophetic spirit' and 'made known future things to men, as clearly as the present things'. An example of this was when an abbot visited Guthlac, but the abbot's two servants asked for leave to attend to some business on the way; Guthlac told him that they had, instead, gone to the house of a widow and had got drunk – which proved to be true. When visitors arrived, who had been talking sceptically about him, Guthlac was able to tell them what they had been saying!

On another occasion, Guthlac healed a man's wounded foot by laying his clothes upon it, and a huge thorn came out of the foot miraculously.

It is evident, then, that Guthlac's life demonstrated many of the spiritual gifts described in the Acts of the Apostles. When he preached and taught, 'it was as though he preached and spoke the words of angelic language'.[70] Whatever he taught 'he confirmed with the divine example of Holy Scripture'.

Abbess Ecgburh, daughter of the king of the East Angles, sent him a lead coffin and winding-sheet to be buried in and asked who should take his place when he died. Guthlac replied that his successor was at that time an unbaptized heathen. This was Cissa, then not even in Britain, but in due course he arrived and was baptised.

Crowland was not free of the cares of the political world. Aethelbald was hunted by Coelred, who wanted to kill him, and came to Guthlac. The holy man prophesied that if he trusted in God, he would become king.

After Guthlac had lived there 15 years he became suddenly ill while at prayer in his church. He endured days of illness, tended by Beccel, who wept as life seemed to be leaving Guthlac. 'My son, be not thou grieved,' Guthlac said, 'for to me it is no sorrow that I am going to the Lord my God'. On the fourth day of his illness Guthlac got up and preached the gospel, Beccel listening, 'and he penetrated him so deeply with his counsel that he never before nor after heard the like.'

Guthlac gave Beccel instructions to wrap his body in the cloth that had been sent although he had refused all such cloth in his time alive. Guthlac revealed to Beccel how, since the second year, God had sent 'the angel of my comfort' to him each morning and evening, and had opened to him 'the heavenly mysteries'.

Guthlac's death was as glorious as his life:
After that he raised his eyes to heaven, and stretched out his arms, and then sent forth his spirit with joy and bliss to the eternal happiness of the heavenly kingdom. Amidst these things [Beccel] saw all the house perfused with heavenly brightness, and he beheld there a fiery tower, from the earth up to the height of heaven, whose brightness was unlike all other, and by its brilliance the sun at midday – all its lustre was turned to paleness. And he heard angelic songs through the regions of the air, and all the island was profusely filled with the exceeding sweetness of a wondrous odour.

---

70   *Life*, 1848 edition, p.73

Guthlac died in about 715AD and his tomb was visited by Æthelbald, who was still being persecuted. In the night Æthelbald had a vision of Guthlac, who told him he would be king of Mercia within a year – as indeed he was; he established a monastery at Crowland (Croyland) in 716AD. After a year his sister moved Guthlac's coffin, and his body was found to be miraculously preserved. A boat man of Æthelbald's was cured of blindness. The monk Cissa began to live in Guthlac's place and in due course also became a saint and was buried alongside Guthlac; both tombs were destroyed by the Vikings but Cissa's remains ended up at Thorney. In 716AD a shrine was built – but we should not assume all this was on the site of the Norman priory.[71] Indeed, there were at least five monastic cells by the time of his death.

Felix's *Life of Guthlac* was written in about 740AD, making it one of the earliest religious texts in the country and was largely based on the accounts of those who knew Guthlac. It is unique in providing a detailed account of a Christian life from such an early date.

Guthlac's sister was Pega, who was claimed to have set up her own monastic cell at what is now Peakirk in 714AD, before dying in Rome in 719AD. When Guthlac realized that his end was near in 714AD, he invited her to his funeral. For this she sailed down the River Welland, curing a blind man from Wisbech on the way. She inherited Guthlac's psalter and scourge, both of which, it was claimed, she later gave to Crowland Abbey. She went on pilgrimage to Rome and died there, c.719. Ordericus Vitalis claimed that her relics survived in an unnamed Roman church in his day, and that miracles took place there.

Even more speculative is the life of Ælfthryth,[72] daughter of Offa, said to have been betrothed to **Æthelberht** King of the East Angles who was murdered in 794 on the orders of Offa of Mercia while visiting his intended wife in Mercia before their marriage. It has been claimed that she then retired to Crowland, where she was walled into a cell to live as a recluse dying in about 795.

Another saint of the era is Werburgh (2), who became abbess of Bardney and lived in about 785AD.[73]

We should mention is Æthelheard, who was abbot at Louth and through the influence of the Mercian King Offa became Archbishop of Canterbury in 792AD. Offa died in 796AD, and when the Kentish men rose in rebellion the new archbishop fled. He returned to Canterbury in 798AD, in the baggage train of a vengeful army. Despite this his biographer concludes that 'Æthelheard appears as an effective and energetic archbishop, concerned both to preserve the integrity and endowment of his see and to ensure the health and discipline of the English church'. His life is important evidence that an influential 'minster' church existed at Louth, possibly as early as the late 7th century.[74]

---

71 Vince (1993), p.104
72 There are various alternatives for this name.
73 J Hutchinson-Hall, *Orthodox Saints of the British Isles*, volume 1, 2014, p.98
74 Caitlin Green, *The Origins of Louth*, 2014, p.80-1

The Danes – and the Growth of the Church 860 –1066

Where could you find a church before the Vikings came?

In Lindsey, there were monasteries at Bardney, perhaps Barrow, Partney (where there were two) and possibly Hibaldstow. Aethelthryth founded two in Lindsey – possibly Stow Green and West Halton where ruins were still visible in the 17th century, with another at Flixborough in the Eighth or Ninth centuries.[75] It has been suggested that there were early 'minster' churches at Grantham, Hough on the Hill, Louth, Edenham (with 8th-century features), Caistor[76] and Wellingore. We are much less confident about any pre-Viking churches in Nottinghamshire. The church at Flawford has been claimed as built on a Roman villa site in the 9th century. Dunham, Mansfield, Orston, Kirkby in Ashfield, Plumtree and East Stoke may pre-date the Danish invasion of the 9th century.[77] Claims for Saxon origins have also been made for Carlton-in-Lindrick, Clayworth, Rampton and East Bridgford.[78]

The problem of Danish invasion started to trouble the region in the early 800s, and in Lindsey especially by 838AD. The Danes overran Northumbria in 866-7AD, killed its princes and captured York in 867AD and then held Nottingham where the Mercians attempted a siege.

There is also a tradition that King Alfred, during his battles against the Danes, held his wedding feast at Gainsborough in 868AD as his wife, Elswith, was the daughter of Ethelfred the Great, a Mercian Earl who lived there.

Mercia was pressed back by 869AD and East Anglia in 869-70AD when the famous King Edmund was killed – soon to become an emblematic saint.

The Danes or Vikings are well known for raiding religious houses, and their victims, by tradition, include Bardney, destroyed in 870AD after landing at Humberston – with some claims that all the monks were slaughtered – and not restored until 1087.[79] It is often claimed also that in the same year the Danes destroyed the church at Stow by fire. The same year the Danes faced Algar, Earl of Mercia, at Lacundon (assumed to be Threekingham in Kesteven) and three of their 'kings' were killed. However, then Danish reinforcements arrived and the next day Algar himself was killed, being later buried at Algarkirk.[80] The Danes marched on Croyland (Crowland), which they destroyed. Also destroyed in 870AD was the large monastery at Medhamstead (Peterborough).

In 873AD the Viking army wintered at Torksey on the Trent and moved to Repton, a key place for the Mercians, the next winter.

---

75   Sawyer (1998), p.66; *The Oxford Handbook of Anglo-Saxon Archaeology*, p.125. The site has also been conjectured as a 'minster'.

76   N J Cooper (ed), *Archaeology of the East Midlands*, 2006, p.170

77   Leicester, p.8

78   Stapleford Cross has been claimed by some as of Saxon origin, dating back to around 700AD, which would make it the earliest post-Roman Christian work in Nottinghamshire apart from the suggested stonework at South Leverton. However, others have dated it to c.1050.

79   How much of Barney was destroyed has been debated, with some historians suggesting Bardney was not 'one' site but a cluster as Crowland was. The evidence against its destruction is that it continued to be the shrine for Oswald but when his remains were removed in 909 there was little of them.

80   *The Gentleman's Magazine,* 1818, p.20

A shadowy figure from this era of whom we know little is St Herefrith, possibly the last bishop of Lindsey or Lincoln in this era who died in about 873AD. A shrine was set up to him in Louth from which his remains were stolen by monks from Thorney Abbey in about 970AD.

When all those dwelling there had been put to sleep by a cunning ruse, a trusty servant took him out of the ground, wrapped him in fine linen cloth, and with all his fellows rejoicing brought him to the monastery at Thorney and re-interred him.'[81] The arrival of the Viking army and the death of Herefrith is an interesting coincidence: could he have been a martyr? Herefrith's comb was still in Louth church in 1486.

Though the Danes and Vikings severely disrupted Church organisation in the region, they proved to be much earlier converts to Christianity than those who stayed at home.[82] They opted to be buried in Christian churchyards and within a generation were commissioning stone crosses to be made. The Vikings who settled in the Danelaw were amongst the first Scandinavians to adopt Christianity. When a Viking army wintered at Repton, Derbyshire, in 873-4AD it left signs of religious belief in transition.

At Edington in 878AD Alfred finally captured the Danish leader, Guthrum, who was converted and baptised with some of his followers. A treaty of 884 established eastern areas as the 'Danelaw'.

Further Danish attacks in southern England in the mid-890s foundered in the face of well-organised opposition. The Vikings certainly had an impact for they destroyed all the monasteries and brought to an end the bishops of Lindsey for a time, but it is probable that many churches continued to function – and most would have been wood and thus easy to rebuild. Yet by the start of the 10th-century most Danish settlers were Christianised.

However, the bones of Oswald were removed from Bardney to Gloucester in 909AD – although later chroniclers said that all but three of the bones had been stolen, and only one arm and some hair made it to Gloucester. They were this removed from Northumbrian influence to be kept deep into Mercia. In the mid-eleventh century, a monk stole one of Oswald's arms from Bamburgh and took it to a monastery at Peterborough, where it was saved from the Danes in 1070 by being hidden in the abbot's bed.

An Interlude of Peace?

Edward fought to reduce the influence of the York Vikings. He retook Nottingham in 918AD, and in 942AD Edmund extended control over northern Mercia. First, in 953 AD Leofwine was appointed the first bishop of Lindsey since 875AD;[83] in the interim the area probably came under York. King Edwy re-established English control after the death of

---

81 From an account written at Thorney c1068-85

82 J D Richards, *Pagans and Christians at a Frontier*, in *The Cross Goes North*, p.383

83 David Roffe has suggested that Leofwine was a suffragan bishop beholden to York, whose long-running claims to include Lindsey are discussed in this section. The unite diocese of 971 is then seen as an attempt to resolve the problem.

Eric Blood-Axe in 954AD and refounded the structures of the Church after the Danish disruptions. In 956AD Oskytel, the bishop of Dorchester (Oxford), was given control over the Southwell area which had for a time been part of the diocese of Leicester, and in 958AD he was given the manor of Sutton (Lound?), near Retford; this territory transferred to the diocese of York when Oskytel became Archbishop. Meanwhile, King Eadwig in 956AD[84] gave land to the Archbishop to establish a church at Southwell, which became the 'mother' church for this area.

From 971AD[85] Leofwine combined Lindsey and Dorchester, in what later became Oxfordshire, and the see of Lindsey seems to have lost its identity within what was to become the huge diocese of Lincoln. The separate see of Lindsey was revived again in c993AD under Sigeforth. There was again no bishop of Lindsey after c1004-1011 when it was re-united with Dorchester, and it was not until the Norman era, in 1072, that church administration was centred on Lincoln. Throughout this era the diocese of York laid claim to Lindsey (giving the role of Paulinus as evidence) despite a Papal Bull against its control in 1061. Thus, Lincoln itself has only a marginal role in the story at this stage.

The recovery of the monasteries was also possible. Thurketel, c.971-984AD, began the revival of the monastery at Crowland.

These changes established Southwell as the centre of the church in the Nottingham region, eventually becoming also a palace of the archbishop, and there is a logic to Laneham evolving also as a house of the archbishop – it was a good calling point on the Trent. By 1000 Southwell contained a shrine to St Eadburh or Edburga who died in about 700AD; she may have been the daughter of King Ealdwulf of East Anglia, became abbess of Repton under the patronage of Wulfhere, King of Mercia but how she came to Southwell is not known. Archbishop Ælfric probably died there in 1051.

One more unsolved problem in the early history of Southwell may here be mentioned — the fate which befell the remains of St. Eadburh. We know that the Norman prelates who followed the Conquest possessed but scant respect for the native saints of the land, but it is not easy to account for the disappearance of a shrine which clearly was an object of frequent pilgrimage in the early 11th century. It has to some extent escaped notice that a discovery of wonderworking relics was made at Southwell in the reign of Stephen; these, however, cannot be connected with St. Eadburh's remains. While a grave was being prepared, there were found the relics of certain saints, and a glass vessel filled with clear water, which restored health to those who tasted it. The matter was brought to the notice of Thurstan, (fn. 61) the then Archbishop of York, but nothing further is recorded in connexion with the discovery.[86]

During the period 950-1066, the senior church posts became dominated by men with land and family connections. Eadnoth, who became Bishop of Dorchester in around 1005, was related to three other bishops; he is believed to have been a friend of St Oswald and the

84 *Victoria County History of Nottinghamshire*, vol 2, p.152
85 P Sawyer, *Anglo-Saxon Lincolnshire,* Lincoln, 1998, p.150
86 'Colleges: The collegiate church of Southwell', in *A History of the County of Nottingham: Volume 2* (1910), pp. 152-161. URL: http://www.british-history.ac.uk/report.aspx?compid=40105 Date accessed: 22 March 2014.

founder of St Mary, Stow[87]

A network of churches was becoming established. To the 'mother' churches which have been identified at Horncastle, Stow, Witham on the Hill, Dunham we can perhaps add West Markham by the 10th century, Saxon era churches around Barrow and Barton in the north, Aisthorpe and Hackthorn in middle Lindsey.[88] In west Nottinghamshire less is known – most of the future county was still underdeveloped.

There was also an established number of monastic sites – Crowland, Bardney, Partney, South Kyme, Hibaldstow, Barrow, Louth, Threekingham and Crowland, which had been attacked by the Vikings, was revived by Abbot Thurketel in 971-984AD.

Owen also observed that springs and 'holy wells' formed a pattern of pre-Conquest religious sites. In Lincolnshire these included St Pancras's well near Scampton, Shadwell or Chad's Well at Barton, Maidenwell and St Mary's at Ancaster.[89] St Helen's Spring at Louth may have been a British Christian cultic site of the 7th century.[90] Less is known of holy wells in Nottinghamshire such as that at Watnall; the better known St Ann's Well at Nottingham may have previously been known as Brodswell or Owswell, which may connect it to Easter rituals.[91] Lady Well at Headon is also well known and there is a St John's Well beneath a house at Welham whilst Southwell was also based on a spring, but we know little of these, or when they originated as religious sites.

Return of the Danes

Relative peace existed from the late 9th century until 980 when sporadic Viking raids resumed and became much more problematic from about 990. However, we should not assume they were all pagan, for Christianity had been the official faith since 965AD although adherence to it may have been superficial for some. Swein Forkbeard appeared for the first time in 994 although he may have crossed to England in raids in 991AD. Swein returned in force in 1003. The *Anglo-Saxon Chronicle* reports that Swein sailed up the Trent to Gainsborough where 'soon submitted to him Earl Utred, and all the Northumbrians, and all the people of Lindsey, and afterwards the people of the Five Boroughs, and soon after all the army to the north of Watling-street; and hostages were given him from each shire'. In 1013 he was thus acknowledged to be the king of England, as well as holding his own kingdom in Denmark where a process of establishing Christianity had taken root. Indeed, two English bishops had already been working in Denmark.[92]

Swein Forkbeard died in 1014 in Gainsborough, and an oft-told legend is that he was struck down by the spirit of Saint Edmund on account of his plundering of English churches. The story is that Ailwin, custodian of Saint Edmund's shrine and remains, was forced to take

87   Hill, p.73
88   D M Hadley, *Northern Danelaw*, p.277, 287
89   Dorothy Owen, *Church and Society in Medieval Lincolnshire*, Lincoln, 1971, p.1
90   Caitlin Green, *The Origins of Louth*, 2014, p.82
91   https://nottinghamhiddenhistoryteam.wordpress.com/2013/01/21/st-anns-well/ accessed 10 March 2019
92   P H Sawyer, *Swein Forkbeard*, in *ODNB*, online edition, accessed 1/2/14.

his precious charges to London in 1010 to preserve them from being stolen. Then in the year 1013, Ailwin had a vision in which Edmund issued a stern warning to Sweyn to leave the English people alone. It was clear that Edmund thought it Ailwin's duty to deliver the message in person to Swein. He had declared himself King of England instead, and so, in a way, Gainsborough where he was often based became a sort-of 'capital'. Ailwin hesitated to deliver Edmund's message, but as 1014 dawned Sweyn increased the pressure by demanding extra 'taxes' from the monks.

This story might be true, or parts of it might be true, or possibly almost none of it is true, but certainly elements of it have been told for a long time. Swein died in Gainsborough on 3 February 1014, but as to what precisely happened when Ailwin arrived there... Many anti-Danish sources paint Sweyn as pagan, but there is some evidence that he followed a moderately Christian line and built a couple of churches in Denmark. Medieval chroniclers like Florence of Worcester's tell of Swein being struck down by Edmund just after planning a raid on his shrine, whilst John of Tinmouth said that Edmund's ghost stabbed him as he sat in a chair. William of Malmesbury in his *Chronicle of the Kings of England* said that he was struck down in his sleep for 'answering rudely' back to Edmund! The most likely explanation is that Swein was poisoned, but however, he died it was certainly a great day in Gainsborough's history.

Æthelred (famous as 'Ethelred the Unready') returned to challenge for the kingdom and brought his army to Lindsey, to drive out Cnut after the death of his father – and succeeded – to an extent:

Meanwhile, after the death of Sweyne, sat Knute with his army in Gainsborough until Easter; and it was agreed between him and the people of Lindsey, that they should supply him with horses, and afterwards go out all together and plunder. But King Ethelred with his full force came to Lindsey before they were ready, and they plundered and burned, and slew all the men that they could reach. Knute, the son of Sweyne, went out with his fleet (so were the wretched people deluded by him) and proceeded southward until he came to Sandwich. There he landed the hostages that were given to his father, and cut off their hands and ears and their noses.[93]

This heralded something of an 'English revival', with Archbishop Wulfstan preaching a sermon which pointed out the connections between declining faithfulness and the decline in English fortunes. However, Cnut returned late in 1015 who by 1016 controlled the whole of the kingdom, being accepted as king in 1017.

Cnut was a 'Christian' albeit one with an eye on the advantages of being 'approved' by the Church and 'His piety was of a very ostentatious type'.[94] He was given to public demonstration, so the famous story of him turning back the waves may have been linked to 'proving' his humility – for of course it was his courtiers who believed he could turn back the waves, not Cnut. Some claims have even been made that the incident took place not on some southern shore but at Gainsborough, with Cnut attempting to stop the passage of the 'Aegir' – the Trent tidal bore.

Cnut's impact on our region was perhaps muted as the people of Lindsey had been

93 *Anglo-Saxon Chronicle*
94 M K Lawson, *Cnut*, in *ODNB*, online edition, accessed 1/2/14

something of allies and the region was well settled with Danes, but further south his relations with the Church were more ambivalent.

The significance of Stow in the region's Christian history has been much debated. From about 1005 a Benedictine abbey was built there and opinions on the church's date vary from about 975 to 1033. Some view it as having been founded by Eadnoth (or Aelfnoth) 'the Younger', founder of several abbeys, who became bishop of Dorchester from about 1007, and was a south fenlander with family interests in Lincolnshire. His promotion owed much to the influence of his relative Oswald, Archbishop of York. He was killed – regarded as a martyr – in a battle against Cnut in 1016. After being burnt down, it was then rebuilt at the time of Eadnoth II from 1034-1050 when the Dorchester diocese included Lindsey. This has perhaps added greater weight to those who argue it must have been a 'mother church' in Lindsey before the cathedral was built.

Earl Leofric of Mercia and his wife the famous Lady Godiva (or Godgifu) funded a monastic community at Stow between 1053 and 1055. Godiva also held the manors of Newark, Fledborough and Stokeham in eastern Nottinghamshire which, with Marton and Brampton in Lincolnshire were to endow it.[95] Tales of Godiva's naked ride through Coventry did not emerge until the 13th century. Stow was a college for 'secular canons' but it was abandoned after the Conquest, although briefly revived by the transfer of Benedictines there by Bishop Remigius in 1091-5.

The worst bishop of the era appears to have been Ulf, the choice of Edward the Confessor in 1049, of who the *Anglo-Saxon Chronicle* said little except he was 'driven out because he did nothing bishop-like' as 'it shames us to tell more now'.[96] The era finished with another dispute between archbishops over Lindsey. Archbishop Ealdred of York seized the Lindsey diocese and 'the church of Stow with Newark' from Bishop Wulfwig, Ulf's replacement in 1053, who had to appeal to the Pope. Archbishop Kensius gave two bells to Stow c1051-60 and also to Southwell, clearly marking his territory. In 1061 the Pope declared that Lindsey – including Stow – was part of the see of Dorchester, but the issue continued to fester until resolved in 1092.

So by the time King Harold marched southwards in 1066 from Stamford Bridge, over the Trent at Littleborough and southwards to meet the Normans on the south coast, Christianity had survived four hundred years of turbulence – and possibly longer. We do not know how many churches there were for many would have been built of wood. At least fifteen in Lincolnshire have pre-conquest features including Barton (where features suggest St Peter's was built in stone by carpenters) and Stow; in other cases such as Holton-le-Clay, it is the graveyard which suggests the early origins whilst Caistor and Castle Bytham may have had 'minster' churches.[97]

In Nottinghamshire there was the principal minster at Southwell, a few scattered churches at villages such as Rampton, West Markham and South Leverton, and perhaps a small number of other churches in places such as Kneesall as the lack of a mention in Domesday is not even an accurate picture. There was probably a church at Laneham, where the

---

95 Hill, p.76
96 Hill, p.73
97 Sawyer, p.159

Archbishop of York had a palace by 1066.[98] It has also been suggested that the name of Misterton is derived from 'mynster', implying an earlier church at the village.[99] At Langar there was a pilgrimage trade to the church of St Ethelburga's, of which little is known. Overall, the region remained one of small, scattered populations served by a thin layer of churches and priests.

---

98   Edward the Confessor issued a writ affecting the archbishop's manor between 1060 and 1065
99   TTS, 2007, p.47

CHAPTER TWO

The Era of Catholicism
1066-1509

For five centuries, the two counties of Nottingham and Lincoln experienced what we might see as the era of Roman Catholicism – for there was no other faith during this time. Despite this dominance, some turbulence surfaced from time to time with reforming bishops like Grosseteste, and eventually in the more significant challenge provided by the Lollards. During this period much of Nottinghamshire came to be dominated by a new generation of monasteries whilst Lincolnshire produced the only native English monastic order – the Gilbertines. Lincoln's greatest figure, though, was actually a Frenchman – Saint Hugh of Lincoln.

Chronology:
1072: New diocesan structure created
1076: Waltheof executed
1087: Bardney Abbey refounded
1103: Worksop Priory founded
1185: Earthquake destroys Lincoln cathedral
1186: Hugh of Avalon becomes Bishop of Lincoln
1189-91: Siege of Acre
1202: St Gilbert of Sempringham canonised
1251: Stephen Langton involved with Magna Carta
1220: Hugh of Avalon canonised
1253: Death of Robert Grosseteste
1255: 'Little St Hugh' controversy in Lincoln
1290: Jews expelled from England
1390: Crusade from Boston to Lithuania
1415: Wycliffe declared a heretic
1456: William Waynflete becomes Lord Chancellor
1520: Completion of Boston 'Stump'

The Normans Arrive

1066 was the year of three kings, but its impact on our region was long term rather than short: in the long, it led to the creation of both Nottinghamshire and Lincolnshire, in

N

River Ouse

GRIMSBY

DONCASTER   Axholme Priory   ■ Hibaldstow

River Trent

Roche Abbey   Scrooby   GAINSBOROUGH   LOUTH ■   Louth Park Abbey
Blyth Priory   Mattersey Priory
Wallingwells Priory   RETFORD   Stow Park   Nettleham
Worksop Priory WORKSOP   Laneham
    Broadholme Priory
Welbeck Abbey   Barlings Abbey
    LINCOLN   Bardney Abbey
Rufford Abbey   Sutton on Trent   Stixwould Priory   ■ Dalderby
MANSFIELD   Kirkstead Abbey   Revesby Abbey
Newstead Priory   Southwell   NEWARK   ■ Wainfleet
    -ON-   River Witham
    TRENT
Beauvale Priory   Thurgarton Priory   Kyme Priory
NOTTINGHAM   SLEAFORD   BOSTON
Lenton Abbey
River Trent   Stow Green Nunnery
GRANTHAM   ■ Ropsley   Sempringham Priory
    River Witham
    ■ Irnham
    SPALDING

✚ Church
✚ Religious house
♦ Archbishop's or bishop's palace
■ Place
▪ Town   Crowland Abbey

STAMFORD

0   10   20 miles   Peterborough Abbey

    Not all religious houses are shown

34

the short it saw Harold march through Bawtry, Littleborough and Lincoln on his fateful journey south. One of the men with Harold in his last days was Leofric, a powerful Mercian who held multiple abbacies including Peterborough, Thorney and Crowland (Croyland)[1] which meant that he held extensive lands in both counties. He died during the campaign, 'God have mercy on his sould (sic),' the Chronicler wrote. 'In his day there was complete happiness and complete prosperity in Peterborough, and he was beloved by all people…' Part of the Norman plan was to redistribute such holdings across their own soldiers, creating a new generation of lords.

By the time the Normans consolidated their control in our region, there was already an established system of diocesan bishops and the beginnings of the parish system over which they overlaid the system of counties with the creation of Lincolnshire and Nottinghamshire. However, we do not know with any certainty how many churches there actually were. The Domesday Book, recording the situation in 1086, recorded 84 churches in Nottinghamshire and 250 in Lincolnshire but Hill thought there might have been nearly 400 by 1100;[2] it is often thought to have understated the numbers.

The arrival of the Normans did not lead to immediate strong control, which as the *Anglo-Saxon Chronicle* explained especially affected the south of Lincolnshire:

This year Earl Waltheof agreed with the king, but in the Lent of the same year the king ordered all the monasteries in England to be plundered. In the same year came King Sweyne from Denmark into the Humber; and the landsmen came to meet him and made a treaty with him, thinking that he would overrun the land. Then came into Ely Christien, the Danish bishop, and Earl Osbern, and the Danish domestics with them; and the English people from all the fen-lands came to them; supposing that they should win all that land. Then the monks of Peterborough heard say, that their own men would plunder the minster; namely Hereward and his gang: because they understood that the king had given the abbacy to a French abbot, whose name was Thorold; that he was a very stern man, and was then come into Stamford with all his Frenchmen. Now there was a churchwarden, whose name was Yware; who took away by night all that he could, testaments, mass-hackles, cantel-copes, and reefs, and such other small things, whatsoever he could; and went early, before day, to the Abbot Thorold; telling him that he sought his protection, and informing him how the outlaws were coming to Peterborough, and that he did all by advice of the monks. Early in the morning came all the outlaws with many ships, resolving to enter the minster; but the monks withstood, so that they could not come in. Then they laid on fire, and burned all the houses of the monks, and all the town except one house. Then came they in through fire at the Bull-hithe gate; where the monks met them, and besought peace of them. But they regarded nothing. They went into the minster, climbed up to the holy rood, took away the diadem from our Lord's head, all of pure gold, and seized the bracket that was underneath his feet, which was all of red gold. They climbed up to the steeple, brought down the table that was hid there, which was all of gold and silver, seized two golden shrines, and nine of silver, and took away fifteen large crucifixes, of gold and of silver; in short, they seized there so much gold and silver, and so many treasures, in money, in raiment, and in books, as no man could tell another; and said, that they did it from their attachment to the minster.

---

1   Croyland is an old spelling of Crowland, but in general, we use the latter.
2   Sir Francis Hill, *Medieval Lincoln*, Cambridge, 1948, p.74

Afterwards they went to their ships, proceeded to Ely, and deposited there all the treasure. The Danes, believing that they should overcome the Frenchmen, drove out all the monks; leaving there only one, whose name was Leofwine Lang, who lay sick in the infirmary. Then came Abbot Thorold and eight times twenty Frenchmen with him, all full-armed. When he came thither, he found all within and without consumed by fire, except the church alone; but the outlaws were all with the fleet, knowing that he would come thither. This was done on the fourth day before the nones of June. The two kings, William and Sweyne, were now reconciled; and the Danes went out of Ely with all the aforesaid treasure, and carried it away with them. But when they came into the middle of the sea, there came a violent storm, and dispersed all the ships wherein the treasures were. Some went to Norway, some to Ireland, some to Denmark. All that reached the latter, consisted of the table, and some shrines, and some crucifixes, and many of the other treasures; which they brought to a king's town, called ----, and deposited it all there in the church. Afterwards through their own carelessness, and through their drunkenness, in one night the church and all that was therein was consumed by fire. Thus, was the minster of Peterborough burned and plundered. Almighty God have mercy on it through his great goodness. Thus came the Abbot Thorold to Peterborough; and the monks too returned, and performed the service of Christ in the church, which had before stood a full week without any kind of rite. When Bishop Aylric heard it, he excommunicated all the men who that evil deed had done.

It will be seen from this that a particular issue was the way the Normans gave leadership positions within the Church to their own kin – systematic nepotism at the point of the sword. There is also brief reference to Hereward, a fenland hero whose stories perhaps had some influence on the later legends of Robin Hood.

The Peterborough monks elected Brand, a man with Lincolnshire connections 'because he was a very good man and very wise'.[3] Brand was able to negotiate some sureties for the monasteries from King William, even after paying a fine for an unwise association with an English rival.

Waltheof (d.1076):

In 1076 William I ordered the execution of Waltheof, Earl of Northumberland, for treason. Waltheof had Danish and English blood, and a Norman wife who betrayed him. Waltheof spent his last days praying and reciting the Psalms, which he knew by heart. He was, allegedly, executed whilst saying the Lord's Prayer and spoke the words '…but deliver us from evil, Amen,' after the axe had fallen.

After he was beheaded, corpse and head were taken for burial in the chapter house at Crowland by the abbot Ulfcytel. When he was replaced by Ingulf and a fire had damaged the buildings, the body was dug up in 1092 and found to be uncorrupted – moreover the head had re-attached to the neck leaving just a thin red line.

---

3   Hill (1948), p.43

In one story, Ingulf recognised Waltheof's face from a dream he had had years before. Miracles began, encouraged further by a vision that the abbot Geoffrey had in which Waltheof was seen walking with St Bartholomew and St Guthlac, who joked that he had been raised from an Earl to a King. Healing miracles were recorded from 1111, many of them occurring at dawn (the time of his execution) with a large proportion being miracles of sight. In contrast, a Norman monk who ridiculed the English pilgrims to Waltheof's shrine collapsed and died. Miracles increased after 1124, when the abbot was also called Waltheof.

He was also known to be a supporter, when convenient, of the monasteries at Crowland, Thorney and Peterborough, and to have supported the building of Lincoln cathedral by gifts of land.

Medieval chroniclers seized on the heroic aspects of Waltheof's story which was, one might say, also good for business at Crowland.

Lincoln and Southwell

The Norman system of counties and redrawn dioceses had a major impact on the region, creating a formal division between the two counties and ultimately separated them into different provinces of the Church. The Normans were to mark the importance of Lincoln as a cathedral city but in Nottinghamshire Southwell remained a distant outpost in the vast York archdiocese whilst Nottingham, the new county town, never had its own cathedral. Nonetheless, a replacement for the Saxon minster at Southwell was begun in about 1110 and a substantial palace erected behind it; no doubt this arrangement helped control an outpost of a huge diocese but perhaps it also marked it out as York's, not Lincoln's.

The manor at Stow had belonged to the bishops since the time of Edward the Confessor. It has been claimed that Stow may have acted as the 'pro-cathedral' before Lincoln took over in 1072-3 when the see was translated there, but this claim seems to lack any solid basis. It has also been argued that Lincoln itself held this honour before the Conquest[4] and as early as the mid-900s, and that the new cathedral replaced a pre-existing Anglo-Saxon structure.[5] The recent discovery of another church within the castle walls has added an extra dimension to this debate. However, it is also perhaps notable that Remigius began a cathedral at Dorchester in Oxfordshire before he moved to Lincoln. The manor, Stow Park, continued in use by the bishops until 1547.

Wulfwig, Bishop of Dorchester and Lindsey, died in 1067, providing an opportunity to place a Norman in this huge diocese. Remigius, a Norman from Fécamp, was chosen. However, unrest and invasion continued including attacks from the Humber by Edgar the Ætheling in 1069 and by King Swein in 1070, with revolt by Hereward in the south; no

4   Hill (1948), p.72
5   D Stocker and A Vince, *The Early Norman Castle at Lincoln and a Re-evaluation of the Original West Tower of Lincoln Cathedral*, in *Medieval Archaeology* (41), 1991.

doubt this influenced the early design for the west end of the cathedral, which shows the intention to build a place of safety.

Turgot (c.1050-1115)

Caught up in the turbulence at the start of the Norman era was Turgot, a young Lindsey 'clerk' perhaps from a minor gentry family who was held as a hostage by the Normans in Lincoln's new castle. He escaped via Grimsby to Norway, where he made a good impression on King Olaf.[6] There he became prosperous but lost most of his property in a shipwreck when returning to England. After some debate it would seem, he became a monk in about 1075. His career continued to be prior and Archdeacon of Durham in 1083 and he helped lay the foundation stone of the new cathedral. He was elected bishop of St Andrews in Scotland in 1107 and probably confessor and biographer of Queen Margaret of Scotland, likely writing this under the influence of her daughter Queen Matilda of England. He died in 1115, with the reputation of one who had shown both pastoral and administrative talents and who helped to build a stronger Church.

The first thing for Remigius was to resolve the boundary of the diocese. When William I took control of England, he treated Thomas of York as the authority over Nottinghamshire and Lincolnshire (despite the Papal bull of 1061). Thomas claimed Stow, Louth and Newark as his but in 1072 the Council of Winchester split the archdiocese broadly along the Humber-Trent boundary and Remigius became bishop of the new diocese covering Lincoln, Leicester and Dorchester – in the Province of Canterbury, whilst Nottinghamshire remained in York. Several writers alleged that a bishopric was Remigius's price for supporting William with men in the invasion.[7] He began a cathedral that – in the Norman fashion – was capable of being defended[8] but if we place value on the arguments for a pre-existing cathedral in Lincoln then we cannot really call Remigius the 'founder'.

The new cathedral was completed by 1092, at which point Archbishop Thomas of York renewed his claims on Lindsey (Stow, Louth and Newark specifically) and delayed its opening. Remigius had to buy support from the king but then died two days before the rearranged event. Robert Bloet was elected the next bishop in 1093 but again needed royal support at a price of thousands of pounds to see off York's claims for Stow, Louth and Newark.[9] Some of this money was then needed by the king to pay off the Archbishop's claims, indicating they had some foundation. This arrangement was confirmed by popes in 1106 and 1177. By about 1100 the deanery of Newark had become part of the Archdeaconry of Nottingham within York archdiocese. In 1109 the new diocese of Ely was created from part of the Lincoln diocese.

The new cathedral and the bishop could be partly funded by the 'episcopal minsters' that Remigius held at Wellingore, Kirton-in-Lindsey, Caistor and Sleaford, as well as perhaps also Grantham and Horncastle. These received dues from the 'parochial' churches founded

---

6   Hill (1948), p.45
7   Hill (1948), p.64
8   Sawyer, p.154
9   Hill (1948), p.66. Chroniclers gave the figure as £3000 or £5000 – several million today.

by landowners as dependant chapels and from them was distributed 'chrism', a sacred oil used in baptism. The parish system therefore partly evolved as, for a time, authority was weak in Lincolnshire and landowners had set up their own from the time of King Edgar.[10] By the time of the Domesday Book, there were 250 churches in Lincolnshire.

By the late 1100s, the cathedral was largely in ruins having been damaged by fire sometime before 1146, and was then further devastated by the earthquake of 1185. One might say this cleared the way for the greatest of the bishops, Hugh, to begin his work. Though it is not the purpose of this book to focus on buildings, we do need to note that the rebuilding began in 1192 and continued after Hugh's death in 1200. There was another catastrophe in 1237 when a tower collapsed and by 1250 the nave had been completed westwards to join the original Norman front. Claims have been made for Richard of Gainsborough, whose tomb slab from 1300 survived in the cloisters, as the major designer of much stonework and the Angel Choir.

The rebuilding of Southwell by the Normans began from about 1108 and continued until about 1150. In 1171 that Pope Alexander the Third created the link between Southwell Minster and the whole clergy and laity of Nottinghamshire. The archdeaconry of Nottingham, which existed from about 1100, then developed its partial separation which led one historian to describe it as 'a semi-independent jurisdiction'.[11] A separate synod met at Southwell, apart from the rest of the York diocese.

The Jews

The Jews were established in Lincoln by the mid-1100s at the time of Henry II and in Nottingham soon after, though to a lesser extent. They were a principal source of capital for building the monasteries – Aaron of Lincoln alone was owed money for Kirkstead, Revesby, Rufford, Louth Park and Roche within our region by the time of his death in about 1185. One chronicler claimed that Bishop Chesney of Lincoln had pawned church furnishings to Aaron,[12] who was active from 1165 to 1185. There were anti-Jewish riots at Stamford in 1189 but the Jews of Lincoln were prepared and took shelter within the upper town; there was a terrible slaughter in York with a Lincoln man, Richard de Malebys, playing a leading role in it.[13] In 1194 the Jews contributed a substantial sum to the ransom of Richard I.

There was probably also a Jewish community in Nottingham by the late 1100s. Although they had a synagogue, they had no place of burial and the dead were taken by the 'winter road' via Ollerton to York. Nottingham had a Jew Lane, but old histories suggest the synagogue there was sold off by force in about 1292.

In 1202 a child murder at Lincoln raised suspicions against the Jews and in 1220 a Jewish man and his wife were murdered, then in 1223 the bishop of Lincoln tried to stop the selling

---

10   Sawyer, p.155
11   R A Marchant, *The Church under the Law*, Cambridge, 1969, p.147
12   Hill (1948), p.218
13   Hill (1948), p.223

of food to them. Understanding the relationship of figures like Robert Grosseteste to the Jews is a complex matter; Grosseteste was worried about the fragility of Christendom at a time of threat from the east, with which Jews were sometimes considered to be bound up. This made them objects of suspicion and prejudice, which combined with Grosseteste's dislike of usury, and so he gathered information on where they lived in his diocese.[14] He perhaps had a softening influence on Simon de Montfort's expelling of the Jews from Leicester in the 1240s, ensuring that they were not killed.

Most seriously in 1255 appeared the events recorded as the murder of 'Little Saint Hugh' in Matthew Paris's writings – reporting that 994 Jews were taken to London as prisoners after the supposed ritual murder by crucifixion of a boy whose body was found in a well. In one of the best-known versions, the boy was kept alive so that Jews from across the country could attend his ritual murder.

However, we cannot dismiss this entire story as pure fabrication, despite 'miraculous' elements in some versions, trials and executions certainly did occur. Both the bishop's brother John of Lexington[15] and Henry III were involved in the executions – perhaps 18 were hung in London, and also the 'informer' Copin, and many of Lincoln's Jews lost everything – it all being forfeited to the king. A commission investigated the murder in 1256 and the cathedral acquired the boy's body no doubt with an eye on the pilgrimage trade.[16] 'Little' Hugh was never actually made a saint (even some Popes were sceptical) but a pilgrimage trade developed, though it seems to have faded away by the 1400s despite a mention in Chaucer.

The issue of the treatment of the Jews came to a head in 1265, when there were massacres in several English cities. In May 1265 records of debts to Jewish traders and bankers were burnt in Lincoln. Henry III took their side and in 1266 ordered compensation to be paid. Finally, in 1290, the Jews were expelled from England.

The Medieval Bishops

The main problem for the bishops from the Normans onwards was how to run such a huge diocese as Lincoln or York. Both prelates had a network of residences – so York had palaces in Nottinghamshire at Laneham, Scrooby and Southwell whilst Lincoln had Sleaford, Buckden and his own London house in the Old Temple. In both dioceses, the archdeaconries became crucial to managing vast territories, with Remigius establishing the archdeaconry of Lincoln. A Lindsey archdeaconry then also developed, eventually becoming Stow and serving the northwest of Lincolnshire. Managing a huge diocese presented many challenges both spiritual and practical; for example, Bishop Walter Coutances, who was only in post 1183-4 – was instructed to ensure that a suitable deputy was provided for rectors who had leprosy and caused 'grave scandal' by still serving at the altar.[17] More typically Bishop Alexander of Lincoln, 1123-48, had to instruct the

---

14   Philippa Hoskin, *Robert Grosseteste and the 13th Century Diocese of Lincoln*, Leiden, 2019, p.156
15   The name derives from Laxton in Nottinghamshire.
16   The Dean and Sir Joseph Banks investigated the tomb in 1791 and found a 3ft 3in skeleton.
17   Owen (1971), p.24

Archdeacon of Lincoln to investigate a complaint from Markby that the priest at Bilsby was the illegitimate son of another priest and had got the Bilsby post through fraud. Some bishops also exercised some quality control on the ministry such as incumbents' literacy – in 1274 the new man at Bicker was told to employ an assistant who could help him with reading. A persistent theme was the need for discipline – Richard Fleming having to forbid Sunday trading on feast days at Holbeach, Sempringham and Marsh Chapel.

Over this 500-year period, the most common system was to maintain standards by 'visitation' – which required bishops to be fit enough to travel. Bishops found missing church fabric and charities being neglected, as well as handling moral offences such as adultery and slander. Both dioceses were huge, so bishops gathered a coterie of officials by the 1200s who tended to become widely hated. Thus, the archdeacons of Nottingham and Lincoln became powerful figures, exacting promises by the churchwardens to keep churches in good condition. The growth of archdeaconry courts then proved lucrative and influential, so it is unsurprising that bishops sometimes faced conflict. So, networks of well-paid officials then surrounded the Church, diluting its focus on the Gospel.

Amongst the bishops, we ought to mention firstly a persistent tradition that Adrian IV, the only Englishman to have been Pope, was curate or Rector at the Lincolnshire parish of Tydd St Mary. Probably known first as Nicholas Breakspear, he seems most likely to have come from St Albans, but he spent most of his career outside England before becoming Pope in 1154. If he held a living at Tydd it may not mean that he ever visited it. Early authors such as Camden accepted the story, but recently it has achieved less credibility. As Archdeacon Trollope wrote in 1871, 'It is painful to contradict a pleasant tradition connected with one's county', yet one must declare this one unlikely and for the future Pope to have been an absent placeholder at best.

A continual problem for the Church was how to ensure that its great leaders – supposedly the bishops – were men of God rather than politicians or administrators. The diocese of Lincoln, being so huge and conferring such power, had a constant problem with this with Robert Bloet, who became bishop in 1094, having risen through royal connections as the chaplain to William I and the chancellor to William II. Indeed, in his rise through politics before the Church he had been married, and later made his son Dean of Lincoln. William of Malmesbury, not an entirely unbiased chronicler, saw him as an administrator and not a churchman who was able to build up the cathedral's finances through vineyards and tolls from Stow Fair. In 1102 Bloet led the siege of Tickhill Castle on behalf of the king. He founded the hospital of the Holy Sepulchre in Lincoln, but this may have been with a mind to his eternal destination. He fell out of favour with Henry I and became embroiled in ruinous lawsuits before dying in 1123.[18] His death was sudden: out hunting, he collapsed into the king's arms and died without absolution – which the chroniclers took as a sign of his ultimate destination.

Geoffrey Plantagenet, Archdeacon of Lincoln by the age of about twenty and bishop from 1173, was not even a priest until 1189 – he just happened to be the king's illegitimate son and enjoyed the diocesan revenues. He was the king's choice, but the Pope hesitated to make one so young (and not ordained) a bishop. Mixing diocesan business with warfare,

---

18   Dorothy Owen, *Robert Bloet*, in *ODNB*.

in 1182 the Pope began to put pressure on him to become a priest and be consecrated as bishop or to resign his post. Geoffrey refused this course and resigned his diocese. In 1189 King Richard pushed him into the post of Archbishop of York, perhaps as a lever to make him become a priest and thus cease to be a rival for the throne. He was ordained at Southwell in September 1189 by his own suffragan bishop, going on to have a tempestuous period at York. He is a good example of how the Church had become the plaything of the powerful – but this was not always to be the case.

Hugh of Avalon (c1140-1200)

Hugh was born in south-east France and, in keeping with his parents' habits, decided from an early age that he was going to be for God and against the Devil. Although stories that he was ordained by the age of ten are unlikely, he was a monk by fifteen and a parish priest by twenty. During this period, he was pursued by an amorous woman and took refuge in the Grande Chartreuse monastery.

Hugh came to England to run a monastery in Somerset called Witham – not connected with the place or river in Lincolnshire. He had been recommended to Henry II, and the two men were to share much time and debate in succeeding years. At Witham, he showed an early commitment to helping the poor and unfortunate, and to standing up to the greedy and rapacious. Possessing considerable personal charm, he was able to challenge King Henry who was diverting Church money into his own coffers. Nonetheless, the king favoured Hugh and wanted him to be a bishop, but it took the prior of Grande Chartreuse's best efforts to persuade Hugh. Even then, he insisted on a free election by the Lincoln canons – he did not like the king having too much influence.

When he became the bishop of Lincoln in 1186 Hugh showed equal zeal for opposing corruption within the church. The Archdeacon of Canterbury performed the ceremony and demanded the customary gift of a horse; Hugh offered no more for the ceremony than he had paid for his mitre – which was of the simplest kind. As a Frenchman knowing little of England, he chose suitable assistants such as Master Roger of Rolleston (presumably in Nottinghamshire) who later would later become Dean of Lincoln. As bishop, he showed a strong focus on pastoral care and the regulation of the clergy whom he wished to be resident in their parishes.

When Hugh came to Lincoln as bishop in 1186, he planned to visit all the properties connected with his new role, including the bishop's manor at Stow. Hugh would have known that Stow was seen as where St Etheldreda was said to have stopped overnight and planted her ash wood staff into the ground, from which sprung a miraculous tree; perhaps Hugh believed this to be the literal truth, or he might have seen in it a story of the planting of the Church into a new area. However, he was warned that the palace moat had been invaded by a huge and vicious swan which had driven away all the other birds, and that no-one dared act against. The servants caught the beast and brought it to him, but instead of ordering it to be roasted he fed it on bread, and it became his devoted friend – even cuddling up to him. The swan stayed at Stow when Hugh was away and seemed to know when he was coming back by its excited flapping. When he slept there, it would guard him zealously and was known to nip the legs of chaplains who annoyed him. After he died it remained on the pond, sad and lonely.

Hugh was involved in several miraculous events during his life. In 1199 he was passing through the town of Cheshunt when people brought to his attention the case of Roger Colhoppe, a sailor who had become mad and violent. The bishop dismounted his horse, blessed some water with his sacramental ring, and gave it to Roger to drink. Hugh then read the first verses of the Gospel of St John and the sailor went peacefully to sleep; when he awoke, his mind was clear and he was cured.

Hugh's behaviour was not always so moral. When he visited the tomb of St Mary Magdalene in France, he appeared to be praying close to her remains – until the monks who were guarding it realised he had bitten off two pieces of her arm to take home with him!

Passing through Alconbury, Hugh was told about a dying one-year-old child who had swallowed a piece of decorative ironwork. Hugh placed his fingers on the child's throat and gave his blessing and on the following Sabbath the child coughed up the piece of metal which was kept as a relic of the saintly churchman. His journeys were not always entirely safe – whilst passing through the Holland part of his diocese he was attacked by a 'ruffian' with a sword but saved by his cousin William who pulled the sword from the man's hands.

On another occasion in 1194 Hugh was at Buckden, where he had a house, and was celebrating Mass. A clerk in the congregation saw a male child 'of supernatural brilliance and whiteness beyond man's imagination' as Hugh elevated the Host. Now, this clerk was not there by chance since he had arrived from Oxford having heard a heavenly voice tell him to go to Hugh and instruct him to – in turn – 'admonish earnestly' the archbishop to reform the abuses that were going on in the Church. Although there was plenty of nepotism in appointments and a good few priests guilty of some carnal sins, the clerk had hesitated to make the journey – until successive voices came to him urging on the task.

Hugh was not afraid of trouble whether with an archbishop or a king; Francis Hill called him 'a strong-minded man of great courage'.[19] He often admonished Henry II and also Richard I, and he was shocked to discover that Henry's mistress 'Fair' Rosamond had been buried close to the altar at Godstow – so he had her moved. The forest laws were a source of much anguish for the poor and Hugh had a famously fractious relationship with the royal foresters. Hugh, calling them 'keepers', famously barred them from the king's room by saying 'Keepers, keep out' and when the king himself muttered at this Hugh replied, 'This saying concerns you too, for when the poor whom these men oppress are let into paradise, you will stand outside with the keepers'. Hugh even excommunicated foresters who mistreated his clergy including the chief forester; this caused a dispute with the king, but Hugh was able to use his wit and humour to defuse the crisis.

Hugh was also a famous defender of the Jews, who were widely persecuted. In 1189

---

19   Hill (1948), p.110

he intervened in a situation in Stamford where Jews were being persecuted, probably following the death of a man, and this was at some risk to himself. There was a similar anti-Jewish riot in Lincoln, where Hugh again intervened.

Hugh personally worked hard on building the cathedral from 1192 which continued until at least 1200. He made extensive alterations, repairing the earthquake damages and extended it eastwards. The choir, transepts and part of the nave all featured his own manual efforts. A hod which he had carried was said to have cured a cripple.

The cathedral was seen as a beacon of God's light in a dark world, and Hugh wanted to keep it that way. One story explained that he worked and prayed to invite the Holy Spirit into the building, while the Dean laboured to keep the Devil *out*. The famous story of the Lincoln Imp and his friend the Wind connects to this time; of course it is still windy around the cathedral to this day, and those in the know understand this is the Imp's patient friend – still stirring things up and trying to get in.

One of the finishing touches on the northern pinnacle of the west front was a statue of a swinesherd playing his pipes. The huge building project was always short of money as the people of the diocese laboured to match the project's needs, and Hugh was grateful for all he could receive. A young swinesherd of Stow kept a few of his coins to give to the bishop and Hugh, mindful of Biblical principles about widows and mites, ordered the statue to be put up to show his gratitude.

In 1200 when he lay dying on his bed in London, Hugh uttered a chastening prophecy on the sons of Queen Eleanor, who he labelled an adulteress. He condemned her for having left her lawful French husband to take on an unlawful English one, Henry II, and that all four of their sons would be wiped out at the hands of King Philip of France 'as an ox plucks out grass by the roots'. Indeed, already three had died.

The dying bishop confessed that 'my evil acts are completely evil, but my good actions are not entirely so'. Dressed in a hair shirt he knelt and waited for his death, praying to the last that 'it is joy to possess [God]; whoever receives him and trusts in him is strong and secure'. As he lay dying, even King John visited him – it was even reported that the wily reprobate was distressed, but Hugh saw little reason to waste his dying words on such a man. Hugh then gave instructions about his burial – including that he should be buried in the simple vestments he wore at his consecration. After he died his corpse was disembowelled on the instruction of the doctors since it would take several days to carry to Lincoln.

The body was then carried from town to town, the first leg being from London to Hertford, accompanied always with candles. There are a large number of miracle stories associated with Hugh's death, which we can consider here without passing judgement for the assumed fact of the stories cemented Hugh's position as Lincoln's greatest saint. It was said that the continuing flame of the candles was itself miraculous. Great crowds gathered at Biggleswade and many who were there heard a sudden crack as the crush caused a break in the arm of a poor man, Bernard. No doctors were available, so the man was taken home in agony but during the night Hugh appeared to him and the arm was healed. Two nights later a tailor of

Stamford who had led a holy and devoted life asked for permission to touch the coffin; he was allowed, and then prayed that God would take his soul to heaven – that night he died. Also, on the journey to Lincoln, a knight's cancerous arm was cured.[20]

The last overnight stop was at Ancaster the next day at the foot of Steep Hill in Lincoln gathered there was the most significant assembly the city ever saw. The kings of England and Scotland both asked to carry the coffin, though the latter was overcome with grief. Three archbishops and sundry other bishops and nobles were also in attendance. The city's Jews came out to mark the passing of their great protector.

When Hugh was laid out in the cathedral, some noticed the unusual whiteness of his skin with just a touch of red, as though he were asleep and not just a corpse. A cry went up that a blind woman had recovered her sight, and clergy were sent to verify the facts. The huge crowd attracted criminals as well as the faithful, and one of these took the chance to steal a woman's purse; he was found a few minutes later, wandering around unable to see, holding up the purse and sobbing that he had stolen it and been struck blind by Hugh. The purse was returned to its owner and that instance sight was returned to the blind thief.

There then followed a series of miracles. A blind man, Simon, who used to stumble around knocking against logs and stones was cured at the tomb one Whitsun, and was afterwards kept in the Dean's house for two years; an oddity of this case was that after his cure the man did not recognise the sound of voices previously known to him. A crippled woman named Mary was brought to the tomb in a basket, where she fell asleep and spent the whole night there. In the morning she woke in agony – she could hear her bones cracking and feel her muscles being stretched as her bent and twisted legs came back to life. A young man afflicted with paralysis who had lived in a hut in St Mary's churchyard in front of the precentor's door was cured at Hugh's tomb – perhaps to the relief of the precentor! A mad girl of Wigford was cured and a dumb boy from the same suburb was able to speak. Many other cures of madness, dropsy and even cancer were reported, including a cure for one of the Knights Templar.

The campaign to have Hugh declared a saint started from almost before he died, but the next local saint was actually St Gilbert of Sempringham, who was canonised in 1202. Then England became too deeply enmired in the complex affairs of King John but those in Lincoln kept a record of the miraculous cures that seemed to result from visits to Hugh's tomb. Gerald of Wales and Adam of Eynsham wrote biographies of Hugh and the latter gave a personal testimony to a commission set up by the Pope in 1219. They logged a number of miracles during Hugh's life and 29 that had occurred at his tomb.

Hugh was declared a saint in 1220 with his feast on 17 November; he had died in the evening of 16 November so for Church purposes this counted as the next day. In 1280 two new shrines were built for Hugh's head and body within the Angel Choir. King Edward I and Queen Eleanor were in attendance as the remnants were placed into a shrine so decorative as hardly to have met Hugh's tastes in life. The head had come away from the torso hence it was placed in a separate casket, being credited with 'sweating wonder-working oils'. At some point a tooth became separate from the head.

---

20   Joseph Clayton, *St Hugh of Lincoln*, London, 1923, p.234, discusses the sources for several legends.

The jewelled reliquary casket for the head was one of Lincoln's greatest treasures and twice a year it was paraded through the streets to celebrate the life of its greatest bishop even though he was a Frenchman by birth. This produced one of the most famous stories about Hugh. In 1364 thieves had watched as the precious reliquary had been returned to the cathedral, and they had perhaps hidden inside to await their chance. Then, in the darkness, they took it – and escaped across the fields to avoid being seen on the highways. Although details of the legend are unclear, somehow the thieves left the head and it remained to offer a clue to the pursuers as to where to follow. So precious was Hugh's head, and so well respected by man and beast (except the robbers) that when it was found it was being guarded by ravens. Although Hugh was known to have been very merciful in his lifetime, his devotees were not so kind – and when they tracked down the thieves, they hung them all.

Stephen Langton (c1150-1228) is important as one of the Lincolnshire men who rose to great eminence – becoming both a cardinal and Archbishop of Canterbury. He was probably born to prosperous farming stock at Langton by Wragby and was noted for his early academic career. Having spent much of his time in Paris, he was consecrated archbishop in 1207 despite the opposition of King John but 'was troublesome to king and pope alike.[21]' John tried to place Hugh, Archdeacon of Wells, as bishop of Lincoln in 1209, but he aligned himself with Langton and was dismissed. Langton was a leading figure amongst the barons' opposition to King John leading up to Magna Carta in 1215, when the reinstated Bishop Hugh of Wells was also present,[22] then fell out with the Pope and was suspended from office until 1218. Langton spent the first half of his time as archbishop in exile but is widely credited with having divided the Bible into chapters.[23] This perhaps makes him one of the most influential persons ever to hail from Lincolnshire. His younger brother Simon Langton was elected Archbishop of York in 1215 but this was blocked by the Pope, so he joined Prince Louis of France in an invasion of England, for which he was excommunicated for a time. Instead, he became Archdeacon of Canterbury in 1227 – alongside his brother who died within a few months. How curious it might have been had two Lincolnshire brothers held both archdioceses.

Robert Grosseteste

One of the best-known early bishops of Lincoln was Robert Grosseteste (c1170-1253) who followed a path from humble origins in Suffolk to being a powerful prince of the Church. In the 1180s he was a member of Hugh of Avalon's household. It is likely his route was aided by a Lincoln man, Adam of Wigford who put him to school in the city and then sent him to Cambridge. For twenty years or more he performed obscure tasks for the Bishop of Hereford, but he was far from idle, for Hereford seems to have been a centre of scientific study and Grosseteste wrote a series of works on astronomy, astrology

21   Maurice Powicke, *Christian Life in the Middle Ages*, Oxford, 1935, p.131
22   He was given the task of publishing the Charter at Bedford and Oxford. Hill, p.198
23   Powicke (1935), p.136

and chronology. This period culminated in one of his greatest works, a commentary on Aristotle's *Posterior Analytics*. He perhaps studied in Paris for a while.

From about 1222 Grosseteste came into contact with the young Henry III, who according to some sources urged him to write about theology. He seems to have made attempts to learn Greek properly and to read the works of the early fathers of the Church. In 1225 the bishop of Lincoln, Hugh of Wells, found him a place in the diocese as rector of Abbotsley in Huntingdonshire, and he began to lecture at Oxford. From about this date he wrote increasingly on theology though maintaining an interest in mathematics. By 1229 he was archdeacon of Leicester, which was in the Lincoln diocese, but by 1231 had decided as a matter of conscience to hold only one benefice in order to care properly for souls. He now knew the perils of wealth – 'how many pricking thorns there are in riches, how many occasions riches offer for sinning'.[24]

By 1231 he was a man with prospects, but he decided to abandon his ecclesiastical and academic careers to become 'lector' to a community of Franciscan friars, probably prompted by a sermon on academic pride.[25] For the next four years he wrote theological books and also another scientific work, but he could also be harsh – as archdeacon of Leicester he advocated persecution of the Jews but not their execution.

In 1235 the Lincoln cathedral canons rather surprisingly chose Grosseteste to be their next bishop. This was a job well within his intellectual reach, and he seems to have used his manor at Liddington in Rutland as a base for his small army of academic translators. Yet his main concern was with the pastoral care of his 2000 parishes, which he toured with a small group of friars, and in which he seems to have been influenced by the work of the Lateran Council of 1215 who emphasised a new focus on individual salvation as the key work of parish clergy.[26]

Grosseteste was supported by the brothers Adam and Robert Marsh. Despite being mainly based in Oxford, Adam was a close adviser on the subject of diocesan pastoral care, helping him to find suitable friars to work in the parishes where he was troubled by absentee clergy. He provided intelligence on individual characters, such as a clergyman who had several children hidden away, often gleaned from fellow Franciscans.

From his surviving letters we can gain insight into his chief concerns as a bishop. In one of the first letters, written in 1235, he lambasted a monk who had presented an unsuitable candidate for a parish living: 'a deacon without the tonsure…wearing clothes of scarlet and rings on his fingers, in dress and behaviour a layman, or rather a knight and, as far as could be gathered from his answers, practically illiterate….who by his behaviour and clothing reveals himself to be more likely to kill souls than cure them'.[27] He refused to appoint priests who had too little learning, deposed seven abbots (including Bardney) and four priors, and condemned licentiousness such as 'the Feast of Fools'. His checks on whether nuns were pregnant scandalised Matthew Paris the chronicler. He also gained a reputation for never passing a dead body in a ditch without ensuring it had a full burial in

24   Hoskin (2019), p.93
25   R W Southern, *Robert Grosseteste*, in ODNB, accessed 29/4/14.
26   Hoskin (2019) , p.4
27   Robert Grosseteste letter to Michael Belet, c. April 1235.

consecrated ground. He told the Pope how he spent his first year as bishop:
'I began to perambulate my bishopric, archdeaconry by archdeaconry, and rural deanery by rural deanery, requiring the clergy of each deanery to bring their people to have their children confirmed, to hear the word of God, and to make their confessions.'[28]

Grosseteste himself then preached to the clergy whilst a friar or minor canon preached to the laity. Before setting out he wrote to his archdeacons telling them to gather the clergy in one place in each deanery: 'I shall preach God's word to them and instruct them as to how they are to teach the people'.[29] He also made unusually strong use of the friars, who he saw as a means of enhancing pastoral care and preaching in the parishes.[30] In 1243-4 he used his archdeacons to censure parish clergy who tried to stop the friars preaching.

In 1236 he sent out a lengthy letter warning priests against errors and abuses such as drinking wine, sharing houses with women, and playing games for prizes – which he said was akin to demon-worship. But his concerns were also practical and pastoral – he instructed his priests to warn mothers against the suffocation risks of sleeping with a baby in the bed; his statutes for clergy also stipulated visiting the sick. In 1236 he wrote to his clergy to warn them against 'making of the house of God a house of merchandise' – having heard that markets were being held in churchyards. His concerns extended to behaviour in the religious houses and the same year he intervened at Kyme Priory to ensure the appointment of a suitable prior; he told Philip of Kyme that being secular patron of Kyme Priory did not give him the right to choose its head. Then he banned celebration of the 'feast of fools' at Thorney and Lincoln – indeed, everywhere – for 'profaning with diabolical inventions a place dedicated to God'. In 1239 he banned drinking festivals called 'church ales'. Disputes with the Dean of Lincoln led to the latter's suspension in 1239.

He reinforced his wishes through regular preaching tours and visitations, starting in 1239, making circuits by rural deanery. He was concerned about his own responsibilities and pursued the visitations 'lest the blood of my sheep is looked for on my hands at the Last Judgement'. His constant activity led the chronicler Matthew Paris to comment that he was a man 'to whom quiet is a thing unknown'.

Several times he rejected unsuitable men who were presented for benefices at a time when clerical status could be somewhat fluid; for example at Healing the advowson was in the hands of a family who seemingly presented one of their own sons, Richard, who enjoyed its income before taking up as a knight.[31] At Rand in 1238 he objected to the presentation of the patron's son as being too young and not suitably ordained.

Grosseteste also became involved in national politics, being one of a committee attempting to manage the erratic king in 1244. His role in national politics was made more complex by his close relationship with Simon de Montfort, which seems to have begun while he was Archdeacon of Leicester. He was tutor to two of de Montfort's sons and personal

---

28 R W Southern, *Robert Grosseteste*, in ODNB, accessed 27 July 2014, drawing on the Chronicles of Matthew Paris.
29 Robert Grosseteste, letter to Robert Hayles, 1236.
30 Hoskin (2019), p.104
31 Hoskin (2019), p.167

confessor to him and his wife; Adam Marsh was also part of this circle. De Montfort led a rebellion against the King in 1258, just after Grosseteste had died, but it was defeated in 1265; some of his followers hid out in Ely where in 1267 they cited 'St Robert' as one of their key influences.[32] Grosseteste's influence on de Montfort in areas like the law, specifically justice and mercy, and theology is well attested. One of de Montfort's early supporters had been John de Crakehall, who had been Grosseteste's steward at Lincoln. One of the miracles attributed to Grosseteste concerned a prophecy of de Montfort's death. Richard of Gravesend, bishop of Lincoln from 1258 to 1279, had formerly been Dean of Lincoln and was also a close associate of Grosseteste's; from 1265-7 he was suspended and in exile due to his closeness with de Montfort. Thus, Grosseteste came to be seen as supporting 'natural law' and liberty, but also hierarchy and obligation, which were fundamental to the de Montfort rebellion; but Grosseteste's main focus was on how such matters helped or impeded the saving of souls.

Grosseteste could be dogmatic and principled, sometimes both at once. He supported the papacy, but not when it conflicted with other principles. He objected to anyone who sought to use influence to appoint unsuitable priests to his benefices, which included aristocrats, other bishops and the pope. In 1245 he attempted to stop members of the Lincoln Chapter doing this by going to the Pope, Innocent IV, to insist on his right to visit the Dean and Chapter. By 1250 his concern was that it was the papal curia who were doing this by trying to appoint a nephew to a Lincoln prebend which had the care of souls and thereby was risking the souls of his people. He told a friend that giving such a job to such a man would risk condemning his own soul to hellfire.[33]

Thus the claim that he 'spared nothing in his determination to free the English church from the exactions of the papal court'.[34] In an extraordinary presentation lasting several days in 1250, Grosseteste effectively surveyed the state of the Catholic Church and found it corrupt – though he blamed the curia and not the pope. Christianity was in decline, he argued. It has been suggested that Grosseteste had a sense of the smallness and fragility of Christendom at this time, which was to be put to test from the south east in the next centuries. Innocent IV effectively rejected his arguments, sending him back to England a disappointed man.

That he was not popular with some clergy might be seen in chronicler Matthew Paris's tale of a Lincoln canon preaching against his 'tyranny'; 'if we should hold our peace the very stones would cry out,' he is reported as saying, whereupon much of the tower fell down – which would place the story in 1237. Yet he also had his lighter side: he said that the three things needed for a good life were 'food, sleep and a good joke' and once advised a depressive Dominican to take a tankard of wine 'as a penance'.

Grosseteste's death at Buckden in 1253 is an extraordinary moment in spiritual history. He asked his physician to define heresy, then supplied the answer himself:
'Heresy is an opinion chosen by human sense, contrary to Scripture, openly declared, and pertinaciously defended; and to defy the gospel by giving the care of souls to those who are inadequate either in learning or in commitment is heresy in action. Many defy the

32   Hoskin (2019), p.180
33   Hoskin (2019), p.66
34   Miss J Plumb, *Early Non-nonconformity in Lincolnshire*, unpublished Sheffield PhD

Gospel in this way, the pope most of all; and it is the duty of all faithful persons, and more particularly the Franciscans and Dominicans, to oppose such a person.'

Accounts relate that the night of his death was marked by strange bells which were heard by the bishop of London and some Franciscan monks travelling near Wantage.[35] His last words were reputed to include the prophecy, 'The Church will not be freed from her Egyptian bondage except at the point of the blood-stained sword'.

He was buried at Lincoln by the archbishop of Canterbury, where people proclaimed him a saint and oil was said to flow from his tomb, but five times the Papacy rejected this claim. Perhaps this was because he refused to appoint the Pope's nephew to a lucrative position as a prebend at his cathedral; this later gave rise to a story in which the spectral Grosseteste appeared to Innocent IV to confront him with having ordered Henry III to throw his bones out of the cathedral and prompt a conviction of his sin.[36] Grosseteste's legacy was championed by his friend Adam Marsh, who in 1259 was urging the Archbishop of York to live up to Grosseteste's principles.[37]

His stand on the issue of the pope, absentee clergy, preaching and corruption led John Wyclif, a hundred years later, to point to Grosseteste as a founder of the English Reformation in that he began the challenge to papal authority. 'John Wyclif grew to admire Grosseteste above all other writers of the more recent centuries' and also 'quoted from him frequently and at length, always with approbation'.[38] He became a popular author for Wyclif's supporters, the Lollards. As early as 1267 he was cited by the rebels in Ely who said they upheld the faith but not the 'desires and will' of those who governed the Church. John Foxe also saw in him a forelight of reformation and he shared an ambition with the puritans to have resident parish clergy. However, another biographer concludes that he would have had 'little sympathy' for Wyclif's views, for his campaign was against abuse of the papal system, not the Papacy itself; indeed much of Grosseteste's anxiety was around the King encroaching into Church affairs although he did object to tyrannical behaviour by the Archbishop of Canterbury in 1250.[39] However, he is also noteworthy as a man who combined the highest scholarship with a focus on pastoral care for the ordinary people. Matthew Paris summarised him as 'an open critic of the pope and king, a censurer of prelates, a corrector of monks, a director of priests, a teacher of the clergy, a supporter of scholars, a preacher to the people….'

Efforts by Adam Marsh and a later bishop, Oliver de Sutton, in 1288 and at other times to have him canonised were fruitless. A critic of governance by both King and Church, there would have been many who were uncomfortable with his legacy alongside which was the issue of his posthumous association with the de Montfort rebellion albeit this was influenced by his ideas of natural law, justice and mercy. A young man who was dumb had undertaken a pilgrimage to Grosseteste's tomb at Lincoln; he suddenly started speaking, telling his parents that there was no reason to stay there praying as 'Robert' had left for Evesham, where 'his brother' Simon de Montfort was to die the next Tuesday – as he did

---

35   The chronicler Matthew Paris records these stories – both parties were travelling towards Buckden.
36   Philippa Hoskin, *Robert Grosseteste and the 13th Century Diocese of Lincoln*, 2019, p.14
37   Hoskin (2019), p.108
38   Robert McEvoy, *Robert Grosseteste*, Oxford, 2000, p.69
39   Hoskin (2019), p.192

in the Battle of Evesham. Grosseteste was also attributed a prophecy about the fate of de Montfort's oldest son.

Some Other Bishops

Oliver de Sutton, the Bishop of Lincoln who conducted the funeral of Queen Eleanor in 1290, was from Sutton-on-Trent and his mother was probably of the notable Laxton family that also produced Stephen Lexington, who became Abbot of Clairvaux in 1243 and Henry of Lexington, Oliver's uncle, who was Dean and then bishop of Lincoln. Oliver became Dean of Lincoln in 1275 and Bishop in 1280, a role in which he excelled. His biographer John de Schalby wrote that 'I cannot deny that he was a man most just, most steadfast and most pure'. The *ODNB* concludes that he was 'an excellent bishop – just, conscientious and deeply devoted to his diocese'. He was very caring towards his clergy and travelled constantly through his diocese. He died in 1299 at Nettleham, with his clergy singing matins around him.

John Dalderby came from a Lincolnshire family – Dalderby is near Horncastle – and became Bishop of Lincoln in 1300 after Oliver de Sutton. At first described as 'a sweet and gentle boy' he was later praised as 'a bright gem of knowledge' by John de Schalby[40]. He was the last bishop of Lincoln to be freely elected by the Chapter of the cathedral. He was noted for his focus on parish clergy, desiring that they should cater for the needs of their parishes, and also for his efforts to complete the great tower of the cathedral. After he died at Stow Park in 1320, a number of miracles were reported in the cathedral in 1322 and 1324 amongst pilgrims to his tomb though efforts in 1326-7 to have him canonised were a failure despite the Dean and Chapter commissioning two 'canonists' to argue the case at Avignon - supported by letters from Edward III and sixteen earls. However, a shrine developed at the cathedral and became a place of pilgrimage. Dalderby himself had failed to get Grosseteste canonised. The Chapter elected their Dean Anthony Bek as Dalderby's replacement in 1320, but he was supplanted by 29-year-old Henry Burghersh at royal command and after the new bishop's uncle and had made a substantial payment to the Pope in Avignon[41].

As an aside and also from this medieval period, we can mention William of Gainsborough (c1260-1307), assumed to have been born in that town about 1260 as he later tried to defend some of its citizens. He became bishop of Worcester.

Another who tried to bring the Lincoln diocese to order was **William of Alnwick** (d.1449), bishop from 1436, whose extensive visitations were conducted at a 'breathless' pace.[42] In his previous diocese of Norwich he had been active in persecuting Lollards, followers of Wyclif's teachings, who we will discuss below. In 1439-40 he was very active resolving the disputes amongst cathedral clergy stimulated by the behaviour of the notorious Dean Mackworth. He was described as 'hard-headed and unyielding' and resented by colleagues at Lincoln for being very tight with money.

---

40 Angelo Silvestri, *Power, Politics and Episcopal Authority in Cremona and Lincoln*, Newcastle, 2015, p.219
41 Silvestri (2015), p.255
42 Dorothy Owen (1971), p.20

Richard Foxe (1448-1528), who enjoyed a starry career as bishop on several sees, was born at Ropsley near Grantham and marked his origins by adding to the endowment of the grammar school there. He sided with Henry Tudor before Bosworth, and thereafter enjoyed royal favour in secular and religious government. His career as bishop of four dioceses was largely a way of financing his political work, which included arranging the marriage of Prince Arthur and Catherine of Aragon. He founded Corpus Christi College in Oxford. Politician-bishops like Foxe might fill an entire chapter for us, but amongst several examples Simon Islip is perhaps worth a mention as he became Archbishop of Canterbury in 1349 after holding livings at Easton, near Stamford, and Horncastle.

One of the last great figures of this era was **William Waynflete** (c1398-1486), who was actually born William Patten but took the name of his home-town of Wainfleet as clerics often did. Waynflete enjoyed an impressive career as an educationalist, bishop and politician having won the support of Henry VI. He became Bishop of Winchester in 1447 largely at the king's behest. Has education career included a role as headmaster of Winchester in 1430, involvement at Eton and King's College Cambridge, and founding several schools or colleges of his own including Magdalen College and its attached school in Oxford and a grammar school in his own home town; this was in existence in 1466 and the buildings were erected probably in the 1480s. Waynflete also supported Ralph, Lord Cromwell, in creating a college at Tattershall which educated the choir and the sons of the tenants for free; this had a charter in 1440 and Waynflete helped draw up the statutes in the 1450s before Cromwell's death in 1456. Amongst these 'political-bishops' we might also mention Thomas Rotherham (1423-1500), whose career included both Lincoln and York, another who tried to ride the tide of intrigue and plot around the Royal succession.

Waynflete became Lord Chancellor in 1456, a time of great complexity in national politics exacerbated by Henry VI's varying insanity. He was seen as a loyal Lancastrian at a time of Yorkist turbulence, leading to his resigning this post in 146-0. But despite his interest in education, he was not progressive in theology: fellows of Eton College had to deny Lollard views.

So, from this selection emerges a wide mixture of saintly men and worldly politicians, the diocese of Lincoln's leadership seemingly veering between God and Mammon and back again. Nottinghamshire continued to have a lesser focus, a backwater of York policed by an archdeacon in Nottingham. Thurstan was recorded as Archdeacon in 1121. The post was sometimes a stepping-stone to greater roles, as with John de Grandison who went on to become Bishop of Exeter, but the county's main links with greatness came with the Archbishop's visits to the palaces at Scrooby, Laneham and Southwell.

The Crusades

The era of the Crusades stretched from 1095 to 1270 as Christianity contended with Islam for control of the holy sites.

During the third crusade, Elias de Amundeville received great help from the brethren of St Lazarus so on his return he founded a hospital at Carlton-le- Moorland. For the third crusade, people gathered at Stamford in 1189, when Jewish merchants were attacked. Guy de Craon, who had lands in North Holland, accompanied Richard I, but died in the Holy Land. William, son of Walter of Metheringham, stopped at Deeping on his way to the Holy Land and granted lands to the priory of Stixwould.

The siege of Acre (1189-91) saw the death of at least eleven Lincolnshire knights including Walter of Kyme and Walter of Ros. A heraldic metal cup, including the Lincolnshire arms, appears to have been made during the siege.[43] According to local tradition, the Nottingham inn *The Olde Trip to Jerusalem* dates from the late 1100s and was where men gathered before setting off. There are also claims that marks in the south door of Worksop Priory reflect crusader knights making crosses in the soft stone before their departure.

Owen[44] gives a list of some of the men of Holland who at least took the cross, but it appears from this that many were too poor to make the journey. Richard of Algarkirk claimed to have been to Jerusalem, but there was no proof. Hubert of Surfleet appeared only to have got to Lombardy. Even wealthy men like William of Stallingborough had to raise finance by leasing their property.

Gerard de Furnival of Worksop made his name as a knight under King John and became a crusader and set off for Jerusalem; he died in Palestine in 1219. However, his body did not rest in the Holy Land – it was brought back to be buried in Normandy. Two of his sons also went to Palestine and Thomas de Furnival died in battle there in 1228. His younger brother, also called Gerard, had Thomas buried and then returned home. Their mother, Maud, was very distressed about Thomas being buried in a heathen land and it seems sent her younger son straight back to the Holy Land. Thomas was dug up and brought back home, where he was buried on the north side of the Priory church at Worksop wearing a helmet 'richly adorned with gems'. A tomb was erected, described as 'a noble carbuncle'.

William de Forz, a knight who led a complicated life, lost his castle at Bytham and promised to make the crusade to make up for his errors. He eventually left in 1242 – but died at sea on the way.

Sir William Neville, constable of Nottingham Castle and justice of the forest, went on the Crusades to Tunis in 1390 followed by a pilgrimage in 1391 when he died, and was buried at what became the Arap mosque in Istanbul. He was buried in a close position with Sir John Clanvowe, causing some speculation about their relationship.

Another non-Christian frontier was in eastern Europe, where paganism still held sway in the late 1300s. In 1390 Henry of Derby, the son of John of Gaunt and future Henry IV, whose birthplace and main home was Bolingbroke, originally planned to take a Crusade to Tunisia, but instead, organised a small force to join a crusade in Lithuania, sailing from Boston or Skirbeck in July 1390 and assisting in the capture of Vilnius. The Teutonic knights failed to capture the castle there, but Henry spent the winter in the company of this group and appears to have had an excellent time of it.

Ultimately the longest effect of the Crusades was to encourage the sale of indulgences

43   L J Whatley (ed), *The Crusades and Visual Culture*, p.79
44   Dorothy Owen, *Church and Society in Medieval Lincolnshire*, Lincoln, 1971

through the practice of funding others to 'take the Cross' on your own behalf. Indulgences were effectively pardons by which people assumed they would gain entry to Heaven and were open to corruption; in the early 1200s a Lincolnshire man, accused of illegally taking control of some land, opted to take the Cross – but then escaped this task by paying money to the Dean of Lincoln.[45] The same approach could then be used for other purposes, for example, the building of a new choir at Southwell, which could be funded by granting indulgences to those who have funds.

Monasteries

The century after the Norman conquest saw a new generation of monastic houses being established or re-established, mostly as foundations by gentry with an eye on their eternal destination. Perhaps the only substantial monastic house certainly still extant in either county when the Normans arrived was Crowland,[46] with even Barrow having suffered once it was placed under the control of Peterborough in 971.[47] Yet between the 12th and 14th centuries there were fourteen monasteries or friaries and two nunneries established in Nottinghamshire and perhaps ninety in Lincolnshire. In Nottinghamshire, they were mainly in the north of the county, perhaps because they were gifted less populated land around Sherwood, and only Broadholme was east of the Trent. Blyth Priory was the first in Nottinghamshire, founded in 1088 close to the Great North Road but reputedly the place where ill-disciplined French monks were sent to repent.

When the Normans conquered England, they brought a new group of landowners who had grown rich on violence. As they faced old age, some of these began to reflect on their eternal destination and paid for chantry chapels and monasteries so that monks would pray for their souls. In Lincolnshire, monastic cells were soon set up at Covenham, Haugham and at South Kelsey,[48] later also Hurst in Axholme and others. The abbey of Bardney was refounded in 1087 by Gilbert of Ghent with the support of Remigius, who was attracted to it by its prominence in the works of Bede.[49] Bardney supposedly still had the head of Saint Oswald and attributed miraculous powers to it 'with a view of drawing superstitious pilgrims to their house.....to sanction the imposture, for deception and falsehood are inseparable, they pretended it was incorruptible and had remained sound for centuries'.[50] They also had a large mound, surmounted by a cross, and claimed as the tomb of King Æthelred though no relics remained of him or Saint Werburga of Mercia.

Crowland was destroyed by fire in 1091 and then rebuilt. Meanwhile, attempts were made to revive the monastery at Stow by transferring monks from Eynsham in the 1090s; however, as soon as Remigius died, his successor Bloet sent them back there and Stow

45   C Tyerman, *The Invention of the Crusades*, Basingstoke, 1998, p.59
46   Although it burnt down in 1091, following which the monks faked a number of charters of their legal rights.
47   Sawyer, p.150. Alkborough, Stow and Spalding may also have still been active with the latter two closing soon after.
48   Owen (1971), p.47
49   Sawyer, p.145
50   T Allen, *History of the County of Lincoln*, Leeds, 1830

became principally the bishop's manor. Partney was refounded as a hospital in 1115 and South Kyme in 1169. Owen says that the peak period for monastic foundations in Lincolnshire was from 1130 to 1200. At the same time new foundations for the military orders like the Templars were established.

Worksop Priory was founded in 1103 by William de Lovetot, a Norman baron. He then made sure he was buried inside the Priory as near to the high altar as possible. His son Richard gave the town to the Priory so that it could be funded from market and other revenues. It was an Augustinian house, as were Thurgarton, Shelford, Felley and Newstead – most of which were 12th century.

In Nottinghamshire, the greatest foundation was the Cluniac house at Lenton, founded in about 1109. This fitted the pattern of a foundation based on the investment of a rich man, in this case, William Peverel, who according to its charter founded it in 'an act of divine worship' and to pray for the souls of various including King William. For three hundred years the monks of Lenton fought a legal battle against the Dean and Chapter of Lichfield over estates in the Peak District. This included a fight in the churchyard at Tideswell, Derbyshire, when lambs were killed or carried off by the monks, and a proctor being stripped and killed in the churchyard at Burton on Trent in 1263 in the presence of the Prior in a fight over control of the benefice – the Prior was subsequently excommunicated. Despite this reputation, Lenton was a regular calling point for medieval kings.

Of the Augustinian houses, some were small though Thurgarton, founded around 1119, achieved fame because of Walter Hilton; less impressive perhaps was that in 1246 one of the canons was imprisoned for abusing Archbishop Wickware whilst in 1286 the Abbot was guilty of an unspecified 'grave offence'. At Felley (founded 1156, replacing a hermitage) in 1276, the Prior was deposed for assaulting one of the canons.

Apart from Lenton, the most important Nottinghamshire houses were around Sherwood. Worksop we have mentioned; Welbeck was founded in about 1140 by Thomas de Cuckney in the Premonstratensian order. In the 1170s the Abbot of Welbeck held with the foundation of Butley Priory in Suffolk, travelling to France to help with preparations, advising on the choice of Prior, and supplying some of the first canons. Houses such as Welbeck were sometimes used by local dignitaries and even the King to deposit valuables. Philip de Ulecotes left his valuables at Welbeck, but there was serious trouble in 1482 when it was found that jewels and plate had been pawned – the Abbot was removed. In 1512 it became the chief house of its order in the country.

Rufford was founded in 1146-7, and the nunnery at Wallingwells has also been dated to the mid-1100s. Broadholme also came from this period, but again we typically know little about it except when there was trouble; in about 1349 the vicar of Lea, William Fox, and two Franciscans abducted Margaret Everingham of Laxton and forced her to wear a green gown whilst in 1383 Isabella of Kent was also abducted. Newstead dates from around 1170.

The role and contribution of the monasteries have been much debated. As well as centres for the spiritual life and religious learning, they provided care for the sick and cover for the traveller. Blyth, a Benedictine house, received extra funds in 1249 to assist travellers on the Great North Road.[51] Because they were successively endowed with land by nobles concerned about their post-death destination, they also became wealthy employers and central to the local and indeed regional economy. Monks played a key role on local society and the economy as at Bridge End where they supervised the causeway but were of course variable in their behaviour. Between 1420 and 1449 there were concerns in Lincolnshire about excessive drinking. At Newhouse and Tupholme monks were known to go out drinking at night, and one of the monks had fathered a child.

Some also carried the Gospel to other lands. In about 1147 the Cistercians of Kirkstead settled a new house at Hovedo in Norway and in the next century an abbot of Hovedo, Lawrence, returned to be abbot of Kirkstead.[52]

The region also gained two notable Carthusian houses when Beauvale was founded in 1343, the last monastery in Nottinghamshire, and the Axholme Priory at Melwood in 1397-8 founded by the Earl of Nottingham. In 1422 there was an unfortunate incident when a monk of Beauvale was imprisoned at Grenoble and the Prior there asked Beauvale to pay for the damage he had caused.

The friars of various orders were later arrivals. Hugh of Wells, bishop of Lincoln in the 1220s, welcomed the Dominicans into the city. Franciscans began to arrive in Lincoln in the late 1220s.[53] Robert Grosseteste at Lincoln was a notable supporter because they emphasised preaching but found it a problem when parish clergy resigned their livings to join the friars. In order to preach, they were generally based in towns and by about 1300 most large towns had a friary – rural examples like Whaplode were rare and short-lived. The Observant Friars house at Newark was established as late as 1507 by men close to the executed William, Lord Hastings, and Henry VII; their connection to the Tudors was so close that the Tudor arms were included in the building.[54] By the Reformation there were fifteen friaries in Lincolnshire and around five in Nottinghamshire.

The Greyfriars house of the Franciscans was founded at Lincoln by Reginald Miller by about 1237. We have noted that Adam Marsh who became an Oxford Doctor of Divinity, was a Franciscan and is recorded (perhaps dubiously) as having 'wrought many miracles' before being buried at Lincoln alongside Grosseteste.[55] He was Grosseteste's greatest friend and confidant, and counsellor to Henry III. He was an adviser to the Franciscans whilst his brother Robert was also on Grosseteste's staff as his trusted assistant in the diocese when Grosseteste was away. According to the *Lanercrost Chronicle,* Adam Marsh (or de Marisco) was the only person who argued against the execution of the Jews at a time of unrest. Grosseteste and Marsh were amongst the leading intellectuals in Europe at the time, helped by Marsh's network of connections which can be appreciated now that his letters have been published; to this we can add William of Sherwood (c1200-67) who became Treasurer of Lincoln Cathedral but wrote significant works on logic and dialectics

51   Victoria County History, Nottinghamshire
52   Hill (1948), p.176
53   Hoskin (2019), p.111
54   G W Bernard, *The King's Reformation: Henry VIII and the Making of the English Church*, Yale, 2005, p.151
55   John Stevens and Sir William Dugdale, *The History of the Antient Abbeys, Monasteries, Hospitals, Cathedrals and ...*London, 1723, p.132

that impressed the famous scientist Roger Bacon who was also a Franciscan. At the same time, in the 1240s, the provincial minister of the English Franciscans was William of Nottingham, who died of plague in Genoa in 1254, whilst another leading Franciscan at that time was John of Stamford.[56] William had joined the Franciscans when they arrived in Nottingham in about 1230 and so also did his brother Augustus, whose career took him to become the bishop of the biblical church at Laodicea. Marsh had his own network of influence which included Boniface of Savoy, the Archbishop of Canterbury from 1249; Marsh died in 1259.

Confusingly, a second William of Nottingham (died c 1336) also became Provincial Master of the Franciscans in 1316. He was a noted theologian with a famous commentary on the Gospels. We might also note that Robert of Sutton, bishop of Lincoln, was a Dominican.

The friars were the evangelistic preachers of their day, often in open spaces such as the Bail in Lincoln, and the churchyard, in Grimsby.[57] Later they gained friary churches and in the later 1300s often preached in parish churches.

The monastic era left us several physical treasures and also some great works. The Prior of Worksop from 1303 was John of Tickhill who commissioned the 'Tickhill Psalter' to be illustrated by numerous artists; this volume contains 482 illustrations of the story of David and Solomon. It remained at Worksop until the Dissolution in 1539, disappeared and was rediscovered in the library of the Marquess of Lothian in the 18th century. Sadly, it is now far from home – it was bought by the New York Public Library in 1932.

The more famous Lincolnshire equivalent is the Luttrell Psalter, commissioned by Sir Geoffrey Luttrell who had estates at Irnham, and produced between about 1320 and 1345. It is remarkable for its scenes of farm and country life and may have been produced in Lincolnshire, perhaps at Lincoln or one of the county's monasteries.

On the literary side, an important figure is Walter Hilton who was born in about 1343 and is likely to have originated from the Lincoln diocese before going to Cambridge and then joining the retinue of Thomas Arundel, who was first bishop of Ely and then archbishop of York. His role seems to have been, at least in part, based around canon law.[58] This was a time of trying to turn back the 'enthusiasms' of Richard Rolle and the Lollards. After a time as a 'solitary' Hilton then went to become a canon at Thurgarton, near Southwell, in about 1386 and stayed there to his death in 1396. Although the prior of Thurgarton was authorised to investigate heresy, Hilton seems to have become more interested in ascetic and mystical theology, but he had a great interest in pastoral matters.

Hilton wrote a number of spiritual reflections, interestingly sometimes choosing Middle English rather than Latin. These included *The Scale* (or *Ladder*) *of Perfection* and *The Angels' Song*. The former was widely circulated and then printed in 1494 since when it has been constantly read. Hilton emphasised the holy life, 'when we turn from all things to God, putting His will and glory before all else, then we find that creation is given back to

56   David McItterick (ed), *The Trinity Apocalypse*, London, 2005, p.14
57   Owen (1971), p.87
58   ODNB, *Walter Hilton*

us, full of his goodness'.[59] He speaks about the renewal of God's image in man and offers practical advice on topics such as prayer and charity. In his next book, Hilton contemplated travelling through the 'luminous darkness' and he also defended the veneration of images. *Scale* became the first book in English to circulate on the continent of Europe.

It has been suggested that the near-contemporary *Cloud of Unknowing* might also have been written by Hilton, although other suggestions include a monk of Beauvale – also in Nottinghamshire. Writers have demonstrated that the two authors knew one another, and that the dialect of Middle English used in *Cloud* and *Scale* suggest origins in the north-east Midlands.[60] It is probable that the author of *Cloud* also wrote *The Book of Privy Counselling*. *Cloud* was not printed in English until 1877 but is now widely available. Both focus on the problem of 'knowing' or 'unknowing' God. Other spiritual works are also likely to have come from Beauvale such as *Speculum Vitae Humanae* in about 1390.[61] This makes Nottinghamshire something of a mystical powerhouse in the late 14th century.

Lincolnshire produced no literature on this level. A Swineshead abbot, Gilbert of Hoyland (d.1172), was a friend of St Bernard, and some sermons and writings of his have survived. Robert Manning, or Mannyng, came from Bourne; he was a canon at Sempringham from 1288 and at Sixhills in 1338, writing *Handlyng Synne* – which he addressed to the people of his home-town, and *Chronicle of England*. The former is a lively work on confession and sin, including a number of fables that are entertaining and also frightening; it is thought to have been based on a work by the intriguingly named William of Waddington, a thirteenth-century poet who wrote *Annual of the Sins*. Waddington's 1260 *Manuel des Pechez* was based on some of Grosseteste's thinking and promoted lay understanding of confession. But, as discussed later, Grosseteste at least brought a group of powerful intellectuals with him into the diocese.

Saint Gilbert of Sempringham and the Gilbertines

Though Lincolnshire did less well in literature, it produced perhaps the greatest English monk. A man of extraordinary achievements, Gilbert of Sempringham is remarkable for the fact that he created a monastic order in England to which he gave his name and is one of the few residents of our district canonised after 1066.

He was born into a privileged local background in 1083, for his father was able to provide him with the livings in the parishes of Sempringham and West Torrington even though he was not yet a priest. However, Gilbert took his role seriously – he set up a school in Sempringham and employed a chaplain, then he started to sort out local discipline by insisting on tithes and making a stand against drinking. He was made a priest by Alexander, bishop of Lincoln, and developed an increasing reputation as a scholarly and serious young man who rejected earthly pleasures. He sold all his possessions and, having been advisor to an anchorite cell, set up his own monastic establishments for both men

59 J Fox, 2002, p.15
60 J Hughes, *Pastors and Visionaries: Religious and Secular Life in Late Medieval Yorkshire*, Woodbridge, 1988, p.216
61 Nigel Saul, *English Church Monuments in the Middle Ages*, Oxford, 2009, p.174

and women. This so inspired Bishop Alexander that he also set up a 'Gilbertine' house at Haverholme near Sleaford in 1139 – Cistercians had abandoned the site in favour of Louth Park.

Gilbert may not have wanted to supervise a network of monastic houses and in 1147 went to France to try to get the Cistercians to take them over, but the presence of women proved an impediment. Despite this, he learnt much from the Cistercians and returned to England with better ideas about organisation. His 'network' began to grow and spread beyond the immediate region to places such as Chicksands, in Bedfordshire, founded in about 1152.

The 'Gilbertines' were not without problems. There was a sexual scandal at the house in Watton, Yorkshire and in 1166 there were fierce arguments between the canons and the lay brethren. Many of their houses were established in areas with a challenging environment, like Haverholme or Alvingham, often near to damp wetlands. Catley, established near Billinghay in about 1154, was in a fenland location and also a very poor foundation with constant money problems. The priory at Malton, Yorkshire, was in a much better location and its church survived to become the parish church.

In Nottinghamshire, the Gilbertine house at Mattersey was founded in about 1185 but it was not always popular locally. In 1275 the Prior was causing resentment by 'encroaching on the roads' and in 1403 the house was trying to earn income by setting up a market. It was also affected by fire in 1279.

Gilbert attracted a number of stories of miracles in his own lifetime. One of the most famous concerns a time when he stayed with a couple who told him their sadness at being childless; sometime later a child was duly born, and the couple attributed this to Gilbert having been present in their cottage. Gilbert was so pleased with the report that he sent a cow to help support the young boy.

Towards the end of his life he agreed to join his own order; received the canon's habit at Bullington, from the hands of Roger of Malton, his chief counsellor and confidant. Bullington was a Gilbertine house founded in the 1150s which suffered from rural depopulation after the Black Death.

In 1188 Gilbert was at Newstead on Ancholme when he was taken seriously ill, and he received the last sacrament – and then began an extraordinary journey on his deathbed to Sempringham as part of a scheme to control his body. He died in February 1189 and was buried in the wall between the nuns and canons at Sempringham. Many miracles were recorded to have occurred there. One lengthy tale was about two brothers who were taking their demented mother to Crowland but lost her in the Fens; whilst at Quadring, Gilbert appeared to one of them and told him where to find her, and to take her to 'his house'. Once at Sempringham she was cured after Gilbert appeared to her in a dream. He was canonised as a saint in 1202 but his biographer notes that there were no further miracles after his canonisation. Perhaps his greatest miracle is his reputed survival to the age of 106![62]

---

62 Most of the stories of Gilbert were recorded in the *Book of St Gilbert*, which was written by one of his own monks.

Despite the shrine to Gilbert, Sempringham seems to have struggled. The first three kings Edward all sent wives and daughters of their enemies to fester at Sempringham but in 1312 the monastery was raided and looted by a group of local lords. The prior and his allies then got together a raiding party to recover their stolen animals.

There was also a convent at Tunstall, on an island in the Ancholme Carrs near Redbourn and thus close to Hibaldstow. It was founded in 1164 but joined with that at Bullington, founded soon after 1148, in 1189.[63]

Relics and Pilgrims

The connection between faith and money was most evident in the 'trade' in saints' relics and associated miracles; the attendant corruption became a key issue in the Reformation and contributed to the wholesale rejection of the miraculous by some reformers of the 16th century. The only monastic houses that possessed relics powerful enough to support a pilgrimage trade in Lincolnshire were Crowland, Bardney and Sempringham but some of the great churches also had relics of note.

By 1155 Grantham had relics of Wulfram (Wulfrianus), Symphorianus and Etritha.[64] Wulfrum had no direct connection with Lincolnshire but at some time after 1086, his arm was moved from Normandy to Crowland (Croyland), perhaps because its abbot Ingulph, had close connections with him. After the fire at Crowland, the relic was moved to Grantham where it was kept in the crypt chapel and became a great attraction for pilgrims. In the 14th century it was moved to a chapel above the porch. In contrast Symphorianus was a second-century Roman martyr and Etritha or Editha a tenth-century princess.

At Lincoln, Hugh's tomb was a major attraction, but so was John Dalderby's around which many tales of miracles clustered – including diseased women, drowned children and men possessed by devils.

Hibaldstow had its shrine to Hygbald's and a pilgrimage trade of sorts and enough to attract destruction of the shrine in the Reformation – but not his body. This continued to lie under the church in Hibaldstow until it was rediscovered in 1866 when the then dilapidated church was rebuilt. The restorers found a large stone Saxon sarcophagus and in it the precious relics of the saint, a tall robust man, lying on the south side of the choir. Here he remains to this day regularly visited by Orthodox pilgrims of several dioceses who ask him for his prayers and venerate his relics.

Apart from the significant shrines, there were others with more local attraction. Notable was the image of St Edmund in a 'ruinous' chapel at Sailholme, which around 1374-5 was said to have worked many miracles including saving the lives of seamen. The Jordan Cross at Rippingale was also the scene of miracles, provoking conflict between the parish, the bishop and the Pope who permitted a chapel to be built; Owen notes no

63   Victoria County History, *Lincolnshire*, p.197
64   D M Hadley, *Northern Danelaw*, Leicester, 2001, p.266

further miracles. The statue of St Petronella at Boultham was popular in 1454. There was a shrine of Anglo-Saxon origins at South Kyme, but only fragments have survived, and its story seems lost.

There was also an outgoing pilgrimage trade. We know few details about this although the Gild of St James at Burgh le Marsh was founded by five men who escaped death by shipwreck on a voyage back from Compostella in 1365.

We might also mention chantries – the practice of leaving large sums of money to pay for priests to say masses for a soul. For example, Robert Dalderby contracted with the prior of Thurgarton to provide two chaplains at St Benedict's in Lincoln whilst several other city churches had chantry priests.[65]

There were also many monuments, stimulating the trade in alabaster carvings, made from gypsum which was mined in Nottinghamshire but also brought in from neighbouring counties. From the fourteenth-century workshops in Nottingham became famous throughout Europe, exporting to Spain in one direction and Iceland in the other.[66] Local examples survived at Holme Pierrepont, Flawford and Mattersey. The county furnished carved altar- pieces to many churches before the Reformation.

Parish Life: The Stirrings of a New Order from 1400

Daily spiritual life operated on a different level where tradition was often more important than theology. There were gifts to the church such as 'soul-scot' whereby a dead man's best animal was handed over at his burial and 'wax-scot' paid to cover the cost of church lighting. Some villages had 'mein-port' where women brought bread to church at Easter, but in 1396 Bishop John Buckingham banned a Nettleham tradition of bringing hard-boiled eggs and bacon to church at Easter. Traditions such as the 'washing of Molly Grime' at Glentham on Good Friday no doubt originated in pre-Reformation practices whose origins are now obscure.

A prominent feature of medieval life was the guild – these could be social, religious or trade- based. A well-known example was the Guild of St John at Spalding, which traced its origins to an image painted by John de Rughton in 1358; various people funded a light to go with this and the image was found to have powerful results, so a few years later a guild was formed to pay for the continued lighting of it. Nottingham had a Guild of the Blessed Virgin attached to St Peter's, whilst Newark had multiple guilds including the Guild of the Holy Richard of Newark and Grantham had a Guild of Corpus Christi. Some smaller places also had guilds like that of Corpus Christi at Gosberton. Boston had as many as nineteen religious guilds.

The Guild of St Mary at Boston was founded in 1260 to fund the saying of masses[67] for the souls of its members and to distribute food to the poor. It was incorporated in 1392,

---

65 Hill (1948), p.152
66 J Fox, *People of Vision*, p.13
67 It had altars in St Botolph's, principally at the east end of the south aisle.

allowing it to elect aldermen. It was aggressively expansionist by the late 1400s and in the early 1500s using gifts such as eels to win the support of Thomas Wolsey, both during and after his stint as Bishop of Lincoln. It became one of the most wealthy guilds, selling its indulgences or pardons across much of the country in a lucrative trade that by 1516-7 had embroiled it in a trade war with the Austin Friars – it then employed one Thomas Cromwell to help in the campaign to win the Pope's support, a description of which was then written up by one of Boston's most famous sons, John Foxe. Cromwell spent six months in Rome, deploying English jelly and music to win attention.[68] Cromwell told the story to Cranmer, who told it to his secretary – Ralph Morice of Boston. Cromwell continued working on and off for the guild until at least 1524, receiving presents of Fenland wildfowl as well as the obligatory eels. The irony of Cromwell, an architect of future reform, grubbing around with one of the most detested aspects of Catholicism, has attracted some amusement – and Foxe clearly had mixed views! Foxe explained that these 'jolly pardons' made up for the losses resulting from the 'decayed' state of Boston's port.

Its success was to gain a 'perpetual jubilee indulgence' which could be granted to those who on Marian feast days completed three circuits of the seven altars in St Botolph's. This was deemed equivalent to the penance of doing a circuit of seven key basilica in Rome or going to Compostela.[69] In the 1520s it was running its own school and from 1530 a choir run by John Taverner – more of these later – and employing nine chaplains.

By 1400 there was growing unease with the Church as more of an economic institution than a spiritual power. Indulgences could be purchased from a variety of institutions by gifts of money and not just from guilds – St Katherine's in Lincoln and the Trinitarians at Ingham also supplied them.[70] There was a growth in personal piety not directly connected to the church in the late 14th century and into the 15th. But also, the parish system did not work well for all people, and this was to be exploited in the next century by Protestant reformers.

As an example, the villagers of Cottam were served by a 'chapel' that was the responsibility of the priest of South Leverton, who was meant to provide for it from the 'fruits' of his benefice. However, Thomas de Langwath failed to provide the customary priest on Sundays, Wednesdays and Fridays until forced to do so by the authorities in 1372.[71] At Dunham-on-Trent in 1309 the churchyard was desecrated by some of the villagers assaulting the priest there, which seems to have been caused by their frustrations – for the Archbishop issued instructions about the regular saying of Mass, the priest not to visit taverns and not to strike parishioners, and only lambs to be grazed in the churchyard. However, we should not assume the people of Dunham were entirely innocent, for in 1315 they were accused of stealing the Archbishop's swans from his manor at Laneham.

Of course, many parishes were faithfully served for decades by committed priests, but we know more about those who did not such as – apparently – Richard Johnson the vicar of Laxton who in about 1471 was taken to Nottingham prison accused of trying to 'ravish' Elizabeth Blyton. One suggestion has been that this was a charge designed to force him

---

68 Diarmaid McCulloch, *Thomas Cromwell*, London, 2018, p31-5
69 R N Swanson, *Indulgences in Late Medieval England*, Cambridge, 2007, p55
70 Swanson (2007), p.465
71 A Calendar of the Register of Richard Scrope, Archbishop of York ..., Volume 11, p.87.

out, for he visited the woman believing her to be alone and was then surprised by a posse of armed men – in which case it was successful as Johnson left the parish.[72]

In Lincolnshire the practice of 'leasing' a parish to someone was very common – by 1518 some 10% of parishes were so leased. This led to abuses, such as when in 1471 the abbot of Thornton leased Kelstern to Thomas Gylby who failed to build a new chancel or repair the rectory by 1496.[73]

In 1518 some 20% of parishes had no resident priest in the Lincoln archdeaconry and the diocese reported 23% of incumbents absent – Hodgett estimated 115 Lincolnshire parishes had no resident priest with an increasing number of plural livings.[74] This had been a problem since the Black Death especially when Bishop John Gynwell (1347-63) had tried to tackle the issue. Absentees were occasionally deprived, as with the rector of Scrivelsby in 1467. Bishop William Atwater took some action after the 1519 visitation although a few, likes Coates by Stow and Sutton in the Marsh, had no priest. In 45 churches, the priest was not maintaining the chancel properly. Few sermons were expected, and few preached.[75]

Whereas the chancel was the responsibility of the priest, the nave of the church was cared for by the parish. When there was no priest, the very fabric of the church began to suffer.

The disarray of the church was yet only hinted at, but exceptional cases indicated deeper problems. In 1393 Lincoln cathedral was closed for a time by the bishop after servants of Dean John Sheppey were involved in a violent assault with 19 named in 1394; Sheppey had been imposed on the Chapter (who had wanted another man) in 1378 and bad relations had persisted. One of the worst was the endless battle between Dean John Mackworth of Lincoln and the Cathedral Chapter from 1412 until his death in 1450. The disputes embroiled Bishop Richard Fleming/Fleming who also received support in the early 1420s from William Of Alnwick – who himself became bishop in 1436, arriving from Norwich with a reputation for dealing strongly with Lollards. Mackworth was from Mackworth near Derby and owed his promotion to Lancastrian support but it was not enough to secure him the diocese of Lincoln in 1431, from which he was thwarted. He broke all the rules, extracted all the money and abused the clergy in public. On his occasional visits to the city he disrupted services, locked the gates, and held Mass when clergy were not expecting it. He seems to have delighted in spreading gossip about the Chapter members and intimidated them with armed men. He turned the Deanery, which he did not use, into stables. In 1435 two of his Derbyshire friends assaulted the Chancellor of Lincoln, Peter Partridge, in the cathedral choir, horrifying pilgrims. He clearly detested Bishop William Grey, in 1437 turning up with great magnificence to outshine his rival, and 'thrived on litigation'. The problem was eventually brought to a supposed settlement by Bishop William Alnwick in 1439, who proposed an effective book of rules for the cathedral, though the Chapter was still unhappy in 1442. Mackworth had to be excommunicated in 1445 and seems to have remained there until 1449 when he exchanged his living at Lincoln for another and vanished from the scene – dying in 1450. Alnwick himself died

---

72 *TTS*, 1981, p.39-41
73 R C Palmer, *Selling the Church*, N Carolina, 2002, p.104-5
74 Gerald Hodgett, *Tudor Lincolnshire*, Lincoln, 1975, p.12
75 Hodgett (1975), p.13

in 1449 and was buried in a tomb that was destroyed in 1644.

In contrast, this was a great age of church building, generated by the last decades of often wool-based wealth. Great monuments such as Newark church were the result of substantial rebuilding from the mid-1300s and its chancel was not completed until 1489. Major building work at Grantham was rather earlier, but additions were still being made at the end of the 1400s and indeed as late as 1550; it is the third highest spire in England for a parish church, at 88m. The spire at Newark, built by about 1350, is reputedly the fifth highest. It is traditionally claimed that Grantham and Newark churches were the result of a rivalry between the towns. The famous tower at Boston was begun in the mid-fifteenth century and not completed until 1520.

The steeple at Louth was not finished until 1515, built over 15 years at great expense with stone brought from Wilsford and with contributions by the parishioners; it became the highest parish church spire in England. Leverton in Lincolnshire was rebuilt from 1492-1534, Leake at a similar period whilst a new tower at Great Ponton was paid for by the wealthy Ellis family in 1519. All Saints in Stamford was rebuilt by the Browne family, wool merchants, from the 1470s. Spilsby and Alford both gained new towers around 1530. Given so much private wealth invested in these churches, it is not surprising that rumours about the closure of churches contributed to the Lincolnshire Uprising in 1536.

Wycliffe and the Lollards: The Dawn of the Reformation?

In 1401 an Act was passed that allowed people to be burnt for holding 'heretical' views – in retrospect it seems astonishing that what was to become almost commonplace in the next two hundred years had never previously been a feature of English life. That a man or woman could be burnt alive on the pretext of protecting the truth of Christ is an uncomfortable problem for us to deal with, and one that had never previously been seen as necessary; in England, not even witches had been burnt.

John Wyclif (d.1384) was been called 'the morning star of the Reformation' because of the challenge he provided to the Roman Catholic Church. His link with our region is that he held the living at Fillingham in about 1342, but it is not known if he ever visited it.[76] He was more influential in his thinking, criticising the clergy privilege, proposing a Bible in the local language, and expounding many doctrinal issues that were to become key two hundred years later – the nature of the Sacramental Mass, the veneration of the saints and many other issues. He was declared a heretic in 1415 and in 1428 his body was dug up, burnt, and ashes thrown in the river at Lutterworth in Leicestershire.

People who supported his ideas became known as Lollards. Their ideas certainly penetrated our region, but much of the activity associated with the diocese of Lincoln was actually at its southern end. Bishop William Grey was one of those troubled by this. In 1382 Nicholas Hereford was excommunicated and kept in prison in Rome until released by a mob but by 1386 was again preaching 'heresy' around London until being arrested

76 Plumb, p6

near Nottingham in 1387. Treatment of him by the constable, Sir William Neville, was so good that he too was also suspected of being a Lollard.[77] By August, he had either been released or escaped. Neville was close friends or a relative with the known Lollard, Sir John Clanvowe, with whom he was buried at Istanbul in 1390. It is suggested that 'there was an important Lollard congregation at Nottingham'[78] perhaps led by William Swynderby who had also preached in Leicester[79]; he was a former hermit, who had been active at Melton Mowbray in 1382.

William Swynderby, Lollard leader

Swynderby is an interesting character and most historians now assume that he came from Swinderby in Lincolnshire. He arrived at Leicester as a hermit and a type of challenging preacher, even a 'revival preacher' in one account,[80] focusing first on the 'adornments' of fashionable women and loose living. It is unclear whether he was ever actually a priest.

This made him unpopular and an attempt was made to stone him, which only caused him to preach, instead, against wealth and the impossibility of buying your way into heaven. He also preached against rich priests and friars. Despite this he had aristocratic protection and was provided with food so he could live as a hermit in the woods, making preaching trips to nearby towns. He joined in with a group of religious misfits at an old chapel by 1382 and attracted some attention after burning an image of St Catherine.

As a result, he was summoned to Lincoln by Bishop Buckingham for preaching without a licence,[81] where he was humiliated and recanted, but later ventured westwards at first to Coventry, where he annoyed the Bishop again, was involved in controversy again in Hereford in 1388-92, and then disappeared via Monmouth into Wales.

In March 1388 a Royal Commission was sent to Nottingham and ordered the Mayor to confiscate Lollard books, and to arrest and imprison those preaching heresies. Six men were arrested in April 1388 including John Bradburne and five laymen though they were released on sureties of £200 (an enormous sum), we know nothing of their punishment.[82] Later that year John de Stoke from Widmerpool was held in the castle before a surety was paid for his release, and then in November orders to re-arrest Bradburne were issued. As Lollards were active in condemning the veneration of images, Thurgarton monk Walter

---

77 C Kightly, *The Early Lollards*, York University D. Phil thesis, 1975, p.7
78 Kightly, p.8
79 One might assume a connection with the village of Swinderby.
80 Black, Merja. *Lollardy, Language Contact and The Great Vowel Shift: Spellings in the Defence Papers of William Swinderby* in *Neuphilologische Mitteilungen*, vol. 99, no. 1, 1998, pp. 53–69. *JSTOR*, www.jstor.org/stable/43346180.
81 A K McHardy, *The Age of War and Wycliffe*, Lincoln, 2001, p.51
82 Kightly (1975), p.9

Hilton wrote a tract arguing in defence of them, sometime between 1385 and 1395.[83]
An early opponent of the Lollards in Lincolnshire was Roger Dymoke, son of Sir John Dymoke of Scrivelsby in Lincolnshire. He was Prior of Boston in 1379 and preached before Richard II in 1391, then two years later wrote a response to the Lollard 'heresies'.

In September 1397 four Nottingham Lollards appeared before Chancery, seemingly including three who had been arrested in 1388.[84] They were forced to worship images and agreed not to despise pilgrimages, then released. Clearly, the Nottingham Lollards were men of substantial standing. After this we know nothing of their cause except that John Lay, a chantry priest at Nottingham St Mary's, was associated with Lollard leader Sir John Oldcastle in 1413.

John Buckingham (or Bokyngham) was the type of career churchman that Lollards disliked, and he disliked them. He lacked a university education, but his political career took him through a succession of exchequer posts to be Lord Privy Seal in 1360-3, and his Church career was equally successful. After being Archdeacon of Nottingham for a few months in 1349, he became Dean of Lichfield and was elected Bishop of Lincoln in 1362 – which he held until 1398. He is seen as a campaigner against superstitious and pagan practice and, in a curious story, he tried to stop the adoration of a cross at Rippingale where the supporters of this cult then took an appeal to Rome. He also took exception to the Lincolnshire tradition of using bacon and eggs for Mass at Easter instead of bread and wine. In 1398 political machinations led to a transfer to the diocese of Coventry and Lichfield, but he refused to move for several months.

Philip Repingdon, later bishop of Lincoln from 1404, for a time shared Wyclif's views on the Sacrament for which he was suspended in 1382; he was a close associate of Nicholas Hereford and had been an Augustinian abbot in Leicester before becoming bishop of Lincoln in 1404. He later changed his views. In 1412 Leicestershire Lollards were summoned to appear at the bishop's house in Sleaford. In February 1414 he called a meeting of clergy in the Chapter House to discuss heresy in Lincoln and ordered penance in the cathedral for those suspected.[85] However, we know little of any cases as most of the records have been lost. The 1416 visitation resulted in imprisonment for the heresy of John Bagworth, rector of Wilsford, and William Smith of Corby.[86]

Lincoln College at Oxford was founded by Bishop Richard Fleming to train priests to combat the Lollards. A few Lollards appeared in Lincoln in the 1400s including Robert Sutton, a cleric who was convicted of heresy, and probably William Hert who in 1432 assaulted a member of the commission that led to Sutton's conviction. Hert had previously been accused, in 1424, of holding unlawful assemblies soon after he had moved to Lincoln. It is hard even to tell who was a Lollard and who not; Franciscan William Russell[87] made an impact at Stamford in 1424 when preaching that tithes were against God's laws – which

83 Jones, W. R. "*Lollards and Images: The Defence of Religious Art in Later Medieval England.*" *Journal of the History of Ideas*, vol. 34, no. 1, 1973, pp. 27–50. *JSTOR*, www.jstor.org/stable/2708942

84 William Dyvet, William Steynour and Nicholas Poucher plus a Nicholas Taillour.

85 J Arnold and K Lewis, *A Companion to the Book of Margery Kempe*, Cambridge, 2004, p.79

86 Owen (1971), p.122

87 *History of the County of Lincoln*, vol 2, p.330

sounds possible – but added there was no sin in clerics having intercourse with women. The same year at Welton Walter Atkirk organised meetings to get people to pay less in offerings to the vicar. There were three probable cases in 1447 at Baumber, Sausthorpe and Wainfleet.

Nonetheless, Lollardy persisted and some have seen a continuity into the Reformation. In 1506-7 a steady stream of Lollards was being identified in the Lincoln diocese, albeit many of them out of the county.

One extraordinary woman who passed briefly through the region but had some influence was **Margery** Kempe (c1373-c1438), a middle-class wife and mother from King's Lynn. Kempe's life story, *The Book of Margery Kempe*, is widely regarded as the first autobiography by an English woman and describes her extraordinary journey to Jerusalem and back accompanied by manifestations which might be called Pentecostal today. Characteristics of her worship included weeping and crying aloud.

Kempe was widely suspected of being a Lollard which some have suggested accounts for her rather pointed devotion to saints and pilgrimages – she hoped to convince others that she was not a 'heretic'. When she was arrested in Leicester (a known Lollard centre) in about 1417, a man from Boston spoke up in her defence saying that 'this woman is considered a holy woman and a blessed woman'. Between June 1413 and February 1414 she met Philip Repingdon at Lincoln who 'treated her kindly' and even suggested she had her story written down – which she did many years later. Her influence in Fenland appears to have been considerable but we know little about her save what was found when her book was rediscovered after being lost for hundreds of years.

This was also an era when it started to become possible to hear 'alternative' preaching, such as when in 1417 the Bishop of Lincoln was troubled by unlicensed preaching in Lincoln, probably by Franciscans.[88]

Under Bishop Chedworth (1452-72) one heretic was burnt whilst Bishop Smith (1496-1514) also burnt people in his diocese.[89] Possible heretics at Brumby in 1517 and Harrington in 1519 do not appear to have been executed.[90]

---

88   Arnold and Lewis (2004), p.80
89   Plumb (PhD), p.12
90   Owen (1971), p.122

CHAPTER THREE

Henry's Imperfect Reformation
1509-1547

The Reformation created great turbulence in the East Midlands, especially in Lincolnshire where a serious revolt against Henry VIII's Church policy erupted in 1536. Ironically this revolt became the catalyst for accelerating change, as Nottinghamshire's more evangelical gentry became trusted with seeing through the dissolution of the monasteries whilst in Lincolnshire it gave Charles Brandon, Duke of Suffolk, the chance to consolidate landholdings around the estates of his wife Katherine Willoughby. Willoughby was by 1545 one of the leading 'godly' women in the nation and planted evangelical preachers across south and east Lincolnshire. It is easily possible to trace lines of continuous influence from the reformers of the 1530s and 1540s to the radical puritans of the early 1600s and the regional leaders of Parliamentary revolt in the 1540s. In Nottinghamshire the group of Hercy-Markham-Denman-Neville expanded to include Whalley and later Ireton; in Lincolnshire the Willoughbys remained significant but with them they brought the St Paul-Wray family whilst names like Irby, Disney and Ayscough also provided a continuous line sometimes crossing the county boundary.

Thomas Cranmer, whose time as Archbishop influenced both faith and language, depended very much on his contacts in both counties.

Chronology:
1509: Henry VIII becomes King
1517: Luther starts the Reformation at Wittenberg
1528: The 'Boston radicals' arrested at Oxford
1533: Archbishop Cranmer approves Henry's divorce
1534: Act of Supremacy makes Henry 'Head' of the Church in England
1535: Execution of John Houghton and others at Tyburn
1536: Large scale monastic dissolutions begin; Lincolnshire Rising
1538: Executions connected to Lenton
1539: The 'Great Bible' published in English; The 'Six Articles' signal a return to conservative religious policy
1540: Thomas Cromwell and Thomas Garrett executed
1541-2: Diocese of Lincoln reduced in size
1543: Robert Testwood executed
1546: Anne Askew (Ayscough) and John Lassells executed
1547: Death of Henry VIII

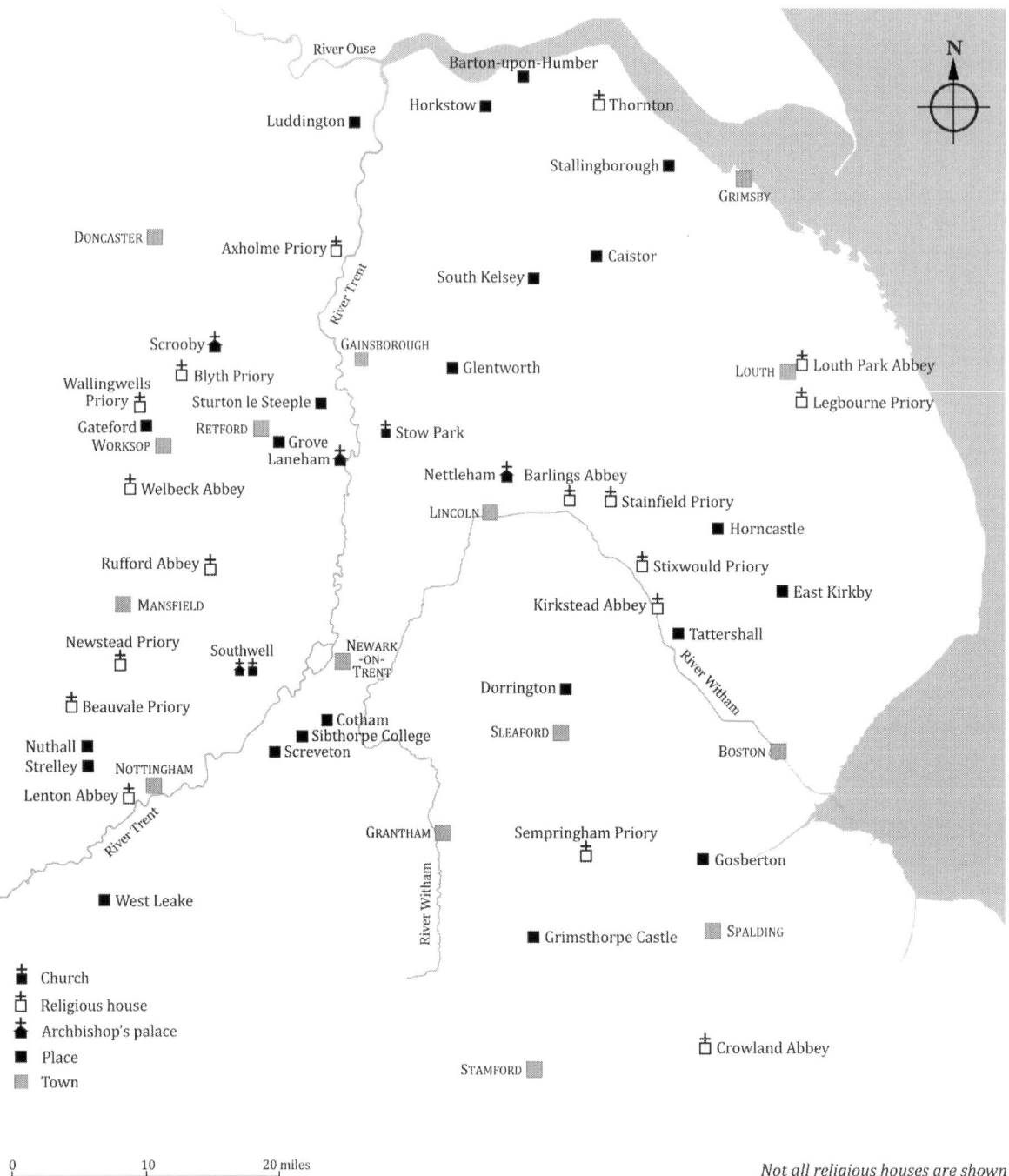

River Ouse

Barton-upon-Humber

Horkstow

Thornton

Luddington

Stallingborough

GRIMSBY

DONCASTER

Axholme Priory

River Trent

Caistor

South Kelsey

Scrooby

GAINSBOROUGH

Blyth Priory

Glentworth

LOUTH

Louth Park Abbey

Wallingwells Priory

Sturton le Steeple

Legbourne Priory

Gateford
WORKSOP

RETFORD

Grove
Laneham

Stow Park

Nettleham

Barlings Abbey

Stainfield Priory

Welbeck Abbey

LINCOLN

Horncastle

Rufford Abbey

Stixwould Priory

East Kirkby

MANSFIELD

Kirkstead Abbey

Newstead Priory

Southwell

NEWARK
-ON-
TRENT

Tattershall

River Witham

Dorrington

Beauvale Priory

Cotham
Sibthorpe College
Screveton

SLEAFORD

Nuthall
Strelley

NOTTINGHAM

BOSTON

Lenton Abbey

River Trent

GRANTHAM

Sempringham Priory

Gosberton

West Leake

River Witham

Grimsthorpe Castle

SPALDING

✠ Church

✛ Religious house

♙ Archbishop's palace

■ Place

▨ Town

Crowland Abbey

STAMFORD

0   10   20 miles

Not all religious houses are shown

Dissent Gathers Pace

In 1500 Lincoln's huge diocese sprawled across much of England making it one of the most powerful religious entities in the country. In contrast, Nottinghamshire remained in many ways a backwater – a branch of the York archdiocese without the wealth or powerful nobility that could be found in its neighbour. Yet in the first few years of the Tudor era a tradition of radical faith began to develop in both counties that was to continue for generations.

Dissent had developed through the influence of the Lollards and in the Lincoln diocese it was Buckinghamshire, at its south end, that often presented the main problems. Lollard ideas were already established well before Luther's works began to trickle into England. In 1506 William Tilfery, 'a pious man', was burnt at Amersham and, according to John Foxe the martyrologist (who was from Boston), his daughter was forced to light the faggots that burnt him. A man named Roberts was convicted of being a Lollard and burnt at Buckingham the same year. Roger Gargrave of Wakefield narrowly escaped death in 1512 when accused of 'heresies' about the nature of the Mass passed to him 'by a certain priest of the county of Lincoln'.[1] Most of the Lincoln records on Lollardy are lost, so we know little about how extensive it might have been.

Whilst Henry VIII, who reigned from 1509, was happily married to Catherine of Aragon those who wanted to see religious change made little progress and lived dangerous lives; many stayed abroad. The Bishop of Lincoln during some of these pivotal years of Henry VIII's reign was John Longland, a scholarly man who had also been identified because of the excellence of his preaching.[2] Coming to the notice of Thomas Wolsey and Archbishop Warham, John Longland took over the see of Lincoln in 1521, at about the same time as Luther's rise to prominence began. From 1524 he also became confessor to Henry VIII. Running the Lincoln diocese was taxing enough on its own, and Longland found it a struggle to meet the court's needs and his diocese's. Among his troubles was the ill-discipline of poorer parish clerks, who got involved in gambling, hunting and other 'unhonest games or play'. Many were unable to distinguish between a Bible story and the life of a saint.[3] Longland fared little better with the monks and became sceptical about the benefits of monasteries and nunneries; the 'poor clerks' at Lincoln were an especial problem. However, Longland was known for his efforts in carefully examining candidates for ordination and institution.[4]

Some churches in Lincolnshire were poor and badly maintained – the roof at Humberston leaked, distracting the worshippers, whilst the chancel at Tetney was not repaired by the Augustinians of Wellow. However, overall Margaret Bowker has concluded it was 'extremely rare' for problems to be long neglected. Much the greater problem was securing resident clergy.[5]

Meanwhile, trade connections yielded religious ideas as well as goods. Martin Luther had

---

1   Dickens, *Lollards*, p.17
2   Margaret Bowker, *John Longland*, in *ODNB*, accessed 27 March 2014.
3   M Bowker, *The Henrician Reformation*, Cambridge, 1981, p.6
4   Hodgett (1975), p.10
5   M Bowker, *The Henrician Reformation*, Cambridge, 1981, p.6

nailed his 95 theses to the door of Wittenberg church in 1517, and rapidly became the most published author in Europe. This became a tide of print that could not be stopped although in 1521 Henry VIII restated his commitment to the Catholic faith. The same year Henry Burnett of Barrow on Humber spent weeks in Amsterdam and Bremen with a group from Hull, absorbing Lutheran influences whilst one had a New Testament in English. Burnett talked too much on his return home and was seen to eat meat on days when it was not permitted. His vicar sent him to Lincoln to be interrogated but he convinced the clergy there that he had done little 'wrong'.[6] In the 1520s Longland became increasingly concerned that heretical books were infiltrating the east coast. Despite this, there seems to have been little heresy of any substance in Lincolnshire or Nottinghamshire before the early 1530s.

Luther's ideas were a clear challenge to the Roman Catholic Church's hegemony. With an emphasis on personal faith in Jesus Christ, rather than justification by works and rituals, much of the Church's practice was under threat of rejection including chantries, the concept of purgatory and prayer to dead saints, and many rituals of the Church year. Personal faith also required access to the Bible in your own language (which had been proposed by Wyclif in the illegal English Bibles of the late 1300s) and that implied a decent education – which in turn implied the option of developing your own understanding independent of your priest. People who embraced these views became known as Protestants only from the mid-1550s in England and are better described as 'evangelicals' before that. The east coast was especially open to. The new ideas as Luther's books and soon Bibles in English were easily smuggled across the sea, but the risk was great as Henry VIII never reconciled himself to 'justification by faith' although he came to reject the idea of purgatory.

By 1527 Henry had convinced himself that he was in error in having married his brother's widow, Catherine of Aragon. Wolsey, Archbishop of York is well known to have experienced his downfall in 1529-30 because of problems in securing the king's divorce. Longland's position also became more complex when Henry VIII began to think about divorce, coupled with the decline in favour of his friend Wolsey. In April 1530 Wolsey set off back to York, stopping at Grantham, Newark, Southwell and Scrooby – he had houses or palaces at the latter two. He was arrested at Cawood in November and then began a journey back to London via Sheffield and Nottingham, but he died at Leicester. The failure of divorce negotiations thus forced a separation from Rome and in early 1533 Nottinghamshire-born Archbishop Thomas Cranmer declared Henry's first marriage null and void and confirmed his second to Anne Boleyn.

The Boston 'Oxford Group' – Cuckoos in the Nest?

To be a reformer in the mid and late 1520s was still dangerous; seemingly most oddly, a group of Boston radicals were arrested in Wolsey's own Oxford college and charged with harbouring heretical books. Thomas Garrett (also Garrard or Gerard) was arrested at Oxford in February 1528,[7] suspected of selling 'heretical' books in London and supplying them to Oxford. He abjured, and was protected by Thomas Cromwell, and by 1535 was

6   Dickens, *Lollards*, p.26

7   Foxe gives 1526, other sources such as *ODNB* 1528. It is curious that Foxe, born in the town where Gerrard had been a schoolmaster, does not mention his origins.

a radical preacher in Yorkshire for Sir Francis Bigod before in 1536 becoming Hugh Latimer's chaplain and chancellor at Worcester – the tide of reform having been favourable to him. Garrett is of interest because he was probably from Lincolnshire originally, was a Cambridge preacher from about 1510 and in 1524-6 he had been a Grammar Master of St Mary's Gild School in Boston, the Gild's highest-paid chaplain, and where he was closely linked to the musician John Taverner (c1490-1545).[8] In 1526 he was a curate at a very reforming church in London, later becoming its Rector in 1537. Garrett's arrest led to an ending of Cambridge's powers to license its own preachers.[9]

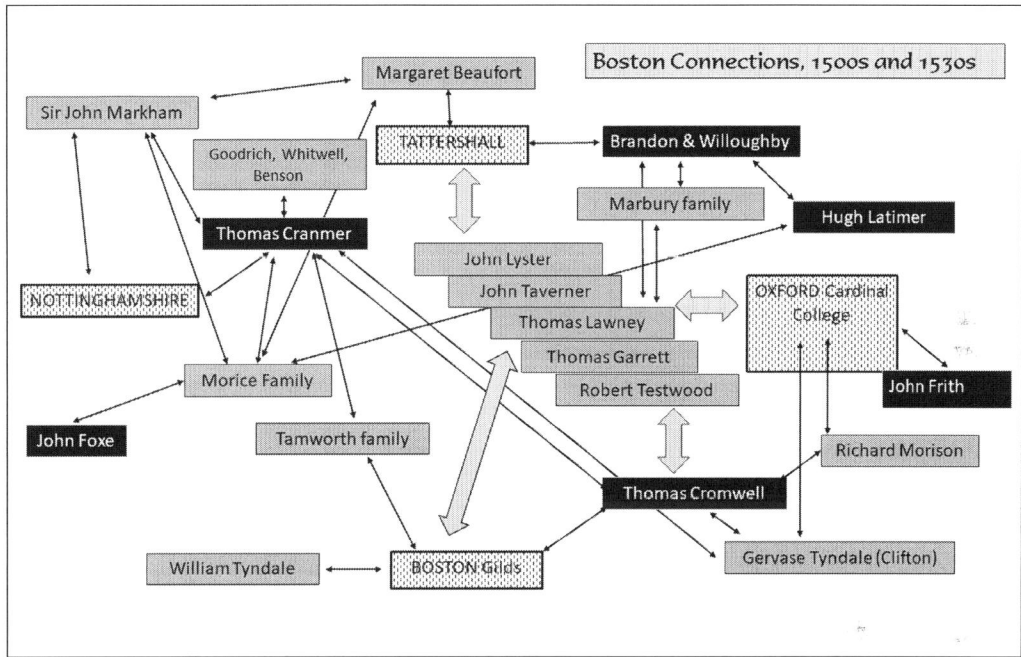

Taverner first came to notice as a choirmaster at Tattershall and sang for the St Mary's Gild in 1524. Wolsey commissioned the Bishop of Lincoln, Longland, to find a choir for his new college of Cardinal College at Oxford and Taverner was the second choice to be choirmaster. He moved to a new job at Cardinal College Oxford in 1526, went back to Lincolnshire in a recruitment drive with Robert Lyne, and enlisted some of his Boston associates – including John Radley, Thomas Lawney and John Lyster – the latter two had also been at Tattershall whilst Radley was from the Boston choir. Robert Testwood, another of the Boston clique who was its choirmaster from 1524-8, became Master of the Cardinal College in Ipswich, Wolsey's hometown. Garrett, now a curate but still also a travelling bookseller, made use of these Oxford contacts and several of them were arrested – Taverner (or 'Tanner') was found to have been hiding books under the floor for Mr Clerke and Lawney was also hiding books. Garrett, who had been staying with Radley, tried to escape abroad but was captured at Bedminster in 1528 and recanted; Taverner was also found to have been 'privy to the letter sent to him by Garret after his flight'. Six were taken into custody, including Lawney, unhealthily imprisoned in the college's cellars. Wolsey and Longland seem to have taken the view that Garrett was the main problem and the others simply misled – or perhaps too valuable to lose.

8   The *ODNB* entry for Taverner mentions this, but not the entry for Garrard.

9   The best overall account of these issues is to be found in M Williamson, *Evangelicals at Boston, Oxford and Windsor*, now uploaded at the Academia website.

The College also included Richard Morison, destined to be one of Cromwell's most trusted agents,[10] whilst listed between him and Lawney was Gervase Tyndale, known to be one of the Lincolnshire-Nottinghamshire group with links to the Clifton family and thereby indirectly to Cranmer. More of his escapades later.

The discovery of the books revealed a nest of 'heretics' within the college Wolsey had himself founded. Taverner's friend John Clerk, whose books he had been hiding, died in custody whilst the future martyr John Frith was also held in custody for a while.[11] The College's more official library included a set of books bequeathed by William Fell, the Archdeacon of Nottingham, in 1528.

What connected Boston to all of this was Thomas Cromwell, who had become well-acquainted with the town in 1517-9 when involved with the St Mary's Gild and who was now working for Cardinal Wolsey as Receiver General and Surveyor of Cardinal College. As MacCulloch has said, 'the arrival of so many suspect men at Cardinal College was neither accident nor carelessness' and nor was the arrival of several *from* Boston – 'an odd place in the early Reformation, with much going on below the surface of its extrovert public religious life'. Clearly, the hand of Cromwell, by this time a supporter of the new faith, had guided them.

It was deeply ironic, and a later cause of much irony to John Foxe, that this was related to the Gild of St Mary which grew wealthy on the sale of indulgences – anathema to good evangelicals. The Gild even employed William Tyndale to say masses from Michaelmas 1521 until Pentecost 1522;[12] then in 1525 it employed 'a startling conjunction of later prominent evangelical names' – Testwood, Garrett, Lawney and Taverner. What might we now speculate as to the connection of these events? Who brought Tyndale to Boston and what influence did he have? MacCulloch even speculates that Boston docks were the route for many evangelical books to enter the country and arrive at Cardinal College. Maybe this is how Garrett got the books that he sold.[13]

After this escapade, Garrett benefited from the Ecclesiastical Licenses Act of 1533, by which Cranmer was able to permit him to preach anywhere in England. In 1536 Garrett was chaplain to Hugh Latimer at Worcester, one of the greatest of the reformers, but Bishop Longland complained that Garrett had been preaching his controversial beliefs in Lincoln diocese.[14][15] Longland was indeed much annoyed by controversial preachers in his diocese especially Garrett in Lincolnshire and Thomas Swynnerton, another of Cranmer's nominees. In May 1536 Longland wrote to Cromwell to complain that their preaching 'on doubtful matters' extended beyond what was legal and 'offends the people'

---

10 Morison's humble origins are unclear but he is believed to have been a northerner in which context it is interesting that his rise was triggered by his writings against the northern risings of 1536; after Cardinal College he linked in with Latimer and Cranmer and by 1539 he was an associate of another future martyr, John Lassells, on the Privy Council staff both having benefited from Cromwell's patronage. His reputation as a 'great heretic' caused him to leave for Europe under Mary and he died at Strasbourg in 1556, where he had gone to study with men such as Sir John Cheke.

11 The others were 'Clerke, Mr Sumnor, Mr Betts and Sir Frithe, Sir Thomas Lawney a priest of the chapel.' (L & P)

12 Williamson, *Evangelicals at Boston, Oxford and Windsor*, p.42

13 The best account of all of this is in MacCulloch, *Thomas Cromwell: A Life*, various pages.

14 Paul Ayris (ed), *Thomas Cranmer – Churchman and Scholar*, p.85

15 *Lincolnshire Historian,* vol 8, 1973, p.36

but also offended the Bishop by encouraging them to read English books; 'Lincolnshire much grudgeth' their presence, he noted – they were perhaps fortunate to not still be there when the Rising broke out a few months later. Swynnerton latter was arrested at Rye in 1537 for questioning the perpetual virginity of Mary where Garrett was also involved, attacking the doctrine of purgatory. Swynnerton and Garrett were the earliest evangelist preachers in the English Reformation whilst the incident shows how both were free to roam the nation. Cranmer also sent Garrett to preach in Calais.

By 1539 Garrett was working as chaplain to Cranmer but in the sharp conservative turn of 1540, which involved the execution of Cromwell, he was a prominent target for the reactionaries. He was burnt in Smithfield without any form of preceding trial. Altogether six died that day, three Catholics and three evangelicals. Garrett became a star of the later Protestant martyrology, celebrated by Bale as a 'pure preacher' and of course by John Foxe.

Lawney at least survived to enjoy a benefice in Kent, where he was able to work for a time with Garrett to develop reform. In 1535 he too was associated with Cranmer in Kent, was accused of heresy in 1536 for denying purgatory and was soon sending reports to staff of the Duke of Suffolk about conservatives; he is referred to as 'sponsored' by the Duke of Suffolk in the 1540s as one of his chaplains.[16] He was known universally as a 'witty man' and once turned aside the Duke of Norfolk's question after the reactionary Six Acts of 1539, 'May priests now have wives or no?' with the response that he did not know if priests would have wives but 'I am sure of it, after your Act, that wives will have priests'. As a recognised supporter of clerical marriage, Lawney would have known the trap being set. He died in 1541.

Meanwhile, Radley left Oxford and then Taverner returned to Boston in 1530 in the employ of the Gild of St Mary which ran the choir. By 1538, though, he seems to have retired from church music for in 1537 Cromwell seems to have helped him secure the post of Boston's collector of customs and subsidies until 1543.[17] However, he was still active in the town and on behalf of the King received the custody of the four friaries in Boston when they were dissolved.[18] He is also reputed to have supervised the burning of the town's rood screen – a detested symbol of Catholicism.

Robert Testwood, Taverner's musician colleague, was in Boston around 1524-9 and also followed a reforming path. He was an early advocate of the Royal supremacy – winning him the enmity of the Bishop of Ely at that time. After the college at Ipswich closed, he wrote to Cromwell for help, but he moved to the college or Chapel Royal at Windsor in 1533 where he became infamous for lambasting pilgrims and broke the nose off a statue of the Virgin Mary. Within a year he was sending information to Cromwell about those who opposed the reforms. However, he exceeded the limits by attacking the theology of the time, again centring on Mary, and was threatened with hanging by the Duke of Norfolk.

To run the story forwards a little, after the fall of Cromwell in 1540, the outspoken Testwood was vulnerable and was soon accused of heresy. He was one of three men burnt

---

16   M Franklin-Harkrider, *Women, Reform and Community in Early Modern England*, Woodbridge, 2008, p.31

17   Williamson, p.40

18   *Lincolnshire History and Archaeology*, 1989, p.36

at Windsor in July 1543, on very slender grounds of averting his eyes during the elevation of the host. It was well reported that Henry VIII soon regretted the executions saying, 'Alas, poor innocents,' whilst his main accuser was himself accused of perjury.

So, the Boston 'nest' of the 1520s produced two of the main martyrs of the evangelical reformation, as well as the man who recorded their stories. Foxe got much information for his work about Lawney from Ralph Morice, whose father had been a prominent figure at Boston, but he seems to have lost his assurance in how to deal with a nest of reformers in his home town who seemingly were happy to take the Papist shilling and indeed the Cardinal's. A late note in Foxe on Taverner comments, 'this Taverner repented hym very much that he had made songs to Popish ditties in the tyme of his blindness'.[19]

Royal Control

Henry cemented the new arrangements by the Act of Supremacy in 1534, which made the monarch Head of the Church instead of the Pope, but he did not accept any reforming doctrines such as justification by faith though he had doubts about purgatory, and the challenge to the belief in the 'real presence' in the Mass had yet to come.

Longland had also continued to play a central role in the divorce case, debating with Queen Catherine of Aragon in 1530, and remained close to Henry though he may also have had doubts about the pace of change; nonetheless, he accepted Henry's supremacy, had done enough to be a target for the conservative 1536 rebels, and publicly denounced the 'bishop of Rome' in 1538.

The king had placed Edward Lee as the new Archbishop of York in late 1531, a man who had worked on the divorce case though who perhaps had some personal doubts about it. He occasionally seems to have flirted with opposition and in 1535 was suspected by Cromwell of doing too little to get his clergy to support the royal supremacy – though in July 1535 he jailed a priest for opposing it. He may be seen as at least a public acceptor of the political reformation. The ambassador Chapuys thought he changed his mind after he became archbishop (rather like Becket) whilst Bernard concluded that 'a reluctance to go ahead' may have been his position.[20] Such was the leader of the Church for Nottinghamshire.

Henry had only reformed Church politics but men like Lee also worried about the reformation of ideas, the theological one. The biggest challenge came from the increasing protests against the Catholic practice and its interpretation of Christianity, accelerating mainly in the far south of Lincoln diocese. In 1532 Thomas Harding was burnt at Chesham for 'denying the real presence in the sacrament'. From the start Longland was keen to root out any of Luther's writings from his diocese (which included Oxford) and he sent four Buckinghamshire 'Lollards' to be burnt at the stake in the same period.[21] At Buckingham he sent one man to the stake for reading the Lord's Prayer in English and another for

19   There is a helpful discussion on this in Williamson, p.40-2
20   G W Bernard, *The King's Reformation: Henry VIII and the Making of the English Church*, Yale, 2005, p.178
21   These were at Amersham, which was also in his huge diocese.

doing the same with James's Epistle. He was less successful in stopping the discussion of evangelical writings at Oxford and continued to worry that the Lincolnshire coast was an import route for such contraband; he also asked the archdeacon of Lincoln to require an oath of orthodoxy from any new parish priest.

New ideas were also trickling into the diocese of York. In Worksop in 1533 Lambert Sparrow, or Hooke, who was of Dutch origins, admitted a range of heresies which were Lutheran in origin including stating that 'there is no priest but God only'. He also denied the real presence in the Mass (making him well ahead of Luther's theology[22]) and proclaimed 'any man may christen another'. He had been selling Lutheran books but recanted and was seemingly pardoned. The next year in the same town, Giles Vanbellaer, also Dutch, had a similar narrow escape from the stake – his offences included having a New Testament in Dutch and saying that the sacrament was only bread.[23] He also recanted. Jennings has suggested that Vanbellaer was active as early as 1529 and Sparrow until 1544.[24]

An ongoing battle was over the Bible in English, which had been begun by Wycliffe and his associates in the late 1300s. Tyndale's New Testament was printed in English in 1526 but Henry banned this in 1530 and Tyndale was executed 1536 near Bruxelles. Intriguingly, Tyndale had been employed by the Gild of St Mary's at Boston to sing masses in 1521; this was soon to emerge as a centre of radicalism.[25] Myles Coverdale produced the first complete Bible in English in 1535. Ironically Cranmer had already begun work on an English Bible in 1534 which was so slow that the 'Matthew Bible' was authorised instead in 1537 with Thomas Cromwell a driving force. Print was making such books accessible, and reading was to become a significant factor in the spread of Reformation thinking. Henry's 'Great Bible' was approved in 1539. However, during the reaction of the 1540s access to the Bible was severely restricted and many were destroyed; in 1542 Cranmer had to block attempts to revert to only a Latin version.

Protestant or evangelical influences trickled into the region via the coast, the rivers and from London. An early example is the life of Robert Plumpton, born to a gentry family at Waterton in Axholme in 1516 and who was buried at Luddington in 1546. By 1536, when he was in London as a law student, he was writing home to try and convert his mother to evangelicalism and sending her the works of Tyndale. The historian Dickens sees Plumpton as a classic example of how young men going to the Inns of Court brought the new ideas back into the country.[26]

'Dearly beloved Mother in the Lord, I write not this to bring you into any heresy, but to teach you the clear light of God's doctrine. Mother you have much to thank God for that it would please him to give you license to live until this time, for the Gospel of Christ was never truly preached as it is now.'[27]

---

22   A radical new understanding of 'communion' rather than the Mass was due to Zwingli, a Swiss theologian largely active in the 1520s but Luther never rejected transubstantiation.
23   A G Dickens, *Lollards and Protestants in the Diocese of York*, p.20
24   S B Jennings, *The Gathering of the Elect*, DPhil thesis, Nottingham Trent University, 1999, p.31
25   D MacCulloch, *Thomas Cromwell*, p.66
26   Dickens, Lollards, p.135-7
27   R W Heinze and T Dowley, *Reform and Conflict: From the Medieval World to the Wars of Religion*, Oxford, 2006, p.207; also covered extensively in Dickens (1959) p. 131-3

Thomas Cranmer and the Church of England

The Catholic Church in England had had many problems, one of which was that it was a career choice for men with their minds on matters other than Jesus's teachings. One such was Thomas Magnus of Newark[28] (1463/3-1550) who enjoyed a rich career as a diplomat and administrator whilst drawing many incomes from the Church. Because of Henry's gratitude for his diplomatic services, by the mid-1530s Magnus held the masterships of St Leonard's Hospital and the college of St Sepulchre in York, and Sibthorpe College, Nottinghamshire, in addition to being vicar of Kendal, Westmorland, and rector of Bedale, Kirkby in Cleveland and Sessay, all in the North Riding of Yorkshire. His eight benefices in the diocese of York alone yielded £814 per annum.[29] In 1529 he founded a grammar and song school in his birthplace. We might say that he was the last great Nottinghamshire 'churchman' of the Catholic era, but the first of the evangelicals had an altogether greater impact.

Thomas Cranmer was probably the first undoubtedly great man of faith to emanate from Nottinghamshire being born in 1489 at Aslockton, a small village between Grantham and Bingham. The family name came from Cranmer Manor near Sutterton in Lincolnshire and his grandfather was the first of the family to live at Aslockton.[30] The family's interests across both counties were crucial in Cranmer's career. The family's parish church was at Whatton, where his father was buried, and the family had many Church connections: his father had close links to the Premonstratensian monastery of Welbeck, Nottinghamshire; two of three sons, Thomas and Edmund, were prepared for a clerical career, and their sister Alice became a Cistercian.

Cranmer's career took him away from his native area, but he retained many personal contacts in the two counties from Boston to Nottingham. Possibly two relatives were monks at Welbeck, until its dissolution whilst sister Alice, who became problematic for him later, remained at Stixwould in Lincolnshire.[31] After the dissolution of Welbeck much of its property was bought by Richard Whalley, one of Cromwell's 'employees',[32] whose sons married the daughters of a Cranmer relative and servant, Henry Hatfield. Another Lincolnshire connection was with the Tamworth family who had houses at Leake and near Stixwould – they had successful careers in the Church and government.[33] His sister Agnes married Edmund Cartwright of Ossington in Nottinghamshire, where he was also connected to the Molyneaux family of Hawton and the Clifton family of Clifton near Nottingham. Perhaps of greatest interest was Sir John Markham,[34] a friend of thirty years with whom he maintained ongoing contacts, who was from a substantial family previously based at 'Great' Markham and later at Cotham; Markham had been in the

---

28 Magnus was, according to legend, found as an abandoned baby on the streets of Newark by some passing clothiers.
29 Alone this would be worth over £250,000 a year today – but he had other incomes as well!
30 A W Pollard, *Thomas Cranmer and the English Reformation*, p.3
31 She became its sacristan. When it was refounded by the king, it was directed to pray for his later queen, Jane Seymour. (MacCulloch, p.207)
32 Wood (1947), p.147
33 D MacCulloch, *Thomas Cranmer*, pps 16-19 provides much detail on his family background. Thomas Tamworth, Cranmer's cousin, was an alderman of the Boston Corpus Christi Gild in 1531.
34 MacCulloch speculates that Gervase Markham, Prior of Dunstable where Cranmer held a hearing on Catherine of Aragon, was of this family. See also *TTS*, 1981.

service of Lady Margaret Beaufort and was an early adopter of 'forward' religion. As early as 1537 Cranmer noted that 'Sir John of long season hath unfeignedly favoured the truth of God's word:' one would love to know the definition here of 'long'. Cranmer also spoke up for Anthony Neville (Nevell) of South Leverton in his home county.

The Markham Family

In the sometimes-dangerous world of evangelical and later puritan faith, family connections were vital and marriages tended to reflect a uniting of faith perspectives.

Sir John Markham inherited some problems from his father, a great knight but also a man known for his temper, but he did gain an illustrious family line linking him to Lady Margaret Beaufort and even earlier to Katherine Swynford. The Sir John of crucial importance to this story married three times – to Anne Neville, Margery Langford of Langford and lastly to Anne Stanhope, née Strelley, who had been living at Rampton. He thus had many connections, fostered also by being related to Sir John Hercy and his many sisters.

He was for a time in the service of Lady Margaret Beaufort, who had interests across Lincolnshire including at Boston, and early in life he grew to know Thomas Cranmer whose home village was but a stone's throw from Markham's at Cotham.

Markham had several connections to the Babington family as well as through his own mother– his son John, who died in 1564, married the daughter of Sir Anthony Babington who was a maternal cousin to Thomas Cromwell. Markham's daughter Frances married Henry Babington, the mother of Anthony Babington who was executed following the famous plot with Mary Queen of Scots in 1586. Anthony was, through his mother, the grandson of Lord Darcy who had been executed by Henry VIII. The Babingtons were patrons of the living of Marnham and may have been responsible for bringing Richard Clifton, the future leader of the Babworth separatists, into the district; ironic, given Anthony's Catholicism.

The Markhams also had links to the Cliftons as Sir John's son, another John, died in 1564 and appointed Sir Gervase Clifton as an overseer of his will. Another close family connection shown in this will was with Charles Brandon, Duke of Suffolk, for the younger John's will of 1564 mentioned 'my leaste standing cupp with the cover that the Duke Charles of Suffolk gave to me'. Another son, Henry, became Precentor of Lincoln Cathedral.

Such complex relationships are complex for the reader but crucial for understanding how the new faith survived and thrived. The Markham marriages connect us to both the radicals of the 1530s and the generation of the 1580s. Sir John's son William married Elizabeth Montagu, daughter of the Judge Sir Edward Montagu of Northamptonshire; her niece married Sir William Wray of Glentworth, who became a significant Lincolnshire radical, and her nephew was a bishop and patron of Worksop's Richard Bernard.

Another local connection was James Morice, who was controller of the customs at Boston and a clerk of works on Cambridge colleges, whose son Ralph became Cranmer's secretary and biographer.[35] Morice had, like Markham, worked for Lady Margaret Beaufort on the Boston tidal sluice in 1502, became controller of customs in Boston in 1504 and weigher of wool in 1509.[36] All his sons became active evangelicals. Very significantly, his sons Ralph and William visited the condemned evangelical James Bainham in prison in 1532 along with Hugh Latimer; William was often in trouble for his progressive views and under arrest at the end of Henry's reign.

Other Cranmer friends were Thomas Goodrich, also from Boston, who became Bishop of Ely and Lord Chancellor in 1552, and John Whitwell who was long his personal chaplain; Goodrich and Whitwell went to school together in Boston. We can also include William Benson, later known as William Boston, another Bostonian and future Abbot and Dean of Westminster whose career was supported by Thomas Cromwell. There were also administrators or surveyors such as Henry Hatfield (a relative on his mother's side) and Henry Stockwith. Closest of all perhaps was his younger brother Edmund, whose clerical career also took him into Canterbury diocese.[37] Henry Rands, later Henry Holbeach, was another Lincolnshire man in Cranmer's circle although it seems they had no connection until Cambridge.

Perhaps Cranmer knew some of these at his grammar school; we do not know where this was, but he hated his 'severe and cruel schoolmaster'.

A Boston Reformer

Chief among Cranmer's friends from Boston was Thomas Goodrich (1494-1554), born to a family in East Kirkby Lincolnshire. He was a friend of Cranmer's chaplain John Whitwell from the age of seven. He was at Jesus College, Cambridge, with Cranmer and then a priest in the diocese of Lincoln in 1523. He was involved again with Cranmer as an advisor on the royal divorce in 1529, winning him the support of the Boleyn family, and he became Bishop of Ely in 1534 as a sure supporter of the Royal Supremacy. Goodrich stood out as a consistent reformer including when this became difficult during the Six Articles controversy in 1539. He faced uncomfortable times in the trial of the Windsor heretics, which included Testwood, and when his associate George Blagge was involved with the martyrs of 1546.

During the time of Edward VI, he continued to be influential, and was appointed Lord Chancellor in 1551. When Mary came to the throne, he paid her homage but effectively became a house prisoner, dying in 1554.

---

35   Ralph Morice was an active protector of radicals in the 1540s.
36   Another Beaufort connection was Thomas Watson, who became choirmaster for the St Mary Guild in Boston.
37   Edmund became Archdeacon of Canterbury and was enriched by the lands of Wingham College, which he managed to acquire illegally when it was dissolved in 1544.

Goodrich's cousin Richard was from Bolingbroke although his father was a merchant of the staple and thus must have been associated with Boston. He became a talented lawyer and was also a committed reformer, he was a friend of Sir George Blagge who narrowly escaped execution in the crisis of 1546. After Blagge's death a few years later, he married the widow but divorce from his previous wife caused some scandalous debate in court. He was elected MP for Grimsby several times. Another Goodrich, John, possibly from Wrangle, contributed some verses in a collection written on the death of the radical theologian Martin Bucer in 1551. Bucer was closely connected to the Duchess of Suffolk.

Cranmer went to Cambridge in 1503, his choice of college perhaps reflecting the connection between Lady Margaret Beaufort and the Markhams.[38] At Cambridge he was with Goodrich, Benson and Hugh Latimer whilst his fellowship at Jesus College was briefly interrupted by a marriage – ending in his wife's death. In 1525 he considered a move to Cardinal College in Oxford, which had recruited others with Boston links such as Taverner; according to Susan Wabuda, he turned back after having actually set off – 'there is the merest hint from some later evidence that the warning came from a member of the Markham family'. Of course, Cardinal College was soon revealed as a centre of Lutheran influence.[39]

We have seen that Henry VIII's need for a divorce from Catherine of Aragon prompted his breach with the Pope. Thomas Wolsey was initially set the task of achieving this and a team of learned clerics were set to work to find a legal and Biblical argument – an opportunity for those with reforming or 'evangelical' opinions. Frustrated by the Pope's failure to support him, Henry drove through the Act of Supremacy in 1534 which made the monarch Head of the Church and made the issue of accepting his Church leadership potentially one where questions of treason came into play. However, in doctrine Henry was never an evangelical, often turning back the tide to reflect his conservative beliefs.

Cranmer himself benefited from being a close advisor in the divorce discussions and his appointment as Archbishop of Canterbury in 1532 owed much to the influence of the Boleyn family, who were broadly supportive of further reform. By this stage Cranmer had already absorbed some of the ideas of the Reformation and on a trip to Nuremburg in 1532 he had met the woman who was to become his secret second wife throughout Henry's reign since the King still disagreed with clerical marriage.

Almost immediately Cranmer was presented with the problem that reformation ideas were running in advance of the king; John Frith was condemned to death for his views on the Mass in 1533. At this stage, Cranmer still disagreed with Frith's views, but his track record of supporting those condemned to die is the most glaring weakness of his time as archbishop. Soon Cranmer himself became more convinced about reform, beginning work on an English Bible in 1534 and he began to approve more radical bishops, such as Hugh Latimer in 1535. We have also seen that he appointed some radicals to preach around the kingdom.

---

38   MacCulloch, p.22

39   Susan Wabuda, *Thomas Cranmer,* 2017, London, 2017. MacCulloch does not mention this story.

Whilst Cranmer rode the tide of change, John Longland found his position increasingly uncomfortable and in 1534 he told the Spanish ambassador that he would 'rather be the poorest man in the world than ever have been the King's councillor and confessor'.[40] Thomas Cromwell rationalised the diocesan geography by splitting the Lincoln diocese with the creation of sees at Peterborough in 1541 and Oxford in 1542 – a profoundly essential change! Eventually, Longland found himself a position just on Henry's side of the fence, denouncing 'the bishop of Rome' as someone who offended God in 1538. He did not oppose the dissolution of the monasteries and he welcomed a Bible in English. Yet he kept control of preaching, by 1540 keeping records on who preached what, and continuing to control the books that were being circulated. As he faced death, he set aside money to build a chantry chapel, whereas by this time the evangelicals were sweeping away any belief in the efficacy of praying for the dead. He also left money for an almshouse in his hometown of Henley. Longland was a man who appears to have been stuck in the middle – not trusted by Thomas Cromwell, disliked by the Lincolnshire rebels, but he took the secrets of Henry's confessional to the grave with him.

The move towards evangelicalism was slow in Lincolnshire. When Richard Quaenus preached the new idea of justification by faith at Stamford in August 1535, he was attacked by Dominicans and had to be defended by Richard Cecil. Then the Abbot of Thame got up and preached a contrary sermon, perhaps more to Longland's taste.[41] It was a warning of what was to come.

Meanwhile, the former Queen had been kept at the Bishop of Lincoln's house in Buckden where Sir Robert Dymoke of Lincolnshire had been a loyal servant. The impediment of Catherine of Aragon was removed in 1536 when she died at Kimbolton Castle. Knowing that she was dying, her friend Lady Maria Willoughby, a Spanish woman married into a Lincolnshire family, broke all the rules by travelling to Kimbolton and forcing an entrance to the Castle where the old queen more or less died in her arms. Lady Maria, a devout Catholic, was the mother of Katherine Willoughby, Duchess of Suffolk from 1533, who was to become arguably the greatest woman in the Protestant history of Lincolnshire.

Cranmer survived the downfall of Anne Boleyn, which might have been a disaster for the evangelical cause, partly through help from Thomas Cromwell. In 1536 he preached a sermon denouncing the Pope as Antichrist, a seminal moment, but there still remained many theological questions to negotiate.

We can see this division in the disputes that took place. In Grantham, for example, the King's schoolmaster Gervase Tyndale objected to the preaching of Rev Dr Stanley in 1535, who had inflamed the congregation's fears of purgatory by colourful allusions to Pompeii. When Tyndale challenged him – the teaching of purgatory being one of the doctrines that had been rejected by the King – Stanley seems to have managed to get Tyndale's pupils to desert him. Tyndale wrote to complain to Cromwell, alleging that he had done good service in reporting on witchcraft amongst friars on behalf of the Earl of Rutland and Cromwell. It is possible that by this stage Tyndale was already working directly for Cromwell and he was certainly well connected – having been at Cardinal College in Oxford with the Boston evangelicals like Lawney and also Richard Morison,

40   Quotation given in Bowker, ODNB.
41   Bowker (1981), p.145

who was one of Cromwell's confidantes, and he was related to the Clifton family of Clifton in Nottinghamshire – who were also connected to Cranmer.[42]

He is probably next seen at Eton in October 1537 where a 'Tyndall' was noted as 'Cromwell's true scholar and beadman'.[43] Tyndale went southwest, where he was involved in 1538 in denouncing Sir Geoffrey Pole and his mother the Countess of Salisbury for actively undermining the king's religious policy by banning local people from having the Bible in English.[44] This came to light after Tyndale was interrogated by the Poles' men, then taken to Lewes to give evidence to Cromwell – with all expenses paid. Hence the suspicion that Tyndale, a clear supporter of the new beliefs, had been sent to gather evidence on its opponents. The outcome was that Sir Geoffrey was arrested, and attempted suicide after a spell in the Tower; his mother was executed in 1541, one of the most prominent Catholic martyrs of the early Reformation.

The new mood of reform encouraged greater spiritual aspiration amidst at least some of the people. It is possible to see this in the protests of the people of St Wulfram, Grantham, who in 1539 complained en masse that they were being neglected by their immoral priests.[45] In Nottinghamshire, one of Cromwell's agents reported perhaps just the simple desire to live in peace:

Here in Nottinghamshire our churches be nothing like furnished with clerkly sermons according to the King's injunctions. The people here did little practise the King's gracious liberty to eat white meats in Lent time. Men say nothing against the King's acts, as long as peace followeth, but when it was said, as at our late musters, we should have war, methought the people but "mely" courageous towards it, saying "How now! an we have war then God have mercy upon us all!" and suchlike dark reasons.[46]

There was some dismantling of Catholic iconography and the rood screen of Boston was burnt in the marketplace in 1538.[47] Churches were ordered to have a Bible; in 1540 even the cathedral was buying bibles for its churches at places such as Gosberton.

Dissolution of the Monasteries

In 1530 there were about 130 religious institutions in Lincolnshire[48] but only about twenty in Nottinghamshire, together with numerous chantries. The Lincolnshire ones were often very poor with 25 on an income of less than £100 a year including six on less than £20. Houses of this size could not maintain enough canons or nuns. Their abuses, most often

---

42 MacDiarmid notes that 'Tyndale was no relation to the Bible translator but was closely related to the Midlands family of Clifton, sires to more than one Cambridge don and kin to Archbishop Cranmer.' *Thomas Cromwell*, p.473-4.

43 Hazel Pierce, *Margaret Pole,* Cardiff, 2009

44 G R Elton, *Policy and Police*, Cambridge, 1972, p.41. Some historians have claimed that Tyndale was related to William Tyndale and others that he was a spy for Cromwell. He was at King's 1535-7. J Chappell and K Kramer (eds), *Women during the English Reformations*,

45 Mary Lucas, *Popular Religious Attitudes in Urban Lincolnshire*, Nottingham, 1998

46 L & P, XIV, I 1094, letter from John Marshall.

47 *Lincolnshire Historian*, vol 8, 1973

48 G Hodgett, *Tudor Lincolnshire*, Lincoln, 1975, p.9

omissions in their duties, were thus not entirely the invention of Cromwell's visitors – in 1525 it was reported that the canons of Humberston went into town to play tennis.

The monasteries may not have been at their best when the King's agenda put them at risk – several of the main Lincolnshire houses, especially Louth Park, had suffered a loss in numbers over the previous century.[49] Indeed, some historians now argue that the policy of dissolution started by targeting smaller houses as the intention was to *reform* the system by only closing these down. As early as 1519 the Pope himself had deputed Wolsey to help reform the monasteries, and so closures had begun. Meanwhile, Henry also had a dislike of religious relics and pilgrimages, with which many of the houses were associated. In 1525 a visit to Stixwould investigated improper relations between the prioress and the seneschal at which Alice Cranmer gave evidence. In 1529 Lord Darcy, who we shall meet again soon, was complaining of the pulling down of abbeys. But a pivotal issue then became the royal supremacy which overlapped with issues of dissolution, and which the 'visitors' who toured the monasteries also investigated at the universities.

The dissolution of the monasteries was organised from London by Thomas Cromwell, who had earlier worked for Wolsey and who mainly relied on regional commissioners; these were usually men of a reforming mind. In Nottinghamshire he relied especially on gentry like Sir John Markham and Sir John Hercy of Grove, who used their minor relatives like George Lassells to aid the work;[50] families like the Lassells and the Whalleys gained much from the dissolution. Markham was already a friend of Thomas Cranmer and John Babington, another of this team, an adherent of Cromwell.[51] A small network of families, of reforming views as they were trusted with the monasteries and most of whom played a role in resisting the Lincolnshire Rising, thus emerge into our story. They knew each other through marriages, land deals and eventually faith. The dissolutions created a fluid land market where people bought and sold to consolidate their holdings; Sir John Markham bought land around Sturton-le-Steeple and Leverton from Sir William Ayscough in 1536,[52] with the two men having married sisters from Strelley. Ayscough's daughter Anne and the Markham-Hercy relative John Lassells both became significant martyrs in 1546.

---

49 Bowker (1981), p.18

50 Hercy was related to the Lassells family, the guardian of George and John, and referred to them as cousins; he was uncle to William Mering and his sisters provided many other family connections, most significantly to the Denmans. Men like Mering were also well known to Cranmer. George named one of his children Hercye Lassells. Although Hercy had no son, he was connected by marriage into many local families and spread his influence and his thinking to the Denmans, Nevilles etc.

51 Dickens, *Lollards*, p.41. This Babington was buried at Rampton.

52 *The Town on the Street*, 1975, p.32

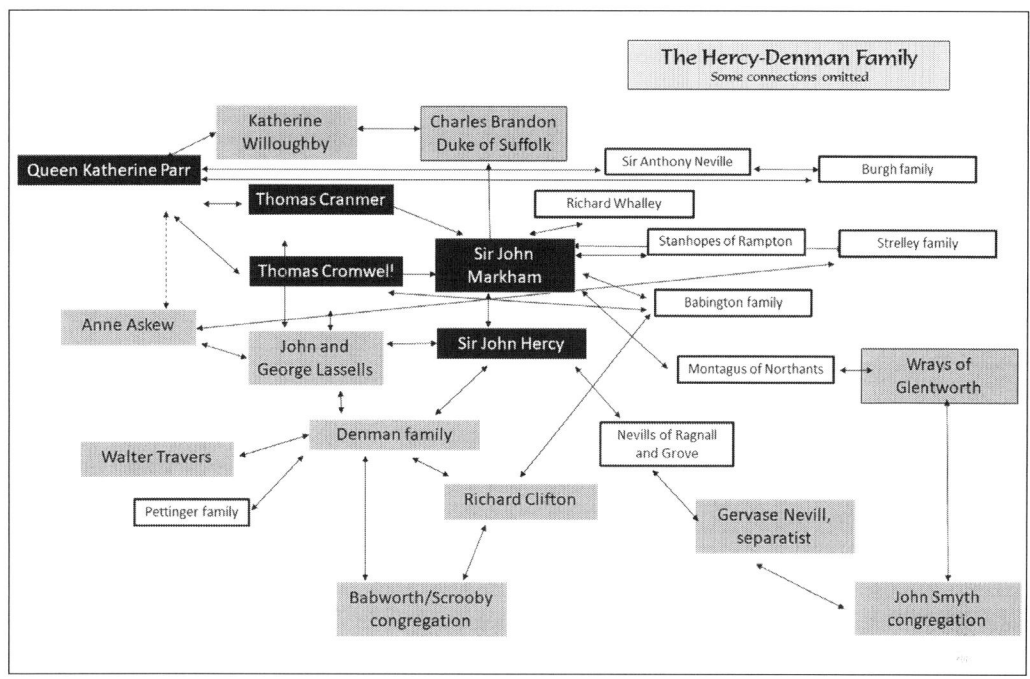

The Hercy-Denman Family
Some connections omitted

Although the initial motivation may not have been for financial gain, many did gain from dissolution, or by providing service at key times, with many being reformers. In general, this had the effect of making the evangelicals more powerful. Edmund Hall of Grantham, who was in the retinue of Charles Brandon, Duke of Suffolk, and was also related to his wife Katherine Willoughby, acquired the manor of Greatford from the abbey of Hyde in 1540 and also other lands taken from the 1536 rebels; evangelical in religion, he fell out of favour during the reign of Mary I but was a witness to Katherine Willoughby's will in 1559 – a sure indication of his beliefs. Richard Goodrich gained lands at Sleaford and also revenues from chantries. The Brocklesbys moved up a notch from yeoman origins, joined the circle of Brandon in 1542 and proved in time to be ardent evangelicals at Glentworth, but Heneages, Tyrhwitts and Dymokes also acted as commissioners. In Lincolnshire it was probably Suffolk, Edward Fiennes Lord Clinton and Saye, and Thomas Manners – who became Earl of Rutland – who gained the most. Suffolk proved adept in consolidating his power by swapping lands in Suffolk for monastic properties in Lincolnshire during 1538-40 which brought him Louth Park, Kirkstead and many others. He sold some to his retinue, such as Grange de Lings to George St Paul who was his legal adviser and Legsby to Matthew St Paul. Fiennes also consolidated his lands around Sempringham. The Heneage family gained Willoughby preceptory in 1542 and also Legbourne Priory; Sir Thomas Heneage seems to have had evangelical inclinations although his brother George Heneage was a noted pluralist, with seven rectories, who became Dean of Lincoln 1528-34 and Archdeacon 1542-9.

Before Cromwell's commissioners even set foot in the monasteries, monks were asked in 1534 to swear an oath under the Act of Supremacy repudiating the Pope's claim to authority in England. Only the Observant Franciscans at Newark and the Carthusians of Axholme (Melwood) and Beauvale had a problem with this. Sir John Markham reported on the Newark situation to Cromwell in early 1534: the friars were preaching in the town to 'move and stir men in communications and in their confessions, considering the credit thy be in amongst the people'. One of them was perhaps John Forest, who had been exiled from London.

The prior of Beauvale, Robert Lawrence, Augustine Webster, the prior of Melwood near Epworth, and John Houghton, previously the Prior of Beauvale for six months but now at London Charterhouse, went to see Thomas Cromwell to argue against dissolution. Although some accounts have said they refused to take the Oath of Supremacy and thereby denied the authority of the King, they tried to exploit a difference between spiritual and secular aspects of church leadership and in fact took the oath with the condition 'in so far as it is lawful';[53] Houghton was placed in the Tower in Spring 1534 and pressure increased on the others.

Henry was irritated by the condition attached to the oaths and ordered fresh oaths to be sworn in April 1535 which Houghton, Lawrence and Webster all refused to swear. When questioned by Cromwell and again later, Houghton denied that a layman could be Head of the Church or a successor of St Peter. Cromwell put one of his staff, John Whalley,[54] in charge of the Carthusians and he reported they were very stubborn – 'they be exceedingly superstitious, ceremonious and pharasaical, and wonderously addicted to their old Mumpsimus'.[55] Ten Carthusians were sent to Newgate and Houghton, Lawrence and Webster sentenced to die for treason. This seems to have been a personal decision by Henry VIII, for Cranmer argued against it.[56]

They were executed on 4 May 1535 at Tyburn by being hung, drawn and quartered. Catholic tradition relates that when Houghton was about to be quartered, as the executioner tore open his chest to remove his heart, he prayed, 'O Jesu, what wouldst thou do with my heart?' A painting by the noted painter of religious figures, Francisco Zurbarán, depicts him with his heart in his hand and a noose around his neck. Lawrence was beatified in 1886 and canonised – made a saint – in 1970, and Webster and Houghton were also made saints. John Whalley was left with the job of resolving any remaining Carthusian issues. Three other monks were executed in June 1535 and at least eight more died in prison with the survivor being executed in August 1540. Two Beauvale monks were sent to Syon for 're-education' in August 1537.

William Trafford was sent to London from Beauvale in 1535 for refusing to accept the supremacy of the King and arrived a few days after Lawrence's execution. Having eventually 'conformed', he was made prior of the London Charterhouse in Houghton's place.[57] By the time dissolution arrived for Beauvale, the Prior there was all packed up and ready to leave when the commissioners arrived.[58]

There seems to have been no other need for harsh punishment though the Sacrist at Beauvale, Nicholas Dugmer, managed to avoid signing the surrender. When challenged by

---

53   Bernard (2005), p.161
54   There were Whalley families in Nottinghamshire and Yorkshire at this time.
55   Bernard, p.162. Was John Whalley related to Richard Whalley of Kirton and Screveton? This remains uncertain, for John was certainly not living in Nottinghamshire.
56   Bernard (2005), p.163
57   Bernard (2005), p.164
58   David Knowles, *The Religious Orders in England*, Cambridge, 1950, vol 3, p.357

the King's commissioners to accept Henry's authority, he replied 'I take him as God and the Holy Church take him; and I am sure he taketh himself none otherwise'. This evasive answer apparently sufficed.[59] One of these commissioners was Sir John Markham, trusted as a reforming friend of Cranmer,[60] who also took part in the suppression of Lenton along with George Lassells and saw the execution of its Prior. Markham was a trusted man in matters of religion – he 'hath unfeignedly favoured the truth of God's word,' Cranmer told the king.

Many years later, living abroad, Dugmer[61] told of a vision he had had at Beauvale:
Our god Father Dugmer told me that when he was young and Sacrist, and one day had washed the Church Corporals, and had laid them in the garden upon the lavender borders to dry, in the midst of his dinner he went into his garden to see the cloths, and he saw our Blessed Lady sitting beside the Corporals tending them, and our Blessed Lord in the likeness of a little child, pulling the lavender knops and, as little children will do, casting them upon the Corporals. 'Then', thought the good Sacrist, 'I may well go to my dinner again, for the cloths are well kept.'[62]

Beauvale Associations

The story of Beauvale did not end with dissolution. In 1538 Sir John Hercy wrote to Thomas Cromwell and asked him to grant Beauvale to John Lassells[63] but the Priory and its lands were awarded to Sir William Hussey, a Lincolnshire landowner, though they embroiled him in many legal disputes during Edward VI's reign. Hussey's daughter Neile married Richard Disney (c1505-1578), of Norton Disney Lincolnshire, by which the Disneys, a reforming family, came to hold Beauvale. Disney's second wife was Jane Ayscough, sister of the famous evangelical martyr Anne, from the Ayscough family we have mentioned before who held lands both at Stallingborough and South Kelsey in Lincolnshire and near to Beauvale at Nuthall; Jane was the widow St Paul, a lawyer in the Brandon-Willoughby empire. Both of Disney's wives can be seen on the memorial at Norton Disney.

The interconnections flow from here to the *Mayflower* itself for Thomas Disney, who was MP for Boroughbridge, married Katherine Smith née Porter, the grandmother of the White girls who married John Robinson and John Carver. Thomas Disney (1579-1623) married as his second wife Elizabeth Denman of Retford and his third Bridget Nevile of Mattersey – all relatives of Sir John Hercy. This established Beauvale and its parish church at Greasley as an evangelical and later puritan enclave which reached its peak when the White family arrived from Sturton-le-Steeple; hence John Robinson, the famous puritan[64] leader, came here to seek a bride who he married at Greasley church, and another sister went on the Mayflower with John Carver. Greasley itself was long a centre of nonconformity.

---

59   David Knowles, *The Religious Orders in England*, Cambridge, 1950, vol 3, p.179
60   D MacCulloch, *Thomas Cranmer, a Life*, p.370 refers to Markham as a boyhood friend of Cranmer.
61   Dugmer died at Bruges in 1575; Wood (1947), p.141
62   David Knowles (1950), vol 3, p.475
63   L & P, Oct 1538, 726
64   The term 'puritan' was an unwelcome label attached to the progressive evangelicals. According to S J Knox in his book on Travers, it was first used in 1564.

Retracing the story to 1535, commissioners were sent out to value ecclesiastical property. Those in Lincolnshire included George St Paul, Anthony Irby and William Ayscough from families that were to prove securely evangelical for a century, but also William Tyrwhitt from one who was not. Dr Legh and Dr Layton were then likely to have begun the second visitation, probably starting with some Trentside houses late in 1535 and leading into the proposals to dissolve the smaller houses in early 1536.

By the Act of 1536, the smaller houses worth £200 or less were dealt with first. Records of the dissolution in York diocese have survived whereas much of Lincoln's has been lost, so we have an incomplete picture of the process itself. Nine of Nottinghamshire's thirteen houses were in the first tranche. Many, but not all, of the smaller houses in Lincolnshire such as Legbourne and Louth Park were closed in 1536 – Lincolnshire had a very high proportion of these although the Cistercian monastery of Stixwould was refounded (perhaps because of its Cranmer connections) with Benedictine nuns from Stainfield by the start of 1537.[65] Then it was closed down again in September 1539.

John Freeman and John Wiseman began work as commissioners in summer 1536. The Abbot of Barlings was sure that his house would be dealt with quickly, so he began distributing valuables and money to the safe-keeping of people such as the vicar of Scothern.

The Observant Friars of Newark, one of only six English houses in this rigorous order, were a centre of opposition. One of the friars attracted Sir John Markham's attention in 1533 by preaching seditious sermons, of which he confessed; in 1534 two of the friars – Hugh Payne and Thomas Hayfield – had set out on a preaching tour across the West Country disguised as priests, speaking out in defence of the Pope before a fruitless attempt to escape to Brittany.[66] They were pursued by John Hilsey, presumably the same man who later arrested Litherland of Newark, and they were captured at Cardiff in secular clothing.[67] They had openly spoken out for the Pope, denounced Hugh Latimer as a heretic and scoffed at the baptism of Princess Elizabeth. Both men denied all charges when arrested, 'abjectly submitted' to the king, and said all the prayers for the king that they could, but Payne still resurfaced in Suffolk in 1537 where he had returned to preaching against the reforms; he seems to have died in the Marshalsea prison in 1539.[68] The visitor Layton had advance intelligence of numerous sexual offences by the friars.[69] In 1536 the friars refused to accept royal supremacy and the order was broken up, many dying in captivity. Their Newark friary was transferred, temporarily, to the Austin Friars, but a few of the friars became involved in the subsequent rebellions.

At Blyth in Nottinghamshire commissioners found four monks guilty of 'disgraceful offences' and one of adultery – this was closed in 1536. When Shelford Priory was broken up in 1536 Cranmer asked for its lands to be awarded to his brother-in-law but Cromwell awarded it to the Stanhopes. Felley also closed in 1536, being converted into a house,

65   Bernard (2005), p.443
66   Bernard (2005), p.155.
67   Hilsey was a former Dominican and then visitor to the friaries who became Bishop of Rochester who was noted for his attacks on fake relics.
68   P Marshall, A Ryrie, *The Beginnings of English Protestantism*, Cambridge, 2002, p.57
69   Bernard, p.262

and the Prior was appointed to the living of Attenborough. Broadholme and Rufford also closed, but others were able to purchase a stay of execution.

As detailed below, the dissolution was then interrupted by the Lincolnshire Rising in October 1536. Barlings and Kirkstead were then early victims, tainted by their links with the Rising. This had a significant impact on Lincolnshire gentry, and also on Nottinghamshire gentry when similar events occurred in Yorkshire. Men like Sir John Markham emerged much stronger from this era whereas others like Lord Darcy and his cousin Lord Hussey of Sleaford were executed. Sir Robert Tyrwhitt I was rewarded with the lands of Stainfield. But perhaps the biggest winner was Charles Brandon, Duke of Suffolk, and ultimately his duchess Katherine, with awards including lands of Barlings and Kirkstead abbeys.

Rufford Abbey was acquired by Sir John Markham in 1537, and he also gained the friary in Newark and Newbo Abbey in Lincolnshire.[70] Its Abbot received a comfortable position as Rector of Rotherham. Rufford was afterwards transferred to the Earl of Shrewsbury by Henry VIII as a reward for his role in crushing the 1536 revolt.[71]

Early in 1537 work began on the three Lincolnshire houses which had been involved in the revolt – Barlings, Kirkstead and Bardney. As the abbots were accused of treason, their 'properties' were confiscated by the Crown and Sir William Parr (the brother of Katherine Parr) charged with disposal of the materials, with the Crown then assuming maintenance of the local dykes.[72] Work on these was completed in 1538.

The dissolution at Lenton was handled by Sir John Markham with Sir John Hercy of Grove, Hercy's 'cousin' George Lassells of Sturton and Gateford,[73] Richard Whalley, John Babington[74] and others of the Nottinghamshire evangelical vanguard. Discussions started in 1536 and correspondence was taken to London by George Lassells in 1537. On the other hand, its cause was defended by Sir John Willoughby of Wollaton.[75] Thus this sensitive dissolution brought together a select group of Nottinghamshire men who had proved their worth during the rebellions; Whalley, for example, had been in Cromwell's employ since at least 1527 and in 1536 was involved in visiting Yorkshire monasteries, helped with the trial of the rebels in York, and had sat on the Commission for the Peace in the North Riding in 1538 – his reward was to augment his lands at Kirketon in Screveton with Welbeck and Sibthorp.

Lenton was the richest house in Nottinghamshire though with many debts, and the Privy Council had received verbatim reports of treasonous discussion there. At Christmas 1536, the worst possible time, Ralph Swenson complained that the king 'will not keep

---

70   S T Bindoff, *The House of Commons 1509-1553*, vol 1, p.570. The Markhams held land around Tuxford and 'Great Markham', also at Ollerton and with their manor of Cotham near Newark. Sir John Markham's mother was a Babington, the daughter of Sir Anthony.

71   J Bramley, *Short History of the Religious Houses in Nottinghamshire*, 1948, p.19

72   Bernard, p.435 – this was the origin of the courts of sewers.

73   L & P, 1538, 726 from Hercy refers to John Lassells, his brother, as 'my cousin'.

74   The Babingtons held land at Kingston upon Soar and other places in Notts. His father Sir Anthony left a will in 1536 whose preamble was a model of the new faith.

75   D Marcombe and J Hamilton (eds), *Sanctity and Scandal*, Nottingham, 1998, p.29

no promise with God himself but pulls down his churches'.[76] This was exactly the same rumour that had triggered the Lincolnshire Rising. Other monks then joined in. One Dan Haughton was reported as saying, 'It is a marvellous world, for the King will hang a man for a word speaking nowadays' to which Dan Relph replied, 'Yea, but the King of Heaven will not do so, and he is the King of all Kings; but he that hangs a man in this world for a word speaking, he shall be hanged in another world himself'. The Sub-Prior then reported, 'I was afraid for my life, for I had heard many of the monks speak ill of the King and Queen, and Lord Privy Seal, whom they love worst of any man in the world'. Indeed, Prior Heath was denounced for calling the queen 'evil' and saying of Henry that 'the devil is in him' and that he would have 'a shameful death'.

Prior Heath was imprisoned in February 1538 under the Treasons Act, and also accused of hiding Swenson's treason, and the next month he and eight monks plus four labourers were indicted for treason – thirteen in all. Several seem to have been executed in Nottingham and their quarters displayed at the Priory.[77] Sir John Markham and John Babington both played key roles in the enquiry. Nicholas Harrison, the priest at Pleasley, had a lucky escape in April 1538 when he was reported to have been sarcastic comments about the King's advisers; Sir John Markham told Cromwell that 'the priest is aged and his wit and memory simple' so he was kept locked up for a time at least.[78] The Lenton site was leased by Michael Stanhope and plundered, but the octagonal Norman font survived in the garden of a local landowner until being given by him in 1842 to the new church of Holy Trinity whilst a replica forms the font at Dunedin cathedral in New Zealand.

Otherwise, 1537 was a year of little change with the only Lincolnshire surrenders being the Carthusians at Axholme and the Gilbertines at St Catherine's Lincoln, surrendered by William Griffiths who had witnessed the executions of the abbots of Barlings and Kirkstead. At Axholme three monks accused their prior of removing property from the house in advance of its closure.

Matters accelerated in 1538 by the end of which the Gilbertines were largely finished. Welbeck, one of the largest Nottinghamshire houses, where Hercy was also commissioned, was surrendered in June 1538 having seen a final moment of glory when it was the rallying point for the Duke of Norfolk when facing the rebels of October 1536. It was sold to Richard Whalley the next year for £500, and eventually became a Cavendish property. Worksop Priory closed in November 1538, and with it disappeared its famous Tickhill Psalter; the priory church was adapted to be the parish one but reduced in size and the lands awarded to the Earl of Shrewsbury. Although the 4th Earl was conservative in his religion, he had played a crucial role in the defeat of the Yorkshire rebels and was well rewarded, though he died in 1538. The Crown swapped Worksop manor for the manor of Farnham Royal in Buckinghamshire, and Farnham's right to provide the monarch's right glove at the Coronation also transferred in time to Worksop. Thurgarton, battered by multiple allegations of sexual offences on visitation in 1536, also surrendered the same month – here as at Worksop some of the priory church was retained for the parish whilst a house was built out of the old cloisters by William Cooper, another of the king's servants on the rise. The Gilbertine Mattersey closed, having only a prior, sub-prior and three

---

76 Bernard, p.385
77 The exact number executed is unclear. It seems unlikely that all 13 were.
78 L & P, 30 April 1538, p.371

canons;[79] when it was visited by Leigh and Layton in 1536 one of the canons was found to be 'incontinent'. It was not surrendered until 1538 and became a manor of the Neville family. Its Prior became Headmaster of Holgate's School in Malton, Yorkshire. Indeed, multiple Gilbertine houses surrendered in autumn 1538, including several smaller ones and the Carthusian house at Axholme (Melwood) surrendered in June 1538.

At Sempringham the Master, Robert Holgate, was a Cambridge scholar with close links to Thomas Cromwell. He attracted much enmity for being the 'nominee' of Cromwell and for having 'taken it upon himself' to be the prior. In fact, he had joined the Gilbertines early in his career, spent years at Cambridge, and by 1529 had become Prior of St Catherine's Without, Lincoln. At this time he may also have been vicar of Cadney near Brigg, from which he seems to have been forced out by a lawsuit from Sir Francis Ayscough.[80] Holgate went to London and a successful career took off. His appointment of Master at Sempringham gave him almost total legal power over the order (though he was not Prior at Sempringham itself). By 1537 he was Bishop of Llandaff and a few months later President of the Council of the North. Holgate profited well from the dissolution of the Gilbertine order. He succeeded Lee as Archbishop of York and is well known for his support of schools, including the struggling school at East Retford which he re-endowed. This grammar school traced its origins to the 1540s, and Holgate was involved when it was re-established and its statutes redrawn in 1551, funded from chantries at Annesley, Sutton-cum-Lound and Tuxford.[81] This school was unusually 'humanistic' in its approach.[82]

Holgate was one of many former monks to marry, though this later embroiled him in a bigamy scandal. His wife had been 'married' at the age of seven, but courts rejected the legality of this; however, after Mary came to the throne Holgate renounced his marriage, claiming he had only made it to prove he was not a Papist. Even more colourfully, the Bishop of Winchester, John Ponet, married a Nottingham woman even before clerical marriage was sanctioned, and she turned out to be already 'married' (through a legal pre-contract) to a butcher there so he had to legally separate from her in July 1550.

Many former monks adapted to a new life. At a lower level from Holgate, a Gilbertine canon Christopher Hudson married a Sempringham Gilbertine nun and became vicar of Dorrington by 1554 but the new Queen Mary then required him to live apart from his wife.

The friaries, such as the Grey Friars in Nottingham, were closed in 1538-9 and the nunnery at Wallingwells in Nottinghamshire was also closed in 1539. With it went the 'comb of St Edmund' and an image of the Virgin said to have been discovered when it was founded. Newstead closed the same year, and someone hid its lectern with the title deeds and two candlesticks in one of the ponds – where they remained for two hundred years. It was bought almost immediately by Sir John Byron. That same year Dr London led a commission in Lincolnshire, assisted by gentry like Sir John Heneage, which acted to suppress ten houses including Thornton Abbey with Crowland probably the last one in December 1539.[83]

79   Wood (1947), p.133
80   A G Dickens, *Robert Holgate*, Oxford, 1955, p.4
81   Jo Moran, *The Growth of English Schooling*, Princeton, 1985, p.183
82   Moran says this school existed in the 1300s and was re-endowed in the 1540s.
83   Hodgett (1975), p.41

Dr London, who handled many local houses, wrote to Cromwell in July 1539 that he had finished his work in many minor local houses and also at Beauvale and Newstead.

Attempts to turn Thornton Abbey into a College were a failure. The former dean of Thornton College then acquired several livings including Haxey and Laceby to top up his considerable pension.

Sibthorpe College, a chantry of several priests in Nottinghamshire, was dissolved and its lands shared between its erstwhile Master, Thomas Magnus, and then the heirs of Richard Whalley.[84] Magnus had once refused Cardinal Wolsey the use of his house at Sibthorpe as 'too poor'. The college at Ruddington was already out of action, though its revenues were being used by private individuals. Tattershall's college closed in 1545.

Some of the monks and priors were given a pension or became parish clergy. Name evidence may not be fully reliable, but it is possible that – for example – Robert Armystede of Clarborough had once been a canon of Worksop or Henry Tingker of Edwinstowe had been the same at Newstead.[85]

By the end of the 1530s attention had turned to the myriad of chantries. For example, in April 1539 Norwell Chantry (Notts) was being handled by Hercy, Markham and Nicholas Denman – the latter a Hercy relative with a similar evangelical outlook. Two friaries in Nottingham were surrendered in 1539 and in 1542 Sir John Markham acquired the former Newark Friary, where his younger brother was amongst the community.[86] In 1540 the Knights Hospitallers were suppressed which included their properties at Ossington (Notts), Willoughton, Temple Bruer and Eagle (Lincs) amongst others; some of this went to the Duke of Suffolk. The work of dissolving the chantries, of which were there were dozens in both counties, extended into Edward VI's reign.

The College and Chantry Commissioners visited Southwell in 1545 but Henry seems to have had it in mind to be the seat of a bishop and had even identified Dr Richard Cox for that role although it did not happen at the time.

It is often said that leading evangelicals enriched themselves from the monastic lands. Yet their leader, Cranmer, generally did not; it was even reported that the evangelical court doctor, William Butts, arranged for some Nottinghamshire monastic lands to be transferred to Cranmer without his knowing.[87] He did indeed take some properties around Aslockton including the advowson of Whatton, where his father was buried, but he soon transferred these to his nephew Thomas; soon after he gained some Lincolnshire lands.[88] William Cavendish who had served under Cromwell became a trusted commissioner; the Welbeck lands were bought from Richard Whalley of Screveton by Sir William Cavendish in 1554. George Lassells clearly used his earnings to buy the Gateford estate and we have seen Sir John Byron gained the Newstead estate in 1540. In Lincolnshire Brandon, Lord

84 Richard Whalley, by then living at Welbeck, lost his office of Crown Receiver for Yorkshire in 1552 for 'malversation'.
85 Wood (1947), p.135
86 Marcombe and Hamilton (1998), p.88
87 MacCulloch (1997), p.168
88 MacCulloch (1997), p.366

Clinton and Saye (Fiennes) and Thomas Manners, who became Earl of Rutland, all did well from the dissolution – Clinton gained the Sempringham lands around Horbling and the family became Earls of Lincoln to reflect their new status in 1572.[89] Such changes affected the social structure of the region especially as Brandon energetically exchanged his own lands elsewhere to consolidate his power in Lincolnshire. He then sold some of his gains to carefully selected acolytes – Westlaby grange and Grange de Lings going to George St Paul, who was related by marriage to Anne Askew who we shall meet shortly.

The era also saw the removal of many ancient relics, of various degrees of confidence in their provenance, but some survived. A clear loss from this era was the golden tomb of St Hugh at Lincoln, which survived until 1540, and also the silver one of John Dalderby. That of Hugh was decorated with silver-gilt, enamel and precious stones including a great amethyst, some of which were hidden away but most were lost when the shrine was destroyed in 1540. 2621 ounces of gold were removed. The arm of St Wulfram disappeared from its place above the north porch at Grantham.

The Lincolnshire Rising and the 'Pilgrimage of Grace'

With a lot of small religious houses and a number of famous shrines, Lincolnshire felt especially threatened by the King's policies including the imposition of the Ten Articles. Bernard has argued that it was the suppression of some ancient religious practices including specific holy days (and the fear of more to come) which primarily sparked the revolt, not the monastic issue, which was more important in the later Yorkshire rising.[90] He writes that, 'it is vital to note that the issue over which anger generated by rumours boiled over into disturbances and then rebellion was that of church treasures and their place in the liturgy'.[91] At the end of September 1536 the monastic commissioners were in east Lincolnshire, royal commissioners were starting work on collecting a levy and the bishop's commissary Richard Rayne(s) was starting work on a visitation of the clergy instructed by Cromwell – with some of the work delegated to Frankish the diocesan registrar. He held a consistory court at Bolingbroke, which upset Simon Maltby, parson of Farforth, enough for him to return home and pray for the Pope and all the cardinals.[92]

The arrival of these officials seemingly added credence to rumours that church treasures would be taken away as well as monastic ones. Specific rumours that the number of parish churches was to be sharply reduced to one in every six or seven miles and that chalices etc were to be replaced with tin ones, were certainly circulating in Lincolnshire. To this we might add a pattern of little 'reformed' preaching in northern areas and some commentary, in the Lincolnshire and Yorkshire revolts, against southern teachings and bishops – though we could hardly call Cranmer a southerner.[93]

89   Both Manners and Clinton built houses on monastic sites they acquired at Belvoir and Sempringham, as Byron did at Newstead.
90   G W Bernard, *The King's Reformation*, London, 2005, p.294-5.p.345
91   Bernard, p.300
92   Bernard, p.312
93   Bernard, p.296

Rebellion started in 1 October 1536, spurred by a sermon from Thomas Kendall the vicar of Louth, with anger directed at Cranmer and Cromwell. Thomas Foster, a 'singing man' at Louth, stirred up the people into action to 'protect' the church's threatened treasures. It was expected that well-loved saints' days were to be abolished, church ornaments removed and changes in teaching imposed – for example about purgatory. They wanted the aspects of the dissolution stopped, but it was the threat to the parish clergy's livings that drove their leadership of the rising.[94] Much was stirred up by Nicholas Melton, who became known as 'Captain Cobbler'.

The mood was stirred further, partly by other priests worried about losing their benefices, on 2 October in Louth and Melton's supporters rang the church bell. They seized the bishop's registrar, John Frankish, and burnt his books with the help of William Morland, an ejected monk from Louth Park.[95] Other books by reformers such as John Frith or New Testaments in English soon followed whilst the bishops who they denounced included reformers like Cranmer and Latimer as well as Longland of Lincoln, more for his support of the divorce than his theology. The bishop's commissioner, Sir John Heneage, in town at the wrong time, was compelled to take an oath of loyalty to the rebels (as was Sir William Skipwith) and later took their letter begging for pardon to London. The 'rich men' of Louth were threatened with hanging if they did not support the rebels. They attacked the commission which was at work at Legbourne – both commissioners were put in the stocks whilst perhaps Morland went off to Alvingham to get horses from the abbot.[96] Morland was one of the most active monks, carrying messages, joining with the rebels at Caistor, and even joining the group sent to collect Lord John Hussey. Arrested later, he maintained he had tried to save the lives of the commissioners and Lord Thomas Burgh's servant. Surveyors were captured at Louth Park and their books also burnt.

In Alford the bells were rung for the 'true faith' and the Cross or Sacrament went before them. The royal commissioners and some of the local gentry agreed to meet at Caistor on 3 October to discuss what to do. The oaths sworn started with loyalty to 'almighty God', then to 'Christ's catholic church' and then the king.[97]

Meanwhile, the rebels considered a move on Caistor, where others were gathering. George Hudswell of Horkstow was elected captain and priests organised more book burnings in the marketplace. With the prospect of Louth rebels joining up with Caistor ones, the gentry agreed to head home and meet at Spital the next day; however, some, for example Sir Robert Tyrwhitt II of Kettleby and Sir William Ayscough, were captured and pressurised to swear the rebels' oath. On Caistor Hill on 3 October, 'Captain Potman' (or Pormon) announced his list of those to be killed headed by Cranmer, Cromwell and the Bishop of Lincoln.

Ayscough was taken prisoner by 'Captain Cobbler', Nicholas Melton, but his brother Sir Christopher Ayscough managed to stay loyal to the king.[98] Ayscough and three

---

94 Bowker (1981), p.155
95 Interestingly the book burners searched out Arthur Graye's copy of one of John Frith's works – these were truly radical to the extent that Frith had been burned for heresy in 1533. Anne Ward, *The Lincolnshire Rising*, 1986, p.11
96 Stories that one, Bellow, was baited to death are dismissed by Bernard who explains he was still working later in the year.
97 Bernard (2005), p.306
98 This Ayscough lived in Grimsby and had had a fierce legal battle with the Abbot of Wellow over access

others were forced to write a letter to the King arguing for mercy for the rebels, and then released. Later he took part in the prosecution of John, Lord Hussey for treason. Lord Burgh escaped across the Trent towards Retford, where he also wrote to the King, Lord Hussey and Lord Darcy (who were cousins). Burgh's servant was killed by the rebels at Caistor instead. Ayscough's sons Francis and Thomas were also captured.

The role of several local gentry was decidedly unclear – had they been leaders of revolt or were they coerced into supporting it? Sir Robert Tyrwhitt[99] seems to have been considered loyal and led a muster at Hambledon Hill whilst Philip Tyrwhitt led at Yarborough Hill, was also described as 'captain of the commons' at Louth, and yet managed to clear his name; Lord Hussey at Sleaford was less lucky. Lord Clinton's inaction was explained by the refusal of his tenants to oppose the revolt. Henry suspected too many of lack of loyalty and thought their 'capture' too easy. Sir John Thimbleby of Irnham raised men in the king's name and used them on behalf of the rebels.[100] Other minor gentry were simply dragged into it and unable to escape, such as Nicholas Girlington.[101] On the other hand, not all the clergy joined enthusiastically – the vicar of Tetney was threatened with beheading if he did not.

At Horncastle on 3 October the crowd were stirred up by William Leach. Perhaps he was connected with Nicholas Leach (Leche), parson of Belchford. A deputation was sent to round up the Dymoke gentry at Scrivelsby; the Dymoke family all submitted, but Sir William Sandon made a greater show of resistance and endured a tough walk to Horncastle before aligning with the rebels. The Dymokes were religiously conservative, with connections in Kent to the Dominicans, and were involved with the rising at Boston.[102] Led by the schoolmaster,[103] the rebels attacked the chancellor Dr John Rayne, one of the bishop's most senior men, who was ill in a chantry priest's house at Bolingbroke. He was taken to Horncastle and beaten to death – 'A great shout of vengeance went up and he was pulled down from his horse and done to death with staves, after pathetically trying to buy them off with twenty shillings for drink'. They also hanged one of Cromwell's servants, who had the unfortunate name of George Wolsey.

Abbot Matthew Mackerell of Barlings supplied food and money, perhaps reluctantly whilst counselling against rebellion, and was said to have been so upset that he was unable to take services due to weeping.[104] Mackrell told a complex but unconvincing story of being forced to join the rebels at Lincoln. With the aid of the vicar of Scothern, the rebels joined up with monks from Bardney, Kirkstead and Vaudney.

Rebels marched to Grange de Lings, north of Lincoln, to meet the men from Grimsby on 5 October, and also mustered at Langworth. Some sacked the bishop's palace at Nettleham,

to the fish trade. Bernard (p.318) reports him to be a loyalist.

99 There were two men called Sir Robert Tyrwhitt active at this time, one of whom was the courtier (I) who was loyal and one was briefly held by the rebels (II) – it is not always easy to distinguish them. The courtier was uncle to Sir Robert Tyrwhitt III. Robert (II) was father of Edward and Philip Tyrwhitt.

100 Ward (1986), p.29

101 Either the father (c1493-1552) or the brother (1514-64) of Lady Anne Wray but he was trusted enough to join Brandon march to the Scottish border in 1542 along with members of the Ayscough family.

102 James, p.220

103 *Letters & Papers*, 1536, 568

104 Bernard (2005), p.316

but most did not enter Lincoln. His chancellor was murdered. When a servant of Cromwell reproved them for this, they bound and gagged him, and wrapped him in the hide of a newly-killed cow before throwing him to starving dogs. But they waited too long around Lincoln and failed to advance on Newark; they dispersed when they heard rumours that the Duke of Suffolk was advancing with an army via Stamford whilst Shrewsbury was gathering troops at Nottingham which became for a time the focal point of resistance, having been at his house of Kirkby Hardwick when he first heard the news.[105] Attempts were made to fortify Newark. Information about the rebellion was sent by Christopher Ayscough, a 'gentlemen usher', to Cromwell, describing some of the atrocities:

'Some of them have gone to Gainsborough, and say they will burn lord Borugh's house and all the town unless he comes in again, for he escaped by reason of a good horse, and his man was slain. They have hanged Mellessent, Cromwell's servant, and baited Bellowe to death with dogs, with a bull skin upon his back, with many rigorous words against Cromwell.'[106]

In fact both men survived, though others were less fortunate. Also, on 5 October George Huddiswell of Horkstow, who had been elected captain of the Caistor group, intercepted lawyer Robert Aske and forced him to swear the oath. Aske became an immediate active participant and was instrumental in carrying the revolt into Yorkshire.

John, Baron Hussey, was at Sleaford when the rebellion broke out and his efforts against it were seen as suspiciously weak, but it is stretching the evidence to suggest that he was a ringleader;[107] even trying to play the role of a mediator would not meet the King's wishes, and he had too few reliable men to ever counter the rebellion. He had developed extensive wealth in monastic service across the country and was known to oppose religious change whilst his wife had spent some time in the Tower for the mistake of referring to Mary as 'Princess'.[108] In 1534 a man associated with the notorious 'Nun of Kent' had dedicated a strongly Catholic book to him[109] and the same year he had discussed action against Henry VIII with ambassador Chapuys – including his cousin Darcy's name in the discussion.[110] Sir Robert Tyrwhitt I, who was a courtier in London, was sent to call on his support – which was not forthcoming. At this point the King's messengers concluded that putting down the revolt was a job for Nottinghamshire gentry, with Hussey claiming to be trapped in Sleaford. Eventually, he dressed himself as a priest and escaped to Sir John Markham's house at Colwick – the motive behind his escape being unclear.

On 6 October rebels in Holland (Lincolnshire) forced the gentry to appear at Boston and swear the oath. Thomas Tamworth, closely connected to Cranmer and whose brother was rector at Leverton (Lincs), fled, and his house was ransacked, and in the account of Anthony Irby JP of Gosberton mention was made that a man named Etton tried to escape and was probably killed. Irby himself later escaped to join Suffolk whilst his son, Leonard, seems to have been evangelical as he was a likely supporter of Lady Jane Grey – and the family were later noted puritans.

105 A C Wood, *A History of Nottinghamshire,* Nottingham, 1947, p.130

106 In contrast Hodgett, p.31, says they suffered no more than two weeks in the stocks.

107 Bernard (2005), p.300, discusses this in detail.

108 One of the ironies is that he was in turn uncle to Elizabeth Hussey, who we shall see later in connection with the radical Martin Marprelate papers.

109 This was *The Mirror of Christ's Passion*, translated by John Fewterer in 1534.

110 Bernard (2005), p.203

On 8 October at Lincoln, George Staines read a list of demands including removal of 'heretic' bishops. The articles agreed on 8-9 October also commented that the closure of the monasteries was 'a great hurt to the commonwealth'.

Shrewsbury could do relatively little, but the Duke of Suffolk was better placed to gather arms and advance from the south while Henry VIII fumed about the inaction of Hussey and Burgh. Sir William Parr was with a small force at Stamford in case the rebels marched south. In Lincolnshire, Hussey was seen as too close to Lord Darcy who made a similarly poor showing regarding the Yorkshire revolt. Hussey was arrested, tried for treason, and executed in Lincoln in 1539; he was suspected of Catholic influences and his wife was too close to Mary, the King's problematic daughter.[111] The weak response to the revolt amongst the Lincolnshire gentry was, though, to prove a turning point for the county's evangelical development.

Letters from the king and Suffolk were received by the rebels in the Chapter House at Lincoln. Henry was angry that the 'rude commons of one of the most brute and beastly shires' thought they could dictate who his ministers should be. Thomas Moigne was accused of misreading the letter to the rebels in the Chapter House by Thomas Ratford, vicar of Snelland. The rebels began to drift away and the captured gentry rode off to Grimsthorpe to meet Suffolk. This was just at the point when rebels in Yorkshire began to arise.

Meanwhile, the King's printers had begun to produce the counter arguments, much of it written by Richard Morison, one of the Cardinal College contingent. 'What foly, what madness is this, to make an hole in the shyppe that thou salest in?' he asked the rebels.[112]

As the Lincolnshire revolt collapsed by mid-October and a new threat emerged in Yorkshire, Shrewsbury marched from Nottingham to Southwell, Newark and up to Blyth and Scrooby to face the rebels at Pontefract. The Duke of Norfolk arrived with more troops, basing some of them at Tuxford by October 25th.[113]

The vicar of Louth, Kendall, escaped to Coventry Charterhouse – where the monks surrendered him. Some of the Lincolnshire rebels, like William Leach, went to join the Yorkshire rebels and then fled to Scotland. Suffolk arrived in Lincoln itself to complete the work of arresting the ringleaders with a few being sent to the Tower – including Mackrell. Although dozens were executed it was 'hardly a bloodbath'[114] with examples being set rather than a wholesale clearance. In the aftermath, it was the priests of east Lincolnshire who paid most dearly. At least 79 were imprisoned, and it is not known that any were pardoned. Twenty six clerics were executed;[115] even the blind priest from Sotby, guilty of being rude about Cromwell, was executed along with his fellow clerics of Louth, Belchford, Alford, Snelland, Scartho, Donington, Cockerington and Biscathorpe. A group

111 Hodgett, p.34
112 W. Gordon Zeeveld. *Richard Morison, Official Apologist for Henry VIII.* PMLA 55, no. 2 (1940): 406-25. doi:10.2307/458453.
113 Wood (1947), p.131
114 Ward (1986), p.32
115 Hodgett (1975), p.37

of twelve were indicted on 5 March 1537.[116] Thomas Moigne, the Recorder of Lincoln, was executed in Lincoln in March 1537. Hussey was indicted at Sleaford with Sir William Ayscough as foreman of the Grand Jury.[117] Abbot Mackrell was in custody as a traitor by October 1536; four of his monks were executed on 6 March 1537 and he followed on 29 March. In 1537, 26 priests, both parish and monastic, and 19 of the commons were executed – with Hussey the leading example.[118] The abbot of Barlings was one of those examined in 1537.

To manage these affairs, Henry used a small group of gentry which included Lord Burgh, Sir John Harrington, Sir William Parr and Sir John Markham at Lincoln in March although Markham was not involved by early May.

Executions also took place in Horncastle and Louth, and then those who had been taken to the Tower. Several monks of Barlings, Bardney and Kirkstead were executed and Hussey was the last to go at Lincoln in June. Yet others survived suspicion – even William Quadring, Sir Christopher Willoughby or Robert Brocklesby, who had been a 'captain'. Hodgett concluded that 'the gentlemen played throughout a somewhat ambivalent role' between trying to avoid direct rebellion and supporting agitation where it might be useful to them[119] whilst perhaps also resentful of the Duke of Suffolk's increasing power in their county. A lot of the support came from the lands of Suffolk's rival Sir Christopher Willoughby, whose son William was heavily implicated.

The early panic of the Lincolnshire rebels prevented most of them joining forces with a Yorkshire band who rapidly captured York and secured Pontefract castle after Lord Darcy, a significant landowner in the region including the manor of Sturton-le-Steeple,[120] surrendered rather easily. Darcy, who had spoken against the king's divorce in 1532, was suspected of being a supporter of the old religion and to have contemplated rebellion in 1535; he was at least guilty of failing to mobilise men quickly and Chapuys had actually expected him to lead a revolt. In the early confusion Sir John Markham of Nottinghamshire rode in to meet Darcy at Pontefract Castle, clearly thinking he was joining the king's men, but found the reverse; he then 'withdrew himself out of the said castle, to his great jeopardy and loss of all his goods'.[121] He presumably went to join the forces of Shrewsbury, a few miles to the south.

One target for the Yorkshire rebels was the home of John Neville, Baron Latimer, at Snape – just across the Yorkshire border. For a time his wife, Katherine Parr – later wife of Henry VIII – was trapped there with her children and, in popular belief, this led to her having a hatred of the North thereafter.

---

116 The list included Nicholas Leche, clerk of Belchford; Thomas Retforthe, clerk of Snelland; Bernard Flecher, yeoman of Fulletby; William Burrowby or Morland, former monk of Louth Park; Robert Sotheby, draper of Horncastle; Robert Leche, husbandman of Fulletby; Philip Trotter, mercer of Horncastle; Bryan Stone, labourer of Miningsby; Thomas Kendall, vicar of Louth; Matthew Makkerell, abbot of Barlings; George Huddeswell, gentleman of Horkstow. All of these were indicted for riotous assembly at Louth Park on 2 October 1536.
117 The others were Guy Kyme of Tetney, Roger Folyot of Ruskington and John Welshman of Sleaford. Moigne was stated to be of North Willingham.
118 Hodgett (1975), p.37
119 Hodgett (1975), p.31
120 Wood (1947), p.131 lists him as holding land in Notts also at Wiseton, Wheatley and Littleborough.
121 Bernard (2005), p.324

When the Northern Convocation met at York under great pressure from Robert Aske on 4 December 1536, Dr Cuthbert Marshall – archdeacon of Nottingham (1528-49) – spoke most strongly for the Pope's claims and was suspected by some of being close to the rebels. Indeed, some historians have identified Marshall as helping to draft, at the very least, one of the petitions of complaint sent to Henry.[122] Three of them, including Marshall, were summoned to court to explain their weak actions in the face of Aske, and all agreed in advance to say they had done so out of fear.[123] Despite the Duke of Norfolk's suspicions, Marshall survived to die in his post in 1549.

The Duke of Norfolk, leading for the king, reached Welbeck and on 2 December Henry wrote to him that Norfolk was 'all desperately' worried but should not hesitate to give the rebels any promise to send them home.[124] At the beginning of December, rebels met the King's representatives led by Norfolk at Doncaster. During the lull in action after terms had been 'agreed', Lord Darcy, one of the oldest of the rebels, wrote to Archbishop Lee hopeful that the country had turned the corner back to Catholicism.[125] Darcy had failed to take Robert Aske into custody, arguing that he had sworn not to and so could not break his word, and when Aske went to London for Christmas under the king's protection, they exchanged secret messages. At a time of tension, potential trouble was also stirring at Lenton Priory leading to one of the most savage acts of the era, discussed above. Aske stayed in London until 5 January 1537 and needed to send no word of warning to Darcy.

Local gentry were heavily involved in the downfall of Lord Darcy. Both he and Aske were in the Tower by 7 April 1537. Darcy was executed in London on 30 June 1537 and Aske was hung in chains at York in July due to his conspiring with Aske. Sir John Babington wrote to Cromwell in July 1537 to report that he'd met George Lassells[126] in London and discussed the belief that Darcy had received warning from the conspirator Aske (then in the Tower with George's cousin Christopher) to stay away. Lassells told how he had been sharing a bed at Gainsborough Old Hall with Thomas Estoft, who described how Darcy had arranged with Aske, who had been invited to London for Christmas by Henry, to set post horses on the road from London to Lincoln so he could be warned if he was in danger and 'again raise the people for his deliverance'.

Lassells' information in the Darcy case seems to have been used by his friends like Sir John Babington at Rampton to put in a request for the Darcy lands at Sturton to be transferred to George Lassells in 1539. In 1540 he finally secured the manor there with lands at Wiseton, Wheatley and Littleborough – but made his main home at Gateford.

Another victim at this time was Henry Litherland who had had a very successful Church career, launching with a role at Lincoln Cathedral in 1522 and taking up multiple benefices in the later 1520s. He had enjoyed a substantial income as chantry priest for St Peter's Altar at Lincoln and had held livings for Alkborough and St Peter's Lincoln; in 1532 he had swapped Alkborough for Belton (Axholme) and also became vicar of Newark. Litherland had courted disaster at Newark in 1534 by preaching against 'heretical' anti-

---

122 M L Bush, *The Pilgrims' Complaint: A Study of Popular Thought in the Early Tudor North*, p.24
123 M H and R Dodds, *The Pilgrimage of Grace 1536–1537 and the Exeter Conspiracy 1538*, p.386
124 Bernard (2005), p.386
125 MacCulloch (1997), p.172
126 The record in L & P confirms Lassells as 'of Sturton'.

papal books and the royal supremacy, for which he was reported by Sir John Markham for having a 'cankered and corrupt mind',[127] whilst also opposing the removal of images and defending the concept of purgatory. Although he had said that the king's words were not Christian, Litherland still managed to become Treasurer at Lincoln in 1535 but it was the Rising that brought him down – he was suspected of being involved in the petition to Henry, had defended threats to Saint Hugh's shrine, and was accused of 'harnessing' men at Crowle to the rebellion. John Horseley was paid £100 to arrest him and he was tried at York. He was executed in 1538 and left bequests to the curates of Belton and Newark,[128] one of perhaps two people with Nottinghamshire connections to be executed after the risings.

The Yorkshire Rising resulted in a toughening of attitudes to dissidents. Before it, a critical priest like Richard Barker was imprisoned but stayed alive. Occasionally clergy and others were caught criticising the King and paid the penalty. George Croft, rector of Broughton, secured the post of Chancellor at Chichester in 1538 but was soon after arrested for denying that the King was Head of the Church, and executed in December. The vicar of Barton-upon-Humber, William Duffield, has been identified as the same person as William Duffy, who was an 'auxiliary' bishop in York and Lincoln from 1535 to 1538 – appointed by the Pope – when he was executed for denying the royal supremacy.[129]

Also executed in May 1538 was John Forest, an Observant Franciscan who seems to have spent some time in Newark during a short-lived release from Newgate; he was suspended over the fire by chains to be slowly roasted at Smithfield, the only Catholic priest burnt in the Reformation. Hugh Latimer, later to be burnt himself, preached at this event and a large Welsh wooden pilgrimage image, the Darvell Gadern, was used to fuel the fire. The same night a 'miracle working rood' in a London church was destroyed by reformers.

The aftermath of the revolt ensured the changed religio-political landscape of Lincolnshire and also eastern Nottinghamshire, although there was some testing of strength in the interim. Sir William Ayscough became very active in chasing out suspected opponents of the King's new religion, such as the chantry priest at St Helen Croft near Wainfleet, on which he was over-ruled by Cromwell. In 1539 local opponents like Sir Robert Tyrwhitt II succeeded in getting him summoned to London, but Ayscough pleaded ill-health and indeed died soon after. Suffolk, through his Willoughby alliance, consolidated his position in the county – he was awarded Tattershall Castle as his seat after the revolt. Indeed, it has been argued that resentment against Suffolk by the rival branch of the Willoughby family, led by William Willoughby, was a factor in the revolt[130] but Suffolk had a track record from then of appointing some interestingly radical clerics who in turn influenced his wife Katherine.

The failed revolts strengthened the hand of men like Sir John Markham and the Duke of Suffolk, expanding the territories acquired through his young wife, who considered

127 Markham was later awarded Newark Friary. Wood (1947), p.131
128 R Hattersley, *The Devonshires*, London, 2014, p.8
129 Margaret Bowker, *The Henrician Reformation*, Cambridge, 1981 p. 139
130 Mervyn James, *Society, Politics and Culture: Studies in Early Modern England*, p.227-233. Willoughby survived the revolt to become Lord Willoughby of Parham despite being identified by Mackerel as a 'grand captain'.

Bishop Longland to be still too close to Rome.[131] His young wife, the formidable Katherine Willoughby, was to use Brandon's Lincolnshire empire to establish radical religion in the county that would ultimately lead to the Great Migration of 1630. Family names like Hercy-Denman, Whalley, Ayscough and Irby were to become established forces in religious reform as the balance of opinion shifted amongst the gentry; the St Paul, Hall, Girlington, Grantham and Brocklesby families were all close associates of Brandon who became leading evangelical dynasties. Bishop John Longland was stimulated enough from 1538 to insist that his clergy preached at least four times a year, as Cromwell had instructed – with limited success.[132] Lincolnshire was plainly a conservative county in 1536 but a radical one by the end of the century whilst Nottinghamshire's gentry emerged as much more influential after the turmoil of the 1530s. Together they set about creating an evangelical heartland in the East Midlands. The fear of a Catholic revolt in the North persisted for long after 1536-8, indeed to the end of the Tudor era.

The rising also did little for the reputation of Lincolnshire. When Robert Singleton wrote his poem *The Pilgrim's Tale* in the late 1530s he chose to make the main character a credulous traditionalist from the county who sets out on pilgrimage to Walsingham, only to have a revelation of the falsity of such places.[133]

The Sting in the Tail: Later Days of Henry VIII

G W Bernard has argued that Henry VIII's later religious policy was to try to steer a middle way between Lutheranism and Roman Catholicism; in this view he perhaps prefigures the later 'settlement' of Elizabeth I. Bernard points out that in the key year of 1540, when Thomas Cromwell was himself executed, religious dissidents of both wings were executed on the same day, but over the next few years the conservatives like Stephen Gardiner were very influential making even Cranmer's position precarious. Indeed, the Six Articles Act of 1539, which confirmed traditional teaching on key doctrines, were clearly intended by Henry to draw a line in the sand on the theological debate as he attempted to stem the flow of religious reform.

The rapid changes caught some unawares – Longland played his hand badly, allowing Cromwell in 1539 to install as Dean of Lincoln John Taylor – a strong reformer who briefly was to return as Bishop under Edward VI. Taylor spent most of his time at Cambridge, where he was Master of St John's. In general, Longland tried to appoint only conservative clergy even at this stage, such as appointing a friar at Goxhill who had already upset Cromwell by his support of the Pope. Longland was severely discomfited when his nephew Richard Pate, who he had made archdeacon of Lincoln when only 24, defected to Rome in 1541 and was attainted for high treason.[134] In Grantham the pace of change was too slow for some, as in 1539 the wardens complained to the visitor Dr John

---

131 Bowker (1981), p.158
132 Wabuda (2002), p.37
133 Gary Waller, *The Virgin Mary in Late Medieval and Early Modern English Literature*, Cambridge, 2011, p.80
134 Pate returned from Rome under Mary I when he became Bishop of Worcester, of which he was deprived in 1559.

London, who had been treasurer of Lincoln cathedral, that 'vicars and priests' there were still breaking the King's injunctions.

James Mallett,[135] precentor and archdeacon at Lincoln, was executed by hanging, drawing and quartering at Chelmsford in 1542 for criticising the royal divorce and hoping the King of Scotland would invade. He had already roused suspicion by his conduct during the Rising. At least three priests from the south of Lincolnshire were also executed in the period 1541-3.[136]

But despite the King's doctrinal conservatism his great friend Charles Brandon, the Duke of Suffolk, appointed some strong reformers to his Lincolnshire livings before his death in 1545 including the Scotsman Alexander Seton to Fulbeck (1539); Seton had been priest to King James V but fled Scotland due to his controversially radical views, so Brandon will have known who he was employing. Seton went off to preach in London on justification by faith alone and in 1541 caused even more problems through his radical preaching – though he then recanted in December in front of the conservative bishop, Stephen Gardiner. Seton was given a second benefice, at Willoughby in 1542, after this but he died at Brandon's London house in 1542-3. Happy to reject the authority of the Pope[137] if religiously cautious himself, Brandon thus linked himself with several ardent reformers amongst clerics and gentry and they formed the basis of a chain of influence that his ardent fourth wife Katherine developed. His business staff included Thomas Marbury and his cousin John, who in turn knew Thomas Lawney, who Brandon made one of his chaplains in around 1540 – although he died soon after;[138] this was the same 'witty' Lawney who had been implicated in the Cardinal College events of the 1520s and who had later been within Cranmer's circle. John Marbury, who worshipped at a London church ministered by Richard Marsh, is an interesting part of this jigsaw.

Another in his circle was John Bale, a former monk at Doncaster who became a key evangelical writer. Brandon was popular with Henry VIII and so his wife, Katherine Willoughby, therefore gained an entry to the Court. There she would have met Hugh Latimer, and he became one of her key influences in the 1540s. Her husband introduced her to reforming families like the Dudleys and the Seymours; she also became a friend and spiritual fellow traveller with Katherine Parr, who became Henry's last wife when Willoughby was one of a small group of witnesses to the marriage.

Katherine Parr is famous as the last wife of Henry VIII, but her connections with our region are much earlier. In May 1529 she had married Edward Borough (or Burgh), son of Thomas, the 3rd baron Burgh of Gainsborough. Her new father-in-law was 'an overbearing bully whose children lived in fear of his temper' and in October 1530 Katherine and her husband had moved to the family's manor at Kirton-in-Lindsey apparently to escape. Her husband died in 1533. As we have seen, she then remarried and became ensnared in the Pilgrimage of Grace when trapped at Snape.

---

135 His relationship to Francis Mallet, Dean from 1554, would be interesting to uncover.

136 Gunn (2015), p.167

137 Bernard (2005), p.39

138 This hints again at the possible connection between these Marburys and the father of Anne Hutchinson in Alford; another Marbury worked for Sir Francis Ayscough which provides another regional connection. Steven Gunn, *Charles Brandon,* Stroud, 2015, p.226

After the death of her husband in 1545 Katherine Parr moved to London and lived at court, where she hoped to marry Thomas Seymour but, through family politics, ended up married to Henry VIII. Her 'zealous evangelical' faith won her enemies, including Stephen Gardiner the powerful bishop of Winchester who tried to force evidence against her from Anne Askew, the celebrated Lincolnshire martyr. Katherine patronised religious books and was the first queen of England to produce a book herself – *The Lamentation of a Sinner* in 1547 with substantial involvement of Katherine Willoughby. She survived the death of Henry.

Round her gathered a group of godly people including Lady Joan Denny, Lady Elizabeth Tyrwhitt, Anne Seymour and Jane Dudley. John Parkhurst, a former chaplain to Brandon who survived long enough to become Bishop of Norwich in 1560, held one of the male offices in the household. After Brandon died in 1545, Willoughby became an increasingly important figure in this evangelical group. He left a gap in Lincolnshire, where Edmund Sheffield was made a baron in 1547; he came from an evangelical background and had been close to Thomas Cromwell, but what might have been a colourful career was cut short when he was killed at Norwich during Kett's Rebellion – an event commemorated by Sir John Cheke.

Katherine Willoughby, with new freedoms and still calling herself the Duchess of Suffolk, gained access to some radical books including Tyndale's New Testament which might have put her life in danger. During 1547 Willoughby sponsored the publication of Parr's *Lamentation of a Sinner* – its printers inscribed it 'put in print at the instaunt desire of the righte gracious Ladie Caterin Duchess of Suffolke'. Eustace Chapuys, the ambassador, thought Willoughby and Anne Seymour to be the stirrers of 'heresy' at the court.[139] She appointed more 'godly' clergy to the livings she controlled in Lincolnshire like Edmund Warter at Theddlethorpe St Helen's,[140] Thomas Sharpneys[141] and Anthony Gilby who she presented to Edenham.[142] Unsurprisingly, John Olde writing in 1547 was clear that the advancing of the godly cause in Lincolnshire was due to 'the helping forwardness of that devout woman of God, the Duchess of Suffolk'. The future pattern was thus being set by 1547, but it was a road that might have ended in disaster – and did for some.

By this stage monasteries and chantries were largely gone, but at the end of Henry's reign work was still progressing on some other vestiges of Catholicism. For example, the gilds were swept away including the Gild of St Mary in Boston, in July 1546, notorious for the selling of pardons and indulgences. Its Guildhall then became the main chamber for conducting the affairs of the town of Boston, but the power of the gilds was transferred into a corporation in 1545 which became influential on the town's religion. This success for the town was seen as helped by the influence of Brandon, the Duke of Suffolk, who had a nearby base at Tattershall and did trade through the port.[143]

---

139 Strype, *Ecclesiastical Memorials*, vol II, Part 1, p,83

140 He was deprived under Mary I as being married, later finding a living in Norfolk

141 He was formerly the priest of St Mary's chantry at Welton le Marsh, then settled at Edenham where he was noted to be a married man.

142 Franklin-Harkrider (2008), p.51. Gilby also fled abroad under Mary I and went on to be a leading puritan figure at Ashby-de-la-Zouch.

143 Gunn, p.232

The Martyrs of 1546

A famous religious radical of the period was Anne Askew, more correctly known as Ayscough, probably born at Stallingborough in Lincolnshire in 1521. Her father Sir William was part of an extensive family that also owned land in Nottinghamshire at Nuthall and South Kelsey in Lincolnshire and he was High Sheriff of the latter. He became a courtier to Henry VIII and was MP for Grimsby in 1529; after a rather ambivalent role in the Lincolnshire Rising, he has attained some notoriety as one of the jurors at the trial of Anne Boleyn. Her brother Edward, who spent some time in Cranmer's household, settled at South Kelsey which Sir Francis Ayscough had earlier acquired through marriage into the Hansard family.

Anne seems to have spent some of her childhood at South Kelsey but when the Lincolnshire Rising broke out her father was captured by the rebels and forced to write a letter to the king. She is described by John Bale[144] as having had a religious conversion – 'in process of time by oft reading of the Bible, she fell from all old superstitions of papysty, to a perfect belief in Jesus Christ'. More dispassionately, her 'resolute disposition, great learning and doctrinal radicalism all reflect her parentage and upbringing'.

What influenced her conversion besides the Holy Spirit? We do not know, but her brother Edward had a place in Cranmer's household in 1539 (after which joining King Henry's) whilst her sister Jane married George St Poll,[145] a steward to Katherine Willoughby, and after he died Richard Disney – both on the reforming wing in religion. Indeed, the link to Willoughby was perhaps crucial as Askew and the Duchess of Suffolk were both key lines of investigation in the crisis of 1546. The Ayscoughs were one of Cranmer's regional connections, but certainly, after 1546, they became one of the leading puritan families of Lincolnshire up until the Civil War.

The traditional story told is that Anne's father arranged for her marriage to Thomas Kyme, a staunch Catholic probably from Friskney, in the place of her sister who had died. This was probably to save on finances after already advancing the money.[146] The marriage was not a success and Kyme threw her out, seemingly after having had two children, although perhaps the final break was after her trip to Lincoln. She probably returned to her family at South Kelsey. Anne then went to London although Catholic writers talked of her gadding about 'gospelling and gossiping'.

Anne's separation seems to have prompted her to seek redress or divorce through the bishop's court at Lincoln. She was warned that if she went to Lincoln 'the priests would assault me'. However, she went there for six days and sat in the cathedral reading the Bible 'to see what would be said unto me' by the 'threescore clerics'; despite this being <u>controversial at </u>the time, only one cleric spoke to her at any length and with 'little effect'.

144 Bale lived close to our area when he was Prior at Doncaster in the early 1530s when his views were already quite radical, attracting criticism for a sermon against praying to saints in 1534.
145 St Paul or 'St Poll' entered Brandon's service as a lawyer in 1537 (Gunn, p,169) and became recorder of Lincoln and its MP in 1542 and was often MP from then until the time of Edward VI. Hugh Grantham, of another evangelical line, joined Brandon as an auditor in 1541. Edward Grantham married Elizabeth St Poll and were at a distance also connected to Robert Brocklesby. Grantham and George St Poll fell out in 1544, and the latter also fell out with Brandon by 1545.
146 Cheryl Glenn, *Rhetoric Retold*, p.152

Although the English Bible had been published, access to it was severely restricted by the Act for the Advancement of True Religion in 1543. This allowed only upper-class men and women (in private) to read the Bible – so Askew was deliberately testing the boundaries.[147] At about this time she started to oppose the office of bishop making her, according to one writer, 'the first non-conformist in the county'.[148]

In London, by perhaps late 1544, she would have met up with her brother Edward Ayscough, now in the royal household alongside John Lassells of Sturton-le-Steeple, after a time with Cranmer;[149] Cranmer had recommended him to Thomas Cromwell in December 1539. Her sister Jane's marriage to George St Paul,[150] (through whom we can connect to the Justice Sir Christopher Wray as overseer of his will), was an alliance of north Lincolnshire reforming families. It was argued that it was Edward who introduced Anne to court ladies 'who were in favour of the Scriptures'.[151] These connections would have provided a link to Katherine Willoughby, Duchess of Suffolk, who was both a Lincolnshire woman and in Katherine Parr's circle, having become strongly evangelical by the early 1540s – perhaps tutors such as John Parkhurst and Pierre Valence were the key. Willoughby employed the St Paul family in Lincolnshire.

Edward also held the manor of Nuthall which the family inherited in 1543 and where they had a connection through marriage to the Derbyshire Foljambes – through which they also were later connected to the Wray family. Through one of these roots, Anne and also Edward knew the evangelical courtier John Lassells, from Nottinghamshire, who had followed a similar career path to Edward.

These connections made her a 'person of interest' to those opposing reform. Spies were set near her lodgings in London to report on her activities – reporting a lot of nocturnal prayer.[152]

In March 1545[153] Anne was arrested under the Six Articles Act (1539) having been spied on by the agents of Sir Thomas Wriothesley. She was examined first by Christopher Dare and then before the Lord Mayor, Sir Martin Bowes, who she seems to have had little

147 'My friends told me, if I did come to Lincoln, the priests would assault me and put me to great trouble, as thereof they had made their boast. And when I heard it, I went thither indeed, nit being afraid, because I knew my matter to be good. Moreover, I remained there nine days, to see what would be said unto me. And as I was in the Minster reading upon the Bible, they resorted unto me by two and by two, by five and by six, minding to have spoken unto me, yet went their ways again without words speaking…there was one of them at last which did speak to me indeed….his words were of small effect.'
148 Miss J Plumb, p.18
149 C Anderson, *Annals of the English Bible*, vol 2, p191.
150 It is thus possible to connect the first great wave of Lincs/Notts 'godly' families of the 1540s with the second wave of 1590-1610; Anne Askew's sister Jane was the grandmother of Sir George St Paul who married Frances Wray I. Jane's first husband George St Paul (Poll) from a Snarford family had done well in the law in the service of the Duke of Suffolk, husband to Catherine Willoughby, as did his brother Matthew St Poll. Jane is buried at South Kelsey along with her brother Sir Francis, whose memorial there certainly has an unusually uncertain expression. Disney was 'earnest in religion' in 1564 according to the Bishop of Lincoln and close to the Earl of Rutland, also a progressive. The S Kelsey connection is through Sir William Ayscough's second marriage to Elizabeth Hansard though some sources say this was Sir Francis Ayscough who thus gained South Kelsey. Jane married Richard Disney around 1560.
151 Anderson, p.191
152 Alec Ryrie, *The Gospel of Henry VIII: Evangelicals in the Early English Reformation*, p.54
153 Whether this was 1545 or 1546 has been debated – I have taken the ODNB date as 1545.

trouble tying up in knots: she ended the discussion with him by saying, 'I will not cast my pearls before swine – acorns be good enough'. One of the 'crimes' brought against her was that she had said she would rather read five verses of the Bible than attend five masses; she readily agreed – 'the one did greatly edify me, the other nothing at all'. Another accusation was her ridiculing private masses for the dead which she said were 'great idolatry'. She was sent to the Bread Street gaol for a while – and then released.

She was next questioned by Bishop Bonner – a fencing match of a debate in which, when Bonner asked her what sort of an answer she had given him, she retorted, 'A poor one… but good enough for the question'. However, it ended with her, seemingly, crumbling, by signing a statement that Bonner had had drafted, although there has been debate over whether she added a postscript. Part of the evidence against her was owning a book by John Frith, who had been burned in 1533.

In June 1545 she was again in custody and brought to the Guildhall, but the evidence was insubstantial. She consistently refused to meet any of her adversaries in private – knowing that claims could then be made of 'confession'. In her public appearances she used the Bible to good effect, often answering by telling her accusers she agreed with scripture. After she went into hiding at home she was betrayed and re-arrested in May 1546; years later her nephew Edward Ayscough implied in a rather confusing account that her own oldest brother, Francis (his father), was responsible for betraying her location in a cottage in South Kelsey despite being a supporter through flesh and faith, but was afterwards haunted by a vision of fire.[154] Despite hiding in the woods, she was then captured, having hidden her Tyndale New Testament in dough.

In May 1546 Kyme was told to appear before the Privy Council with her, but in June before the Privy Council she denied he was her husband. He was sent back to Lincolnshire. Following this, she was taken to the Council at Greenwich and then imprisoned in Newgate where she was refused access to ministry from Hugh Latimer.

It would seem likely that her privileged connections had put her in great danger, for Wriothesley and Sir Richard Rich had hoped that she would implicate other reformers at the court including even Queen Katherine Parr. It has been suggested, for example by the Jesuit Robert Persons, that it was Katherine Willoughby who connected Askew with the Queen.[155] In the Tower she was visited by court ladies such as the wives of Edward Seymour and Sir Anthony Denny. She was also connected to another group around the Earl of Surrey through her Lincolnshire cousin, Thomas Hussey,[156] although he does not seem to have been very religious.[157] Anne Askew's significance can only be understood by seeing how she was connected through family to so many gentry families of the two counties so that others, like that of George St Paul – married to her sister Jane – would have been at risk with her condemnation.

154 Edward Ayscu, *A Historie Concerning the Warres between England and Scotland*, cited in Macleod, *The Heretics*

155 Parr and Willoughby knew each other well enough for Parr to quote Willoughby in a letter in 1547 – 'as my Lady of Suffolk saith, 'God is a marvellous man'. Parr survived and by 1550 she had a notable radical, Robert Cooche, as her wine steward; of him we know little, but as early as 1550 he was questioning paedobaptism.

156 Alec Ryrie, *The Gospel of Henry VIII: Evangelicals in the Early English Reformation*, p.55

157 S T Bindoff, *History of Parliament*, 1982. Accessed online 26/7/14.

Several of the ladies suffered arrest but were eventually released and even the Queen's escape was a narrow one. Elizabeth Tyrwhitt, who had married into the Kettleby, Lincolnshire, family and was a great friend of Parr, was one of these. Her husband, Sir Robert Tyrwhitt I, did not agree with her evangelical views – 'my wyffe is not sayne in Dyvinity, but is half a Scripture woman' – he wrote.[158] She took a dislike to Katherine Parr's last husband, Thomas Seymour, which was rather confirmed in the scandal over his behaviour with the Princess Elizabeth which led to Lady Elizabeth becoming her governess for a while. She survived the various crises of her life and continued in her faith, in 1574 publishing *Morning and Evening Praiers, with Divers Psalmes Himnes and Meditations* which included content that she had originally shared with Princess Elizabeth. In 1577 the evangelical printer John Field dedicated a book to her.

At the end of June 1546 Anne was convicted of heresy – illegally as without a jury – and sentenced to be burnt at Smithfield with three others including John Lassells of Nottinghamshire. Again, she referred to scripture to confound her enemies, saying that 'I have searched all the Scriptures yet I could never find that either Christ or his Apostles put any creature to death'. She was condemned for a belief that was to become a core Protestant doctrine: 'this is the heresy which they report me to hold, that after the priest has spoken the words of consecration, there remains bread still'. Anne's opinion was now that 'I believe faithfully the eternal Son of God not to dwell there'. Then she turned her incisive logic to the problem: 'And as for that ye call your God, it is a piece of bread: for a more proof thereof….let it lie in the box but three months, and it will be mouldy….. whereupon I am persuaded that it cannot be God'.

The day after her conviction Anne was taken to the Tower. She was tortured, illegally, at the hands of Wriothesley and Sir Richard Rich, who hoped to harvest evidence on the other evangelicals including perhaps Katherine Willoughby, dowager duchess of Suffolk, the Queen, and the ladies Denny, Fitzwilliam and Hertford; this caused disquiet even in the officials of the Tower itself. Sir Anthony Knevet, lieutenant of the Tower, made a pretence of 'pinching' her on the rack but Wriothesley and Rich racked her until 'her bones and joints were almost plucked asunder'.

The torturers wanted to know the source of her funds, but Askew argued that her maid went out and collected it from apprentices in the street, although money had been delivered by liveried servants claiming to be from Denny and Hertford. After two hours lying on the floor while the lord chancellor argued with her, she was allowed to recover in bed in a house and then taken to Newgate.

Knevet went to see King Henry personally, perhaps knowing his own life was at risk if he were held at fault for such a doubtful proceeding, and the King ordered the torture stopped. When he returned to the Tower with this news, the other warders were 'not a little joyous'.

Due to the torture, Anne was unable to walk to the stake and had to be carried on a chair; she was accompanied, bravely, by Nicholas Throckmorton, Katherine Parr's cousin. Bishop Shaxton, a former evangelical, preached a sermon at the execution but

---

158 ODNB, *Elizabeth Tyrwhitt*, accessed 13 August 2018.

Anne Askew provided her own commentary – although this may have been enlarged in Foxe's account. When asked to recant she said, 'I come not hither today to deny my Lord and Master'. John Loud recounted that before she died she had 'an angel's countenance and a smiling face'. Three others died with her, including John Lassells, their deaths hastened by pouches of gunpowder tied to them. German merchants[159] who witnessed her death told John Bale that she suffered with an 'angel's face' and at her death 'there was a pleasant cracking from heaven'. Bale noted none of the martyrs had any relics with them – only 'a bundell of the sacred scriptures enclosed in their hartes'. Another witness said that 'methought it seemed rather that the angels in heaven rejoiced to receive their souls into bliss, whose bodies their popish tormentors cast into the fire'.

A century later Bathsua Makin, a tutor to Charles I, wrote that she 'so seasoned the Queen and ladies at court…that the seed of reformation seemed to be sowed by her hand'.

Her writings were published as *Examinations* and this has perhaps led to her having the greatest fame amongst the martyrs, save Cranmer himself.

Of the three men who were burnt with Anne Askew, one was John Lassells,[160] a courtier who had been born most probably at Sturton-le-Steeple.[161] The three Lassells children – George, John and Mary – seem to have become orphans and were taken into the care of Humphrey Hercy at nearby Grove, to whom they were related. After 1520 Lassells' guardian then became the early evangelical stalwart Sir John Hercy of Grove; in 1538, Hercy referred to John as his cousin.[162] Dickens suggests that Lassells became an evangelical through influences at the Inns of Court, but the influences may have been much earlier for Hercy was a leading evangelical.[163] Lassells was employed by Thomas Cromwell in 1538 after he had lost his previous post because of his evangelical views. At least two examples survive in the State papers of letters between Sir John Hercy and the Crown conveyed by John to and from London.[164]

In 1539 Lassells secured a post in the king's household where he soon joined up with others who shared his views. However, in September 1540 Lassells cautioned them not to be too forward as at that time the Howard family and Bishop Gardiner were in the ascendancy following the fall of Thomas Cromwell. One wonders about Edward Ayscough's links to

159 Or possibly Dutch
160 This name varies in its spelling – Foxe spells it 'Lacels' and his brother was typically 'Lascelles'
161 A G Dickens, *Lollards and Protestants in the Diocese of York*, p.33, refers to the Lassells 'seat' at Sturton.
162 *Letters & Papers*, 1538. Hercy was much involved in the dissolution and by 1547 was one of Edward VI's commissioners for the visitations throughout the diocese of York (identified as such by Dickens, though often mis-spelt as 'Hearn'). Doubtless Hercy was involved in the dissolution of chantries at Tuxford and elsewhere which funded the revived school at Retford.
163 A G Dickens, *Lollards and Protestants in the Diocese of York*, p.237
164 Of particular interest is 1054, 23 May 1538: 'I have been informed that Sir Edw. Eland, chaplain to Dr. Knolys, vicar of Wakefield, has been teaching young folks seditious songs against your Lordship and others, which he has confessed, on examination. I enclose his confession and a song learned by heart by boys and others. Sir Edward denies that this was the song he taught, which he cannot report, but pays that he had it of one Byrkeheyd, of Bole, who is now at London, and my cousin George Lassells knows him well. Let me know your pleasure in this by your servant John Lassells, to whom I beg you to continue good lord, and have pity for the poor men of Cottam, sore vexed by Ant. Nevyll, who, besides his own matter, threatens them with consilement with a lunatic priest put to them by the abp. of York's officers. They showed themselves loyal at the commotion time. I wish you would be pleased to take the Lady at Doncaster away, and send some good preachers into the country. Grove, 23 May'

this group at court. Then the cautious approach was disrupted when Lassells' sister, Mary Hall, told him about the youthful sexual antics of the new Queen, Catherine Howard, when they had shared a 'dormitory' in Lambeth at the dowager Duchess of Norfolk's house. Lassells passed this on to Cranmer, a fellow Nottinghamshire man – leading to the downfall of Catherine Howard and her family. Hall was interviewed by the Earl of Southampton to whom she described 'misconduct' – about which she had told no-one except her brother; she was one of the few to escape any censure. Howard was alleged to have committed adultery at various places on the royal progress to York including Gainsborough and Lincoln Bishop's Palace, though not at Grimsthorpe where Katherine Willoughby was no doubt warned in advance.

Lassells was a young man who was certainly radical in religion. His older brother George Lassells had been reformer enough to play a key role in the dissolution of Lenton and had acquired the manor of Sturton in 1540 after its previous lord, Thomas Darcy, was executed in 1537 for his role in the Lincolnshire Rising;[165] as we have seen, George provided key evidence in that case. Sturton was to be central to the story of the Pilgrims, producing both John Smyth and John Robinson. George later sold off some of his land around Sturton – including to the White family, from whom John Robinson later found a wife. In 1546 clear links between Lassells and Anne Askew were established; it has been suggested Lassells was the 'instructor' of Askew and one historian of the reformation, Dickens, considers Lassells to have been the key figure amongst the court evangelicals; 'Lascells and not Anne Askew was the leading spirit of the group'.[166]

Lassells was also said to be a patron of Richard Laynam,[167] a radical priest, who prophesied the overthrow of Henry VIII. Association with Anne Askew did not help him and he was arrested in May 1546, professing his willingness to die for his beliefs. He was openly an opponent of the Catholic Mass and wrote a defence on his position from his cell: 'The Masse is the vnquietnes of all Christendome, a blasphemy vnto Christes bloud, and a shame to all Christen Princes'.[168] Lassells and Askew took the view that the words of Jesus, 'this is my body,' were misunderstood – it having been falsely assumed that he meant the bread in his hand rather than the body itself in which he dwelt. 'The blessed and immaculate Lamb is present to the eyes of our faith,' he wrote – as recorded by Foxe – in 1546, and 'I do differ from the pope's church, that the priests have authority to make Christ's natural presence in the bread, for so doth he more than our Lord and Saviour did'.

After being condemned to death, Lassells:
'…mounted up into the window of the little parlour at Newgate, and there sat, and by him sir George.[169] Master Lascels was merry and cheerful in the Lord, being come from

165 W H Burgess, p.6, says that George Lassells was in London in 1539 to press a claim for Darcy's lands at Sturton.

166 Dickens, *Lollards and Protestants*, p.33

167 Historical sources first report this individual in Wiltshire but at a time when surnames often came from places that of 'Laynam' is interesting – especially when connected to others from Nottinghamshire where there is a village with this name.

168 Foxe, 1563 edition, http://www.johnfoxe.org/index.

169 Sir George Blage or Blagg(e), who had been arrested for an off the cuff remark but was pardoned by Henry VIII. Blagge was also from a Lincolnshire family closely connected to Cranmer's friend Thomas Goodrich, and was the brother of Cranmer's London business agent; he was pardoned by Henry in 1546 and so escaped execution. Richard Goodrich of Bolingbroke and Louth married Blagge's widow after an unseemly divorce.

hearing the sentence of his condemnation, and said these words, 'My Lord Bishop would have me confess the Roman church to be the catholic church, but that I cannot, for it is not true'.

Whilst in the Tower Lassells feared that Anne Askew had confessed and repudiated her beliefs. He communicated this to her, and she replied: 'O friend, most dearly beloved in God, I marvel not a little what should move you to judge in me so slender a faith as to fear death, which is the end of all misery. In the Lord, I desire you not to believe in me such wickedness'.[170] In the end Lassells was burnt alongside Askew on 16 July 1546, a day which is still used to commemorate Askew by the Church of England though Lassells seems to have been forgotten.

Two figures on the fringes of the Askew and Lassells story were Edward Crome and Nicholas Shaxton, who for a time was bishop of Salisbury. It was Shaxton's influence that brought the reformer Crome to the prebend of South Grantham in 1537, and he was known to Cranmer. Shaxton was a victim of the conservative reaction of 1539 and lost his see but Crome, as throughout his career, managed to survive although sometimes banned from preaching. In the crisis of 1546, he argued backwards and forwards on the issue of transubstantiation – and survived; several of those known to him, like Askew, did not. Indeed, some have blamed him for Askew's demise, although others have argued his complex policy of obfuscation allowed evangelicalism to survive. Ralph Morice's brother William, a gentleman usher at Court, was also arrested and detained until Henry's death.

Famously, the Queen and her circle – including Willoughby – escaped serious trouble because they were warned by Dr Butts, Henry's physician. They destroyed the most incriminating books and Parr won over Henry. When he died in 1547, it appeared that the evangelical group would now be safe and indeed in power.

Family Links

It is almost impossible to explain the many connections between the evangelical and later puritan families of the two counties. Let us take one example, the Whalleys of Screveton. Thomas Whalley who was born in 1535 was married to Elizabeth Hatfield, whose father was a cousin to Thomas Cranmer – Cranmer's mother was a Hatfield; Elizabeth's sister also married one of the Whalleys. Thomas's father in law Henry Hatfield connected him to Cranmer whilst his mother-in-law Alice Hercy was sister to the very central evangelical figure of Sir John Hercy whose estate was at Grove near Retford. Alice Hercy's second husband was Robert Markham to whom her uncle Sir John was also connected to Sir John Markham – these two men having married sisters. Hercy's father Humphrey and then Hercy himself was clearly related to, as well as guardian of, George and John Lassells. Sir John Markham was married to one of the Babingtons. Other marriages connect the story to the Ayscoughs and from there into a wider circle of Lincolnshire evangelicals.

---

170 C Anderson, *The Annals of the English Bible* vol 2, p.198

Thomas and Elizabeth Whalley had a son, Richard, who married Frances Cromwell; through this link the family were related to Oliver Cromwell. Through the Hercy-Markham link they connect through Hercy's sisters to the Neville and Denman families and then by marriage to the later puritan author Walter Travers; Hercy himself had no children. The Whalleys also presented Richard Bernard to the living of Worksop. They are one of the many families who, involved in early evangelical culture, became significant figures in the Civil War era.

CHAPTER FOUR

A Time of Turbulence
1547-1558

In a few short years, England varied from the strongly evangelical short reign of Edward VI to the repressive restoration of Catholicism under Mary, and eventually back to something of the middle ground under Elizabeth. Mary's era produced the most famous martyr of the era in Thomas Cranmer but this decade of change also contributed much to three of the greatest literary endeavours in which people from our counties were heavily involved – the Book of Common Prayer *(1549 and 1552 editions), Foxe's 'Actes and Monuments' and the 'Geneva Bible'.*

Chronology:
1547: Edward VI becomes King
1549: Martin Bucer arrives in England; first *Book of Common Prayer* issued
1552: Second *Book of Common Prayer* issued
1553: Forty-Two Articles for the new canon law published; Edward dies and is replaced by Mary
1554: Heresy laws revived; John Foxe flees to Strasbourg
1555: Hugh Latimer executed
1556: Thomas Cranmer executed
1557: New Testament of *Geneva* Bible completed
1558: Queen Mary dies

King Edward 1547-1553: A False Dawn for Protestantism

In the short reign of Edward VI, Protestantism advanced rapidly. The 1543 Act restricting access to the Bible in English was abolished, along with the conservative Six Articles. The Bible was again widely available in English from June 1549. Action against the chantries progressed, undermined by direct action but also by the official rejection of the doctrine of purgatory that had given them all a purpose. Historian Susan Wabuda has highlighted that the return of free access to the Bible in English was due to the campaigning of Katherine Parr and Katherine Willoughby.[1]

Evangelicals like Willoughby lost no time in campaigning against saints, processions and pilgrimages. Some shrines had been demolished in the 1530s but not all, so old shrines,

---

1   S Wabuda, *Preaching during the English Reformation*, Cambridge, 2002, p.104

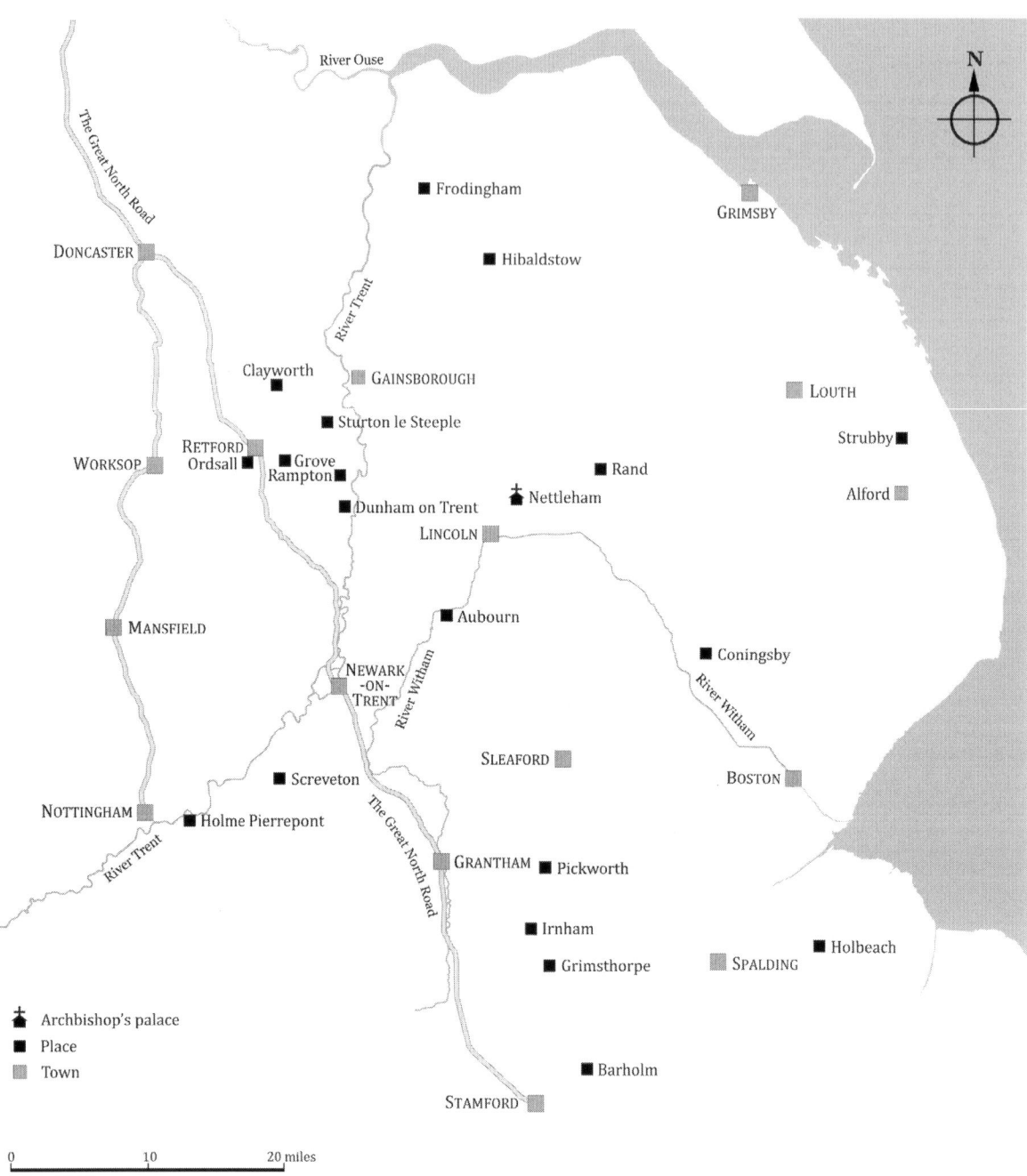

River Ouse

The Great North Road

DONCASTER

Frodingham

GRIMSBY

Hibaldstow

River Trent

Clayworth

GAINSBOROUGH

LOUTH

Sturton le Steeple

Strubby

RETFORD
Ordsall

Grove

WORKSOP

Rampton

Rand

Alford

Dunham on Trent

Nettleham

LINCOLN

MANSFIELD

Aubourn

River Witham

Coningsby

NEWARK
-ON-
TRENT

River Witham

Screveton

SLEAFORD

BOSTON

NOTTINGHAM

Holme Pierrepont

River Trent

The Great North Road

GRANTHAM

Pickworth

Irnham

Holbeach

Grimsthorpe

SPALDING

Archbishop's palace

Place

Town

Barholm

STAMFORD

0   10   20 miles

such as St Petronilla at Boultham, were destroyed.[2] Perhaps it was at this time that three fine alabaster figures were hidden beneath the altar of Flawford church in Notts, including one of Mary and one of St Peter. Perhaps the same happened with St Hygbald at Hibaldstow. Meanwhile, the removal of Catholic elements from church buildings continued. Wall paintings were covered over – in June 1550 the Mayor of Boston discussed whitewashing the church of St Peter's. Some fine examples have since been recovered to an extent at Blyth, Corby Glen and Pickworth.

Given the origins of the Lincolnshire Rising in fears that churches would be closed, it is ironic that an Act of 1549 provided for exactly that – although rather than isolated rural churches, this dealt with the extreme excess of churches in Lincoln, the population of which had not multiplied. The Act reduced the city's parishes from around 40 to 14 or fewer with many old churches being demolished. In Boston several chantries, chapels and churches closed such as St John's (which was still standing but, derelict, in 1626) so that the town had just one church.

Meanwhile, the new faith was spread by the efforts of the King's Commissioners. In the diocese of York they included Sir John Markham and Sir John Hercy, who went about issuing instructions – in the Deanery of Doncaster they advised that drunken celebrations of 'Plough Monday' should cease and set out instructions on the High Mass, with the bread being a 'token'. In Kesteven, the work of the Commissioners did not really get going until 1553, when in a week they disposed of vestments and ornaments worth £158 from Grantham, Wellingore, Folkingham, Stamford and Ancaster.[3] In places like Grimsby even the bells were removed. Nonetheless, much survived, to face renewed threats in the 1560s and 1640s.

During 1547 Henry Holbeach was confirmed as the first married bishop of Lincoln. His birth surname was Rands[4] and it is assumed he took the name 'Holbeach' from the place of his birth. He had been a monk at Crowland in the 1520s but in the 1530s became a friend of the great Protestant, Hugh Latimer. This introduced him to the Brandon-Willoughby circle, and he had preached at Brandon's funeral in 1545. In 1542 he was Dean at Worcester (having been Prior) and led the destruction of the shrines of Oswald and Wulfstan. He likely married in 1544. He moved from being bishop of Rochester to Lincoln, but supervised an exchange of properties that turned out 'so inequitable was the exchange that [it caused] the see of Lincoln from being one of the richest in England became one of the poorest'.[5] He helped Cranmer with the new Prayer Book but died of the sweating sickness at Nettleham in August 1551. Hajzyk suggested that later bishops did not like the Nettleham palace as it was 'haunted by the influence' of Holbeach.[6] It was finally demolished around 1630.

Katherine Willoughby set out to evangelise south and east Lincolnshire. She was already recognised in 1548 as a 'bright spectacle to womanhood' by Nicholas Lesse, an important translator of religious works who seems to have died in about 1550. Sabuda notes that 'he

---

2 R E G Cole, *Notes on the Ecclesiastical History of the Deanery of Graffoe*, p.36
3 E Duffy. *The Stripping of the Altars*, London, 1992, p.477
4 His son Thomas Rands was an important diocesan official in the 1580s
5 *ODNB, Henry Holbeach*, 27 July 2017
6 Helena Hajzyk, *The Church in Lincolnshire 1595-1640*, unpublished PhD, Cambridge, 1981, p.9

accorded her compliments that spoke to her ministry of the Word which previously would have been unimaginable if applied to a woman'.[7] Lesse showed his support for a woman doing such things, which was a 'reproach' to those who hated to hear that 'a woman should once have the evangelie in her hande or in her mought'. She supported the Bible printers John Day and William Seres and paid for a new edition of Tyndale's New Testament in 1548. Through this work she became one of the 'brekars of this heavenlye foode and breade unto the people', Lesse wrote. He continued to explain that 'the common people hath received already many comfortable and spirituall consolations, instructions and feelinges'.[8] Day and Seres went on to print her coat of arms in six of their books. She also supported Day in sponsoring George Bancroft's 1548 attack on the style of the Church's communion services – a topic on which Willoughby was influenced by Martin Bucer.

Her connections included Hugh Latimer, who often preached at Grimsthorpe, indeed one of his sermons celebrated how households like hers had replaced the monasteries as 'that same is a religious house....that house pleaseth God'. There was also Martin Bucer, a leading German theologian who had come to England in 1549 and was a leading critic of images. These two probably helped her move to their new teaching in rejecting transubstantiation, though she had been aware of this from the 1546 executions of Lassells and Askew. Latimer came to Grimsthorpe after losing his position as court preacher in 1550 and preached his first Lincolnshire sermons in Stamford that year, developing his practice of starting and finishing with the Lord's Prayer to help people learn it.[9] One of her chaplains was still John Parkhurst, and he obtained some very attractive livings but had to flee the country when Mary took the throne. By this stage Willoughby controlled some sixteen benefices, mainly in east Lincolnshire.

Willoughby also supported the licensing, in 1550, of the Austin Friars church in London for use by foreign Protestants without having to use the *Prayer Book* and thus by 1550 she was in the advance guard of Protestant progress.

Bucer stayed with the widowed Willoughby for some time in summer 1550; the friendship caused an associate to joke that Mrs Bucer should hurry to England. She provided him with a house in Cambridge, and a cow and calf for his support. Then she sent her two sons by Brandon to Cambridge to hear the great man's lectures.[10] However, he became ill and Willoughby was one of several people who nursed him and attended at his death in February 1551.

The sweating sickness was a danger to all that year and Katherine Willoughby took her two sons out of Cambridge and placed them at Buckden, where they had to keep in separate rooms. Almost immediately afterward she was rocked by the sudden death of her two sons at Buckden with both famously having a presentiment.[11] The oldest son Henry, at this stage Duke of Suffolk, was sitting 'merrily' at supper when he turned to his governess and said, 'We shall never sup together again in this world, be you well assured'. Late that night he fell

7   Wabuda (2002), p.104
8   Lesse's extended comments can be found in his introduction to the translation of Johann Aepinus's *Fruitful and Godly Exposition.*
9   Hill, *Tudor and Stuart Lincoln*, p.61
10   Constantin Hopf, *Martin Bucer and the English Reformation*, p.22-3, Oxford, 1946
11   This was recorded by Thomas Wilson, an evangelical hardly given to superstition. Wilson's funeral sermon blamed Willoughby for greedily supporting enclosures which hurt the poor.

ill and died before seven the next morning. His brother was not told of his death, but Charles declared 'Well, my brother is gone, but it makes no matter for I will go straight after him' and so died within half an hour of his brother. Henry spent less than half an hour holding the title of 3rd Duke of Suffolk, believed to be still the shortest peerage ever.

Thomas Wilson, the boys' tutor, attempted to steady the Duchess, for whom the deaths were almost a mortal blow. He advised her that two so good should return to their Maker and she should not regret His choice:
'How could your Grace think, that when you saw ancient wisdom in the one, and most pregnant wit in the other, marvellous sobriety in the elder and most laudable gentleness in the younger, both of them most studious in learning, most forward in all feats, as well of the body as of the mind, being two such and so excellent, that they were long to continue with you?'

Sir John Cheke, an eminent Cambridge academic, wrote their epitaph. Not only were they bright young men but they were friends to the king in the faith so their loss was mourned by theologians too, such as Peter Martyr who wrote to Heinrich Bullinger in Zurich about them – that Henry 'was a youth of such hopes' that 'would shortly have been a great support both to the state and the church'. Perhaps the events helped to bring Katherine closer to William Cecil a near neighbour from Stamford who was rapidly rising in the service of the State. His second wife Mildred Cooke, reputedly to be one of the cleverest women in the kingdom, became a close friend. A month after the deaths she wrote to them, struggling to manage her faith and the reality of their deaths:
'I give thanks, good Master Cecil, for all his benefits which it hath pleased him to heap upon me; and truly I take this last (and to the first sight most sharp and bitter) punishment not for the least of His benefits, inasmuch as I have never been so well taught by any other before to know His power, His love and mercy, mine own weakness and that wretched state that without Him I should endure here. And to ascertain you that I have received great comfort in Him, I would gladly do it by talk and sight of you. But as I must confess myself no better than flesh, so I am not well able with quiet to behold my very friends without some part of these vile dregs of Adam to seem sorry for that whereof I know I rather ought to rejoice'.
Cecil himself was a rising star at this stage, but also interested in evangelical issues. Late in 1551 he and Richard Morison hosted debates about the eucharist issue and transubstantiation, in their own houses. This was part of Edwardian movement to 'set up the gospel theme of liberty as the one standard of salvation' by denying 'the authority of custom, throwing off the accretion of church tradition'.[12]

By 1552 Katherine was recovered enough to go hunting in her own park and send Cecil a buck. Perhaps later that year, or early in the next, she remarried for love to Richard Bertie, a clever and religious man who held a senior position in her household, but was nonetheless, a clear social inferior – she intended to remain mistress of own destiny. But royal fortunes thought otherwise.

The Goodrich family are of significant interest in this era. We have already mentioned Thomas Goodrich, who was Bishop of Ely during Edward's reign and still with a focus

---

12   D MacCulloch, *Tudor Church Militant*, London, 1999, p.134

on reform; he was progressive in his views on the Mass, and active in the work on the Prayer Book. His cousin Richard Goodrich (?-1562) was born at Bolingbroke, had a legal career and was MP for Grimsby. He was related to Cranmer and also had close connections with Cecil, for whom he did some legal work. Perhaps as a result, he gained some Lincolnshire properties from the dissolution including at Sleaford in 1547, which he sold and some chantries in 1551. A strong evangelical, he joined his cousin on the commission during Edward's reign which looked at the Church's legal issues. He also took part in the prosecution of resistant bishops such as Heath, Gardiner and Tunstall.

We know only a little of the radical fringes of the Protestant reformation at this time including little of whether ideas such as Anabaptism reached our region. Nicholas Bullingham, archdeacon of Lincoln and with legal training, was asked to join a commission on anabaptists and other heretics in 1550. Thomas Cole, possibly from Grantham and the brother of William Cole (see later), was arrested in January 1551 and accused of denying original sin along with other 'freewillers'. He recanted and went on to be a Marian exile and to have a controversial career in the Elizabethan church.[13]

Meanwhile, in the early stages of Edward's reign, Cranmer was busy on the *Book of Common Prayer*. By this stage he was publicly accepting the revised understanding of the symbolic nature of the mass, a bitter conversion after the executions of 1546 when he had hidden from view. When the *Prayer Book* was published in 1549 it drew on both medieval English and European reformist ideas. The prose that he wrote has echoed down the centuries so that today even people with no church engagement can speak some of his phrases, making him perhaps second only to Shakespeare as the father of English. His words have been used for generations to marry and to be buried: 'to have and to hold from this day forward, for better for worse, for richer for poorer, in sickness and in health…'. and then proceeding to 'O God, from whom all holy desires, all good counsels, and all just works do proceed; Give unto thy servants that peace which the world cannot give…'.and the phrasing of 'dust to dust, ashes to ashes'.

By 1550 the pace of reform was growing but Cranmer still had to struggle against those who wanted even greater change, like Bishop John Hooper of Gloucester, whose arguments about vestments presaged another debate that was to come. In 1552 he issued a revised *Prayer Book* and in 1553 he published the forty-two articles that became the new Church of England's canon law. But King Edward died in the summer of 1553, the rule of Lady Jane Grey proved to be just a puff of smoke, and Cranmer faced the arrival of Queen Mary with some clarity over his likely fate – indeed many of those who by this stage shared his views fled across the Channel.

Queen Mary 1553-1559: The Protestant Diaspora

Mary's policy was to restore Catholicism and Catholic worship with all ceremonial. Some grasped this chance with both hands – in Grantham they revived the cult of St Wulfram

---

13 Another 'freewiller' was Robert Cole who was been suggested to be a third brother, though Michael Pearse believes him to have been from Faversham.

and built a new silver and copper shrine, perhaps with one eye on the trade it would bring. Saints' days and festivals returned to the calendar with such ceremonials as 'creeping to the cross'. In Lincolnshire, which appears to have remained highly conservative despite the efforts of Garrard (Garrett), Willoughby etc, this return was welcomed. Many had never quite abandoned the old feast days.[14] Parishes like Cadney retrieved all their 'Popish trumpery' from the gentlemen to whom they had 'sold' it.[15] At Irnham, a nun Elizabeth Thimbleby produced a cope and chasuble for the church's use – these were then 'reclaimed' by the Catholic Richard Thimbleby when Elizabeth took to the throne, and reported as being 'defaced' by him.

When Mary came to power seeking to restore Catholicism those clergy who had married provided an easy target. Given its earlier conservatism, it is surprising that around 13% of clergy in the archdeaconry of Lincoln and Stow were deprived,[16] at least 70 in Lincolnshire. Bishop John Taylor of Lincoln was displaced by John White (1554-6) and then Thomas Watson (1556-9) but one historian dissociates them from the terrors of the period and judged of Watson that he 'cannot be charged with cruelty'. Matthew Parker, the Dean of Lincoln and a future archbishop, was deprived and also John Aylmer the Archdeacon of Stow. In any event, more died for their faith under Henry VIII in our two counties than under Mary when no-one was burnt in Lincolnshire or Nottinghamshire; however, it is also the case that many fled rather than put her clemency to the test. Taylor bravely walked out of the Catholic Mass being celebrated in the House of Lords in 1553 and was sent to the Tower, but there is less certainty of his final fate – Foxe amending his account to say that Taylor was sent to Ankerwyke House in Bucks where he died. Others went the reverse direction – Francis Mallet, Mary's former chaplain who had been put in the Tower for celebrating Mass with Mary before she became Queen, was made Dean of Lincoln in 1554.

In the archeaconry of Nottingham probably fewer than twenty clergy were deprived – mostly these were men of 'advanced' Protestant opinions who had indicated this by getting married. There were several in the area around Retford where the influence of the Hercy-Denman family was proving significant. William Denman, a Cambridge graduate, had been ordained at Grove Chapel by the Bishop of Hull in 1551, Grove being the home of Sir John Hercy his uncle. He became rector of Ordsall from 1550; he was summonsed in 1554 and deprived in 1556 due to being married and fled to Europe. After his period in exile, he was restored to the living at Ordsall in 1559 by Royal Commission under Elizabeth and left a remarkable monument in his church, now lost, but which ended with the words: 'At length, being dead, I lie under this heap—Dead! Ah! Mistake!—I live a blessed life; the earth has my carcass; my Spirit inhabits Heaven'.

John Wilson, vicar of Dunham and Sutton-on-Trent,[17] was another married clergyman who was charged and deprived in 1554 on the same day as Denman and Thomas Brumhedde[18]

---

14 Duffy (1992), p.405
15 Duffy (2005), p.549
16 Bowker (1981), p.174
17 Wilson seems only to have been appointed to Sutton in 1553, leaving by 1554.
18 This is evidently the same family one of whom left Wheatley to go with Smyth to Holland. Bromheads were in several villages around and owned land at Bole in the 1520s.

at Rampton.[19] Christopher Sugden in Newark also lost neighbours at Winthorpe and Thorpe, but there was no strong geographical pattern to the deprivations.[20]

William Pierrepont, of the prominent local family, was rector at Holme Pierrepont until deprived in 1554 and was appointed by Hercy to replace Robinson at Grove but he was reportedly soon in trouble again – one of his offences was being married and he was forced to make a profession of chastity in front of his wife before being 'restored'. It was safe enough for him to be appointed to a living at Tollerton, North Yorkshire, in March 1558. Suggestions that he fled to Frankfurt by 1556-7, therefore, seem unlikely, but this may have been a relative Edmund or Edward.[21]

The Hercy-Denman link was fundamental to the growth of radical Protestantism in the Retford area, so their appointee at Grove, Robinson, was also deprived. Similarly, the 'godly' Richard Whalley lost his appointees at Screveton and Barnby-on-Dun. Whalley had done well out of the Reformation thus far – Worksop Priory and the chantry of Sibthorpe had come his way. But Whalley had already run into problems during the Somerset protectorate which had ended with a spell in the Fleet prison and then the Tower in 1551 and 1552, and then having to give evidence against Somerset. While in the Tower he was allowed to see his wife without the supervision of its Lieutenant, who rather conveniently was Sir John Markham. Still, he produced perhaps 25 children and a family name of national significance in the Civil war era as we shall see. He had a bumpy ride during Mary's reign, although he managed to host the evangelical William Ford at Welbeck and married two daughters into the Cranmer family.

Gentry like Whalley and Sir John Markham made a judicious decision to lower their profile during Mary's reign, but for the most part her focus was on the clergy. Markham's son Thomas was an MP and made some objection to the restoration of Catholicism – ironically both his wife and son became Catholics during Elizabeth's reign. However, Markham's daughter Isabelle, who had inspired some famous love poetry by her future husband Sir John Harington, was a marked woman due to having been a lady in waiting to Princess Elizabeth; both she and Harington went to the Tower, according to an old family history, but sadly this romantic tale is not quite true.[22] Harington was an evangelical in 1538, when he attracted the support of Henry VIII by composing an anti-monastic hymn that the King liked. But Harington was sent to the Tower for his role in supporting the Seymours in 1549 during Edward's reign and again in 1553 and 1554 under Mary when he supported the Wyatt rebellion, and perhaps saw Isabelle while her father was its Keeper; they married in 1559, after the death of Harington's first wife. In another little connection, Harington's book on Cicero was dedicated to Katherine Willoughby, both having common friends in the Parr family.

George Monsonne, a long-serving rector of Clayworth, had got married and was ordered to apologise for his marriage 'and other offences' in Clayworth church, after which he

---

19   Collinson, *Reformation Studies,* p.120
20   Wood (1947), p.140
21   Edmund was Master of Jesus College from 1551 to 1557 and held various Church livings.
22   Her son later reported that 'she was glad to sojourn with one Mr Topcliff'. Most likely this refers to Richard Topcliffe, later a famous torturer.

was restored to his position in 1554.[23] Nicholas Holme at Sturton-le-Steeple was also deprived for being married but thought better of it, recanted, and enjoyed a brief time as vicar of East Retford from 1556.

William Denman was not alone in crossing the Channel. Most who went were clergy or gentry with the money to travel; in the case of Katherine Willoughby, it would seem the departure was carefully planned with funding in place. A famous exile was the brother of Thomas Cranmer, Edmund, who was of course born in Nottinghamshire, and who had become Archdeacon of Canterbury in 1535. He was deprived in 1554 due to being married. He moved abroad to live at Emden and died in 1557.

Another refugee was John Plough, born in Nottingham, who held the living at St Peter's in the city from 1539 to 1550 which had previously been held by an uncle who bought the advowson for 'one term' from the prior of Lenton in 1538 or before. A well-known radical, he fled by 1554 to Basle when Mary took the throne and wrote several anti-Catholic works – all now lost. However, he got to know Edmund Grindal, later archbishop of York and Canterbury, and returned in 1559 to the benefice of East Ham, dying about 1562.[24]

John Staunton (Stanton) was another Nottinghamshire refugee and it is likely he was the uncle of William Stanton, who was hung for treason at Tyburn in May 1556 after being captured at the coast while trying to escape following the failure of Wyatt's Rebellion.[25] John Staunton was in Frankfurt by 1554 where he was supporting John Knox and in Geneva in 1555.

John Aylmer the archdeacon of Stow from just before the death of Edward in 1553, and Nicholas Bullingham archdeacon of Lincoln from 1549, fled abroad. Aylmer had a lucky escape – his ship was searched but he was hidden behind a secret compartment in a wine barrel. Aylmer was a marked man – he had denied transubstantiation, he was a married priest and he had a connection to the failed Lady Jane Grey, but he survived to become Bishop of London after stopping in Strasbourg for a while before touring the universities of Europe. Bullingham, also a married man, reached Emden by 1555 – perhaps in a state of some poverty; he had a wife from Washingborough which had marked him out, and in a later sermon he showed some bitterness against the clergy who had 'forsook unnaturally their wives and married benefices' during Mary's reign.

Gilbert Berkeley, a former Lincoln Franciscan friar, had now also travelled so far in his views that he went abroad to Frankfurt in 1554 – returning to become Bishop of Bath & Wells in 1560.

---

23   A G Dickens, *The Marian Reaction in the Diocese of York*, vol. 1, p. 26
24   Dickens, *Lollards and Protestants in the Diocese of York*, p.194
25   Jennings (1999), p.32

The Early Life of John Foxe:

The famous author of what became known everywhere as *Foxe's Book of Martyrs* was born in Boston in about 1516 although his father died when he was young. His mother remarried, to Richard Melton of Coningsby, and it seems likely that young Foxe's abilities were recognised by the rector of Coningsby, John Hawarden. Through his influence Foxe went to Oxford and began an academic career but his interest in evangelical Christianity sparked rumours and he left Oxford although this also meant he could avoid the almost compulsory ordination.

Foxe filled in with acting as a tutor for a Protestant family and married in 1547 before returning to Coningsby for a time. There it seems likely his stepfather was a Catholic and there was some animosity, so Foxe decamped to London. There he survived with more tutoring and translating works of Luther. Closely associated with the Duchess of Richmond, he was becoming better known in Protestant circles but when Mary came to the throne in 1553 his position became perilous.

After his short academic career and an uneven one as a tutor, he fled abroad in 1554 eventually settling in Strasbourg – though it is wholly typical of him that he diverted on the way to see Erasmus's birthplace. At Strasbourg, he met up with Anthony Gilby, Katherine Willoughby's protégé, and became embroiled with John Knox in arguments over the use and acceptability of the Prayer Book. In 1555 he abandoned Strasbourg for Basle, along with Knox. Here he worked as a printer, developing his interest in the history of martyrs which was to prove so fruitful. Other key associates were John Bale, the former prior of Doncaster, and John Aylmer, who also helped to record the lives of the martyrs. Especially influential was Matthias Flacius, who argued that the 'true' church in history had been, but a few isolated groups united by the Holy Spirit. He began collecting stories of the recent martyrs of the English Reformation.

Foxe's use of Protestant networks abroad is a key indication of the importance the survivors of this generation were to have over the Elizabethan era but in the dispute over the Prayer Book, it also indicated the divisions that were to come.

William Cole of Grantham fled to Zurich by 1554 and lived in a community there before moving to Frankfurt, Basle and Geneva. For some of this time he was with John Foxe of Boston and later the famous Scottish preacher, John Knox. During 1558 he helped with the famous Geneva Bible translation but seems not to have returned to England until 1564 – he became president of Corpus Christi College in 1568 though many of the fellows were unhappy about this as he was married. Cole's apparent brother Thomas also went to Frankfurt, having been specifically exempted from Mary's general pardon at the accession. At Zurich Cole met up with John Parkhurst, another one of the Brandon-Willoughby circle. Anthony Wolmer of Swineshead also left for Aarau, returning to be minister at Bloxham.

Anthony Gilby and The Geneva Bible:

This famous translation of the Bible was produced by a network of Englishman working in Geneva where it was published in full by 1560 although not printed in England until 1575-6. Thereafter it became very popular and was famously taken to America on the *Mayflower* as well as being used by Cromwell's troops in the 1640s.

The New Testament, which was completed by 1557, was largely the work of William Whittingham and Anthony Gilby, the former minister at Grimsthorpe and Edenham, who led on the Old Testament. William Cole of Grantham was also a significant contributor.

Both Gilby and Whittingham eventually returned to England and enjoyed the patronage of the Earl of Leicester, who set them to evangelise the county around his seat Ashby. Those associated with the Geneva Bible were often nonconformist on their return to England though Cole became increasingly conservative during his long career which took him via a stint at Colchester to be Archdeacon of Lincoln in 1577 and Dean in 1599.

Anthony Gilby was born in Lincolnshire in 1510,[26] graduated from Christ's College in 1535, and appointed to Edenham, by Willoughby, where he burned eleven mass books during Edward VI's reign.[27] He fled abroad to Basel and then Frankfurt where John Foxe lodged with him for a while – Foxe, of course, came from Boston so they may have had some family knowledge of each other. He helped set up an English church in Geneva in 1555. He was an important assistant with Coverdale and others in the work of translation that led to the publication of the *Geneva Bible* in 1560, which also involved Anthony Mayhew of Pembroke College and Lincolnshire who died in 1559 just after returning to England. Henry Hastings, the Earl of Huntingdon, found Gilby a niche as a lecturer at Ashby-de-la-Zouch from where his influence extended over much of Leicestershire. In 1578 he published a provocative view of the Church of England called *'A View of Antichrist, His Laws and Ceremonies in* Our English Church, unreformed'. Ashby became a puritan enclave and had many links to puritans in Nottinghamshire and Lincolnshire as we shall see.

Some Lincolnshire laymen, such as Anthony Meres of Auborn and from a Kirton-in-Holland family, also faced problems though not clergy themselves. Meres' property was sequestrated at the same time as Willoughby's in 1555; when he returned in 1559, he was an enthusiastic defacer of Catholic remnants in his parish church. Sir Christopher Kelke, of a family from Barnetby-le-Wold and living in York, was accused of being a 'Lollard' in 1555. His cousin was Roger Kelke, who fled to Zurich in 1554, but who returned under Elizabeth; he became master of Magdalene College in 1559 and eventually archdeacon of

---

26   The precise place appears to be unknown. Surname evidence might point to Gainsborough or possibly Boston.

27   Harkrider, p.88. Most historians leave this part of Gilby's life blank, eg 'It is not conclusively known where Gilby first settled as a Minister of the Gospel'. (R Danner, *Antony Gilby Puritan in Exile* in *Church History* 40 (4), 1971, p.412

Stow in 1563. Kelke's mother was Isabell, daughter of Robert Girlington of Frodingham or Normanby, and great aunt to the Wray children who were to prove greatly significant religious radicals. Less certain is the case of Robert and Lucy Harrington, possibly from Lincolnshire, who escaped to Frankfurt.[28] The Harringtons were well known in radical circles for the famous martyr John Bradford wrote to them from the Tower whilst another martyr, Laurence Saunders, asked them to care for his widow; Lucy died, and Robert had married the widow Joanna by 1556.

Thomas Wilson (1523/4-1581) was a well-known Marian refugee who went into exile in Padua with Sir John Cheke, a famous Greek scholar. Wilson was born at Strubby near Alford. He seems to have come into contact with Brandon, the Duke of Suffolk, when he was acquiring the lands of Bullington and Kirkstead priories. After gaining his MA, Wilson in 1549 became tutor to the two sons of the Duke and Duchess of Suffolk and probably their cousin, until the two boys died at Buckden in 1551 – Wilson wrote some poetry in their honour. He was also a friend of Martin Bucer. He wrote his famous book on rhetoric while staying with Sir Edward Dymoke at Scrivelsby in 1552 and then settled at Washingborough by about 1553. His links with Bucer and Katherine Willoughby would have made him a marked man when Mary's reign began.

Soon after he went into exile and by 1555 he was in Padua studying law with Cheke, and possibly also another exile John Tamworth, a Lincolnshire relative of Cranmer's whose family had lands near Boston and who later became its MP. When Wilson went to Rome to pursue a legal case he fell out with Cardinal Pole in 1558 and was ordered to return to England; when he did not, he was arrested as a Protestant and tortured in Rome but escaped during a riot in 1559. Back in England by 1560 he enjoyed a good career in politics and diplomacy with Cecil's support and in 1571 became MP for Lincoln, never losing his focus on the battle against the Papacy.

Moving in high political circles, he was repeatedly involved in the examination of Catholic prisoners starting with John Hales in 1564 and culminating with the Duke of Norfolk and other Ridolfi plotters in 1571 which led Wilson to call for the execution of Mary Queen of Scots, who he questioned at Sheffield. He undertook several diplomatic missions. He became a privy councillor in 1571. Late in life he held the parsonage of Mansfield and was appointed Dean of Durham in 1579, drawing on the revenues but still being a layman.

Wilson largely forsook his native county for its position limited his ambitions. He wrote, 'As it is much better to be born in Paris than in Picardy, in London than in Lincoln. For that both the air is better, the people more civil and the wealth much greater and the men for the most part more wise'.

The medieval heresy laws were revived in November 1554 – three laws having been abolished under Henry and Edward – and few were prepared to risk the penalties: Thomas

28   L Garrett, *The Marian Exiles: A Study in the Origins of Elizabethan Puritanism*, Cambridge, 1938, p.178

Armstrong of Corby recanted his heresy when challenged. Burnings started in 1555. As we have seen, many escaped abroad but a famous victim with strong Lincolnshire connections was Hugh Latimer, one of Katherine Willoughby's closest associates with a long record of preaching in the county, who was burnt at Oxford in October 1555 with Nicholas Ridley. At the stake, Latimer is said to have uttered the famous words, 'Play the man, Master Ridley; we shall this day light such a candle, by God's grace, in England, as I trust shall never be put out'.

The most significant victim of the Marian policy was Archbishop Thomas Cranmer. We know that one of Cranmer's sisters was still a Catholic and lobbied for him during his last days; this may have been Alice, the former Stixwould nun who he had made prioress of Minster in Sheppey, and this might have led to his being moved from gaol in Oxford to Christ Church. By the time of his execution on 21st March 1556 Cranmer seems to have made a radical change of position, rejecting the repentance he had made – perhaps this time under the influence of a Protestant sister.

Cranmer's last hours are amongst the most famous in English Christian history. At the stake he rejected the body that had weakly betrayed his beliefs: 'Forasmuch as my hand offended, writing contrary to my heart, my hand shall first be punished there-for'. He deliberately put his hand first into the flames, repeating that 'this hand hath offended', and using the final words of Stephen, the first Christian martyr by declaring 'Lord Jesus, receive my spirit … I see the heavens open and Jesus standing at the right hand of God'.

In December 1556 Thomas Watson was nominated Bishop of Lincoln. He had been close to Stephen Gardiner but achieved ignominy through his treatment of John Rough. During Edward VI's reign Rough, a noted Protestant, had intervened to save Watson from a treason charge after an incautious sermon but under Mary I Watson refused to return the favour, calling him 'a pernicious heretic', and Rough was burnt at Smithfield. Watson had already attained such notoriety that he needed an armed guard to protect him while preaching at Paul's Cross and as a persecutor of Protestants at Cambridge in 1553-4, supervising the digging up and burning of the remains of respected Protestant theologians like Martin Bucer in Cambridge. When Mary died, the position of such men became very insecure.

The Greatest Escape

As we have seen, the main effect of the Marian persecution was to drive a generation of leading clergy out of the country – from which they were to return with a stronger reforming agenda after 1559. As to the gentry, they generally kept their profile low and no doubt practiced their own variations of Christianity in the privacy of their homes whilst paying lip service at church. This left one clear regional figure with a marked record of evangelicalism who also had an acrimonious relationship with Stephen Gardiner, the influential Bishop of Winchester.

Katherine Willoughby's views had already brought her within a whisker of disaster in 1546. She had been a fervent Catholic in her earlier years, but her views began to change after her marriage and when she joined the household of Katherine Parr, Henry's last wife. As the only child of the 11ᵗʰ Baron Willoughby d'Eresby who had in 1533 become the fourth wife of Charles Brandon, Duke of Suffolk, she was one of the richest and most influential women in the country – with a second husband who would not curtail her activities. Brandon, along with Cranmer and many others, had been a godparent to Prince Edward, reflecting his close relationship with Henry VIII. After he died in 1545, she had married Richard Bertie, probably for love, in 1552; it is believed Hugh Latimer conducted the ceremony in July 1552.[29] She survived the crisis of 1546 and enjoyed some good years under Edward VI though devastated by the deaths of her sons; but now under Mary, she was known as the step-grandmother of Lady Jane Grey, who was executed for her part in a plot to keep Mary off the throne, too closely connected to the Seymours and someone with public views on the Mass that would now, once again, constitute heresy.

The hardline Catholic Bishop Gardiner became her famous sparring partner. During the reign of Edward VI, he was shut in the Tower of London, and attracted Katherine's attention as she passed by. She told him that it was a good day, 'for it was merry with the lambs, now that the wolf was shut up'. During Edward's reign she had also developed close links with Latimer and Ridley, who were later martyred under Mary in 1555, and Latimer was invited to preach at Grimsthorpe as well as tutoring her sons; he preached regularly in Lincolnshire from October 1552 to January 1553 and seven sermons on the Lord's Prayer formed the core of a publication of his work dedicated to the Duchess in 1552. Believing in propagating the Word, she was involved in printing Latimer's sermons and Tyndale's biblical translations; the edition of Latimer's sermons was dedicated to her by Augustine Bernher who edited them. Willoughby had also made use of other reformers like Roger Ascham and John Cheke to educate the children. She had appointed like-minded clergy under Bishop Henry Holbeach.

When Edward died in July 1553 and Mary took to the throne, Katherine was an obvious target, but the intention of Gardiner and Mary was to bring her to repentance. Her husband, Bertie, was ordered to appear before the Bishop of London who told him, 'I shall make you an example to all Lincolnshire, for your obstinacy'. Particular bad feeling had been caused by the story that Katherine had dressed her dog up in fine robes like a bishop and called it 'Gardiner' though her husband Bertie later protested she had not been responsible for this. When she and the bishop had been at a dinner, it had been decreed that each person should sit next to the one they loved most, but Bertie was absent; Katherine sat next to Gardiner and said 'forasmuch as she could not sit down with my lord who she loved best, she had chosen him whom she loved worst'. She sent money to imprisoned Protestants such as Ridley. Now the summoning of Bertie to speak for his wife was a deliberate insult given their different social standings, especially as Willoughby always clung to her title of 'duchess'.

Bertie was released to return home and persuade his wife to yield, but instead, they escaped down the Thames at dead of night with this grand lady dressed 'like a mean merchant's wife'. Thus the 'traditional' version of the escape, but as Harkrider explains it was well enough prepared for the Willoughbys to have conducted a furniture sale in advance and for her husband, Bertie, to have been on a preliminary trip into Europe – Bertie's mother sent them revenues from their estates. She took with her devout members of her household

29   Harkrider, p.71

such as Robert Cranwell and Margaret Blackborne. They went to Wesel in 1554 where the minister of the French church in London was already a contact of the Willoughbys. At Wesel, the Willoughby group expanded to almost a hundred people and included Miles Coverdale, the famous early translator of the Bible, and held their own services based on the 1552 *Prayer Book* with the former bishop of Bath and Wells, William Barlow, as their minister. Coverdale helped her secure a place at Weinheim in 1556, with Barlow and possibly John Bale.[30] When a messenger arrived from Mary I to demand her return, he was soundly beaten. After many adventures and a time in Germany, they went to Poland in 1557 where again her contacts from the Strangers' Church had proved fruitful.[31] They assisted the King of Poland by helping run a part of modern Lithuania.

In exile, Katherine pined for England and desired to 'sing our songs to the Lord in our native land'.[32] But exile also solidified her views, and she became convinced that she and her fellow believers were 'the elect in Christ'.[33] In exile, she met up with John and Thomas Turpin, Lincolnshire gentry, at Wesel, children of whom she later brought up within her household – one became keeper of deer at Grimsthorpe and the other estate manager at Spilsby.[34] John and Alice Pretie, who she met at Wesel, later also joined the household. By February 1559 she was corresponding with her old friend Cecil – who had managed to survive the challenges of Mary's reign – about her return to England, and already becoming annoyed at what she was hearing about the new Queen's lack of reforming policies.

The Dangerous Career of a Printer: A Historical Dispute

We have already encountered William Seres and John Day as Protestant printers active from 1546-7 during the last days of Henry VIII and the reign of Edward VI. They were closely involved with Katherine Willoughby, who used them to print an edition of Tyndale's New Testament and other works. Their interest was clearly in highly progressive works and in 1548 they printed ten books arguing against transubstantiation. Day also printed Lesse's translation work that praised Katherine Willoughby in 1548 and Hugh Latimer's *Sermon on the Plough* – Latimer was becoming a key Willoughby associate of course.

An interesting part of this story though is that the printers had close ties to William Cecil who was of course from a Stamford family and whose wife was a close friend of Willoughby's. Cecil had already helped to arrange the printing of Parr's *Lamentation of a Sinner* for Willoughby in 1547. Seres at least seems to be a servant of William's by 1548 and developed Lincolnshire connections. He was involved with Cecil and Lawrence Eresby in the purchase of an old London chantry in November 1548 that became Stationer's Hall in 1554.

---

30 Harkrider (2008) suggests Willoughby appointed Bale one of her chaplains.
31 This and the stories about Gardiner are told in John Foxe, *The Christian Historians of England*, volume 8, p.569-573
32 Franklin-Harkrider (2008), p.118
33 Ibid, p.63
34 Baldwin, p.174

However, things changed under Mary I and it has been claimed that Day fled to Lincolnshire where he continued printing in secret near Stamford from October 1553 to at least May 1554 under the name of 'Michael Wood of Rouen'.[35] Evenden has shown how Day rented two acres of land from Sir William Cecil at Barholm, just outside Stamford and only a few miles from Willoughby's house at Grimsthorpe – although, of course, she had fled abroad. Roger Alford, an associate of Seres, was collecting rents in the county at the same time – which Seres also did on behalf of Cecil.

This view has been challenged by another historian, who has argued that the name of John Day was a mere coincidence and that the property rented at Barholm was not suitable for a printing press.[36]

October 1554 John Day was arrested and taken to London. There he was imprisoned with the future martyr John Rogers who, according to Day, told him that 'thou.... shalt lyve to see the alteration of thus religion, and the Gospell frely to be preached agayne'. Meanwhile, Seres and another associate, Roger Alford, were employed by Cecil as rent collectors around Stamford. Seres and Alford both helped Cecil in hiding some of his property in case he was arrested by Mary's regime.

Also arrested was Sir William Cooke, Cecil's brother-in-law, who was 'committed to a vile prison'. Cooke was actually from Essex but was clearly being used by Cecil to support the reforming view in Lincolnshire where he became MP for Stamford in 1559 and Grantham in 1563. Day was later released and, in Evenden's version, returned to Lincolnshire until late summer 1556 when his tenancy ended at Barholm in July. Both he and Seres went back to London at about the same time where they printed a few books that were not immediately problematic.

After the death of Mary, John Day prospered and because of this was able to become the printer for the enormous task of producing John Foxe's *Actes and Monuments* from 1563. He had, himself, come close to being one of its martyrdom stories, but now he got to produce a text in which his own experience was a small part of the story.[37]

35   Elizabeth Evenden, *Patents, Pictures and Patronage: John Day and the Tudor Book Trade*, Aldershot, 2008, p.32-40

36   Peter Blayney, *The Stationers' Company and the Printers of London, 1501–1557*, Cambridge, 2013. The analysis in *ODNB* favours a connection with the Wood works but is silent on the Lincolnshire connection. The *ODNB* article on Seres is written by Evenden and provides substantial evidence to support *his* presence in Lincolnshire.

37   Additional information from E Evenden, *Patents, Pictures and Patronage*, Aldershot, 2008, pps 18, 32-40

CHAPTER FIVE:

Unhappy 'Settlement'
1558-1580

In 1559 the Act of Uniformity *was passed which was meant to define the Elizabethan 'settlement' of the disputes over religion. All were expected to conform to the practices and beliefs set out in the* Book of Common Prayer, *and to attend communion at their parish church: but some of both Protestant and Catholic views found they could not – hence the word 'non-conformist' was to be a defining term. In 1565 the Government decided to clamp down on those clergy who would not conform to expectations to wear the surplice and the cornered cap, prompting what became known as the 'Vestarian Crisis' – although the controversy continued for many years. Men such as Archbishop Grindal, at York from 1570, found themselves struggling to bring the Protestant reformation to northern parts whilst at the same time fighting off factious puritans who wanted more reform. However, 'a succession of radically protestant bishops' in both Lincoln and York kept puritanism alive within the Church.[1]*

There were many in the Church who wanted to go at a faster pace than Queen Elizabeth. In the Midland counties they did this by rejecting any trace of old rituals – including the surplice (prompting a crisis over vestments) – then by increasingly rejecting the Book of Common Prayer *which they replaced with a passion for sermons and open prayer of 'prophesying'. As we shall see, such people became known as 'godly' or 'puritans',[2] sometimes 'precisians', and powerful puritans who had the right to present a minister to a benefice chose like-minded men. Where this did not happen, men and women stopped attending communion and thus risked legal redress. A pivotal moment came when Grindal, who had been promoted to Archbishop of Canterbury, frustrated the Government in 1577 by defending the 'prophesying' with the result that he was deprived of some of his powers and came close to being removed altogether.*

---

1   P Collinson, *Elizabethan Puritan Movement*, 1967, p.60
2   The term 'puritan' was first used in the mid-1560s; we shall use it throughout here to avoid confusion, though to speak of puritans in 1561 is technically misleading.

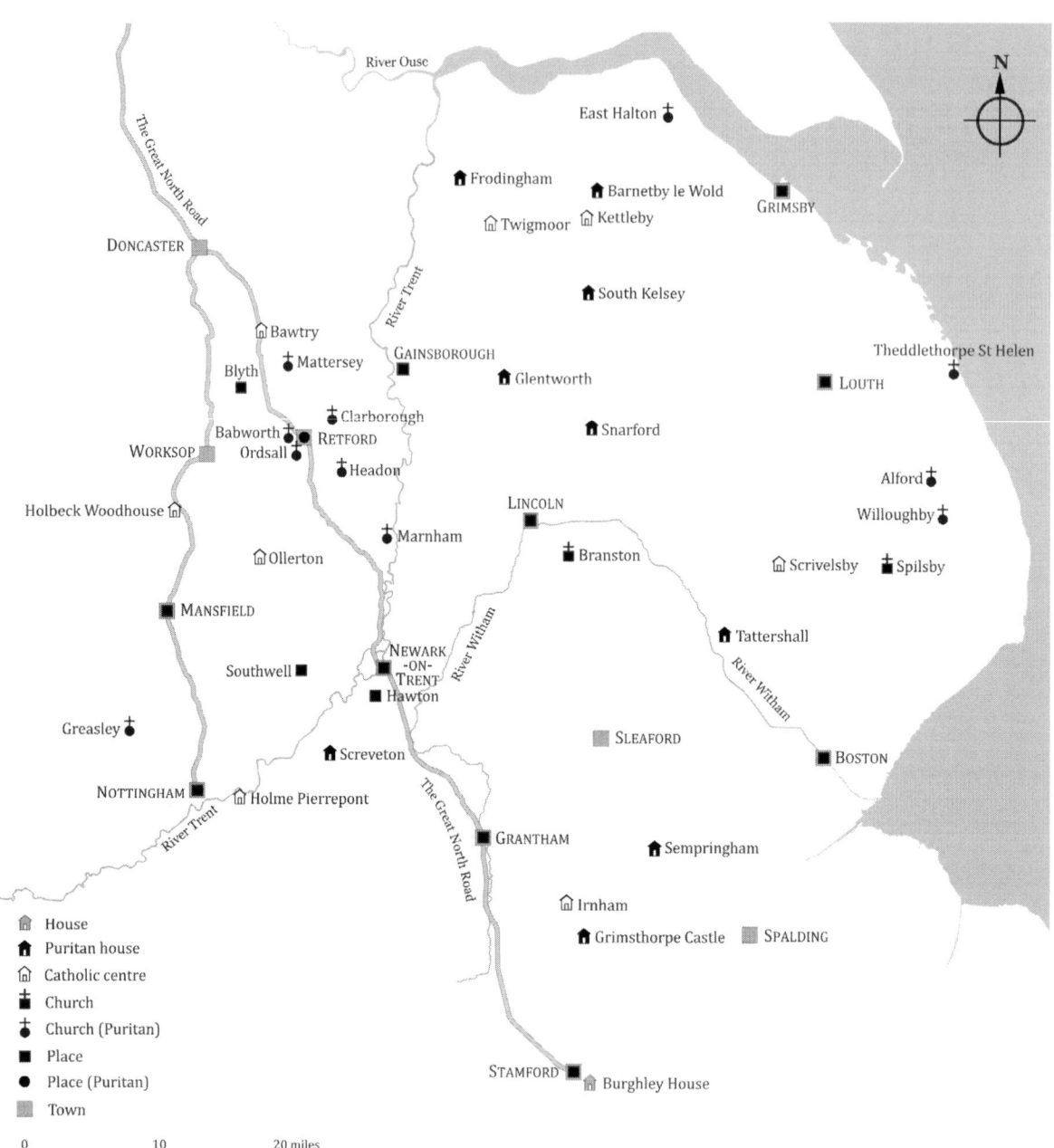

River Ouse

The Great North Road

East Halton

Frodingham

Barnetby le Wold

GRIMSBY

DONCASTER

Twigmoor

Kettleby

River Trent

South Kelsey

Bawtry

Mattersey

GAINSBOROUGH

Theddlethorpe St Helen

Blyth

Glentworth

LOUTH

Clarborough

Babworth   RETFORD

Snarford

WORKSOP

Ordsall

Headon

Alford

LINCOLN

Willoughby

Holbeck Woodhouse

Marnham

Branston

Scrivelsby

Spilsby

Ollerton

Tattershall

MANSFIELD

River Witham

NEWARK
-ON-
TRENT

Southwell

Hawton

SLEAFORD

River Witham

Greasley

BOSTON

Screveton

NOTTINGHAM

Holme Pierrepont

The Great North Road

GRANTHAM

Sempringham

Irnham

Grimsthorpe Castle

SPALDING

	House
	Puritan house
	Catholic centre
	Church
	Church (Puritan)
	Place
	Place (Puritan)
	Town

0   10   20 miles

STAMFORD

Burghley House

N

The Unhappy Settlement

In 1558 Elizabeth I came to the throne of a country that stood on the brink of the sort of religious conflict that plagued Europe for centuries. For the Protestants it seemed they were truly delivered from evil – 'Wherefore now is our season if ever any were of rejoicing. For if the Israelites might joy in their Deborah, how much more we English in our Elizabeth, that delivereth our thrilled conscience,' Katherine Willoughby wrote.[3] 'Do the will of Him that hath raised you up [in] spite of His and your enemies,' she wrote in January 1559 to the Queen. But the dowager duchess's mood was swiftly changed, in less than two months, and before she had even got back to England, she was complaining of Sir William Cecil and other advisers, 'How long halt ye between two opinions?'

An early effort to influence Elizabeth's thinking was by Lincolnshire lawyer Richard Goodrich, who sent her *Divers Points of Religion Contrary to the Church of Rome.* He argued for her to use Parliament to legalise the split from Rome and to imprison the Catholic bishops, which the Queen at first hesitated to do.

The Elizabethan period was one of interesting development for the two counties. Nottinghamshire developed a strong tradition of radicalism growing from roots in the northern parts of the county; Lincolnshire, one of the most conservative areas in 1536, also became more radical – especially in the east and around Gainsborough. As Harkrider concluded in her study of Katherine Willoughby, 'by the end of Elizabeth I's reign, Protestantism had clearly made inroads into this conservative county'. All this reflected the established influences of Willoughby and the Hercy-Denman group around Retford, new influences like the Wrays from the 1580s, and the persistent faith of minor gentry like Whalley, Irby, Armyne and Ayscough. Families such as St Pauls, clients of Willoughby, were committed to reform in successive generations and politically influential whilst Robert Monson, who replaced the old George St Paul as a Lincoln MP, was also a puritan in outlook.[4] The explanation of both trends lies in local activity as much as national

3   Collinson (1967), p.24
4   Hill (1956), p.69

policy. The seeds of the '*Mayflower*', the first Baptists and the 'Great Migration' were sown at this time and by these people – and watered by the Elizabethan church's alternating tolerance and repression.

The famous 'Settlement' enforced by the Act of Uniformity of 1559 was intended to prevent conflict and to maintain royal authority, which it largely managed to achieve. The Settlement was enforced by a proclamation against breaches of it on 22 September 1560. Compared to other countries, very few died for their faith under Elizabeth although we should not underestimate the sacrifice of those who did. Others were fined or went briefly to prison, but many learnt to pay lip service to the new rules whilst living by their own: national policy was inconsistently asserted by Church authorities. Puritans with wealth discovered how to play the system – for a time.

Elizabeth's solution was a Church that was generally Protestant in its doctrine but retained some of the features of Catholicism in its structures and services. The use of the *Book of Common Prayer* was an issue for the more evangelical Protestants, for it defined the words to be used and the vestments to be worn in all services at all times – there were to be no other words spoken except in a sermon. The puritans disliked surplices, bowing at the name of Jesus and the use of wafers rather than bread for Communion. The name given to the altar/table, whether it was of wood or stone and its position all inspired disagreement, to which the government added confusion by issuing some conflicting messages. Puritans disliked kneeling at Communion.

All were meant to conform or be fined (although not effectively so until 1572), but many more radical Protestants had been in exile abroad and their ideas were more progressive than the Queen's; therefore the stage was set for a battle of wills which, in general, Elizabeth won. Her opponents on the progressive Protestant side became castigated as 'puritans' because they wanted every last vestige of Catholicism purified, with those who wanted the abolition of bishops called Presbyterians. Most of these believed the work of the Reformation could be continued by further reforming the Church of England. Later we shall meet the 'separatists', who wanted to abandon the Church of England altogether and form separate churches.

Visitations were arranged to assess the situation. The diocesan visitation of 1559 showed Lincoln in a bad state. Churches were in disrepair, there was a lack of curates, some had no services or prayers in English. One reason for the lack of priests was that the patron of the parish could retain its revenues if there wasn't one whilst many of the livings were poorly rewarded and hence it was difficult to recruit good clerics. Over the Trent in East Retford, the vicar of this significant market town was notably poorly paid compared to his counterpart in rural Clarborough.[5] Problems such as this led to the Elizabethan expansion of the universities to provide a new generation of educated, Protestant priests.

Clergy were expected to subscribe to the new settlement in 1559 and most did so. Those who could not and were ejected included the Bishop of Lincoln, Thomas Watson, and the 'Marian' archdeacons of Stow and Lincoln John Harrison and Owen Hodgson, but only a tiny number of clergy appear to have been deprived although, with some records missing,

---

5   Marcombe, p.164

this figure may be open to reinterpretation. Visitors appointed to deal with related offences included Sir Francis Ayscough who, with ten other Lincolnshire gentry, petitioned William Cecil on behalf of the exile Nicholas Bullingham to regain his post as archdeacon of Lincoln. Instead, he was consecrated Bishop of Lincoln in 1560, those who provided the sureties for his 'first fruits' including Robert Brocklesby of Glentworth, a puritan family on the rise of whom we shall hear more soon. Bullingham moved to Worcester in 1571 when he was replaced by Thomas Cooper. Bullingham also married again – choosing a widow who had herself been in exile in Antwerp.

John Aylmer returned to become Archdeacon of Lincoln in 1562, setting out on a campaign to remove Catholic symbols from churches, and a step up perhaps from his previous role at Stow but his career was held back for having published an attack on bishops – although he became Bishop of London in 1576. Later puritans saw Aylmer as a worldly turncoat, especially for his role in attacking those behind the *Marprelate Tracts* as we shall see later. In his turn, Aylmer was replaced as archdeacon until 1581 by William Cole, a Marian exile who had been born in Grantham and contributed to the Geneva Bible, but who now showed perhaps a careerist focus on conformity.

The visitation in Nottinghamshire was held at St Mary's in Nottingham, Southwell and Blyth. In Nottinghamshire, probably only a handful were deprived at disparate places such as Fledborough, Farnsfield and Headon,[6] and also the archdeacon of Nottingham himself, Robert Pursglove (also known as Sylvester), who retired to run a school at Tideswell and was replaced by William Daye. A few other priests lost their places to make way for returning exiles as in Ordsall and Newark. Nottinghamshire had escaped the worst excesses of the Marian era and now it enjoyed similar benevolence under Elizabeth – with only ten clergy presented for nonconformity between 1574 and 1601, yet it was far from quiescent.[7] There was also the odd 'scandalous' priest to be got rid of, such as the vicar of Wollaton who had rushed communion so as to return to gambling, lost all his money gambling in Nottingham, defaulted on his debts and tried to seduce a girl of fourteen. William Underne was deprived in 1564.

The Unlikely Career of William Underne

William Underne's career in the Church is the very antithesis of the 'godly' yet he survived to die as a prebend of Southwell. We first hear of him as holding the living of Wollaton, which he acquired from the executors of the Willoughby estate about 1557. However, by 1559 his parishioners were in open revolt and in 1560 condemned him as 'an evil man in his conversation and lying'. The first sign of a problem seems to have been a twelve-day gambling spree at Christmas 1557, but this became a habit and he was described as 'a common gamester at the alehouse'. He was also notably bad at gambling – losing heavily at the alehouse and then again on a trip to Nottingham in 1558. On one occasion he 'borrowed' a horse and disappeared for months, prompting the circulation of a pamphlet by noted author William Birch which was accused of libel.

---

6   Wood (1947), p.142
7   Jennings, p.27

The Wollaton parishioners complained that babies were dying unbaptised due to Underne's absences, but he clearly had some other vices. He was accused of 'canvassing a young maid of 14 or 15 years old in a blanket or window cloth at midnight' and of living with a woman at Bingham.

He seems to have left Wollaton in about 1560 and moved to Lowdham, but was not deprived until 1564. Only two years later he managed to get another living at Upper Langwith, which was in a different diocese, but was still on the Nottinghamshire scene sufficiently to be accused of fraud by the Archdeacon of Nottingham; both Underne and his wife were excommunicated in 1570 for failing to appear at Greasley to answer charges.

Despite all this, and perhaps helped by a change in Archbishop, Underne then emerged as vicar at St Mary's in Nottingham in 1572. His honeymoon here was brief – he was in trouble again by 1573, indeed may have already been in prison. In 1574 he was declared an outlaw for non-appearance to meet a debt of £66 owed to a goldsmith in London. He resigned in 1576 and went to live at Staythorpe, but retained an income from a Southwell prebendary until his death.[8] However, he did not go quietly – in 1580 he was again in trouble for £10 debt, and in 1581 he was suing Trinity College, Cambridge, over the manor of Staythorpe. He had a brother, Edward, who was made a deacon in 1560 and was later rector of Boultham in Lincoln, with whom he also had a nasty legal battle.

At the same time, some of those who had been deprived under Mary returned to the same or different livings. Edward Mawde took over at Blyth whilst Thomas Curwen, ejected from the Whalleys' living of Screveton under Mary, resurfaced at Car Colston with the same patron in 1562. Christopher Sugden regained his place as the ill-named Perpetual Vicar of Newark, having been removed in 1554. In Ordsall, William Denman returned.

Around Retford, David Marcombe has identified the appointment of growing numbers of ex-Cambridge clergy after 1559 as evidence of Protestant sympathies in local patrons.[9] The practice was led by Sir John Hercy, who had been sufficiently worried at the start of Mary's reign to take legal advice on the division of his lands; he died in 1570 without a child so his lands were divided between his sisters and their various children including the Nevilles and Denmans. Hercy had been patron of the churches at West Retford, Grove, Babworth and Ordsall. Hercy was evidently popular locally, with Rev Edward Hodgson writing that 'he hath been accustomed ever to do good'.[10]

Rev William Denman, who had been appointed to the benefice of Ordsall in 1550 by Hercy, fled as a married priest at the time of Mary, now also became lord of the manor of West Retford in 1572 – taking over patronage of the benefice from his uncle Sir John Hercy of Grove and appointing his brother Francis to the living in 1578. Between them, and with the help of many local relatives, they succeeded in gathering other puritan clergy

8   S W May and A Bryson, *Verse Libel in Renaissance England and Scotland,* Oxford, 2016, p.149-51
9   David Marcombe, *Small Town Life: Retford 1520-1642*, Nottingham, 1993, p.170
10   Marcombe (1993), p.156

in the district.[11] William Denman died in 1588 whereupon Francis became Lord of the Manor of West Retford.

His appointment of Nicholas Pettinger, who also held Babworth, to West Retford was also a Protestant move and Pettinger was married to Elizabeth Denman. Denman's nephew John married the sister of Walter Travers, a prominent puritan from Nottingham. We will return to Travers below. Jennings argues that Hercy was responsible for appointing puritans such as Robert Lilley or Lylley at Babworth in 1557, Edward Hodgson in East Retford, Nicholas Pettinger at West Retford from 1559 and William Pettinger at Mattersey.[12] Marcombe has explained that the Denmans were influential in bringing ministers like Richard Clifton, Nicholas Watkins of Clarborough from 1577, and George Turvin to the Retford area[13] though, in fact, Clifton first arrived at Marnham through the Babingtons and then moved to Babworth in 1587 to replace Lily. Through family connections they linked to other local puritans like Sloswicke and Darrell. They, in turn, maintained close relations – Lily's sister married Hodgson – and provided some of those involved in separatism, including two Pettingers, who were both in Leiden by 1613 and Humphrey Denman who was in Amsterdam and received a legacy from Walter Travers in 1634.[14] Mary Pettinger, baptised at Carlton-in-Lindrick in 1561, married Richard Jackson in Doncaster and was the mother of Susannah Jackson – the future wife of New England's Edward Winslow.[15] Richard Jackson signed the lease at Scrooby Manor in 1604, so the Pettingers form a useful bridge between the early Hercy-Denman evangelicals and later separatism. Other members of the Jackson family held roles with the Spalding Court of Sewers which may explain the separatists' links with people in Boston. From Watkins' parish went two of the Southworth family whilst Anne Peck of Sutton-cum-Lound left £7 in his safe-keeping when she left England.

Walter Travers came from a Nottingham goldsmith family of committed evangelicals. His older brother Robert was a Cambridge theologian and died in Geneva in 1575 – a key Protestant city. Travers himself was born in about 1548 and went first to Christ's College at Cambridge, aged twelve, then to Trinity, from where he presented an address to Queen Elizabeth in 1564. The Travers family were puritans of some standing – a sister married John Denman of Retford (cousin to William and Francis) whilst another brother, John Travers, was married to the sister of Richard Hooker – a leading puritan figure who became a rival of Walter Travers. John later became rector of Farringdon in Devon and remained a puritan agitator there for many years until his death in about 1620; one of his sons became a chaplain to Charles I but another retained the family attitude by being ejected from his Cornwall living in 1662. Yet another brother, Humphrey, became vicar of both north and south parts of Grantham in 1580.[16]

---

11   Marcombe (1993), p.181

12   Stuart Babbage, *Puritanism and Richard Bancroft*, London, 1962, p.47 – though some appear to be after his death and are not recorded as presented by Hercy in CCED.

13   D Marcombe, *Small Town Strife*, in K Holland, *Mender of Disorders*, p.48

14   Jennings, p.

15   This research is discussed at greater length in S Allan's 2017 book on Susannah White Winslow and at the website, http://mayflowerhistory.com/white-susanna/

16   S J Knox, *Walter Travers, Paragon of Elizabethan Puritanism*, London, 1962, p.14

However, John Whitgift was appointed Master of Trinity in 1567 and in 1570 forced Walter Travers out for nonconformity – he also left for Geneva. These departures mark out the Travers brothers as in the vanguard for further reformation. In Geneva Walter mixed with great figures of ecclesiology – Thomas Cartwright and the Scot Andrew Melville. There amidst the Calvinists he wrote his major work, *Ecclesiasticae disciplinae et Anglicanae ecclesiae ab illa aberrationis, plena e verbo Dei, et dilucida explicatio*, arguing for a Presbyterian model of Church based on New Testament evidence – and without bishops. This was translated from Latin into English by Thomas Cartwright. Unable to find a job in England, Travers effectively became a Calvinist minister in Antwerp, a key base for the Merchant Adventurers, where his cause was supported by William Davison, the ambassador to the Netherlands and later the patron in 1584 of William Brewster. His 'ordination' there by Antwerp ministers in 1578 was to be a persistent source of controversy since he was ordained on the Presbyterian model and never ordained by a bishop. After some of his supporters left Antwerp, Travers was attacked by Nicholas Loddington of the Merchant Adventurers for not using the Prayer Book. Davison stood up for Travers, and enlisted the support of more powerful men like Sir Francis Walsingham. Patrick Collinson concluded that 'the Antwerp congregation seems to have powerfully influenced the domestic puritan movement in a Presbyterian direction'.

Travers left for England in 1580 and was replaced in Antwerp by Thomas Cartwright, another very well-known reformer. By 1581 he had secured a post at the Temple Church in the middle of London, with the help of Lord Burghley (Cecil), but his innovations were not entirely welcomed and this placed him in a highly visible position when Whitgift became Archbishop of Canterbury in 1583. We shall hear more about him in the next chapter.

During the early 1560s, much of the trappings of Catholicism were cleared away from the churches, though areas of Lincolnshire were slow to change.[17] The first instructions were issued in 1559, with the intention of sweeping away rood screens and idols – Witham on the Hill burnt its rood screen and sold its vestments straight away and at Wilsford the rood was burnt in 1560. But from the start parishes played a game – Welby sent some 'popish peltrie' to be burnt at Grantham but clung on to its missal, vestments and handbells until 1565. Stallingborough and Langtoft did much the same even though the former was within the Ayscough influence. When Bishop Bullingham arrived at Ashby near Horncastle in 1561 he found that nothing had been done at all, and his own men set to work tearing books and breaking furnishings. Market Rasen itself suspected, or claimed, that a royal servant had gone off with its best treasures. Many of the parishes had hidden away their treasures during Edward's reign and got them out again during Mary's – so perhaps they now thought they could do the same. At Folkingham they reported they had burnt all the rood figures in 1560 but at Epworth, although Mary had been done away with, Mr Maw the churchwarden was unable to say where she had gone.[18]

In Lincolnshire, Archdeacon Aylmer, Thomas Tailor and Thomas St Paul were key

17   See list of sources in Harkrider, p.113
18   Edward Peacock (ed), *English Church Furniture, Ornaments and Decorations*, 1866, p.78-90,

assistants in this with the former leading on the removal of many 'idols' from churches from 1562. In cases like Hacconby we have many lively details of what happened; in 1562 the parish burnt or destroyed its crosses, censers, pyx, chrismatory, mass books, processioners and the reredos whilst the holy water stoup became a pig trough for the priest's swine and the sacring bell was attached to a horse's harness.[19] At Carlton-le-Moorland in 1563, Thomas Disney took away the 'Popish' books and three years later the rood loft was sold and defaced. In Alford, Francis Spanning removed the rood images and other 'such like trash.[20]' At Edenham figures of Mary and Joseph from the rood were defaced and burnt whilst a copper cross with figures of Mary and John was defaced by none other than Richard Bertie, husband of Katherine Willoughby, dowager duchess. Bertie had acted more quickly in other respects – the stones from the altar had been broken and used for paving in 1562. Alkborough's wardens burnt Mary and John in 1565. The rood screen, and figures, was a prominent target in many churches but at Pickworth and Corby Glen the whitewashing of wall paintings helped create a hidden treasure for future generations. Stone altars and altar rails also went – at Barkston the altar was broken up and the stone used for paving. The Bishop acted to clear the 'nest of unclean birds' at Lincoln cathedral in 1565, using financial impropriety as his excuse, and to clear Catholic recusants from the diocese.[21] He was also suspicious of Grantham, where the corporation were still lamenting their pilgrimage trade.

Fillingham only destroyed its rood screen when Archdeacon Kelke arrived – but he was not in post until 1563; many of its books, copes etc, had mysteriously gone away. Although 1565 was the peak year for clearing away unacceptable ornamentation, there were some survivals such as the stained glass at Belton (Axholme) which stayed until 1595. Archdeacon of Lincoln, John Aylmer, was so horrified by the state of the religion in Lincolnshire that he lobbied for an extra commission in 1565, 'for undoubtedly this country hath as much need of it as any place in England'. Other villages like Kelby in Heydour reported destroying everything 'yesterday'. So Bullingham's commissioners acted with suspicion – they would not believe items had been destroyed unless they had names, dates and evidence; the picture that developed was of 'a slow and reluctant conformity imposed from above'.[22] Duffy, a Catholic historian lamenting the losses, notes that some parishes failed to comply with the expectations of 1565 and delayed their actions until the next visitation in 1566 – only a quarter seem to have promptly met the demands made in 1559. In 1566 Bassingham was forced to hand over various items stashed in the 'safe-keeping' of its people – but only because Anthony Meres forced the issue and destroyed some of the items himself.

Vestments were an easily disposable target. Some went for bedspreads. At Cumberworth vestments were sold to parishioners who used them as costumes for players. Books also had to go, though at Bardney the wardens reported that their priest had 'taken away' the mass book and they knew not where. But for the advance guard of the Reformation, now being termed 'puritans', these disposals were not enough and from 1565 the issue of conforming to prescribed vestments including a surplice became a confrontational point in the Church.

19   Duffy (2005), p.585
20   Harkrider, p.132
21   Hill (1956), p.98
22   Duffy (2005), p.573

A leader of the opposition was Thomas Cole, who is believed to have originated from Grantham and to be the brother of William Cole, the Marian exile and later Archdeacon of Lincoln. Despite having had a brush with authority in 1551, he had the credibility of having been an exile and a powerful backer in the Earl of Leicester – through whom he was helped in securing the archdeaconry of Essex and also became Dean of Bocking. He was brave enough to denounce human invention in religion before Elizabeth, but then attracted Archbishop Parker's attention for refusing to conform to vestment rules in 1564. Both Essex as a whole and Bocking, in particular, developed a radical and even separatist reputation before Cole's death in 1571. The issue became a battleground for Archbishop of Canterbury Matthew Parker, who in 1566 took a decidedly conservative step in publishing his *Advertisements* which re-emphasised conformity to the rules about wearing of vestments and specifically the surplice. Parker had been briefly Dean of Lincoln from 1552 before being removed under Mary in 1554. The Protestant Reformation in England had now tackled questions of the Papacy, doctrine in great detail, styles of worship and the form of churches; from 1566 the battle between progressive reformers and conservatives was to be almost entirely over the matters of the outward forms with some growing focus on church governance.

Now we must meet a family that was to have great significance over the next eighty years. The Brocklesby family had made some progress up the economic scale by acquiring monastic lands including Robert's purchase in 1543, having assisted with the commissions of the 1530s, much like the Lassells across the Trent who 'managed to establish themselves in the ranks of the gentry in the wake of the dissolution of the monasteries'.[23] For our purposes, the first important figure is Robert (I), who died in 1553 but left two sons who inherited his lands at Glentworth – Robert (II) – and at Kirton, Richard; plus a third Edward who went to Eton and then entered the Church. The elder Robert Brocklesby's will named a supervisor who was one of the closest servants of Brandon.[24] His associations included the Girlingtons, Halls, Ayscoughs, St Polls and Granthams – though relations between all of these were not always smooth.

Anne Girlington married Robert (II) but he died in 1557 leaving her with one son. He bequeathed 'two partes' of his lands at Glentworth to his wife and the rest to his son Edward, who died at some point in the next eight years. Through either the efforts of Anne or her second husband, Christopher Wray, who was a rising lawyer from Yorkshire, the Glentworth estates were bought back. Anne's background is worth examining for as the mother of a great dynasty of puritans it has been suggested Anne was from a Catholic family but the Girlingtons, of Frodingham, were related to the Kelkes of Barnetby – one of whom had been a Marian exile whose cousin had been accused of being a Lollard in 1555. Anne's aunt Isabelle was mother of eleven children including numerous Tyrwhitts by her first marriage and the four Kelke brothers by her second. The oldest of these married Jane St Paul, a daughter of another upcoming reforming family. Thus, her cousin was the exile in Zurich and Basle, Roger Kelke, who enjoyed the favour of Sir William Cecil and became Master of Magdalene College in 1559 and archdeacon of Stow in 1563.

Anne Girlington's connections therefore constituted a large portion of the reforming families in Lincolnshire and into Derbyshire through Sir Godfrey Foljambe, almost all of whom had connections to Charles Brandon, Duke of Suffolk, and thus to his widow

23   Stephen Taylor, *From Cranmer to Davison: A Church of England Miscellany*, p.53
24   Gunn, p.226

Katherine Willoughby. Girlingtons and Tyrwhitts had been in campaigns with Brandon in 1542, whilst St Paul and Brocklesby families provided justices and commissioners in his service.[25] Matthew St Paul (Poll) had been Brandon's attorney and his brother George also active in his service – both gained monastic lands.

Anne Girlington's brother-in-law through her first marriage was Edward Brocklesby. After Eton he attended King's College; he fled to Emden at the time of Queen Mary along with Nicholas Bullingham, then the archdeacon and in future the bishop of Lincoln, to whom the Brocklesbys were clearly close with one writer suggesting family connections.[26] In fact, Bullingham was married first to Margaret Sutton of Washingborough (through whom he was connected to the Disneys), another family to whom Anne Girlington was connected by marriage. When Bullingham was proposed for the bishopric of Lincoln in 1560 his sureties included Sir Francis Ayscough, who had petitioned for his restoration as archdeacon in December 1558.[27] Others included Richard Brocklesby, of Kirton.

Edward Brocklesby was first appointed vicar of Congresbury but by 1561 was in London at St Nicholas Olave; it is possible that his brother Richard was living nearby at St Thomas the Apostle. In 1563 Brocklesby was appointed to Hemel Hempstead, largely due to Bullingham's personal support.[28] Brocklesby attracted Archbishop Parker's attention in 1565 because of his lack of conformity and it is most likely that this was because of his continuing prominence in a London parish; Parker was then working on his controversial *Advertisements* which included some contribution from Bullingham. In April ecclesiastical commissioners visited Brocklesby's Hertfordshire parish and found plenty of evidence against him. He had declared the 'churching of women' to be 'superstitious', Mary to be 'a lumpe of sinne as other women are', he refused to wear a surplice or to use wafer bread in communion.

This refusal meant that on 8 May 1565 Edward Brocklesby became the first cleric to lose his position under Elizabeth due to his opposing the use of the surplice – but his radical position is further emphasised by the fact that he was a Marian exile in Emden. It was perhaps less his activities in Hemel Hempstead than in the vacant parish of St Martin Olave in London that brought him into trouble;[29] he was deprived on 8 May 1565. This was the first round in the 'vestments controversy' where Parker and other conservatives attempted to quell the nonconformists.

After his deprivation Brocklesby had good enough advice to be able to appeal his requirement to pay the 'first fruits' and to win his case, perhaps with the support of Grindal.[30] By this time his brother Robert had died, probably in 1557, and his sister in law Anne Girlington had married again to the rising young lawyer Christopher Wray with the family estates being left partly to Anne and the rest to their young son who had died by 1566; Wray was able to complete the purchase of the estate, from which a hugely influential family of puritans was born.

---

25   S Gunn (2015), p.118

26   Taylor, p.54

27   Taylor, p.55

28   Taylor, p.56

29   F J Bremer and T Webster (eds), *Puritans and Puritanism in Europe and America*, vol 1, p.34, Santa Barbara, 2016

30   Stephen Taylor, *From Cranmer to Davidson: A Church of England Miscellany*, p.52

In 1568 or 1569 Edward Brocklesby became rector of Branston, Lincolnshire, on the presentation of Christopher Wray. In 1571 he was collated by Bullingham to the prebend of Sexaginta Solidorum in Lincoln Cathedral. He died in possession of both preferments in 1575. This pattern shows an interesting light on Wray's early career – established in Lincolnshire, connected to religious radicals by marriage and location, and apparently not afraid to risk having his cards marked by supporting a nonconformist. Yet historians have universally labelled him as 'conservative'.

The Wray family itself is said to have originated from Carlton, Coverdale, Richmond. Sir Christopher's brother Richard maintained a line at Kelfield, Yorkshire. Wray was born at Bedale in 1523, though he was bedevilled by rumours that he was the outcome of an illicit liaison in a belfry at Hornby, North Yorkshire, between an errant Rector and a serving maid. He attended the college at Cambridge that became Magdalene and then launched onto a successful legal career to become Lord Chief Justice in 1574. He was involved in many famous cases including defending Bishop Bonner in 1565 and in a famous session at Bury St Edmunds in 1583, convicting both three separatists and seven recusant Catholics; however, we must tread warily regarding his personal opinions. Although at various times MP for Boroughbridge, Grimsby and Ludgershall, he was less successful in politics. Nonetheless, Elizabeth granted a share in the profits from the coinage to help fund his new house at Glentworth. Somehow Wray managed to juggle the demands of a legal and political career with maintaining a household which was intimately connected with radical, nonconformist religion, producing three children who sponsored the next generation of puritan leaders.

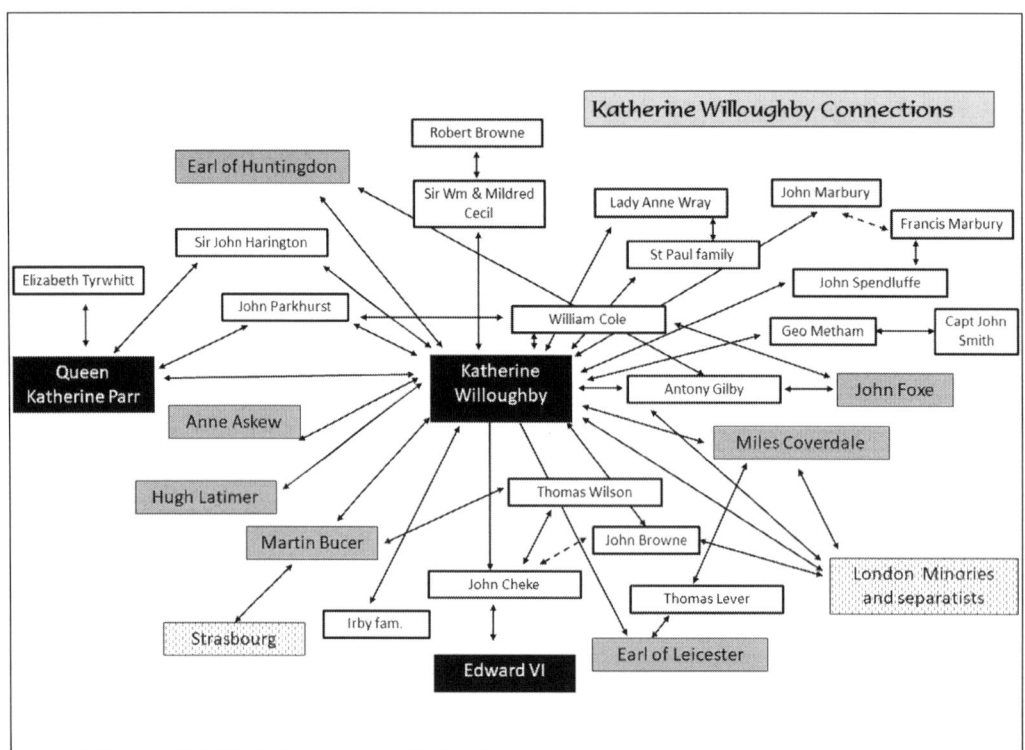

They were to be the next generation, but in the 1560s Katherine Willoughby was still the most progressive force Lincolnshire – and outside of it. When she returned from exile Katherine had been eager to encourage further religious change in England and especially Lincolnshire, which clung to the old ways. Her husband supported her in this work, and they had links with like-minded nobles in other counties, such as Henry Hastings, the Earl of Huntingdon, at Ashby-de-la-Zouch (who had taken over her support for Anthony Gilby) and Robert Dudley, Earl of Leicester. However, she was not in step with Queen Elizabeth, whose famous 'Settlement' of 1559 was too conservative and protected too much that the more committed evangelicals – on the way to puritanism – disliked. For Willoughby the Gospel was 'a route sufficient and only to be followed'.[31] Ritual behaviour such as bowing at the name of Jesus or using communion wafers rather than bread she despised.

Her network at home and abroad was extensive – Coverdale, Bale and many others returned alongside her from exile. John Parkhurst, who had been her family chaplain in the early 1540s and had been at Zurich, returned to be appointed Bishop of Norwich in 1560 where he proved himself a poor administrator if tolerant of some nonconformity. Patrick Collinson has also identified a group of 'mostly proletarian exiles' who had gathered under Willoughby's covering at Aarau and been ministered to by Coverdale and Thomas Lever; two of these are especially interesting for William Betts may have been one of the famous Hadleigh congregation whilst Thomas Upcher was from Bocking in Essex – a village which might be claimed as the first separatist centre in England.[32] These (with one doubt) were ordained by Grindal in 1560, along with their colleagues from Aarau Robert Pownall and Walter Richardson. Thus, the dowager duchess's network grew.

She was unhappy with much of the Settlement, comparing its services to idolatrous worship of Baal.[33] John Strype (1643–1737) later credited that the reformed faith was advanced 'by the helping forwardness of that devout woman of God, the duchess of Suffolk', and added that:

'She was very active in seconding the efforts of government to abolish superfluous Holy Days, to remove images and relics from the churches, to destroy shrines and other monuments of idolatry and superstition, to put an end to pilgrimages, to reform the clergy, to see that every church had provided, in some convenient place, a copy of the large Bible…in inculcating upon all the reading of the Scriptures, and especially the young, the Pater Noster, the Articles of Faith, and the Ten Commandments in English'.

Willoughby made use of the Suffolk house at the Minories in London, where she established Miles Coverdale, the famed Bible translator who she had known for many years including at Wesel, as a preacher and tutor. This was close to Holy Trinity, Minories, a non-parochial church which thereby 'enjoyed the patronage and protection of a radical of the highest rank'.[34] Its unusual status meant that parishioners appointed their own ministers and people could attend from other parishes – which they did, as it was staffed with radical preachers like Crowley and Gough. Indeed, Coverdale preached a series of sermons there over the winter of 1567-8 when separation was in the air.

---

31 Franklin-Harkrider (2008), p.113

32 An Upcher had been accused of holding a conventicle in his house at Bocking in 1550, but it must have been a younger one ho was made deacon in 1560.

33 Harkrider, p.116

34 Patrick Collinson, *Archbishop Grindal*, London, 1980, p.178

What had prompted a lot of the trouble was Archbishop Parker's *Advertisements* which caused a crisis over vestments in 1566. In London, many clergy were either suspended from their livings or resigned in protest and in the Minories, where Suffolk House stood, they found a shelter.

The Catholic Thomas Harding wrote 'now last of all creepeth forth one Browne at London, with his unspotted congregations, otherwise called Puritans'.[35] Browne's group split into several sections and, after a time in prison, he went back to work as the chaplain to Willoughby; in the 1570s he reappeared as an associate of John Field and Thomas Wilcox, also linked to the Minories, who in 1572 ignited considerable controversy and prison sentences with their *Admonition to the Parliament*. Willoughby's former rector at Edenham,[36] Anthony Gilby, provided a link with these two and the puritan stronghold of Ashby-de-la-Zouch.[37] Browne was twice arraigned before the Star Chamber and in a letter c.1572-3 Willoughby needed to defend him as 'of true heart and humble obedience' to the queen.[38] By 1574 he was holding Presbyterian views aligned with Thomas Cartwright though cautious about actual separation.

Another man stirring the pot in London associated with Willoughby was Master Pattenson (or Patinson), who was suspended from preaching in 1567 after calling the Bishop of London Edmund Grindal 'a traitor and antichrist'.[39] He told Grindal that he ministered to any congregation:[40] '….wheresoever I do meet with a congregation that are willing to hear the word of God preached at my mouth,' he declared.[41] Grindal told Pattenson that 'I sent for you [from the Gatehouse gaol] because the Duchess of Suffolk hath been a suitor to me for you, that you might be at liberty'. However, the sureties the bishop asked for offended Pattenson who 'did not want to make the preaching of the Gospel subject to a popish licence'.[42] 'Her grace told me of no such sureties, neither do I mind to put in sureties to break the commandments of God,' Pattenson complained. When Grindal threatened him with seven years in prison, Pattenson retorted 'you know not whether you shall live seven days or not'. Pattenson spent three months in the Gatehouse and sent a copy of this interview to the Duchess.[43]

Miles Coverdale, closely associated with Willoughby at this time and perhaps living some of the time at her house, preached some of his last sermons here,[44] and several leading puritans such as Nicholas Crane and William Bonham, Thomas Wilcox and John Field congregated here at the end of the 1560s. As persecution began to increase such people

---

35 Thomas Harding, *A Detection of Sundrie Foule Errours*, Louvain, 1568, sig 332r (cited by Collinson, 2013)

36 Harkrider (p.51-2) argues this forcefully but no presentation deed exists. Assumptions that Gilby was in Leicestershire are equally uncertain and Gilby does not appear in CCED at all.

37 ODNB, Anthony Gilby, 27 Dec 2018.

38 Harkrider, p.118

39 T George, p. 26

40 Michael Watts, *The Dissenters*, vol 1, Oxford, 1986, p.22

41 Albert Peel, The First *Congregational Churches*, p.8

42 Albert Peel, *The First Congregational Churches*, p.8

43 We know little of Pattenson. Perhaps he was at Christ's College 1557-8 and there was a Richard Pattenson as vicar of Walthamstow 1563-7, but there was also a 'Master Patinson' active in a group of puritans forming a 'classis' at Kettering, 1557.

44 Hodgett, p.154, seemed unable to believe that *the* Coverdale had stayed at Grimsthorpe – but the relationship was well established.

began to meet in houses and on a ship[45] and in June 1567 a hundred were caught at the Plumbers' Hall pretending to be holding a wedding. The suggestion of a sequence of activity here owes something to John Stowe's account written in 1568, which refers to them as having first 'kept their church in the Minories', then in a lighter at St Katherine's Pool, then in Thames Street where John Browne was arrested, and then in several other places culminating it would seem in Plumber's Hall in 1567.

In 1568 John Browne, seemingly a former Marian exile in Padua,[46] Strasbourg and Frankfurt in 1557-9, was arrested for running a 'separate' congregation at Thames Street close to Holy Trinity, the Minories, in London – the significance being his position as 'a protegé of the powerful Duchess of Suffolk'.[47] He was at least at times one of her chaplains and in 1571-2 Archbishop Parker wrote to the Duchess asking her to surrender him.[48] While Crane was imprisoned in 1569, he received funds from the Minories churchwardens and both he and Bonham returned to lecturing at the Minories that year. Another, Seth Jackson, died in prison in 1570, but his will called this the 'congregation of Christ'. This group were to be hugely influential over the next twenty years and the link to Willoughby cements her position as one of the greatest Lincolnshire influences on Tudor religion.

Grindal's other tactic was to try to bribe them into submission. In April 1569 he released some prisoners, conditional on 'good behaviour', and Bonham and Crane took up lectureships at the Minories. Trouble immediately ensued, although Grindal was able to escape to become archbishop of York in 1570.

What might have been a powerful congregation had, by 1570, split into four or five as Browne lamented to the Duchess, in one of which Pattenson was still active. Many were in prison and stayed there for a decade.[49] Pattenson died in gaol in the 1570s. On some occasions they were accused of being 'anabaptists'. John Browne's group, sometimes called the 'Brownings', provided people who joined the more famous congregation of Fitz. Browne was still working closely with Willoughby in 1572, when Archbishop Parker sent her a letter requiring the presence of her chaplain Browne 'to answer such matter as he is charged withal'. In 1573 Browne visited Field and Wilcox in prison and was again referred to as her chaplain.

Such events around Willoughby posed challenges for her friend and neighbour, Burghley. We often see him playing a complex game between the factions. When a group of four dissentient ministers were hauled up before Star Chamber in May 1573, he, thus, found that one was a friend of his sister-in-law and another a chaplain to Katherine Willoughby,

---

45   Collinson, *Grindal*, p.178

46   Wilson and Cheke had also been to Padua in exile. But another Browne had been running a secret congregation in Islington in 1555, and this Browne became a roving preacher in 1556. MacCulloch (1999), p.180

47   M Watts (1986), vol 1, p.22. T George, *John Robinson and the English Separatist Tradition*, p.25. The Minories was eventually brought under control from 1576 by John Aylmer, the bishop of London, who had previously been Archdeacon of Stow and later Bishop of Lincoln. It is important not to confuse this Browne with Robert Browne who came a few years later from a house close to Willoughby's in Lincolnshire. The possibility of a connection is intriguing.

48   White (1971), p.28; E M Tomlinson, *History of the Minories*, 1907.

49   Watts (1986), vol 1, p.23

a close Lincolnshire neighbour with whom his family was often linked. Burghley, like Archbishop Parker, could see the advantages in silencing such rebels but feared the accusation of behaving 'as in Popish times'.[50] When he finally agreed to a proclamation against the works of these rebels, not a single copy was handed in.

Katherine Willoughby and John Browne had a narrow escape from disaster in 1574 when a confidence trickster named Humphrey Needham suggested there was a plot by Browne, Willoughby and puritan leader Thomas Cartwright to set up an illegal press in Southwark and even to murder Archbishop Parker and Lord Burghley.[51] Some of the evidence included forged letters allegedly written by Browne, who was hauled in for questioning along with other London radicals such as Nicholas Standen. Although Burghley was briefly deceived by this 'puritan plot', sometimes called the Undertree Conspiracy, the fraud was soon uncovered and the conservative Archbishop Parker badly damaged in the furore thereafter. It is interesting that along with Willoughby and John Browne, Thomas Cartwright and other later radicals were named in this. Crane, one of the Minories 'graduates', died in prison in 1588.[52]

Katherine Willoughby also had a wide influence on the evangelical faith in Lincolnshire, contributing to 'the slow transformation of the county's religious climate through a variety of domestic, educational and religious institutions'.[53] One way of doing this was to use her powers of patronage to appoint clergymen of the correct type – generally university-educated married men who would live in their parishes and evangelise the people. She controlled 16 benefices, mainly in east Lindsey, and made appointments to another six. Men like John Booth, appointed to East Halton, set about removing saints' images and disposing of vestments. Some, like Roger Rowth (Belleau, Scremby, Aiby), had a track record of unlicensed preaching but were later licensed as diocesan preachers. Reginald Grome of Theddlethorpe St Helen opposed the use of robes and the liturgy, having succeeded the noted Hull preacher Edward Dawes. The efforts of Libeus Sadler at Willoughby in the Marsh were welcomed by George Metham, another acolyte from a Yorkshire family brought to Lincolnshire under Brandon's influence. She prevailed upon the Catholic Sir Edward Dymoke to help her secure the living of Fulletby for Edward King in 1566.[54] At Well,[55] Richard Catterton was the Willoughby client with John Gray as the godly parson.

An especially active Willoughby appointment was apparently John Booth at East Halton.[56] He encouraged the destruction of many 'superstitious' articles. William and Edward Booth, the local gentry, participated in destroying the pyx, cruet and two bells during the 1560s. Upon Willoughby's death in 1580 her son Peregrine continued some of her policies, appointing Richard Alleyn and Joseph Gibson who were soon in trouble for nonconformity.[57]

---

50   Collinson, *Elizabethan Puritan Movement*, p.148
51   Collinson, *Elizabethan Puritan Movement*, p.154-5. Nicholas Standon and Bonham were also named.
52   Peel, p.27
53   Franklin-Harkrider (2008), p.112.
54   Franklin-Harkrider (2008), p.125. He seems to have been at Blaby in 1561. He moved to Essex in 1578.
55   Thomas Wraie was rector here in 1558.
56   Franklin-Harkrider, p.129. Clergy Database says Halton Holgate, but the patron – clearly his relative – was Booth of Killingholme.
57   Franklin-Harkrider, p.89

Anthony Gilby

Gilby (1510-85), a Lincolnshire man who had briefly been at Grimsthorpe and Edenham, settled in the 'godly' enclave of Ashby-de-la-Zouch in Leicestershire as lecturer after his period of exile. Here he was protected by the Earl of Huntingdon, one of the greatest puritan powers in the country. By 1570 Gilby was running 'exercises' at Ashby for the education of the region's clergy which attracted the disapproval of Queen Elizabeth. Gilby's regional influence was such that Aylmer described him as 'Bishop to Leicestershire' and closed down the 'exercises' that he was leading – which Gilby promptly replaced with fasts held before communion. His views are clearly seen in the title of his 1578 book, *A View of Antichrist, his Laws and Ceremonies in our English Church, unreformed*. In his last months, in 1584, he was an important voice against Whitgift's Three Articles. Huntingdon was appointed President of the Council of the North in 1572, allowing him a brief alliance with Grindal who was then still Archbishop of York, and also sat as a member of the High Commission; this meant that Huntingdon had many opportunities to support evangelical religion including through establishing town lecturers in Nottinghamshire and elsewhere.[58]

Willoughby formed close links with other protestant gentry across Lincolnshire including William Pelham, Harrington, Heneage and Wingfield. She also had contacts with many women who held her beliefs, including Elizabeth Fiennes and Elizabeth Vane. She also supported reform and promoted her interests through carefully chosen men of business such as John Spendluffe around Alford and Edmund Hall in Kesteven. Richard Catterton, bailiff at Alford manor, was a godly believer. They died as they lived, leaving clear messages; John Spendluffe's tomb stated that 'Though I lie here enclosed in earth, yet I do live by Christ'. Katherine Willoughby died in 1580 and was buried at Spilsby; her tomb represents one of the great memorials of Christian faith in the district. It was inscribed with messages giving her views on sin and salvation – ironically mostly in Latin – including the words of John 3.16. An early biographer, Augustine Bernher, described her as 'God's instrument for the spread of the Gospel'. Her funeral was attended by Lady Anne Wray – mother of the next generation of Lincolnshire Christian pioneers – and by Mildred Cecil, Lady Burghley. Various writers have explored her influence on Elizabethan literature – it has been suggested that she was Paulina in de Vere's 'The Winter's Tale' (with a 'bondless tongue') whilst her son and his wife feature in 'Twelfth Night' (as Sir Toby Belch[59] and Maria) and in 'The Taming of the Shrew'. Her widower, Richard Bertie, moved to Bourne.

Mildred, Lady Burghley (1526-89), is perhaps more interesting than her husband in terms of local impact on faith and had strong connections with Willoughby. She follows a clear pattern with Willoughby and the Wray siblings (see next chapter) of well-educated and committed godly patrons of religion. Mildred had connections with many leading puritans such as John Strype and Roger Ascham. She funded scholarships at St John's Cambridge, even paying for their winter firewood, and was highly educated in Latin and Greek.

---

58 Cross, M. (1960). Noble Patronage in the Elizabethan Church. *The Historical Journal*, 3(1), 1-16. Retrieved from http://www.jstor.org/stable/3020441

59 Their wedding in 1578 accounted for 500 gallons of wine and both were fond of drinking.

The Gathering Storm

During the 1570s the 'Elizabethan settlement' became more burdensome for religious progressives, the 'godly' who were to be termed 'puritans,' although there was often still room for local 'interpretation'. As we have seen, it was possible for men like Brocklesby, with useful connections, to refuse to conform and still return to a benefice whilst in areas like Retford. Local gentry were effectively protected by radical local gentry and Church leaders – both Archdeacon of Nottingham and Archbishop of York being tolerant; the archdeaconry court in Nottingham was fairly inactive except when responding to interest from Grindal.[60] A brief experiment with having a suffragan Bishop of Nottingham from 1567 to 1570 had little effect; Richard Barnes was given the job but, after he moved to Carlisle in 1570, he was not replaced.

We have seen that Matthew Parker's *Advertisements* had raised the pressure on the puritans in the 1560s, but in our region their application was never consistent. Edmund Grindal, Archbishop of York from 1570-6 was a man progressive enough to form a friendship with the Earl of Huntingdon whilst his Archdeacon of Nottingham from 1565 unto 1590 was the somewhat doubtful John Lowth; the Bishop of Lincoln from 1571 to 1584 was Thomas Cooper, who held 'exercises' and 'prophesyings' to edify his clergy and fell foul of Elizabeth as a result. Nonetheless, issues of the *Prayer Book*, vestments and compulsory church attendance meant that a battle over style of worship was developing.

Puritans were also behind a drive for a more educated clergy and the resurgence of Cambridge especially at this time. Concerned about absent or incompetent clergy, puritan laymen on the town corporations arranged for 'lecturers' to teach and educate the townspeople – and these were of course normally puritans reflecting their own views. Boston employed Melchior Smith where he apparently 'sowed discord' before departing – having been 'head hunted' by the Corporation – to Hull in 1561, where he caused further unrest by ignoring pastoral work and the *Prayer Book* in favour of preaching, whilst conservatives stirred up accusations about his rather turbulent 'marriage' including his wife's attempt to throw herself in the River Hull.[61] Nonetheless, he remained in post to his death in 1591 and was succeeded by his son.

Boston's corporation had controlled the rectory of St Botolph's since 1545 and also controlled the post of lecturer. They had enjoyed the robust services of Melchior Smith as lecturer and preacher to 1561 and in 1568 they were able to appoint Henry Holland as lecturer and borough preacher, and then in 1571 elevated him to vicar of St Botolph's. Thus, they could ensure they had a man to their taste. In Lincoln, where poor benefices had failed to attract good preachers, by 1583 the council was calling for a learned preacher who could instruct the people[62] and Mr Jermyn was appointed. However, the city was divided between a progressive and a conservative faction, which was to cause problems for John Smyth a few years later, and Jermyn was given a hard time by those who said they would rather hear tales of Robin Hood. The bishop saw the conservatives as 'the hidden hand of the papacy' and the issue gained the attention of the Privy Council.

---

60   Collinson, *Archbishop Grindal*, p.201
61   *Lincolnshire Historian*, vol 8, 1973, p.37
62   Hill, p.101

Education was a key concern for the evangelicals and the Willoughby circle promoted schools. Katherine Willoughby and her heirs had the right to appoint the schoolmaster of Spilsby Grammar School, founded in 1550, which originally used a chapel on the Eresby estate and was funded from chantry properties of the Willoughby family. She also founded a scholarship at St John's Cambridge for suitable young men. John Spendluffe endowed two scholarships to Magdalene College, Cambridge – a puritan foundation – and helped fund the schools at Horncastle and Alford, where his brother was the master. William Cecil supported the grammar school at Stamford, which had been founded in 1532.

Kirton-in-Lindsey's opened in 1577 whilst that at Alford was endowed by Francis Spanning in 1565 for the 'godly and virtuous education' of the town's youth. By 1594 33 places in Lincolnshire had schoolmasters, increasing to 77 by 1604 or even 85 if other sources are included.[63] Nottingham had had a grammar school since 1513, we have seen how Newark and Retford gained them, and Mansfield's was founded about 1561. Sir Christopher Wray and his wife of Glentworth[64] also endowed scholarships to the universities – both they and Spendluffe supporting Magdalene College in Cambridge.

But conformity problems did start to surface. Archdeacon Lowth seems to have got off to a slow start in his role, although he was unique in having his own archdeaconry court and a local High Commission Court. He did slowly respond to Archbishop Grindal, notably from 1572, and brought in cases about Sabbath breaking as well as failures to comply with the *Prayer Book*.[65] For example, in 1574 two Mansfield men were brought before Archdeacon Lowth for nonconformity and dismissed his labelling of them – 'Master Archdeacon knoweth no more what a puritan is than his ould horse'. That same year Elias Oakdene[66] at Greasley became the first of the Nottinghamshire clergy to be cited for not wearing a surplice – this was to become a long-term rebellious parish.[67] For a while Lowth organised the hearings at Mansfield as this was easier for him when living at Hardwick.

In Lincoln diocese, Cooper had been made bishop in 1571 and his visitation of 1574 identified only five nonconformist clergy with issues such as wearing the surplice foremost. Cooper, though, was far from an assiduous persecutor of non-conformists but 'a scholar in favour of prophesying and who recognised the value of good preaching'.[68] He sent some problematic and uneducated clergy to the religious 'exercises' for their own benefit. In 1577 he took action to ensure that less educated parish clergy could benefit from the expertise of better educated neighbours but in such a vast diocese he had little chance of knowing what was actually being said and discussed in the prophesying in many of the market towns such as Grantham.[69] These became popular and were attended

---

63 Hodgett, p.147
64 V Morgan, *A History of the University of Cambridge*, vol 2, p.192 says that Sir Christopher retained the right to nominate the two fellows and six scholars in his lifetime and this then passed to the Dean and Chapter of Lincoln, with the concurrence of his heirs, and assuming a preference for scholars from Kirton that seems to have rarely been met.
65 Marchant (1969), p.151
66 Oakdene had the same problem with William Underne at Greasley that Lowth had at St Mary's Nottingham.
67 Wood (1947), p.163
68 Miss J Plumb (PhD), p.54
69 Collinson, *Elizabethan Puritan Movement*, p.171

by gentry and their wives as well as clergy, and often many of the townspeople also. Under pressure, he closed the 'prophesying' in Lincoln which was used by 'base persons' but permitted others to continue for a time. He also restored the palace at Nettleham. The less conciliatory Wickham was appointed in 1584.

One of the battlegrounds for the puritans was the *Book of Common Prayer* – they disliked much of its content including its rubric, and favoured exposition of scripture and spontaneous prayer which was called 'prophesying'. Nottinghamshire fell within the diocese of York where Edmund Grindal was appointed archbishop in 1570; Grindal was a reformer; he was seen by many as having been slow to control puritan and arguably separatist activities within his previous diocese of London. He was chosen for York, though, not because they needed a man to control puritans but because it was still a centre of Catholicism. When the Earl of Rutland visited York in 1560, he had found it 'no so forward in religion as I'd like'. So Grindal encouraged 'prophesying' to develop more effective Protestant clergy; in running York, he was literally 'looking the other way' and many of the canon laws were not enforced until Neile took over.[70]

Grindal was tolerant, even encouraging, of puritanism and 'preaching exercises' or prophesyings were established in the Nottinghamshire towns of Retford, Southwell, Nottingham and Mansfield whilst he was early in his days at York.[71] Clergy who incurred his wrath for their misdemeanours were sent to the exercises as a penance.[72] In Mansfield during the 1580s, the preacher or lecturer lodged with the schoolmaster and was paid 20s a year.[73] Burghley perhaps saw appointing Grindal to Canterbury as a way of winning over puritans who disliked Parker, so despite his record the Queen appointed Edmund Grindal to succeed Parker in 1575.

John Lowth (Louth) was Archdeacon of Nottingham from 1565 to 1590, a man with a curiously mixed career. He was born in 1519 at Sawtry, where his father had been killed by tenants of the monastery for whom he worked – John was about three at the time. Although Lowth may have intended to show his reforming credentials through this, another interpretation is possible if you know that his father had literally bullied the rector out of their parish.[74]

As a young man at university he had been converted through reading the works of John Frith, who was burnt at the stake in 1533. Marchant suggests his reformist direction was confirmed whilst at Lincoln's Inn, where he might have been at some risk. He was (self) reportedly an eyewitness at the burning of Anne Askew, John Lassells and two others in 1546, providing some evidence about this for John Foxe. Lowth wrote to Foxe after his *Actes and Monuments* had been published, hoping that future editions might include some details of his own life. Lowth is the source of the story that Askew was spied on by a 'Papist' named Wadloe, who she won over.

---

70 *The Church under the Law*, p.131
71 Collinson, *Grindal*, p.207; *Elizabethan Puritan Movement*, p.174
72 Collinson, *Elizabethan Puritan Movement*, p.173
73 Marion Gibson, *Possession, Puritanism and Print: Darrell, Harsnett, Shakespeare and the ...*, p.23
74 Marchant, *The Church under the Law*, Cambridge, 1969, p.150

His account of her execution seems more concerned to promote his own reputation for he mentions he felt 'a little dew, or a few pleasant drops upon us' and then spoke out: 'I could not, for fear of damnation, stand by and say nothing against their cruelty; therefore I with a loud voice, looking to the council, say, 'I ask a vengeance of you all that thus do burn Christ's member'.

Lowth's early memoirs have survived as the *Reminiscences of John Louth* but it is generally considered their details are not to be trusted regarding their own author's part in the proceedings. For example, the Protestant William Forde was apparently saved from depression and suicide, during Mary's reign and while staying with Richard Whalley at Welbeck, by an uplifting letter from Lowth. Forde had been plunged into depression and tempted by Satan having heard a Catholic mass being celebrated at nearby Woodhouse. However, this does provide a clue that Louth may have been at Attenborough during this period.

From 1549 to 1553 he was vicar of St James, Louth, perhaps indicating a direct link with family origins there. During Mary's reign, he claimed to have narrowly escaped detection for being a heretic. Then during Elizabeth's reign, he became a notorious pluralist. He accumulated several incomes without having been ordained; after going through this procedure he later lost her certificate, causing a few problems. He was vicar of St Mary's in the town for from 1568 and Archdeacon of Nottingham from 1570, and other benefices like Hawton for many more. He employed Thomas (a failure) and Humphrey Lowth (a relative success) as registrars for the archdeaconry, keeping the money in the family.

When appointed Archdeacon of Nottingham in 1570 he was living at a vicarage in the town, but he lost this in 1572 and so lived, instead, at Hardwick Hall. Acquiring the living of Hawton in 1574 he moved there, soon moved to another living at Gotham and finally settled at Keyworth. At this time St Mary's was the finest church in Nottingham and Lowth held the living from 1568 to 1572 when William Underne brought a case against him and unseated him presumably on a legal technicality. Lowth tried excommunicating Underne but this was rejected by the Chancellor of the diocese. No matter, for within the year Underne was in Nottingham gaol.

Lowth's desire to acquire vast income led him into a confrontation with his Archbishop, Grindal. The first round of this was his insulting treatment of Grindal over his own appointment to Hawton in 1574. In the crossfire from this case, Richard Morley, rector of Teversall, was accused of adultery with the wife of Francis Molineux, the patron of Hawton. At this point Grindal became suspicious that Lowth had never been ordained.

Grindal used the ecclesiastical courts through the High Commission and the Court of Chancery to bring Lowth to heel, also putting him into York Castle gaol for eleven days on a charge of slander after he compared the High Commission to the Spanish Inquisition.

At this point Grindal brought up the issue of Lowth's doubtful ordination but he was able to put together enough witnesses to avoid this serious charge. Lowth was perhaps saved by Grindal's translation to Canterbury, dropping his resignation of Hawton at the last moment.

Archbishop Sandys was much more congenial to Lowth but after his death in 1588 Lowth was again accused of exceeding his authority.

Yet despite this Lowth was good for radical religion in the county, to the extent that historian Ronald Marchant labelled him 'the blind eye'. Marchant also noted that after 1581 Lowth 'succeeded in reducing the officiality of the archdeaconry into chaos…'

Elizabeth immediately asked Grindal to suppress the prophesying and in 1576-7 Archbishop Grindal fought a battle in defence of this against the Queen and her government – and lost; his letters to her on the subject represent considerable bravery in defence of spiritual exercises and plentiful preaching. But all bishops then received a letter telling them to put a stop to it with a specific letter being sent to Cooper at Lincoln; only licensed preachers were to be allowed. Cooper 'played along' at the game of seeming to do something but Grindal would not and was suspended in 1577 until 1582;[75] he died in 1583.

Thus Cooper was under suspicion too. In 1579 Arthur Hall, MP for Grantham, threatened to tell the Queen about the exercises being tolerated by Bishop Cooper but a few years later Bishop Chaderton agreed to the requests from county officials for a whole day of 'exercises' at Louth – provoking the fury of Justice Anderson who saw this as plainly against the 'statute of conventicles'.[76]

In several places in the diocese of Lincoln holding a public fast became common as an alternative to prophesyings. In June 1580 the magistrates of Stamford were prompted by Robert Johnson, puritan rector of North Luffenham,[77] to plan a public fast with several 'godly learned preachers'. Burghley, whose house was nearby, found out their plans and cautioned them to use a single preacher from their own diocese and with Bishop Cooper's sanction. They went ahead anyway, with Johnson preaching without authority and Lord Zouche present to give some aristocratic support.

Elizabeth wanted to bring all this back under her control and the man chosen to impose this was John Whitgft, a merchant's son from Grimsby. As we shall see in the next chapter, Whitgift's approach was to impose the 'Three Articles' of royal supremacy, the Thirty-

75 Collinson, *Archbishop Grindal*, 1979, p.236

76 P Collinson, *Richard Bancroft and Elizabethan Anti-Puritanism*, Cambridge, 2013, p.212. Hall was MP for Grantham from 1571 and must surely have been related to Edmund Hall, also MP for the town and one of the Willoughby faction. He led the life of a 'reprobate' and was several times imprisoned.

77 Collinson, working from a Catholic pamphlet of the period, reports him as being rector of Loughborough. His involvement in Stamford was not accidental, for Johnson came from a wealthy family in the town and by 1591 was Archdeacon of Leicester. He founded educational charities at Uppingham and Oakham. Fuller's *Worthies* reported that 'he could surprise a miser into charity'. He was the grandfather of Isaac Johnson, who married Lady Arbella or Arabella Clinton of 'Great Migration' fame.

Nine Articles, and the *Book of Common Prayer* – which of course encompassed vestments as well. To back this up he enhanced the powers of the High Commission and used his authority to ban problem clerics like Walter Travers from preaching – in his case in 1586. However, the 'prophesyings' continued at least in the diocese of Lincoln except with one preaching rather than a 'panel' and under the name of 'exercises' and were still occurring in 1614; indeed, Collinson thinks the Nottinghamshire ones continued uninterrupted until the late 1620s.[78] John Darrell, the 'exorcist', seems to have had no trouble finding them as he travelled around.

John Foxe and the *Acts and Monuments*

We have seen that Foxe settled in Basle during Mary's reign. In the later 1550s, he began gathering stories of the English martyrs and published his first substantial work in 1559 before returning home to England where he began work on the next epic and was ordained a priest in the Church of England. The first edition of *Actes and Monuments*, nearly always called *Foxe's Book of Martyrs,* appeared in 1563. Meanwhile, he remained on the evangelical wing of the church, standing with those who opposed any 'Romish rags' worn by priests. However, it was never entirely Foxe's effort – Miles Coverdale and Thomas Becon contributed, and Edmund Grindal played a significant role in the early work. He drew on some of the writings of Thomas Cooper – later to be Bishop of Lincoln – about the Mary era, and also received inputs from John Bale. This allowed them to add specific personal details – such as how the news of Mary's death was received by the exiles in Zurich.

Prompted by Catholic attacks on his first edition,[79] Foxe wrote a new and expanded version (it was about 2300 pages) which appeared in 1570. Meanwhile, his old patron and pupil, the duke of Norfolk, became embroiled with Mary Queen of Scots for which he was sent to the scaffold by Queen Elizabeth in 1572; Foxe stood beside him when he died. Foxe, through connections with Archbishop Parker, became an advocate of an historical interpretation of the English faith which believed it had once been pure and apostolic but corrupted after 1066 by foreign bishops and practices such as transubstantiation.

The new edition made Foxe famous, but he was also highly esteemed for his pastoral work in London and his charitable efforts. The Church of England decided that an edition should be placed in every parish church. In 1570 he preached at Paul's Cross, an evangelical sermon confronting Catholicism. Such was his growing reputation, that sick people were brought to him – but his son later reported that Foxe turned them away.[80] Foxe's real interest was in spiritual healing and in April 1574 Foxe commanded demons to depart from Robert Briggs, who suffered from seizures and spiritual despair. After two attempts, Briggs' seizures ceased and the case attracted huge interest.[81]

---

78   Collinson, *Elizabethan Puritan Movement*, p.209

79   One of the criticisms was that Foxe had repeated the unproven allegation that King John was poisoned by a monk. In Lincolnshire this deed was claimed by both Swineshead and Sleaford.

80   T S Freeman, *John Foxe*, ODNB online edition, 16/2/14

81   It also attracted the attention of a Nottingham clergyman, John Darrell, as we shall see.

In July 1574, demons were apparently cast out of two girls in London; Foxe was involved, but not in the actual casting out. This prompted a response from Archbishop Matthew Parker who was 'probably motivated by fears of a vast increase in the prestige and charisma of as independent and potentially troublesome a figure as Foxe'.[82] Parker put pressure on the girls and one of their mothers in prison, following which they confessed to being frauds. Parker published a thinly veiled attack on Foxe and denounced as frauds all those claiming to cast out demons.

Foxe, though, had a status that placed him above petty criticism because of the huge success of his writing. Patrick Collinson, one of the most important historians of this period, has concluded that 'No book except the Bible itself has had more influence on the protestant consciousness which the English people were to develop of themselves, of their past and present place in the divine scheme of things…'.[83]

Foxe died in 1587 and for a century his work continued to be popular, but after that it was increasingly chopped up into sensationalist material that was ripe for criticism when it fell out of fashion in the 1800s. More recently there has been a revival of interest and an understanding of the huge influence Foxe has had in shaping Protestant culture in Britain. That he did so appears to have been at least in part the result of a Lincolnshire country parson noting the talents of a young lad.

William Cecil, Lord Burghley

A more influential Lincolnshire figure in the Government at least was William Cecil (1520/1-1598). Although most associated with Burghley House, just outside the county boundary, he was a significant influence in Lincolnshire whilst his mother was from a Bourne family with lands at Burghley. He was also arguably a quiet protector of Katherine Willoughby in later life, having enjoyed her support at the start of his career. Cecil's career in government had developed in the early 1550s under Edward VI, when he promoted John Knox the famous Scottish preacher as a royal chaplain; he became involved in discussion with godly clergy about the *Prayer Book* and other topics. When Mary came to power he was not radical enough to be at significant risk, but also radical enough that he chose to align himself with Princess Elizabeth although he was still elected an MP. In 1558 the new queen made him Secretary, and he became one of the dominant figures for the next 40 years, as Treasurer from 1572.

Although only cautiously progressive in religion, he was shaped by a fear of a Catholic alliance against England and sympathetic to Protestants in continental Europe which also influenced his approach to Mary Queen of Scots. At first, he was tolerant of Catholic practice, but as missionaries started to arrive from Douai he approved their execution for treason rather than any crime of religion.

---

82   ODNB
83   P Collinson, *Archbishop Grindal*, p.80

The ODNB sees him as of strong convictions but realistic: 'His personal commitment to the reformed faith was whole-hearted, but his determination to see it triumphant was conditioned by an acute awareness of the great risks involved in imposing a new religious order on a profoundly traditional society'. Although conservative in his attitude to church structures, he favoured a concept of the clergy in keeping with puritan views – educated, active and preaching. He disliked aspects of Parker's attack on the nonconformists. He was a supporter of Grindal and, at first, of Whitgift – but he came to dislike Whitgift's harsh imposition of conformity (as we shall see next), which the Queen agreed with, and lost influence over Church policy as a result.

The Roman Catholics

At the start of Elizabeth's reign, many Catholics adopted a policy of minimal compliance, attending the parish church but maintaining private beliefs. They became known as 'church Catholics'. There were no Catholic martyrs in the first decade or more of Elizabeth's reign and only five before 1577 – mainly connected with the revolt in the North in 1569 which had serious implications for Catholic life. The position of the Catholics in the nation was often affected as much by politics as by religion, a situation made more complex through Elizabeth being Head of the Church. Mary Queen of Scots was a risk to her on both counts, and notable for our story is here brief 'imprisonment' at Worksop Manor in 1568 and the increased tension caused by the 'Revolt of the North' in 1569 – though this did much to create a long term understanding that in the Diocese of York at least the Catholics were a bigger threat to Elizabeth than the puritans.

However, in 1570 the Pope issued the bull, *Regnans in Excelsis*, which created a wholly different relationship as it encouraged Catholics to rebel against Elizabeth although it was suspended from 1580-4. From 1574 missionary priests began to enter England and in 1575 the English College was founded in Rome. In 1579 this was placed under the control of the Jesuits and from 1580 their priests also began to enter England. For the first half of Elizabeth's reign, the issue of Catholic nonconformity remained relatively modest, but from 1580, Pope Gregory's decision to support the removal of Elizabeth by force ensured an increasingly bitter struggle and turned well-meaning priests into political activists who could be deemed traitors.

Notable survivors from Mary's reign included Bishop Thomas Watson of Lincoln who was sent to the Tower in 1559 and deprived by Elizabeth in July for refusing to take the oath. He remained in and out of house arrest until 1565 when he was sent to the Tower again until 1574. A further attempt at keeping him in house custody collapsed when he was found to have been in contact with various recusants and exercising bishop functions. In 1580 he was sent to Wisbech Castle, itself an old bishop's palace, where he died in 1584. Around eleven of Watson's Lincolnshire clergy were deprived for similar reasons.

From 1559 most Catholics kept a low profile and generally attended their parish church, with occasional Mass in a private chapel; they became known as 'Church Catholics'. The survival of Catholicism depended, almost as progressive evangelicalism did, on wealthy local patronage. However, from 1570 attendance at church was more strictly enforced and recusancy more commonly challenged; local Catholics were not helped by Papal policies.

In Lincolnshire, the Dymoke, Thimbleby and Tyrwhitt families are examples. Sir Robert Dymoke died in prison in 1580, apparently paralysed by a stroke. Sir Robert Tyrwhitt III of Kettleby was perhaps the leading Catholic in north Lincolnshire but had few problems until 1580 when he was put into the Fleet prison; he died in 1581. His son William Tyrwhitt, whose home for many years was at Twigmoor was a Catholic centre for many years, was arrested for his Catholicism in 1580 and sent to the Tower; briefly released, he returned to his practice and was arrested again after Bishop Cooper lodged a complaint. Whilst held in the Fleet prison he was rumoured to have heard masses. Although some degree of freedom was later restored, he remained a 'marked man' for the rest of his life and was largely exiled from Lincolnshire although he was buried at Bigby in 1591.

In this context we might also consider William Byrd, Lincoln Cathedral's most famous musician and who derived some income from Lincolnshire rectories. He was organist and choir
master from 1563 to 1572, when he left for the Chapel Royal, but by the early 1570s was increasingly drawn to Catholicism. Curiously he replaced in this job Robert Parsons, who had drowned in the Trent at Newark – and who also enjoyed revenues from Lincolnshire rectories including Stainton as well as probably harbouring Catholic beliefs. In 1577 Byrd's wife was cited for refusal to attend church services. By 1594 he had largely retired from public life to Essex where he spent much time arranging music at Catholic country houses and he was fined regularly, but nonetheless, was still wealthy when he died in 1623.

In Nottinghamshire, some of the Pierreponts at least were long term Catholics and Sir Henry was probably arrested in 1567 for attending an ambassadorial mass. Other gentry families who remained Catholic included a branch of the Markham family at Ollerton, the Molyneuxs at West Markham, Booths of Fledborough and in the north the Mortons of Harworth and Bawtry who were related to the Dallisons of Lincolnshire. Dr Nicholas Morton of Bawtry was a preacher at Canterbury under Queen Mary but then left for France; he returned to be involved in the 1569 Northern Revolt but managed to escape its aftermath. His nephew Robert Morton[84] of Bawtry was executed at Lincoln's Inn in 1588 with Hugh More of Grantham. However, a 1577 list of recusants contains only fifteen names.[85]

84 For an interesting discussion of possible links between these Mortons and George Morton who went to New England in 1623, see: http://www.pilgrimfathersorigins.org/bawtry-chapel-and-george-morton-research.html
85 Wood (1947), p.161

CHAPTER SIX

Coercion and Reaction
The Whitgift Era
1583-1603

Archbishop Grindal was replaced in 1583 by John Whitgift from Grimsby, an implacable opponent of the puritans. The new archbishop required all clergy to assent to three articles accepting the royal governorship, the Thirty-Nine Articles, and the Book of Common Prayer. *Those refusing the required oath were suspended.*

Through his actions he hastened the development of separatism – leaving the Church of England – by using the Court of High Commission to pursue puritan clergy. By the Act of Seditious Sectaries, 1593, the Government made some elements of 'puritanism' an offence and risked turning a spiritual debate into a political struggle. The term 'puritan' now became common, though it was at first intended as an insult.

Chronology:
1580: Jesuit mission to England begins
1582: Robert Browne leaves for Middelburg
1583: John Whitgift becomes Archbishop of Canterbury; *Three Arti*cles imposed
1584: Subscription Crisis and Travers controversy
1586: Babington plot with Mary Queen of Scots; Richard Clifton appointed at Babworth
1588: Hugh More executed
1589: First 'Marprelate' tracts appear
1590: John King becomes Archdeacon of Nottingham
1593: Seditious Sectaries Act; execution of Barrow, Greenwood and Penry
1597: Francis Johnson's plans to settle in America abandoned
1600: John Smyth appointed lecturer in Lincoln

Whitgift's Church

John Whitgift (c1530-1604), a merchant's son from Grimsby, held the highest office in the Church of England from 1583 to 1604 as well as also having been Dean of Lincoln from 1571. His is not a glorious tale and he can be accused of a cruel, almost tyrannical streak in persecuting puritans who stood out against the uniformity expected by Queen Elizabeth.

N

River Ouse

Barton upon Humber

The Great North Road

Kettleby
Twigmoor

GRIMSBY

DONCASTER

River Trent

Ashby cum Fenby

Wharton
GAINSBOROUGH

South Kelsey

Ludborough
South Somercotes

Scrooby

Glentworth

Market Rasen

LOUTH

Sutton cum Lound
Clarborough
Sturton le Steeple

Snarford

Babworth
RETFORD

Beesby

WORKSOP

Headon

Saxilby

Hemingby

Alford
Well
Willoughby

Holbeck Woodhouse
Walton

Thoresby

LINCOLN

Edwinstowe
Ollerton

Marnham

Scrivelsby

MANSFIELD

South Collingham

Blankney

Tattershall

Boothby
Graffoe

River Witham

NEWARK
-ON-
TRENT

Greasley

Nuthall

SLEAFORD

BOSTON

Silk Willoughby

NOTTINGHAM

Holme Pierrepont

Attenborough

River Trent

The Great North Road

GRANTHAM

Horbling
Sempringham

Kegworth

Osgodby
Irnham

Edenham

SPALDING

Little Casterton

STAMFORD
Burghley House

House
Puritan house
Catholic centre
Church
Church (Puritan)
Place
Place (Puritan)
Town

0   10   20 miles

Whitgift began to roll back some of the tolerance of puritan preaching and practice that existed in the Church into the 1580s[1] to create a Church that was more Catholic in style. Although in his early career at Cambridge in 1565 he supported those who would refuse the surplice, yet within a short while the proffered patronage of Archbishop Parker and Lord Cecil caused a change of mind.[2] Edward Dering, a puritan, wrote that 'Dr Whitgift is a man whom I have loved, but yet he is a man, and God hath suffered [him] to fall into great infirmities'. His patron Andrew Perne wrote that 'neither he nor any of his will lose sixpence for the wearing of a surplice.....but will rather wear three surplices'.[3] Whitgift certainly had the heritage of a reformer – at Cambridge he had mixed with John Bradford and Nicholas Ridley, both of whom were martyred, but was himself sheltered by Perne. Any puritan streak was seemingly of a pale colour.

However, in 1564 Whitgift was still prepared to sign his name against a motion indicating he still opposed surplices. Signing his name brought him to the attention of Cecil, but within a few months he seems to have changed sides and won Cecil's support. By 1570 he had begun to tighten control in the university where he was vice-chancellor but still showed interest in some Lincolnshire connections – he tried to support Roger Kelke to get the mastership of St John's College.

Then, also in 1570, Whitgift was plunged into the controversy over Thomas Cartwright, who lectured at Cambridge against having bishops in the church – favouring a 'presbyterian' view. Whitgift, no doubt working with Cecil's close interest, engineered the ejection of Cartwright from the university; he left for Geneva, probably with Walter Travers who lost his fellowship at about the same time.[4] Cartwright returned in 1572, prompting a further bitter row. Cecil himself was on a journey, which in his old age led to disillusion with Calvinism before his death in 1598.[5]

When Whitgift was Dean of Lincoln from 1571, he tended to go there in the summer months, also picking up the living at Laceby. From 1573-5 there developed a crisis in the national Church when Cartwright, John Field and others led an attack on what they saw as the Papist elements that remained, with first Cooper and then mainly Whitgift responding. Part of the argument was really around who considered what to be significant or 'indifferent': for example, some considered the wearing of a surplice to be of no real significance, whilst others considered it an impurity that needed to be rooted out. In the midst of this, Whitgift signalled a closer relation between Church and State, emphasising that the State might be used to 'discipline' unruly elements within the Church. This, of course, was to become a fundamental issue. In the debate, Whitgift won the support of Elizabeth, Cecil and other key figures, but he persuaded few puritans.

Having been supported by Archbishop Parker, Whitgift became Bishop of Worcester in 1577 where he had to use the Protestant armoury against extensive Catholicism, and

1   Marchant (1969), p.136
2   Collinson, (1967) p.123
3   Collinson (2013). p.20. Puritans insinuated he and Whitgift were lovers but they had a clearer target in assaulting him as a 'turncoat' who spun so fast that he was the preacher both when Bucer's bones were dug up for burning under Mary and again when what was left was re-interred under Elizabeth.
4   *ODNB*, John Whitgift, accessed 30 July 2019.
5   MacCulloch (1998), p.213

then Archbishop of Canterbury in 1583 to replace Grindal who died after a period of being placed under house arrest for disagreeing with Queen Elizabeth about puritan 'prophesyings'.

As Archbishop Whitgift followed on from Parker with an increasingly firmer line on issues such as use of the *Book of Common Prayer*, which he held was fully in line with Biblical worship. By the Three Articles of 1583, he attempted to enforce discipline on clergy throughout the province of Canterbury. Clergy were ordered to affirm the royal supremacy, accept the Thirty-Nine Articles and subscribe to the Prayer Book as containing nothing contrary to the Word of God. This meant to wear the surplice, use the sign of the Cross and many other ritual behaviours. In 1584 the screw was tightened by asking clergy to 'subscribe' to the new expectations of conformity. The result has been termed the 'subscription crisis'. Many would not accept that the *Prayer Book* contained nothing contrary to the Word of God – this issue had been debated since the 1550s by exiles in Frankfurt. This policy was supported in 1586 by legislation giving the Archbishop and the Bishop of London control over publications.[6] Nonetheless, some parishes retained a strong puritan influence and the impact in the Province of York was more muted – Nottingham St Mary's was effectively a nonconformist church under Robert Aldridge from 1578 to 1616; the pressure from Whitgift had the reverse effect of his intentions, for it solidified the mutual understanding within a hardening puritan caucus.

Whitgift was especially concerned about radical religion in Essex where Mark Wyersdale, who had been born at East Deeping and then entered the Church after Magdalene College, became vicar of All Saints, Maldon, in June 1584. This was one of the most radical puritan centres in England, and possibly Wyersdale took the job to provide protection for his predecessor, George Gifford, who had been removed by Aylmer, by now Bishop of London, for nonconformity and organising a 'classis' of radical ministers around Braintree. Wyersdale seems only to have stayed here until 1586-7, then apparently going to Cambridge before being given livings in Leicestershire and Costock (Notts) by 1595.

Whitgift also faced some opposition from Parliament in 1584 and 1586 as well as William Cecil who had become Lord Burghley in 1571, but in 1587 won a test case, for which Sir Christopher Wray of Glentworth was one of the judges, which gave the monarch full power over religion. Whitgift revived the ecclesiastical courts and the High Commission and added another set of articles intended to force clergy to promise to answer questions without knowing what the questions were; this was another area in which Burghley had doubts and where some of the House of Commons began to show a commitment to the puritan interest. As a microcosm of this struggle, Whitgift and Burleigh disagreed over the place of Walter Travers at Temple Church – a dispute which Whitgift won. Burghley supported Travers for the mastership of the Temple in London against Whitgift's wishes and advocated 'the spirit of gentleness....rather than severity' rather than the searching out of faults in 'simple men'.[7]

The crisis caused by this prompted a conference in December 1584 held by Whitgift and Bishop Cooper, which was attended by the Earl of Leicester and Sir Francis Walsingham. Travers spoke for the puritan cause with Thomas Sparke, who was born at South

6   Greasley, p.19
7   Collinson, p.271

Somercotes in Lincolnshire and had been Archdeacon of Stow 1575-82. The puritans protested about a range of issues including the use of the *Apocrypha* and the sign of the cross in baptism, but it is generally considered they made poor use of this opportunity to debate with Whitgift.

The Subscription Crisis – so named because clergy had to subscribe – forced the puritan wing into organising themselves. In the Lincoln diocese several sent their doubts to Bishop Cooper. In the end twenty-three Lincolnshire clergy were suspended but only after they had been to London to complain;[8] they asked that 'we be restored to our flocks and people in such sort as with all peace of conscience we may go forward with the Lord's work in building up his house in our several places'.[9] They included James Worship of Boston. When Cooper moved to Winchester in 1584, they carried on in their own parishes saying they had been authorised by their old bishop, running rings round Archdeacon Barefoot. The nonconformists circulated a letter from John Field, the Presbyterian leader, which was blamed on John Huddlestone, vicar of Saxilby. Huddlestone was suspended for not wearing a surplice.[10] Hugh Tuke, of Silk Willoughby, was suspended in 1584 for refusing to use the sign of the Cross at baptism or wear a surplice; Tuke, who has been referred to as 'the father of Lincolnshire puritans',[11] had been presented by Bartholomew Armyn – one of a notable puritan family who protected him at various times for many years. Richard Allen (or Alleyn) at Edenham was also suspended but at the same time there were over 100 parish preachers actively filling the gaps.[12] At least five Willoughby appointees were suspended, including four in the Marsh area, and even Anthony Hunt at West Deeping – who had been appointed by William Cecil. The same individuals crop up repeatedly – John Somerscales, vicar of Alford and then rector of Beesby, was suspended for refusing the *Prayer Book* but was still around to journey to London in winter 1589 to meet Walter Travers, the Nottingham radical discussed below, and others.[13] Around the country only nine clergy were taken to the full conclusion of actual deprivation. Richard Holdsworth, at Boothby Graffoe was suspended in 1584 but the Earl of Huntingdon who was Lord President of the North placed him immediately in Newcastle to strengthen puritan faith in a notorious region.[14]

James Worship, fairly safe in Boston, was in trouble again in 1590 but died in 1592. Thomas Wooll was appointed by the corporation as his successor and maintained this nonconformist stance by refusing to wear the surplice in 1604. None of this helped with the problem that Lincolnshire had of recruiting enough clergy to fill its poorly paid parishes, or of maladministration by patrons who retained revenues during an interregnum. Around 1588 the parishioners of Grainthorpe had to petition for their parish clerk, John Maltby, to be at least appointed curate by Bishop Wickham which he duly was; Maltby was not

---

8   Collinson, *Elizabethan Puritan Movement*, p.252. A list is provided in Brook, *Lives of the Puritans*.
9   Seaver, p.106
10   Davies, 1989, p.2. Collinson mistakenly places him at Saxby.
11   Hill, p.113
12   Miss J Plumb, p.49. Allen was a preacher throughout the diocese. In 1569 he appears to have been vicar of Skillington. Harkrider, p.131, reports that as late as 1615 he was still being invited to take puritan funerals in other parishes.
13   A colleague from Theddlethorpe St Helen was also suspended. The list shows a wide distribution but with clusters in the Marsh, west of Lincoln (Torksey, Saxilby) and the south of the county.
14   Seaver, p.106. His son, also Richard, rose through the ranks to be Dean of Worcester and Master of Emmanuel College.

university educated but he spent his small income on books and provided a good service – being promoted to the living of Aby nearly twenty years later.

In Nottinghamshire there were at first fewer problems. An effective harbinger of what was to come was Robert Lilly (Lylley) who, having been rector of Babworth since 1559, was cited for lack of a surplice in 1581 – Nicholas Pettinger also having been rector of this parish. As with Greasley earlier, this further marks out Babworth as a radical church years before Richard Clifton arrived to begin the movement that led to the *Mayflower* voyage. In 1584 John Savage at Sutton Bonington and Thomas Hancock, curate at West Retford, were cited over the surplice – the latter being another of the Hercy-Denman network around Retford. In 1587 George Higgins at Eakring was cited for not using the *Prayer Book*, whilst Nicholas Halam at West Bridgford and Richard Barton at Edwinstowe were surplice offenders.

The crisis forced a sharper identification of groupings. The Armyne family (Armyn) of Osgodby were becoming leading puritans in the south of Lincolnshire, forced to defend their appointees. Sir William was 'a vigerous suppressor of vice and debauchery, a Religious Gentleman and one that kept a very well Ordered family'. His son William was born in 1593 and his initial education put in the hands of Tuke. Armyne's monument at Lenton (Lincs) declared 'Mallem mori, quam foedari' – which has been translated as 'I would rather die than defile my Name and Honour with Sin'.[15] Such deepening attitudes in this family and others were to prove revolutionary when confronted with Charles I and Laud.

Whitgift's powers increased during the later 1580s, when he and Aylmer attempted to get printing under control, and in the early 1590s. The *Marprelate* controversy of 1589-90, which we shall cover below, gave him plenty of ammunition to proceed against Cartwright and others. In 1593 he secured the execution of two puritan separatists, Barrow and Greenwood, under an anti-Catholic Act of 1581 and then twisted some further Commons legislation so it became oppressive of puritans whether 'Brownist' or more conventional. This law of 1593 made Protestant 'sectaries' liable to be banished. It is not surprising that, only 15 years later, Smyth and Helwys of Nottinghamshire began to formulate ideas of separating religious belief from the law altogether. By the time Whitgift died in 1604, he had bequeathed a nation where small but deeply entrenched groups were accustomed to struggling for change; with Elizabeth dead as well, King James had the chance to resolve these tensions.

The Puritan Resistance

The opposition to Whitgift was small, often localised, but determined and resourceful. Nationally it was strong in areas like London, Essex, parts of the Midlands like Northamptonshire, around Ashby-de-la-Zouch, in northern Nottinghamshire, Nottingham itself and parts of Lincolnshire. For a few, the issues mattered enormously; for most, the issues were not so vital.

---

15   Cliffe (1984), p.76

In Nottinghamshire around Retford the gentry had enjoyed several decades of relative freedom to manage the clergy as they wished. They accordingly brought in those who would play by their own rules, such as Richard Clifton who arrived first at Marnham in 1586; Marnham remained a puritan hotspot for three decades although Clifton moved in a year to Babworth when Robert Lilley died.

Headon, close to Hercy's old home at Grove, is now a tiny hamlet but from the 1580s it was a centre for religious radicalism held by the Wasteneys (Wasteneys) family[16] and also influenced by the Nevills at Grove, whilst some land also belonged to relatives of John Robinson's wife.[17] It was held by puritans from 1579 with Thomas Hunt as vicar and Francis Nevill as rector; Nevill being one of the families linked to Hercy whilst Sir John Hercy's sister Barbara had married into the family. Religious life appears to have been chaotic; in 1589 a presentment bill concerning Headon complained that:

> Our service is not done according to the *Book of Common Prayer*; our church and chancel are out of repair; Edward Formary committed fornication with Frances Mynnett; Mr Hunt does not wear the surplice; Wm Harper is a usurer; Mr F. Nevyll does not bestow the 50th part of our parsonage amongst the poor.[18]

Robert Southworth was the curate in 1590 and then the vicar of Headon from 1596; he was in trouble for not wearing a surplice in 1590 and later presented to the courts in 1595, 1601 and 1602 for similar offences but each time he was simply 'dismissed.[19]' Southworth fortified his position by marrying Jane Wasteneys. Eventually, under James I, Southworth was deprived of his living but replaced by another puritan, Thomas Hancock.

Hancock was curate at Scrooby in 1590, the village where William Brewster, the future 'Pilgrim', held sway. Scrooby was an appropriated benefice, with tithes and patronage granted under Elizabeth I to one 'Webster'. This meant it was served by a stipendiary curate who was not subject to induction by a Bishop – he needed only a basic licence. William Brewster's brother, James, held the living nearby at Sutton-cum-Lound, and was also a puritan, and Scrooby was within his parish. Hancock was prosecuted over the surplice issue in 1591 and in 1592 was again in trouble – this time for officiating at the wedding of Southworth at Scrooby without banns or licence. By 1593 Hancock had moved to be curate at the Denman stronghold of West Retford, where he was again in trouble, next became vicar of Elkesley and then replaced Southworth at Headon after he was deprived.[20] Hancock moved in 1623 to Todwick, near Worksop, where the patron was one of Southworth's wife's family who was still living at Headon.[21] Hancock is a clear example of how puritan clergy could, with local gentry support, persist in their views against a conservative Church.

---

16   They also held Bilsby Lincs – which had links with Wheelwright.

17   http://southwellchurches.nottingham.ac.uk/headon-cum-upton/hhistory.php

18   http://southwellchurches.nottingham.ac.uk/headon-cum-upton/hhistory.php

19   R Marchant, *The Puritans and the Church Courts in the Diocese of York*, London, 1960, p.138-9

20   Marchant, p.144

21   In 1620 Hancock was still at Headon when he was fined 6d in a sessions held at Laneham for riot – along with a large number of others. Todwick was clearly a Wasteney property and a previous incumbent had been William Wasteneys from 1579-91. Goodall explains that the manor was then leased to the Sandys family and controlled by Samuel Sandys in 1602, which helps explain the involvement of the Sandys family in the Mayflower discussions.

Scrooby had long been an archbishop's palace, especially attractive for its hunting and is acquisition was south by both Elizabeth and James I. It became a great favourite of Archbishop Sandys, who used it regularly for his extensive family from 1576, and Sandys employed the senior William Brewster as bailiff of the estate.[22] The younger Brewster went to Cambridge in 1580 but stayed for barely a year. He joined the service of William Davison, a religious radical of some standing whose significant political career came to a sudden ending with the execution of Mary Queen of Scots. Sandys then leased the manors at Scrooby and Laneham to his own son Samuel, and the family retained both properties on advantageous terms until well after the Restoration.[23] Thus, the elder Brewster became bailiff to the Sandys family and continued to be so after the Archbishop himself died in 1588.

William Brewster returned to Nottinghamshire in 1590 and replaced his father as bailiff at Scrooby Manor, still leased to Samuel Sandys, on his death. He assumed he would also become postmaster, but this created an upset with Sir John Stanhope, the Postmaster General, and the subsequent row included a local lawyer made good, Samuel Bevercotes. Only after the intervention of Davison did Brewster become postmaster, a managerial role more related to maintaining the postal system on the Great North Road. By this stage the Sandys family had long lost interest in Scrooby, but the children of the former archbishop held long leases on advantageous terms of archdiocese's surrounding estate.

Scrooby's position as a chapel, not a parish church, allowed Brewster some freedom in having puritans preach, perhaps partly protected through James's presence at Sutton. This is perhaps why Robert Southworth and Jane Wasteneys were allowed to marry there in the early 1590s – with another puritan, the curate Thomas Hancock officiating[24] – although Jane had already been married. In 1591, when churchwarden William Throope said that 'one of his horses could preach as well as the curate,' Thomas Hancock, sued him. In 1598, Brewster was in trouble with six others for 'gadding' about to hear better sermons elsewhere and 'publicly repeating' what he had learnt in afternoon sessions at the church[25] – usually presumed to have been from Richard Clifton at Babworth. But Brewster defended himself by arguing that the settlements of Scrooby and Bawtry had clubbed together to hire one minister between them, so shuffling between the two was necessary – he made no mention of Scrooby.[26] The churchwardens at Scrooby also reported the curate, Henry Jones, for not wearing a surplice in 1598.[27]

Such complex local networks suggest that the patrons of the Anglican benefices were successful in gathering and protecting like-minded clergy. People like Brewster and the Denmans were minor compared to Katherine Willoughby, but by the 1580s a new family was emerging with connections across the region.

---

22 Sandra Goodall, *The Scrooby Puritans in Context*, University of Arizona PhD, 2015, p.126-7

23 I. J. Gentles and W. J. Sheils, *Confiscation and Restoration: The Archbishopric Estates and the Civil War*, York, 1981), p.45-50

24 Venn Cambridge database confirms as curate 1590-2

25 Jennings (1999), p.86

26 Archdeaconry of Nottingham, Retford Deanery, AN/PB 292/7/46, 5/17/1598 cited in Goodall, p.133

27 Jeremy   Bangs: http://sail1620.org/dev2013/articles/the-pilgrims-leiden-and-the-early-years-of-plymouth-plantation-chapter-1

We have previously mentioned the Wray family in connection with Edward Brocklesby. By the 1580s the children of Sir Christopher Wray and Anne Girlington were becoming forces in their own right, each one radical in religion. They were Sir William (c1555-1617), Isabel (1567-1622) and Frances (1562-1634); Isabel successively married as Foljambe, Bowes and Darcy. Frances married Sir George St Paul, the grandson of Anne Askew's sister Jane, and later the 1st Earl of Warwick. How this brother and sisters came to be progressives in Christianity is surprising because their father, Sir Christopher, had been Lord Chief Justice under Elizabeth. He had been legal adviser to the City of Lincoln and MP for Grimsby in 1563, which he gained with the support of Sir Francis Ayscough – a known evangelical. His supposed conservatism in religion was instrumental in seeing him appointed as Speaker of the Commons in 1571, though he soon lost control of debate as puritan influence grew. Returning to the law as a judge, he took part in prominent cases against both Catholics and puritans – presiding in the case of the Jesuit Edmund Campion and also over nonconformists in Norfolk and Suffolk; he was involved in the trial of Mary Queen of Scots. Officially he was recorded as 'indifferent' in religion by Bullingham's measure, meaning not especially active regarding the reforms. Perhaps he was best known for his advice about the most important choices a man should make in life: in his friend, his wife, his book, his secret, and his expression and garb. When he died in 1592 his children pursued a very clear puritan course, plainly derived from their mother's side, which ultimately was to connect with the godly community on both sides of the Atlantic.

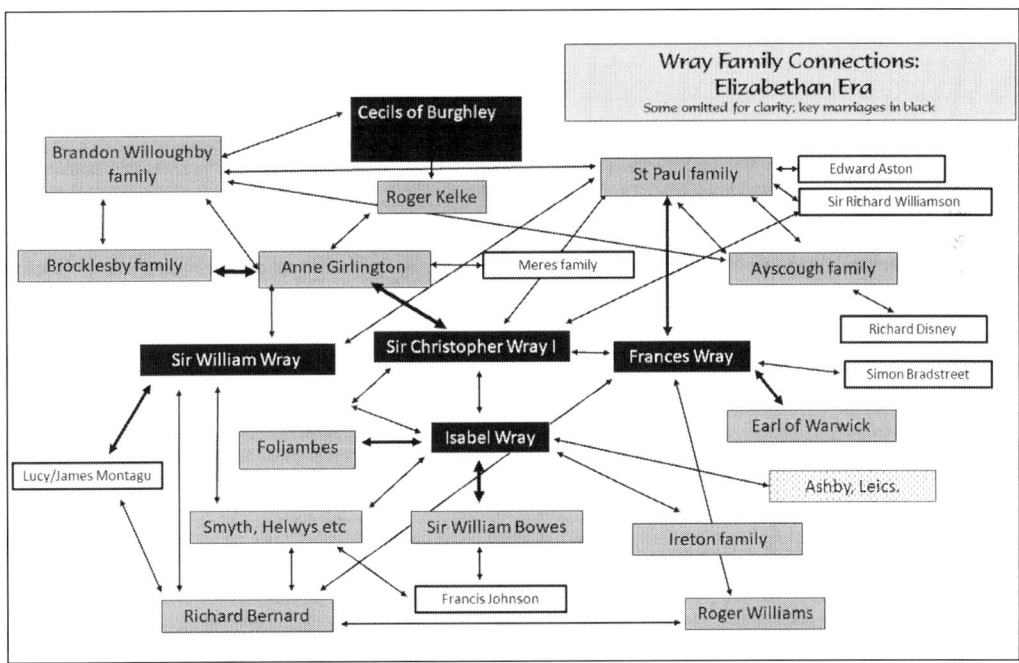

The radicalism, though, came through his wife Lady Anne Girlington who had ensured that her deprived relative through her first marriage was found a safe haven at Branston. The Girlingtons were well connected with Lincolnshire evangelicals and we should remind ourselves that Lady Anne was one of the chief mourners at Katherine Willoughby's funeral. The three Wray children were brought up with a formidable set of evangelical connections, all reinforced by marriage; it is unlikely that their father had no say in any of this.

William, Isabel and Frances became central figures to the puritan movement in the north Midlands. By 1586 Isabel was married to Godfrey Foljambe of Chesterfield and already involved in radical Christianity.[28] Her interest in radical religion may explain why a woman said to be possessed, Katherine Wright, was brought to her house at Walton near Chesterfield having previously been chained to a post for her own safety. After various ministers had attempted to cast out the demon, John Darrell was said to have accomplished the act. We shall say more about Darrell in the next chapter, but for the time being Isabel linked him with the highly influential group of puritans under Arthur Hildersham at Ashby-de-la-Zouch.

Hildersham, who went to the same Cambridge college as John Smyth and Richard Bernard, was one of another network supported by Isabel Wray, including like-minded men such as John Ireton, the rector of Kegworth 1581-1606.

When Isabel's father in law, also called Godfrey, died in 1585, he left instructions for his son to found a grammar school in Chesterfield. By the time of his own death in 1595, the younger Godfrey was displaying more radical intentions by setting aside funds to pay for a preacher or lecturer in Chesterfield as well as a schoolmaster; he wanted:

> 'a venerable honest man and learned in the Scripture, who shall continually, diligently and sincerely exercise himself in preaching, and explaining the Word of God in Chesterfield, in the parish church there'.[29]

Godfrey intended the revenues of the rectory and parsonage at Attenborough to pay for the preacher, the schoolmaster, funds for the Cambridge colleges of Jesus and Magdalene, and the residue to go to the poor of Chesterfield. However, Isabel made a conveyance of the Attenborough property to William and Mary Ireton, leading to a legal dispute against Chesterfield Corporation and the Cambridge colleges in 1610. Lands at Ashover continued to support the charity. The Chesterfield preacher role inevitably became a puritan position, as did the similar role they funded in Mansfield; George Tuke, probably one of the noted Lincolnshire family of clerical puritans, was appointed to be the lecturer,[30] and in 1607 began a law case against Thomas Helwys (a separatist pioneer and later Baptist) that also seems to have been linked to Foljambe's will.

Godfrey Foljambe was given custody of his grandmother, Lady Constance, causing a dispute when he stopped her annuity due to her continued recusant ways in 1590. Godfrey was buried at Chesterfield on 14 June 1595, leaving his widow Isabel (who had no children) with control for life over the 'best part' of his estates. One of his last acts must have been to appoint Robert Houghton to be vicar of Tickhill that year – Houghton had been one of the first scholars at the new puritan college of Emmanuel in 1584, which the Wrays supported financially; he later moved to St Mary le Wigford in Lincoln, became headmaster of Lincoln Grammar School and was a diocesan preacher and also held the living at South Kelsey where the Ayscoughs resided. The advowson of Tickhill was later passed by Isabel to Francis Foljambe.

---

28 Isabel's father was a supervisor of her father in law's will, as was Robert Manners. Her husband named John Manners in his own will as his cousin.

29 R Mellors, *Attenborough Then and Now:*
   http://www.nottshistory.org.uk/articles/mellorsarticles/attenborough1.htm

30 S Glover, *History of the County of Derby*, vol. 2, p.282. He became rector of Heath in Derbyshire in 1606.

Foljambe's death left Isabel, despite the lack of children, with a life interest in his Derbyshire estates (covering much of the Peak District) and Walton Hall near Chesterfield, which was always her favourite home. The estate included eleven manors,[31] largely in Derbyshire, houses in Derby and at Walton and lands at twenty-seven other places as far west as Bakewell. Annual income was to be £3000 – a huge sum. Clearly, the marriage settlement had been carefully drafted using her father's skills. In 1599 Isabel married again and became Lady Bowes by which time her circle included influential figures for the future such as Thomas Helwys. Sir William Bowes had shown his radical leanings by applying for bail in favour of the separatist preacher Francis Johnson at Cambridge in 1589. He may have known Johnson from their origins on the Yorkshire/Durham border, where the Bowes family was also acquainted with the then bishop of Durham – Tobie Matthew. Sir William and Matthew worked together as justices and as border commissioners. The Bowes family organised preaching exercises, which were hardly legal, at Barnard Castle in which Matthew participated in 1593 and 1596. These connections were to prove useful, but the border disputes with King James of Scotland were to prove detrimental to Bowes's later political career.

Isabel's brother Sir William built up the family estates in Lincolnshire at Ashby, near Grimsby, and Glentworth, but he was often at Wharton near Blyton. He was at various times elected as an MP for the borough of Grimsby or the County of Lincoln. He was rather denigrated in the family history as 'he does not seem to have made any figure in the world, though he brought honour to his name by two good marriages he made'.[32] In 1602 he received a book dedication from Simon Patrick, also from Lincolnshire, of a translation of *The Estate of the Church, with the discourse of times, from the Apostles untill* [*sic*] *this pre sent: Also of the lives of all the Emperours, Popes of Rome, and Turkes: As also of the kings of France, England, Scotland, Spaine, Portugall, Denmarke, &c. With all the memorable accidents of their times. Translated out of French.* This was from the French of Jean de Hainault, and memorably included a discourse between the Pope and the Devil.

Frances Wray married her brother's friend, Sir George St Paul (1562-1613), who had homes at Melwood Grange,[33] Epworth, and Snarford in Lindsey. He was also 'an ardent puritan'[34] and supported the same causes as Sir William in Parliament. This is perhaps unsurprising since his grandmother was Jane Ayscough, sister of the famous Protestant martyr Anne[35] and his grandfather a lawyer in the retinue of Brandon and Willoughby. After she was widowed, Jane had married Richard Disney – also of Lincolnshire, and with lands at Beauvale close to the other Ayscough property at Nuthall. The St Paul family had been active in the service of Katherine Willoughby and also for the diocese of Lincoln.

---

31 This was at St Helen's and the site later became a marble factory

32 C Dalton, *The Wrays of Glentworth*, vol 1, 1880, p.65

33 Therefore, on land formerly held by Melwood Charterhouse, whose prior was Augustine Webster, martyred in 1535.

34 A Thrush and J Ferris, *History of Parliament: The House of Commons 1604-29*, online edition, 4 June 2014

35 Anne was burnt at the stake in 1546 along with John Lascelles, another member of the local puritan gentry.

Elizabeth Hussey and the *Marprelate Tracts*

Another forward-thinking Lincolnshire woman was Elizabeth Hussey, daughter of Sir Robert Hussey of Linwood near Blankney. By 1550 she was married and living in Surrey at Molesey as Elizabeth Crane, with a similar-minded husband Anthony and they were probably both involved in the Presbyterian congregation at Wandsworth with John Field in 1572 – possibly the first congregation in England to have a structure with elders.

By 1588 she was giving shelter at Molesey to a printing press which produced the first of the highly controversial *Marprelate Tracts* which satirised conservative figures in the Church – an early one was called *Epistle to the Terrible Priests* and it claimed to have been 'printed oversea in Europe within two furlongs of a bouncing priest'.[36] It insinuated that Whitgift was homosexual whilst Bishop Bullingham's preaching was lampooned. Probably four of the tracts were printed at her house before the press began a tour of the Midlands aimed at keeping out of official clutches. The *Marprelate Tracts* were supposedly written by 'Martin Marprelate' and annoyed the Church authorities most intensely – they are one of the most famous examples of satire ever.

In 1589 she married another ardent puritan, George Carleton, a Northamptonshire puritan MP.[37] In April 1589 he was questioned about the secret press and on 1 October 1589 Elizabeth was also questioned about her involvement. Collinson says that 'she kept what was virtually a puritan salon in her London house'. In 1590 this landed her in Fleet Prison for a while and she had to affirm her loyalty in front of the Star Chamber, receiving a very substantial fine and imprisonment.

Growing Dissent

Having noted the Wray family, we can see how the geographical spread of the puritan interest now grew. Sir William Wray and his friend Sir George St Paul had interests in the western and northern parts of Lindsey especially, and also in Gainsborough where they had some legal disputes with the Burgh family. His sister Isabel had moved to Chesterfield where she lived all the rest of her life, from where her interest extended westwards to Buxton but also into Nottinghamshire around Mansfield and through wider connections southwards to Ashby-de-la-Zouch. This network gradually interlinked with the existing puritan gentry families in the southern and eastern parts of Lincolnshire and then, eventually, with similar groups in Essex.

In the centre of all of this the Hercy-Denman area around Retford remained solidly puritan in outlook. In the opinion of one historian, David Marcombe, '400 years of

---

36 'Over sea' was a weak joke about being at Mole-sea.
37 Carleton was superintendent of Wisbech Castle, where various Catholics were held prisoner. Collinson p.386 speculates whether he wrote some of the Marprelate tracts himself, although they are now generally attributed to Job Throckmorton.

mismanagement from York had created vacuums of authority' probably made worse by the weak impact of a conservative incumbent in East Retford from 1508 to 1550. However, Marcombe later qualifies this by arguing that there was some protection of non-conformity by sympathetic York archbishops, Grindal (1570-5) and Sandys (1576-88); the Archdeacon of Nottingham, John Louth[38] from 1565 to 1590, was also tolerant of puritans and influential local gentry like William Denman patronised and protected those who fitted their criteria.[39] Sandys 'did little to restrain any but the worst excesses of the more Puritan ministers....'[40] It was also always the case that Catholic recusants were the greatest fear in the North, as was proven by the Rising of the North in 1569 when Catholic nobles tried to replace Elizabeth with Mary Queen of Scots, partly instigated by Nicholas Morton of Bawtry. In comparison, a few country parsons refusing to wear a surplice was a minor consideration.

However, under Whitgift and a less tolerant archdeacon of Nottingham from 1590 to 1610, John King, a new policy was introduced and York under John Piers from 1589 was also less tolerant of puritan nonconformity. King, who became Bishop of London in 1611, may be best seen as a rigidly orthodox evangelical – not prepared to brook dissent from either wing. Nonetheless, Jennings cites the example of Watkins at Clarborough 1577 to 1618 – a known nonconformist cleric who survived forty years with only minor problems despite persistently ignoring ritual requirements. Richard Barton, in trouble at Edwinstowe in 1587 for not wearing a surplice, was reported in 1592 to have never worn a surplice in years of ministry and indeed vowed never to wear one, but he was also in trouble for neglecting to distribute charity money; despite this he stayed at Edwinstowe until his death in 1625. He must surely have been related to Brian Barton, Rector of South Collingham cited in 1595, who also went on to survive in the ministry for years despite refusing to wear a surplice, sign the cross or use rings in marriage. Thomas Towler, cited at Hayton in 1596, similarly enjoyed a long career. John Reyner (Rayner) of Rampton was also cited in 1596 for not using the sign of the cross – a church that had a minister ejected for being married at the time of Mary. These all appear to be examples of what Sandra Goodall called 'negotiated conformity'[41] but it had boundaries – Barrow and Greenwood died in 1593 for crossing the boundary of separation.

One of his associates, George Turvin of East Retford, was in trouble for his puritan leanings in 1592 and repeatedly for the next ten years although the risks of losing his job eventually caused him to conform. The Rector of West Retford from 1578-96 was Francis Denman, who took on as curate in 1591-2 Thomas Hancock – the former curate from Scrooby, who was promptly prosecuted in 1593 for the usual offences such as not wearing the surplice.[42] Francis Denman was in repeated trouble from 1593-5 for his refusal to conform but was independently wealthy. In 1598 Zachary Jenkinson, curate at West Retford, was disciplined. So, there was already a strong pattern of dissent which ultimately reached its high point when thirteen Retford people got into trouble in 1605 for going to Sturton to listen to John Robinson preach – a group including local notables John Denman and John Sloswicke.

---

38 Louth was an eyewitness to the execution of Anne Askew and wrote a record of her death.
39 Marcombe (1993), p.179
40 John Adair, *Puritans*, Stroud, 1998, p.87
41 Goodall (2005), p.80
42 Marcombe (1993), p.182

We have seen that Babworth was evangelical long before Richard Clifton's ministry after 1586.[43] The advowson was in the hands of the Hercy family until 1570, and then their relatives by marriage the Denmans. Clifton was born at Normanton, Derbyshire, the eldest son of Thomas Clifton of Normanton and his first wife. On 12 February 1585 he had been instituted to the vicarage of Marnham in Nottinghamshire. The patron there was Thomas Babington; the Babingtons were connected with Normanton and also with Rampton; they had been leading evangelicals for two generations including being involved in the dissolutions such as at Lenton – indeed they acquired Marnham from the Priory of St John of Jerusalem. However, Thomas died and Anthony Babington, his successor, was executed for the Babington Plot in 1586 which had supported Mary Queen of Scots – he was castrated and disembowelled while alive.[44] Anthony was the twelfth child of Henry Babington and Frances Markham, preceded by nine girls and two boys who died. This may explain why Clifton was instituted to the rectory of Babworth, near Retford, on 11 July 1586, probably with the helpful influence of William Denman who seems to have left his books to him and it was in many ways a much better living. In 1591 the rectory of Marnham was taken off the Babington family as it had been held by Anthony. It later passed through marriage to Sir William Cope who appointed John Herring in place of Henry Aldred who had been there since 1594 but was deprived in 1602. Marnham remained a puritan stronghold, though on occasions a turbulent one.

Meanwhile, Clifton maintained the puritan approach at Babworth: in 1593 he was cited for lack of surplice, not observing holy days and fast days, and not using the sign of the cross.

The Travers Controversy

The extended Hercy-Denman family included Walter Travers, a great writer on church government born in Nottingham. He was not a great success in Antwerp and by July 1580 he was back in England and living under the protection of Lord Burghley as tutor to his son; Burghley was of course closely connected with Lincolnshire and at the very top of Government, but he and his wife were well linked with puritans and helped to get Travers a suitable lecturing post at the Temple Church in London, in 1581. This was despite being told by Whitgift that Travers was an enemy of the government.[45] Burghley often helped Travers until his death in 1598. At Temple, Travers introduced many reforms including the taking of communion standing whereas Archbishop Parker had ordered that it be taken kneeling.

Travers was then involved in December 1584 in a controversial but fruitless debate with Whitgift, chaired by the Earl of Leicester, about reforms in the *Prayer Book* – where he provided a public challenge to the two archbishops over matters such as the use of the Apocrypha. In the debate, Travers was assisted by Dr Thomas Sparke, a cleric who had been born at South Somercotes in Lincolnshire and from 1575 was chaplain to Bishop Cooper of Lincoln.

---

43   S B Jennings (1999), p.52
44   F Madden etc (eds), *Collectanea Topographica et Genealogica*, Volume 8, London, 1843, p.351
45   Collinson, p.271

He was Archdeacon of Stow from 1575 to 1581 and was 'much esteemed for his gravity and exemplary life and conversation'. We will meet him again at the Hampton Court Conference.

However, Whitgift was also a man with growing power and, as Archbishop of Canterbury, was able to block Travers' preferments – his Presbyterian views and ordination being key factors. For a time, Richard Hooker preached in the mornings at Temple, Travers in the afternoons – with very different views on Church governance. It was Richard Hooker, himself related to Travers by marriage, who got the permanent master's post at Temple in 1585 and took part in a public theological battle against Travers – who was banned from preaching by Whitgift in 1586. By 1588 Travers was effectively the leader of Presbyterianism in London if not England – years later Fuller wrote that 'Allowing Mr Cartwright for the Head, Mr Walter Travers might be termed the neck of the Presbyterian party'. Between the two of them they were probably responsible for a powerful statement of Church organisation, the *Book of Discipline,* which was published in Heidelberg in 1574.[46] But as Whitgift acted to suppress Presbyterianism and the movement lost momentum, Burghley found Travers a post at Trinity College in Dublin in 1594. He left Dublin in 1598, never securing another permanent post, yet living on until 1635. Ten years later, his views on Presbyterianism finally became fashionable.

Walter Travers' younger brother John was also a noted puritan who married the sister of Richard Hooker, a fellow puritan but on matters of church government certainly Travers' rival. Based in the West Country, he was often in trouble for nonconformity. A grandson was ejected from his living in 1662.

Thus far the disputes had been about styles of worship and then about church governance, sometimes called polity. But in the 1590s some differences over theology also began to emerge that challenged the Calvinist dominance. William Williams, the rector of Asgarby near Sleaford from 1592, rejected Calvinism and was a 'proto-Arminian'. He preached a provocative sermon in Sleaford in 1598 and was denounced to the bishop for being in contravention of the Lambeth Articles, which Whitgift had introduced to clarify aspects of the Thirty-Nine Articles. It was reported that he could be found in Sleaford market and also spoke at a meeting at the *Angel Inn*, arguing for baptismal regeneration and that 'an elected man might fall away from grace totalle'. Silenced by Chaderton in November 1598, he went off to Cambridge to seek support from Whitgift. Williams defended himself by arguing that Whitgift also disagreed with predestination and seems to have escaped prosecution since he also held the benefice of Aswarby until 1634.

The existence of such views in the 1590s is intriguing. The views were called Arminian as they derived from the views of Dutch theologian, Jacobus Arminius. He rejected the rigidly predestinarian teachings of Calvin, arguing instead that Man was condemned by his own choice to sin and that all were capable of repenting. These views had been expounded by French theologian Peter Baro at Cambridge in 1595-6. Baro's son Peter, known as Baron, lived at Boston as a physician and, according to John Cotton, spread

---

46   Collinson (2013), p.83

'that which was then called Lutheranism, since Arminianism'.[47] Cotton complained that he 'leavened many of the chief men of the town with Arminianism, as being himself learned, acute, plausible in discourse and fit to insinuate into the hearts of his neighbours'. Baron's brother Andrew also lived in Boston, and he received some protection from Cecil rising to become Mayor in 1610. He died there in 1630.

Otherwise, Boston had a strong puritan element, though not always dominant. As in Lincoln, there were strong factions. There had been a town preacher since 1571, a role eventually held by John Cotton from 1612. In 1590 the corporation, which had unusual powers over church life, agreed to remove the rood screen (perhaps a surprising survival) and in 1591 decided to sell the organ, but others used legal action to block this. By the end of the century many other towns had a preacher or lecturer, free from parish duties, and often well paid; the city of Lincoln introduced a mayoral chaplain in 1571 and a Wednesday lecturer in 1578 whilst in 1600 they decided to employ a city lecturer on the high salary of £40 a year – which they awarded to John Smyth of Sturton in Nottinghamshire.

However, radical Presbyterianism declined in the 1590s. Francis Marbury (1555-1611),[48] a former 'hothead' himself who was the son of a Lincolnshire lawyer and MP William Marbury,[49] had caused so much aggravation in the 1570s that John Aylmer, then Bishop of London, put him in prison for two years in 1578. His offences included criticising bishops who appointed ignorant clergy and then refusing to grovel in front of Bishop Aylmer, who called him 'an ass, an idiot and a fool'. Aylmer sent him to the Marshalsea Prison to enjoy the company of 'Papists'. Ensconced in Alford as schoolmaster and curate from 1585 he transgressed again in 1590 after again criticising the ignorance of clergy – and bishops, but independent wealth and the school income gave him a degree of independence. Alford was becoming more radical, with lectures established from 1589 but it was hardly isolated – this was still Willoughby country. From 1594 he showed greater intention to conform and was allowed to preach again. In 1596 he noted that no ministers favoured a presbytery in the area of the Lindsey coast – 'for men have enough to do to stand by that religion which her blessed Majesty hath approved unto us by her express laws'.[50] In 1602 he published *A Frightful Sermon necessary for the Time* which he then delivered at Spital. Later he gained some livings in London from 1605. Anne inherited her father's youthful vigour with little of his later compromise. Marbury was named as an executor of the will of John Spendluffe (an associate of Katherine Willoughby's) along with John Somerscales, the puritan vicar of Beesby, who had also been vicar of Alford.

The puritan influence in this era left an enduring legacy of schools, some of which survive to this day. The Lincoln school was established in 1567 in the old Grey Friars buildings. One of them, Rev Francis Trigge of Welbourn, also left money to found the famous library in the room above the porch of St Wulfram's Church, Grantham, in 1598. Though some

---

47   Cited by Coggins, p.137

48   Marbury is of great significance in his own right but also as the father of Anne Hutchinson. It is interesting that Brandon had a Thomas Marbury in his service in the 1520s in London, who had clear evangelical associations by the 1540s, and perhaps he was a key influence. He attended the church of Richard Marsh, a reformer and a chaplain to the Suffolks. His cousin John also worked for the Suffolks. This continued in the 1560s with Willoughby. What was the connection?

49   Usually reported as born in Market Rasen or Burgh on Bain (*History of Parliament*) whereas Francis was born in Alford or London.

50   Collinson, p.433

have seen this as the first 'public' library, it was more to support the puritan ministers of the district. Trigge, who was buried in 1606 at Welbourn, preached and wrote against the impact of enclosures on the poor; he left money for the poor of both Stamford and Grantham, the latter jointly with his mother Elizabeth Hussey of Honington. He also published, about 1599, *A Touchstone whereby may easilie be discerned which is the true Catholike Faith* which is considered 'an early example of covenant theology'.[51] At his death 'a memorable story concerning the prediction of his death' circulated, which as a puritan he might not have liked![52] Trigge is also closely linked to the case of the murderer of the Market Rasen vicar, which we will deal with later.

The First Separatists

The first 'separatists' were men and women who rejected the Church of England and refused to attend its services, as the Elizabethan laws demanded. Non-attendance on Sundays and saints' days cost a fine of 12d, rising to £20.[53] Their precise motivation varied: as we have seen, puritans focused on aspects of ritual and worship whilst church governance was the issue for Presbyterians. However, there were also emerging issues of doctrine, although some of these took a long time to affect England. There was, for example, almost a century between the first emergence of Anabaptism[54] in Zurich in 1525 and its arrival as a substantive influence amongst English puritans. It was established in Amsterdam by the 1530s, spread into northern Germany through the 'Mennonites' and then to Strasbourg.

The Anabaptists developed new views that further differentiated them from the core of puritan or protestant thinking – divisions which were to emerge when the Clifton and Smyth groups reached Holland. Thinkers such as Hubmaier began to emphasise free will and human spirituality. The Schleitheim Confession of 1527 argued that churches should be entirely separate from the state, and John Denck wrote in favour of religious freedom for all – 'everyone among all peoples, may move around in the name of his God' – opinions that were to cause problems for Thomas Helwys.[55] These views were further developed by Balthasar Hubmaier, who wrote about the burning of heretics: 'it is clear to everyone, even the blind, that a law to burn heretics is an invention of the devil….a Turk or heretic is not convinced by our act, either with the sword or with fire, but only with patience and with prayer'.[56] Unsurprisingly, anabaptism struggled to establish itself in England and it was heavily persecuted in many areas of Europe. The name 'Anabaptist' was then badly damaged by the hideous events in the revolt at Münster in 1536-7, a problem that it struggled to escape from.

We have already seen that the activities around the Minories in London in the 1560s gave rise to what has been called the Plumbers' Hall congregation, around 1567. Although the

---

51   Hajzyk, p.285
52   A Wood, *Athenae Oxonienses: An Exact History of All the Writers etc*, London, 1813, Volume 1, p.759
53   R Kershaw, *Baptised Believers*, Nottingham University MA dissertation, 1995.
54   This term simply means 'baptised again' since most of the first Baptists had already had an infant baptism.
55   Stephen Greasley, *Early Baptists*, 2009, p.12
56   B Hubmaier, *Concerning Heretics and those who burn them, 1524,* in Greasley, p.12

congregations at Bocking in Essex and elsewhere came earlier, they do not offer the same continuous line.

Influential among the London-Minories group was John Browne, so it is confusing that the best-known early separatist was also a Browne. Robert Browne, born at Tolethorpe Hall in Rutland in the 1550s but was effectively a man of Lincolnshire due to his links with Stamford where his family was powerful and had connections with the Cecil family of Lord Burghley. It is, of course, interesting that he had a close geographical link with Katherine Willoughby, whose own links to separatism are discussed above, but any link to her chaplain John Browne is unclear. The role of Robert Browne has been much debated as later congregationalist historians, including William Bradford, sought to downplay his role due to some aspects of his career. They looked for the origins of separatism in London congregations under Robert Fitz or even in Mary's time, under a Mr Rough. However, none of these earlier examples provide a continuous link to the present day although they do prove that Browne was not the originator of the thinking.[57] Collinson concluded that he was 'remotely ancestral to the Congregational churches of later years'.[58] Later both John Smyth and John Robinson made efforts to claim the martyrs of Mary's time as part of their own tradition.[59] White's conclusion is that 'he may not actually have played a critical part' in the growth of separatism and the later separatists unfairly labelled 'Brownists' 'owed little if any of their distinctive ecclesiology to him'.[60]

Browne went to Cambridge where he was exposed to the radical teachings of puritan Thomas Cartwright in 1570. This was also the university of the three separatist martyrs of 1593: Barrow, Greenwood and Penry. Although he could have got an easy career in the Church, by 1578 Browne was discontented with the state of the Church of England and disillusioned with the ecclesiastical structure – especially with bishops, who he denounced as 'ravenous and wicked persons'. Bishops, he thought, should not appoint pastors.

In 1579 he insisted on preaching without a licence having 'disposed' of it, and magistrate Sir Robert Jermyn asked Burghley to stop him 'going to farr'.[61] Even though his brother went and got a licence for him, he insisted on destroying it. Eventually, he was banned from preaching anyway.

By 1581 he was aligned with a Presbyterian view,[62] the opposition to bishops, and living in Norwich where he had his own separate congregation of about 40 people.[63] He developed the idea of a covenant community, members committing themselves to God and each other. In setting up illegal conventicles in Norfolk and Suffolk he was risking arrest or worse, but seems to have been protected by Lord Burghley; on 19 April 1581 the Bishop of Norwich complained to Burghley that Browne had private conventicles of 'the vulgar sort of people'.[64] Browne rejected the idea of a national church in favour of 'gathered

57   B W White, *The English Separatist Tradition*, Oxford, 1971, p.3
58   Collinson (2013), p.29
59   White (1971), p.18
60   White (1971), p.44
61   T George, *John Robinson and the English Separatist Tradition*, Macon, 1982, p.36
62   A 'tradition' cited by Miss J Plumb in *Early Non-conformity in Lincolnshire*, unpublished Sheffield PhD in Lincoln library, is that Presbyterianism started 'in Folkingham'.
63   Burrage, *Early English Dissenters*, p.94
64   White (1971), p.49

churches' of the visibly godly. Nonetheless, he was arrested after preaching in Suffolk and twice imprisoned before he led a congregation to Middelburg in the Netherlands in 1582 but this quickly fell apart; he quarrelled with his friend Robert Harrison, calling his wife a reprobate whilst Harrison accused Browne of 'leaning to antichristian pride and bitterness'. He returned to England, via Scotland, in 1584, although his wife was in Stamford by February 1584.

Meanwhile, Whitgift had become Archbishop of Canterbury in 1583, increasing the tempo of persecution, and he vowed to campaign against 'wayward and conceited persons'. In 1586 he acted to shut down radical writings by suppressing puritan publishing. This did not prevent him being satirised as 'Beelzebub of Canterbury' and 'a most bloody oppressor of God's saints' in the tracts supposedly written by 'Martin Marprelate' and in which a Lincolnshire woman, Elizabeth Crane (nee Hussey) was involved.

Browne's writings were condemned in 1583. Two men had already been hung under Sir Christopher Wray as judge for circulating Browne's writings[65] and Browne himself was arrested in 1585, but Burghley somehow managed to engineer a submission by Browne that was enough to satisfy Archbishop Whitgift; perhaps his worldly responsibilities were weighing on him. On 7 October he made a statement bowing the knee to Whitgift and his Church. Others condemned him as 'a slipperie shifter'.[66]

As a result, by 1586 Browne had fallen out with other separatists and, indeed, accepted a living in the Church of England at Little Casterton where his family had influence, although he moved to a nearby parish in Northamptonshire, Achurch-cum-Thorpe in 1591. He seems to have lived relatively quietly until 1617 when he failed to conform to the *Prayer Book* and in 1623, when sued for restitution of conjugal rights by his second wife. His nonconformity seems to have reawakened and he was ejected from the Church of England in 1631. He died in Northampton prison in 1633, having been arrested following a fight over a debt. Although Browne's behaviour was such that the later separatists disliked being called 'Brownists', his views on church government were very influential both on those who formed the first nonconformist congregations and those who went to America. He believed that church membership should be restricted to the personally committed, and that the ministry 'should be firmly subordinated to the covenanted community'.[67]

The term 'Brownist' was used to label other separatists like John Greenwood and Henry Barrow. By 1589 some 52 separatists linked to these two were in prison. In prison in 1590, Barrow repudiated the name – 'We are no Brownists, we hold not our faith in respect of any mortal men....' Barrow even denied that baptism was necessary for salvation. Sir William Bowes, future husband of Isabel Wray, was involved when Francis Johnson and Cuthbert Bainbrigg were taken into custody in 1589 at Cambridge – proving his own

---

65 Elias Thacker and John Copping at Bury St Edmunds, in June 1583, having been rooted out by Bancroft. Wray and his fellow judge, Sir Edward Anderson, gave Bancroft a copy of the separatist writings of Harrison, which Collinson thinks 'perhaps ironic' – Babbage (p.21). Lincolnshire's Oliver Pig, perhaps from Boston, was also arrested at Bury in 1578 and was an important intermediary between Presbyterianism in London and Suffolk. Collinson (p.127) reports him as a leader of the conference movement in Suffolk, in 1582 an intermediary between John Field in London and Suffolk radicals, and curate at Rougham. A third man was executed at Thetford.

66 T George, p.44

67 White (1971), p.62

radical credentials. Bowes was among 68 who signed a petition to have both men re-instated as fellows of the university.[68] Bowes, with Sir Henry Knyvett, tried to intervene with Burghley when Francis Johnson[69] had been imprisoned and had offered bail. Johnson and Bainbrigg were at Christ's College, where Johnson was a significant influence on John Smyth, the future separatist, and perhaps also therefore on Richard Bernard.

Francis Johnson left for Middelburg in the Netherlands, although he made occasional returns to England. Other separatists fared less well. Henry Barrow was martyred in 1593 with John Greenwood; John Penry followed soon after, all at Whitgift's instigation. Barrow, in particular, wrote in detail about the reasons for separation and, given the links between Church and State, this could be seen as sedition – as it was when Helwys wrote about it twenty years later. Perhaps the young Thomas Helwys who may have witnessed the executions in April 1593,[70] and his contemporaries from Nottinghamshire and Lincolnshire who were at Cambridge at the time must have been influenced by these events.

A shadowy figure linked to Barrow was James Forrester (or Forster), who later became vicar of Mavis Enderby from 1606-26. A Cambridge graduate, his early roles seem to have included some curacies and being chaplain to the Earl of Lincoln, but the chronology is unclear. He then moved to London, where he assisted Barrow in preparing his book *A Brief Discovery of the False Church* for publication in 1589 but was at some point arrested and placed in the Bridewell prison. He was also in trouble in 1592 for practicing as a physician illegally and gave 'absurd and inadequate' replies when challenged. In 1593 he addressed a separatist meeting at a 'garden house' near the Bedlam Hospital. He then made the leap to be vicar of Mavis Enderby, through the patronage of the Earl of Lincoln, and in 1610 published *The Marrow and Juice of Two Hundred and Sixty Scriptures* which was a fierce attack on separatists, recording himself also as a chaplain to the Queen.

In 1591 Francis Johnson was pastor at Middelburg in the Netherlands to the church where Travers had once ministered, but only after reading one of Barrow's books did he fully commit to separatism. By late 1592 Johnson had returned to be pastor of a separatist congregation in London and was arrested several times. It was clear that radical puritans were seeing that it was not possible to remain within the Church of England. Men like Henry Ainsworth, who had also left for Amsterdam earlier in 1593, were influenced by Henry Barrow, John Greenwood and others.

Whitgift faced up to these new challenges by, in 1593, adapting an Act for taming sedition from Catholics into laws that could also be used against nonconformists and especially separatists, sometimes called the Act against Puritans, the Seditious Sectaries Act or more formally An Act for Retaining the Queen's Subjects in Due Obedience. Refusal to attend the parish church, or going to something else, became a felony and could result in three months in prison or banishment. By July 1593 some of Johnson's

---

68 Scot Culpepper, *Francis Johnson and the English Separatist Tradition*, p.30
69 Johnson was from Richmond, North Yorkshire, close to Bowes' own home. Bowes acted with Sir Henry Knyvett, whose motivation is not known although they may have known each other from trips to Scotland.
70 A third, Penry, was executed in May.

followers had already fled to Amsterdam, where they were not entirely welcome.[71] However, Johnson and his brother were kept in prison until 1597 when they crossed the Atlantic in an attempt to create a new Church in Newfoundland; this failed and they returned, then they went to Amsterdam instead. Henry Ainsworth, who had been living in Amsterdam, joined Johnson's 'Ancient Separatist Church of Amsterdam' as a teacher. Johnson again emphasised the idea of the covenant. Briefly, early in the next century, men such as John Smyth came within Ainsworth's orbit but the 'Ancient Church' fell apart in 1610.

Most who disliked the religious policy had not yet fled across the sea. Whitgift's Act soon ensnared those in north Nottinghamshire or Lincolnshire who disliked aspects of the Church. Christopher Browne, curate of Londonthorpe at Grantham, was soon in trouble for preaching a form of separatism and had to give assurances before he could take up a post as vicar of Horbling in July 1593 – a living that persistently appointed radical clergy due to the Clinton influence.[72] David Allen, the vicar of Ludborough and under the protection of the Wray family, was accused of 'Brownism' in 1596 but retained his place.[73] Pressure intensified with appointments such as Richard Bancroft as Bishop of London in 1597

William Brewster and several others from Scrooby[74] were presented in 1598 for not attending their own church and Brewster for publicly repeating sermons – often assumed to be those of Richard Clifton at Babworth, and the same year his curate Henry Jones was denounced for not wearing the surplice in 1598. In the afternoons at Scrooby they did 'confer with one another', implying an approach not unlike a modern church housegroup. In his defence Brewster put out an argument about one curate being shared between the two chapels at Scrooby and Bawtry.

> Scroobie and Bawtrie being not far distant one from the other have joined together to maynetaine one preacher betweene them, who preacheth at one Towne one Sundaye and at the other Towne on the next sundaie by a continuall course, so that if their preacher preach at Bawtrie he with other of the parishe of Scroobie go thither to hears him, and otherwyse he doth not absent himselfe from his parish Churche on the Sabothe daye.[75]

Those in the laity who opposed the direction the Church was taking protested by not attending it – or going to churches they preferred. In 1598 six were cited for not attending Sutton-cum-Lound church, with many more to follow. In all these moves we can see a development of a 'covenant' approach to church 'membership', where some of a congregation were deemed to have an 'elect' status that did not apply to others – but it was not yet separatism. Such concepts angered those perceived as not in the elect, and

71   White (1971), p.96
72   Hajzyk p.370; Lincoln Record Society 1959, p.55. Clinton was made Earl of Lincoln in 1572 and controlled lands around Tattershall and Sempringham. Presumably Browne did not survive long as Simon Bradstreet was there in 1594.
73   Plumb, vol II, p. 306
74   Those named were Rowland Stringer and his wife; Richard Jackson and his wife and family; Anthony and Edward Bentham; William Bradley and John Bett. Of these, it is Jackson who is the most interesting name due to his family's connections with Boston.
75   Archdeaconry of Nottingham, Retford Deanery, AN/PB 292/7/46, 5/17/1598

they complained. This was made clear by the behaviour of William Hieron[76] vicar at Hemingby from the mid-1590s to 1601; he was plainly a puritan as he did not use the sign of the cross in baptism and had to be 'persuaded' to use the *Prayer Book*, which he then did so poorly having condemned it as 'a few dead lines'; in his preaching he made clear that the congregation consisted of those who were regenerate and those who were not (which seemingly included his parish clerk) – to the displeasure of many as 'no man dare controwle him'.[77] Those who insisted in kneeling for Communion he 'hath lifted them up with his hands'.[78] Hieron's personalised preaching – calling the unregenerate 'thieves in gaol' – was a pattern that attracted censure more than simple nonconformity; such an approach was seen as divisive. Hieron got into trouble as his parishioners complained in 1595 and 1597 and the clerk added that he had had to persuade Hieron to use the Prayer Book at all – which he did badly. Hieron called the prayers 'a few dead lines' but was also suspected of concealing alms for the poor. He preached about being the only godly minister in the diocese and refused the 'popish' practice of taking sick communion to a dying parishioner. The bad feeling that resulted at Hemingby was soon to boil over in a case at Stamford.

It was not only the nonconformist clergy who experienced trouble, for the eccentrics and the venal also persisted. John Robotham of Manton in Lincolnshire engaged in legal battles with his parishioners, even issuing summonses during services[79] – although there were perhaps few, since the people retorted in 1577 by accusing him of not preaching quarterly and missing prayers and even Easter communion to play bowls. At Folkingham in 1597 the churchwardens complained their parson, Hoskins, had only been resident for forty days in the last year so that parents had to walk to the next parish for baptism; he appeared in the pulpit wearing a sword and dagger, and carrying a cudgel!

But Elizabeth was old and without a child and her heir James VI of Scotland, was a Protestant king of a Presbyterian country. The deprivation of Brian Vincent in Newark in 1602 was perhaps a last call to conformity. The puritans of Nottinghamshire and Lincolnshire were optimistic about what might happen next; one of them, John Robinson of Sturton-le-Steeple, preached to his Norwich congregation on 'This is the day that the Lord has made' to greet the new king. But things were not that simple.

---

76 This surname is better known because of Samuel Hieron (c1572-1617), William's almost exact contemporary and a great writer and nonconformist originally from Essex. Samuel had close links to Sir Francis Barrington who was a near neighbour in Essex of the Rich family (Warwick), had links to the Wrays and Whalleys, owned land in Lincolnshire and was a strong puritan. It was at their house that Roger Williams so upset Barrington's wife, Joan, by an unwanted proposal of marriage to Jane Whalley. So, a connection is possible. Samuel was uncle to Walter Hieron of Stapenhill, Derbys. who was the father of Derbyshire clerics John and Samuel, who were both deprived in 1662. Walter Hieron's parish was a great puritan centre and was involved in one of the Darrell exorcisms (see chapter X); Walter probably knew John Smyth (Wright, p.16). However, there were also Hierons at Loscoe near Mansfield.

77 Judith Maltby, *Prayer Book and People in Elizabethan and Early Stuart England*, Cambridge, 2009, p.72

78 K Fincham, *The Early Stuart Church, 1603–1642*, Stanford, 1993, p.127

79 LAO, 69/1/7

The Catholics

Of course, Mary Queen of Scots is well known because of her many 'plots'. One of these involved the Babington family, who had strong Nottinghamshire connections originally at East Bridgford. Sir Anthony Babington came from a Derbyshire family who had bought into Nottinghamshire though his mother Mary was the granddaughter of Thomas Lord Darcy (executed after the 1536 rising), former lord of the manor at Sturton-le-Steeple. He had been actively involved in Catholic activities since 1580 and first met Mary while she was Shrewsbury's prisoner at Sheffield Castle. After his father's death, his mother married Sir Henry Foljambe whilst another relative, Lady Constance Foljambe, was also a Catholic, causing problems for her puritan grandson. The execution of Babington in 1586 led to the family's loss of the rectory of Marnham and posed significant problems for their relatives, the Pierreponts.

Mary was executed at Fotheringhay in 1587. In her last moments she was assigned to the care of Richard Fletcher, who was nominally at least the rector of Algarkirk in 1584-5 amongst other benefices.[80] Fletcher employed a famously hectoring style in a fruitless attempt to convert the condemned Queen, and then presided over her funeral at Peterborough where he was Dean.

The 'Catholic threat' became more dangerous after the opening of the   mission to England in 1580 and a massive increase in the level of fines for non-attendance – penalties were again increased in the 1590s. In the mid-1580s a Spanish agent reported that five Lincolnshire gentry could mobilise 2000 men for the Catholic cause.[81] The threat of invasion by Spain in 1588 brought fears to fever pitch, and the defeat of the Armada was widely seen as due to God's intervention against the forces of Anti-Christ. In 1589 Edmund Hellwis, of Askham in Nottinghamshire, published his own commemoration of this entitled *A Marvell Deciphered*; this eulogised Elizabeth and was dedicated to the Lord Chamberlain. Edward Hellwis is believed to have been the older brother of Thomas Helwys, the future separatist and Baptist leader.

Sir Robert Dymoke of Scriveslby had maintained a dual life as a 'Church Catholic' but in 1579 received into his house the priest Richard Kirkman (and possibly Edmund Campion), who had arrived back from Rheims and was acting as a family tutor. This led to a hardening of his own position as a Catholic and a summons to Lincoln by Bishop Cooper in July 1580. In September 1580 Sir Robert Dymoke died in Lincoln Castle as a Catholic prisoner; meanwhile, Kirkman had escaped, but he was captured at Wakefield and executed at York in 1582. In an alternative version, Sir Robert had reportedly lost his faith in God as a result of being confused by too many Protestant sermons, and was introduced by friends to the Jesuit Robert Persons, later reverting to Rome.[82] Anne Dimock, a maid of honour at the court, had become a Catholic under the influence of Father Persons, eventually going to a convent in Rouen.

Edmund Campion was in England by 1580 and spent Christmas with Gervase and Henry Pierrepont at Holme Pierrepont and Thoresby in Nottinghamshire before going

80   Algarkirk also enjoyed the brief services of Tobias Matthew in 1584.
81   Hill (1956), p.107
82   Richard Simpson, *Edmund Campion, A Definitive Biography*, London, 1867.

to Derbyshire. There he briefly stayed with Lady Constance Foljambe and possibly even visited Walton before it became the home of Isabel Foljambe née Wray. Lady Foljambe had previously hosted Mary Queen of Scots in 1569. Lady Foljambe was arrested for recusancy in 1588 and died in 1600, reduced to poverty.[83] The two Pierreponts were arrested in 1581 following the discovery of Campion and had a narrow escape from execution. Gervase was lodged in the Marshalsea prison where he was found in 1584 to have been holding illicit masses, for which he was tortured on the rack. In 1589 he was under arrest at Banbury with John Thimbleby and then from 1589 to 1591 Thimbleby was held under house arrest by the Lincolnshire gentleman, Edward Billesby of Bilsby. Henry Pierrepont was accused of recusancy again in 1592 by Sir Thomas Stanhope but took advantage of local politics to get the support of the Earl of Shrewsbury. He died a natural death in 1616. Campion himself was captured in Berkshire and sentenced to death as a traitor by Sir Christopher Wray in 1581.

Hugh More, a 25-year-old 'gentleman' from Grantham, was executed for treason by hanging at Lincoln's Inn Fields on 28th August 1588. Although he had been educated a Protestant, More had converted to Catholicism and illegally left the country for Rheims and Douai – centres of training for Catholic mission. According to some, More was 'persecuted to death by his own father' and died because he refused to attend church as his penance.[84] A Catholic source described that he was 'a high born layman of extremely heretical parents and was for many years numbered among heretics' himself. He was executed the same day as Robert Morton, a Catholic priest born in Bawtry who had also been to Rheims – and who was also hung. More was beatified in 1920 whilst the last of his family was Rev Gabriel More of Elston. More's father Richard was elected MP for Grantham in 1589, a year after the execution; we know little of his actual religious views though in 1584 he did request a different pew at St Wulfram's because his was 'most unfriendly placed ... amongst boys and apprentices'.

Eustace White was born in Louth in 1559. He converted to Catholicism and travelled to Rome for training, returning with unfortunate timing in 1588 when the link between Catholicism and treason was most obvious to most minds. He was arrested in 1591 following a chance conversation and taken to London, where he was tortured by Richard Topcliffe who taunted him that the sound of invading Spanish drums could be heard from his cell. He was executed at Tyburn with four others, two men standing on his arms whilst he was 'drawn'; he was declared a saint in 1970.[85]

In 1592 a new commission was set up to root out Jesuits and recusants with many of the best-known local evangelicals listed in its ranks – including Clinton, Lord Sheffield, Bartholomew Armyn and even Sir Christopher Wray. However, few names were discovered – in Nottinghamshire, only fourteen were listed.[86] Punishments were generally not severe, with the first policy being to place recusants into the household of more reliable persons.[87] A few years later, in 1597, Cecil was informed that Twigmoor in

83 A Godfrey Foljambe also left England for France in 1583.

84 J H Pollen, *Acts of English Martyrs hitherto Unpublished*, London, 1891, p. 323

85 Another 1591 martyr, Brian Lacey, has been variously suggested to have been a priest from Louth or a gentleman from Yorkshire but generally mentioned as being betrayed by his own brother.

86 Wood (1947), p.161

87 Wood (1947), p.163

the North was still a dangerous Catholic centre – it had links to the Dymoke and Tyrwhitts who also made Bigby a centre for Catholicism.

On 23 April 1600, a meeting took place at Mr East's house in Aldersgate, London, that involved several Lincolnshire recusants – Edward Forset from Bilsby ('Billesby'), John and Richard Thimbleby. Forset was married to Anne Billesby, suggesting that Thimbleby's previous captor had somehow 'gone native'. They received a letter from the priest Persons, delivered by a servant of Gervase Pierrepont, and admitted being in correspondence with Scottish Catholics. The meeting was betrayed by enterprising apprentice boys and the main characters arrested.

Richard Topcliffe (1531-1604): A Man from the Dark Side

The history of the faith in this area is not without its darker moments and, in this era, Richard Topcliffe (1531-1604) was one of the darkest. Born in Lincolnshire at Somerby[88] as a grandson of the Burgh family of Gainsborough, he then married Jane Willoughby of Wollaton, Nottinghamshire. He had his own land in Nottinghamshire also, notably around East Markham, where he sold off the manor. His uncle Edward was the first husband of Katherine Parr. As an orphan by age 12, he was in the care of his uncle Sir Anthony Neville[89] of South Leverton who was married to one of the Burghs; Neville was one of the circle of Cranmer, Markham and Hercy, perhaps from which association he was able to come into possession of Mattersey Priory. From these connections, Topcliffe became known to Princess Elizabeth and entered her service at the start of her reign. A significant role in helping against the Northern Rising led him, by the 1570s, to be seen as something of an expert on Catholic 'recusants'.

He was an MP from 1572 and effectively the torturer employed by William Cecil, Lord Burghley, in tracking down and extracting information from Catholics. He became active in Derbyshire especially as 'popishe beasts' were present around Buxton. This work increased from 1580 when the Jesuits became more active, after 1581 when anti-Catholic legislation was strengthened and escalated after about 1588 when he became notorious for the use of torture. Another factor might have been his close involvement with the Earl of Shrewsbury, who was the custodian of Mary Queen of Scots at Worksop. Such was his zeal for his work at the Tower of London that even Protestants started to protest, and he took his work 'under cover' at home where he boasted he had machines even more fearsome than 'the rack'.

In 1592 his over-confidence led him to attempt to blackmail Archbishop Whitgift; his relationship with Queen Elizabeth was soured by bragging about 'intimacies' with her and there were rumours was also allegedly a rapist.[90]

---

88   Although he was sometimes referred to as 'a Yorkshireman'. It might have been better if he had been.

89   His son was secretary to three successive archbishops – Parker, Grindal and Whitgift.

90   T M McCoog, *The Society of Jesus in Ireland, Scotland and England*, Researchgate, 2012, p.46

Topcliffe tried to persuade one victim to claim to be Whitgift's illegitimate son. However, in 1592 the priest Robert Southwell was arrested and tortured by him, restoring his reputation but his treatment of Southwell exceeded the level of brutality that was acceptable, and he spent a time in prison. In 1593 he accused the sheriff of Derbyshire of harbouring Catholic priests. Altogether he was involved in more than fifty torture cases – the vast majority of those of his time.[91] By 1596 he was in trouble and spent his own time in prison, emerging just as wicked and described as 'hoary and a veteran in evil'. He increasingly lived at Somerby where he died in 1604; his later years were clouded by lameness, a son with criminal tendencies and a nephew who was suspected of being a Catholic.

It is also worthy of note that Topcliffe's land interests in Lincolnshire kept him in a protracted legal battle with Sir Christopher Wray.

Catholic martyrs from this era include[92] Robert Widmerpool, from the village of that name, executed at Canterbury in 1588. William Anlaby stayed with the Tyrwhitts in Lincolnshire and was martyred in 1597 after he had left the region. Roger Dickenson, martyred in 1591, and Mark Barkworth, similar in 1601, both supposedly came from Lincolnshire. Richard Yaxley of Boston was a martyr at Oxford in 1589 and Eustace White of Louth was executed as a traitor at Tyburn in 1591 and. Others prospered – Richard Smith of Welton, born 1567, ended his days as the 'Bishop of Chalcedon'.

Thomas Hunt and Thomas Sprott were executed as traitors at Lincoln in July 1600 after being caught with holy oils at the *Saracen's Head*.[93] Their arrest was an accidental result of a search for two robbers and was unfortunate in occurring at a time when the assizes were being held and a judge available. Judge Glanville pronounced the sentence and a few days later was apparently thrown by his horse, dying from some horrible injuries.[94] Two years later William Smith of Edlington was in trouble for saying that 'they died not for treason, but for their conscience'.[95]

There were many lesser Catholic connections and Thomas Rands, a senior Lincoln diocesan official had family connections with recusants at Tydd St Mary.[96] When Rands prepared a diocesan list of recusants in 1601 it was such a 'blatant underestimate' that it angered his bishop, Chaderton. Of nineteen who attended at Buckden to pledge conformity, eleven were from Lincolnshire. An example might be the career of Richard Read as vicar of Barton upon Humber, who was presented by the Crown in 1584 but managed to survive undetected as a 'Catholic' until Chaderton's visitation of 1598 – resigning in 1599, having also preached at Goxhill, Barrow and Ferriby. He managed to continue unlicensed preaching until 1621.[97]

91 F Brownlow, *Richard Topcliffe: Elizabeth's Enforcer*, 2003 and in R Dutton and others (eds), *Theatre and Religion*, p.161-5
92 Thomas Sherwood, executed in 1578, has been suggested, but I am unclear on the Lincolnshire connection.
93 Hodgson p,184 says executed.
94 Challoner, *Memoirs of Missionary Priests*, vol 1, London, 1842, p.377
95 Holmes (1980), p.39
96 Hajzyk, p.14
97 Hajzyk, p.421

A Murdered Parson

William Storre, vicar of Aisthorpe and Market Rasen in Lincolnshire from 1597, was murdered in 1602. He became involved in an argument over the annexation of common land by his local landowners (which presumably included at least associates of the St Paul family) but inflamed it by some stinging remarks from the pulpit. The son of one local landowner, Francis Cartwright, became incensed and called Storre 'a scurvie, lowsie, paltrie priest'. Later he threatened to cut him up and hang his 'quarters' on the maypole. Storre stuck to his position and after seeing him out walking a few days later, Cartwright went out and got a sword or knife from the cutler's shop, with which he mortally wounded his vicar on a road south from the town just after eight o'clock in the morning. Many people witnessed the vicar bleeding to death, and the town's bells were rung in panic according to a pamphlet published soon after. This described Storre's leg and arm being cut off. Storre must be the most unusual martyr in our history and left five children.

A testimonial to Storre was signed by many influential people ranging from determined puritans to closet Catholics: George St Paul, Philip Tyrwhitt, Sir Edward Ayscough (the same family as Anne Askew, another martyr) and more.

The murderer, Cartwright, fled abroad. His cause was defended by Francis Trigge, a 'godly preacher of Leadenham' and Welbourn who was an opponent of enclosure and depopulation until his death in 1606. Whilst abroad, Trigge's 'daily Letters quickened and seconded that good worke the Lord had already begun in me,' Cartwright wrote later. News of the murder reached Archbishop Whitgift who complained to the Privy Council that such a man had been released on bail – there was a clear element of him being 'protected' by fellow gentry here and many of these were puritan landowners.

However, Cartwright was pardoned in 1603 by 'corrupt dealing' according to one of the pamphlets produced as a result of Storre's widow's lengthy battle for redress – the illustration of the murder in one of these is unique for this period. Cartwright then did penance in the House of Convocation in front of the Archbishop and others and for a time he was sent to live with Rev Henry Hooke rector of Nettleton, who later became Archdeacon of York 1617-24. At Nettleton, he courted a wife – prompting an incident in which he was beaten by other locals.

Cartwright was, though, widely detested and got into a fight in Grantham in which he killed another man, Riggs, who had attacked him and for which he was given a year in prison. Cartwright alleged that the man was unhinged and had attacked him for the purpose of getting himself killed. During this period, Cartwright was taken out in chains to watch the burial of his only child. In his later confession, Cartwright described receiving great spiritual support at this time (while he must have been in Lincoln Gaol) from ministers Buddle and Atkinson; these were on very opposite wings of the Church, George Buddle an opponent of puritans from Wickenby and Robert Atkinson the puritan vicar of the godly stronghold of Glentworth.

After his release Cartwright went to sea and had many adventures, gaining an especial dislike of Turkish pirates and describing the terrible fates of those Englishmen he knew who converted to Islam. Returning to England, he had a miraculous escape from accidental death and settled in London where he also received spiritual support while in Lambeth from Daniel Featley and Thomas Goad – both very interesting and important figures!

Cartwright published his own pamphlet in 1621, *The Life, Confession and Heartie Repentance of Francis Cartwright, Gentleman; for His Bloudie Sin in killing of one Master Storr*. Perhaps this was an attempt to move on with his life. In this he certainly aimed to show repentance: 'Secondly, that since I have beene deeply branded with shame of the world outwardly, and with the terrors of God, and scourge of conscience inwardly, my example may be a dreadfull thunderclap of warning and affright to all, presuming and persevering Sinners, whom the hand of God will surely finde out, and deeply wound with the Darts of his vengeance.' You can read this online.

The story is a reminder of the importance of enclosures in the period. The issue was often seen as a form of the rich robbing the poor, and many of the 'godly' were on the side of the rich or actually took part in the enclosures; a few years later they were to condemn King Charles for trying to do something similar in the drainage of the Fens and Carrs. Trigge was independently wealthy and funded charities for the poor in Stamford and Grantham; he is most famous for the library that bears his name at Grantham.[98]

98 Read Cartwright's whole text at: http://tei.it.ox.ac.uk/tcp/Texts-HTML/free/A18/A18070.html

CHAPTER SEVEN

The Exorcists and the Supernatural
1586-1650

In the early years of the Reformation, any supernatural aspects of Christianity came under suspicion as reflecting 'Papist' tricks to deceive the uneducated. Calvin himself declared that the supernatural gifts had ceased. However, over succeeding decades there was a gradual rediscovery of the lost gifts of prophecy, healing and the casting out of demons. The latter has become best known because of its ready adaptation into drama, but the period up to and including the Civil War also saw great interest in prophecy. Nottinghamshire has produced the most famous 'exorcists' of this era while Richard Bernard, of Epworth and Worksop, has produced one of its seminal books on the subject.

Chronology:
1586: Eckington case
1596: Stapenhill case
1597: Leigh and Nottingham cases
1599: Darrell and More convicted
1629: Richard Bernard publishes book on witchcraft
1642: Carlton-in-Lindrick prophecies published

John Darrell is a figure of some controversy and notoriety in Christian history, and some disagreement, but is one of the best-known Nottinghamshire figures from this era. A puritan, he adopted an approach to the supernatural that brought him criticism and even accusations of being on the side of the Catholics, spreading across the last years of Elizabeth and into the time of James I. Much of his story is uncertain and confused because Darrell's case became central to a legal and propaganda war between different factions within the Church of England.[1]

Darrell was born in the Mansfield area in about 1562, his father was a farmer and miller,[2] and he was able to attend Queens' College, Cambridge until about 1582 and then the Inns of Court, but after this he returned to Nottinghamshire to farm.[3] The Law was not a success – 'the Lord did draw me another way, by laying his hand upon me, in causing a strange and extraordinary sluggishness to fall upon me'. However, university may have

---

1   Harman Bhogal, *Miracles, Cessationism, and Demonic Possession: The Darrell Controversy and the Parameters of Preternature in Early Modern English Demonology* in *Preternature: Critical and Historical Studies on the Preternatural* , Vol. 4, No. 2 (2015), pp. 152-180

2   Marion Gibson, *Possession, Puritanism and Print: Darrell, Harsnett, Shakespeare and the Elizabethan Exorcism Controversy*, London, 2006, p 16-23

3   T S Freeman, *John Darrell*, in ODNB, accessed 27 July 2014

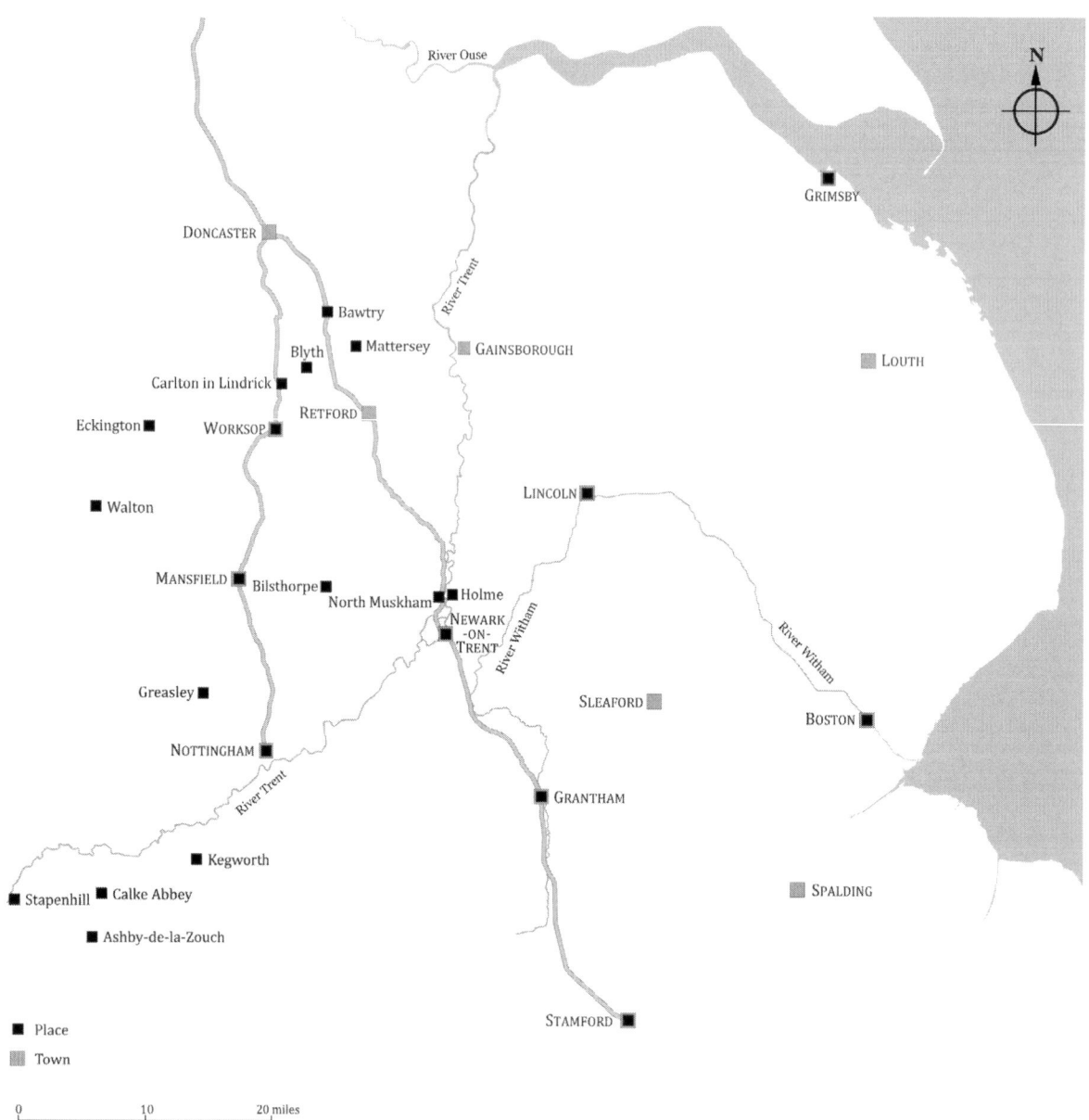

N

River Ouse

GRIMSBY

DONCASTER

Bawtry

Blyth
Mattersey
GAINSBOROUGH
LOUTH

Carlton in Lindrick
RETFORD

Eckington
WORKSOP
River Trent

LINCOLN

Walton

MANSFIELD
Bilsthorpe
North Muskham
Holme
NEWARK
-ON-
TRENT
River Witham

River Witham

Greasley
SLEAFORD
BOSTON

NOTTINGHAM
River Trent

GRANTHAM

Kegworth

Stapenhill
Calke Abbey
SPALDING

Ashby-de-la-Zouch

STAMFORD

■ Place

▨ Town

0   10   20 miles

184

helped form some connections for life since the college was also used by the Huntingdon and Bowes families, and Richard Rothwell – who we shall meet soon, and it helped him with links to the regional puritan leader Arthur Hildersham with whom he stayed.[4] His was something of an unusual career path but certainly brought him into touch with puritan thought for by 1586 he had gained a local reputation as some form of spiritual leader. In between, he married Joan Gadsby in 1583/4. Around 1588 he seems to have been ordained and received payment for preaching Mansfield in 1589, where he lived until at least 1591.

In 1586, a young Derbyshire woman from Ridgeway near Eckington,[5] Katherine Wright, was reported locally as being demon-possessed and to be chained to a post for her own protection.[6] She had lived with an abusive stepfather at Eckington although he had stopped beating her after she reported a vision of a child without feet. Some claimed that she then used 'fits' to ensure the beatings did not resume. Her plight came to the attention of Edward Beresford who provided a shelter for her – and he was connected with the Earl of Shrewsbury. To cure the 'possession', they arranged for a 'conjuror' – who summoned up a devil for which he was arrested.

This came – or was brought – to the attention of Isabel Foljambe (nee Wray), a wealthy local puritan from Lincolnshire who was living at Walton near Chesterfield.[7] Perhaps it was her who called in various godly ministers to help, but to no avail. Then John Darrell and Thomas Beckingham of Bilsthorpe[8] were called in, although one source suggests it was Beckingham who called in Darrell.

Darrell was reported to her to be 'a man of hope for the relieving of those that were distressed in this sort'.[9] We do not know where Darrell learnt about possession or how to battle against it, but he was probably familiar with the John Foxe cases of 1574, relied on open prayer, and did not initially use fasting. The use of informal prayer – prophesying – alone would have marked him out as a puritan on the radical fringe of the Church. However, Beckingham was not convinced that Katherine Wright was possessed and withdrew, but nonetheless, the exorcism was done in the house of a relative of Beckingham's. The two men also fell out over the suggestion that Darrell 'lay on' Wright during the lengthy exorcism; the implication was that this was indecent, whilst Darrell made a poor attempt at defending himself with confused responses including the Biblical example from the ministry of Paul and also that it was for 'restraint'. He pointed out that his wife was present throughout. Wright, though, later gave testimony that 'he lie upon my belly, saying that he would by so lying press the devil out of me'.

---

4   T Webster, *Godly Clergy in Early Stuart England*, Cambridge, 1997, p.25

5   Variously cited as Whittington, Eckington and Brampton – all near Chesterfield. Collinson opts for Eckington. *Athenae Cantabrigienses* is the only source to specify Ridgeway.

6   K M Bardell, *Sorry Rogues and Sorcery*, 2005, drawing on C Rickert, *The Case of John Darrell* in *Humanities*, 9, 1962.

7   T S Freeman, *Isabel Wray*, in ODNB. There are slight differences in Freeman's two accounts between these sections as to how Darrell became involved with Wright and also over the name of Isabel's husband. In one he is Godfrey, in the other Geoffrey.

8   Beckingham was a local 'godly' minister at Bilsthorpe where he had been a 'man of note' since 1573 – whereas Darrell seems to have had no real status and was never clearly a beneficed clergyman – although Rickert credits him with official positions at Mansfield, Bulwell, Ashby and Nottingham. The two fell out and Darrell thought Beckingham had gone mad although he was still at Bilsthorpe until 1599.

9   These words are from Samuel Harsnett, one of his main accusers and later an archbishop.

Wright was cured on the second attempt – apparently – and then Darrell was involved in an attempt to prosecute Margaret Roper of Eckington for having engineered the possession. For puritans who put their trust in the Bible, the casting out of demons was quite in line with what the New Testament said, but there was no similar precedent for the accusations of witchcraft since this never occurred in any of the cases involving Jesus; coupled with this, it was uncomfortably close to some 'superstitious' practices in Catholicism which puritans argued were used to give priests a hold over ignorant people. Darrell also seems to have erred in that, throughout the various cases, he failed to close off the 'victim' against further possession.

The local Justice of the Peace, Godfrey Foljambe, Isobel's husband, was unimpressed by Darrell and dismissed the witchcraft case; some sources have suggested Darrell was imprisoned by Foljambe,[10] although the extent of his displeasure may have been exaggerated by Darrell's enemies. Wright then required a second exorcism, this time from eight devils. Nonetheless, Darrell sent an account of the Wright case to Isabel, Lady Foljambe. Isabel, later Lady Bowes, remained interested in his ministry and later also brought Richard Rothwell – a Lancashire preacher and occasional exorcist – to Mansfield. The exact relations between these three may never be fully understood but, given later controversy, it is possible Godfrey Foljambe thought that the puritan cause might be put at risk by behaviour that was closer to Roman Catholic practice. In 1600 Wright may have suggested that Darrell had told her to fake fits.[11]

Isabel Foljambe's connections were useful to Darrell who moved first to Bulwell and then to Ashby-de-la-Zouch in 1592, where he took up a small farm having sold his property at Mansfield. Ashby was a significant puritan stronghold – he preached there in 1593-4 and caused upset by condemning the ringing of the church bells on the Sabbath for the Queen's anniversary. The Earl of Huntingdon had gathered many key puritans such as Anthony Gilby and Arthur Hildersham so Darrell's location there is a sure sign of his standing. In the intervening eight years he seems to have lived a 'holy life' with little that could be used against him later; having been almost invisible for a decade Darrell returned to prominence with another exorcism in 1596.

In 1596 William Walkden, minister at Clifton Campville near Burton-upon-Trent, became concerned about witchcraft affecting a young relative at Stapenhill;[12] he asked Darrell for help with his thirteen-year-old grandson Thomas Darling[13] who he thought was possessed. Interestingly, though accounts do differ, Darrell seems to have tried to avoid any direct involvement with the actual exorcism and kept away while others prayed successfully for deliverance.[14] Rickert suggests that he was unconvinced about the boy's possession.[15] Again, a local woman, Alice Gooderidge of Stapenhill, was accused of witchcraft – she

10 Bardell (2005), p.86
11 Bardell (2005), p.86
12 Stapenhill, on the edge of Burton, was not a backwater: Walter Hieron, its curate 1605-16, was the nephew of Samuel Hieron of Devon, a leading puritan; William Bradshaw, a puritan polemicist, lived here under the protection of Alexander Redditch. Wright, p.16, suggests links between them and John Smyth.
13 Darling's uncle was Edward Wightman, who was the last man to be burnt for heresy in English history at Lichfield in 1612. Gibson (2006) provides a good account of the various family relationships.
14 Gibson, p.37
15 Rickert, p,15

died in prison, though this was in no way Darrell's action. Darrell's behaviour was hardly that of a man seeking to profit from exorcism. The case was publicised that year by Jesse Bee and John Denison in *The Most Wonderful and True Story of a Certain Witch named Alice Gooderidge*.

Stapenhill was only a few miles from Ashby-de-la-Zouch and was the home of Walter Bradshaw, a leading puritan writer who had got into trouble for distributing Darrell's pamphlets at Cambridge, and from 1605-1616 the curate was Walter Hieron of a famous puritan family.

This further incident brought Darrell to renewed attention in radical puritan circles and he was invited in March 1597 to Leigh, Lancashire where a group of people were gathered at the house of Nicholas Starkie, and where a man had already been hung over the case.

Darrell took with him George More, who was minister at Calke Abbey in Derbyshire, and who probably went with him to act as a guide and support.[16] The Starkie family had suffered many child deaths at Cleworth Hall with accusations of witchcraft; it was suspected this was organised by Catholic relatives on Mrs Starkie's side who wanted to inherit the property. Now seven were said to be possessed – all connected to Starkie. Yet Starkie did not turn to the puritans first for he lived in a very different district where Catholicism was still very influential, so he tried a Catholic priest and then a 'cunning' man, Edmund Hartley. Eventually, partly through the influence of the infamous Dr John Dee,[17] Starkie turned to 'godly men' who identified Hartley as part of the problem, and he was hung for witchcraft. However, the seven were still possessed so Starkie asked for Darrell – and he had to ask three times; Darrell consulted the congregation at Ashby before going. When he arrived with More, the young people attacked them and abused them verbally.

Darrell attended them with George More and the local minister, Mr Dickons or Deacon.[18] A group of around thirty or more gathered for open prayer and fasting over two days – practices that were both to attract criticism. Of the seven possessed only one, Jane Ashton, was not completely delivered and she became the subject of much accusation and counter-accusation; one theory was that she was put up to her 'fits' by local Catholics. This 'mass exorcism' attracted attention and in an age when the printing press began to be truly influential, stories started to circulate. However, Darrell did not seek publicity – others wrote about him first and he only went into print himself when rumours and accusations began to spread.

In October 1597 a young man in Nottingham, William Sommers, was believed to be possessed. On 5 November Darrell went to Nottingham at the invitation of the mayor to try to depossess him with the approval of Robert Aldridge, the minister of St Mary's.[19]

---

16   Gibson, p.40. Calke was a strong puritan centre, where More held regular fasts. By 1610 the minister at Calke was another radical – Julines Herring – who maintained More's practice of holding fasts. He moved to Shrewsbury in 1618, fell out with Archbishop Laud, and in 1637 went to Amsterdam as minister of the English Reformed Church

17   Whose butler was a cousin of Thomas Darling

18   Bardell (2005), p.87. It is possible this is the Deacon who wrote the subsequent book.

19   T Freeman, *Demons, Deviance and Defiance* in Lake and Questier, *Conformity and Orthodoxy in the English Church,* 2000, c1560-1660, p. 34. Rickert suggests that he held an official position at St Mary's.

John Ireton, the puritan rector of Kegworth, recommended him to the mayor[20]; Ireton had an interest in the supernatural and once challenged the Archdeacon of Derby to a debate about possession and exorcism, supporting the practice. Sommers had been a servant lad at Langley Abbey near Ashby and then with Anthony Brackenbury[21] at Holme near Newark, whose wife's brother had employed Sommers at Langley. He was been sent back to his parents in Nottingham due to having fits or faking them in about 1589; he had also been unsuccessfully apprenticed to a musician.[22] Sommers accused an old woman of bewitching him. According to one local source, Darrell was at Mansfield at this time but was called to Nottingham by his 'sister' but most other sources say he came from Ashby-de-la-Zouch, where he was living in 1593; an early historian of Nottingham reported that the boy learnt about Darrell and then started calling his name, so that Mr Aldridge of St Mary's sent for him.[23] Sommers was seen by several to have a lump under his skin which moved around his body. What Darrell perhaps did not know was that the case was deeply woven into Nottingham politics.[24]

The exorcism in November 1597 was witnessed by an enthusiastic crowd and included prayer and fasting, but no rituals or set prayers. Some of the scenes were spectacular – Sommers' 'bodie doubled, and his heade betweene his legs, and the suddenly he was plucked upon an heape'.[25] Witnesses also described the strange and mobile white swelling under his skin. Darrell was appointed assistant preacher at St Mary's. However, Sommers claimed to have been repossessed and displayed his symptoms again – and his sister also claimed possession. The pair of them began denouncing individual citizens of the city and thirteen were accused, though only two were kept in gaol. One of them, Doll Freeman, was a relative of William Freeman, a Nottingham alderman, who launched his own claims against Sommers. Sommers confessed to fraud, having been at risk of being accused of witchcraft himself, and Darrell was in an uncomfortable position.

These events had now reached the ears of Bishop Bancroft in London, and the Archbishop of York appointed a commission to investigate. By this stage, the commission was a well-established mechanism for bringing recalcitrant puritans to heal. Darrell and More were clear opponents of the Church leadership – More had proclaimed that spontaneous prayer was more effective than the Prayer Book whilst there were fears people would say that if Darrell 'is the only diviner of signs and wonders…his ministry shall have my only applause'.[26] But the commission, of which Ireton himself was a member,[27] decided that Sommers had indeed been possessed and cleared Darrell, but this was not the outcome wanted by the archbishop or Bancroft. Darrell was deprived of his licence to preach and, with George More, summoned to London by Archbishop Whitgift. Sommers does not appear well from any of this and was quite happy to allege that Darrell had met him in an

20 Freeman, in Lake and Questier, p.36. Ireton was a friend and helper of Arthur Hildersham.
21 We will meet Brackenbury again later as the owner of a coal barge used by many of the separatists to escape from Gainsborough.
22 J Orange, *History and Antiquities of Nottingham*, 1840, p.688
23 The suggestion in Orange's book was that Aldridge must have been Darrell's father in law – and thus the 'sister' was actually sister in law.
24 Collinson (2013), p.154
25 Marion Gibson, *Possession, Puritanism and Print: Darrell, Harsnett, Shakespeare and the Elizabethan Exorcism Controversy*, London, 2016, p 1–2.
26 Lake and Questier, p.38
27 Charles Cooper and Thompson Cooper, *Athenae Cantabrigienses*: 1586 – 1609, Volume 2, p.441

alehouse at Ashby years before and taught him how to fake possession.

Darrell and More were not an equal match for men such as Samuel Harsnett, an acolyte of Bancroft's, who more or less led the Church's campaign. Harsnett saw the actions of these men as a threat to order in the Church whilst Darrell saw Harsnett as a man who was trying to destroy godly works and would likely go to Hell.[28] Harsnett was able to exploit the apparent confusion of puritans engaging in practices linked with Catholicism; men such as Whitgift and Bancroft were resolutely doubtful about the supernatural, and painted them as doing the Pope's bidding, but it was disorder they feared most. 'Darrell was not opposed by Whitgift and Bancroft because he was an exorcist, but because his exorcisms sanctioned, even sanctified, crucial puritan practices and dogmas', Freeman has written.[29] More insisted that spontaneous prayer, 'prophesying', was more powerful than reading from the Prayer Book – just what they did not want to hear. Supporters from the Midlands came to London for the trial and Rickerts suggests that Darling visited Darrell in prison.

In May 1599 they were convicted of fraud by the court of ecclesiastical causes, but the real battle was in the press. It has been suggested that Darrel spent a year in the Gatehouse prison, and More was put in the Clink.[30] In 1599 Harsnett published his own denunciation of the exorcists, *A Discovery of the Fraudulent Practises of John Darel*. Despite the importance of the case, first Darrell and later More were quietly released and the former returned to Nottinghamshire; one of the conditions of their release was that they did not engage in fasting.[31] But Darrell did not go down quietly, for he continued to write and argued persuasively against those who said that Biblical accounts had been mistranslated and were really metaphorical: 'Nay then let us conclude, because these texts of Scripture be metaphorical, therefore all the Scripture is metaphorical…'[32] He and his supporters 'repeatedly accused the Church of England of denying the existence of demons and the facts of exorcism'.[33] In reply, Harsnett repeatedly linked Darrell and his group to Catholics such as the Jesuit William Weston, who wrote a *Book of Miracles* about his exploits as an exorcist which he believed to be effective in recruiting new believers. Matters cannot have been helped when Thomas Darling, who had gone to Oxford, accused its vice-chancellor of being a 'Papist' and also the Bishop of London; for this he was tried by the Star Chamber and sentenced to have his ears cut off.[34]

More wrote his own account which was published in 1599. He agreed with Darrell about possession but was more radical about miracles, which More argued continued to occur after the apostolic era whereas Darrell was cessationist on this. 'If the Church of England have this power to cast out Devils, then the church of Rome is a false Church. For there can be but one true Church, the principal mark of which, as they say, is to work miracles, and of them this is the greatest, namely to cast out devils.'

---

28   Gibson (2016), p.15
29   T Freeman, *Demons, Deviance and Defiance* in Lake and Questier, *Conformity and Orthodoxy in the English Church, c1560-1660*, Woodbridge, 2000, p. 35
30   G J Gray, *Athenae Cantabrigienses 1589-1609 vol II*, Cambridge, 1861, p.380. This concludes that 'it cannot be doubted that Darrel was an egregious rogue who richly deserved his punishment'.
31   Freeman, in Lake and Questier, p.43
32   Darrell, *Survey of Certain Dialogical Discourses*.
33   Rickert, p.5
34   Rickert, p.31

In 1601 two new books emerged both by John Deacon and John Walker, both attacking Darrell from a puritan perspective – arguing that he was deluded, but not a fraud. Deacon represented the anti-supernatural wing of puritanism that argued the 'gifts' had ceased after the Apostles and denied that 'possession' even existed. At the time they were intriguingly called 'Sadducees'. They thought Darrell's activities made the puritan cause look ridiculous and wanted to keep the focus on Church reforms.

Who was John Deacon?

Deacon has been identified as a Magdalene College graduate who was a clergyman from 1577 with a benefice in Leicestershire, who then took up the curacy at Bawtry in 1594 (where he was presented in Nov 1594 for preaching without proper licence) and Scrooby in north Nottinghamshire 1598,[35] or he might have been the preacher at Leigh in Lancashire with a very similar name who was an active observer in Darrell's Lancashire work. There are a lot of problems with this, including why he would have given up a rectory for a curacy.

Harmon Bhogal, who completed his PhD thesis on this issue,[36] relies on the evidence from Marchant (1960) that the Bawtry Deacon is the man. The local link is certainly attractive, but in his own account, *A Brief and True Discourse….*, George More plainly identified 'Mr Dickoms' as Starkie's minister at Leigh in Lancashire who penned an account of the proceedings. Rickart takes the view that the books were mainly Walker's work. On the other hand, in their 1601 book *Dialogicall Discourses*, one of the debates takes place on a journey from Mahgnitton to Eirtwab – which is strong evidence for a connection with Bawtry! John Deacon also published in 1616, *Tobacco Tortured*, which explained the 'pernicious effects' of smoking for which it blamed the Gunpowder Plot and the enclosures.

A note added to *Venn*'s Alumni for Deacon suggests that actually he was both – giving him now as preacher at Leigh in 1597 as well as being in Nottingham in 1586 and at Ridlington in Rutland.

These men took a moderately critical position – they thought Darrell was deluded rather than a fraud and should be allowed to continue to minister; however, one historian considers they distorted and misquoted Darrell.[37] Both men were confident 'cessasionists' but it is also clear they resented Darrell's local success which they perhaps saw as disrupting their own more stoical efforts and distracting the godly people which they called 'intermeddling'. Fostering superstition and false miracles would only encourage Catholicism, they argued. Darrell replied with two publications of his own, and in the view of one historian he got the better of the argument: 'Deacon and Walker seemed out of their depth and their

---

35 T Freeman, *Demons, Deviance and Defiance* in Lake and Questier, *Conformity and Orthodoxy in the English Church, c1560-1660*, p. 51. Gibson (2016) takes a similar view.

36 H Bhogal, *Rethinking Demonic Possession: The impact of the debates about the John Darrel case on later demonological thought, with particular reference to John Deacon and John Walker*. PhD thesis, 2013, Birkbeck, University of London

37 C H Rickert, *The Case of John Darrell*, University of Florida PhD thesis, 1962, p.65

pomposity makes their works unattractive reading'.[38] A more charitable view is perhaps that they thought Darrell gave Bancroft and Whitgift the chance to attack puritans in general. Darrell attacked his attackers by accusing them of denying the Biblical records of witchcraft and labelled them as 'Sadducees'.

Although Harsnett held the power, the accession of James I in 1603 created some doubts. James had great interest in the supernatural and in 1597 had published *Daemonologie*, a book which set out his views. In February 1603 the allies of Bancroft launched a sermon and pamphlet campaign to argue that supernatural possession had ceased after the time of the apostles; seemingly they jettisoned the Holy Spirit along with witches and demons. By the time he got to London, Harsnett and Bancroft seem to have developed a strategy for convincing James that belief in witchcraft was a trick of the Catholics and therefore potentially dangerous to his position on the throne, and so the 'cessassionist' view dominated.[39] Harsnett published a book on 'Popish impostures' that deliberately blurred the distinction from the puritans; thus we can see that in succeeding years the most radical puritans could be accused of being Jesuits.

Of course, beliefs in witchcraft persisted whatever Harsnett might have thought. In 1583 a man at West Burton had been accused of making wax images of his mother-in-law and her family in an effort to bring harm upon them. Within a few years and a small area, K M Bardell found several cases. In 1606 a North Wheatley woman was accused of poisoning, murder and witchcraft; in 1608 a Walesby (Notts) woman was found watching in the church porch on St Mark's Eve to predict the death of a neighbour; and in 1616 three North Muskham women were accused of using incantations.[40] Anne Cook of Mattersey was in trouble in 1622 for predicting when people would die and Elizabeth Tuttie of the same village was sent for trial in 1629 for witchcraft.[41] An accusation of witchcraft causing the death of the vicar of Worksop is discussed later.

Before he went to ground again, Darrell left a lasting impression on the Church of England for under James I the regulations were changed so that by canon 72 exorcism could only be practiced with a licence from the bishop. Another puritan practice, open prayer, which was called 'prophesying', was also banned. Once Bancroft became Archbishop of Canterbury exorcism could lose a clergyman his living. In Freeman's view, by these new laws 'the Church of England paid a high price'.

Darrell remained a nonconformist puritan; in 1607 he was at Teversal and his family was accused of not attending communion, perhaps because he preferred churches elsewhere. The same year there were complaints that churchwardens had allowed him to preach at Greasley (where John Robinson got married) and Sutton-in-Ashfield;[42] both were known puritan churches.[43] It is now certain that Darrell was the 'John Dayrell' who in 1617 published *A Treatise of the church – written against them of the separation commonly called Brownists*. This was his only 'authorised' publication, and he took up a firm stance

38   Gibson (2016), p.146
39   Lake and Questier, *Conformity and Orthodoxy in the English Church*, C. 1560-1660, p. 59
40   Martyn Bennett, *Society, Religion and Culture in Seventeenth-Century Nottinghamshire*, 2005, p.93
41   Holland (2004), p.13
42   Lake and Questier (2000), p.55
43   Gibson (2016), p.173

in defence of the Church of England against the separatists. He 'certainly knew John Smyth and John Robinson'[44] and their areas overlapped, if not their careers, and they may even have met at Greasley.

Darrell is now quite a well-known figure, the subject of several books and regularly appearing on websites. Some condemn him as a 'fraud' but this is perhaps harsh. There is no evidence he sought to profit from the excommunications, he did them very rarely, and for long periods he maintained a low profile. He was certainly a godly man, and his actions were certainly exploited by others for political purposes. A few years later Bishop Joseph Hall, who held the sees of Exeter and Norwich, wrote of him that 'in our age Mr Dayrel, a godly and zealous preacher, through the blessing of God upon his faithfull devotion, performed those famous ejectments of evil spirits, both at Nottingham and Lancashire, which exercised the press and raised no small envy from gainsayers'.[45] Hall may even have known him, since he was from Ashby and born near there in the 1570s. He seemingly gained no benefit from the exorcisms, in fact, quite the reverse, so he may not have been a 'fraud'; perhaps in his own lack of experience he was himself open to being misled.

Another figure of this era was Richard Rothwell, born about 1563 in Lancashire and who died at Mansfield in 1627. In his youth he was amongst the 'gayest of the gay' and continued to be so even after being ordained:

> He continued several years a stranger to religion, when he preached learnedly, but lived in profaneness, addicting himself to hunting, bowling, shooting, and filthy and profane conversation. We are told, that in Lancashire there were two knights at variance with each other; one having a good park, with an excellent store of deer; the other good fish-ponds, with an excellent store of fish; and that he used to gratify himself by robbing the park of the one, and presenting his booty to the other, and the fish-ponds of the other, and presenting the fish to his adversary. On one of these occasions, it is added, the keeper caught him in the very act of killing a buck, when they fell from words to blows; but Mr. Rothwell, being tall and lusty, got the keeper down, and bound him by both his thumbs to a tree, with his toes only touching the ground, in which situation he was found next morning.[46]

Eventually, Rothwell had a conversion experience after being chastised by a godly minister for his profane habits, including playing bowls with 'Papists', and he became a powerful preacher. 'When he preached the law, he used to make men tremble, yea sometimes to cry out in the church, opening the depths of Satan and deceitfulness of the heart, so that he was called the 'rough hewer'.[47] For a time he was a military chaplain in Ireland and lecturer in a chapel in Lancashire. Rothwell refused a benefice as he wished to be free to preach, but he did accept a position as a chaplain to the Earl of Devonshire where he contested with the philosopher Hobbes.

---

44 Gibson (2016), p.145
45 This was published in *The Invisible World* in 1659, three years after his death.
46 The *Lives of the Puritans*, vol 2
47 Joseph Hunter, *Hallamshire – the History and Topography of the Parish of Sheffield*, London, 1819, p.243

He seems to have come to the notice of Lady Isabel Bowes (née Wray) through working for the Devonshires as a chaplain, and she set him to work with miners on the lands in the North around Barnard Castle. Rothwell's biographer reported that this followed the funeral of Lady Bowes' husband Sir William at Barnard Castle in 1611, after which her chaplain Beriah Dyke reported the lack of a minister in the district but declared himself unfit for the task and recommended Rothwell. As a peeress she was entitled to appoint her own chaplains and met with Rothwell. When she expressed concern as to the reception he would get, he told her – 'Madam, if I thought I should not meet the devil, I would not go: he and I have been at odds in other places, and I hope we shall not agree there'. However, after much success in County Durham, Rothwell began to suffer from an unexplained illness in the head and perhaps for this reason Lady Bowes brought him to Mansfield.

Rothwell was in Mansfield as a lecturer in 1621 as the incumbent of the Church of England was ineffective due to drink; he may have been there earlier as Gregory Sylvester, a mercer, left 10s a year in a will of 1616 if he stayed in the town to preach. 'He was a known nonconformist and was preacher at a church where the vicar was a conformist, yet he had complete freedom to preach there and in other churches thereabouts.'[48] It was perhaps the influence of Isabel Wray that allowed Mansfield to be, in Marchant's view, 'the centre of a puritan area' which also included Sutton-in-Ashfield where Darrell had been allowed to preach in 1607 and which had Ezekiel Burton as its puritan curate. This was despite, or because of, the long-term failures of Mansfield's parish clergy – back in 1598 the churchwardens had been complaining of the ruinous state of the church whilst Brian Brittaine, the vicar, had failed to deliver weekday services or attend the sick.[49]

Rothwell's most famous case involved a John Fox 'near Nottingham'.
> 'This man was possessed with a devil, who would violently throw him down; and take away the use of every member of his body, which was changed as black as pitch, while those fits were upon him; and then spoke with an audible voice within him, which seemed sometimes to sound out of his belly, sometimes out of his throat, and some-times out of his mouth, his lips not moving;'[50]

Fox was struck dumb but was able to carry on correspondence with godly men such as Rev Henry Lanly of 'Traswell'[51] and 'Mr Bernard of Batcomb' – Richard Bernard, formerly of Worksop.

> '…many prayers were put up to God for him, and great resort, especially of godly Ministers, to him: amongst the rest Master Bernard of Batcombe, then of Worksop; and Master Langley of Truswel, betwixt whom and John Fox, I have seen divers

---

48   Marchant, p.170

49   Diocesan Presentment Records

50   Words from a broadside published c1810-30 and therefore not an eyewitness account! http://digital.nls.uk/broadsides/broadside.cfm/id/16634/transcript/1

51   This would be Henry Langley, curate of Epworth in 1604-06, preacher licensed in York diocese, and rector of Treswell 1611-36 although during this era a number of his parish were refusing to attend church which questions his 'godly' credentials. His link to Epworth – home of Bernard – is interesting, as is the possibility that he also attended Christ's College. He received a legacy from the puritan Sir John Stanhope of Melwood Park in about 1627.

passages in writing, he relating by pen his temptations, and they giving answers when he was stricken dumb.'[52]

Casting the demon out of Fox was a long and drawn-out affair during which Rothwell had a 'lengthy discourse, by way of question and answer' with the demon. Eventually, it left and Fox recovered after a short time when people thought he was dead.

In his last months, Rothwell seems to have occasionally lost his reason.[53] On his death bed, Rothwell recited a psalm and his last words were, 'Blessed is he that hath not bowed the knee to Baal'.

The Darrell cases produced several works on the supernatural, but on witchcraft the one book linked to our region that stands out is Richard Bernard's *A Guide to Grand Jury Men*, published in 1629 long after he had left Nottinghamshire, the title indicating its purpose to help those on juries in witchcraft cases. We note elsewhere that there was a witchcraft furore in Worksop after the death of Bernard's successor. Bernard wrote this book after he had become involved in a witchcraft case at Taunton, feeling the need to defend himself against accusations that he did not believe in such things. In the book he explained his own personal experience dating from his time in Nottinghamshire, including an exorcism case. 'He wanted to equip readers from a variety of backgrounds and life circumstances to understand and respond correctly to the presence of evil in the world,' one historian has concluded.

An interesting side effect of this issue was that fasting (clearly a Biblical practice) was frowned on by Church authorities. We have seen this used in place of 'prophesyings' and now it was seen as part of exorcism. The release of Darrell was dependant on not engaging in public prayer and fasting. However, some 'godly' ministers continued to gather in fasting and prayer to combat the persecution of the reformers such as Harsnett, promoted to Archbishop of York in 1628, who in 1631 was ill and had gone to Bath to take the waters. The puritan leader Thomas Hooker observed that 'Prayer is a great force; it will bring punishment upon a man, and he shall not know who hurt him'. Samuel Harsnett, by this stage Archbishop of York, fell ill and died at a 'House of Entertainment' on his way back north to Southwell.[54]

Few other supernatural cases have surfaced. In 1623 there was a case of a boy at Wysall in Notts who could cure people by 'stroking' – those who went to him were presented. Similarly, we know of occasional people who consulted a 'wizard', such as Robert Shawe of Bramcote in the same period.

Interest in the supernatural increased during the 1630s and 1640s and printing made possible the publicising of new revelations – which were either received with awe or mocked mercilessly. An interesting case of prophecy is related in a 1642 pamphlet, *The*

---

52 The report was written by Stanley Gower in his life of minister Richard Rothwell and appears in Clarke, *The Lives of Two and Twenty English Divines*, 92-94. Gower was a disciple of Rothwell, later based at Attercliffe, and both men were associated with the patronage circle of Isabel Bowes. See also Joseph Hunter, *The History and Topography of the Parish of Sheffield in the County of York*, 242-243. It is unclear whether the Fox exorcism occurred before or after the passing of Canon 72 in 1604, which forbid such activities without direct episcopal approval. Cited in Tan, p.219

53 *Lives of the Puritans*, vol 2

54 Lake and Questier, p.43

Wonderfull Work of God, declared by a Strange Prophecy of a Maid. This booklet relates how James Turner, a servant to Sir Francis 'Thorney' (presumably really Thornhagh), married Margaret Holbeck of Blyth at Carlton (we assume Carlton in Lindrick in November 1641. 'Thorny' provided a feast as Turner was 'beloved of all the inhabitants'. This was described as 'near Worsop' – which could be either Warsop or Worksop but has been assumed to be the latter.

The next day Turner's sister, aged about 16, and a friend visited Thorney's house and Anne Thorney with whom they discussed clothes – though Miss Turner expressed little interest in such frivolities. Two days later both Miss Turner and Anne died in the same afternoon.

Rev Faber proposed they be buried in the same coffin, which Sir Francis negated, and Mrs Turner decided to have one last look at her daughter. Some twenty hours after the death, she unwound the grave clothes at which the girl sat up and started speaking! 'My dearest mother,' she began, 'why have you sinned so sore against God? You have made me sorrowful many times, but bee you content, God hath forgiven all, for I am sent as a messenger unto you, and within five days I shall return againe to the place I came from'.

The girl then delivered a set of sombre prophecies. Firstly, that England would be judged for its sin of pride. Secondly, that there would be desolations, wars and sorrows. Thirdly, that signs and visions would be seen. Lastly, that the end of the world was nigh. Despite these messages, most people agreed the girl was much more cheerful than usual!

Rev Faber asked her what had happened, and the girl described meeting a 'comely old man' near a bridge, who took her to a 'fair and costly fort' – more of a palace in fact! It was full of angels and glorious singing. He told her that she must go back to deliver the prophecies, but the girl was reluctant so struck a bargain that she could return to the palace after five days.

On the fifth day she took communion, warned against 'the Whore of Babylon', lay down, said the Lord's Prayer, and died.

The story was dismissed by an early historian of Worksop as fabrication as he could not identify Faber or any marriage records, but possibly the marriage took place at an extra-parochial chapel. 'Thorney' is likely to be Sir Francis Thornhagh (1593-1643) or his son Sir Francis (1617-48) who held lands nearby at Osberton, Fenton and elsewhere, whilst Anne may have been a daughter in law as the booklet refers to her as 'Mrs'. The warnings issued were well-timed as the nation was engulfed in civil war in 1642, during which the younger Thornhagh died at Chorley in 1648, being later buried at Sturton-le-Steeple.[55] Both Thornhaghs were moderate puritans, who sided with Parliament, with the elder educated at Emmanuel College Cambridge. This also introduces the possibility that the pamphlet is an allegory, providing some hidden commentary on the events of the time.

Also missing from the dialogue of clergy after the Reformation was the appearance of angels, the consensus being that they no longer appeared in visible form. Despite this,

---

55 http://www.nottshistory.org.uk/articles/tts/tts1934/thornhagh1.htm

a pamphlet appeared in 1659 called *The good angel of Stamford, Or an extraordinary cure of an extraordinary consumption, in a true and faithful narrative of Samuel Wallas recovered, by the power of God, and prescription of an angel* [sic]. This purported to tell the tale of a disabled Stamford shoemaker who shared a beer with a passing stranger in a rainstorm and was miraculously restored to health. The stranger was dressed in purple and white – suggesting a non-puritan outlook perhaps – and was unaffected by the rain.

Later in the 1600s some 'prophets' became considerable figures, including Anne Wentworth (1629-1693), a London Baptist believed to have been born in Lincolnshire. Her writings were prompted by a distressing marriage and Hanserd Knollys, the highly regarded Baptist preacher from Lincolnshire, at first supported her but later changed his mind.

CHAPTER EIGHT

The Crisis of Separation
1603-1608

James I arrived in England to be confronted by a list of puritan demands for reform of the Church of England including the abolition of surplices and pluralism. They got nowhere – after the Hampton Court Conference James issued orders for all clergy to 'conform' by 30 November 1604.

Following on from Hampton Court, conservative leaders of the Church amended Canon Law to try to stamp out the practices they did not like – 'fasting, exorcism and spiritual healing seemed to divide puritans and later dissenting groups from the established Church'.[1] By doing this, they accelerated division, stimulated separatism, and ensured conflict.

Yet only a few were ever suspended or deprived, and a mere handful fled to safety in other countries. For the most part, Church leaders focused on a few 'fractious' leaders of dissent and looked the other way for many of the rest – the greater fear remained of Catholicism. This explains why a handful of the regional leaders were 'deprived' and remained so, whereas others maintained a strangely persistent ministry in the Church of England. Separatism and Presbyterianism remained minority interests. In fact, under the leadership of George Abbot, the Church of England became remarkably tolerant of dissent until the later 1620s. Despite this, there emerged two groups of people from Nottinghamshire and Gainsborough who decided to quit England to pursue a purer church in the Netherlands; many of their fellow puritans chose to remain, and for the most part continued to enjoy a degree of freedom. Given the events of the 1590s, formal separation from the Church of England was still seen as a major risk.

Key Events:

October 1602: John Smyth loses post at Lincoln

March 1603: James becomes King of England in addition to Scotland

January 1604: Hampton Court Conference disappoints puritans

April 1604: riot at Marnham involving leading puritans

November 1604: 'Subscription crisis' as conformity enforced

March-April 1605: clergy deprivations in North Nottinghamshire

Spring 1606: John Smyth decides on separation from the Church of England

September 1607: Archbishop Matthew preaches against separatists at Bawtry

Late 1607-early 1608: first escape attempt via Boston

March 1608: Joan Helwys and others in court at York

May 1608: second escape attempt via Stallingborough

---

1   Freeman in Lake and Questier, p.62

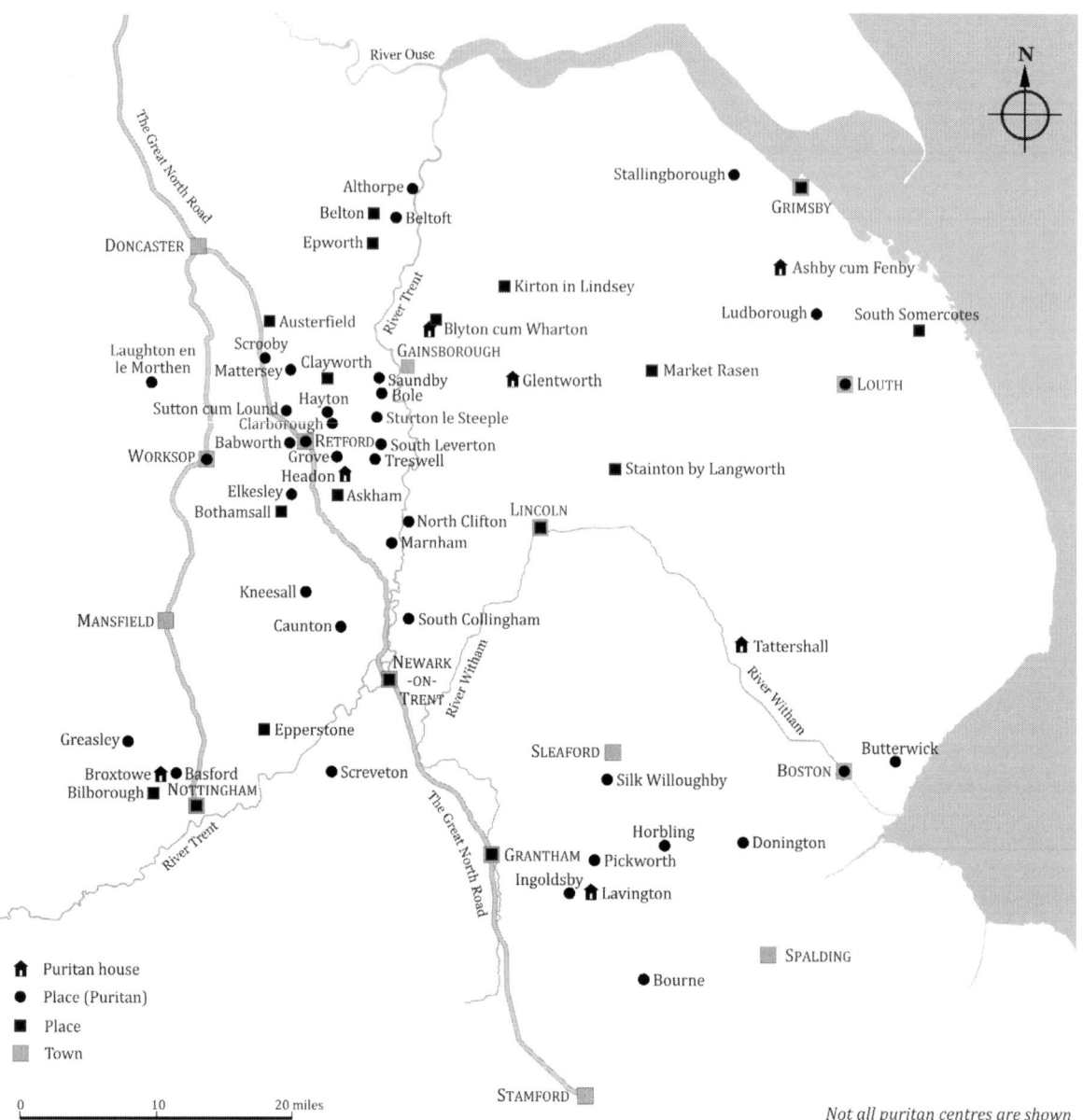

River Ouse

N

The Great North Road

Althorpe

Stallingborough

GRIMSBY

Belton Beltoft

DONCASTER

Epworth

Ashby cum Fenby

River Trent

Kirton in Lindsey

Ludborough South Somercotes

Austerfield

Scrooby Blyton cum Wharton

Laughton en le Morthen

Mattersey Clayworth

GAINSBOROUGH

Market Rasen

LOUTH

Saundby

Glentworth

Sutton cum Lound

Bole

Hayton

Clarborough Sturton le Steeple

WORKSOP

Babworth RETFORD

South Leverton

Grove Treswell

Stainton by Langworth

Headon

Elkesley

Askham

Bothamsall

North Clifton

LINCOLN

Marnham

Kneesall

MANSFIELD

Caunton South Collingham

Tattershall

River Witham

NEWARK -ON- TRENT

River Witham

Greasley

Epperstone

SLEAFORD

Butterwick

Broxtowe Basford

Silk Willoughby

BOSTON

Bilborough NOTTINGHAM

Screveton

Horbling Donington

GRANTHAM Pickworth

River Trent

Ingoldsby Lavington

The Great North Road

SPALDING

Bourne

Puritan house

Place (Puritan)

Place

Town

STAMFORD

0   10   20 miles

Not all puritan centres are shown

198

A Disappointing King

On his way to London, King James was presented with the Millenary Petition by a group of puritan ministers, asking for 'the redress of divers abuses'. In Norwich, John Robinson, a young Nottinghamshire cleric from Sturton-le-Steeple, preached a sermon reflecting his hopes of the new king, 'This is the day which the Lord hath made'. James made no apparent decision but agreed to a conference in 1604.

Supporters of the petition included Sir William Bowes and his wife, Isabel Wray. They were angered by criticism of the petition from Oxford University and Sir William commented on this in a letter to the Earl of Shrewsbury, a near neighbour, in December 1603. Sir William wrote that he had consulted Isabel about the matter because 'she is verie wise, especiallie in thinges of this kind'. Sir William repeated his wife's comments and she added a postscript to the letter, comparing Oxford's *Answer* to the warning to Hezekiah in 2 Kings 18: 19–36. She also prayed that God would give the king a change of heart so that he would support the petition. Shrewsbury was surprised to be given the opinion of a woman and replied to Lady Bowes that 'your indiscrete comparison bewrayes the weaknes of your womanhode, thoughe much disagreeing from the modestie of your sex'. As was customary at the time, he used the example of Eve when seeking to put a woman in what he took to be her correct place, and warned Sir William against listening to his wife's opinion complaining that puritan ministers were stirring up 'simple women'. Isabel, daughter of a chief justice, was far from simple.

So puritan hopes that King James would bring more radical religious views with him from Scotland did not last long – it was the disappointment of Elizabeth over again. Yet there was still the hope of the conference. At the Hampton Court Conference in January 1604, puritan voices were outgunned by an array of conservatives and nonplussed by the king's condemnation of Scottish Presbyterianism. The puritans clearly had some discussion on who would speak for them, with the first proposal including Walter Travers, and possibly John Ireton of Kegworth and Arthur Hildersham, but in the event none of these took part. Four moderate and ineffective men were chosen to represent the puritan voice one of whom, Thomas Sparke, said nothing. Sparke we have met before at the ineffective conference of 1584; he had been Archdeacon of Stow and was Lincolnshire born, but disgraced himself in the eyes of the reformers – he arrived wearing robes 'such that Turkey merchants wear,' then 'spake verie sparingly', abandoning his position as a spokesman for the reformers in a private audience with James and repudiating the name of 'puritan' as 'odious'! John Rainolds, another puritan spokesman, had been nominally Dean of Lincoln in the 1590s but was more focused on his Oxford career; he led most of the puritan argument, prompting James to suspect Presbyterianism and to leave the room shouting, 'No bishop, no king'.

Others who were involved included Gervase Babington (1549/50-1610), usually cited as having been born in Nottinghamshire,[2] who was Bishop of Worcester at this time having previously held the sees of Llandaff and Exeter. Babington was a career Churchman but also a strongly committed Calvinist, and he occasionally stood this ground against

---

2   The Babington family had land in Leicestershire, Derbyshire and increasingly in Nottinghamshire. His most likely birthplace was Kingston on Soar.

Whitgift (whose funeral sermon he preached) and later Bancroft. James Montagu, Sir William Wray's brother-in-law, attended as Dean of Lichfield.

The puritans won some minor battles but lost the war. James stopped the practice of private baptism by women, for example. Arguably the greatest legacy of the conference was the King James Bible.

The defeat of the puritans was underlined when Whitgift died in 1604 and was replaced as archbishop by Richard Bancroft, who succeeded in imposing a new array of canon laws which securely established ritual, vestments and the *Book of Common Prayer*, backed by the promise of sanctions for the nonconformists. But by this time puritanism was soundly established and many were not to be cowed, even by threats of removal from well-paid benefices. Those who felt unable to conform now faced a choice. Clergy were told they had to conform to the *Prayer Book* by the end of November 1604, amidst other canon law requirements: in the archdeaconries of Stow and Lincoln alone, 194 parishes reported they did not have a Prayer Book whilst in 28 churchwardens reported their minister for not wearing a surplice – and in 13 *they* were in trouble for *not* reporting their clergyman for this.[3] 746 ministers of the Lincoln diocese put their names to a protest against Bancroft's actions,[4] probably led and delivered by Robert Atkinson[5] who was safely established in the puritan stronghold at Glentworth, where he was vicar 1600-26, complaining that the Church 'has been dangerously corrupted, and sundry Popish errors broached'. Atkinson, who had previously been vicar of Blyton (another Wray living), was cited for nonconformity in 1604 and excommunicated until he swore to obey the law; he was a lecturer at Market Rasen in 1614 (part of the Wray-St Paul influence) and at Lincoln in 1615 – evidence of renewed strength of the puritans there. However, many bowed the knee – South Witham, Hareby, Withcall, Quarrington and Sibsey all soon managed to have a surplice.[6] At Ludborough the churchwardens pretended that the questions were so many and so hard that they could not answer them and did not understand what the 'Cannons' [sic] were, until threatened with excommunication when they revealed their minister, David Allen, to be a nonconformist who did not use the sign of the cross.

The caution the King showed was wise as he risked conflict with a changing Church landscape: the proportion of university-educated clergy had rapidly increased – from 33% to 80% between 1603 and 1610 alone in Lincolnshire.[7] That this did not result in huge numbers of deprivations after 1604 was because the policy was clearly was not rigidly enforced – it was of 'sporadic enforcement and enticing moderates to subscribe'.[8] This can be coupled with a less frenetic atmosphere after the death of Bancroft in 1610 and a King who, after recovering from the Gunpowder shock in 1605, was reluctant to persecute his enemy's enemies systematically; in 1614 he declared that 'no state can

3   Babbage (1962), p.342, p.349. The slack churchwardens included Bolingbroke, Hagworthingham, Fulletby, Dunstry, Edlington, S Ormsby.
4   Collinson, *Elizabethan Puritan Movement*, p.464
5   Atkinson was a graduate of Queens' but there is a twenty-year gap in his ministry before he began a series of Lincolnshire cures until Glentworth from 1601.
6   Babbage (1962), p.342
7   H Hajzyk, p.173
8   V J Gregory, *Congregational Puritanism 1585-1625*, unpublished PhD, Cambridge, 2003

evidence that any religion or heresy was ever extirpated by the sword or by violence, not have I ever judged it a way of planting the truth'. However, he did have Thomas Helwys, the Nottinghamshire Baptist pioneer, in prison at the time he framed these words.

There were numbers of entrenched radical clergy in both counties. In Lincolnshire many of them signed the petition to James I and the leaders appear to have been David Allen (Ludborough), Robert Atkinson (Glentworth), Simon Bradstreet (Horbling), Hugh Tuke (Silk Willoughby), John Jackson (Bourne), Charles Richardson (East Barkwith) and John Fisher (Ingoldsby). Also included was Edmund Lynold (Lynold) – who was deprived at Healing as late as 1637. Sir William Wray delivered a supporting petition from Lincolnshire gentry.[9] News that 'the silenced ministers of Lincolnshire exhibited a petition to the Parliament' was heard as far away as Devon.[10] Many of these flirted with deprivation through nonconformity for years, protected by gentry such as Sir William Wray and Sir William Armyne.[11] All six livings controlled by the puritan Sir George St Paul had clerics who refused to conform although two were also noted for neglecting their parishes![12] To these we can add the thirteen advowsons held by the Bertie-Willoughby family and another twelve by the Clintons to understand the depth of puritanism in Lincolnshire. John Smyth referred to Wray, saying that 'a multitude of faithful ministers' had 'rested under his shadow' – although not everyone he appointed was equally 'godly'. Sir William Armyne presented to Silk Willoughby, Lenton (Lincs) and Pickworth – where the spectacular medieval wall paintings have now been famously recovered from their puritan whitewash. One of the later Armyne clerics, Seth Wood, succeeded his father Tempest Wood at Lavington and commented of his generation of Armyne that 'he was to such good men as lived under his wing and protection a shadow from the heat and a refuge from the storme of that persecution which scorched others very sore' – although it may have helped that Lady Mary Armyne had good links with Bishop Williams.[13]

Of course, many were far from radical. Thomas Westfield, at South Somercotes from 1600-5, was a chaplain to the 1st Earl of Warwick – a noted puritan as discussed later – but developed into a Laudian and became a royalist bishop of Bristol. He was an emotive preacher and became known as the 'weeping prophet' on account of his emotive delivery. Certainly, some did eventually conform under pressure – the incumbents of Healing, Saltfleetby St Peter and East Barkwith being examples.[14] For many though the issues were around where they drew the line on what was 'indifferent' or a matter of principle – for some it was women doing baptisms, for others it was the clerical cap or kneeling at communion. There were also many career clergy like Richard Gymney, rural dean of Newark, who was dismissed from this post in 1606 for exceeding his authority; he had risen on the coattails of the infamous John Lowth from about 1576.

9   V J Gregory, p.213

10   Seaver, p,61

11   The Armyne family seat was at Osgodby Manor near Lenton (Kesteven) – not to be confused with the village of Osgodby in Lindsey. The house was demolished in 1947 but there is a family memorial in the church.

12   Hajzyk (p.322) says Bassingham, Faldingworth, Legsby, Swallow and West Torrington with Swallow and Snelland the 'neglected' parishes.

13   Cliffe (1984), p.185

14   Lesley Rowe, *The Worlds of Arthur Hildersham*, unpublished Warwick PhD, 2009.

Bishop William Chaderton[15] in Lincoln was hesitant to deprive 'nonconformist' ministers of their livings,[16] tending to focus more on the 'extremists' like John Smyth.[17] During the 1601 visitation only one Lincolnshire cleric was cited for not wearing the surplice, but by 1604-5 this had increased to 45 whilst 61 ministers in Lincolnshire were rebuked for not conforming with the *Book of Common Prayer* – but it is a measure of the system that only two were ever deprived.[18] In October 1604 George Eland[19] preached a sermon in Lincoln Cathedral in favour of conformity that puritans considered 'very dangerous and heretical'. The same month, Chaderton cited 93 to appear at St Benedict's in Lincoln to answer charges.[20] Puritans were good at the use of delay – the vicar of Calceby tried to win time by protesting that his surplice was not 'comely' enough.

With so many poor livings, Lincoln was a challenging diocese for finding good parish clergy. Any bishop who chased out all the puritans would then create another problem for himself. Around thirty signed a petition in November 1604 against subscribing to the *Prayer Book*[21] and in December 1604 Chaderton summoned about the same number of nonconformist clerics to Huntingdon but did not proceed to deprivation. Chaderton had many clergy who were very poor and some drunkards, but there were unsung heroes such as John Maltby at Grainthorpe who gave much from the little that he had and 'is in our towne and countrye very well beloved'.[22] Refusing to wear surplices was so common that Thomas Wooll the vicar of Boston offered to sit on his as a cushion and deemed it a 'popish rag'. Men like Edmund Newton of Sleaford, in 1604, were allowed to make 'intermediate obedience' by agreeing to wear a surplice though refusing to subscribe to the articles whilst in 1605 John Jackson of Bourne also slipped through this way.[23] Another trick was for the curate to wear a surplice, but the vicar or rector not to.

By January 1605 King James was annoyed that Chaderton had made little progress but in February 1605 Alexander Cooke of Louth was deprived – it being reported that he would 'rather lose his living than wear [the surplice]'.[24] Cooke then petitioned the King to let him stay in his vicarage until August. He went to Yorkshire and in 1617 resurfaced as vicar of Leeds as successor to his brother without appearing to have changed his principles.[25]

---

15 Chaderton's grand-daughter Elizabeth Jocelin became famous for *The Mother's Legacy to her Unborn Child*, which she wrote in anticipation of her death from childbirth – which indeed occurred. She was largely brought up by the bishop's household.
16 T D I Escrick, *Messenger, Apologist and Non-Conformist*, p.35
17 Hajzyk, p.53
18 S Davies, *Quakerism in Lincolnshire*, Lincoln, 1989, p.2. Hajzyk, p.55
19 A relative of Chaderton's, who became Chancellor and enriched himself with multiple livings. When he preached again at Lincoln in 1629, one man said, 'he would rather heare a ewe of his owne lowe'. (Hajzyk, p.157)
20 Babbage (1962), p.163
21 Babbage (1962) p. 126 says the leader of this was John Burgess, whose details are unclear, but was perhaps Rector of Waddesdon in Herts.
22 In Holmes (1980) p.61
23 Hajzyk, p.56
24 Babbage (1962), p.164
25 R A Marchant, *The Church under the Law*, Cambridge, 1969, p.133. Cooke's brother was vicar of Leeds and so he went to live there, becoming vicar in his own right in 1615 on Archbishop Matthew's presentation, despite twice refusing to subscribe. In 1610 he had published a notable book on the story of Pope 'Joan' and another in 1625. Archbishop Matthew pushed his appointment through against local opposition (in favour of Prince Charles's chaplain) and despite Cooke's refusal to wear a surplice or subscribe. In 1622 he was still causing problems for criticising bishops and the confirmation ceremony.

In February George Pike of Donington was deprived, though he seems to have been soon re-instated in May and on promising to conform and survived until his death five years later;[26] he was then replaced by William Symonds, a nonconformist lecturer from Christ Church, Newgate Street. In 1605 there were 31 Lincolnshire cases heard but few made a principled fight of it and Chaderton removed only eight[27] though there was clearly some intention to be tolerant. Others were made of sterner stuff, such as Simon Bradstreet[28] at Horbling, in trouble in 1604 for not wearing a surplice, which he had never done since instituted in 1595; in 1605 he excused himself from attendance for a 'special infirmity' and he was not conforming in 1607 and still not in 1611 – nor up until the time he died in 1621. John Jackson at Bourne was another who pleaded for time, claimed to be ill in 1605, and surviving until being suspended in 1611; he died in 1615. David Allen, the recalcitrant incumbent of Ludborough, also found excuses not to attend in 1605 and lived until 1615. Robert Atkinson – safely positioned at Glentworth – carried on as before. At Ingoldsby, there was John Fisher, another surplice prevaricator. Brian Burton of Langton by Partney was in trouble in 1607 but survived until death in 1612. But Chaderton also had to manage the new recruits – William Bourne of St John's College was initially refused ordination as he would not subscribe to the Three Articles.[29]

The Formation of a Separatist Movement: 1603-1605

As we have seen and shall continue to see, many of these nonconformists had no intention of leaving the Church of England; like Brian Barton at South Collingham they battled it out for years. So, from where did the impetus to separate and flee to the Netherlands come from? The American historians have tended for good reason to concentrate on those who made it across the Atlantic and led the new colony – Brewster and Bradford in particular – but the key figures in the movement as a whole were John Smyth (c.1570-1612) as arguably the prime mover, Richard Clifton, John Robinson and Thomas Helwys – none of whom ever reached America. These were the spiritual leaders. One historian thinks that John Smyth was '(perhaps *the*) principal leader...'[30] which as we shall see seems to be supported by the evidence.

First, we also need to be clear that 'separatism' was not invented in our region. There were congregations in Bocking, Essex, and Faversham, Kent, fifty years or more before those at Scrooby and Gainsborough, and these also rejected predestination as Smyth and Helwys later did.[31] We have also noted Katherine Willoughby's associations in London.

26 CCED database, accessed 26 August 2018. Usher, Roland G. "The Deprivation of Puritan Ministers in 1605." *The English Historical Review*, vol. 24, no. 94, 1909, pp. 232–246. *JSTOR*, www.jstor.org/stable/549652.

27 Holmes (1980), p.93. Hajzyk argues that only two were deprived (p.55) whilst Usher only one – Burgess, probably John Burges of Waddesdon who resurfaced as a prebendary of Lichfield.

28 He was the father of the more famous Bradstreet, discussed below. In July 1605 Bradstreet wrote to his bishop to 'give me leave and leisure to go somewhat slowly that I may go the more surely. I have and do still desire and endeavour the Lord his good direction for the good of his Church and the lawful contentment of my superiors'. (Babbage, p.220)

29 Hajzyk, p.48

30 J R Coggins, *John Smyth's Congregation*, Herald Press, Ontario, 1991, p.16

31 T George (1982), p.10

What is clear is that the movement for separatism grew out of an impressive concentration of puritan clergy in north Nottinghamshire – those who either worked or were born there. If we attempt to list, not even exhaustively, some clergy just from a few miles around Retford we see a remarkable concentration:

- Richard Bernard at Worksop
- Richard Clyfton at Marnham and Babworth
- James Collie at Worksop
- Roger Edwards, Marnham
- Thomas Hancock at Scrooby, West Retford and Headon
- Robert Lilley at Babworth
- John Nayler, North Clifton
- Robert Southworth at Headon and also as curate at Grove
- James Brewster at Sutton-cum-Lound
- Hugh Bromhead at North Wheatley and Bole
- Henry Gray at Bawtry and Headon
- Nicholas Watkins at Clarborough
- John Smyth, born at Sturton, at Lincoln, North/South Clifton and Gainsborough
- John Robinson, born at Sturton
- Robert Gifford, at Laughton (Worksop)
- Francis Chapman, at West Markham
- Richard Rothwell, preacher at Mansfield
- Ezekial Burton, curate at Sutton-in-Ashfield and then Sutton-cum-Lound
- Brian Barton, South Collingham
- John Viccars, born at Treswell
- Robert Hargreaves, Marnham, N Collingham and Kneesall
- Luke Bacon, Kneesall and Caunton (unofficial)
- George Turvin at East Retford and Babworth, though latterly conforming
- Thomas Toller, perhaps from Sutton-cum-Lound, at Hayton and later of Sheffield
- John Wasteneys at West Burton
- Edward Hodgson, East Retford
- William Pettinger, Mattersey
- Nicholas Pettinger, West Retford
- Francis Denman, West Retford
- Alexander Smith at Elkesley
- William Snape, curate of Sutton-in-Ashfield, 1615-20

As well as individual puritan ministers, there were clearly puritan parishes. Marnham had Richard Clifton briefly as its priest in the 1580s but in 1608 had Roger Edwards, clerk, preaching there without a licence – a man who also preached at South Leverton (where the wardens – regular offenders – claimed not to know about his licence) and Treswell in 1613. By 1619 Marnham also had Robert Hargreaves, also without a licence, who was cited for not using the sign of the cross in baptism, not using a ring in a wedding, nor wearing a surplice.[32] Yet by 1621 Hargreaves had been ordained priest and the following year was vicar of Kneesall.[33] Hargreaves and Ash the vicar of Marnham, were cited for holding 'private religious exercises' at Ash's vicarage. Many of these villages had Retford

32   Marchant, p.183
33   According to Marchant, but not found in Clergy Database.

as their market town and it was 'a notably Protestant community' where cases of non-attendance at church increased significantly between the 1590s and 1610.[34]

The Key Players: John Smyth (c1570-1612)

John Smyth perhaps plays the leading role in this drama and is justifiably famous as the pioneer of the English Baptist denomination. He is thought to be the fourth son of John Smyth from Sturton-le-Steeple, intriguingly the same origins as the martyr John Lassells and John Robinson.[35] Whitley reported that he was 'a Sturton lad from the Habblesthorpe district of his uncle Thomas' where the Helwys family also held land.[36] Why did two such key figures originate from one village? The vicar was John Quippe, said to have been an unlikely figure to be their inspiration, who was apparently at odds with the latest of the Lassells family, another George – in 1594 they even came to blows.[37] The Lassells family, fifty years after the martyrdom of John, do not seem likely to have been Willoughby-style patrons of godly men: in 1605, John Robinson's father was dragged into a case where Lassells was accused of buying sex from a woman. Quippe though seems to have influenced a generation of clergy at least two of whom proved to be of rebellious puritan inclinations; given that we know there was a school here in 1601 it may be that Quippe had educated both boys in godly principles.[38]

A focal point in the story is Cambridge from where many returned with progressive and radical views. This was part of a tradition stretching back more than a hundred years and had included Robert Browne, the Stamford man who set a pattern by escaping to the Netherlands in 1578 to avoid trouble; Smyth and the later separatists always hated the nickname of 'Brownist' which William Bradford said was 'akin to calling the disciples Judasitts'.[39] At Cambridge from 1586, Smyth was influenced by his tutor Francis Johnson, a leading influence in Christ's College, who later became an early 'separatist' and formed a puritan community in the Netherlands. We cannot be certain whether Smyth went to Christ's College *because* Johnson was there, or if he became a puritan as a consequence; it had been a puritan college since the 1560s producing graduates such as Arthur Hildersham in 1586 who became one of the leading nonconformists in the East Midlands. While Smyth was at Christ's, Richard Bernard also came up from Epworth and became Smyth's sizar[40] – remaining one of his close associates for several years. Smyth was ordained in 1594 by the Bishop of Lincoln, William Wickham, and became a fellow of his college. In 1597 Smyth objected to the burial service, the churching of women and the surplice but in any event lost his fellowship at Christ's when he married in 1598.[41]

---

34 David Marcombe, *English Small Town Strife*, in Holland (2004) p.44-5
35 S Wright, *The Early English Baptists*, Woodbridge, 2006, p.13
36 W T Whitley, *Thomas Helwys....*, London, 1935. *Miscellanea Genealogica Et Heraldica* vol. 4, p.133. Kreitzer has found evidence of a Smyth who worked for a Helwys there. The 1538 record of musters has five Smyths at Sturton.
37 N Bunker, *Make Haste from Babylon*, London, 2011, p.121
38 It has been argued that Robinson attended grammar school in Gainsborough; no evidence for this has yet surfaced and the assumption seems based on the lack of any other secondary school in the area in the 1900s.
39 William Bradford, *Dialogues*
40 A sizar was an undergraduate who financed his education by taking on some basic jobs, such as a servant to an older student or fellow
41 Burgess, *Smyth, Helwys and the First Baptist Church*, p.47

This apparent meeting of Smyth and Bernard at Christ's is interesting, especially as the latter became sizar to the former. Bernard's education was funded by Frances Wray and Sir George St Paul her husband; thirty years later Bernard recalled this when writing 'for whoever tasted more deeply than my self of the charitable liberality, and singular bounty of that right honourable lady, the lady Francis, Countess of Warwick Dowager, lately deceased, who first sent me into and planted me in the University'. That Smyth also referred to Sir William Wray, her brother, as his 'patron', the same man that soon employed Bernard as tutor to his children, makes this circumstance seem far from coincidental. But, intriguingly, Bernard's dedication also referenced James Montagu who, as Bishop of Bath and Wells, was credited by Bernard with helping his later move to Somerset having known him at Cambridge. Montagu had been a student and then a Fellow at Christ's in 1585-95 – but was also Sir William's brother-in-law through his marriage to Lucy Montagu in 1580. The Montagus were a prominent Northamptonshire puritan family and James's aunt Elizabeth had married William Markham, the son of Sir John Markham Cranmer's friend. So, both men were intimately connected with both Lincolnshire and Nottinghamshire puritanism.

We do not know for certain what Smyth did between then and 1600. There is a presentment record of a schoolteacher at Sturton in 1601, named John Smyth MA. There is a fair chance this was Smyth, but it would hardly have been the sort of post he wanted. Could he have held this role and his certain role in Lincoln? Possibly: it was a ferry crossing and a few hours ride to Lincoln from his home village.

As a puritan on the radical wing, Smyth became the well-paid lecturer in Lincoln,[42] based at the corporation church of St Peter at Arches, on 27 September 1600 but his religiously radical views were always likely to cause problems in the divided city. Hajzyk records that Smyth was the choice of Sir William Wray who wanted to strengthen puritanism in the city[43] although he was elected narrowly 8-7 by the council.[44] The puritans had managed to gain control of the council and ousted the previous lecturer by including rules that he had to live in the city and not hold a benefice;[45] Smyth arrived into a tense situation. This post was funded by the corporation to provide more frequent preaching. He was already developing the popular view that the reformation of the Church of England had been incomplete and needed to go further, but some of his preaching was personally critical of others in the city.

Life does not seem to have been easy for Smyth in Lincoln and the naming of a daughter in January 1602 Mara – 'bitter' – may have reflected his mood; she was baptised at St Peter at Gowt's.[46] It seems his preaching across Lincoln exceeded his authority[47] and some city luminaries felt personally attacked by his sermons. A split council elected a mayor from the rival faction who complained to Archbishop Whitgift and Smyth lost his licence to preach. In Hajzyk's analysis, Smyth came up against a group of 'Church

---

42 W T Whitley, The Works of John Smyth, p.xli – a salary of £40 a year
43 Hajzyk, p.424
44 Hill, p.110
45 P S Seaver, The Puritan Lectureships, Stanford, 1970, p.95
46 J D Bangs mentions a reference to a John Smyth as a schoolteacher in Sturton in 1601; it is possible that the same John Smyth held both posts, or it provides a clue as to the background of Smyth.
47 White (1971), p.119

Catholics' such as Leonard Hollingworth who he criticised – but in 1602 they gained control of the mayoralty.

Matters came to a head on 13 October 1602 and Smyth lost his post in Lincoln having never regained his licence. He was condemned for being a 'factious man in this city by personal preaching and that untruly against divers men of good place'.[48] Puritan behaviour was widely tolerated, but preaching *against* people often caused trouble. An arbitration panel of Sir William Wray and Edward King, on one side, and Lawrence Stanton – the Dean – and Sir Philip Tyrwhitt on the other failed to resolve the issue. Lord Edmund Sheffield who, despite having married a Catholic, was a puritan sympathiser, resolved the issue by awarding Smyth £50; his rivals then appointed Thomas Luddington to the post on £30 a year. Smyth later said he was happy with the compensation he eventually received.[49] Smyth dedicated his second book to Sheffield in 1605.

In spring 1602 Smyth preached without licence at West Burton (where Robinson also preached) and in 1603 at North Clifton with the permission of its puritan vicar; Smyth may still have been teaching at Sturton – and it was conveniently close by ferry to Marnham, another centre of puritan influence where he became involved. He was charged with unlicensed preaching by Bishop Chaderton in December 1602. Somehow in March that year Smyth secured a licence, under 'false pretences', from the unlikely source of Archbishop Whitgift, to preach throughout the province of Canterbury, but the Bishop of Lincoln – with better personal knowledge – objected[50] and the licence was revoked in September 1603. In between he was noted as acting as a 'painful preacher of God's word' at North Clifton.

In 1603 he published *The Bright Morning Starre*, his four Lincoln sermons based on Psalm 22, dedicated to Sir William Wray who had attempted to help him during the dispute in Lincoln, and perhaps more often. Wray was 'my approved good friend and benefactor' and 'a principal professor and protector of religion in these quarters (for what a multitude of faithful ministers are debtors to your flesh)…'.[51] On 18 April 1604 Smyth appeared at sessions in Newark for being part of a 'riot' that was linked to a dispute over the induction of Smyth's friend John Herring to the nearby living of Marnham after Henry Aldred had been deprived in January 1604[52]; this was a short ferry boat trip from North and South Clifton where Smyth was said to be 'clerk'. Charges against Aldred included assault and imprisonment. Numerous persons, mainly clergy, were involved and Smyth stood surety of £10 for Herring; Herring left Marnham and was inducted at Basford in March 1605. Also involved in the dispute was a Newark curate, Godfrey (or Geoffrey) Pye and Richard Jackson, who – as Smyth did – preached illegally at Greasley. Then on 5 October 1604 Smyth, Herring, Jackson, Godfrey Pye, Henry Bannister and eight others were charged with 'riot and rout', perhaps over the same or a similar case.[53]

---

48 Champlain Burrage, *The Early English Dissenters in the Light of Recent Research*, Cambridge, 1912, p.227

49 Watts (1986), p.73. Edward Reyner, another Wray cleric, became city preacher in 1627.

50 S Greasley, p.30

51 John Smythe, *A Bright Morning Starre*, 1603, p.1

52 One might infer from this that Aldred was a nonconformist, but he was clearly opposed by the local puritans at a church which was traditionally nonconformist. He had been recommended for the living in 1595 by Topcliffe, the torturer.

53 Marchant p.150 and ODNB. Stephen Wright, *British Baptists and Politics 1603-49*, unpublished PhD, King's College, p.50-6. Wright (2006), p.14-15

We have seen that in 1603 Smyth was probably schoolmaster at North Clifton,[54] noted by the churchwardens as both their curate and schoolmaster as 'a painfull preacher'; this was a living held from 1588 by John Nayler, who in 1614 was cited for not using the *Prayer Book*.[55] He then left this place, perhaps as a result of the troubles at Marnham.

Smyth was presumably living at Gainsborough as a daughter was baptised there in March 1604 and on 23 August he was accused of preaching in the town without a licence.[56] The defence given was that he did so on request as the vicar, Jerome Phillips, who was absent; interestingly, within two years Sir Gervase Helwys gave Phillips the lucrative post at Saundby. Late that year Smyth discussed the new canon law requirements with Richard Bernard and others, hesitating for nine months or so over them.[57] For a time, he supported himself working as a physician and seems to have often been in Nottinghamshire visiting Thomas Helwys; they perhaps met through Helwys's connections with Lady Isabel Bowes (Wray).

Smyth– albeit fractious – must have at this time still been resolved to stay within the Church of England. In this context it is interesting that other local puritans like Clifton and Bernard lost their livings in March 1605, as also did Robert Southworth of Headon (who was presented more than anyone else in Nottinghamshire) and Henry Gray of Bawtry.[58] Smyth's second book, *The Patterne of True Prayer*, dedicated in March 1605 to Lord Sheffield of West Butterwick who had supported him during the dispute in Lincoln, was conciliatory on the use of set prayers as in the Prayer Book (Smyth had been accused of being against this), but March 1605 probably marks the time when separation began.[59] He hoped it would help in the 'clearing of myself from unjust accusations'. In it, he noted that 'persecution is a great discouragement to a minister, and it driveth many a godly man to his dumps'. He specifically referred to 'faithfull ministers' being attacked by malicious men and hoped they would be preserved from 'tyrants and wicked men'. Quite a provocative text for the time!

By March 1606 he was again, or still, suspended from preaching and on 2 March preached despite this at Gainsborough, so that a letter had to be sent on his behalf on 3 March which referred to 'your former favour in sparing to suspend him'. Now suspension seemed inevitable!

The Key Players: Richard Bernard (1568-1642)

Richard Bernard, an Epworth man of relatively humble origins who played a key part of this drama whilst at Worksop, had 'preached widely against false religion' in west

---

54 Marchant, p.156
55 Marchant, p.181
56 White (1971), p.120
57 Coggins (1991), p.32
58 Marchant, p.149. Gray was likely a 'placing' by William Brewster in a place where he had some influence. In 1606 Gray was prosecuted for 'pretending' to be curate at Headon but in 1607 he became a diocesan preacher and moved away from the separatists. Goodall (2017) notes that he was still curate at Headon in 1614.
59 Richard Bernard, in 1608, used this book to explain that Smyth had once attacked separatism. See White (1971), p.118

Lindsey, perhaps while acting as tutor to the Wray children; his first publication (a translation of Terence) was dedicated to Sir William Wray's sons who were 'nephews to the virtuous and true religious ladies' Lady Bowes and Lady 'Saintpoll' who were 'his very bountifull patronesses'. He and John Smyth are the most evident beneficiaries of the Wray family, who funded his university education at Christ's in Cambridge, where he was sizar to the slightly older John Smyth; the presence of these two together is most interesting for Smyth also refers to Wray as his 'patron' but never specified precisely how this was so.

Bernard reflected on the influence of the Wray family on his life from the perspective of 1635, when dedicating *The Ready way to Good Works* to Sir John Wray, William's son:

> For who ever tasted more deeply than my self of the charitable liberality, and singular bounty of that right honourable lady, the lady Francis, Countess of Warwick Dowager, lately deceased, who first sent me into and planted me in the University. How bountiful likewise was the hand of that noble lady Isabell, the Lady Darcy, to many, and to me in particular, while my abode was in those parts, with my loving parishioners at Workesop. I cannot but commemorate so transcendent goodness of these your right honourable Ants to you, so noble minded friends towards me, imitating therein your Worthy Father, and your blessed Mother, Sister to that my honourable good Lord, the Right Reverend Father in God, James the Lord Bishop of Winchester.

His preaching in West Lindsey on the text 'O King we will not serve thy gods, nor worship the golden image which thou hast set up' (Dan 3, 16-18) would have been controversial. Perhaps this was what Chaderton was thinking of when he complained at the end of 1604 about the 'knights' of Lincolnshire petitioning on behalf of those 'not conformable' so that there was a risk that 'neither will any of the ministers conform themselves, neither shall we have any peace in our churches'.[60] This comment might equally have applied in some districts west of the Trent.

Bernard had clearly left a recalcitrant puritan group around Epworth. Two members of the Glew family were presented for nonconformity, including going to Althorpe church and in 1604 six from Belton were excommunicated for their offences.[61] One of those in trouble was Thomas Bernard – perhaps a relation. Robert Broughton of Beltoft seems to have been the 'elder' of this group which was happier when they had Henry Langley as their perpetual curate from 1606 to about 1610 so that none of the group were presented in 1607. Thomas Granger, of Butterwick and Horbling, also came from Epworth.

Richard Bernard was presented to the living of Worksop in 1601 by Richard Whalley, one of the influential Nottinghamshire puritan family. He moved into the old priory gatehouse, which was for a short time the vicarage, providing a place to lodge his growing family. Bernard certainly had the best set of children's names, though the evidence suggests he lost impetus as his family expanded: Bengallevel, Cannanuel, Besekiell, Hoseel, Masakiell, Mary, and Benjamin. Of these Mary has achieved the greatest fame, helping to form the

---

60   Babbage (1962), p.129, quoting from Cecil MSS.
61   Joy Lloyd, p.191-5

state of Rhode Island by founding Providence with her husband Roger Williams.

Richard Bernard was deprived on 9 April 1605. It seems likely that he went to Gainsborough for a while as he mentions serving a congregation there in one of his book dedications but ultimately Archbishop Tobie Matthew persuaded him back into the Church in 1607 – though he was never a conformist.

Although Bernard's time out of favour was to prove a short one, he was a man with a large family. This perhaps explains his comment, written from Somerset in 1634, that 'how bountiful likewise was the hand of that noble lady Isabell, the Lady Darcy, to many, and to me in particular, while my abode was in those parts, with my loving parishioners at Worksop'.[62] After Worksop he moved to Somerset, arranged no doubt by his patron Sir William Wray's brother-in-law James Montagu who was Bishop of Bath and Wells.

Bernard was one of many radicals from Epworth. A generation or more had established what we now might see as a puritan outlook in many areas such as south Axholme. Henry Langley, perhaps another Christ's College man, enjoyed the support of Sir John Stanhope of Melwood Park – who left him a legacy in about 1627. Langley moved to Belton in 1606 and then Treswell in 1610 but Robert Coakes of West Butterwick still asked for Langley at his funeral in 1620. Robert Broughton of Beltoft was another of puritan mindset whose list of requests in his will of 1604 included there should be 'no jangling of bells and such like' at his funeral and that he should be buried outside of the church and 'rather on the northe syde'.[63] His wife was not to lend any of his books to 'Papists'.

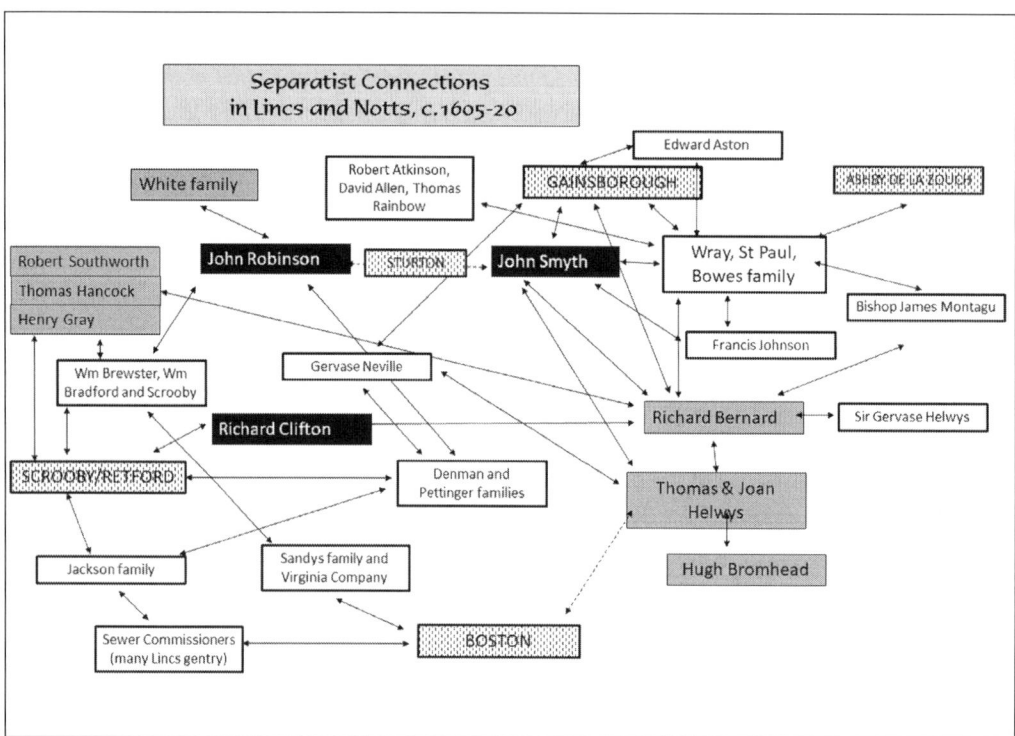

---

62   Dedication in his book *The Ready Way to Good Works*, published in 1635.
63   Joy Lloyd, *The Communities of the manor of Epworth in the Seventeenth-Century,* Sheffield PhD, 1998, p.191. He also made a bequest to Richard Bernard.

The Key Players: Thomas Helwys (1575-c1618)

One of Smyth's contacts was Thomas Helwys,[64] from a family associated with Askham near Retford. One of the family, John Helwys, had been something of a well-connected pluralist with various livings at East Retford in 1497, Ordsall, Hayton and Headon (both vicar and rector for a time from 1503).[65] The Helwys[66] family were prominent in Nottinghamshire with a mixed record on the national stage. One of them was probably the Edward Hellwis who wrote a celebration of Queen Elizabeth, *A Marvell, Deciphered*, in 1589. They also had connections in Lincolnshire, at Worlaby and Gainsborough, where some of the family were baptised. Thomas's cousin Sir Gervase Helwys (1561-1615) was baptised in Askham, near Retford,[67] in 1561, and his uncle Geoffrey (1541-1616) became Sheriff of the City of London in 1610. Gervase seems to have lived in Gainsborough or at nearby Saundby from 1595 into the early 1600s but is also described as 'of Worlaby'; in 1605 he was able to appoint George Turvin as Clyfton's replacement at Babworth (Turvin had been presented five times), in 1606 he appointed Jerome Phillips (previously vicar of Gainsborough) to Saundby, and in 1613 Gervase himself was appointed Lieutenant of the Tower where he became implicated in the death of Sir Thomas Overbury, for which he was hung on Tower Hill in 1615. His death achieved great attention for he died repentant and expressing confidence in his salvation. In 1618 Phillips added the living of Althorpe, which also had a puritan tradition, and published a sermon called *The Fisherman* in 1623, which records that it was preached at a synod at Southwell.

Achieving some wealth, Thomas's father Edmund leased Broxtowe Hall near Nottingham from about 1585. Thomas was therefore probably born at Askham.[68] Edmund, clearly a godly man as demonstrated in his will, died in 1590. In 1591 Thomas and his sister Anne were involved in a legal battle over this will, which was generous to Anne in providing for her to live at Broxtowe Hall. Then from 1592 he was involved in another protracted legal battle over leasing some of the Broxtowe property, in which he was alleged to have tried to transfer some of it to his housekeeper Joan Ashmore[69] perhaps under her 'evil counsel and persuasion'.[70] Thomas was sent to Gray's Inn to study in January 1593 (he may already have been in London) and returned to Nottinghamshire the following year, where he married Joan Ashmore his housekeeper in 1595[71] at Bilborough church.

---

64 One problem here is the spelling of the name and its pronunciation. He was admitted to Gray's Inn as Elwes, recently the normal version of the family name.

65 http://www.nottshistory.org.uk/articles/villagepacks/broxtowehall.htm, 15 Nov 2014. John Helwys was buried in East Retford in 1511.

66 There are many different spellings – Elwes being a common variant.

67 The Helwys family holdings included Saundby, Notts – close to Gainsborough and Sturton. There is a tomb to John Helwys, his father, at Saundby and made from local alabaster. Sir Gervase Helwys, sometimes spelt Elwes, married Elizabeth Tyrwhitt, daughter of Edward Tyrwhitt of Stainfield, whilst her mother was born Faith St Paul, daughter of Sir Thomas St Paul..

68 F C Atton, 1962. Some sources say Broxtowe, but it was not leased in 1575.

69 L Kreitzer (2019), p.54

70 Kreitzer (2019), p.59

71 His marriage ceremony appears to have been unusual for the time and there were later accusations in 1596, 1598 and 1613, that he was not properly married and a fornicator. Larry Kreitzer has shown that this relationship was attracting negative comment in 1592 when Joan may still have been a child (and Thomas barely 17) – at least in law. He also has shown that the marriage register for Bilborough records them as marrying in Dec 1595 yet the churchwardens presented them for suspicion of fornication as not known to be married in 1596 and 1598. Perhaps they were married at the Broxtowe chapel rather than the parish church, or even at the Hall; marriages were not always public occasions at that time. Ashmore was probably related to the Basford miller Henry Ashmore who was cited in 1598 for breaking Sabbath laws.

Helwys enrolled at Gray's Inn the same day as Edward Stanhope, one of the Rampton family Stanhope's father was a supervisor of the will of Helwys's father which stipulated provision of a monument for him in Bilborough church.[72] Helwys's career in this may have been influenced by Sir Thomas and Edward Stanhope[73] whilst he also seems to have worked for the Earl of Shrewsbury – perhaps as some form of land agent. In 1596-8 he was again living in and around London and maintaining his legal battles over the Broxtowe leases.[74] During his time in London he may have witnessed the execution of the separatists Henry Barrow and John Greenwood. Helwys's cousin Thomas Elwes of the Leverton-Habblesthorpe[75] branch of the family was also admitted to Gray's Inn, in 1597, with the older Thomas acting as a financial guarantor. Professor Larry Kreitzer also thinks it likely that Thomas Helwys spent some time in the Fleet prison in London in early 1597 for contempt of court in his ongoing dispute over the leasing of Broxtowe Hall, from which he does not emerge in a good light.[76] In 1598 he was living in Middlesex.

Somehow Helwys was transformed from an argumentative young litigant with a questionable morality to a fully committed puritan gentleman prepared to risk all for his faith. Perhaps this happened back at Broxtowe, where Helwys became connected with Richard Bernard, the puritan-inclined vicar of Worksop who moved from his home at Epworth[77] in 1601, and the two began to meet at Broxtowe. By 1600 the connection had also been made to Smyth who had arrived in Lincoln. Around there were already many of like mind – at Markham Francis Chapman, another one of the Cambridge group; at Laughton, Robert Gifford was 'more intent on preaching than on conformity to rituals';[78] whilst at North Wheatley and Bole was Hugh Bromhead, who later went to the Netherlands as one of the Smyth and Helwys group. Bromhead clearly came to have an intense dislike of the Established Church:

> 'Babylon, the mother of all abominations, the habitation of devils, and the hold of all foul spirits, and a cage of every unclean and hateful bird'.[79]

It is an interesting possibility that Bromhead was related to Thomas Brumhedde who was deprived of the living at Rampton in 1554 by Mary for being married.[80] The family were long established landowners in the district, especially at Bole and Wheatley. There is also the question of 'Hugo Bromhead' and his wife of Bole, presented as 'Popish recusants' in 1607, though this seems perhaps a deliberate error. Wright says that Bromhead was clerk

---

72 L Kreitzer, *Thomas Helwys and His World (1)*, Oxford, 2019, p10

73 J G Clayton, *Thomas Helwys, A Baptist Founding Father*, in *Baptist History & Heritage*, Jan 1973.

74 L Kreitzer, *New Light on the Early Years of Thomas Helwys*, Oxford, 2018, p.9, p.65

75 This provides an intriguing possibility of a link to John Smyth, who has also been associated with this now 'lost' village, especially as one 'William Smyth' was bequeathed 40s by this Helwys's father as his servant in 1591.

76 One of Helwys's lawyers in this was Samuel Bevercotes (Bevercotts), of the Nottinghamshire family, who was buried in Ordsall church in 1603. He was legal advisor to the Stanhope family was involved in the argument over the replacement of William Brewster (senior) as postmaster at Scrooby in 1590. Kreitzer, p.9.

77 Kenneth Gibson, *Richard Bernard*, p.165-8 suggests Bernard held a living at Epworth 1598-1601. CCED indicated he was curate from 1597.

78 *The Works of John Smyth*, p. liv. Bradford said that he was 'persecuted' but remained within the CoE. In 1607 he was presented for moving the altar into the 'body' of the church and other offences, and again in 1615 and 1619, and his churchwardens were also presented for failing to present him.

79 Letter to Sir William Hamerton, 1609; Hamerton is described as 'beloved Cousin'.

80 A G Dickens, *Reformation Studies*, p.120. A Thomas 'Brumhead', perhaps a brother of Hugh, was father to a child christened at North Wheatley in 1608.

to the 'peculiar' of Bole. Bromhead and his wife were among the group who later applied to join the Waterlanders in Amsterdam with Smyth, as was Gervase Neville (Nevile) of the Ragnall branch of the family (and so a descendant of Sir John Hercy), although all seem to have either died or decided against by 1615. Helwys would easily have come into contact with all these since his family held land across east Nottinghamshire at Saundby and Askham as well as at Gainsborough and Worlaby. It has been suggested that Nevill had returned to the Church of England by 1611.[81]

The Key Players: Richard Clifton (c1553-1615)

Richard Clifton (often spelt Clyfton) at this time held the living of Babworth. He is usually cited from Normanton near Derby but with a brother who farmed at Everton (very close to Scrooby), he may have had some other local connections.[82] On 12 February 1585 Clifton was instituted to the vicarage of Marnham near Newark, Nottinghamshire. On 11 July 1586 he was instituted to the rectory of Babworth, near Retford, in the same county, indicating that he was trusted by the Nottinghamshire puritan gentry. He seems to have known the Jessops at Hayton,[83] and in 1593 was nominated as a supervisor of Richard Jessop's will; it has been suggested his brother was Francis Jessop, later to be found with the Pilgrims at Amsterdam.[84] In the same year, Clyfton had a brush against authority when he was challenged for not wearing a surplice or using the sign of the cross at baptism.[85]

It has been argued that by 1602 Clyfton was the pastor of the leading puritan radicals in Nottinghamshire.[86] As such his circle included William Brewster at Scrooby, whose brother James Brewster held the living at Sutton-cum-Lound where he was also in regular rebellion against his Church masters; in 1603 he was in trouble for conducting a wedding at Scrooby without using the correct service, for which William was a witness.[87] He was also involved in a dispute over apparent misuse of his post as Master of Bawtry Hospital, where he had turned the chapel into a stable perhaps out of puritan disregard for medieval chantries. In 1603 Robert Markham of Gainsborough was given as the curate at Scrooby and he then moved to Owston Ferry in 1605 – in 1607/8 the people of Scrooby were petitioning as they had no minister at all.

Clyfton seems to have also known Thomas Toller, who was vicar, preacher and lecturer at Hayton in 1588 until placed in a Sheffield benefice by William Jessop of Hayton in

---

81 Watts (1986) thought that Neville was one of the few separatists to have been possibly economically motivated following a land dispute. Possibly he eventually became a Catholic as the book *Prophane Schism* of 1612 referred to 'Master Nevil' as 'now be further run backward than ever he was forward'.

82 Marcombe (1993), p.184

83 There was also an Edmond Jessop who became an Anabaptist but returned to the CoE by 1623, but is usually given as from Ackworth near Doncaster, but it has also been suggested this name was an alias for John Etherington.

84 *Collections of the Massachusetts Historical Society*, series 4, volume 1, Boston, 1852, p.61

85 Bunker (2011), p.136. There was also an Edmond Jessop who became an Anabaptist for a while and later wrote *A Discovery of the Errors of the English Anabaptists, 1623;* however, this is likely to have been a pseudonym.

86 James Hanbury, *Historical memorials relating to the Independents, or ..., Volume 1*, London, 1839, p.185

87 Jennings (1999), p.57. As Minister at Sutton, James Brewster was technically responsible for any curate based in the 'chapel' at Scrooby.

1598; both men were supervisors of Richard Jessop's will in 1593. Toller was described by Collison as 'one of the most zealous Puritan ministers of the time, strong in his opposition to ceremonies, though not going the extreme length of separation'.[88] In 1607 he was in trouble for ignoring the *Prayer Book* and not conforming, surviving as Archbishop Tobie Matthew always supported good preaching if not openly separatist. Toller was in trouble again in 1619 and once more in 1635, a habitual flouter of the rules on surplices, being forced in 1635 into resigning the vicarage and becoming an assistant to retain some position. Toller's career is an example of how many puritans repeatedly flouted expectations in what Sandra Goodall has called 'negotiated conformity'.[89] Brian Barton, Thomas Hancock and Robert Southworth did much the same, as did Mark Wyersdale at Costock who was restored to his benefice for another few decades. The implication is, therefore, that those who left for Holland did so more because they had feared the greater risks that separatism might bring rather than the routines of persecution for those who stayed within the fold. As Goodall concludes, 'the pursuit of a narrow and exclusive religious theology *not* persecution was the primary motivation for their removal from England to Holland'.[90] Yet a man like Helwys would have well understood what had happened to separatists in 1590s London whilst the father of Smyth's patron had sent some to their deaths at Bury St Edmunds.

The Jessops continued to be influential supporters of the puritan cause in Sheffield for a generation, with Francis Jessop finding a place for Rowland Hancock in the school and as a preacher there until most of the Sheffield clergy were cleared out in 1662. The vicar of Sheffield during this radical period was Fisher, uncle to John Cromwell of Clayworth and Barnby Moor. Another of the Sheffield deprived, Bloom, found a place at Wyham on the Hill with Sir W Ellis.

From about 1602 Clyfton's influence included the very young William Bradford, who had been born at Austerfield in 1590 and was an orphan though with moderately well-connected relatives. We have few sources to describe his youth but much later Cotton Mather said that at about the age of 12, after an illness, he began to read the Scriptures and came under Clifton's influence; for this he received 'the wrath of his uncles and…the scoff of his neighbours'. He later joined the Scrooby congregation – conveniently several miles closer than the Babworth church!

In February 1605 the churchwardens at Babworth had to admit they had no surplice nor the latest *Prayer Book*.[91] Clifton was presented for nonconformity on 15 March and finally deprived of Babworth on 12 April 1605 as one of four removed in a batch to which we can add the 'homeless' John Smyth. Clifton may then have done some work as a lecturer or preacher at Sutton-cum-Lound in the intervening period and then at Scrooby and Bawtry.[92] Yet men like Clifton were very much in the small minority – others like Nicholas Watkins at Clarborough survived in their positions for years by promising future conformity – he was cited in 1604 for not subscribing, but there is no record that he ever *did*.[93]

---

88   P Collison, *The Church under the Law*, p.471

89   Sandra Goodall, *The Scrooby Puritans in Context*, Arizona University PhD, 2015, p.80

90   Goodall (2017), p.5

91   Marchant (1969), p.182

92   This claim has been based on the banns for marriage of 'Henry Cullandt'. Marchant also reports Clyfton
     as having preached at Sutton before going to Holland.

93   Marcombe (1993), p.186

Other members of Clifton's circle were probably Robert Southworth and Thomas Hancock. Let us recap these, as although they may be seen as peripheral to the separatist saga, they are perhaps more typical. Southworth was a Cambridge man and first in trouble in 1590 as curate of Headon for not wearing a surplice and not following the Prayer Book; he continued to have problems almost annually until 1607. In 1592 he married Jane Wasteneys, one of the leading Headon family, in a ceremony at Scrooby that was illegal because banns were not read – and there is some uncertainty about what had happened to Wasteneys' first husband William Riggs.[94] The service was conducted by Thomas Hancock, a puritan and no doubt associate of William Brewster, who later moved to Retford. When Southworth became vicar at Headon his patron was Oliver Southworth of Clarborough, himself the nephew of a previous Headon clergyman – Henry Southworth. In 1602 Southworth added the curacy of the nearby benefice of Grove – a puritan church. On 15 March 1605 he was presented (the same day as Clifton) and then deprived, but in 1607 made an appearance as unlicensed curate at Scrooby, perhaps then maintaining himself as a teacher. He was presented nine times up to 1607, when he was excommunicated. Southworth, Smyth and Bernard knew each other well enough to discuss separation while walking near Worksop.[95]

Thomas Hancock attended Christ's College and Corpus Christi in the early 1580s and, perhaps after a time in Suffolk, was curate at Scrooby from 1590-2 and then at West Retford. Of course, Scrooby is where his preaching was compared to that of a horse by lone of his churchwardens. He was, of course, a nonconformist and had been presented for refusal to wear a surplice; he was temporarily excommunicated in 1593. He followed the typical pattern of moving around various puritan livings, being vicar of Elkesley in 1598 and then succeeded Southworth at Headon when the latter was deprived in 1605. In 1620 Hancock was fined for taking part in a riot, and in 1623 was presented to the living of Todwick by the Wasteneys where he lived until his death in 1647. Thus Hancock, like Brian Barton, managed to have a long and largely uninterrupted ministry career.

The Key Players: John Robinson (c1575/6-1625)

John Robinson came from the Nottinghamshire village of Sturton-le-Steeple, born perhaps four years after Smyth. Robinson is usually said to have been educated at Gainsborough[96] before going to Corpus Christi College, Cambridge in 1592. He would certainly have been aware of the execution of three of its graduates in 1593 for challenging the Church of England. Robinson was elected to a fellowship in 1597. From this training he was able to become famous as the 'pastor of the Pilgrims', described by John Cotton as 'a man of the most learned, polished and modest spirit'.[97]

94 Bangs, p. 25, notes that John Wastenes, minister of West Burton, was cited for allowing John Smyth to preach there in 1602. It may be assumed that there was a family connection between West Burton's minister and the Wasteneys of Headon.
95 John Smyth, *Works,* 2:334
96 This is the most likely place if Robinson went to a town school, but there were nearer schools in villages including his own.
97 John Cotton, *The Way of Congregational Churches Cleared*, 1648, p.7

Robinson moved to Norwich and in August 1603 criticised the magistrates and also its 'unlearned' priests – a classic puritan tirade; at some point he also preached in 1603 at the church of West Burton, close to Sturton and a puritan stronghold.[98] Despite this he ministered 'occasionally' at St Andrew's Norwich in 1604 whilst actually living in a different parish.[99] He returned briefly to Nottinghamshire to marry his wife Bridget at Greasley in February 1604; she was originally also from Sturton, daughter of Alexander White of Wybornedale[100] in that parish and the sister of Katherine Leggatt (nee White) – one of the *Mayflower* pilgrims who married her second husband John Carver at Leiden. Carver may also have been from Sturton. [101] At the time of their marriage Bridget was living at Beauvale Abbey, presumably with her brother Charles, which was in the parish of Greasley.[102]

Robinson married at Greasley as Bridget seems to have moved there with her brother Charles after the death of their parents and, by the next generation, they were certainly involved in coal mining.[103] Bridget's sisters Jane (later Thickens) and Frances (Jessop) as well as her brother Roger all went to Leiden.

Here again we see hints of the connections that sustained the faithful fellowships. The mother of the White family, Eleanor Smith,[104] was related through marriage to Thomas Disney (1579-1623) who had held Beauvale, who was successively married to Elizabeth Denman and then Bridget Nevile, of Mattersey. These are all familiar names in puritan circles. However, this influence could not protect Robinson in Norwich and in late 1604 he was deprived of his curacy for refusal to subscribe to the articles.

With James I taking a tougher line after the Hampton Court Conference, Robinson was unable to secure another post in early 1605. Then in May 1605 he returned to preach at Sturton-le-Steeple, attracting a number of visitors, seventeen of whom were then in trouble for non-attendance at their own church – these included John Denman and his wife Anne and others of the Denmans, amongst nine from East Retford[105] and four from the Moorgate part of Clarborough parish.[106] This was only two months after Clifton and the others had been ousted from their churches and those charged included many of the prominent Retford puritans; it seems likely that many of the Babworth congregation had gadded to hear Robinson. They were fined 6d each. It was Anne Denman, sister of Walter

98 Bangs, p. 27

99 The full evidence for this is given in Goodall (2015), p.177

100 Bunker (2011), p.120, refers to 'Wybern Dale' as land occupied by the Whites, rather than their home.

101 There are no parish registers for Sturton. However, the certificate of musters for the '30th year of Henry VIII' in Sturton lists a John Corver and a Richard Carver – along with George Lassells, several Smyths, a Legett and Thomos Whyt. Six years later a list of those who contributed 'benevolence' to their King includes a John Carver. Lists are given in full in J Ford, *The Town on the Street*, pps 30-32.

102 J Ford, *The Town on The Street*, Sturton, 1975, p.102

103 Bunker (2011), p.110. Some genealogists say that John Robinson's mother Ann was born in Greasley, married there, and three of his siblings were born there. This tends to suggest the village as a significant puritan cluster.

104 Genealogists seem to agree she was born in Sturton in 1545. The surname is interesting!

105 T George, *John Robinson and the English Separatist Tradition*, p.79; Marcombe (1993), p.183. The Denmans were consistent – we can add Nicholas Denman for not attending church in 1593. John Broome (Browne) – the former Babworth warden – and his wife also attended (Babbage, p.375). Plus John Ellis, Simon Bullivant, James Denman and his wife of Ordsall, Mr and Mrs Robert Denman, Mr and Mrs Richard Brownley and Mr and Mrs Peter Hansford of East Retford as listed in Jennings (1999), p.86.

106 Marcombe in Holland (2004), p.49

Travers,[107] who then disrupted the Easter service at Babworth in 1606 and also a baptism at St Swithun's when Turvin used the sign of the cross. The incident shows that Robinson was already influential in the puritan community and Marcombe speculates that some of this group may have attended the conventicle at Scrooby.[108]

The Crisis of 1606-7 to autumn 1607

Robinson struggled as to whether to separate from the Church of England; he broadly accepted its theology, but not its ceremonial or the use of bishops. After making a final decision whilst visiting Cambridge and listening to Paul Baynes, he came back to Sturton and in 1606 formally joined the separatists by uniting with Clifton in the Scrooby congregation.[109] However, we do not know when either Robinson or Clifton actually left England for the greater freedoms of Amsterdam in advance of the others' final decision to do likewise.[110]

On 2 March 1606 Smyth 'prophesyed' at Gainsborough in the apparent absence of the vicar Jerome Phillips and got into trouble with the bishop; two of the Willoughby family, Sir Thomas Darrell, Sir Gervase Helwys, Robert Somerscales and Sir William Hickman, who was related to the Phillips by marriage, signed letters of support but to no avail.[111] The defence was that he had only read some public prayers and a few Psalms as the minister had not arrived; he did not wear a surplice. A second letter of additional support from the parish then pointed out that his wife was unwell, so Smyth had been unable to attend the Archdeaconry Court, that he had spent too long expounding the Psalms, but not 'one word' of disturbance had been uttered. The case was heard at Huntingdon in June 1606. Wright suggests that Smyth may have been the author of *A defence of the Ministers reasons for refusal*, published in 1606, specifically at least its section on kneeling.[112]

This shows that separation was not inevitable. It was possible if not actually permissible for puritans to preach in different churches: Southworth also preached at Sturton with the permission of the Vicar and wardens, who had previously let Robinson preach. Elkesley, Greasley and Sutton-in-Ashfield permitted John Darrell and Brian Barton to preach there.[113] Robinson also preached at South Leverton (Jan 1608) and Treswell (Feb 1608) before leaving for Holland.[114] There were thus puritan churches as well as ministers, and puritans wanted their own people to minister to them and were prepared for trouble if

107 Anne Travers was born in Nottingham and was John Denman's first wife. John Denman was the son of Thomas's marriage to Mrs Elizabeth Pettinger, from another Retford puritan family. Elizabeth's daughters by her first marriage, Elizabeth and Dorothy, went to Leiden by about 1610. John and Anne's son Humphry was in Amsterdam in 1634-8. John's children by his second wife included Mary, who went to Massachusetts where she married in 1645 and died in 1707, and John who settled near New York and died in 1691.

108 Marcombe (1993), p.184

109 Some claims have been made that Scrooby only became a meeting place after Smyth and the Gainsborough congregation had left.

110 Hanbury (1839), vol.1, p.185

111 Lincs Archives, Cor/B/2, no.19 and no 20. Wright (2006), p.17

112 Wright (2006), p.16

113 Marchant (1960), p.155

114 Marchant (1960), p.156

not; in Easter 1606 Elizabeth Denman of East Retford disturbed the service at Babworth, probably reflecting the loss of Clifton.[115]

Most probably in 1606[116] Isabel Wray, Lady Bowes, and her husband Sir William hosted what was effectively a 'summit meeting' of the disaffected faithful at her home near Coventry.[117] Isabel's views we know, but Sir William also had 'form' in this area. With his main interests in Durham he was involved in Border affairs from 1590 and much concerned by the 'gangrene' of Catholicism which he told Burghley was 'molesting the foote of this kingdom'. In 1594-5 he accompanied the Earl of Essex on a visit to Cambridge and was awarded an MA, having largely had a diplomatic career. By November 1595 he was seeking the hand of Isabel Foljambe (Wray) who was 'not only a staunch puritan but the sister of one of Burghley's officers'.[118] He had petitioned for the release from gaol of Francis Johnson, one of the first separatists, and offered to stand bail for him and Johnson was a significant influence on John Smyth. However, Bowes' strong puritan line in discussions with James VI of Scotland caused him to be 'chastised' by Elizabeth and unpopular when James came to England. In March 1603 he was troubled by claims of debt in London, despite having extensive interests in Teesdale mining. His retirement to Walton was the result.

Those attending included Smyth, Clifton, probably Robinson,[119] Helwys[120] as the only lay guest perhaps and Bernard,[121] plus other reformers such as John Dod and Arthur Hildersham. Another possibility was the attendance of John Barbone of Charwelton, who may have been the father of the famous Praise-God Barebone who gave his name to the Barebones Parliament.

What happened at this conference – or indeed if there were more than one – has been much disputed often with anger by parties at war with each other. John Cotton wrote about it in 1648, seemingly using the memories of William Brewster who must have had things secondhand from Robinson or Clifton. He wrote of Smyth that 'it is true, he had found helpe by the conference (which he himself requested) with Mr Dod, Mr Hildersham and Mr Barbon, before he left England'. In Cotton's account, Smyth 'had promised then he would win over his tutor Johnson' from 'the errors of his rigid separation'.[122] Cotton says that the reverse happened, and Smyth himself was convinced to separate by Johnson; he promised another conference, but this did not take place. Bernard, in *Plaine Evidences*, told a similar story.

The issue was whether to separate from the Church of England, which was vehemently

---

115 Marchant (1960), p.156
116 Wright (2006), p.16 suggests 1605 but the ODNB goes for 1606.
117 White (1971) cites Smyth, Works, ii, 534 for this, in *Parallels, Censures etc.* The site has not been found but Coventry was a radical centre and long served by the radical Humfrey Fen. However, I have not been able to trace any Bowes, Wray or Foljambe linked to Coventry. See also S Culpepper, *One Christian's Plea*, Baylor University PhD, 2006
118 C M Newman, *The Bowes of Streatlam*, York, 1991, p.73
119 Timothy George, *John Robinson and the English Separatist Tradition*, p.83; George is confident that Robinson was present, but the evidence suggests he was present at *a* meeting with Bernard and Helwys
120 The presence of Helwys at this meeting has been debated – he would have been the only lay guest. Kreitzer (2019) contains a discussion of his relationship with others in Isabel Bowes's circle through a law case against him brought by George Tuke which also involved Ireton at Attenborough. This case suggests links between Helwys and members of this key circle in 1600.
121 White (1971) says Bernard not at this particular conference.
122 John Cotton, *The Way of Congregational Churches Cleared*, 1648, p.7

argued by Smyth and Helwys, one of the few laymen present, who probably brought Bernard with them. Smyth wrote that the meeting was 'about withdrawing from true Churches, Ministers and Worship corrupted'.[123] John Cotton later suggested that it was Smyth who led on calls to separate and persuaded Clifton to agree, and Smyth later wrote that this was the first time he decided on full separation[124] but Bernard's version written in 1610 suggested Smyth was more equivocal. Wright thought that Smyth 'converted' Clifton.[125]

Smyth wrote that 'I did not conferre with them about the separation' and denied receiving advice – 'but rather thought I had given instruction to them'. Smyth expressed his satisfaction with proceedings saying, it was claimed, 'I praised God for the quiet and peaceable conference'.[126] In fact, Bernard alleged Smyth promised to go to Amsterdam to persuade Francis Johnson to return to the Church of England, which partially matches Cotton's non-eyewitness version also.[127] Smyth's version has him full of separatist views by this time.[128] Later Clifton wrote that 'I and divers others had once purposed to commit our souls' to Smyth who 'was dear to me'. Robinson perhaps did not play a leading role and later Bishop Joseph Hall in response to Robinson referred to Smyth and Robinson as 'Mr Smyth and his shadow' although he referred to both as 'ringleaders' in separation. Writing in 1610, Bernard indicated Smyth 'fell in love' with separation 'warily and secretly at the first'.

In 1617 John Darrell of Mansfield (or Dayrell) commented on the bitterness caused by the split in his *A Treatise of the Church*; Darrell had been a friend of all the leading puritans including Hildersham and Lady Bowes, but now Smyth had refused communion with his erstwhile friends who refused to separate, and 'Did not then some of the chief of you *in my hearing* magnify Mr Francis Johnson?'[129]

Smyth was also accused of practicing medicine without a licence in November 1606 and attended a hearing on this in January 1607. His delayed response to the medical charge may reflect his illness at this time, for Bernard described him as suffering 'sickness nigh unto death,' during which he stayed with Helwys. It has often been suggested that this illness was stress related to the separation. On 25 February[130] 1607 he preached illegally at Basford, of course in the diocese of York; the claim was that he did this as the priest had been absent (an excuse he used at Gainsborough) but both he and John Herring, the vicar, were cited for this with Smyth being described as 'late of Gainsborowe'. Herring was, of course, an old friend. Kreitzer has shown that Helwys had left Broxtowe by this stage (certainly prior to November 1607) and settled in a house at Basford – Smyth himself later referred to being 'troublesome and chargeable to him' whilst sick at 'Bashforth'.[131]

---

123 Smyth *Works*, II, p.534
124 Whitley, p.332
125 Wright, PhD, p.10
126 Smyth, *Parallels, Censures, Observations*, p.2
127 White (1971), p.122
128 Smyth, Works, ii, p.534
129 Darrell, *A Treatise of the Church*
130 Wright, p.18, says 19th, Kreitzer says 25th.
131 Kreitzer (2019), p.70

He may have stayed in Radford between these two homes.[132] In May 1607 Helwys and his wife were cited for not taking communion at Bilborough although they still attended at Basford in 1607[133] where they were cited for not taking communion at Easter in March 1608, by which time they had presumably gone to Boston as we shall see.[134]

Smyth was fined 2s6d for preaching at Basford, where Helwys's home had presumably provided a lodging during several months of illness; John Herring, the vicar, was presented for 'suffering a minister to preach without seeing his licence'.[135] Herring would certainly have known whether his friend Smyth had a licence or not. He then must have renounced his Anglican ordination and drawn up a covenant based probably on the ideas of Francis Johnson. Greasley concludes that this covenant was probably drawn up at Gainsborough where Smyth had declared himself a pastor.[136] Both Bernard and Bradford confirm that something of this order took place, but neither tells us exactly when.

Wright concluded that Smyth separated in Spring 1607.[137] He mentions the 1607 writing of Francis Mason who referred to 'Brownists' having 'made an actual separation', but the context of this does not refer directly to any specific group – and there were already 'Brownists' in the Netherlands. Wright also mentions that in May 1607 Edward James lamented his 'friends...have severed yourselves from our assemblies' and was known to Smyth.[138] More certain is Henoch Clapham's *Flyer* in late 1607 which knew that in the 'furthest part' of Lincolnshire and Nottinghamshire people 'are flatly already separated;' indeed they were, as Smyth had already decided there would be 'no religious communion to be had but with members of a visible church'. Clapham, probably from Lincolnshire, was a former separatist of the 1590s who had changed his views.

Shortly after this Richard Clifton was excommunicated for a final time on 24 April arising from his failure to defend charges of 'pretending' to be the curate at Scrooby.

Smyth referred to himself as 'Pastor of the Church of Ganesburgh' in a letter to Richard Bernard in autumn 1607, and he was criticised for being 'made minister by tradesmen'.[139] Bradford wrote that 'in one of these churches (besides others of note) was Mr John Smith, a man of able gifts, and a good preacher, who afterwards was chosen their pastor'. Who were these 'tradesmen'? The term clearly excludes gentry like Wray, so perhaps it is men such as the furrier John Murton who described how several stood up in covenant and 'these became a church'.

Smyth's relationship with Richard Clifton and John Robinson, who became closely involved in a congregation meeting at Scrooby, and how far this was a separate church has been much debated. Writing later, William Bradford referred to 'two distinct bodies or churches' under Smyth and Clifton implying that distance was the factor, yet Coggins

---

132 Kreitzer (2019), p.168
133 Greasley, p.43
134 Kreitzer (2019), p.125
135 This citation is also interesting for referring to Smyth as 'late' of Gainsborough, implying that he may have been living at Broxtowe – so what of the Gainsborough congregation?
136 Greasley, p.33
137 Wright (2006), p.19
138 Wright (2006) and Smyth, Works II, p.532; where James lived would be interesting to discover.
139 Bunker (2011), p.107

refers to Bradford himself as 'a member of the original Smyth congregation' as Clifton's later writing suggests was indeed the case.[140] Coggins' conclusion is that this was a 'single congregation' meeting in different places, of which only the regular use of Scrooby is clear.[141] Bradford though says 'but in this *other* church besides other worthy men, was Mr Richard Clifton'. Did he mean Babworth or Scrooby? We cannot be sure.

This interpretation tends to place Smyth as the dominant leader, at least until they reached Amsterdam. Nonetheless, Clifton was certainly active, even reading the banns at Sutton-cum-Lound in July 1607 for a couple who married in Amsterdam in July 1608.

White sees that 'the Gainsborough-Scrooby Congregations were organized as replicas of Johnson's Congregation in Amsterdam' and differences emerged only later.[142] Most probably we would side with the interpretation of William Bradford, writing many years later, who wrote that 'these people became two distinct bodys or churches, and in regard of distance of place did congregate severally'. Bradford made clear that Gainsborough was a separate church, for he wrote 'in this *other* church....besides other worthy men, was Mr Richard Clifton, a grave and revered preacher, who by his pains and diligence had done much good, and under God had been a means of the conversion of many'.[143]

Where did Robinson fit into this? By his own account he 'refused to join' with Smyth in 1607 although separating from the 'parish assemblies' that year. He was a separatist by 1610 when he published *Justification of Separation*, but prior to 1610 his position is less certain. In 1608 Joseph Hall thought he had 'made a secession, rather than a separation from our church' and Bernard thought him 'not so schismatical as the rest' in 1610.

During all this turmoil, by 1607 Smyth had written and published *Principles and Inferences concerning the Visible Church* which outlined his thinking on what a 'true' and by necessity separated church should be like. Coggins assumed this was written in England but published in the Netherlands, and Wright identifies this as at Middelburg by the end of the year.[144] Wright concluded that Smyth had therefore reached Middelburg by the end of 1607, though many others had not; however, even here it was possible that Smyth simply arranged for it to be published there as safer.

Robinson's memoirs suggest he already had clear differences from Smyth. Coggins thought that by the time they were in Holland 'the Robinson congregation was, in fact, a breakaway faction of the Smyth congregation'.[145] Robinson was still living in Norwich in January 1607, when a daughter was baptised.

Both were well capable of pastoring an independent church in 1608. Clifton was, we already know from Bradford, 'a grave and revered preacher' who was assisted by

---

140 Coggins (1991), p.31
141 Coggins (1991), p.58. Coggins points out that the known membership of the two groups did not divide strictly geographically since even some who lived in Scrooby were linked to Gainsborough, where only Murton and Smyth are known to have lived. He also concludes that they did not meet in the same place every week.
142 White (1971), p.124
143 William Bradford, *Of Plimouth Plantation*, p.
144 Coggins (1991), p.37
145 Coggins (1991), p.22

Robinson. Smyth was 'a man of able gifts and a good preacher'.[146] Smyth though was also restless and constantly changing: 'I will every day as my errors shall be discovered confess them and renounce them,' he wrote in 1608.

We must also be cautious about ascribing fixed notions of where they met; as Bradford says, 'they…continued together about a year, and kept their meetings every Sabbath in one place or another,' before going on to explain how they were watched and harried. Meeting every week in Brewster's house at Scrooby seems unlikely in this context. However, when writing more specifically about Brewster, Bradford wrote that 'they ordinarily met at his house on the Lord's day, and with great love he entertained them when they came, providing provision for them to his great charge'.

It has often been said that some protection was afforded Smyth's Gainsborough group by the Hickman family.[147] Sir William Hickman had bought the manor and the Old Hall in 1596, and the Hickmans were Protestant stock of the finest vintage. Hickman's maternal grandfather was said to have smuggled Gospels (in French) into England during Henry VIII's time and his parents, Anthony and Rose, had sheltered Bishop John Hooper, John Knox and John Foxe at the time of Queen Mary. Anthony was imprisoned in the Fleet Gaol in 1554, then they had lived in exile in Antwerp. Their son William bought the Old Hall in Gainsborough from the de Burgh family and was knighted by James I. In 1605 Hickman was one of those who signed the letter defending Smyth after his illegal preaching in the town.

In recent times the tradition that the separatists worshipped together in secret at the Old Hall under Hickman's protection has been challenged. We know that Smyth himself spent much time with Helwys, who was latterly at Basford but where they met in Gainsborough has never been established by documentary evidence. Although Hickman clearly supported Smyth at times, his relations with the other local puritans was complicated by a very bitter dispute with their commercial interests over tolls in the market and on the river, which Hickman had expected to control as part of his purchase of the Old Hall estate. This had even involved the alleged murder in 1598 of one of Hickman's men by a man in the employ of a group including Sir George St Paul, Sir William Wray and Nicholas Girlington – Wray's mother being a Girlington; the rather dubious figure of Richard Topcliffe also became involved in this dispute.[148] Defenders of Hickman took the view that his actions helped to lower the price of food for the poor.[149] By 1607 Hickman was still at odds with this group both because of financial disputes such as the market tolls and his prosecution of John Noble for wearing a hat in church – an incident which may reflect the enmity between the men as much as religious sensibilities. Who was at fault in this dispute has also been debated, although Holmes clearly sided against Hickman in

---

146 Though this did not stop Bradford consigning him to obscurity – 'afterwards…falling into errors…and [with his congregation]..bury themselves and their names'.

147 For example, R M Bartlett in *The Pilgrim Way* writes that 'the Hickmans were friendly towards John Smyth and his followers and invited them to meet in the Old Hall…'. What we can dismiss is any ideas that the *Mayflower Pilgrims* met at the Old Hall, for there is no evidence that Brewster, Bradford etc were ever part of a Gainsborough congregation.

148 In 1598 Hickman complained that Martin Furser had been killed by St Paul's men who were oppressing him along with Wray, 'his brother' (St Paul), and Girlington.

149 Sir William Killigrew to Robert Cecil, 5 July 1598; but Killigrew was associated with the Hickman family in London so may not have been a dispassionate commentator.

commenting on him 'aggressively insisting upon….manorial rights in order to increase their rake off from the trade of….Gainsborough'.[150]

It has been suggested by one historian that by 1623 most of Hickman's associates were from Catholic families.[151] Sir William's son Willoughby Hickman married a daughter of Sir John Thornhaugh of Fenton, a Parliamentary family, but himself avoided taking up arms in the Civil War although he did accept a baronetcy from Charles I in 1643, making him suspicious to the stauncher Protestants and resulting in him being fined by Parliament, whilst his son William gained 'the reputation of a persecutor' under Charles II's anti-nonconformist Clarendon Code.[152] Almost to a man, Lincolnshire's puritan families supported Parliament.

So, might Hickman have provided shelter, at risk to himself, for Smyth – a man who was a close associate of the Wray-St Paul faction? Certainly, he signed a letter, but that was before Smyth decided to separate – a decision in which none of the key local gentry joined. Smyth was also made minister 'by tradesmen', which would be a demeaning label for Hickman, and perhaps this points more to men like Thomas Seamer or John Murton who might have provided premises. We should also bear in mind that the key figures in this whole era then published much about the events of these two years, often bitter in tone, without ever listing Hickman as one of their associates, but offering praise to the Wrays in their book dedications.

More obvious supporters of the puritan cause in the town included Sir Richard Williamson – who might have been included in a description as a tradesman, and arguably Edward Aston. Williamson had started life as a Gainsborough draper's son but prospered as a London lawyer (seemingly being prodded into this career by Sir Christopher Wray)[153] and was a member of the Council of the North. His nephew, Gervase Nevyle at Grove and Ragnall near Retford (linked to the Hercy-Denman faction), was also a puritan; living at Scrooby but apparently associating with the Gainsborough group, he was imprisoned for attending conventicles and later went to Holland.[154] Williamson, John Noble and Edward Aston a lawyer were also involved in a commercial legal battle with Hickman in 1607-10. In contrast, Hickman making Noble remove his hat in church was a symbolic dividing point for puritanism.[155] Possibly protection was also provided by Sir Gervase Helwys who was Sheriff of the County in 1607. Aston knew Helwys well enough to stand bond for his wife in 1608. Williamson led the legal battle against Hickman in 1609-10. The other Justice in Gainsborough at the time was Sir Thomas Darrell; by 1604 his son Edward had married the wealthy heiress Francis Denman and thereby became Lord of the Manor of West Retford, perhaps *the* puritan stronghold in the area.

---

150 Holmes (1980), p.69
151 Hajzyk, p.320 (referencing LAO COR/B/2 no.19). William Hickman's daughter Frances married into the Rokeby family, who had a number of Catholics.
152 *Sir William Hickman* in *History of Parliament*, accessed 17 Oct 2019
153 History of Parliament, https://www.historyofparliamentonline.org/volume/1604-1629/member/williamson-sir-richard-1563-161516; accessed 3 August 2019
154 G F Willison, *Saints and Strangers: Lives of the Pilgrim Fathers and their Families,* p.54. There is some evidence he was in Amsterdam by 1601.
155 Paul Howitt-Cowan, *William Hickman, the Pilgrims and the Old Hall*, Friends of the Old Hall Association, 2010

Alternative Paths:

We can see that no one of higher social standing decided to join Smyth in separation. His leading supporters were clergy and minor gentry like Helwys and Neville. Major social forces, such as the Wrays, did not separate though men like Helwys continued to try to persuade them.

We can see how the Wray influence spread through the career of Edward Rainbow (1608-84), who became bishop of Carlisle. Sir William appointed his father Thomas Rainbow as his vicar at Blyton (and the Wrays later provided him the living at Wintringham), and Rainbow married the daughter of puritan nonconformist David Allen, the rector of Ludborough. Thomas was very unusual in being a graduate MA of Edinburgh University in 1593 so his connection to the man of the same name who was labelled as 'schismatic' at Christ's College in 1590 for taking communion, sitting, and coming to chapel without a surplice is uncertain – but probable.

Rebecca Allen was well-schooled by her father and knew Greek, Hebrew and Latin. Their child Edward was named after and given a Wray godparent, Edward Wray of Rycot. Frances Wray identified Edward as one of her potential puritan leaders and nominated him for a Wray scholarship to Magdalene College Cambridge – these were set up by her father, the Chief Justice. By 1630 Rainbow, who had known Bishop Williams from an early age, was master of the school at Kirton-in-Lindsey, returning to Magdalene and becoming its Master in 1642. Unusually for one with such a background, he was dismissed from his Mastership in 1650. However, his fortunes were restored at the Restoration and he became Bishop of Carlisle in 1664, where his condemnation of immoral living made him some enemies who blocked him from becoming Bishop of Lincoln. Along the way he seems to have moved away from puritanism and died as 'an orthodox but moderate Anglican, sympathetic to nonconformists'.

Thomas Rainbow, rector of Treswell who died in 1661, may be a relative; he seems to have died under the stress of conforming.

Bernard's Dilemma

Richard Bernard survived in his position at Worksop until 9 April 1605 when he was finally deprived of his Church of England living for his views, including refusal to wear a surplice. This was highly unusual – we need to remember that the deprivations of 1605 affected only a small proportion of the radical clergy of Nottinghamshire. Possibly this was because Bernard was considered 'fractious' – he had divided the town by his thinking about an inner congregation. Though some supported him, like the Carlile family, others would not have been happy about their implied second-class status.

For a time, he was associated at Gainsborough with Smyth, indicated in a book dedication which refers to a congregation at Gainsborough.[156] However, this may refer to a time before he went to Worksop when he was preaching in west Lindsey.

Whereas Bernard and others thought Smyth had prayed with relief at not separating, Smyth maintained he had prayed at the end of the conference at night because of 'the resolution of my doubts'.[157] For his part, Smyth later argued that Bernard agreed with separation at other meetings[158] only to renounce this. He claimed that Bernard showed 'readiness to embrace this truth we profess, first at Sir William Bowes his house when it was opposed by some adversaries'. For some time after Smyth went to live with Helwys due to illness, perhaps caused by the stress of separation; in his own words he explained that he 'doubted nine months' and perhaps this was that time. Robinson was also a prominent voice for separation but Hildersham spoke against.

This confusion about what happened forced Bernard to defend himself. Bernard himself later claimed, 'I was much moved….but I was not removed'. Whitley's history of separatism talks of Bernard behaving like a 'Tax Inspector' by sending Helwys 'a list of his doubts and objections to the course Helwys was taking….and set them on a sheet ruled in double column for replies to be annexed'.[159] Smyth implied Bernard was also a coward, writing that he had told him and Robert Southworth whilst walking near Worksop, that 'you could easily die upon the tree for truth, but you could not without great horror think of being burned…' He told this story to illustrate how Bernard was planning to 'dispatch your estate and to get away to safety' – implying a decision to separate.

For a time, Bernard seemed to be a separatist. Robinson, in his preface to *Justification*, lambasted him for having discussed and agreed separation with himself and Helwys 'in fear and trembling'. His covenant group of 'one hundred people' was such that 'the whole country ringeth of it' but 'alas yet again you have revolted from all this truth'. White notes that he said as much at a meeting at Bowes' house with Smyth and another radical, which might have been at Walton or Coventry, when he seemed to be considering exile. This was not the 'summit' Coventry meeting (so does this explain the confusion over his attendance?).[160] White sees Hildersham as influential in his decision, because Smyth refers to Bernard coming back from a meeting 'from Mr Hildersham' (presumably therefore at Ashby) and stopping at Broxtowe where he accused Smyth of 'choosing not a fit adversary to debate' by selecting Clifton (rather than Bernard himself), who was not known to have been university educated.[161] Smyth though thought Clifton would 'approve his sufficiency to be superior to your diving witt'.

In 1607 the new Archbishop of York, Tobie Matthew, persuaded Bernard to return to his old 'living'. Smyth complained that Matthew 'hath so bewitched you with his flattery, eloquence and angels, that your covenant is profaned and cast in the dust, men of your

---

156 *A Large Catechisme* of 1602 mentions his 'friends and wellwishers' at Worksop, Gainsborough and Epworth.
157 Smyth, Works II, p. 534
158 Coggins (1991), p.40
159 W T Whitley, *Works of John Smyth*, p. lxv, 1915
160 White (1971), p.130
161 Smyth, *Parallels and Censures*, in Works, vol 2, p.2

covenant must shift for themselves'. Bernard was dubbed a 'chameleon' and his former friends hinted he really wanted the increased income if he secured the living of Saundby. For a time, Bernard had his own covenanted congregation at Worksop, perhaps in the autumn of 1607.[162] Arthur Hildersham of Ashby-de-la-Zouch led the opposition to Smyth's plans, and Bernard returned to Worksop where 100 or so formed a covenant group with him – with perhaps only thirty from Worksop itself.[163] Robinson later suggested that he did this only to stop them going off to join Smyth[164] but it was also Robinson who suggested later that it was Smyth who persuaded Clifton to separate. Clifton was excommunicated in March and April 1607. In the same year, Bernard published *The Faithfull Shepherde*, perhaps his most enduring book and the next year began to publish attacks on the separatists whilst not fully conforming himself.

But Bernard's congregation did not endure, and several from Worksop and nearby Warsop went to Holland. A bitter pamphlet war then broke out, with Bernard defending his position in 1608 with *The Separatists' Schism*[165] to which Smyth replied with Parallels in 1609 and Robinson with *A Justfication* in 1610; to which Bernard then replied with *Plaine Evidences* also in 1610. Smyth commented that 'your covenant is profaned and cast in the dust' with its members abandoned. Bitter correspondence between Smyth, Helwys and Bernard was published by the latter as *Christian Advertisements* in June 1608 having originated about six months earlier. By 1613 he was in Somerset.

Bernard declared 'the Church of England is apostolicall, the separation schismaticall' for a key argument was that the Church of England was descended by apostolic succession from the disciples whereas any separatist church was descended from.....nobody, hence it had no authority. Bernard took the chance to point out to Smyth 'of his purpose to go to Amsterdam to reclaim his tutor Mr Johnson'.

Smyth responded that Bernard had accused him of 'divers untruths' and 'therefor herein I indite you as a publique slanderer'. Smyth accepted the charge that he had 'doubted 9 months' but denied that he had ever separated and then returned to the Church. On this point he appealed to Gainsborough. As to what had happened at Coventry:

> Whereas you say I became satisfied at Coventree after conference had with certayne Ministers, and hereupon kneeled downe and praised God: I answer. I did not conferre with them about the Separation as you and they know wel enough in your consciences: but about withdrawing from true Churches, Ministers, and Worship, corrupted: Wherein I received no satisfaction, but rather thought I had given instruction to them: and for kneeling downe to praise God I confesse I did, being requested to perfume the duty at night after the conference by the Ministers: but that I praised God for resolution of my doubts, I deny to death and you also are a slaunderer: I praised God for the quiet and peaceable conference, and such like matters, and desired pardon of the Lord for ignorance, and errors, and weakness of judgement, and any disordered caryage: if the Ministers that heard my prayers and praises of God did misconstrue my meaning let them look unto it.

---

162 T S Freeman, *Isabel Wray*, ODNB, accessed 1 April 2014. Wright, thesis, p.11, suggests there were about 100 of whom only about 30 were from his own Worksop parish.

163 Wright (2006), p.20; the estimate comes from Ainsworth and Robinson.

164 John Robinson, *Justification of Separation*, 1610, p.60

165 No copies of this seem to have survived, a major loss for our story.

Although she ceased to support him, Helwys maintained enough affection for Lady Bowes who had hosted this controversial event to dedicate *Declaration of the Faith* to her in 1611, stating that 'I know there is none in the land that hath better means to procure a cause of religion to be handled according to the judgement of the best'.[166]

Arrests encourage preparations to leave: 1607-8

It is not surprising that when Archbishop Tobie Matthew, on his archepiscopal visitation, visited Bawtry in September 1607 he preached an anti-Brownist sermon; Clifton had been cited for being the 'pretended curate' of the town in March that year whilst John Slacke of Cantley and Henry Fletcher, curate of Austerfield, had also been involved there in a problematic wedding service. Matthew was well informed by Peter Haworth, the vicar of Everton, who had Richard Clifton's brother John in his parish: 'If some order be not taken with Mr Clifton, their teacher, and John Clifton, his brother, I doubt a great many will be infected with their pestiferous opinions'.[167] His problems were not solved when Clifton left, for Roger Drue appears to have returned by 1609 to recommence his nonconformity.[168] Meanwhile, Robert Southworth was excommunicated on 25 September.

> Persecution was engineered by **Dr Robert Snoden** who was originally from Mansfield Woodhouse and also a Christ's College graduate. In 1603 he became a member of the York High Commission, was appointed a Justice at Southwell, and also acted as a commissary for Matthew in the Nottingham archdeaconry. Perhaps the Archbishop thought that Snoden's local knowledge and evangelical reputation would help tame the schismatics. He preached in front of James I at Newstead Abbey in 1612 but his attempt to become Dean of Lincoln in 1613 failed. However, he leapfrogged up the ladder by landing the see of Carlisle in 1616, causing some court gossip:
>
> > 'I remember I wrote to you that Dr Carleton was Bishop of Carlisle, and so both himself and all his friends believed and gave out. But I hear one Snowdon, an obscure fellow, is come in at the window and shut him out'.[169]
>
> Snoden died in 1621.

Matthew had arrived in York in summer 1607 with a reputation as a 'godly' man, but one who drew the line at separatism. In September he travelled to Southwell, where he preached, then went to Nottingham and Bawtry where he preached against separatism – seemingly with Clifton in mind.[170] Tolerant of nonconformity, Matthew detested separatism as 'branches torn from the vine'.[171] This visit to the separatist heartland inspired him to set up a High Commission and he took personal control of the licensing of curates in the district – he appointed Thomas Brittain to Bawtry in December 1607 and in 1609

166 Newman, p.414-5
167 Babbage (1962), p.62
168 Jennings, p.65
169 John Chamberlain to Sir Dudley Carleton, 26 October 1616
170 R Oates, *Moderate Radical*, Oxford, 2018, p.203
171 Oates (2018), p.204

appointed a curate to Scrooby – by which time Brewster had long gone.

Helwys' wife Joan and two Nottinghamshire laymen had been arrested and Joan was imprisoned at York for three months for non-attendance in 1608 – John Drew(e) of Everton[172] and Thomas Jessop of Mattersey[173] were also arrested and perhaps stayed in custody for longer. Drew's fault was to have not received communion at Easter 1607 whilst Thomas Jessop had been absenting himself from his church in order to go to Babworth since 1603 and also did not take Easter communion in 1607. Jessop argued with his judge about kneeling at communion and called him 'like a painted wall'.[174] Joan Helwys ('Helwish'), Thomas Jessop and John Drew were brought before the consistory court in York on 22 March 1608,[175] where they denied being 'Brownists' and were returned to prison having refused to take the ex officio oath.

It may then have been Helwys who began the planning to move to Amsterdam – perhaps being the 'harbinger' of the group that Bishop Hall noted there in 1607, and hence clearly having been apart from his wife at the time she was arrested as both had been absent from church since September (Michaelmas) 1607; Robinson always acknowledged Helwys' role in organising and funding the move. Kreitzer comments that Helwys's absence when his wife was at York 'remains one of the great mysteries of the case' but it may simply be that Helwys was away when his wife was captured. Meanwhile, others were also still antagonistic – four from Bothamsall were reported for not going to church and said they would not attend where the minister was not a preacher.[176] Hugh and Anne Bromhead were cited as 'recusants one month' in October 1607 which coincides with Robert Southworth's excommunication in September and the Helwys' absence from church;[177] perhaps this indicates that people had begun to leave for the Netherlands, or Boston, by this time. To add more precise evidence, Helwys was cited for absence from church on 29 September 1607. Gervase Neville (Nevyle), who was 'said to be of Scrooby' but with a family from Grove and Ragnall, was brought before the commission in York on 10 November 1607 as a 'dangerous schismaticall Separist Brownist' and asked questions about separatism and conventicles. He started by accusing the archbishop of being part of an 'antichristian hierarchy,' refused to co-operate and was sent to gaol. The situation with Nevyle was more sensitive as he was related to Sir Richard Williamson, who was a member of the commission.[178] After this he was sent to prison.

In December 1607 William Brewster, Richard Jackson[179] and Robert Rochester were also sought by the archbishop's officers (perhaps including Snoden) amongst several other

---

172 Cited for not taking Easter communion, 1607.
173 Cited in 1603 for attending Babworth and in 1607 for failure to take Easter communion at Mattersey. He argued he did not take it as unsure whether standing or kneeling was correct.
174 Babbage (1962), p.376
175 Kreitzer (2019), p.173 discusses that this date has often been given incorrectly.
176 p.376
177 Wright, PhD, p.11
178 Bunker (2011), p.184
179 Wright (thesis) cites Jackson as 'clerk of Norwell' but perhaps also of Scrooby, as the same person involved in the disturbance at Marnham, p.9. He remained at Norwell until 1633. However, Sue Allen has now shown him to be the husband of Mary Pettinger of Carlton-in-Lindrick (married 1591 at Doncaster) and father of Susannah White Winslow, *Mayflower* Pilgrim, who rented part of Scrooby from 1604. His brothers John and Robert were clerks to the Court of Sewers at Spalding successively from 1586-1607 and 1607 to 1624/5. Any connection between the two remains to be explored.

laypeople – this appears to have been a deliberate tactic by Archbishop Matthew and may have accelerated the move to another country.[180] Heavy fines were issued against Brewster and Jackson.

Gervase Neville appeared again before Matthew at York on 22 March 1608, the same month in which Robinson seems to have preached his last known – and illicit – sermon in England.[181] Drew, Jessop and Joan Helwys were questioned the same day. Neville was sent to York Castle but was later permitted to go to Holland as were Drewe or Jessop.[182] Larry Kreitzer has shown that Drew, Jessop and Neville were released on order of the Privy Council made on 25 May 1609.[183] Drew and Jessop became significant figures amongst the early Baptists.[184]

Joan Helwys appears to have been released at an unknown earlier date, presumably after 22 March 1608 when a bond for her reappearance was entered. We know she was with Thomas in May at Stallingborough, and when her case was discussed again on 5 July 1608 she was not present and therefore presumably the bond provided by Edward Aston,[185] the Gainsborough lawyer, and Michael Faux,[186] began to be a problem for them; Thomas Helwys was also mentioned at this time. Their case came up again in August 1608 at York when warning was to be sent to the parish churches of Aston and Faux at Gainsborough and Woodall. On this occasion it was made clear that Thomas Helwys had been issued with a 'monition' on 26 May 1608 to appear at York in August – possibly this was a result of his appearance before the Lincolnshire justices on 13 May after the incident at Stallingborough (discussed below) as it was, in fact, served upon him.[187]

Both Thomas and Joan were discussed by the High Commission again at York on 4 October 1608. By this stage, it must have been well known that both had left the country and therefore, as far as the Archbishop was concerned, there was no longer any pressing problem. From this complex legal history, we can see that none of the separatists suffered long term imprisonment and were generally permitted to go free in presumably confident knowledge that they would then leave the country.

Matthew was an unenthusiastic persecutor 'using the threat of coercion to start a conversation that he hoped would end in cooperation, if not full conformity'.[188] This was his policy with Richard Bernard. Matthew returned to Southwell in May 1608 to oversee

---

180 Marchant (1960), p.161
181 Bunker (2011), p.187
182 Kreitzer (2019), p.178
183 Kreitzer (2019), p.178
184 Kreitzer (2019), p.179
185 Aston's connection to local puritan circles is confirmed by his being a tutor and/or guardian to the children of John Otter of Clarborough, his brother in law, along with Thomas Southworth of Welham. Otter's will of 1606 mentioned Nicholas Watkins, Richard Southworth and others, and mentioned that his house in Moorgate was rented to William Parnell. Otter's son's will in 1640 was also witnessed by William and Edward Southworth. Aston played a leading role in the fight against Hickman in Gainsborough.
186 Probably Michael Fawkes of Farnley, who owned land at Woodall near Rotherham. Although he was a conformist, his father was a recusant in 1604 and his son an ardent Royalist so the connection is puzzling except that his wife was from Teversall in Notts.
187 Kreitzer, p.182
188 Oates (2018), p.205

the examination of separatists, yet he continued to tolerate the preaching exercises at Mansfield in 1609 and more widely in Nottinghamshire in 1613 – even preaching at exercises himself in Retford and Nottingham.[189] He also encouraged exercises around Doncaster. For more Catholics were brought to the High Commission than separatists.

Going Away: 1608

In 1607-8 Smyth, and around 40 others from the Gainsborough group went to the Netherlands. Smyth left behind forever the landscape of his birth, but not with any sense of loss; he said that the Trent valley was full of 'infinite sorts of sinners…adulterers. Theeves, Murtherers, Witches, Conjurers, Atheists, Swaggerers, Drunkards, Blasphemers'.[190] They were not going to an entirely foreign land as some members of the 'Ancient Church' were there already, possibly including Thomas Willason of Bevercotes from as early as 1603.

According to Brewster, Clifton's church 'began to fly over to Holland' in autumn 1607 and in February 1608 more got over to Holland. William Brewster resigned his position as postmaster in September 1607. Clearly, others were expecting them to go – in February 1608 William Crashaw, a Sheffield man who knew Robinson, asked if they would 'soon go to the Church of the Low Countries'.

The original plan for members of both groups seems to have been to leave in 1607 via Boston, where a vessel might be hired to take them all to the Netherlands. There, after a period of 'long waiting' according to Bradford's account, they arranged to be picked up by a boat to take across the North Sea – in other words, manifestly *not* from the conventional port of Boston. The Bradford telling of this story is that the ship's master betrayed them before they could get far down to sea, they were offloaded into open boats where they were 'rifled and ransacked', held for a month after which most were released but '7. of ye principall were still kept in prison, and bound over to ye Assises'.[191] Bradford says they were made 'a spectacle' of in Boston, but the magistrates 'used them courteously' although they were held (briefly) until orders came from the Council. Then it is assumed the seven were taken to Lincoln, where they would have been held in the castle [192] for the assizes. Writing of Brewster, Bradford later said that 'he was the chief of those that were taken at Boston and suffered the greatest loss'. In fact, the surviving document lists a William Bingham, gentleman, first.

---

189 Oates (2018), p.213

190 John Smyth (1609) with acknowledgement to Bunker (2011), p.127, for this excellent quotation.

191 Bradford reported in his much later account, *Of Plimouth Plantation*, that seven were arrested. But this account does not seem to suggest that Bradford himself was there.

192 There has been a dispute over whether the manuscript should be read as seven or some.

Scotia Creek

The memorial to the failed escape attempt was erected at Scotia Creek, but Wheeler's *A History of the Fens of South Lincolnshire* makes clear that this was named after a steamer that used to berth there in the 1830s – long after the Pilgrims! So we can be clear that they did not arrange a meeting at 'Scotia' Creek but before the building of the Hobhouse Drain in the early 1800s there was a more substantial waterway that led almost up to Fishtoft called the Graft – a 'creek of considerable magnitude'. This was used by fishing boats at least, so it might have been a good place for the Pilgrims to link up with their boat – or to be unloaded for arrest. The artificial straightening of the river here has changed the scenario significantly, but a map of 1815 shows 'Smack Creek' in the vicinity before the river was altered. An interesting name, but maybe one that will have trouble replacing the more exotic sounding Scotia Creek in the guidebooks…

The church at Fishtoft is dedicated to St Guthlac and had a statue of him with a whip – it was said that as long as he had his whip, rats and mice would not disturb the village. You can guess whether or not he still has his whip!

The main independent evidence for this escape attempt is a document which records charges related to not attending church at Boston or 'other places' and holding illegal assemblies and conventicles at Boston; this has no clear date so we can only estimate these events as late in 1607 or early in 1608. The document is filed with the Spalding Court of Sewers records, an apparent oddity; one theory for this is that the clerks of this court, which dealt with drainage issues, changed from John to Robert Jackson during 1607 – were both brothers of Richard Jackson, who had married Mary Pettinger of Carlton-in-Lindrick at Doncaster in 1591.[193] These Jacksons were at Scrooby in 1604 where they were cited along with Brewster and others, and their daughter Susannah later became a *Mayflower* passenger and eventually husband of Edward Winslow; Winslow wrote to Robert Jackson at Spalding in 1623 as a 'kinsman,' enquiring about the health of his father in law Richard Jackson. We should note also that the Spalding Court of Sewers held regular meetings at Boston but also that its work routinely involved gentry from across the county – Isaac Johnson, Richard Bellingham, Sir Christopher Wray, Edward Ayscough, Atherton Hough and Sir Anthony Irby all crisscross its records.

The list – which is of fifteen abbreviated names which must be guessed at – included probably Clifton, Brewster and Helwys as well as Leonard Beetson who remained in Boston during John Cotton's era and became a 'schismatic' churchwarden.[194] It does not include John Smyth, who had possibly already left, or Robinson. Robert Rochester of Scrooby was also listed – he had been fined along with Brewster in April 1608. Helwys's servant Edward Armfield was also there and stayed with him to Amsterdam where he married Margary Orghan probably from Kersall;[195] when Helwys split from Smyth,

---

193 The Pettingers were part of the Denman circle of puritans around Retford.
194 Kreitzer suggests he had been churchwarden at 'Walesbury' in Notts until 1607. However, he was cousin to Richard Whittingham, whose will of 1614 showed close links to Cotton and Simon Bradstreet. He died in 1625.
195 Kreitzer (2019), p.146

Armfield stayed in Amsterdam.[196] All were accused of 'plotting and intending to scandalise and bring into contempt the true and pious religion established in this kingdom', holding unlawful assemblies and not attending church. Bradford reported that 'the greatest part' of those arrested were set free and only seven kept in prison for the assizes. By December 1607, Brewster and Richard Jackson had failed to attend court and eluded the constable.

An interesting debate might be whether this implies they had all been active or resident at Boston for some time in advance of the attempt to escape that ended in failure? We already have noted Bradford's 'long waiting'. Unless 'seditious intent' includes planning to leave the country, the document makes no direct mention of an escape – rather it is focused on non-attendance at church and unlawful conventicles. The list also includes Samuel Letsham, who had been living in Boston since at least 1602.[197] John Coppyn was a merchant at Boston, where he was still living in 1616.[198] Other names are more problematic – it was headed by William Bingham, a gentleman, but who was he?[199] He seems most likely to have been William Bingham, originally of Danbury Essex; his son William married Lucy Ayscough, the daughter of Sir Edward, probably in 1634 – she was the widow of John Welcome who died at Goxhill in 1627 but who had interests at Market Stainton. Thomas Gosse may have been from Brant Broughton. Bradford's phrase implies they stayed at Boston for some time; we cannot be sure, but it is reasonable to suppose that the Court of Sewers document provides additional evidence that members of both Gainsborough and Scrooby groups must have been in Boston for several months as they formed conventicles with others in the town. Some of these they must surely have known or had contacts in advance, which may have been through the Jackson family – but this can only be speculation.

Robinson, Brewster and Helwys stayed behind 'to help the weakest over before them'. However, it is also possible that Helwys went to Holland in 1607 where he may have laid preparations for those who were to settle there, and then returned.[200] Whitley, writing a Baptist history and therefore potentially biased, wrote that Helwys made all the business arrangements and rented an old bakehouse in Amsterdam where the separatists began to settle in July 1608.[201] In fact, most had clearly left weeks before this date.

Helwys was influential in covering much of the cost of the move to the Netherlands in Spring 1608 but was largely left out of the story by Bradford, and it is because of Robinson's writing that we know 'it was Mr Helwys who above all others….furthered this passage into strange countries; and if any brought oars, he brought sails…'.[202] Helwys and his wife were cited for not attending church at Basford as late as April 1608[203] and cited

196 Kreitzer (2019), p.146
197 A Daniel Letshem was an English student at Leiden in 1625.
198 A man of the same name was hung for being a Brownist at Bury in 1583, under the instruction of Sir Christopher Wray.
199 One William Bingham of Tattershall left a will in 1657, others were from Market Stainton whilst a third was married in Gainsborough in 1597. This could be the same person or a son.
200 Greasley cites evidence from Bishop Joseph Hall about a 'harbinger' of the group; Helwys, as one of the wealthiest, might have been a likely contender.
201 Whitley, *Works of John Smyth*, p.lxxiv-lxxvi. Adam Taylor says that most had arrived in Holland n 1606. Others that it was the Gainsborough group who went first, in late 1606. The bakehouse was not rented until 1609.
202 John Robinson, *Of Religious Communion Private and Publique*, Amsterdam, 1614, p.14
203 Bangs, p.38

to appear in July.[204] By this stage, Helwys and his servant had not attended church for months. On 6 April a John Armefield of Epperstone was cited for refusing the sacrament – Helwys's servant.[205]

What we know about how they left is mainly from the account given by Helwys when he was interrogated by Sir Roger Halton and Thomas Hatcliff, with details supplied by Bradford and written down much later. The plan was to escape from the coast north of Grimsby. Helwys hired the *Francis*, under the command of Henry Spencer and with a probably sympathetic owner,[206] to collect the women and children at Gainsborough on 9 May. At this stage there were ten women, three children and two men though eventually there were 'four score' – so perhaps they collected others at places like West Stockwith which might have been convenient for Bawtry or Scrooby. Indeed, in his evidence Spencer seemed very confused about what happened at Stockwith. However, Robert Barnaby's evidence suggested that more than eighty people filled the boat at Gainsborough on 10 May. Spencer said he only knew it to be going to Grimsby or Stallingborough with goods belonging to 'Sir Gervase Elvish'. Meanwhile, most of the men walked overland to Stallingborough Creek via Caistor, where they lay overnight, and then they met at a sheepcote near Stallingborough for a last night. The choice of Stallingborough is of great interest due to the connection between this location the Ayscough (Askew) family who were committed local puritans at this time.

Memorial…in the wrong place

At Immingham, there is a memorial to the successful escape of the 'Pilgrims'. This is currently in a park, where the fact that it has the wrong date – 1609 – can clearly be enjoyed. However, it was first put up in the wrong place in 1924, for it was assumed the escape had been from Immingham Creek and this was where the monument was originally sited. Later an oil refinery covered this site, so it was moved into Immingham town. This was ironic because the correct site at Stallingborough Creek was and still is perfectly accessible to the public!

The plan was for the groups to meet on land at Stallingborough, where there was as Bradford said 'a large common a good way distant from any town,' and then get aboard a Dutch vessel using a small boat for the transfers. It seems though that women, and perhaps some men, landed so as to sleep better at night, since the weather was poor. Helwys and his wife were at the sheepcote together for at least part of the night. On 12th May around a dozen men met them at Stallingborough and went out first to the waiting Dutch boat, whose master said they were from Amsterdam. Before they could all get to the Dutch ship armed men arrived, so most of the women and children were left behind to the horror of the men and with no possessions or money – although some men still on land were able to escape.

---

204 Wright, PhD, p12

205 Wright, PhD, p.12

206 The boat was owned by Anthony Brackenbury of Holme, who, in the 1590s, briefly employed the Sommers who was involved in one of the Darrell exorcisms and had himself lived at Ashby for a while according to family historians. He was brother in law of Thomas Gray, of Langley Abbey near the puritan centre of Ashby. The 'cover story' was that it was needed to transport goods for Sir Gervase Helwys.

The authorities plainly did not know what to do with a group of women and children who were homeless and had just watched their men and possessions sail away. No-one wanted to take responsibility and in the end this helped them, as Bradford explained: 'To be short, after they had been thus turmoiled a good while, and conveyed from one constable to another, they were glad to be rid of them; though in the meantime the poor souls endured misery enough'. A local legend is that the women and children were then sheltered in Immingham church; there is no known evidence for this, though given Bradford's version it *might* be. Helwys and the faithful Armfield were left to face the authorities and a series of inconclusive hearings before they were allowed to leave – we do not know how they got to the Netherlands themselves.

Those on the Dutch vessel endured a terrifying 14-day passage due to storms during which they were driven almost to the coast of Norway. When the ship was on the point of sinking, again according to Bradford, the 'Pilgrims' prayed, 'Yet Lord thou canst save,' and indeed saved they were. Robinson, Clifton and Brewster seem to have arrived in Amsterdam after this, in August 1608.[207]

A Nottinghamshire couple, Henry 'Cullandt' of 'Nottinghamshire' and Margaret 'Grymsdiche' of Sutton-cum-Lound were married in Amsterdam on 5 July 1608, having previously had their banns read by Clifton at Sutton.[208] So it is pretty clear that people were established by this stage.

They were hardly a united group: Clyfton and Smyth had had some differences over excommunication, and Smyth also had similar differences with Robinson. This may explain why Robinson came to be more closely linked to the Scrooby group than Smyth's at Gainsborough though he was also in the area for less time than the others – he was still in Norwich in January 1607.[209]

Among those 'left behind' was Bernard, at Worksop. Whereas Smyth believed churches could ordain their own ministers, Bernard was reluctant to renounce his own ordination and he had Archbishop Matthew who appeared keen not to lose him – after a conversation, also involving Arthur Hildersham, he was restored to his living in 1607. Bernard wrote a book against bishops which was published anonymously and his own 'covenanted' congregation had agreed not to hear 'dumb ministers', to watch over each other, and to observe the Lord's Supper – they were thus semi-detached from the Church of England.[210] In the unhappy aftermath of his decision not to separate, John Smyth drew attention to his preaching from Daniel 3, 16-17, so often that 'every man conceived that he would have been a ring leader to reformation'.

He exchanged letters with Helwys and Smyth during the torrid months of 1607-1608.[211] He became a fervent writer against the separatists, with works such as *Christian Advertisements and Counsels of Peace* (1608) with attracted the ire of Henry Ainsworth and Smyth, who called him a 'chameleon' who 'pretended zeal for the truth and faith of

207 Zachary Clyfton's family Bible which states August.
208 *Transactions of the Baptist History Society*, vol. 3, 1912-3.
209 Greasley, p.40
210 Coggins (1991), p.40
211 Coggins (1991), p.38

Christ'. This was ironic coming from Smyth, a man who changed his position many times over his life and was accused of being 'as changeable as the Moon' by Joseph Hall in 1610. Robinson argued that 'the Prelate of York hath so bewitched you with his flattery, eloquence and angels'.[212] Smyth accused him of having coveted the livings of 'Sawenby' (especially well paid) and Gainsborough:

> 'I do proclaim you to the whole world to be one of the most fearful apostates of the whole nation…I have noted your vehement desire to the parsonage of Sawenby, and your extreme indignation when you were defeated of it; further, your earnest desire to have been vicar of Gainsborough…'.[213]

He wrote a pamphlet urging against bishops 'but there was weakness in his character, and when it was proposed to print it, he dared not fix his name'.[214]

Although Bernard defended the Church of England he remained very much on the puritan wing, skirting the boundary for much of his life; he refused to use the sign of the cross whilst at Worksop in 1608 and 1611.[215] Despite this, in July 1608 Matthew confirmed his diocesan preaching licence, and Bernard dedicated some of his writings to Matthew. After moving to Batcombe in Somerset in 1613, he got into trouble for refusing to genuflect and for departing from the set prayers despite having a Bishop who would have known what to expect. This long-distance move is itself interesting, for in a 1635 dedication to Sir John Wray Bernard referred to 'your blessed Mother, Sister to that my honourable good Lord, the Right Reverend Father in God, James the Lord Bishop of Winchester'. This was James Montagu who, as Bishop of Bath and Wells, had brought him to Somerset.[216]

However, Bernard is also interesting as a writer of many faith books including *The Faithfull Shepherd* and *The Isle of Man* (1627) which has been seen as an influence on John Bunyan. He also showed an interest in the supernatural, claiming to have exorcised a demon whilst at Worksop. In 1627 he published *A Guide to Grand Jury Men* which denied that a 'good' witch could exist and argued for the execution of all who had signed up with the Devil.[217] He wrote this book to defend his own position after being involved in counselling one of the accused in a witchcraft trial at Taunton.

Even in his old age he was helping to raise money to help the 'godly' who had been deprived by Laud.

Bernard may not have crossed the Atlantic, but his influence did. His connections in New England included John White of Dorchester and John Cotton.[218] His fourth son Masakiell

---

212 John Robinson, cited in Kenneth Gibson, *Richard Bernard*, in Bennett (2005), *Society, Religion, and Culture in Seventeenth-century Nottinghamshire*, p.169

213 John Smyth, *Parallels, Censures and Observations*, 1609.

214 *The Works of John Smyth*, p.lx.

215 Kenneth Gibson, *Richard Bernard*, in Bennett (2005), p.168

216 Montagu was from a Northamptonshire puritan family had been a graduate at Christ's College, where Bernard was personally known to him, and was notably connected with many leading puritans including Hildersham as well as related to the Markhams. His sister Lucy married Sir William Wray in 1580 – cementing a great alliance of Midlands puritans. One of the same family was the famous Earl of Manchester, Parliamentary commander in the Civil War, and nephew to the bishop. James was a significant figure in preparing the King James Bible.

217 R L Greaves, *Richard Bernard*, in ODNB. Accessed 1 April 2014.

218 S Hardman Moore, *Pilgrims: New World Settlers and the Call of Home*, Yale, 2007, p.46

sailed to New England with the puritan rector of Colyton/Northleigh,[219] Joseph Hull, and several others from Batcombe; his daughter Mary emigrated in 1631 with her husband Roger Williams[220] who she had met in Essex. They would become the founders of Providence, Rhode Island, and the first Baptist church in America; they also took with them views on religious tolerance derived from writings of Smyth, Helwys and Murton. He was also a close friend of Sir Henry Rosewell of Forde Abbey, to whom he jointly dedicated a publication in 1629, saying 'I have….much honoured you in my heart for your true love to Religion, and your good respect for God's Ministers…'. This is a significant connection, for Sir Henry was a great supporter of the Massachusetts Bay colony and in 1640 was fined for holding conventicles in his private chapel.[221] In 1635 Bernard reconfirmed his links with the Wray family by dedicating a new book to Sir John Wray, son of Sir William, and used this chance[222] to praise the two sisters who had supported him: 'I cannot but commemorate so transcendent goodness of these your right honourable Ants,' he wrote, perhaps betraying his northern roots in his spelling, for their being 'noble minded friends towards me, imitating therein your worthy Father, and you blessed Mother'. He linked the latter to his other patron James Montagu, brother-in-law to Sir William Wray.

---

219 Close to Batcombe in Devon. Masakiell is believed to have returned to England by about 1644.
220 A curious coincidence is that Williams grew up at St Sepulchre's in London, worshipping in the same congregation as Lincolnshire's Captain John Smith, the famous explorer of America
221 Cliffe (1984), p.168
222 This time he was cited by the wardens, implying some factionalism within the parish. Jennings, p.83.

CHAPTER NINE

The Gunpowder Plot and Catholicism
1603-1640

The Gunpowder Plot, which involved people from Lincolnshire, had a significant impact during the reign of James I. His successor Charles was visibly more open to Catholic influences and his Church moved closer to these in its practice.

Chronology:
1603: James becomes King of England as well as Scotland
1605: Gunpowder Plot
1606: Tobie Matthew appointed Archbishop of York

Small elements of Catholicism persisted across the two counties, usually linked to specific gentry in an area, but except for the crisis caused by the Gunpowder Plot the focus tended to be on capturing Jesuit priests whilst those 'Church Catholics' who paid lip service to conformity were generally tolerated. Several Lincolnshire families were actively Catholic including that of Anthony Monson at Carlton where Mass was said regularly, and prophecies of change delivered. In Nottinghamshire Henry Pierrepont and his wife were Catholic, but this did not prevent him being knighted in 1603. Most families continued as usual with only occasional challenge. Nottinghamshire Catholicism seems to have been increasing or was better detected, for the 1603 list included 64 names.

The arrival of a new king is a time of potential weakness, and some elements tried to exploit this. Ollerton was the home of one branch of the Markham family who, by the 1590s, had shown interest in reverting to Catholicism. One of them, the soldier Sir Griffin Markham, was certainly a Catholic (although he resented the Jesuits) and saw the accession of James I as an opportunity; however, he was equally motivated by the desire to reclaim family lands in Nottinghamshire which had been lost to others. He hatched a bizarre plot to kidnap the new king, imprison him in the Tower, and demand both freedom of religion and return of his lands. His twin brothers seem to have done their best to avoid being involved. Markham was sentenced to death at Winchester in 1603 but, on the scaffold with the axe ready, this was commuted to exile for life for him and two others.

In or before 1595 he had married Anne, daughter of Peter Roos of Laxton. Her husband banished, Anne contracted a bigamous marriage with her manservant, James Sanford. This irregularity was soon common knowledge, and she was forced to perform penance at Paul's Cross in November 1617. Markham himself wandered Europe as a soldier and spy and was last heard of in Vienna in 1644.

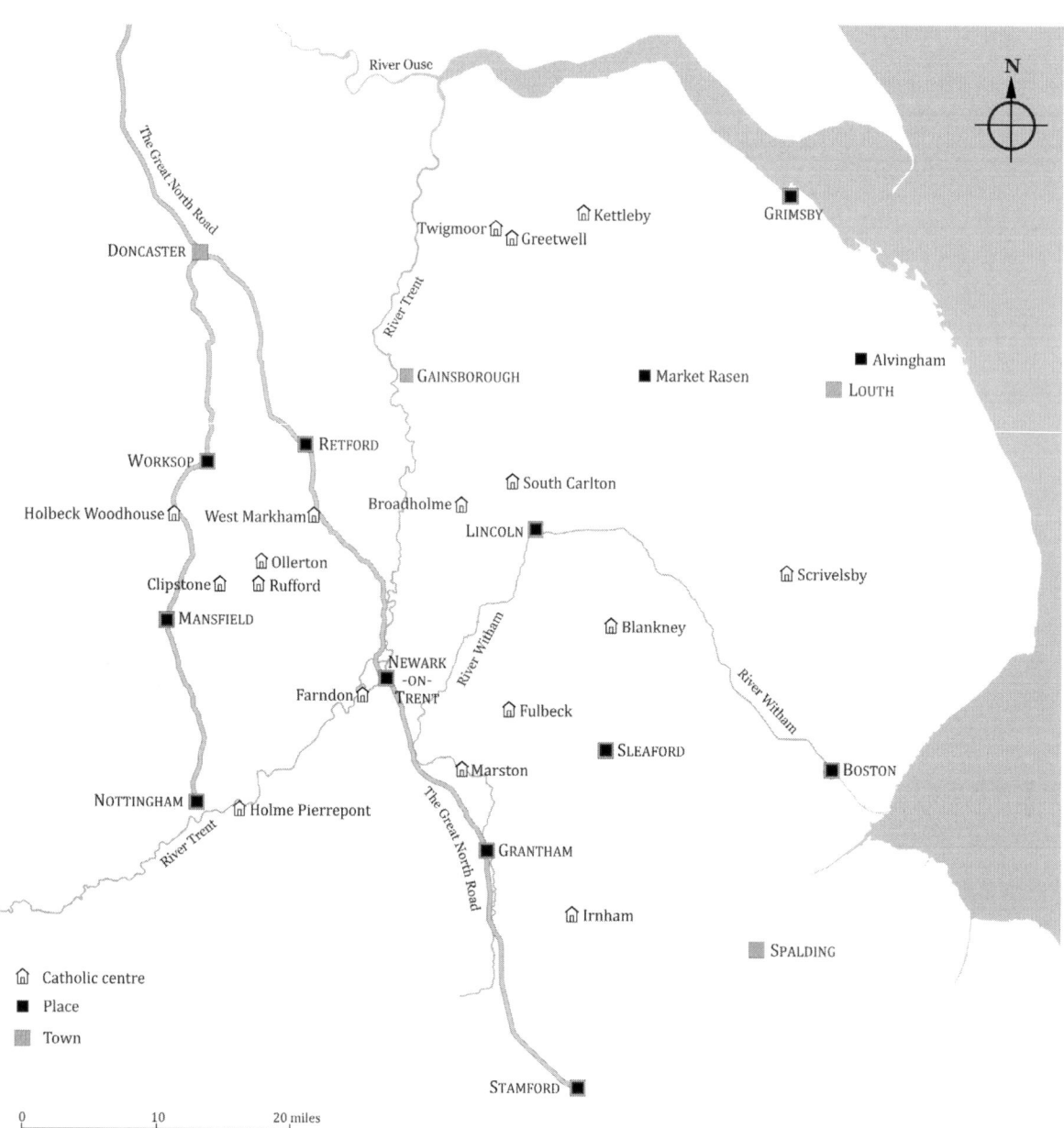

River Ouse

N

Twigmoor Kettleby
Greetwell

GRIMSBY

The Great North Road

DONCASTER

River Trent

GAINSBOROUGH Market Rasen

Alvingham
LOUTH

WORKSOP RETFORD

South Carlton

Holbeck Woodhouse West Markham Broadholme

LINCOLN

Scrivelsby

Ollerton
Clipstone Rufford

Blankney

MANSFIELD

River Witham

NEWARK
-ON-
TRENT

Farndon

Fulbeck

River Witham

Marston

SLEAFORD

BOSTON

NOTTINGHAM Holme Pierrepont

River Trent

The Great North Road

GRANTHAM

Irnham

SPALDING

Catholic centre
Place
Town

0   10   20 miles

STAMFORD

We have already mentioned that Twigmoor (Twigmore), an isolated place between Scunthorpe and Brigg, was a centre of Catholicism during Elizabeth I's and James I's reigns. The manor belonged to the Tyrwhitts; in 1580 the young Lord Sheffield was living nearby in Sir Robert Tyrwhitt III's house at Kettleby, when his tutor became alarmed that the Tyrwhitt sons were converting Sheffield to Catholicism and he was resorting to 'the Church of Twigmore' for masses with Robert Tyrwhitt. Five of them were arrested and imprisoned; it is likely at least one died in prison and Sir Robert died in 1581. But Sheffield's marriage to a Catholic woman of this family, conducted with Catholic rites, was to cause him much trouble.

In 1597 Anthony Atkinson wrote to Sir Robert Cecil for permission to use armed ships from Hull to root out the recusants. 'This place is one of the worst in Her Majesty's dominions and is used like a Popish college for traitors' one of Cecil's agents wrote, who pointed out that 'great woods, caves and vaults' aided the Catholic agents.[1] Hajzyk has suggested that Twigmoor benefited from being in a diocese where Catholics were less actively pursued compared to the situation in York, where they were regarded as a greater threat. One of the Tyrwhitts provided financial support for Father John Gerard, a Jesuit priest, from 1598 to 1606.

Fugitive priests said Mass there in 1604. John, or Jack, Wright lived here and became involved in Catesby's 'Gunpowder Plot' of 1605, because of which he moved his family away. He had been involved in a plot in 1601 and was said to be one of the best swordsmen in the land. Thomas Percy, also recruited by Catesby, was Wright's brother-in-law. Also involved were Ambrose Rookwood, who married Elizabeth Tyrwhitt in 1599, and her cousin Robert Keyes; these were both executed in 1606. Keyes was the son of the rector of Staveley near Chesterfield, and his mother was a Tyrwhitt.

Rookwood was educated in France and a known Catholic, indicted for recusancy in Middlesex in 1605; after this he moved North. He was recruited into the conspiracy by Robert Catesby. They then recruited Jack Wright, a Yorkshireman living at Twigmore, in 1604; he seems to have been a committed Catholic and had endured prison, though Father John Gerard thought he became a Catholic only in 1601. Christopher Wright was brought in during 1605; it is possible he had been involved in secret approaches to Philip of Spain in 1603.

The plot to blow up the House of Lords and the King with it was hatched by Robert Catesby, who was from Northamptonshire. The story of how Guy Fawkes was discovered in the cellars and nearly a tun of gunpowder revealed is of course well known. The conspiracy discovered, most of them fled north, Rookwood having prepared a sequence of horses in case of flight being needed. The conspirators were cornered at Holbeach House in Staffordshire. During the fighting, Rookwood was injured by gunpowder but survived to be captured. Both Wright brothers died in the fighting. Rookwood's wife, Elizabeth Tyrwhitt, was also arrested.

On 31 January 1606 Winter, Keyes, Rookwood and Fawkes were executed in London. They left behind a controversial legacy, one that even Catholics at the time had struggled

---

1   Anthony Atkinson to Robert Cecil in *Cecil Papers*, 12 July 1597.

with. It proposed an unprecedented level of violence and once again connected belief in Catholicism with a plot to kill the Monarch. The Tyrwhitt family were perhaps fortunate to survive this disaster and a later family history blames Rookwood for the disaster: 'this unhappy and infatuated man had been bred amongst the most bigoted Romanists in England Flanders...beloved of all who knew him' – but blindly led into conspiracy by Catesby.[2]

Stories about Twigmore site have continued to circulate, such as that it was riddled with underground hides and in 1940 a complete underground stable was discovered. In general, the heavy Lincolnshire element to the plot has tended to be glossed over due to a focus on Fawkes or Catesby.

Perhaps one effect of the Gunpowder Plot was to ensure the appointment of Tobie Matthew as Archbishop of York in 1606, having previously lost out for Canterbury to the more conservative Bancroft. Matthew was much more of a puritan in his heart, valued preaching, and encouraged 'preaching exercises'. He was clearly tolerant of men like Richard Bernard of Worksop, who subscribed to the Three Articles in 1608 and yet never truly conformed. He was similarly tolerant in 1607 of Thomas Toller and Robert Gifford as he needed good preachers even if they were known to be nonconformist. Even as late as 1616 he supported Lady Grantham's[3] proposal for preaching exercises in Nottinghamshire – as long as they were led by conformists, although none of them conformed for long.[4] One view is that 'under his rule little was done to curb even the most persistent offenders'[5] so that only those who delivered 'factious' preaching or took a separatist line forced his hand.

Puritans complained that in the Lincoln diocese at least, it was easier to be a Catholic nonconformist than a Protestant one. Four men from Grantham summonsed for 'gadding about' in 1611 complained that no one would have bothered had they been 'Papists'. Perhaps this explains why Sir Thomas Grantham, regularly elected to Parliament, used his position to accuse others of being Catholics and to complain that the diocese of Durham never identified any 'recusants'. Their low profile was because the 'Church Papists' kept up a pretence of conformity, just as many puritans did, but by the 1630s there was indeed more tolerance of Catholicism. Some like the Dymokes even controlled their own parishes – ten in the case of this family.[6] A significant influence around Grantham was Sir George Manners, who became 7th Earl of Rutland in 1632. The Manners family had been widely suspected of Catholicism, though James I was not aware of this when he stayed at Belvoir in 1604 – though Sir George lived much of his life at Fulbeck. In May 1610 he was given responsibility for collecting fines from Lincolnshire recusants – two of whom were his brothers; in 1624 he was again chosen to manage land seizures from Catholics, not without some local opposition. Sir Thomas Grantham felt it necessary to denounce the 6th Earl as a Catholic that same year.

---

2   R P Tyrwhitt, *Notices and remains of the Family of Tyrwhitt*, London, 1862, p.101
3   The wife of Sir Thomas Grantham, a family close to that of Col Hutchinson
4   R Oates, *Moderate Radical*, p.214
5   Cliffe (1984), p.146
6   This included Horkstow, where the parish was very poor and had no Bible in the early 1600s! (Hajzyk, p.330)

In 1612 King James was concerned enough to order precautions against an armed revolt in Lincolnshire.[7] In 1617 there were five recusants being held at Lincoln Castle, leading to complaints they were receiving too much liberty. Puritans helped to uncover these – for example in 1618 Sir Thomas Grantham informed the King that the widow of Robert Carre was a Catholic.

Nonetheless, Lincolnshire retained strong Catholic elements especially in areas of the county where Catholic families like the Tyrwhitts retained influence. Charles Dallison of Greetwell, who was Recorder of Lincoln from 1637, was typical of these, suspected most of his life of being a 'Church Catholic' – attending Church to cover his true views. Inevitably men such as these came to be Royalist supporters, Dallison was knighted by Charles in 1641; Dallison's son and two daughters all converted to Catholicism – the latter becoming nuns. Those who supported Laud in the 1630s, like Sir John Monson of South Carlton, were seen as secret Catholics. It was mainly lower gentry or the humble classes who were cited for recusancy such as Matthew Gooche at Alvingham in 1609; he was from a known recusant family in a village where the schoolmaster was also cited for Catholicism.

Also significant is the Thorold family, which had several branches including at Marston and Blankney. Thomas Thorold converted in about 1622 and went to Rome in 1629; he spent some time in England as a Jesuit priest from 1635 and by the 1640s was one of the leading clerics in English Catholicism under the alias of Thomas Carwell. Clifton Thorold was the son of Anthony Thorold and joined the English College in 1638 whilst another Anthony, from the Grantham branch of the family, went to Flanders in 1646. Under the Thimbleby family, Irnham was also was a centre of Catholicism and the family line there continued in the faith until its extinction in 1712. During the Stuart era the Thimbleby family married into other Catholic families such as that of Lord Aston. Richard Thimbleby, who died in 1623, had a son (also called Richard) who became a Jesuit and three daughters who became nuns; the family was continued by Elizabeth through her marriage into the Conquest family. Sir John Thimbleby was knighted at Belvoir in 1624.

Thomas Doughty, who had Lincolnshire origins, became the first Carmelite missionary to England in about 1614. He became based at London, to an extent protected by the Spanish ambassador, and is claimed to have been the person who 'converted' George Calvert, Lord Baltimore – although Calvert came from a family who only reluctantly conformed. He supported Baltimore in a plan to create a Catholic colony named Avalon in Newfoundland.[8]

In Nottinghamshire, there was a similar pattern of small clusters of Catholics, often based around a local family of significance. The Markhams of Ollerton (notably George Markham) and eventually a cluster around Holbeck Woodhouse near Welbeck developed.[9] The Cavendishes of Welbeck also followed Catholic inclinations. Sir Charles Cavendish (1553-1617) was widely suspected of being a Catholic and a 'bad influence' on the 7th Earl of Shrewsbury who was married to his sister, who was known to be Catholic; another

---

7   Hill (1956), p.110

8   Baltimore's project at Avalon failed and he was then ordered out of Virginia due to his religion. He did not live long enough to see the success of the colony of Maryland, intended to practice free worship, for he died in 1632.

9   Kate Holland (ed), *Mender of Disorders*, Nottingham, 2004, p.8

sister, Frances Pierrepont was also Catholic, and all of these sided with the Royalists in the Civil War.

By 1608 Catholics also included Rutland Molyneux of West Markham and Farndon, who had gained the Bevercotes estate through marriage. The following year he was involved in a serious accusation of harbouring 'the most notorious recusants' by Lady Anne Markham of Bestwood, which was attributed to the bitter relations between local gentry at that time[10] which had included one of the Markham boys being killed in a duel which was witnessed by Thomas Helwys's father. Lady Markham's dislike of Molyneux was because she had hoped to secure a pardon for her husband Sir Griffin by luring the fugitive Father Gerard to her house, but Molyneux had given him a warning so that he escaped to Harwich. Molyneux was also harassed by Francis Chapman who was chaplain to Sir John Holles and vicar of West Markham, who wrote to St John's College to try to force him out of a leasehold property on account of being 'evil to the state, the college and his neighbours'.[11] The Molyneux family later moved to Fledborough.

Sir John Holles of Haughton was asked to search out Catholicism in Nottinghamshire and on this basis ransacked the home of his old enemies, the Talbots, at Rufford Abbey – finding little.[12] The Countess of Shrewsbury, Jane Talbot, was well known for her Catholicism and Rufford ideal for harbouring priests, but her views led to the Countess being 'closely confined' from 1613-15 and her refusal to swear allegiance led to a £20,000 fine for her husband. Holles complained that most of the 'granges' in the district harboured Catholics. In 1612-16 Anne Vaux, noted for sheltering Father Garnet at the time of the Gunpowder Plot, was living at Broadholme near Thorney (Notts) and was regularly cited for not attending church. Holles himself suffered a setback when disgraced in the collateral damage from the Overbury affair, which led to the execution of Sir Gervase Helwys in 1615.

Other Nottinghamshire Catholics included Lady Elizabeth Gilby at Hayton in the 1620s. In 1603 only 54 Catholics were reported in Lincolnshire, but the Bishop estimated 222 a fairer number with as many as 80 gentry.[13]

In 1633 a boy named John Sherwood died at the house of Marie Hodgson, a known Catholic, in Holbeck Woodhouse, and was buried at night at Cuckney probably due to his being a Catholic. There was a Catholic community around Clipstone throughout this period.

10   *Calendar of State Papers*, August 26, 1609.
11   St John's College: SJCR/SJAR/1/1/Clayton/3/3/1
12   Alexander Thomson, *John Holles*, in *The Journal of Modern History*, June 1936, p.154.
13   Hajzyk, p.409

CHAPTER TEN

Paths Diverge
Baptists and the Mayflower
1608-1620

Once in the Netherlands, the separatists from Nottinghamshire and Lincolnshire soon split again into different factions. The restless John Smyth began the English Baptist denomination by his rejection of infant baptism and also embraced the 'free will' Gospel interpretation of Arminius known as Arminianism – controversial in that this was soon also in the ascendancy in England amongst those seen as closet-Catholics. Meanwhile, the erstwhile Babworth congregation, with others, gathered anew at Leiden under John Robinson's leadership. From here, several provided the leadership for the 'Mayflower' voyage in 1620.

Ironically, both groups became influential in the development of Christianity in the United States – one as Congregationalists and the other as Baptists. However, it was the Baptists who developed, again from continental thinking, a radical new view of religious tolerance.

Chronology:
1607: Captain John Smith arrives in Virginia
1608: Separatists mostly arrive in the Netherlands
1609: John Robinson moves to Leiden; Smyth decides on believers' baptism
1610: Helwys and Smyth split
1612: John Smyth dies whilst Helwys moves back to England
1614: Captain John Smith maps coast of New England
1616: Richard Clifton dies in Amsterdam
1620: The Mayflower sails to America

Smyth's Journey

The Nottinghamshire and Lincolnshire people did not arrive in a country devoid of puritan compatriots. Francis Johnson, who Smyth knew well from Christ's College, and Henry Ainsworth already had the 'Ancient Church' there since 1597, but nonetheless, Smyth kept separate from them and might have emerged as the key leader of the new exiles; Clifton wrote that he was the one who 'to whose charge both I and diverse others had once purposed to have committed our soules' until they found disagreements arose. Clifton remained in Amsterdam after Robinson left for Leiden in 1609 and eventually joined the Johnson 'Ancient Church'. Later Clifton was dragged into a 'pamphlet war' with Ainsworth that delighted critics in England, and later also with John Smyth.

In the Netherlands doctrinal issues developed that ultimately drove wider splits in the separatist body, however, far they had ever been one in the first place. Smyth had anticipated this, warning his congregation that they would encounter challenges and that 'we are like men set upon the ice, and therefore may easily slide and fall'.[14] Smyth may have reached Amsterdam before the others, for he had time to reflect on his differences from the Ancient Church in *The Differences of the Churches of the separation*, published in 1608; he disagreed with them about the use of translated scripture in 'spirituall worship' (which he thought had the effect of 'quenching the spirit'), church officers and gifts to the church. By September 1608, there was no chance of them joining together.[15]

Smyth probably came into closer contact with the rejection of child baptism (known as 'paedo-baptism') through his connection with a group called the Mennonites, a type of group that he would have had little previous connection with. The specific Mennonite group was called the 'Waterlanders'. A year or two after arriving,[16] perhaps in 1609, Smyth's congregation moved into a 'bakehouse' – a former hard tack bakery with living quarters – which had been acquired by Jan Munter of the Mennonites.[17] This was more than just a 'bakehouse' for its Mennonite function was to provide food and housing for poor church members – and it now did this for Smyth's congregation until 1632 – but it would have been too small to accommodate all those who had crossed the North Sea.

One immediate result seems to have been that Smyth got to consider the issue of baptism, which had been hugely controversial since the horrific events at Münster in 1534-6. Smyth's publication of *The Character of the Beast* in 1609 showed that he had already become a believer in adult baptism by March 1609, provoking a dispute with Clifton.

The apparently revolutionary idea about baptism was more common in Holland and almost unknown in England. Baptists – or Anabaptists – had been present in Europe since the 1520s but had often provoked extreme reactions, especially after the dreadful events at Münster in 1534-5.[18] Smyth's close contact with anabaptists, the Mennonites, perhaps changed his mind. Other English Anabaptists were around – Leonard Busher appears to be one, and he was still in the Netherlands when he contacted the Mennonites for help in 1642 from Delft, having also written importantly on religious liberty. Men like John Hancock and Henry Martin may have joined Smyth or the Mennonites having previously left the Ancient Church in the 1590s.[19] In 1610 Smyth appears to have had about forty in his congregation, reduced to about thirty by January 1615 when he applied to join the

---

14   W R Estep *The English Baptist Legacy of Freedom and the American Experience*, in *Pilgrim Pathways*, p.264
15   Wright (2006), p.28
16   James R Coggins suggests by February 1609 when they 'formally broke' with Robinson's group.
17   Mary S Sprunger in T M Safley (ed), *Reformation of Charity – Secular and Religious in Early Modern Europe*
18   Anabaptists seized control of the city in 1534 leading to some frenzied events and a year-long siege led by the local bishop.
19   Keith L Sprunger, *Dutch Puritanism*, New York, 2016, p.83

Mennonites.[20]

Coggins took the view that the Scrooby-Gainsborough groups 'split' by early 1609 due to Smyth criticising Robinson, also over the use of Biblical translations. Quite where baptism fitted chronologically within a number of issues including apostolic succession is not possible to clarify. Perhaps the real factor was Smyth's endless search for greater and greater 'purity'. In 1609 Smyth criticised Clifton for sticking with infant baptism, telling him that 'you are subtly blind and lead the blind after you into the ditch.[21]' To Smyth, baptism was not simply washing in water but 'it is baptism of the Spirit, the confession of the mouth, and the washing with water'. The first two of these could not be done by an infant. Sprunger suggests that Smyth refused to join the Johnson church because of the translation issue and split from the others in 1610.[22] White thinks that Smyth's conversion to baptism attracted some members to split off from the Ancient Church in 1610, which to an extent was troubled with anabaptists itself in 1609.

Once people started to reject the 'baptism' they had received from the Church of England, questions developed over who might then perform the baptism of the believers. A principle at stake was that of 'apostolic succession' – should there effectively be a spiritual 'line of descent' and in the absence of one could a man baptise himself?

John Smyth resolved this problem by 'baptising first himself, then Mr Helwys, then the rest' according to the version recorded by John Robinson. This seems to have been done between late 1608 and March 1609 from the evidence in Smyth's and Clifton's written dispute which was boiling over during mid-March 1609.[23] It may have simply been done by sprinkling water from a basin.[24] Smyth baptised himself because he thought no other Church could do this, but this led eventually to a breach with Helwys, when Smyth revised his views, and proposed another baptism.[25] This created an irreparable breach with Clifton, Robinson, Brewster and others.

Clifton and Smyth's dispute in March 1609 was written up by Smyth in *The Character of the Beast* and to which Clifton replied in *A Plea for Infants*. Bradford later wrote of Clifton, 'Much good had he done, and converted many to God by his faithful and powerful ministry, and truth in preaching and catechising; sound and orthodox he always was, and so continued to the end'.[26] By denying the validity of these forms of baptism, Smyth also denied the controversial label of 'anabaptist'. Edward Southworth and Bromhead met with Clifton to try to persuade him, but eventually it was Southworth who left to join Robinson.[27] He died in 1616.

Given that Smyth and Helwys also began a journey from rigid Calvinism to a 'free will' or Arminian view of salvation, this has led to debates as to how far Smyth's changing views reflected Mennonite influence. In Coggins' view, Smyth had begun his journey to

---

20   Sprunger, p.83
21   Whitley, p.680
22   Sprunger, *Dutch Puritanism*, various pages
23   Coggins (1991), p.63
24   Champlain, p.238. White cites Joseph Hall's comment of 'in a bason'.
25   Wright (2006), p.33
26   Nathaniel Morton and others, *New England's Memorial*, Boston, 6th edition 1855, p.471
27   Coggins (1991), p.66

believers' baptism by early 1609 with no Mennonite influence but that this was evident by the time he published *The Character of the Beast* later that year.[28] For example, the issue of the limiting of the authority of magistrates over religious matters begins to appear in his work: this was a Mennonite theme, and contrasted with the others who still argued the role of the magistrate was to impose *rightful* religion. Coggins concluded that the confessions of faith published by both Smyth and Helwys groups showed they 'had travelled some considerable way together in accepting Mennonite theology'.[29] Both showed wide acceptance of free will and the universal possibility of salvation, rejecting 'original sin'. This view was associated with the theology of Arminius, and so was called Arminianism, but Smyth doubtless was aware of it before he got to Amsterdam; the theologian Peter Baro taught a version at Cambridge and his son Peter Baron clearly did so when living at Boston. As we have seen, in 1598-9 the Aswarby vicar William Williams was accused of preaching 'universality of grace to every sinner' and that 'God did not violently drawe or inevitably force any man to receive grace'. Williams was also involved in an argument about whether the 'elect' might 'depart from grace given' but was silenced by Bishop Chaderton in November 1598 – though he then went to Cambridge to get support from Whitgift. Smyth would surely have been aware of all this as Baro had been effectively sacked from Cambridge in 1596. Though he soon split with Helwys and Murton, elements of Smyth's new thinking informed their own as they began the General Baptists.

What sort of church did Smyth lead in the Netherlands? He rejected any use of books in services, disdaining the approach of the *Book of Common Prayer*; instead, services could include praying, tithing, prophesying (interpretation?), the singing of psalms, baptism and celebrating the Lord's Supper.[30] He rejected the use of the Bible in English in services since the translation was a 'work of man'. Smyth's services are known because Hugh and Anne Bromhead were writing to contacts in London in July 1609. The morning service had a series of speakers, each for up to 45 minutes, with no music apparent. Bromhead (and his wife Anne) also sent a letter to their cousin Sir William Hamerton in autumn 1608 which described the services in Helwys's church – four hours long, with much reading from the Bible and prophesying upon it.[31]

The core of Smyth's new church was himself, Helwys, John Murton, Thomas Piggott, possibly from Axholme, and Thomas Seamer[32] but there were 39 signatories of a confession of faith.[33] However, the four listed here, with about six others, all split from Smyth by 1610.[34] There was also Hugh Bromhead and his wife, Gervase Neville and a Robert 'Southworth' or perhaps 'Southwood' – and therefore possibly the deprived minister of Headon, a topic which has been hotly debated.[35] Members from Worksop and Warsop were probably refugees from Bernard's abandoned congregation. Stephen Wright has suggested Ursula Bywater was connected with Rev Thomas Bywater, a Christ's

---

28 Coggins (1991), p.73

29 Coggins (1991), p.77

30 Ibid, p.20

31 Champlain, p.236

32 This was a Gainsborough name. Thomas Seamer married Jane Hailes at All Saints, Gainsborough in 1592, and their first child was also called Thomas.

33 B Evans, *Early English Baptists Vol 1*, p.211. Coggins (1991) says that 43 agreed the confession of faith in 1610

34 Sprunger, *Dutch Puritanism*, p.81

35 Wright (2006), p.25-6

College graduate c.1593, who was imprisoned for a book which challenged religious opinions in 1605[36]; he was known to have been a chaplain to Lord Edmund Sheffield and later Lord John Hunsdon.

Smyth published two further works in Amsterdam: *The Differences of the Churches of the Separation* (which perhaps provoked the split with Robinson) and *Parallels, Censures, Observations* (which attacked conformists like Bernard) almost simultaneously in 1609. Parts of the latter were written whilst still in England and include his discussions with Bernard and others including 'AS', prompting a further reply from Bernard.

The Robinson Congregation

Almost immediately after their arrival, Robinson got into a doctrinal dispute with Francis Johnson due to his preference for the French style of Protestantism but also with Smyth we may assume. Robinson seems to have become uncomfortable with Johnson's more centralised proposals for church government – 'polity'.[37] On 12 February 1609 the application of Robinson, Brewster and others to move to Leiden was accepted; by 24 March Smyth had already heard of their move[38] and they had done so by May 1, all of which suggests a dispute must have arisen late in 1608 probably as a result of Smyth's differences from Johnson with Coggins suggesting Robinson took a middle position on key issues.[39] Coggins believes that around two-thirds of the 'pilgrims' went with Robinson and abandoned Smyth.

Robinson held strongly to the idea of infant baptism which became a defining issue in his split with Helwys and Smyth. He was being criticised by his old friend Richard Bernard and in 1610 was forced to publish *A Justification of Separation* in response. In 1611 he bought a house in Leiden that also served as a church. At first, he was resolutely opposed to links with non-separatists but gradually moderated his views, although he always refused to link up with Helwys and Smyth.

Smyth and Helwys Separate

By early 1610 Smyth had decided that self-baptism was wrong, perhaps influenced by criticism such as in John Hetherington's *A Description of the Church of Christ with Her Peculiar Privileges*. He applied to join the Waterlander Mennonite church around February 1610 which he saw as a 'true' Church. The Amsterdam bakehouse had been rented from a

---

36 Bywater offered advice to King James, handing it to the King while he was out hunting, which was passed to the Privy Council. He was accused of falsifying scripture. He had been ordained in the Diocese of York. Sheffield, who needed a robust puritan since his wife Ursula Tyrwhitt was a Catholic, sacked him in the midst of the ensuing crisis. Bywater was alleged to be bitter at his lack of personal promotion. So, Bywater was in the right territory, but other sources have Ursula as a widow of Thomas Bywater who had died by 1615 – an interesting coincidence of names.

37 Wright (2006), p.31

38 Smyth, *Works II*, p.664

39 Coggins (1991), p.58

Mennonite, and the Mennonites rejected the predestination beliefs of the Calvinists. This caused a defining split with Helwys who refused to join the Mennonites (though he is still listed there as a 'leader') and he effectively founded the first English 'Baptist' church in 1610 with around ten others when he divided from the Smyth group, which was rather larger.[40] Initial members included John Murton and Thomas Seamer; they condemned the Smyth faction as 'heathen and publicans'. Smyth explained his belief that baptism was for those 'which hear, believe, and with penitent heart receive the doctrine of the Holy Gospel....and no unspeaking children.[41]' Smyth also favoured the washing of feet and the laying on of hands, the latter act being seen as linked to the receiving of the Holy Spirit.[42]

Smyth's group was much the larger and included Gervase Neville and Hugh Bromhead. However, by 1611 Neville was striving 'to build up the succession of Rome', according to Helwys, seen as meaning a complete reversal in his position.

By 1610 Smyth, Helwys and Murton had also begun to reject Calvinism under the influence of Arminianism, perhaps via the Mennonites.[43] That Helwys still had some relations with the Mennonites himself can be seen by his advice to them to block the membership of Smyth etc. In article five of his belief code, Smyth stated that God's grace was freely available to all – not limited to an 'elect'. He wrote that 'original sin is an idle term.....there is no such thing,' and continued that 'God doth not create or predestinate any man to destruction'. He now believed that God 'has ordained all men (no one being reprobated) to life....God imposes no necessity of sinning on any one; but man freely, by Satanic instigation, departs from God'. After he died in 1612, his *Propositions and Conclusions* rejected original sin and predestination outright. He believed that to argue Christ died only for some was to limit the power and authority of Christ.

Forty-three of Smyth's group signed the Mennonite confession of faith although only 32 signed the application to join them. The Mennonites then interviewed the English on their beliefs, following which a poll was taken of the congregation – most of whom agreed to accept the English, but delayed a final decision to consult with other Mennonites.

Meanwhile, Smyth had contracted consumption and knew that he was dying. In this context he wrote *Called the Retraction of his Errours and the Confirmation of the Truth* in which he showed a new tendency towards tolerance and forgiveness, but delayed a final decision to consult with other Mennonites.

Thus, when Smyth died in August 1612, relations with the Waterlander Mennonites were still not fully resolved, passing the leadership to Thomas Pygott who also published his more conciliatory final writings. The remaining people applied to join the Mennonites

40   There may have been Anabaptist groups in England in the 1590s, but it is clear that Helwys started the church that has been continuous since. See Burrage, p.233. Various 'traditional' claims have been made to a Baptist church on Axholme by 1599. Stories that John Smyth had actually been baptised by 'Elder John Morton' in the River Don near Crowle and had walked to Epworth in his wet clothes were, as Kershaw argues, a forgery and the stone making the claim at Crowle Chapel therefore erroneous. The error was 'proved' by documents 'discovered' at West Butterwick in 1866 which were used to dupe minister Jabez Stutterd. Further falsifications were published in 1879-81 by John Clifford.

41   C Douglas Weaver, *In Search of the New Testament Church*, p21

42   C Douglas Weaver, p.24

43   Watts (1986), vol 1, p.46

in November 1614 but only in January 1615 were the remnants, twenty-six of them, admitted to that fellowship although an English identity was evident until 1642.[44] The Bromheads stayed with Smyth, but it seems that Hugh had died by 1615 although his wife lived to merge with the Mennonites.[45] Occasional new arrivals, such as Swithin Grindall in 1615, were baptised into the Mennonites. Pygott became a full member of the Mennonites in 1620 although language always proved a barrier; he died in about 1639. Another lay leader was John Drew ('Druw') who was in active correspondence with Baptists in Lincoln in 1630 and was still alive in 1640; he resigned from his position with the Mennonites as his Dutch language was insufficient. A few more joined in the 1640s but gradually the remnant lost their English identity.

One link for the Smyth congregation which is an intriguing mystery is the connection to the influential radical and 'leveller', Richard Overton. A man of this name applied for baptism in 1615 in Amsterdam, though presumably too old to have been the later Leveller, and several Overtons/Overtooms were baptised by the Mennonites around 1640.[46] The family were reputedly of Lincolnshire origin, and Overton the Leveller was certainly a Baptist with some agricultural interests. His pamphlet *The Arraignment of Mr Persecution* showed Baptist thinking in arguing for toleration of Jews and Catholics.

The Helwys Faction

Helwys and a few others split with Smyth sometime in late 1609 to early 1610. Helwys, Murton, William Pygott and Thomas Seamer with their families formed a new congregation, perhaps ten people in all. The remaining members of the Smyth group then applied to join the Waterlanders, which Helwys tried to prevent in March 1610. The Helwys group responded by excommunicating the Smyth group.

The defining issue was Smyth's decision that they should apply for another baptism by the Waterlanders. This was because his original decision to baptise himself was based on the lack of a 'true Church' to do the baptism, but by 1610 he had concluded the Waterlanders were such a Church. However, as far as we know Smyth was never re-baptised by the Waterlanders – he and his followers were thus also accepted as a 'true Church' by the Dutch, despite him having written to them to say they admitted their 'error' that 'they began to baptise themselves'.[47]

The Waterlanders saw the Smyth baptisms as 'disorderly' but not erroneous, an argument that failed to convince Helwys. It is strange that such a fine line appears to have divided

---

44 Coggins (1991) lists some of those still with Smyth and the Dutch version of their origins. John and Ales/ Alice Arnefield from 'Eppestown', therefore Helwys's servant; Alexander Hodgkin and Jane Southworth from Worksop; Margaret 'Mauritze' from 'Scheckbye' which we might see as Skegby; Jervase Nevill from Scrooby; Frances Pygott, Dorothea Thomson, Thomas Pygott, Mother Pygott, Ales Pygott from 'Axen'; two Thomsons from 'Lauwe' and Margaret Pygott from 'Bafford' which must be Helwys's servant from Basford.

45 Coggins (1991), p.111. About 28 were accepted without baptism, four new members were baptised and four rejected.

46 However, ODNB and other sources doubt the date of this and suggest he made his confession much later.

47 Smyth, *Works*, 2:681

them after so many years together, but there were perhaps other issues lying beneath.

Helwys, who had some other subtle differences from Smyth on theology,[48] concentrated on defining the beliefs of his own group and in 1611 produced his *Declaration of Faith of the English Church Remaining at Amsterdam* with 19 articles. This was especially intended for readers in England. He rejected Calvinist predestination ideas in article 5 – 'God hath predestined that all who believe in him shall be saved'.[49] In article 9 Helwys rejected any control of the church by secular authorities. In fact, he produced four works in 1611-12, some of which attacked the positions of his fellow separatists including Smyth, although the two men were fellow Arminians. Probably in 1611,[50] Helwys's *'An Advertisement or Admonition unto the Congregations'* addressed the Dutch, pointing out 'errors' by the Mennonites, and called Smyth an apostate, largely for trying to join them. Helwys blamed the Mennonites for the split in the English; he argued against the succession issue by showing that no Anabaptist could prove the line of 'succession' from Christ. Also, in 1611 he published another pamphlet denying that any unbaptised child could be condemned. Helwys, Pygott, Seamer and Murton sent a letter to the Waterlanders rejecting 'succession' in baptism and ordination.

In 1611 Helwys published *A Short and Plaine Proof...*[51] which he dedicated to Isabel Bowes (Wray), back in England. This rejected predestination and attempted to woo this influential woman away from Calvinism. Here we see Helwys the evangelist for his cause, with an eye on the English audience.

For Helwys there was clear pain in the situation. He complained that 'our wounds are yet fresh and greene' from the separation and condemned Smyth as a 'wicked man'. He told the Waterlanders that 'you have made our friends into enemies'. Within this we can read his desperation – a small band of laymen, none with academic knowledge of theology, in a land where they knew little of the language. One can see here perhaps the belief that returning to England might offer the prospect of survival as a group, despite the risks.

So, Smyth and Helwys were far from friends when the former died, but there is no doubt there had been great love between them, as Helwys acknowledged even in 1611:

> Have we not neglected ourselves, our wives, our children and all we had and respected him? And we confess we had good cause so to do in respect of those most excellent gifts and graces of God that then did abound in him. And all our love was too little for him and not worthy of him'.

It may be tempting to weigh the relative influence of Smyth and Helwys, with the former of greater fame than the latter. Though one stayed to build a new Church in a new land, and the other to do the same task in the old country, both were crucial. We can easily agree with one writer that 'the General Baptist tradition, through the ideas of founders John

---

48 Coggins (1991) provides a useful summary of these – including a dispute over the bodily nature of Christ, an interpretation of 'apostolic succession', and attitudes to Old and New Testaments.

49 See the debate on the views of Robinson, Smyth, Helwys, etc in Timothy George, *Predestination in a Separatist Context* in *The Sixteenth Century Journal*, 1984, p.73

50 Coggins (1991), p.98

51 The full title was *A Short and Plaine proofe by the Word and works of God that God's decree is not the cause of anie Man's sinne or condemnation. And that all men are redeemed by Christ. As also That no Infants are Condemned.*

Smyth and Thomas Helwys, implanted Baptist ideas that still characterise the Baptist identity in the 21st century'.[52] Most importantly Helwys held to Smyth's conversion to a religion free of legal restraint and to Arminianism: 'God would have all men saved,' he wrote.

When Helwys and John Murton put their views into print, Robinson responded, insinuating that as non-clerics they knew little. He called them 'double washers' and said, 'they know not what they speak'. Murton published *A Description of what God hath predestined concerning Man....* was published in 1620.

The fledgling communities were bolstered by occasional extra migrants and through marriage. This gives us some evidence as to who they were, such as when 'Henry Cullandt' married 'Margaret Grymsdiche' at Amsterdam on 5 July 1608, both being from Sutton-cum-Lound which also produced Margery Dale.[53] John Murton, a key member of Smyth's congregation from Gainsborough, married Jane Hodgkin[54] of Worksop on 23 August 1608; Rosamond Horsfield also came from Worksop as did William Jepson – both moving on to Leiden with the Robinson group. A week later Francis 'Pigett' [sic] of Axholme married Margaret 'Struts' of Basford. The Piggotts were a significant family in the group, and Thomas Piggott returned to England with Helwys and Murton as well as editing Smyth's last work and writing a short account of his last days. They were related to Dorothy Strutt, also of Axholme. It has been suggested that Thomsons of Louth became Baptists at Amsterdam in 1609.[55] Others who moved to the Netherlands included the Bannister family from Retford, John Williams and James Hurst of the same town. Margaret Morris of Scrooby was there by 1615.

Families were split by the migration, but often consistent in their theology. Anne Southworth, in trouble at Clarborough in 1620 for not attending communion, was sister to Thomas and Edward who were at Leiden.[56]

Virginia

We now need to make a short diversion to consider events in North America where a key figure is John Smith (c1580-1631), who is conventionally distinguished from the Baptist by calling him Captain Smith. He was born at Willoughby in east Lincolnshire, was possibly taught by Francis Marbury at Alford, and probably attended Louth Grammar School. After his father died, Smith became the ward of George Metham; Metham was certainly one of the puritans, from a family closely connected to the Brandons and Willoughbys – it was probably his father who was standard-bearer at Brandon's funeral. The Methams were regular visitors to Katherine Willoughby.[57] The older George died in

52   C Douglas Weaver, p.31
53   The banns were reported by Richard Clyfton as having been read by him at Sutton, presumably Sutton-cum-Lound. Both were also of Sutton.
54   This family was noted as living long in Amsterdam.
55   Baptist Quarterly article – *The Midland Churches of 1651*
56   Marcombe (1993), p.250, but much debated. In 2017 Sue Allan's research concluded these Southworths were indeed from Clarborough.
57   Harkrider, p.123

1589 and left a will testifying to his saving faith in Christ as well as his 'best animal' to Peregrine Bertie.

It was, therefore, his son the younger George who married Mary, daughter of Sir William Skipwith of South Ormsby, in 1574; Skipwith carried the 'great banner' at Katherine Willoughby's own funeral in 1580, at which at least one of the Methams had also participated. Unsurprisingly, Skipwith was listed as 'earnest in religion' in 1564. The Methams were also related to another Brandon-Willoughby client family, that of Thomas Seckford. The elderly Skipwith went to live with Metham at Hanby until his own death in 1586. These were the people with whom the Smiths were connected.

Smith would clearly have been brought up surrounded by 'godly' influence and then his early military career involved some time with Peregrine Bertie, grandson of Katherine Willoughby, from 1599. A complex career via Transylvania and Morocco eventually delivered him to the shores of Virginia in May 1607, where he was to be governor of a new colony – soon interrupted by his capture by native Americans. The story of his release through the influence of Pocahontas and her marriage to an Englishman in 1614, is well known, and of course, has been badly distorted. He returned to England in 1609 having been injured in an explosion, but he had helped to establish the colony.

The Virginia Company, although originally formed as two separate but related concerns of London and Plymouth (which was to cover the northern territory), was founded in 1606. This is why the Pilgrims named their new colony of 1620 'Plymouth' rather than the coincidence of having stopped at Plymouth in Devon for repairs. The many members of the Virginia Company eventually included several with Lincolnshire connections including Sir Thomas Grantham and Sir Anthony Irby, who eventually sold his share to the Earl of Exeter – Thomas Cecil of Burghley House. Irby's father-in-law, Sir Edward Barkham, was also a member of the Virginia Company and his brother-in-law – also Sir Edward – was Boston's MP in 1625 and 1626.[58]

In 1614 he surveyed and mapped the coast of New England, building links with Sir Ferdinando Gorges, leader of the Plymouth Company. In 1616 Smith published *A Description of New England,* but his help was famously rejected by the later colonists, who thought it easier (and cheaper) to use his outputs rather than the man himself. In later life he became an ardent advocate of colonisation in New England and placed a high priority on the religious conversion of the American natives. Indeed, Pocahontas is widely regarded as the first true Christian convert amongst them.

One of the interesting sidelines of the story is that three of the sons of Archbishop Edwin Sandys, who had been Archbishop of York from 1576 to 1588, developed close connections with the Virginia Company. Thomas Sandys was an early traveller to the area, his brother Sir Edwin was on the Council of the Virginia Company from 1607 and its treasurer in London from 1619 (a post he secured with the help of the Earl of Warwick) whilst George was a treasurer and resident in America from 1621 to 1631. All had childhood connections to Scrooby and William Brewster certainly knew this family as Samuel held the leases at Scrooby, Laneham and Askham, and Brewster owned a book by George Sandys as well

58 The Barkhams had made their money in London but bought the manor of Wainfleet in 1597, also holding lands at Fishtoft and Skirbeck.

as having connections to them via William Davison; in addition, Samuel Sandys knew the father of Edward Winslow, one of the *Mayflower* passengers whilst Davison's son, Christopher, was also involved with the Virginia Company. In November 1617 Sir Edwin, as an 'assistant' or director of the Virginia Company, was involved in discussions with the Leiden separatists (specifically Brewster and Robinson) over their possible journey to America – by this stage, he had significant investments in Virginia.[59] Another involved in the Virginia Company was Lord Edmund Sheffield.

Robinson's Church and The Trip to America

By rights Clifton should have been a significant leader in Holland but, at some time after his arrival in about August 1608, he joined the Ancient Church instead. Robinson left Amsterdam for Leiden with around 100 people, perhaps the majority of those who had fled in 1608.[60] Others came and went but overall their community flourished with many arrivals from Norwich in particular.[61] In 1611 the congregation purchased an estate with living quarters and a meeting hall at Leiden.

Robinson's church was reckoned to have 300 members by 1620. William Brewster was the leading deacon. Requirements for membership included an experience of conversion. Services consisted of a sermon followed by an open time of 'prophesying'.

Despite this success, they were no longer content in the Netherlands. The fellowship was already planning to go to Virginia and early in Brewster made contact with Sir Edwin Sandys in London, no doubt on the basis of the connections previously mentioned but also perhaps because Sandys had written a book favouring tolerance in religion – separatism was still dangerous and permission to go to Virginia would need to address this issue. So, 1617 Carver and Robert Cushman went to London to meet Sir Edwin Sandys of the Virginia Company – and in November Sandys wrote positively to Robinson and Brewster. The Virginia Company was hoping to open extra colonies to help with the viability of Jamestown and a patent was granted in 1619 in the name of John Wyncop, a chaplain and tutor to the Countess of Lincoln (who was related to Ferdinando Gorges), but he died.[62] Cotton's history says that by 1619 'they foresaw Holland would be no place for their Church and their posterity to continue there comfortably'.[63] Problems included the language, Sabbath-breaking by the Dutch, the cost, children's education and that they would cease to be English.

The plan was for William Brewster to lead forty whilst Robinson stayed in Leiden, supporting them by letter. They worked in the way of puritans – through contacts, including those made at Cambridge. Sabine Staresmore was their man in Southwark, and he arranged a meeting in February 1618 with Sir John Wolstenholme of the Virginia Company and

---

59   Theodore Rabb, *Edwin Sandys*, in *ODNB*, accessed 24 Sept 2019.
60   Coggins (1991) reports several from Worksop, Scrooby, Ackworth and also the Southworths now thought to be from Clarborough, and several from Norfolk.
61   Coggins (1991), p.66
62   Peggy Baker, *The Plymouth Colony Patent*, Pilgrim Hall, 2007
63   Cotton (1648), p.8

also the East India Company. Wolstenholme then sought the support of the Chancellor of the Exchequer, Fulke Greville, a puritan who would support the colonisation idea. They used Sir Robert Naunton to persuade the king that letting the puritans go to form a fishing community would cause no harm; famously, James was supposed to have joked that 'Tis an honest trade; 'twas the Apostles' own calling'. They were further helped by factions who feared the Dutch and the Spanish in the Americas.

The affair dragged out over two years, during which other puritans sailed for Virginia and met, often, with death. However, when the pilgrims eventually landed, they did so in the wrong place and outside Virginia Company jurisdiction – instead, in an area nominally administered by the Council for New England. In 1621 this Council provided a patent for a settlement for seven years, known as the Second Peirce Patent. Signatories included the Earl of Warwick and Lord Edmund Sheffield. The charter was renewed in 1629, again signed by Warwick.

The *Speedwell* brought the pilgrims across to Southampton where she joined up with the *Mayflower* and both set out on 5 August. At Dartmouth they stopped to repair the *Speedwell*, but this was ineffective for both had to turn back to Plymouth and the *Speedwell* received a vote of no confidence. The *Mayflower* left Plymouth in September 1620 with 102 passengers of whom roughly half were separatists from Leiden and just below half adult men. Those who survived were destined to be the subject of obsessional genealogy for centuries, but the real legacy they took with them was a stubborn Protestantism that formed the backbone of a nation.

Endless print has been expended on the origins and later lives of the *Mayflower* passengers, which is beyond the purpose of this book. Our greatest interest will be in those who had come directly from the Babworth congregation, of which William Brewster and William Bradford were to prove the most significant. But Robinson had chosen as leader his brother-in-law, John Carver, who had married Katherine Leggatt – neé White in Sturton – by about 1609. Carver's own origins are obscure and there remains the possibility that he also had origins or connections in Sturton; we can only speculate as to why Robinson identified Carver, who was a deacon of the congregation, and not Brewster, as the original leader. Both Carvers died in 1621.

As is well known, the *Mayflower* mistakenly went further north than intended, first sighting the land at Cape Cod, perhaps 250 miles out of their way. In December 1620 William Bradford of Austerfield first saw running water in the Americas and, befitting his origin, the first published account used a northern word to refer to it: 'We saw two becks of fresh water'.[64] Water, in two different ways, represented life. In 1623 Bradford married Alice Southworth, widow of Edward Southworth, who was from Clarborough.[65] Bradford went on to be a significant leader in the New World, the first historian of the colony, and was governor many times up to his death in 1657. Alice's children by Edward, Constant and Thomas, made their way to New England by about 1628.

Brewster became the religious leader in Plymouth Colony, there being at first no ordained clergyman. When John Cotton wrote about him in 1648, he described 'Old Mr Brewster'

64 *Mourt's Relation* (1622)
65 Marcombe (1993), p.259; Marcombe in Holland (2004), p.49

as 'a man of long-approved piety, gravity, integrity'.[66] Significantly, Brewster took a library to New England with him and used his experience of political affairs to maintain relations with England. However, as elder he was kept apart from civil affairs, leaving the younger William Bradford to fill the space as governor repeatedly from 1621. Bradford is also important to our story as the first chronicler of the New England settlement, most especially in *Of Plimmouth Plantation* which told the story up to 1646 – although he died in 1657. Though the importance of Plymouth was later overshadowed by the rapid growth of Boston, it is of huge importance as the first settlement established in New England by separatists – though there were many others who joined them.

The legal status of the new colony was an important question and a patent was authorised in 1621. This was signed by the 2nd Earl of Warwick, stepson of Frances Wray, and Lord Edmund Sheffield of West Butterwick, a long-term associate of the puritans in our area but who suffered from having a Catholic wife, Ursula Tyrwhitt, and considerable financial problems not helped by his colonial speculations.

Robinson stayed in the Netherlands and never returned to England. In his old age Robinson became more moderate and Richard Bernard noted that he was the one 'yet nearest the truth unto us, as I hear, and not so schismatical as the rest'.[67] Robinson died in 1625 and was buried in the churchyard near his home; his congregation in Leiden gradually withered and joined the Dutch Reformed Church – but his legacy lived on in America. Some of the Leiden group may have rejoined the Amsterdam congregation but Bridget Robinson lived at Leiden Pieterskerkhof until her death in about 1640. The oldest son, Isaac Robinson, went to New England in 1631; he helped found the town of Falmouth and became a Quaker.

One other local connection with the early colonists was William Blackstone, who is most likely to have been from Horncastle and went to Emmanuel College, Cambridge. Ordained but disliking bishops, he emigrated in 1623 as part of a Robert Gorges expedition and settled in Massachusetts, leading an unconventional and isolated life. Despite being an ordained clergyman, he refused all Church appointments though he did occasionally read a service. He died in 1675, famous for having granted land for the settlement of Boston, and for his large library. He sold his land at Boston in 1634 and moved close to Providence where he was also a friend of Roger Williams, an influential minister in New England. Although he preached occasionally he would never join a church and so was perhaps the ultimate separatist: 'I came from England, because I did not like the lord-bishops; but I can't join you, because I would not be under the lord-brethren,' he told Cotton Mather, although he was conventional enough to use the *Prayer Book* in a service at Rhode Island.[68]

66   John Cotton, *The Way of Congregational Churches Cleared, 1648,* p.5
67   Sprunger, p.137
68   Robert Charles Anderson, *William Blackstone* in *ODNB*, accessed 17 Nov 2019.

CHAPTER ELEVEN

After the Departure
The Church in England
1608-1625

The departure of the 'Pilgrims' and future Baptists to the Netherlands did not result in a flood of separation from the Church of England. The rest of James's reign was marked out by an ongoing but restrained struggle with the puritans at a time when Catholics were still seen as the greater threat. King James's oldest son, Prince Henry, was a committed Calvinist with many puritan influences and seemed to offer the hope of a 'better' Church, but he died in 1612, probably of typhoid. Prince Charles offered a less certain future.

Chronology:
1612: John Cotton appointed to Boston
1613: Richard Bernard moves to Somerset
1616: Frances Wray marries Earl of Warwick
1617: Disputes in Nottingham; death of Sir William Wray
1621: John Williams becomes Bishop of Lincoln
1622: Isabel Wray dies
1624: Disturbances at Collingham
1625: Death of King James

Nonconformity Continues Unabated

Many more radical puritans remained in the Retford and Gainsborough area than had left in 1607-8 and they continued to battle on issues such as not kneeling at communion, although after 1620 refusal to attend midweek services for saints' days became the most common offence in Nottinghamshire.[1] Nonconformity continued much as before: in 1609 John Herring, an associate of Smyth, preached without a licence at Greasley, a church with a pattern in this respect. Edwards, his associate from the fracas at Marnham, was excommunicated for preaching without a licence at Marnham in 1608, again offended at South Leverton in 1610, and yet was still preaching without a licence at Treswell in 1613. In 1610 27 parishioners of Treswell refused to attend the sermons of a new vicar and were fined 1s each.[2]

---

1   Jennings (1999), p.68
2   N Bunker, *Make Haste from Babylon,* London, 2011, p.106

Belton ●
Epworth ■
Owston ●

Blyton ●
🏠 Wharton
GAINSBOROUGH

Gringley on the Hill ■
Saundby ■

Sutton cum Lound ●

Clarborough ●
RETFORD ■
Grove ■ South Leverton ●
Treswell ●

Elkesley ●

WORKSOP ●

North Clifton ●
Marnham ●

Kneesall ●

Caunton ●
South Collingham ●

MANSFIELD ■

Sutton in Ashfield ●

Selston ●

Southwell ■

NEWARK
-ON-
TRENT ■

Greasley ●
Nuthall 🏠

🏠 Screveton

NOTTINGHAM ■

Attenborough ●

Costock ●

River Ouse

Alkborough ■

GRIMSBY ■

🏠 Ashby cum Fenby

Ludborough ●

Market Rasen ■

LOUTH

Glentworth 🏠

Faldingworth ●
Snarford 🏠 Wickenby ■

Donington on Bain ●

LINCOLN ■

Revesby ■

Timberland ●
🏠 Tattershall

Butterwick ●

SLEAFORD ■

BOSTON ■

Silk Willoughby ●

Donington ■
Horbling ●
Sutterton ●

GRANTHAM ■
🏠 Sempringham

Osgodby ●

SPALDING   Moulton ■

River Trent

River Trent

River Witham

River Witham

The Great North Road

The Great North Road

DONCASTER

N

🏠 Puritan house
● Place (Puritan)
■ Place
　 Town

0   10   20 miles

STAMFORD ■

258

Preaching without a licence also occurred at Barton and St Peter's Nottingham in 1612. In September 1609 William Barlow, the Bishop of Lincoln, sent his chaplain Robert Johnson[3] to preach at Paul's Cross against 'lawless sectaries'; yet Barlow was in some ways tolerant, and even attempted to reinstate the infamous Arthur Hildersham in Leicestershire. In his 1611 visitation he also pursued some puritan objectives by seeking out absentee clerics and drunken ones.

The action after the Hampton Court Conference had mainly affected Nottinghamshire. Those deprived already included Richard Clifton at Babworth, Richard Bernard, Henry Gray the curate in Bawtry, Robert Southworth vicar of Headon and also some time curate at Grove. Clifton and Southworth were deprived on the same day in March 1605 with Gray a few days later and Bernard soon after that though he conformed in 1607 – loosely. Hugh Bromhead a curate at Wheatley and clerk to the peculiar of Bole, also left. To these may be added John Robinson, a Nottinghamshire man from Sturton who had been a curate in Norwich. National figures such as Arthur Hildersham (1605) and John Dod (1607) were also deprived but decided not to separate and yet found other places. But it is quite possible to overestimate the impact of these deprivations; a small pension was payable to the family and most deprived ministers of standing generally found an alternative place whilst it is quite clear that many nonconformists were able to persist in their nonconformity for years. This is what now continued to happen.

That the persecution extended to include non-attendance and 'gadding about' was described by William Bradford who wrote of his fellows being 'hunted and persecuted on every side'; he continued that 'some were taken and clapped up in prison, others had their houses beset and watched day and night, and hardly escaped their hands; and the most were fain to flee and leave their houses and habitations, and the means of their livelihood'. But very few went to prison after 1608.

Where a puritan was deprived or the priest was not to their taste, puritans formed their own illegal groups called 'conventicles' such as that at Donington-on-Bain in 1607.[4]

At Silk Willoughby in Lincolnshire Hugh Tuke, who had survived pressure from Whitgift in 1584, survived again in 1604-5, was described as 'unconformable' in 1611, and survived again in 1612 because local gentry like Sir William Armyne (1562-1622) of Osgodby spoke up for him – he was tutor to one of Armyne's sons. Armyne protected others like Tempest Wood. Tuke received a summons to Buckden by Bishop William Barlow but the gentry rallied to protect him. Armyne wrote to the bishop to say that Tuke was an honest, godly and peaceable man. Thomas Tuke, Hugh's son, also made a dedication to Armyne 'partly to demonstrate my gratitude and devoted affection to you, who has always been a constant patron to my nearest and dearest friends'.[5] The Armynes, like the Wrays, were puritan for several generations (fostered by Cambridge educations) and the younger Sir William (1593-1651) led such a life that at his funeral it was preached by Seth Wood that

---

3   Johnson also became Archdeacon of Leicester and founded Uppingham and Oakham grammar schools.
4   Plumb, volume 1, p.79. Donington on Bain was held successively by the father and sons combination of Thomas Kent (who also was vicar of Scamblesby, died 1623), Timothy Kent (died 1624) and Thomas Kent (1624-38). Timothy's sons were also clergy.
5   Cliffe (1984), p.36. Silk Willoughby church has two famous examples of graffiti by another of the Tuke offspring.

he kept his body as 'a Temple of the Holy Ghost' and 'could not endure any vice should be master over him'.[6] Their policy was clearly noted in this valedictory sermon, that 'in all those places in his dispose he planted men of very good reputation, and abilities to preach the Gospel...'.

Thomas Tuke

The name of Tuke is fairly unusual, though sometimes also spelt as Tooke. In the light of what we know of other Tukes, the career of Thomas Tuke is interesting for it is likely that he was a son of Hugh.[7] By age at least this is quite possible, for he was of age to make the impeccably puritan choice of Christ's College in 1599 and then sought a church career in Kent.

His first publication was a translation of a work of William Perkins. Then he published, in 1607, some sermons entitled *The True Trial and Turning of a Sinner*, apparently while living at Cuxton in Kent. In 1612 he began a series of posts on London and was presented to St Olave Jewry in 1617. He continued writing and produced the clearly puritan work, *A Treatise Against Painting and Tincturing of Men and Women: Against Murther and Poysoning: Against Pride and Ambition: Against Adulterie and Witchcraft, and the Roote of these, Disobedience to the Ministrie of the Word*, in 1616 – this commented on the Sir Thomas Overbury affair which led to the execution of Sir Gervase Helwys of Nottinghamshire. He also wrote *Concerning the Holy Eucharist and the Popish Breaden-God* (1625).[8]

After 1618 he wrote little and perhaps his views changed, for in 1643 he was sequestrated and imprisoned as a Royalist. He is known to have 'retired to the country' but in 1650 emerged preaching sermons for the Countess of Lincoln at Tattershall – which were published. In the context of debate over his origins, this appearance in Lincolnshire is intriguing.

His son Thomas was present at the landing of Charles II in Dover and gave the new monarch copies of the Bible and *Book of Common Prayer.*

The name of Tuke appears in many puritan locations across the region with Ephraim as curate of Saundby 1625-32, George Tuke[9] a lecturer in Chesterfield (and perhaps Mansfield) and the colourful Lemuel (or Samuel) enjoying a fifty-year career that involved both separatism and congregationalism.

---

6   Cliffe (1984) citing Seth Wood, *The Saint's Enterance into Peace and Rest by Death*, p.16-18. Wood later held the family living at Lenton (Lincs) from 1639; a predecessor Tempest Wood was his father. He took a London living in 1654.

7   The *ODNB* makes no comment on his origins, unusual in itself. J T Cliffe (1984), p.36, states that he is Hugh Tuke's son.

8   This appears to be noteworthy as the first known occasion for use of the word 'stupider'. Ammon Shea, *Bad English: A History of Linguistic Aggravation*.

9   He was born in Essex and later returned there.

Thomas Granger was born at Epworth in 1578 and, after Cambridge (which he reached at the relatively mature age of 20) as a sizar at Peterhouse, he returned there as curate in 1606 but within a few months became vicar of Butterwick near Boston. His pathway is similar to Richard Bernard's, who was also from Epworth, and one wonders if he was similarly sponsored. In 1607 he was presented for teaching an unlicensed school and he soon proved himself a nonconformist: in 1609 he was cited for various offences around ceremonials including taking a baptism without wearing a surplice. In a series of books published from 1616 to 1621 he emphasised the importance of Scripture as a guide, not the Church, and emphasised a strong Calvinism. It has been suggested that he had a separate congregation at Butterwick, where he at first encountered a 'vulgar ignorant people' and he favoured almost total separation of the godly. In 1621 he moved to be vicar of Horbling – central to the puritan group which formed around Sempringham and where he was a successor to Simon Bradstreet.

Both at Butterwick and Horbling, Granger supplemented his income by acting as a schoolteacher. This is a useful reminder that small schools, often of only half a dozen pupils, existed even in some of the smaller villages.

Puritans were not always popular, as perhaps John Smyth in Lincoln was not whilst James Ashton at Moulton from 1597 to 1619 was quite happy to point out and denounce individual sinners in his congregation.[10] This was what became known as 'fractious' preaching, perhaps reaching its zenith in the crisis at Stamford in 1631.

Especially where deprivation was a risk, tensions could run quite high. We know that Smyth and others were involved in a 'riot' at Marnham, and puritanism was a factor in a riot at Revesby in 1607 and more directly at Tattershall in 1610 when the unwanted priest of Stixwould was dragged out of the pulpit by local puritans.

Certainly, Marchant's argument in *The Puritans and the Church Courts in the Diocese of York* is that Nottinghamshire puritan ministers often managed to survive in post for lengthy periods if they avoided being too fractious. Ezekias Burton had a safe post as curate at Sutton-in-Ashfield and then succeeded the puritan James Brewster at Sutton-cum-Lound (including Scrooby chapel) in 1614 under the patronage of Lord William Cavendish, was accused of non-compliance in 1616 and 1618, but surviving to accumulate five citations up to 1646.[11] In the period 1610-9 the village of Sutton supplied a high proportion of lay nonconformists troubling the authorities.[12]

Some lay families also maintained a lengthy repudiation of nonconformity. The Iretons at Attenborough were frequently at war with the Church, perhaps protected by their association with Lady Isabel Bowes. In 1608 German's wife refused to be churched, in 1616 he kept his hat on in church, and in 1620 when the minister was absent, he arranged

10   Holmes (1980) p.62
11   While he was at Sutton a son, Hezekiah, was born in 1632. He also became a clergyman, was admitted to one of the Wray fellowships at Magdalene where he met Samuel Pepys. He became interested in psychic research but died, relatively early, in 1681. His widow married the Bishop of Gloucester.
12   Jennings (1999), p.66

for a 'stranger' to take a service. In 1636 he was still refusing to kneel at the altar. From such stock came Henry Ireton, Cromwell's son in law. Lady Bowes's influence also lay behind the presence of Richard Rothwell in Mansfield, preaching from 1621 in the town where the vicar was a notorious drunkard; when mercer Gregory Sylvester died in 1625, he left 10s a year for Rothwell if he continued in the town. The drunken vicar outlasted Rothwell though and died in 1628, following which Mansfield had more puritan ministers in Price and Firth.

Then we have characters such as Gervase Lee, a onetime-friend of Archbishop Sandys, with property at Southwell and Norwell Park, who was hauled before the Star Chamber in 1608 for his poetic satire on the clergy of Southwell – from what has survived, we know that part of this made comments about veneration of the Virgin Mary. Sandys had made him a justice in the archbishop's liberties in Nottinghamshire which he was for more than three decades but in 1617 he also complained of libel; attempts were being made 'by all base means practised to deprave your said subject and to bring infamy and disgrace upon him, not only in the county where he dwelleth, but also to draw your highness's favour from him'.[13] Other glimpses of nonconformity can be seen in cases like Sarah Hatchet of Grove, cited in 1609 for 'in her own stall did teach divers maids of the same parish the catechism'.

Richard Bernard left Worksop in 1613 and James Collie, a puritan curate, filled his place. The benefice was awarded to Oliver Bray who was not; Collie clung on, not letting his successor into the vicarage, so Bray presented him for peaching without a licence. Collie's ally, Christopher Carlile, who had told Bray he was unfit for the church, was also presented and was no doubt one of those who would not hand the church key to its vicar. Collie called Bray a 'dumb dogge' and said children baptised by him were damned. One parishioner told Bray, 'You have made many men of Worksop to go to the Devil'.[14] When Bray suddenly died in January 1615 Margaret or Ann Patrick was accused of poisoning him and tried at East Retford although the result is unknown. Bray was replaced by William Carte, a puritan and Collie resurfaced in 1617 as vicar of East Retford where he spent many decades.

Bernard's new home was at Batcombe in Somerset, where he had been brought through the influence of James Montagu, Bishop of Bath and Wells. Montagu had been one of the first to raise a concern about Arminian teaching in the 1590s by Peter Baro and remained a solid puritan.

In 1611 a group of dissenters was found to have been meeting in Michael Murre's house in Clarborough, in 1613 a separatist was reported to have visited Treswell and in 1617 two people from Babworth were cited as 'Brownists' – the term used for the contacts Hanserd Knollys made in Gainsborough at a similar time.[15] In 1616 Henry Wilde of Gringley was in trouble for saying 'he was not to owe any submission to anye prelate in England'. In 1616 and 1618 a woman from Farndon and a man from South Leverton were accused of separatism.

---

13 *History of Parliament*, accessed 31/8/19.
14 A T Hart, *The Man in the Pew*, 1966, p.171
15 Marcombe (1993), p.258

South Collingham is an excellent example of a nonconformist centre persisting for years. Brian Barton, rector of South Collingham, arrived in 1595 and had an excommunication and 32 years of court appearances up to his death in 1626; he was linked to the cases of many laypeople – for example, those cited for attending the wrong church or not having a child christened. The result was that the local population was 'disturbed' and that Barton was running 'in effect a separatist congregation'.[16] Thinking spread up the road where in North Collingham in 1610 Thomas Pacy (Paice) was reported for saying that kneeling down to pray 'offereth the sacrifice of fooles & his prayer is abhominable the sacrifice of fool'.[17] In 1619 a woman from Newark who attended Barton's church was referred to the High Commission for being a separatist and three from South Collingham were charged with 'schismatic opinions' of whom one was sent to York Castle.[18] The same year Edward Taylor of Laxton was cited for attending Barton's church and telling his own vicar that he preached false doctrine. North Collingham descended into chaos in 1624 when it ended up with two rival sequestrators, or temporary clergy, allowing James Piercy, to seize the opportunity; when he was ousted by an archdeaconry official and replaced by a conformist, ten of the congregation were cited for refusal to kneel for communion. Some parishioners were, as at Marnham, indicted for riot and the eventual victor Greene or Groome spent years presenting his puritan enemies for nonconformity – and they accused him of being drunk and a 'sordid debauched priest' in 1625. South Collingham also exported its activities – Towne[19] from there preached illegally at Barnby le Willows in 1628.

Clergy also continued to be cited for Prayer Book offences from 1610-19 including Burton at Sutton-cum-Lound, William Snipe (or Snape) at his previous home parish of Sutton-in-Ashfield, Worth of Selston, James Nayler at North Clifton and Alexander Smith at Elkesley; perhaps Smith had learnt his lesson, for in May 1606 his parishioners, grieving the loss of Hancock, complained that he read his sermons from a book and in 1607 the irrepressible Brian Barton was cited for preaching there, prompting a visit from the Archdeacon.[20] Smith cannot have learnt well, for in 1612 a parishioner was summoned for calling him a fool. In 1620 Robert Hargreaves was cited for preaching without a licence at Marnham and then in 1621 cited along with Robert Ash, the village's vicar, and Nayler of Clifton for holding 'exercises' (the new name for 'prophesying') at the vicarage. Hargreaves then went to Kneesall in 1622 when he continued his refusal to conform.

What was happening at Marnham was a private religious meeting or 'conventicle', and they were increasing. John Brigham was accused of holding private sermons in his house at Tiln (Notts) in 1618 and Hugo Vasen of Sutterton (Lincs) was holding a conventicle in his house in 1623, apparently on good terms with the vicar Edmund Diggle and also often travelling to Boston where he was friendly with successive vicars, Wooll and Cotton. Nearby at Donington Christopher Browne was a 'separatist' though less is known about this case.[21] In 1624 the vicar of Caunton, Richard Hughes, was holding private meetings at his house for a small group of parishioners.

---

16   Marchant (1969), p.180
17   Kendall (2004), p.8
18   Jennings (1999), p.93
19   Perhaps Robert Towne, ordained in 1616.
20   George Yardy, *People and Parliament: Representative Rights and the English Revolution*, London, 2008, p.198
21   Hajzyk (181), p.363

It remained a narrow line between nonconformity and separatism. Lady Grantham asked Archbishop Matthew about funding preaching exercises in Nottinghamshire in 1616, his concern was that they should be conformist. In 1621 he allowed Ezekiel Rogers, part of the Essex group that included at various times Frances Wray, the Whalleys and Roger Williams, to revive preaching exercises in East Yorkshire.

William Howat of Farndon was another who survived excommunication. Mark Wyersdale of East Deeping in Lincolnshire, as discussed in the last chapter, was able to hold the living at Costock (Notts) where stayed in post from 1595 to his death in 1639 despite at least seven citations, and then was replaced by another member of his family – possibly his son.

Dissent also bubbled away on Axholme, where the group in Belton were now all in trouble again in 1611 having lost the curate Langley. The two Glews were again guilty of offences whilst William Chessman additionally disturbed services by forcing his way in despite being excommunicate. What has been shown by Lloyd in this case is very much how dissent was related to the specific character of the services being provided. In the 1623 visitation, Haxey found one man excommunicate, Owston twelve and Belton had fourteen excommunicate, ten suspended and another nine presented for not coming to church whereas Epworth only managed one suspended and two presented for not attending prayer. The Belton cases again included the Glews.[22]

In East Retford, John Watt was in trouble in 1623 for a stack of offences including not following the *Prayer Book* and not meeting corpses at the church stile but more significantly he had refused to wear the surplice and allowed 'strange' ministers to preach.[23]

Much of this was because bishops did not enforce rigorous compliance. Bishop Neile continued this in Lincoln from 1614-17. When he arrived with a reputation for pursuing radical puritans, Neile was told by his staff that 'lecturing hath brought many of God's holy and good ordinances into contempt, as public prayer, reading of the scriptures and receiving of the blessed sacraments'. He soon identified ten places and sixty clergy which he saw as centres of resistance, including John Cotton at Boston who he soon visited. Neile continued to allow the 'limited subscription' permitted by predecessors and although 28 were cited on the article relating to the *Prayer Book* in 1615, he deprived no-one. After he moved on in 1617 his successor, Montaigne, who became Archbishop of York in 1628, rarely visited the diocese although he was a greater opponent of Calvinistic puritans; the poet Milton called him a 'swan eating and canary sucking prelate'. Tobie Matthew, Archbishop of York from 1606 to 1628, was notably moderate.

We have already seen that there were some in Boston who were happy to join in conventicles with the separatists in and around 1607. That such people were still active in the 1620s can be seen from the visits paid to Boston by Alexander Leighton, a radical Scottish minister, who had abandoned his Church career to train as a doctor – and went to Leiden University to do so. There he stayed from 1617-9 with Thomas Brewer who had set up the 'Pilgrim Press' with Brewster, where he also became friends with John

---

22   Lloyd, p.198
23   Marcombe (1993), p.186. Interestingly, Watt moved to East Retford from Bawtry Chapel, formerly a Brewster outpost of puritanism.

Bastwick and knew John Robinson; of course, Brewster's involvement with the Press led to him being forced into hiding in 1619. Back in London, Leighton joined Henry Jacob's separatist church, had works printed by the Ancient Church in Amsterdam, and made trips to Boston and Leicester. By 1629 he was pastor of the English church in Utrecht. Leighton was to prove very controversial during Charles's reign, so he makes an interesting visitor to Boston.

Sometimes the puritans caused resentment. We have noted the factionalism that divided Nottingham over the exorcism cases, and this flared up again in 1617. The town's puritans had been 'gadding' to St Mary's church and had been occasionally cited for it, but they had enjoyed some protection from Robert Aldridge until his death in 1616. A rival faction gained control of St Mary's and brought in Oliver Whittington, who had already confronted nonconformists at Gotham. When he died, he was replaced by the similar Ralph Hansby. A group of puritans led by the town preacher, Richard Caldwell,[24] instead, gathered around George Coates the minister at St Peter's; some prominent citizens led by Anker Jackson (whose daughter married Coates) were accused of forming a conventicle and lampooned around the town in a drunken ballad written by William Whittington. The drunken riot led to a hearing before the Mayor, Thomas Nixe, who let them off with being bound over to keep the peace – then was himself revealed to have demanded the piper play 'the song of the Puritans of Nottingham' during a drunken revelry in a Lenton alehouse.[25] Anker Jackson sued for libel, but the result is not known. In 1621 more than twenty were charged over failure to attend a midweek festival in Nottingham. St Peter's, however, became so popular that a gallery had to be added in 1625. Perhaps George Coates was related to Grace Coates, who was cited at Basford in 1624 for preaching.[26]

An attractive position for a puritan was as a 'lecturer'. Lincolnshire had six – Lincoln, Grantham, Alford, Louth, Horncastle, Grimsby and Market Rasen – and they were meant to provide at least quarterly sermons although Sleaford had to do without after being refused a licence.[27] More conservative clergy disliked them including Bishop Neile of Lincoln (1614-7) who was unhappy with public prayer and reading of the scriptures. 'Combination lectures' provided a chance for clergy to get together, most often on market days, but those attending were not always the puritans. The Market Rasen lectures caused a dispute between conservatives like Buddle of Wickenby and radicals like Atkinson, Allen and Tuke. Bishop Barlow (1608-13) refused to have lectures extended to Sleaford. George Buddle of Wickenby, Lincolnshire, published a critique of 'evangelical fasting', *A Short and Plain Discourse,* in 1609 and dedicated it to Barlow. The Wray sisters and Sir George St Paul funded a regular 'sermon' at Welton where there had been 'never a settled preacher in the memory of any man'.[28] All these roles were eventually suppressed by Archbishop Laud.

When Sir George St Paul died in 1613, his funeral oration was delivered – as requested – by Dr John Chadwick the rector of Faldingworth. Chadwick referred to the 'six learned and

---

24   Caldwell was paid £10 a year. He later became rector of Normanton on Soar.
25   C J Sisson, *The Lost Plays of Shakespeare*, London, 1936, p.196
26   George Yerby, *People and Parliament: Representative Rights and the English Revolution*, London, 2008, p.194
27   Plumb (PhD), p.87
28   Edward Reyner, Funeral Oration, 1613

profitable preachers…who were brought up in the universities at his cost and charge'.[29] Chadwick preached on Psalm 37 v37 and gave a detailed description of St Paul's gracious last days, surrounded by his friends:

> '….as many of his good friends and divers Reverend Ministers in whose godly discourse, devout prayers and good company he much rejoiced, acknowledging God's goodness that those Beloved in his Life should be with him at his Death….. He was a right and true hearted Jonathan and such a friend may I say he was as, I fear, I shall never find till my soul rest with his.'

St Paul's widow, Frances Wray of Glentworth, now became one of the most eligible widows in the country. Her suitor, the Earl of Warwick, was divorced from his first wife because of her adultery and as devour puritans they considered no marriage could go ahead while the errant wife yet lived; they finally married in 1616, so Frances became Countess of Warwick. She then spent much of her time in Essex at Leez Priory, in an area where Warwick had established many puritan ministers. Warwick and his son, the future second Earl, also developed their interests in America. This relationship helped to cement the links between Essex and East Midlands puritanism, which reached its high point in the sailing of the 'Winthrop Fleet' and perhaps the marriage of Roger Williams to Mary Bernard of Worksop.

Her sister, Isabel Wray, who was by now Lady Darcy, died in 1622 and was buried at Rawmarsh. According to the claims of Richard Rothwell's biographer, who had been with him for several years, the text preached at her funeral was Matthew 26.13: 'Wheresoever this Gospel shall be preached in the whole world, there shall also this, that this woman hath done be told for a memorial of her'.[30] Rothwell's biographer wrote, 'Oh that God would raise out of the ashes of this Phoenix some more such mothers in Israel'.

Meanwhile, Sir William Wray, Smyth's patron, had died in 1617. His son Sir John, who lived largely at Wharton, was also a patron of the godly religion and was described by Bernard as 'of more than ordinarie zeale for holiness and religion'. Despite this endorsement, the family history credits European travel for developing this in him; 'whither he travelled I know not, but he returned with a strong hatred of Papists and a love of hearing his own voice'. He continued the pattern of supporting godly clergy, such as Thomas Coleman and maintained a network that was to include marrying a daughter to Captain Sir John Hotham the Younger, who was to achieve fame and infamy at Hull during the Civil War. Another son, Sir Christopher Wray, was more influential in NE Lincolnshire from Ashby-cum-Fenby and became the father in law of Sir Henry Vane.

The years after 1608 show how successful some villages were in persisting with their puritan styles of worship despite persecution, and sometimes with running inner congregations or conventicles. Kneesall and the two Collinghams are examples of this, and in these cases they all showed an interest in radical structures as the century progressed – Kneesall had Quakers, South Collingham an Independent congregation and North Collingham a Baptist

---

29   Thrush and Ferris, *ibid.* Full text also available in J. Wilford, *Mems. and Characters* (1741), pp. 179-83.
30   Gower, *Rothwell*, p.70 (Neman)

church which perhaps had more than local significance.

The Hampton Court Conference had focused on styles of worship and it was the imposition of the Prayer Book and various rituals that forced the separatists to leave. But in 1611 George Abbot became Archbishop of Canterbury, replacing the more disciplinarian Whitgift and Bancroft, and he proved remarkably tolerant of nonconformity whilst puritan gentry across the country happily sheltered their hand-picked radical clergy without serious problem. Meanwhile, in York Tobie Matthew 'followed the same kind of laissez-faire policy and under his rule little was done to curb even the most persistent offenders'.[31] Indeed Matthew was 'an indefatigable preacher and patron of the preaching ministry'.[32] In Lincoln, John Williams from 1621 also proved a generally tolerant bishop. Until the late 1620s, the more extreme puritans enjoyed as much freedom as at any time, providing they avoided too public a challenge to authority, so it might even be argued that those who had gone abroad had jumped too soon.

However, in 1625 Charles I became King and the relationship with his archbishop Abbot soured in 1627. Problems and persecution for the puritans increased dramatically from 1628 when William Laud effectively replaced Abbot – who was in disgrace. In 1632 Richard Neile became Archbishop of York and the following year Laud was confirmed at Canterbury. Neile and Laud brought not only a sharper focus on conforming to ritual but a new theology, arminianism, which was a complete shock to puritan sensibilities (though less so, of course, to the General Baptists); for all the issues they had had with Whitgift, this theology had not really been a concern. This new battle led to new departures for America and ultimately to the execution of Charles I.

The Wray Family

As we noted in the last chapter, the Wray family were Lincolnshire landowners with a strong interest in puritan matters and close links to John Smyth in particular. Frances Wray was linked to many of those who were to become radical puritans or separatists and paid for the university education of Richard Bernard – the one who stayed. After the death of Sir William Bowes, Isabel Wray remarried John, Lord Darcy, in 1617, who was of Aston, Chesterfield. For a time, she was close to those who became the Baptists such as Helwys (see below) but also financed 'preachers where there were none'. From her base near Chesterfield, she supported clergy who were otherwise 'silenced' such as Rothwell, Baynes[33] and Beriah Dyke,[34] her personal chaplain; the former was highly successful in Durham. According to Gower, she gave £100 a year to 'maintain preachers were there were none, nor any means of them, and all her Preachers were silenced men by reason of Non-conformity....she would lay out all her interest to get them their liberty, and then she

---

31 J T Cliffe, *The Puritan Gentry*, p.146

32 P Collinson, *Archbishop Grindal*, p.290

33 The most likely person is Paul Baynes one of the Christ's College puritans, who was ejected from his position in 1608.

34 Dyke is commonly referred to as the father of the Dykes who became writers, but I cannot match this with the Christian name given in the *Works of John Smyth*. Daniel and Jeremiah Dyke were the sons of William Dyke, who died in 1608, and was certainly a puritan clergyman. Jeremiah's son Daniel went to Emmanuel, became a 'tryer' for Cromwell and eventually a Baptist.

would dispose of them where there needed in the North, or in the Peak in Derbyshire, or other places, and allow them pensions'.[35]

However, neither Isabel nor any of her husbands achieved lasting political influence. Bowes was already unpopular with King James even before he became king of England, and Isabel's reported friendship with Lady Arbella Stuart would not have helped. It has been suggested that Isabel tried to arrange for Arbella to stay at one of the houses of her brother-in-law Sir George St Paul during her captivity after 1610.

Isabel's brother was Sir William Wray, who Gervase Holles described as 'a simple honest man' and a strong puritan. He was elected as MP for Grimsby in 1604 and formed a Parliamentary alliance with his brother-in-law, Sir George St Paul (or St Poll) to promote many puritan causes – mostly with little success. In 1604 they promoted a Bill against 'scandalous and unworthy ministers' and for reform of the ecclesiastical courts. In 1606 he was trying to win legislation on Sabbath observance and to control 'pluralities' and ministers who did not live in their parishes. He wanted legal action to develop greater learning amidst the ministry. He had some direct control over eight parishes. He died in 1617.

His friend and relative by marriage to Frances Wray, George St Paul (1562-1613), had homes at Melwood Grange near Epworth [36] and Snarford in Lindsey. He was also 'an ardent puritan'[37] and supported the same causes as Sir William in Parliament. His involvement with the Bill against 'scandalous clergy' in 1604 was 'to make fit the ground and to weed'. After Guy Fawkes' failed plot, St Paul was on a committee to consider the Jesuits. In 1607 he was supporting the free preaching of the Gospel and in 1610 was supporting typically puritan proposals to stop clergymen holding several benefices and to restrain 'excesses in apparel'.

St Paul liked reading the works of Bishop Jewel and condemned Catholicism as 'ambition, human policy and heathenish superstition'. Although his funeral oration said that he spent his days 'looking at nothing but how to provide for the good of God's people' he was astute in finance and challenged Sir William Hickman for control of the Gainsborough market; Hickman was involved in a lengthy and bitter battle with the people of the town over the market and river tolls.[38] Holmes blamed this on Hickman's 'most aggressive extension and exploitation of his manorial rights' which he pursued through 'crooked manipulation of his authority as a justice of the peace'. The town's cause was championed by Sir Richard Williamson, a local man with a successful legal career, with Hickman's bailiff being taken to Lincoln assizes in 1608; the following year, Hickman tore up railings around the marketplace, prompting another legal case which went to Star Chamber. Williamson came from the Gainsborough commercial class and it has been suggested he began a legal career at the suggestion of Sir Christopher Wray.

St Paul attempted to help the puritan clergyman David Allen of Ludborough who got into

35   Gower, *Life of Richard Rothwell*
36   Therefore, on land formerly held by Melwood Charterhouse, whose prior was Augustine Webster, martyred in 1535.
37   A Thrush and J Ferris, *History of Parliament: The House of Commons 1604-29*, online edition, 4 June 2014
38   Holmes (1980), p.31-2

problems for not using the *Prayer Book* and left him £5 in his will. Allen held lectureships at Market Rasen, Louth and Grimsby and was rector at Ludborough from 1594 to 1614, and was found even by Neile's visitation to be 'an apostolic man'.[39] He was reported by his own churchwardens in 1604 for the usual offences connected to the surplice and the Prayer Book, winning a reprieve from his bishop in 1605 and 1606 whilst thinking it over.[40] Allen is a classic example of partial conformity, for he was said to have never used the sign of the cross but despite this retained his living at Ludborough.[41] Allen also broke a rule by inviting others to preach in his church, organised parish fast days (perhaps inspiring Buddle of Wickenby to publish an attack on the practice) and had 'abstinence prayer' sessions from eight o'clock to four. During the deprivation of Cooke at Louth, various puritans went illegally to his church instead, including one of the Spendluffe family.[42] Like Viccars at Stamford, perhaps Hinchcliffe at Timberland and Bernard at Worksop, he seems to have had an 'inner congregation'.[43] His brother Walter was also active in Wolds parishes and as a lecturer.

Allen's daughter Rebecca was fluent in Latin, Greek and Hebrew because her father taught her well. She married Thomas Rainbow, who had been appointed by the Wrays as vicar at Blyton and gave birth to Edward Rainbow who was named after Edward Wray and eventually became Bishop of Carlisle – having taken a Wray scholarship to Magdalene along the way.

St Paul also laboured hard as a magistrate, seeing public service as a Christian duty. His funeral sermon mentioned that he 'dearly loved' the President of Corpus Christi College, which in 1613 was John Spenser, a friend of the leading puritan Richard Hooker, but a man who in 1604 had stood firmly against the dissension in the Church. Spenser and St Paul had been at the same college.

St Paul's only child, a daughter, had died in 1597 and much of his wealth was spent on charity and the church. He controlled six livings, all of which were held by nonconformists. He supported ten old men and old women and young tradesmen in Market Rasen for 30 years (then added an extra twenty) where he also funded a schoolmaster and supported a hospital. He began every Monday with prayer in his study. St Paul's last words were reported as 'Now is my comforter come, and hell gates shall not prevail against me, and by the power and the comfort of the Spirit I know I shall finish my course with joy, and after receive the crown of life'.

After his death in 1613, his funeral oration was delivered – as requested – by Dr John Chadwick the rector of Faldingworth. Chadwick referred to the 'six learned and profitable preachers...were brought up in the universities at his cost and charge'.[44] His wife Frances helped finance the Cambridge education of the puritan rector of Worksop Richard Bernard in one of his book dedications in 1635, *The Ready Way to Good Works*. Bernard's first

39   Hajzyk (1981), p.265; Allen had links to Elizabeth Morison, wife of puritan Henry Clinton 2nd Earl, who in turn had links through her father to Thomas Cromwell and Hugh Latimer.
40   Babbage (1962), p.222
41   Hajzyk (1981), p.252
42   Babbage (1962), p.176
43   Hajzyk (1981), p.277
44   Thrush and Ferris, *ibid.*

book was dedicated to the children of Sir William Wray and he credited his book, *Christian Advertisement*, to St Paul and his wife Frances née Wray. In 1628, Bernard dedicated *Ruth's Recompense* to Frances Rich, Countess of Warwick, as she had by then become. St Paul and Frances built a magnificent alabaster tomb for themselves at Snarford, but Frances was never buried there.

St Paul's widow, Frances Wray, remarried to Robert Rich, 1st Earl of Warwick, also a puritan, in 1616; he in turn died in 1619. Some of St Paul's lands passed to his sister Faith, Lady Tyrwhitt, who had married into another notable Lincolnshire family.

Wray Family Patronage:

The Countess of Warwick, as Frances had now become, continued to support the university education and careers of suitable young men such as Edward Reyner, who graduated in 1621, became a teacher[45] and then became master of Sir George St Paul's school in Market Rasen. Frances then made him lecturer at Welton. A puritan of impeccable credentials, he was a friend of John Cotton and was influential enough not to be too troubled by minor nonconformities, becoming lecturer in Lincoln 1626 – a position which he held until war came calling. Reyner was tempted by the offer of a cathedral prebend but having accepted it then regretted it; he got Lady Armyne, to whom he was related, to negotiate his way out of this with the bishop.[46] 'I have had many countesses, ladies and others, who have been suitors to me to get preferment for their friends,' Bishop Williams wrote, 'but you are the first that ever came to me to take away'.[47] In 1639 he turned down an offer to be minister to the English congregation in Arnhem. Reyner's journey eventually led to him making the decision to separate and become effectively a congregationalist 'after many hours spent in prayer with tears'. The conditions of the Civil War era led to a short-term residency in Yarmouth but he returned to Lincoln in 1645 where he could still preach at the cathedral and St Peter at Arches. War itself came to Lincoln in 1648 when he famously escaped being killed by Royalists as one of the officers had been taught by him at Market Rasen.

Reyner died in 1660. His son was ejected from Emmanuel College in 1662 and went to Nottingham to practice medicine.

Frances 'was a person of a shining conversation, and eminent bounty, of which, though we have not a particular account, yet we cannot but name one instead of all, which is, that she was a great benefactress to Magdalen College in Cambridge, which her father had before her much improved, by not only completing the buildings, but adding three fellowships and six scholarships in 1624.[48]' She endowed the College with lands at Alkborough – hence that village still has a Countess Close and a College Farm; she also endowed charities in her father's home country at Bedale, where her name is still visible

---

45 Given in *ODNB* as at 'Aserby', presumably Aswarby.
46 Hill, p.116
47 *Congregational Magazine*, vol.15, 1832, p.529
48 *Magnia Britannia in Lincolnshire*, vol.11, p. 1453; some sources give the date as 1625.

in the parish church's list of benefactors.

Her stepson, Robert Rich, who became the 2nd Earl, also had puritan sympathies which made him distance himself from Charles I and drew him to the New England colonies as well as Virginia. In 1628 he helped to get a patent for the Massachusetts Bay Company. He opposed Charles in the Civil War and commanded the Parliamentary navy, providing some help to the colony of Rhode Island in 1643 and therefore aligning with the supporters of religious liberty.[49] Here again one small family proves to have connections across the globe.

---

49 Rhode Island had been set up by the husband of Mary Bernard, daughter of the Wray family protegée Richard Bernard of Worksop.

CHAPTER TWELVE

The Baptists Planted in England
1612-1660

The Baptist denomination was planted in England by men who had come from Nottinghamshire and Lincolnshire, with Lincoln an early centre of growth. Their central belief that separated them from others was that the christening of infants was not based on Biblical precedent, but only the baptism of believers was scriptural. The Baptists soon took their ideas to America, where they became the largest Christian denomination. But perhaps of even greater significance, they brought with them their thinking about religious tolerance, wrote about it, and passed these ideas through Roger Williams into the bloodstream of the new America.

Chronology:

1612: Helwys and Murton start a congregation in London

1615: Estimated date of Helwys's death, usually assumed to have been in prison

1620: John Murton completes *A Description*

1623: Baptists arrested in Lincoln

1626: At least five Baptist congregations known to be active

1629: Roger Williams marries Mary Bernard

1644: Williams publishes *The Bloudy Tenent;* Henry Denne becomes a General Baptist; Hanserd Knollys becomes a Particular Baptist

---

The Church planted:

After the split with Smyth, Thomas Helwys returned to England in 1612 and lived in Spitalfields or Stepney. This aligned with an outburst of writing in 1611-2 in which he set out many of his positions. He and his followers intended to 'lay down their lives in their own country for Christ and his truth'[1] – which he did indeed do. This move probably coincided with the publication of Helwys's last significant work, *The Mystery of Iniquity* of 1612, in which he attacked the concept of 'hierarchies' in the Church, labelling all bishops as hell-bound, and began to shift to be critical of the spiritual authority of the King although insisting on loyalty in other respects. He reiterated that magistrates, including the King, had no authority over the Church. He also ended by saying it was wrong to flee your country because of fear of persecution. Trouble was inevitable: it made few

---

1   M R Bell, p.58

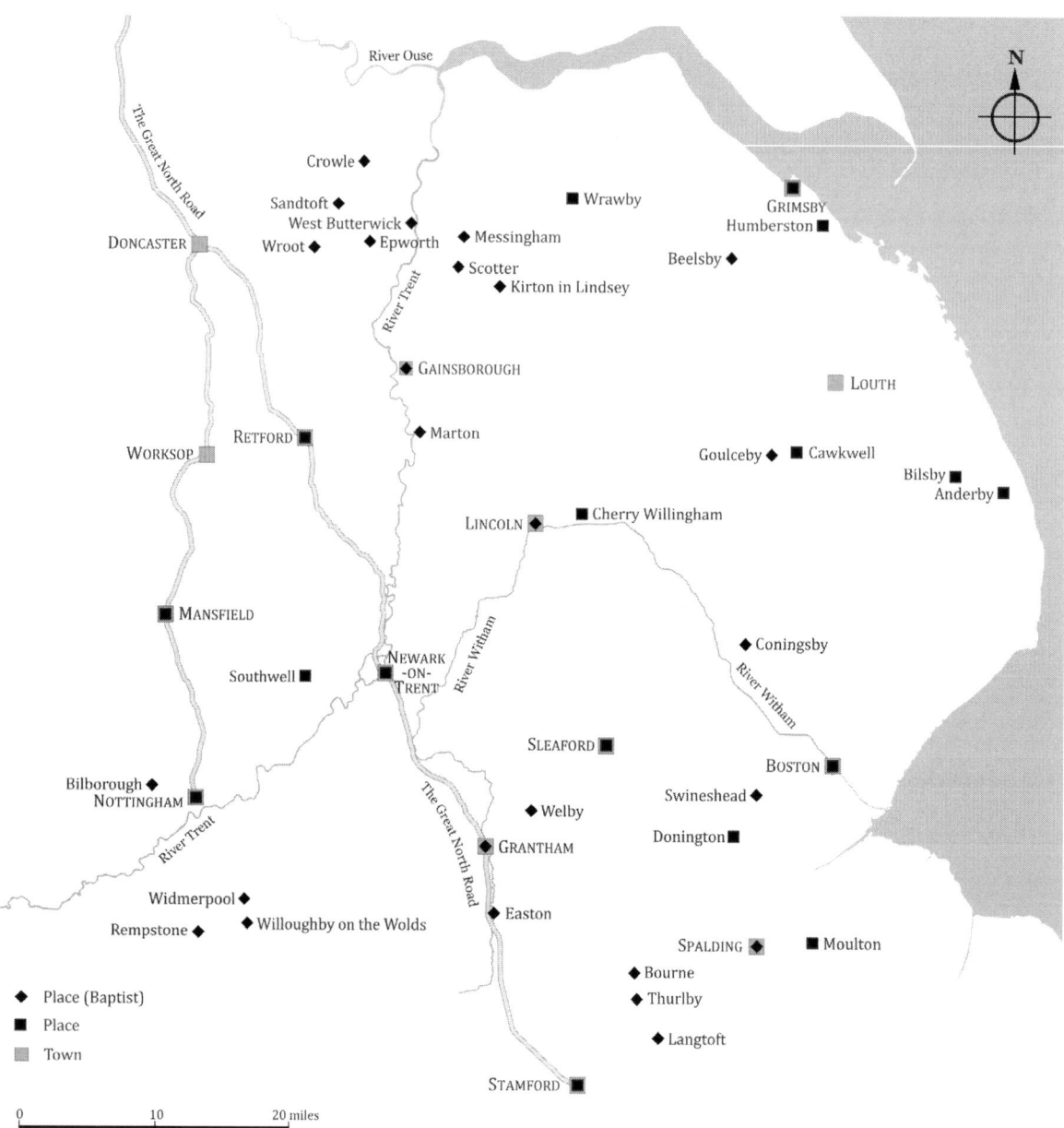

Crowle ◆

Sandtoft ◆
West Butterwick ◆
Wroot ◆   Epworth ◆

■ Wrawby

GRIMSBY ■
Humberston ■

◆ Messingham

DONCASTER ■

◆ Scotter
◆ Kirton in Lindsey

Beelsby ◆

◆ GAINSBOROUGH

LOUTH

WORKSOP ■   RETFORD ■

◆ Marton

Goulceby ◆   ■ Cawkwell

Bilsby ■
Anderby ■

LINCOLN ◆   ■ Cherry Willingham

MANSFIELD ■

◆ Coningsby

Southwell ■

NEWARK
-ON-
TRENT ■

SLEAFORD ■

BOSTON ■

Bilborough ◆
NOTTINGHAM ■

◆ Welby

Swineshead ◆

Donington ■

◆ GRANTHAM

Widmerpool ◆

◆ Easton

Rempstone ◆   ◆ Willoughby on the Wolds

SPALDING ◆   ■ Moulton

◆ Bourne
◆ Thurlby

◆ Langtoft

◆ Place (Baptist)
■ Place
▨ Town

0   10   20 miles

STAMFORD ■

274

friends as it attacked every other Church that had existed and laid into John Robinson especially. Helwys argued that, by leaving England, the separatists had turned against the responsibility for witnessing to the Gospel in their own land, for reasons of personal safety. Helwys famously provoked further trouble by sending a copy of his book to King James, to which he added a personal note.

Robinson took exception to this criticism and others returned the assaults: Helwys was accused of having wrecked his own position in Holland so that he had to return to England. Also, in April 1612 what was to be the last burning at the stake which occurred in England, of 'Baptist' Edward Wightman, and it seemed this had turned public opinion against such things.[2] In fact, the identification of Wightman with Baptists is misleading and his 'heresies' were unusually radical.

In coming to England, Helwys knew he risked considerable opposition from all sides. Baptists were widely derided as 'anabaptists' and tainted by historic events at Münster, whilst their new Arminian position meant they could be condemned as 'Catholics'. They were also often associated with the Family of Love or Familists and the suggestion that they were 'antinomians', unfettered by concepts of sin. How numerous Familists were in our region is hard to establish, but John Cotton was aware of them in Nottingham led by a Mr Townes and there were around forty still there in 1669.

An indication of what was happening with Helwys is perhaps that the archdeaconry of Nottingham again became interested in his marriage in February 1613 when a search was made at Bilborough for records of his wedding; given that he had long left Bilborough, this can only have been prompted by his arrest. On 6 May 1615, he is mentioned in probate as formerly of 'Stebinheath' or Stepney, so we must assume he had died by this time.[3] Joan Helwys survived until probably 1626, leaving three daughters and two sons – her son Thomas being a servant in Canning Street.

Helwys had trusted for supernatural help – 'in all things we hope and wait for wisdom and strength' – and his work flourished after his death and does so to this day with around 43 million Baptists in the world. His view on predestination has become dominant in British Baptist life, if not American, broadly summarised by Watts as 'while no one was predestined to death, some were predestined to life'.[4] Helwys thought that 'the Lord creates no man to damnation' and that he 'would have all men saved' – if they wanted it.

Conventionally it has been said that Helwys probably died in Newgate prison in about 1615, close to the time when his cousin Sir Gervase was executed on Tower Hill over problems while he was in charge of the Tower. Sir Gervase was clearly fully aware that Thomas's reputation was well known, for in his final speech he denied that he was an Anabaptist, which he considered 'a fond, ridiculous, foolish and phantasticall opinion'. Indeed, the Lord Chief Justice had asked him if he was one. However, Larry Kreitzer has

---

2   Wightman had had some connection with Darrell in the Thomas Darling case but later developed a variety of radical opinions which were labelled as heretical. Some of his children, fittingly, emigrated to Rhode Island in 1660. However, it is not technically correct to say – as has often been given – that he was a 'Baptist'.

3   Kreitzer (2019), p.268

4   Watts (1986), p.299

challenged the view that Helwys died in Newgate, or indeed was taken to prison at all; all we know for certain is that he died by 1615.[5]

With Helwys soon dead or out of circulation, 'leadership' (insofar as they believed in this) of the Baptists passed to John Murton from about 1613. Although Helwys has been traditionally viewed as the leader of the Baptists, Stephen Wright has argued that they, in fact, favoured a collective style of leadership in which perhaps the younger John Murton emerged as a leader of comparative influence with roots in the Lincolnshire town of Gainsborough. Murton seems to have been in Newgate prison by 1613, so the London Baptists made little progress. However, Murton survived long enough to write, including *A Description* in 1620. Murton was born in Gainsborough in 1583 and married Jane Hodgkin of Worksop[6] in Amsterdam in 1608, presumably just after both left with the Helwys group for the Netherlands.[7] Murton sided with Helwys when the church split in 1610 and worked as a furrier before returning to England in 1611. His writing earned him the enmity of Robinson, who condemned him as 'better suited for wielding a shovel and a pick than for discussing theology'. Yet modern critics, like Durso, see him as 'quite able to hold more than shovel and pick'. Thomas Seamer had also returned and may have been the link that supported new Baptists in Lincolnshire.

Sometime before 1624 the London church was strong enough to expel sixteen members and it seems to have continued in Lambeth.[8] A small number of Baptist congregations sprang up and in 1626 both London and Lincoln churches were communicating with the Waterlanders in Holland. In 1630 Jane Murton, assumed to be John's widow, applied in Amsterdam to join the Waterlanders.

Helwys' role may appear to have been brief, but it was influential. He had, it would seem, seeded a new Church in England, which by 1626 had branches in London, Tiverton, Lincoln, Sarum and Coventry. Though it may never be possible to prove continuity between Helwys's handful of returning migrants and the General Baptist Church that grew soon after, it seems strongly likely. His church was also very unusual at the time for holding an Arminian theology, though Calvinistic Baptists were soon to emerge.

Baptists and Religious Freedom

Robert Browne of Tolethorpe had begun to develop ideas of religious toleration but as late as 1607 Smyth still thought it reasonable for princes to build churches and command their subjects to enter them. Yet by 1612 he was able to write 'the first unequivocal plea for religious freedom for all Christians ever to come from an Englishman'.[9] Smyth argued in Proposition 84:

'The magistrate is not by virtue of his office to meddle with religion, or matters of

---

5   Kreitzer (2019), p.304-6
6   Champlain, p.258
7   Keith Durso, *No Armor for the Back – Baptist Prison Writings*, Mercer, 2007, pps.32-48; this provides good coverage of a largely forgotten but interesting character
8   Wright (2006), p.59 and p.61
9   Watts (1986), p.48

conscience, to force and compel men to this or that form of religion or doctrine; but to leave Christian religion free, to every man's conscience, and to handle only civil transgressions, injuries, and wrongs against men'.

Helwys followed this. He brought *The Mystery of Iniquity* with him from Holland and published it in England. He formed a Baptist congregation at Spitalfields and then tried to present his book to King James. He attached his famous letter to the monarch, saying that 'The king is a mortal man, and not God, therefore hath no power over the immortal soules of his subjects to make laws for them, and to set spiritual Lords over them…'. John Robinson was unimpressed by Helwys's pugnacious attitudes, blaming his 'natural confidence' causing him to 'date and challenge king and state to their faces'.[10]

After Helwys died, the reputation of the *Mystery of Iniquity* has grown – fitfully. Although seen as 'savage, its contents mediocre…repetitive and tedious, with little literary merit'[11] it yet contains ideas of great importance. Helwys argued that the King had no right to govern in spiritual matters, and from there moved to argue that no man had the right to force another – 'Men should choose their religion themselves'. To an extent it can be argued that this view was a development of Smyth's suggestion, in his Proposition 84.[12] As in many things, Smyth had changed his mind on this. Helwys now wrote:

> 'For our Lord the king is but an earthly king, and he has no authority as a king but in earthly causes….Men's religion to God is between God and themselves….. Let them be heretics, Turks, Jews, or whatsoever, it appertains not to the earthly power to punish them in the least measure'.

He also wrote:
> 'The king is a mortal man and not God, therefore hath no power over the immortal souls of his subjects to make laws and ordinances for them, and to set spiritual laws over them'.

Helwys and John Murton developed an idea that could be seen in the writings of John Smyth but was emphatically not there in the work of John Robinson. Thus, the thinking of the Baptists did not emerge amongst the colonists of New England for many years, with the exception of Rhode Island.

The distinctive addition that Helwys and Murton made was to extend tolerance to all religions, specifically including non-Christian ones, though this certainly did not mean that they accepted all religions were of similar value. The ideas of religious freedom were shared with another Baptist, Leonard Busher, a Gloucestershire man who went to the Netherlands in about 1606, and later with Roger Williams.[13] Busher's only published work was entitled *Religions Peace; or, a Plea for Liberty of Conscience, long since presented to King James and the High Court of Parliament then sitting, by L. B., Citizen*

---

10 Robinson, *Of Religious Communion*, p.41
11 Greasley, p.72
12 Greasley, p.81
13 J. Stern, 'A Key into The Bloody Tenent of Persecution: Roger Williams, the Pequot War, and the Origins of Toleration in America' in *Early American Studies*, 2011, 9(3), 576-616. Retrieved from www.jstor.org/stable/23546670

of London, and printed in the year 1614; it is now thought likely that Busher was pastor of his own congregation rather than one of the Smyth-Helwys congregation, but he did send one of his manuscripts to John Robinson, who failed to reply. Murton, it is conjectured, was unaware of his writings.[14] In '*Religion's Peace*' Busher argued that 'error and heresy cannot be killed by fire and sword but by the word and Spirit of God'. Together these Baptists produced the most sustained printed arguments for religious tolerance that had yet been seen in England.

It is difficult to trace the origin of these ideas, but an anonymous separatist in England in the 1570s had got to a similar place, arguing that 'The queen's highness hath not authority to compel any man to believe anything contrary to God's word…the soul of man for religion is bound to none but unto God and his holy word'.[15] However, the congregation of John Smyth had come into close touch with Dutch Mennonites such as Pieter Twisck, who in 1609 published the first history of religious toleration.[16] Twisck met Robinson in Leiden in 1617, influencing Robinson to becoming more accepting of toleration. Murton drew his thoughts from the Mennonite Twisck, whilst Roger Williams then based much of his famous work *The Bloudy Tenent* (1644) on that of Murton.

In 1613 a petition, *A Most Humble Supplication of Divers Poor Prisoners* was submitted on a scrap of paper to Parliament, signed by 'those most falsely called Anabaptists', and was rejected when the Commons met in April 1614. Its central point was that Protestant sectaries were treated more harshly than Catholic ones.

In 1615 the Baptists produced another work, *Objections Answered by way of Dialogue*. There is uncertainty about who wrote this – perhaps Murton, though Stephen Wright believes it was Helwys because its author would have had to have been adult in 1603.[17] It offered a systematic view of religious liberty and attacked the role of the bishops and any form of 'compelled' religion. In *Objections answered by way of dialogue*, Helwys (or possibly Murton) said that it was 'heinous….to force men and women by cruel persecutions, to bring their bodies to a worship whereunto they cannot bring their spirits'.

It is more confidently believed that Murton was soon in Newgate where he spent most of the time between 1613 and 1626.[18] He was imprisoned in 1615 for his *Persecution for Religion Judged and Condemned* (a different title for *Objections*). He wrote at least two works there, with *A Humble Supplication the King's Majesty Loyal Subjects…* (1620) apparently written in milk as there was no ink, then smuggled out to friends who read it by firelight. Murton's thoughts are exceptionally interesting even though part of his mind was occupied in debate with Robinson; he disagreed with him on infant baptism, fleeing from persecution, and whether it was acceptable for magistrates to promote Christianity by force. He argued that a true church consisted only of baptised believers who had repented and 'publicly confessed their faith in Christ' – so babies, who had neither sinned nor repented, did not need baptism. He denigrated earthly learning as often resulting in

---

14   William R. Estep, *The English Baptist Legacy of Freedom and the American Experience* in J Y Briggs (ed), *Pilgrim Pathways: Essays in Baptist History in Honour of B R White*, Mercer, 1999, p.270
15   Watts (1986), vol 1, p.25
16   Jeremy Bangs, *Dutch Contributions to Religious Tolerance*, in *Church History*, 2010, p.585-613
17   Wright (2006), p.45
18   Kreitzer (2019), p.303; Wright (2006), p.46

the persecution of those who know the truth by the Holy Spirit.[19] He used James's own words against him, from 1609: 'It is a sure rule in divinity, that God never loves to plant his church by violence and bloodshed'.

His other work was *A Description of what God hath Predestinated*, was also printed in 1620. As Coggins has pointed out, none of the Helwys-Murton writings concentrated on baptism per se: they wanted to talk about how someone was saved, and about authority over religious belief. Baptism became more of a topic later, when immersion became the theme.

It is to Roger Williams that we owe the story of Murton writing secretly from prison:

> The author of these arguments against persecution … being committed (a) prisoner to Newgate for the witness of some truths of Jesus … and having not use of pen and ink, wrote these arguments in milk, in sheets of paper brought to him by the woman, his keeper, from a friend in London as the stopples of his milk bottle. … In such paper, written with milk, nothing will appear; but the way of reading by fire being known to this friend who received the papers, he transcribed and kept together the papers, although the author himself could not correct nor view what himself had written. … It was in milk, tending to soul nourishment, even for babes and sucklings in Christ … the word of truth … testify against … slaughtering each other for their several respective religions and consciences.

Addressing the King, Murton wrote, 'It is not in your power to compel the heart; you may compel men to be hypocrites, as a great many are, who are false-hearted towards God and the state, which is sin both in you and them'.

Murton, unsurprisingly given his supposed lack of formal education, separated spiritual wisdom from earthly knowledge. 'The Spirit bloweth where it listeth (John 3:18) and is not tied to learning,' he wrote. He disagreed with the view that the Holy Spirit only spoke to or through educated clerics; in Murton's view, the key 'offices' were of preaching, then 'reading and interpreting'. He was explicitly spiritual in advocating a freedom in worship – 'worship Him with our souls and our spirits, and…according to the truth of his Word'. Like Helwys he was an early advocate of religious freedom which he tried to combine with loyalty to the king; his time in Newgate shows this was not entirely successful. In *A Description of what God hath Predestinated*' in 1620, he roundly criticised the Calvinist views on predestination and perseverance. He could not imagine anything 'more repugnant to the nature of God' than that men were sent to hell for doing the things God might have compelled them to do. Greasley, himself a Baptist minister, argues that Murton moved Baptist theology back closer to the Smyth position on free will.

Murton said history would judge on the issue of compulsion in religion:

> 'Will not succeeding ages cry out against the cruelty of the learned Protestants herein, as well as they cry out against the cruelty of the learned Jews and papists? Yes, we are assured they will, as many millions do in other nations this day'.[20]

Murton died in about 1625 or 1626, having perhaps considered some formal unity with the Mennonites, and his wife Jane then returned to Amsterdam where she joined the

---

19   As set out in the heading to Chapter V.
20   Durso, p.48

Mennonites in 1630, not needing baptism as having been baptised by Smyth.[21]

The ideas about tolerance of Helwys and Murton were later found in Roger Williams, a puritan who married Mary, the daughter of Richard Bernard of Worksop, in 1629 and migrated to New England. They founded Providence and the state of Rhode Island, which practiced freedom of religion. There he briefly became a Baptist and therefore a woman from Nottinghamshire was involved in the first 'Baptist' church in the Americas.[22] The Providence Island Company was supported by many English puritans including the 2nd Earl of Warwick and Sir Thomas Barrington, from an Essex family with whom Williams had close connections.[23] Warwick even declared his intention of moving to Rhode Island[24] whilst Barrington's son later said that he supported the venture for the good of the kingdom and to propagate the Gospel.[25] For a time, Anne Hutchinson of Alford found a home there, having been rejected by the rigid expectations of the New Englanders. As Jeremy Bangs has said, Murton may be seen as 'one of the sources for religious freedom in Rhode Island', the colony that Williams created.

Having both a son and a daughter in New England, Richard Bernard was very interested in its affairs and exchanged some letters with Cotton, who he felt was too exclusive in his church policy regarding new arrivals: 'Take them in, if bad to make them good, if godly minded, to make them better,' he advised. Bernard was also a correspondent of Thomas Gorges, who in 1641 wrote to him from the new colony of Maine, about John Wheelwright – a Lincolnshire man who had met with some opposition during the Hutchinson fracas. 'I told him,' Gorges wrote about Wheelwright, 'for the civil we steered as near we could to the course of Ingland. For the Ecclesiastical we forced no man to the common prayer book or to the ceremonies of the Church of Ingland but allowed the Liberties of Conscience'.[26]

Roger Williams and the Development of Ideas of Liberty

Williams came to know the fairly obscure writings of Murton through his possession of a section of text which Williams referred to as *Scriptures and Reasons written long since by a Witness of Jesus Christ, close prisoner in Newgate, against Persecution in Cause of Conscience* which was actually a part of the 1620 *Humble Supplication to the King's Majesty* edition which was bound up with *Persecution for Religion Judged and Condemned* and printed that year. Williams then supplied a copy to John Cotton in about 1635, which Cotton responded to.[27] Their discussion forms a part of Williams's 1644 book. How far Williams understood the connection of this with friends of his father in law can be debated, but if he knew who had written it, he would surely have known the

---

21 Sprunger, *Dutch Puritanism*, p.84. Her maiden name was Hodgkin and she is assumed to have been the sister of Alexander Hodgkin, who had remained with the Smyth-Mennonite group in Amsterdam.

22 This has been much debated; some see John Clarke, from Suffolk, as the founder of the first true Baptist church which was also at Rhode Island.

23 Barrington subscribed over £1000 in 1631, but the Company was soon in financial trouble.

24 Cliffe (1984), p.204

25 Cliffe (1984), p.117

26 Abby Chandler, *Law and Sexual Misconduct in New England*, Basingstoke, 2015, p.1

27 Guggisberg, H. (1977). Religious Freedom and the History of the Christian World in Roger Williams' Thought. *Early American Literature, 12*(1), 36-48. Retrieved from http://www.jstor.org/stable/25070810

connection. Given that he seems to have known enough to add details of how the text was smuggled out, it is likely he knew at least some of the background.

Williams came back to England in 1643-4 to acquire a charter for Rhode Island in which he developed thoughts on freedom of religion. Thus, in *Queries of Highest Consideration* (1644) he ridiculed state control of religion and in *The Bloudy Tenent of Persecution* (1644) he specifically used and defended Murton's the *Humble Supplication*. He said that it was 'in vain' to allow ordinary people to 'search the Scriptures' if 'they should be forced to believe as the church believes'. On 9 August 1644 Parliament voted to burn Williams's books but the tide was clearly shifting and within weeks a new toleration began to emerge. In 1653-4 Williams returned to England on business and stayed at Sir Henry Vane's estate at Belleau. On 1 April 1654 he wrote to friends at Providence and Warwick about Vane's efforts to support the settlement whilst staying for ten weeks in the care of his wife: 'Under God the sheet anchor of our ship is Sir Henry, who will do as the eye of God leads him'.

These ideas did not take root in Massachusetts as Anne Hutchinson, Elizabeth Hooton and others found. Thus, when Sir Richard Saltonstall wrote to John Cotton and others in about 1650-1, he was able to echo almost the very words of Helwys and Murton:

> 'Truly, friends, this your practice of compelling any in matters of worship to do that whereof they are not fully persuaded is to make them sin, for so the Apostle (Rom. 14 and 23) tells us, and many are made hypocrites thereby, conforming in their outward man for fear of punishment'.

Saltonstall went on to give a warning: 'I hope you do not assume to yourselves infallibility of judgement when the most learned of the Apostles confesseth he knew but in part and saw but darkly as through a glass'.[28] Cotton refuted the charges.

Nonetheless, this strand of thinking influenced Williams, Sir Henry Vane, John Milton and later John Locke, and from there influenced the American Constitution and the United Nations Declaration of Human Rights. The doctrine of religious liberty is arguably the greatest contribution of our region to global civilisation, championed by three men from Sturton, Broxtowe and Gainsborough.

Baptists Continued

Although Smyth, Helwys and Murton were soon absent from the scene, the Baptists soon picked up (or gathered in the pre-existing) adherents in Lincolnshire and Nottinghamshire with Robert Godfrey of Wrawby being cited as an Anabaptist in 1616 and claims of a Baptist group east of Brigg within a few years. But we do not know whether these had connections with Helwys in London or Anabaptists overseas. In 1620 a reference was made to Baptists in 'divers counties' – but we don't know where.[29] They did not, it would seem, immediately have visible 'clergy' of their own for as Murton wrote in 1620, 'ever disciple that hath ability is authorised, yea commanded, to preach, convert and baptise…'

---

28   John Adair, *Puritans*, Stroud, 1998, p.241
29   Wright (2006), p.58

The origins of the Lincoln church are, inevitably, obscure; in 1616 Richard Lollie of Lincoln, an apprentice to William Bristowe, was accused of being re-baptised along with members of four other households.[30] Ruth Johnson was presented that year for being absent from church, and her husband Thomas emerged as the Baptist leader in the city a few years later; he was 'presented' regularly from 1623-38. In 1618 Thomas Lauton or Lawton, an apprentice in the same house as Lollie in Lincoln St Benedict's, was in trouble for anabaptism. Plumb suggests that a man named Pigott brought Smyth's ideas from Gainsborough; Thomas Piggott had been present in Amsterdam, but it has been suggested he remained in Amsterdam as the English Baptist leader there. Thomas Seamer seems to have been the most likely connection given his known presence with seven others in Gainsborough in 1631 and excommunicate status.[31]

In 1623 in Lincoln St Swithin's ten confessed to being Anabaptists and having seventeen of their children of at least twelve parents taught by Peter Finch,[32] an Anabaptist schoolmaster,[33] who seems to have been there since 1621.[34] One of his pupils was said to have been the daughter of the mayor, Mr Ward, although Lincoln did not have a mayor of this surname. Another was the child of Stephen Mason, an alderman and gentleman, who had been mayor in 1615 – and was followed by Robert Mason in 1616. Four of the parents were influenced into signing a confession. Members like the Cawtons and Bells were related to the Coddingtons at Harmston and South Hykeham. Links to this group, which included a musician of some standing, may explain a Baptist licence at Cherry Willingham in 1672 and there might also be familial connections to the early Baptist group at Kirton-in-Lindsey. The Lincoln Baptist church was certainly in existence by 1626[35] when they were one of a handful nationally corresponding with the Mennonites[36] and another school was being run by a Mrs King by 1629 whilst Finch was still around in 1638. In 1641 14 'anabaptist recusants' were identified.[37]

Thomas Johnson (d. c1648), a wealthy baker[38] who was able to live in the Cathedral Close eventually, became the established leader and his son Jonathan succeeded him; he was presented at every visitation after 1623 with his wife. All three of his children were presented at some point for being Anabaptists. Jonathan was probably leader by 1651 and was involved in the pamphlet war against the Quaker Martin Mason in 1659. When the younger Johnson died in about 1670 one of his trustees was alderman and mayor of Lincoln.[39] Another was Stephen Mason, a wealthy farmer of Cherry Willingham, who died in 1629, and also wealthy was Martha Kent, wife of an alderman – two of the Kent family were mayors in the 1630s.

30   Hajzyk (1981), p.370
31   Wright, p.59
32   Kershaw (1995), p.8
33   Plumb, vol.1, p.93. Plumb also reports a claim from the minister at Burgh that the deeds for the chapel dated from 1612.
34   Hajzyk (1981), p.371
35   Plumb, p.88-90.
36   Kershaw (1995), p.8. Additional information from Kershaw's article in *Baptist Quarterly*, https://biblicalstudies.org.uk/pdf/bq/37-2_087.pdf.
37   Wright (2006), p.70
38   Bob Kershaw has suggested that this was at the site of the 'Green Dragon'
39   *Lincoln: Gentlemen, Musicians and Bakers* in *Baptist Quarterly*, http://biblicalstudies.org.uk/pdf/bq/37-2_087.pdf

In 1634 Archbishop Laud was warned that 'in Lincolne there are many Anabaptists', but this seems to be an exaggeration.[40] They numbered at least fourteen, and that they considered linking with the Waterlanders suggests a lack of confidence in their own strength.[41] However, in Lincoln at least, the Baptists included people of some social influence.

Baptists followed the established pattern by spreading perhaps through family or trade links to Cherry Willingham, South Hykeham and probably Kirton-in-Lindsey.[42] By 1623 there were small groups at Scotter, Messingham and Marton, whilst another group was at West Butterwick, a home of the Sheffield family; the Scotter group appears to have been the strongest outside Lincoln lasting until at least 1640 when it had eleven, up from seven or eight in 1631.[43] Reports indicate Baptists at Alvingham in 1616 and 1637.[44] At Wroot in 1633 the Archbishop of Canterbury visitation found Dutch and Walloon congregations with English members.[45]

An interesting case is Gainsborough. Hajzyk[46] found records of persistent 'Brownism' there from 1623-40, with separatists led by a Richard Brown and 'anabaptists' led by Thomas Seamer – about 14 in all. Of course, a Thomas Seamer had gone with Smyth and Helwys to Holland; Gainsborough records indicate the christening of a Thomas Seamer, son of Thomas, in the town in 1593 – so it was an established local family. Hanserd Knollys famously had 'conference and very good counsel' there with 'Brownists' – were they the Baptists? Kreitzer suggests that a famous 'anabaptist petition,' which he dates to 1609, could have originated in Gainsborough *before* Helwys returned to England – for it gives clear prominence to William Barlow, bishop of Lincoln; this is quite a revolutionary suggestion, but wholly possible given North Sea trade. In February 1631 a Thomas Seamer, perhaps the same one, was charged with standing excommunicate along with seven others.[47] Overall, Seamer seems the most likely explanation for the origin of the Lincolnshire Baptists. In 1635 Gainsborough had ten excommunicated and included two 'Brownists' and one 'Anabaptist'.

Isolated examples are known from Coningsby (1625), Aswarby, Metheringham (1630) and Eagle (1630) whilst in 1638 Mr Breen of Beelsby was in trouble for 'preaching in a tubb at night in the house of Mary Wright'.[48] In 1641 only 14 Baptists were listed in tax records for Lincoln[49] but the 1640 list of excommunicated persons in the Stow Visitation gave 27 at Gainsborough, 43 at Belton, 19 at Epworth, 14 at Haxey and 12 at Owston and West Butterwick.[50] The importance of Axholme is clear and this may reflect protection by Lord Edmund Sheffield (1564-1646), who was a puritan sympathiser; Epworth, Crowle

40   Holmes (1980), p.41
41   Champlain, p.275. Possibly this is the same Jonathan Johnson who debated with Quaker Martin Mason in the 1650s (Plumb, p.129).
42   Kershaw (1995), p.9
43   Wright (2006), p.69
44   Hajzyk (1981), p.373
45   Plumb (PhD), p.107
46   Hajzyk (1981), p.374
47   Wright (2006), p.59
48   Plumb (PhD), p.167
49   Holmes (1980), p.41
50   Kershaw (1995), p.26

and West Butterwick were well established and still listed as Baptist churches in 1673 with 100 members at Epworth.[51] The claim that Crowle was the first Baptist church in the country was, sadly, the result of a Victorian forgery.

A characteristic of the Baptists was their strength in rural areas. They also developed in south Nottinghamshire around Widmerpool, clearly feeding off established family rebellion but also part of the curiously rural nature of Baptist strength at times. Samuel Brett became one of the leaders, perhaps following a father who had been in trouble for condemning his own parish church at Willoughby-on-the-Wolds in 1624. But, in general, there were fewer Baptists in Nottinghamshire although a congregation existed at Rempstone in 1654. Of course, there is also the famous story of Col John Hutchinson, who was the governor of Nottingham Castle, and who agreed to disperse 'anabaptists' meeting there on the instigation of local Presbyterians in summer 1644. Finding not them but some papers, his wife Lucy was impressed by their arguments against 'sprinkling'; when she was pregnant in 1646, Lucy expressed doubts about christening to her husband and they became Baptists.[52] However, this did not result in a sustained Baptist congregation in Nottingham and larger towns like Worksop never had an established Baptist congregation.

The Baptists were soon enmired in further doctrinal dispute as the 'Particular' Baptists split from the 'General' in 1633 or possibly 1638; the former believed that atonement was limited to particular persons and believed in full immersion which was practiced from about 1640-1.[53] The 'General' group who were Arminian believed in the laying on of hands, but there were disputes about this from about 1645. The congregation at Langtoft and Thurlby was in dispute about this in 1656. What sort of a Church were they? Perhaps not all were like the church run by Thomas Lambe in London – 'his church gatherings were noisy and chaotic. Everyone was allowed to participate and often the congregation voted on who they wanted to hear preach'.[54]

During the Civil War era identities became very fluid and some Baptists became Levellers and later Quakers, but others moved in the reverse direction. Henry Denne had once been 'a great time server, a High Altar man' before the war according to the author of *Gangraena*, Thomas Edwards. He then left his ministry as a curate in the Church of England at Pirton and became a General Baptist in 1644 at the Bell Alley church in London. They recognised his talents and sent him north to plant churches in the Fens at Warboys and Fenstanton. This he managed to combine with being given the parish living at Eltisley through the influence of the lord of the manor. By 1644 he was in prison for preaching against infant baptism, where he met Dr Daniel Featley the author of an anti-Baptist work, *The Dippers Dip't*. According to Denne, Featley abandoned the argument once forced on the defensive and so Denne took to print to continue it. Late in 1645, Denne was in Kent where 'he dipped many' and preached in houses.[55]

51   The church here appears to have been a victim of the falsified history of the Baptists in this area and believed their foundation to have been in 1607. The Misterton church was reported in one document to have been founded by William Brewster in 1610, who ministered here for ten years before going to America!

52   J H Wood, *A Condensed History of the General Baptists of the New Connexion*, London, 1847, p.123

53   C Douglas Weaver, *In Search of the New Testament Church – the Baptist Story*, Mercer, 2004, p.20

54   Bell, p.42

55   Wright (2006), p.160

In 1646 he was arrested at Spalding for baptising two (or four) women in the river – one of the women told the magistrates; he admitted preaching there but denied the baptisms. Once he had turned away from tithes and altars, he became a carter to finance his travelling ministry as a Baptist, apparently living at Caxton.[56] He established General Baptist churches in the counties of Huntingdon, Cambridge and Lincoln, as well as Kent where his family originated. There has been some debate about whether he preached the idea of an 'inner light' before it was popularised by George Fox, the Quaker.[57] Denne was one of the first General Baptist 'Messengers' with a commission to 'preach the Gospel where it is not known, to plant churches where there is none, to ordain elders in churches remote, and to assist in dispensing the holy mysteries'.[58] His prominence is perhaps shown by the vehemence of the published attacks on him by the London Particular (ie Calvinist) Baptists in 1646.

It has been suggested that for a time at least Denne was a 'Universalist', believing that all would be saved, and was 'justly' imprisoned at Cambridge until being released through 'influence'.[59] 'He taught that Christ died for Judas as well as Peter, and for the Turks and Pagans also; all sins were forgiven when Christ shed his blood'.[60]

Denne served in the army from 1647 and had a brush with death in 1649 when he was involved in the 'Leveller' mutiny at Burford, narrowly escaping being executed although he later published *The Levellers Discovered* to condemn the others such as Lilburne, who was stuck in the Tower, and they retorted by calling him 'Judas Den'. In some interpretations he had behaved bravely, being one of the few officers to stand by the men at Burford. He appeared at the trial in a winding sheet, somehow earning a pardon after saying that 'he rejoiced to suffer with willingness under so righteous a sentence'. Three others were shot. Nonetheless, by 1653 he was back in the General Baptist mainstream, being sent out by the influential church at Fenstanton in Cambridgeshire as missioner.[61] Perhaps Denne's influence explains the spread of the Baptists north of Spalding towards Grantham. The church at Bourne is well known, but in 1651 there was a congregation at Thurlby and another serving Easton, Welby and Westby by 1655; the elder of this was William Everard whose brother Robert became a Catholic. Bytham was served by visitors from Grantham. Surfleet and Swineshead had Baptists by 1651. Here is another example of the Baptists laying down roots in rural areas.

However, from 1654 Denne was active in Kent, remaining there until his death in 1666 though his influence in the strength of the General Baptists in South Holland is perhaps important.

In the new atmosphere of religious ferment, the 1640s saw some leave the Baptists. Lawrence Clarkson's career included a short time ministering in Lincolnshire and then some occasions of preaching at Spilsby and Horncastle while chaplain to Col. Twistelton's

56 Watts (1986), p.112-3
57 Watts (1986), p.205. This view is criticised in T Underwood, 'The Baptist Henry Denne and the Quaker Doctrine of the Inner Light', in *Quaker History*, 1967, 56(1), 34-40. Retrieved from www.jstor.org/stable/41946524
58 Underwood, *English Baptists*, p.120 cited by Watts, p.283
59 H N Brailsford, *The Levellers*, London, 1976, p.37
60 Brailsford (1976), p.37
61 J H Wood, *The Condensed History of the General Baptist of the New Connexion*, London, 1897, p.176

regiment. He was arrested in January 1645 following the familiar allegations of naked baptisms in Suffolk conducted with Hanserd Knollys. He later became a 'Seeker' and acted as chaplain to the Lincolnshire Regiment in 1647; he ended up as a 'Muggletonian,' widely condemned as a heretic.

In 1647 Samuel Oates was preaching the Baptist faith around Stamford and also distributing the Leveller publication, *Agreement of the People.*[62] Oates was accused of holding meetings in barns and stables, but also of breaking into churches and using the pulpit. In 1649, while based in Rutland, his infamous son Titus was born. He faced many allegations – common against Baptists – that 'he dips women naked, in ye night, fit for works of darkness'.[63] In Essex it was claimed that he was responsible for impregnating many previously childless women.[64] In 1653 he was asked to resolve a dispute in the congregations at Thurlby and Langtoft with their pastor, Robert Wright. Kershaw suggests that it was Oates as much as Denne who was a successful 'church planter'; it was possible he set up the Thurlby-Langtoft churches himself, another at Easton-Welby-Westby by 1653 and even that at Swaton and Bourne. Kershaw speculates that the Coningsby church was set up by John Lupton, a possible Oates convert, who became a messenger and died in about 1670.[65] However, William and Elizabeth Lupton were cited at Lincoln in 1625, and Elizabeth was cited for being an anabaptist at Coningsby in 1635, so a close causal link with Oates seems unlikely.[66]

Another key Lincolnshire figure in the growth of the Baptists was Hanserd Knollys (1598-1691). Born at Cawkwell near Louth, Knollys grew up in the Church of England as his father was vicar of Grimsby and Scartho. Richard 'Knowles' was one of those summonsed to the High Commission in 1635. Some of the events of Hanserd's young days marked him out including being rescued from drowning by his father at the age of six – perhaps an experience similar to that of John Wesley. His father also advised him against strong drink and making vows, whilst young Hanserd felt convicted of sin after a fight with his brother. Knollys himself went to Cambridge and there came under puritan influence after a sermon convinced him of the need for repentance, before returning to his home county to teach at Gainsborough. There he met a 'godly old woman' who introduced him to a 'Brownist' and attended meetings where the Brownist used to 'pray and expand scriptures in his family'.[67] Despite this separatist influence he was ordained in 1629, was given the living of Humberston in 1631 and married Anne Cheney of Wyberton.

Here Knollys had a spiritual experience. Whilst praying with a dying woman, he felt 'the Devil set upon me with a violent suggestion, that the scriptures are not the Word of God'. He prayed that the woman would recover to confound the tricks of Satan – and she did.[68]

However, Knollys could not leave the touch of the puritans behind and found some

62   Holmes (1980), p.198
63   Andrew Bradstock, *Radical Religion in Cromwell's England*, London, 2011, p.12
64   Ute Dreher, *A case study of Lawrence Clarkson* (1615-1667), Durham theses, Durham University, 2000. Available at Durham E-Theses Online: http://etheses.dur.ac.uk/4328/
65   Kershaw (1995), p.22-3. Oates is most famous as the father of Titus Oates, the informer who appears to have been one of the least lovable characters in a century not lacking for candidates.
66   Wright (2006), p.70
67   Kershaw (1995), p.14
68   Howson, p.58

problems in the Laudian Church. By 1633 he was having problems as he did not wish to wear a surplice, sign the cross or admit the unrepentant to the Eucharist. He decided that his ordination in an erratic Church was invalid and resigned his living in 1633. Although the bishop of Lincoln from 1621 to 1641, John Williams, tolerated these issues and allowed Knollys to continue preaching in east Lincolnshire, but he soon attracted persecution; a man who stood witness against him on his arrest in 1636 changed his mind and 'was so greatly terrified in his conscience that he set open the doors and let me go away'.[69]

Knollys played down his own impact during this period. 'Though many had been reformed and moralised, yet I knew not…..how to convert any souls to God'.[70]

One day Knollys was out in the woods at Anderby, praying.

> After prayer I walked and meditated under the wood-side till sunset, and then went homeward, resolved not to preach till the Lord made my call to that great work of preaching the Gospel clear to me. As I was going home, an answer to my prayers was given me in these words, 'Go to Mr. Wheelwright, and he shall tell thee, and show thee how to glorify God in the ministry;' but I heard no voice, nor did I see any vision, only those words were plainly and articulately spoken into my ears and understanding: at which I was astonished and said, 'Lord, let me not be deluded nor deceived;' then was brought to my mind that passage of Cornelius sending to Peter, who should tell him what he ought to do ; whereupon I was fully persuaded it was an answer to my prayers from the Lord, and I was filled with such joy, that I went on my way rejoicing, leaping and praising God.

At some time in 1633-5 John Wheelwright and Knollys met, perhaps at Wood Enderby,[71] and this became one of the most intriguing relationships of Christian Lincolnshire – and indeed America. Wheelwright told Knollys that he was held back by a reliance on works and explained the 'covenant of grace' to him. Wheelwright was another Cambridge graduate who was vicar of Bilsby in Lincolnshire from 1623 to 1633 when he was removed on doubtful charges of corruption. Knollys's own conversion was completed through the text of Acts 26, 16: 'But rise, and stand upon thy feet: for I have appeared unto thee for this purpose, to make thee a minister and a witness both of these things which thou hast seen, and of those things in the which I will appear unto thee.'

A man with a new faith, Wheelwright 'began to preach the doctrine of free grace, according to the tenor of the new and everlasting covenant, for three or four years together, whereby very many sinners were converted, and many believers were established in the faith'. Denounced to the High Commission, Wheelwright escaped because the man who came to arrest him was 'so greatly terrified in his conscience that he set open the doors and let me go away'. He was related through marriage to Anne Hutchinson who had such a challenging impact on the early settlers in New England. He attracted attention for his puritan views and then left for New England in 1636. He formed the first Congregationalist church in New Hampshire.

---

69 Kershaw (1995), p.15
70 Hanserd Knollys, *The Life and Death of…Hanserd Knollys, Written with His Own Hand to the Year 1672*, London, 1693, p.9
71 Kershaw (1995), p.15

Knollys went to London and then, by 1638, to Boston in New England, losing a child along the way. His associations with Wheelwright and the Hutchinsons made Knollys unwelcome in Massachusetts and he was banished almost as soon as arriving. He pastored a church at Piscataqua (now Dover in New Hampshire) but got into problems with a rival pastor, Thomas Larkham, causing a riot and ending up with a heavy fine.

There he and John Wheelwright attracted some opposition and sexual scandal was alleged against Knollys for a 'filthy dalliance' by trying to seduce his two maids – which he denied. As well as being criticised for being an Anabaptist, he was alleged to be an antinomian – 'free to live a scandalous life' as free from the laws of God,[72] both of which he denied. He returned to England in December 1641, becoming for a time a preacher in the Parliamentary Army with which he became disillusioned. A spell in unlicensed preaching culminated with him being stoned out of the pulpit in Woodbridge, Suffolk. However, by 1644 he was becoming aligned with the Particular Baptists in London, who had been gathering together since about 1638, and elsewhere, refusing to have his infant son baptised, and where he formed a 'Particular Baptist' congregation in 1645 – one of the first – and said to number a thousand within a year.[73] For a time, he was with Edward Montagu, the Earl of Manchester, in the Parliamentary army where a conservative critic complained 'he did a great deal of mischief'.[74] It has also been suggested that he had links with the General Baptists around Wainfleet.[75] He baptised Henry Jessey, a future Baptist leader to whose church he had briefly belonged, in June 1645.

Also in the early 1640s, **Henoch Howet**, probably of Sleaford but a Baptist in Lincoln in 1630,[76] appears to have been a key Baptist influence on Thomas Lambe and they were both cited in 1640, at times being linked to the Bell Alley church in London along with Samuel Oates and Henry Denne. Lambe and Howet were arrested in 1641 after a Baptist meeting in Whitechapel. Lambe became a pioneer of baptism by immersion. Howet published a book on sin in 1645 when he was described as an 'Anabaptist' of Lincoln. Howet was still active as a Baptist in 1654 when he was castigated in the Quaker pamphlet *The Walls of Jericho Razed to the Ground* by Edward Burrough.[77] In 1655 he published a riposte, *Quaking Principles Dashed to Pieces by the Standing and Unshaking Truth*. Burrough replied, including the comment that 'a great part of which book of his is not worth mentioning'. James Nayler also responded in *The Boaster Bared and His Armour Put Off*.

On 14 February 1645 Knollys was 'stoned out of the pulpit' at Debenham in Suffolk by a mob, encouraged by a constable. In May he was hauled before the Committee of Examinations of the Westminster Assembly and accused of being an 'antinomian', thus

72 B H Howson, *Erroneous and Schismatical Opinions: The Question of Orthodoxy regarding the Theology of Hanserd Knollys*, Leiden, 2001, p.2
73 Howson, p.64
74 T Edwards, *Gangreana*, vol 1, various pages
75 Kershaw (1995), p.18
76 Murray Tolmie, *Thomas Lambe, Soapboiler, and Thomas Lambe, Merchant, General Baptists*, in *Baptist Quarterly*, vol 27.
77 Howet also features in Roger Williams's discussion of George Fox. (*The Complete Writings of Roger Williams*, vol 5, various pages.)

confusing him of being a General Baptist to which he reacted with some fury.[78] Knollys took the popular argument that 'free grace' believers 'take liberty to live in sin, and walk after the flesh, fulfilling the lusts thereof'. He had moved some way from the point of agreeing with Wheelwright.

At this stage Knollys seems to have flirted with the extreme in Suffolk when he was arrested with Lawrence Clarkson after six women were baptised. It was alleged that the women were naked, and that the ministers enjoyed their favours during the rite; Clarkson turned it to laughter by asking the judges what they knew of the 'pleasures' of such acts in the water – in winter! Such arrests were linked to the suspicion about 'free grace' that caused so much trouble in America, but Clarkson soon rejected the Baptists and by 1649 had taken some extreme views that led him into being a 'ranter, pantheism and actual sexual libertinism'. In London in 1645, where Knollys could command an audience of a thousand, he prayed from the pulpit for the release of the Leveller, John Lilburne.

In 1646 Knollys subscribed to the *Appendix to the Confession of* Faith, which set out the Calvinist Particular Baptist views. He continued preaching in London and Southwark, attacking General Baptists when he could as well but also those that supported child baptism. Perhaps he rubbed shoulders here with John Spittlehouse, who he may have taught at Gainsborough, and who was a member of a General Baptist congregation in London in 1652. In January 1649, a period of greater tolerance, Knollys was allowed to preach in Suffolk.

In the 1650s Knollys was seen sometimes as a 'Fifth Monarchist' and as a 'hyper-Calvinist'; this was a belief in predestination that was so rigid that it saw no reason to share the Gospel with non-believers. Yet, from 1658, he bizarrely combined his role with the Baptist congregation in London with being the Church of England vicar at Scartho – a post in which his son succeeded him to make three generations. This was a time of growth for the Baptists, and Knollys was especially active preaching in Suffolk, and possibly planting churches in Cornwall.[79] Kershaw has argued that he was behind the planting of Baptist congregations in Wold villages like Goulceby but Thomas and Richard Drewry have also been linked to this congregation, in 1651. In 1656 he published a book on the Song of Solomon, drawing on preaching done at Lord Francis Willoughby's house in Gainsborough in the 1640s.

Knollys was compromised by the Venner Revolt – Venner being a Baptist – against Charles II in 1661 and was imprisoned for 18 weeks. Some of his congregation were 'Fifth Monarchists' which did not help his cause. After this he spent time in Holland and Germany.

He was arrested again in 1670 but perhaps his most important contribution was to help consolidate the Baptist church through meetings in London. Knollys was also involved in healing and in his autobiography wrote of his own miraculous healing following anointing with oil and prayer in 1670.[80] Healing seems to have been more common in the Particular Baptists than in the General Baptists. In 1684, well into his eighties, he was imprisoned

78   Wright (2006), p.158
79   Howson, p.68
80   Jane Shaw, *Miracles in Enlightenment England*, London, 206, p.38

again yet was still able to preach to the other inmates. In 1689 he prayed for his friend Benjamin Keach who was ill, that his days would be added to, then he prophesied that Keach would outlive him; he did – by 13 years.[81] Knollys is therefore important in our Baptist story, for people with our local links – indeed it is true to say that people with specifically Gainsborough links – formed both the General and the Particular Baptists.

So, by 1660 the Baptists were established in Lincolnshire and had something of an uncertain foothold in rural Nottinghamshire. Although they benefited from the freedoms of Cromwell's England in the 1650s, they had also been the group most prone to competition from the Quakers as George Fox often liked to point out. But we must conclude that the Baptists were one of the great Christian history developments from our region, and especially so their contribution to religious liberty.

---

81   Howson, p.60

CHAPTER THIRTEEN

Charles and Laud
try to Rollback the Puritan Tide
1625-1633

Under Charles I from 1625, and especially with William Laud's influence, nonconformity in the Church shifted from questions of 'form' – worship, robes etc. – to also include matters of doctrine with the rise of Arminianism, which Calvinists saw as indistinguishable from a 'Popish' teaching of 'good works'. Ironically the first Baptists were also Arminian to some extent and had to face abuse as a result.

The 'forced loan' crisis of 1626-7 followed by the promotion of William Laud to be Bishop of London in 1628 and then Archbishop of Canterbury in 1633 destroyed the possibility of compromise. Moreover, it created an opposition to the King based on both his abuse of power and his religious policy. The prosecution of nonconformists increased during this period, notably after 1631 when the rules on 'gadding' and altar rails began to be more tightly applied. The King's need for money forced him into a parallel conflict over the extent of Parliamentary power, causing a critical convergence over the issues of Religion and Politics in which the gentry of the two counties took sides through choice or necessity.

Chronology:
1625: Charles I becomes King
1627: Forced Loan crisis begins; Grantham altar dispute
1628: William Laud becomes Bishop of London; Irby overturns Boston election; Tobie Matthew, Archbishop of York, dies
1629: Charles's 'personal rule' begins
1631: Stamford case reaches courts
1632: Richard Neile becomes Archbishop of York
1632-3: new regulations on altar rails enforced
1633: William Laud confirmed as Archbishop of Canterbury; John Cotton resigns Boston benefice

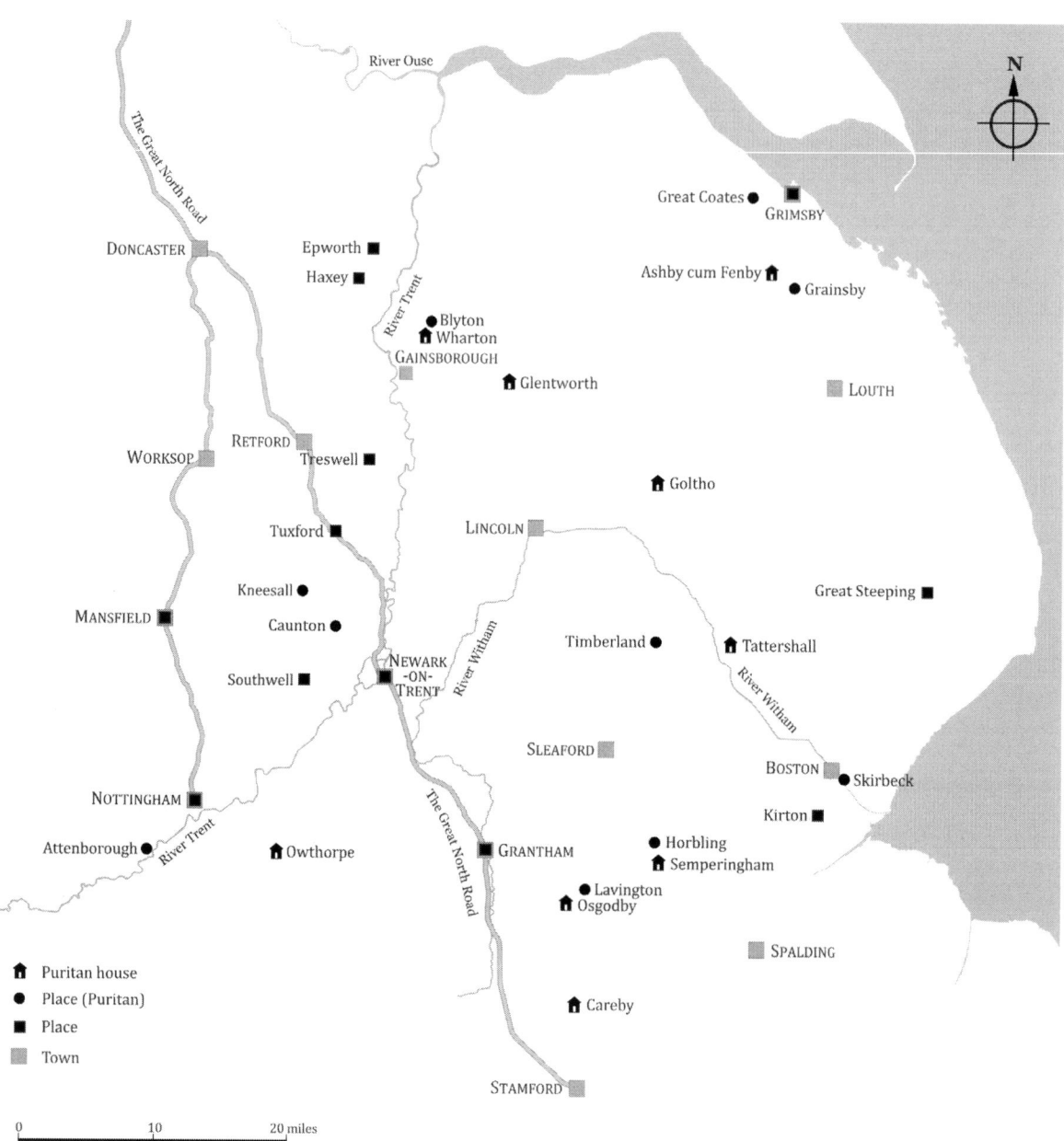

The Great North Road

River Ouse

DONCASTER

Epworth ■

Haxey ■

River Trent

● Blyton
🏠 Wharton
GAINSBOROUGH

🏠 Glentworth

Great Coates ● ■ GRIMSBY

Ashby cum Fenby 🏠 ● Grainsby

LOUTH

WORKSOP

RETFORD

Treswell ■

Tuxford ■

🏠 Goltho

LINCOLN

Great Steeping ■

Kneesall ●

Caunton ●

Southwell ■

MANSFIELD ■

River Witham

Timberland ●

🏠 Tattershall

River Witham

NEWARK
-ON-
TRENT

SLEAFORD

BOSTON ■ ● Skirbeck

Kirton ■

NOTTINGHAM ■

Attenborough ●

River Trent

🏠 Owthorpe

The Great North Road

GRANTHAM ■

● Horbling
🏠 Semperingham

● Lavington
🏠 Osgodby

SPALDING

🏠 Puritan house

● Place (Puritan)

■ Place

▨ Town

🏠 Careby

0   10   20 miles

STAMFORD ■

292

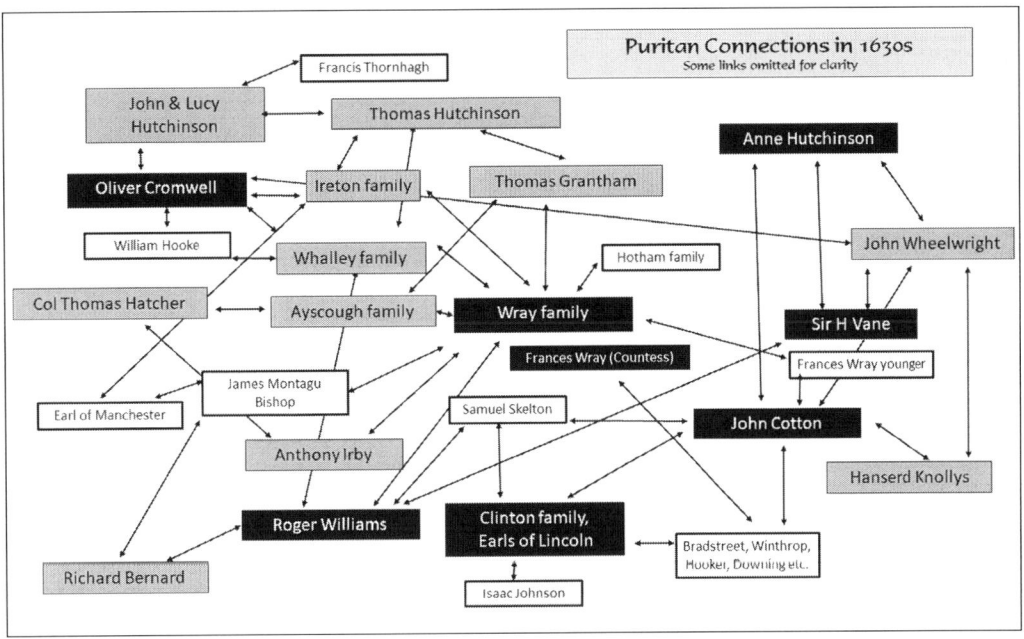

Charles and Laud: Sowing the Seeds for Disaster

When Charles I came to power in 1625, he supported clergyman with ritualistic intentions such as William Laud, who became Bishop of London in 1628 and Archbishop of Canterbury in 1633. Laud actually became the dominant figure much sooner than he arrived at Canterbury for his predecessor, George Abbot, was out of favour with Charles I from 1627 and Laud held much of the national influence that should have been his – indeed Laud knew from 1626 that he would be the next Archbishop of Canterbury.

It was already clear that the Church of Charles and Laud would be a very different one, even to that of James. As early as 1606 Laud had been accused of 'Popish' tendencies, by 1615 he was accused of Arminianism and being a 'crypto-Catholic' and whilst still only Dean of Gloucester he caused a dispute about the position of the altar (or 'table'). In his early career he had developed an intense rivalry with John Williams, the Bishop of Lincoln, and Williams became an 'obsessive fear'[1] that marked out much of Laud's life.

As his influence grew Laud fed the new king's preference for prayer over preaching. Laud was an advocate of strong bishops, detesting Presbyterians and therefore suspicious of puritans in general who he feared harboured such views; he also thought Calvinism damaging to the State and the authority of the King. These groups, in turn, became increasingly suspicious of Laud and his patron Neile, both of whom were named as Arminians in Parliament in 1628, although both denied this in 1629. In the midst of the forced loan crisis and Charles's dispute with Parliament, Laud's status as both politician and Church leader gave him great power and yet also sowed the seeds for his downfall. Charles's dissolution of Parliament in 1629 helped to solidify the mutual suspicions. Yet

---

1   Anthony Milton, *William Laud*, in *ODNB*, accessed 29 August 2019.

this was also Laud's intention, for he had told Charles that if the Church 'had more power, the Kinge might have more both obedience and service'.

The forced loan crisis came about as Charles had dissolved Parliament in 1626, though was the normal mechanism for raising money through taxation. He then attempted to raise money through trying to force wealthier citizens to 'lend' him money and imprisoned some of those who challenged him. Charles used the Church to support his case, arranging for sermons on the Divine Right of Kings to be preached – which Laud supported. The crisis is important in the region's Christian history as it widened the divisions between the puritans and the increasingly Laudian Church – and the King.

Too many Irbys

The Irby family of Gosberton, Whaplode and Boston commonly used the same Christian names for all their oldest sons, making their family a significant challenge for the reader. In our story we meet:

- Anthony Irby I (d. 1575) of Gosberton, who featured in our account of the Lincolnshire Rising
- Sir Anthony Irby II (1547-1625) was son of Thomas Irby of Whaplode, was an MP for Boston on seven occasions, and a major puritan figure. He left £10 to John Cotton in his will. Left most of his estate to his grandson (IV) and buried at Whaplode.
- Sir Anthony Irby III (1576-1610), has little involvement in the story and was buried at Whaplode
- Sir Anthony Irby IV (1605-1682), who first married Frances Wray and had a significant career in Parliament stretching from 1628, through the Civil War era, until his death in which he repeatedly represented Boston. His career included being a Commissioner of Sewers and Recorder of Boston.

The 'godly' almost entirely sided against the forced loan, with notable opponents including Theophilus Clinton, the Earl of Lincoln, who organised a campaign against it that landed himself and some of his staff before the Star Chamber and the Earl himself in the Tower of London. His father in law, Lord Saye and Sele, also refused to pay. Many Lincolnshire gentry and MPs also refused to pay, indeed it was rumoured that only three people in the whole county had agreed,[2] though they were not always as badly punished – Sir Anthony Irby managed to avoid prison. However, those who were gaoled for at least a time included many of Lincolnshire's puritan gentry such as Sir John Wray, Sir Thomas Grantham, Sir Edward Ayscough and Sir William Armyne, although he tried to evade arrest. Men like Armyne were not swayed by 'the corruption of Court-Flattery' and cared for 'his Country's welfare and never forsook it'.[3] One of his chaplains commented that Armyne was 'alwaies too brave a spirit to endure vassalage'. Armyne had a fine memorialist in Seth Wood, who provides us with a summary of the solid puritan practice of appointing good men to parish practice:

---

2   Hill (1956), p.119
3   *A Remonstrance of the True State of the Kingdom*, 10 in BL Thomason Tracts, cited by Cliffe (1984) p.153

'…in all those places in his dispose he planted men of very good reputation, and abilities to preach the Gospel, and gave proportionate encouragement both for countenance and maintenance.'[4]

Sir John Wray was briefly imprisoned until released on health grounds to 'house arrest'; Grantham was exiled to Dorset and Kent. The Mayor of Boston William Anderson and ten of the town's leading citizens refused to submit to the loan (Anderson was imprisoned) and these included at least three who soon left for New England – Atherton Hough, William Coddington and Thomas Leverett.[5] It also included Edward Tilson, a former mayor, who was accused additionally of hosting the radical Scottish preacher Alexander Leighton – who also knew Brewster and Robinson from Leiden.[6] In Nottinghamshire around a quarter of the gentry refused to pay but Nottingham itself assented – resistance stiffened during 1626 and also strengthened to the similar demands for Ship Money after 1635. Of that country's gentry, Sir Thomas Hutchinson, a moderate puritan, tried to evade the King's demands.

Although one-time Lincolnshire MPs such as Sir John Wray, Armyne and Grantham[7] were all imprisoned for opposing the forced loan in 1627, yet the King's need for money was so great he was forced to call a new Parliament in which they were re-elected in 1628. Thomas Hatcher of Careby, whose wife was Katherine Ayscough and who was also related to Armyne, was elected for Stamford, a known sympathiser of those who had been in prison and a puritan – he became Colonel Hatcher in the Civil War.

Bishop Williams seems to have strengthened his own position by securing the election at Boston his two of his staff, firstly William Boswell (who seems not to have been a loyalist) in 1624-5 and then Richard Oakley (1624, 1626 and 1628), in exchange for permitting the corporation to demolish a church. Oakley's election in 1628 was overturned by Sir Anthony Irby, of clearer puritan tendencies since he had been married to the younger Frances Wray III[8] at Glentworth and went on to fight for Parliament in the Civil War; given this, it seems unconvincing that the election of Boswell and Oakley at Boston was in exchange for the bishop tolerating 'the almost wholesale non-conformity which characterised the town'.[9] Opposition to the forced loan was much less in Nottinghamshire – only a quarter of the gentry refused to pay it; the generation of Ireton, Whalley and Hutchinson had yet to fully emerge and for a time staunch royalists like the Earl of Newcastle held sway.

---

4   Seth Wood, *The Saint's Entrance into Rest and Peace by Death*, London, 1651, p.18

5   J C Hotten, *The Original Lists of Persons of Quality; Emigrants; Religious Exiles etc*, London, 1874, p. xiv, names amongst others Thomas Leverett, Edmond Jackson and John 'Coppyn' – the latter being one of those arrested with the 'Pilgrims' twenty years earlier.

6   Leighton was arrested in 1630, branded and had his ears cut off for criticising the Queen and other offences.

7   Sir Thomas Grantham (1573-1630) had a strong record of denouncing Catholics in his region, including the 6th Earl of Rutland in 1624. John Hutchinson, a figure of great importance in the Civil war, lodged with him as a boy, and Sir Thomas Hutchinson – his father – was Grantham's friend. In 1629 Thomas Paybody dedicated a book to him and Hutchinson – *A Just Apologie for the Gesture of Kneeling in the Act of Receiving the Lord's Supper*. Paybody had been Lady Lucy Grantham's chaplain and was presented to the living of Panton.

8   We might term her Frances Wray III, daughter of Sir William and niece to Frances I, Countess of Warwick. Frances Wray V married Sir Henry Vane. She died in 1627, not long after marrying.

9   Hajzyk (1981), p.133

Therefore, Parliament of 1628 reflected a significant development for the Lincolnshire puritans where the connected gentry of Sir Christopher Wray, Ayscough, Clinton, Armyne, etc. dominated the polls.[10] Their intransigence contributed to their being no Parliament called for the next eleven years. Tensions were further increased by Charles' personal rule from 1629.

The term 'Laudian' began to be used for a new phase of 'high church' practice, too similar to Catholicism for the comfort of the puritans. As Archbishop, Laud also increased censorship of publications. As Laud attempted to build a more powerful Church, persecution of nonconformity accelerated; ceremonial conformity became almost another obsession. Samuel Harsnett became Archbishop of York in 1629 and then Richard Neile, in many ways Laud's patron, in 1632; they pursued the Laudian approach of more rigorous discipline. Neile, as we shall see, acted in 1635 to improve enforcement by officials in the southern part of his diocese through appointing Edward Mottershed.

Both bishops in our area were out of step with the policies of Laud and King Charles at the start of the reign. Tobie Matthew at York, who died in 1628, had long been on the opposing wing and his national prominence had suffered: 'as he found himself edged out of politics, Matthew became more committed to protecting his godly flock'.[11] Despite this, action against nonconformists had increased in the 1620s with Jennings judging there to have been a 63% increase in puritan-related offences in Nottinghamshire in that decade.

Bishop John Williams of Lincoln (1582-1650), a Welshman who held the see from 1621 to 1641, was an intense rival of Laud's from the 1620s. He had joined the clergy from Cambridge in 1605, as 'a Calvinist with liberal inclinations'.[12] Williams was academically gifted – he could use nine languages – and a good enough preacher to impress James I. He held the prebends of Lufford, Asgarby and Kelsey in Lincolnshire from 1613, became Dean of Salisbury and then Westminster, and was clearly ambitious. He was given the task of bringing into the Church of England Lady Katherine Manners who was to marry Buckingham, the king's favourite. Despite his political machinations, Williams failed to capture the see of London for which he hoped and, instead, was given Lincoln – a huge task, out of the limelight, and with a ramshackle palace in Buckden which might as well as have been nowhere; Williams however, conspired to keep the deanery of Westminster as well. In doing so he made an enemy of William Laud, who became linked to the future King Charles I, who he also alienated. Despite performing the last rites of James I and preaching at his funeral, Williams was in a weaker place. Certainly, up to at least 1625 he was more interested in Westminster politics than his diocese, but after that he was forced out of his political career.

Williams was certainly aware that there were puritan ministers in his diocese and that some officials wanted them out or persecuted more forcefully – income could be derived from fining them. Many of them were entrenched in livings which were in the gift of puritan gentry – such as Great Coates, which was held by the Barnardistons of Suffolk, and where Thomas Biggen was curate and 'preacher of God's word' in 1621 whilst the

---

10 A typical family connection was the marriage of Sir Christopher's daughter Alice into the Yorkshire branch of the Ayscough family.

11 R Oates, *Moderate Radical*, Oxford, 2018, p.155

12 Brian Quintrell, *John Williams*, in ODNB, accessed 14 June 2014

Rector for many years was Abraham Smith – who had been rector in 'godly' Winterton and then ejected from West Halton in 1614 on the suit of the Bishop of Norwich.[13] Williams's general tolerance of puritans allowed conventicles to flourish and puritan interests to strengthen in Lincolnshire in a way that they had in Nottinghamshire thirty years earlier.[14] Edward Reyner, a 'gentle rebel but a puritan radical', was largely untroubled.[15] Williams's tolerance led to him making enemies of diocesan officials Henry Allen, Sir John Lambe and Dr Robert Sibthorpe. Lambe had been brought into the diocese of Lincoln by Neile and was appointed a commissary by Williams in 1623; he was indeed an expert church lawyer, but hardly of Williams's type – he had been on a pilgrimage to Rome and supported unlimited Royal authority. With Sibthorpe, he favoured a more ceremonial church and tended to an absolutist view on how it should be run. Lambe won the King's favour and from 1629 was on the High Commission. Another appointment with disastrous consequences was of John Pregion, principal registrar.

Williams told them he would not persecute puritans and that 'they might complain of him if they could to the council table, for he was under a cloud already'.[16] Williams refused to back Lambe's actions against conventicles in Leicestershire; comments made at this meeting by Williams were relayed to enemies in London in 1628 by Lambe and became the basis of his eventual downfall. In 1628 Williams preached in Westminster, reasserting his Calvinist views and condemned the Arminianism of Sibthorpe. His policy was to communicate 'with dissentient Brethren that did not conform, whom he gained first with kindness and then brought over with Argument'.[17] In 1631 he opened Lincoln College, Oxford, built from the proceeds of his many Church offices.

Williams tried to appoint only clergy who were well educated but controlled under half the livings in his see. He tried to manage them through his visitations and in some parishes, such as Aby, the people were prepared to complain to the bishop. He tried to make his diocesan officials 'live by honest gains' and not to accept bribes but failed; his registrar Pregion was accused of extortion and begetting an illegitimate child.[18] He had to deal with problems such as Edward Collingwood, the curate at Stow, who broke the rules on allowing 'clandestine' marriages by permitting couples to wed whilst wearing gloves and masks. There was also a problem with the rector of Epworth, Richard Massey, who had been there since 1597; in 1634 he was hauled before the Commission due to being separated from his wife – 'it being alleged that Massey was an ancient and grave minister, and was willing to receive home his wife and give security for her good usage'.[19] In 1635, he was sued for alimony by Sir John Lambe (see above) and by the time of the 1640 Visitation he was described as 'excommunicate'. Nonetheless, the churchwardens were presented for failing to stop him celebrating communion whilst Matthew Heath of Epworth was excommunicated for calling him 'an old rogue' – which seems a reasonable accusation. Nicholas Massie, perhaps his son, was presented 'for begetting a bastard on Alice Standrige of Owston'. This chaos seems to have been ended by Massey's death that year. But turbulence was common in this area – in the same year, a man at Belton was

13 The living remained in the patronage of the bishops of Norwich for many years.
14 Hajzyk (1981), p.98
15 Hajzyk (1981), p.136
16 Plumb (PhD), vol.1, p.94
17 Cliffe (1984), p.147
18 Holmes (1980), p.60
19 Both cases from the Calendar of State Papers, 1634

presented for forcing his way into the church and disrupting the service[20] whilst at Wroot another abused the minister, Mr Newland, who was presumably a curate. Lloyd has also argued that drainage schemes contributed to a worsening of relations between minister and parish in villages such as Haxey in the 1630s; certainly, there was strong feeling against the Dutch engineers being brought in by the King.[21]

Williams also had problems with new clergy pursuing Laudian excesses and, one case, in particular gave him great trouble. In Grantham,[22] Peter Titley arrived in 1625 full of ritualist zeal, immediately banishing the town's lecturers from his pulpit. He introduced complex ritual and in 1627 moved the altar back into the chancel where some said he was remote from the congregation and inaudible. One version suggests that he got an old image from a dissolved abbey and included it in the altar.[23] There were some claims that he did this because the altar was being abused by the town's people – in one version, someone slept on or under it during a service! He argued that being above the chancel steps made it more visible. Some of the people, led by Alderman Whitley, forcibly moved it back although in the battle Titley was said to have lifted a form or bench and used it to knock down half a dozen opponents. Then Titley declared he would replace the 'old trestle' local people favoured with a stone altar that no-one could move[24] although it has also been argued that Williams introduced this as an allegation in his own provocative response.[25]

A later 'poem' marked the events:
>What mischiefs did in Kirks arise
>By setting tables altar wise,
>How Grantham's Vicar by the rabble
>Was bang'd about the communion table.

Williams was called in by the town's aldermen to mediate in 1627; they actually went to Buckden to find him, offering a compromise that it should not be fixed, but capable of being moved to a more audible location for communion. Williams declared himself indifferent to the issue but rejected Titley's arguments and hinted that he needed 'some more experience in the cure of soules'. Williams' *Letter to the Vicar of Grantham* became central to national argument, being debated in Parliament in 1629 (when it was alleged Titley had said all who refused the forced loan would be damned) and in front of the king in 1633.[26] If Titley did say this then it was raising the temperature still further as the sometime Grantham and Lincolnshire MP, Sir William Armyne, was a strong puritan (with friends in the Ayscoughs and Wrays) and an opponent of the forced loan – and indeed was imprisoned in 1627 on account of this.

---

20 Kershaw (1995, p.27) reports that John Norfolke, a significant Axholme Baptist in the 1670s, was excommunicate at Belton in 1640.
21 Lloyd, p.207
22 The town had the benefit of a library above the church porch, a gift from Francis Trigge, the puritan clergyman of Welbourn.
23 William Hurd, *A New Universal History of the Religious Rites, Ceremonies and Customs of the Whole World*, London, 1799, p.625
24 Holmes (1980), p.29
25 K Fincham and N Tyacke, *Altars Restored: The Changing Face of English Religious Worship, 1547-c.1700*, Oxford, 2007, p.179
26 Antony Milton, *Laudian and Royalist Polemic in Seventeenth-Century England: The Career and....*, Manchester, 2013, p.57

Williams suspected that Titley had been put up to this by his enemies, Laud and Neile. The main evidence for this is that Titley was certainly rewarded by Neile in 1632 when he was promoted to a canonry at Southwell with financial sureties supplied by people close to Neile – although he died in 1634. However, he has also been identified as being vicar of Tuxford 1621-7.

Another factor to mention here is that Neile in his Province of York actually began enforcing new expectations about the railing and positioning of the altar in 1632-3, before Laud did in Canterbury.[27] In 1633 Laud ruled that the 'altar' should be at the east end and behind a rail but Williams would only order the provision of a rail. Williams defended his views[28] in 1637 in another pamphlet, *The Holy Table Name and Thing*, but in doing so was dragged deeper into a dangerous conflict. We shall return to this in the next chapter.

One of those involved in Grantham was William Howe, who described himself as 'preacher and curate' at Grantham in 1623-4. Titley clearly did not trust him, setting out his duties in specific detail so that he could not use his own ideas about catechising for example. Through the patronage of the Earl of Lincoln he was moved to the safer place as curate at Tattershall in 1634.[29] He was the father of Obadiah Howe, who became the vicar of Boston in 1660.

In Lincolnshire especially, Laud's reforms faced entrenched opposition led by powerful puritan families – often now in their second or third generation. Almost all of them featured a few years later in the Parliamentary opposition to the King. Men like Sir William Armyne roundly hated Laudianism – 'those pretty bawbling fooleries…he ever thought a Cappe and a Congy a sorry thing to please Almighty God with'.[30]

Responses to Laud's reforms by laypeople were various – they could form their own conventicles, 'gad about' to more suitable churches or protest in other ways. In the period 1609-34, after the separatists had left for Holland, only John Bingham of Tiln was presented for holding a conventicle.[31] However, others certainly met; at Kneesall it would appear that the puritan Luke Bacon was replaced by William Clough and started preaching at Caunton instead, whilst parishioners held their own conventicles from 1628-33.[32]

New centres of puritan strength were also developing. The case of Boston is well known, but south-west Nottinghamshire was another with a belt of puritan influence flowing across to Ashby-de-la-Zouch. At Attenborough German Ireton was no ordinary man. His father William Ireton in 1592 took a lease at Norton Cuckney but he moved to Attenborough in about 1595 as the result of Isabel Wray's planning after her first husband's death. Ireton took the rectory revenues and was meant to maintain a preacher and schools from these. After the arrangement expired in 1605 German and his widowed mother maintained possession leading to a lengthy legal battle over the terms of the Foljambe inheritance there including

27 Kenneth Fincham, *The Restoration of Altars in the 1630s* in *The Historical Journal*, vol. 44, no. 4, 2001, pp. 919–940. *JSTOR*, www.jstor.org/stable/3133545.
28 Williams took the view that the table was a place of 'laud and thanksgiving' not an altar of sacrifice.
29 Hajzyk (1981) p.341, but a local listing of the church says 1627. Henry Hough had been curate in 1614.
30 Seth Wood, *The Saint's Entrance into Rest and Peace by Death*, London, 1651, p.18
31 Marchant (1960), p.178
32 Marchant (1960), p.187

the 'impropriation' of the rectory – for which German Ireton spent some time in prison;[33] he also failed to repair the chancels at Attenborough and Bramcote. German married Jane Warburton and his son Henry was probably born in 1611; a less famous younger brother John became mayor of London. Between 1608 and 1636 he was regularly in trouble for typically puritan behaviour – his wife refusing to be 'churched', wearing a hat in church in 1616, arranging for strangers to preach in 1620 (when he also locked the church door) and refusing to kneel at the altar in 1636.[34] Between 1610 and 1619 Attenborough provided a high proportion of the county's lay nonconformity cases.[35] The legal case was resolved by transferring the rectory and the advowson for the vicar to Sir William Bowes and some other nominees in 1611. Meanwhile, Henry Ireton spent a little time at Oxford without taking a degree, being remembered as 'a stubborn and sawcy fellow'.[36] Just across the Leicestershire border, John Ireton had been the puritan minister at Kegworth until 1606 and a key influence on the famous Hildersham of Ashby. Nearby at Owthorpe lived John Hutchinson who the Ireton boys knew in childhood; thus, the next generation, whose actions were to be momentous, were nurtured in Nottinghamshire puritanism.

Another cluster of radical puritans gathered around the figure of the 4th Earl of Lincoln, Theophilus Clinton (1599-1667), who succeeded to the title in 1619 in the footsteps of a father who left him many financial problems; his grandmother had been one of the Hastings family of Ashby-de-la-Zouch. In the 1620s he was a prominent supporter of puritans and visitors to his Sempringham house included John Cotton. Samuel Skelton held the spiritual reins at Sempringham as curate and as Clinton's chaplain; he was later chosen to be a pastor at Salem in America.[37] Anthony Tuckney also served as a chaplain; he was the son of William Tuckney, minister at Kirton-in-Holland, and a graduate of Emmanuel. He became a lifelong trans-Atlantic friend of Samuel Whiting and succeeded Cotton in Boston. Needing to rescue his estate, Clinton in 1619 hired Thomas Dudley as his steward – who was, of course, the father of Anne Bradstreet neé Dudley. The vicar of nearby Horbling was Simon Bradstreet the elder, father of Anne's husband Simon; Horbling was a strong puritan living and Bradstreet's successors included Thomas Granger. Clinton was a strong puritan influence in southern Lincolnshire whose father in law, Lord Saye and Sele, showed his opposition to the monarch and enthusiasm for American colonies. Clinton was also an influential figure in the strong anti-government puritanism in south Lincolnshire; he refused the forced loan and led resistance to it.

Cotton's Boston

This brings us to Boston, where John Cotton gathered a group 'to follow after the Lord

---

33 It would seem Ireton did not meet the terms of the Foljambe agreement and also failed to pay £18 due to the king. The same Foljambe trust had led to complications over funding George Tuke's lectureship in Chesterfield and the school.

34 David Farr, *The Ireton Family and Benefice of Attenborough*, in *Thoroton Society*, vol 110, 2006.

35 Jennings (1999), p.66

36 Athenae Oxonienses. An Exact History of All the Writers and Bishops, vol 1, p.81

37 Skelton was the son of the Rector of Coningsby (d 1602) and married Susanna Travis whilst curate at Sempringham. He became minister of the church at Salem. Another William Skelton held the living of Coningsby until 1679 and John Skelton those of Stixwould and Scrafield until 1685.

in the purity of his worship'.[38] Cotton was the most important of the second wave of separatists that came mainly from Lincolnshire; he was born in Derby in 1584 of godly parents and was another Cambridge product, starting his degree at Trinity but moving to Emmanuel to do his MA, where in 1603, he was noted as not following the Prayer Book. Whilst at Cambridge, Cotton became 'disconsolate' but eventually 'the Grace of God made him a thoroughly renewed Christian and filled him with a sacred joy'.[39] During this period he was influenced by Richard Sibbes and William Perkins.

Thomas Wooll, the previous vicar of Boston who had moved to Skirbeck, the man who had offered to use his surplice as a cushion, led the group that went to Cambridge and recruited Cotton despite some reluctance. The Corporation controlled the advowson and they clearly wanted a trusted man to help in their choosing. In the interim, the curate Benjamin Alexander held the position[40] – his previous record as curate at Torksey confirmed he was also a puritan. The mayor's chaplain, John James, was born in Boston was also a noted puritan, cited in 1609. Several of the town's people were cited along with the separatist leaders following the failed escape to Holland in 1607-8, and the charges made clear that the holding of conventicles was practiced in the town.

So, it is evident that Cotton came to a town that was already a leading radical centre. Some historians have argued that its radicalism stretched back to 1485 when the rectory was held by the absentee Priory of St John of Jerusalem allowing the vicar, his three curates, 18 chantry priests and 11 stipendiaries some 'independence'.[41] As we saw in chapter three, there was certainly radical influence in the town in the 1520s.

A gifted academic, Cotton chose parish work over the college life as indeed the statutes of Emmanuel encouraged. He even consulted his brethren as to who he should marry.[42] On his wedding day in Cambridgeshire in 1613, he received a 'second assurance' of God's love; 'God made that day a day of double marriage to me' as he experienced 'sacred joy'. Like other puritans, Cotton emphasised the importance of preaching without which 'the people are as ignorant as those that never heard of the name of Christ' and a minister who did not preach was not a 'lawfull minister'.[43] Cotton lived up to this by preaching for two or more hours at a time and putting on public lectures several times a week; by some accounts a Sunday service could last five hours. Since his Cambridge days he had believed preaching was important in changing a man's heart.

Cotton's career to this point is interesting because he is another example of a puritan minister of a major church who enjoyed some impunity. He had been selected by the puritan elements within the corporation of Boston in 1612 who controlled the living,[44] and showed himself consistently nonconformist, abandoning the surplice and much of the

38   John Cotton, *The Way of the Congregational Churches Cleared*, 1648, p.20

39   J Rosenmeier, *Spiritual Concupiscence – John Cotton's English Years*, Lincoln, 2012, p.47-49, quoting from Cotton Mather. I am indebted to this magisterial work for much of the detail on Cotton's time in England.

40   Rosenmeier refers to him as also a mayor's chaplain.

41   *Lincolnshire Historian*, vol. 8, 1973

42   Holmes (1980), p.43

43   Holmes (1980), p.53

44   Rosenmeier (2012) notes Mather's claim that Cotton got the job only because the Mayor voted for him twice in error.

Prayer Book and 'following after the Lord in the purity of worship'. Saints' days were not commemorated. When Bishop Neile visited in 1614 he thought all Cotton's sermons were 'poisoned with some error or other;' as Cotton criticised non-resident and non-preaching clergy, implying also criticism of bishops, this reaction was hardly surprising – and perhaps underlined by one man who fell asleep during a Cotton sermon, and dropped 'downe from the loft into one of the pewes, to the well example of others'.[45] Neile sat through an afternoon service of five hours, but Neile had other enemies too – he soon fell out with Lincolnshire's puritan MPs.

Cotton seems to have gathered his own 'inner group' of up to 100 strong puritans with the semblance of a covenanted congregation by 1614-5 – perhaps as Bernard appears to have done at Worksop, Robinson at Norwich and Viccars at Stamford – but he was a reluctant separatist and less 'factious' in his preaching than Smyth or Viccars. Writing in 1648, he referred to 'scores of godly persons in Boston' who had 'entered into a covenant with the Lord and with one another, to follow after the Lord in the purity of His worship'. He escaped problems in 1616 as Thomas Leverett was 'piously subtile' enough to convince legal officials that Cotton was 'conformable'.[46]

Stained glass windows and statues were removed from the 'Stump'. Atherton Hough, who later went to New England with Cotton, tried to knock the statue of St Botolph from the Stump as he thought it was the Pope. Bishop Montaigne became concerned and sent Robert Sanderson, who was at Wyberton in 1618-9, to investigate and to preach against factionalism from Cotton's own pulpit. Sanderson preached from Romans 14:3, a clear comment on the division between 'inner' and 'outer' congregations.

Cotton brought in curates and schoolmasters to develop them further, not always with success: Tristram Hinchcliffe went on to Timberland, appointed by Theophilus Clinton, where his version of an exclusive Calvinist approach confused the villagers and excluded most from communion; the High Commission took an interest in his nonconformity in 1634-5.

However, there seems also to have been an Arminians in Boston led by Dr Peter Baron, son of the famous theologian Peter Baro, which was established well before Cotton's arrival. Baron had been elected an alderman in 1609, despite some opposition, became Mayor in 1610 and has been said to have had the support of Burleigh.[47] One of the town's puritan MPs sponsored a Bill for his naturalisation. 'Though he was a physician by profession (and of good skill in that), yet he spent the greatest strength of his studies… in promoting the Arminian tenents.'[48] Even earlier, there had been a dispute at Sleaford in 1598-9 when William Williams, vicar of Asgarby and Aswarby, was accused by eleven of his colleagues of Arminian heresies; Bishop Chaderton banned him from preaching or acquiring any new books, but Williams fought a strong case and was still in the ministry in 1640.[49] By 1618 Cotton appears to have been moving away from strict Calvinism himself: 'Cotton stressed the demonstration of God's justice and grace in the decree of

---

45   Hajzyk (1981), p.157
46   Holmes (1980), p.95
47   Rosenmeier (2012), p.92
48   Rosenmeier (2012), p.96
49   Hajzyk (1981), p.225, who speculates the links between Arminian thought in Boston and Sleaford.

predestination and portrayed reprobation as non-election. He argued that God offered salvation to all and that those who are condemned are damned for refusing to do what they can do.'[50] Cotton began to accept a dual approach, perhaps under the Baron influence, with a covenant of grace for the elect and one of works for the others.[51]

In 1621 Boston again chose strong puritans as its two MPs – Sir William Armyne of Osgodby, whose father of the same name[52] was already MP for Grantham – which the younger Armyne then became in 1625, and Sir Anthony Irby. His grandson Sir Anthony (1605-88) whose first wife was Frances, daughter of Sir William Wray of Glentworth, succeeded him as MP in 1628. Another MP in 1628 was Richard Bellingham, also a puritan, who went to America with John Cotton in 1634. Richard Oakley, a close associate of Bishop Williams, was also elected in 1628 – this the town was represented by people who opposed the King both in politics and religion.

Despite all the flouting of legal requirements, Cotton enjoyed relative peace until 1621. It was only when some of his congregation broke crosses off the town's maces and defaced the royal coat of arms in 1621 that Cotton got into serious trouble. Atherton Hough, who later went with him to America in 1633, admitted breaking the hands off a carving of the Pope[53] whilst others had broken the crosses off some new maces. The Privy Council sent the Solicitor General to investigate but to an extent Cotton's was protected by the borough's independence. He also escaped a challenge of his refusal to kneel at prayer. Sanderson was sent back to the town and in April 1621 he preached once more against division and the defacing of the church, 'delivering his sermon in a controlled rage'.[54] In the summer of 1621 Cotton was 'silenced' and unable to preach until June 1622. Although Cotton was told he would have to receive the sacrament on his knees before the bishop, this was never enforced. Perhaps what saved him was that Bishop George Montaigne moved to London and the new bishop, Williams, was more tolerant: as Rosenmeier observes, 'we may wonder if it had not been for Williams whether Cotton would have lasted in Boston'. Williams had the ear of King James but, disliked by Prince Charles, he was not on sure foundations and had his own problems from 1624 – accused of being soft on nonconformity.

Cotton also took in what were effectively postgraduate students for further training. One of these was Ralph Levett, a Christ's College graduate. He was with Cotton in 1624 then became the private chaplain to Sir Christopher Wray at Ashby-cum-Fenby. Some of his letters to Cotton about this experience reflect the challenges of the puritan life – he consulted his mentor on how to deal with dancing and card-playing at Christmas, and also how to respond when invited to draw a name out of a hat by young ladies at Valentine's! Despite these perils, Wray provided a safe place whilst Laud was increasing the pressure on nonconformity. He married Anne Hutchinson, the sister of John Wheelwright's second wife at Bilsby, Wheelwright's church, in 1632.[55] By 1633 he had become rector of the

---

50   F J Bremer, *John Cotton*, in ODNB online, 25/8/16
51   M W Winship, *Making Heretics – Militant Protestantism and Free Grace in Massachusetts*, Princeton, 2009, p.32
52   Died in 1622.
53   *The New England Historical and Genealogical Register*: Volume 28 1874, Volume 28, p.133
54   Rosenmeier (2012), p.134
55   His wife's brother William was married to Anne, who became the famous Anne Hutchinson.

Wray manor at Grainsby, through the influence of Lady Frances Wray II,[56] and soon also Little Carlton – both parishes with few people. His son took over at Little Carlton.

In 1625 Cotton was again in discussion with his bishop, Williams, because he had upset some by refusing to kneel. Cotton assured his bishop that he was reflecting on the arguments and gained more time to continue doing so. Like many others, Cotton became expert at stringing out his nonconformity by May 1633, when he already knew he was going to New England, he was still able to write to Williams to say that he had studied and rejected the arguments of others: 'in things pertaining to God and his worship, still I must, as I ought, live by mine own faith not theirs'.

Cotton was not alone in his efforts. In 1629 his cousin Anthony Tuckney, from Kirton-in-Holland where his father had been vicar, was appointed town preacher. Tuckney had been-chaplain to Clinton and was close to future emigrants like Isaac Johnson and Samuel Skelton. When Tuckney's wife died, Cotton attributed this to the division amongst the people. Tuckney's career was eventually to take him to London and the mastership of Emmanuel College in Cambridge, holding the Boston living until 1660.

Yet it was not only the puritans who believed in preaching. Robert Sanderson, now at Boothby Pagnell, 'emphasised the centrality of the effective preaching of the word'[57] and also lived at a time when the clergy became much more educated. Sanderson had passed through Oxford and then been presented to the living of Wyberton, Lincs., by his cousin – choosing to move almost immediately to Boothby Pagnell. In 1631 he became a chaplain to Charles I on Laud's recommendation and in 1633 was also presented to the living of Muston, near to Belvoir, by the Earl of Rutland. The King visited twice in 1634 and 1636 and was impressed by Sanderson; 'I carry my ear to hear other preachers, but I carry my conscience to hear Dr Sanderson'. Sanderson may have been unfashionable to puritan opinion in Lincolnshire, but he would yet have his day in the sun.

Another challenge for the Church authorities was the rise of millenarianism. Tempest Wood, who was vicar of 'Lavington' or Lenton (Lincs) 1601-39, and the father of Seth Wood who wrote Armyne's memorial; he was one of the first 'millenarian' scholars and wrote an unpublished meditation on Revelations. The teaching was that earthly government was corrupt and would be swept away for a 'new millennium' – not a view that would endear itself with Charles. It is believed he was the Lincolnshire cleric who was reported in 1629 for saying that Christ and the saints would return to reign on earth and to eat and drink.[58] This view won over the more famous Thomas Goodwin, but was a radical suggestion that earthly kings might indeed be replaced. One of the earliest millenarian texts, Robert Parker's *The Mystery of the Vialls Opened*, was not published until 1651 though Parker had died in 1614; its survival was due to Sir John Wray who had held a copy – and by the 1650s works denouncing 'earthly monarchy' had become more acceptable! The movement evolved into the Fifth Monarchists in the 1640s.

---

56   *Correspondence of John Cotton*
57   Holmes (1980), p.53
58   Bernard Capp, *The Fifth Monarchy Men*, London, 2012, p.149

Hell, Whores and Heresy in Stamford

Bishop Williams tended to defend his puritan clergy but, as with Smyth in an earlier generation, was reluctant to help those that were 'fractious' and provoked trouble. John Viccars (1604-60) is one example. Born in the puritan heartlands of north Nottinghamshire, at Treswell, he went via Cambridge to be vicar of St Mary's Stamford in 1627.[59] However, he was much too progressive for some of his parishioners, who promptly denounced him for heresy. Viccars had divided his parishioners into the godly and the ungodly, holding prayer meetings and days of fasting that attracted others from outlying areas – refusing communion to those he considered 'hell hounds'. He complained of 'whorish Dalilas' and 'painted Jezebels' in the town. At first Williams made him apologise and read a sermon whilst wearing a surplice, but this did not prevent further trouble.[60] Viccars had an 'inner' congregation of much the same sort as Bernard at Worksop and Cotton at Boston and those not on the inside resented it.

Bishop Williams had cautioned Viccars about this, but the parishioners complained again to the Crown. Viccars had some strange opinions, especially on marital relations; he thought that 'if a man Knowe his wife after her conception with Childe, or when shee is past Childe bearing, it is both murther [murder] and adulterie'. It was also adultery for a man to sleep with his wife three days before or after taking the sacrament. He condemned other priests who did not preach twice on a Sunday to 'the fire in hell' and also those who didn't attend twice. Closer to the puritan view, he thought that the 'common prayers' were not enough for salvation and launched personal attacks on individuals in his sermons. He also had his devotees and the women among them refused to work for 'ungodly' masters and were castigated as 'the newe nunnery of Stamford'.[61]

It seems to have been the last point that caused most trouble, for his attacks included noted aldermen and innkeepers of the town. 'Factious' preaching always caused trouble. He made an enemy of William Camock, the Laudian rector of St Michael's and was seen to be putting the peace at risk. However, not everyone was against him as he organised a fast before he went to London and preached some long sermons, including at least one of six hours or more.[62]

Wanting to put pressure on Williams, Laud selected Viccars as an easy target for the revived High Commission. Several local people appeared as witnesses in his defence at the High Commission in 1631 and supported arguments that his accusers were drunkards and reprobates. The senior clerics who listened to the evidence had some doubts and the Bishop of St David's accused Viccars of having turned 'the pulpit into a place to vent his malice upon the poor people of Stamford'. One historian called him 'an arrogant

---

59   Viccars was related by his sister Helen's marriage to William Sampson, a writer born nearby in South Leverton who wrote a play with Gervase Markham. Sampson's widow then married Obadiah Grew, an Anglican on the puritan wing who debated with Hanserd Knollys. William Sampson and Helen had two sons; William became rector of Clayworth whilst Henry became a nonconformist minister in Suffolk and later a physician. He was buried at Clayworth.

60   Holmes (1980), p.118

61   *Cases in Star Chamber and High Commission*, p.205; Holmes (1980), p.43

62   T Harris, *Britain's First Stuart Kings*, p.330-2. 'Vicars' is also mentioned in correspondence between Edward Reyner and John Cotton, along with Langley of Treswell, but the actual issues have been lost.

prig'.[63] Bishop Williams did not defend Viccars, the 'personal' style of his attacks was unacceptable – an offence he shared with John Smyth. He was defrocked, fined £100 and imprisoned but recanted after a few years and was restored to the ministry in 1635 although forbidden to preach in Stamford. Then he set out on a massive project to examine manuscript versions of the Psalms in as many eastern languages as he could find, including spending many weeks in libraries across Italy – including the Vatican. On his return, he and his brother Samuel funded the printing of *Decapta in Psalmos* which looked at ten languages and for which he had to pay to have Arabic and Syriac typeface created. This he dedicated to Laud in a 'grovelling' introduction, but it probably helped him to win the living of South Fambridge in Essex in 1640. His comfort did not last long – in 1644 his trip to Rome came back to haunt him and his living was sequestrated on the basis that he was a Roman priest. An irony!

In some ways the case of Viccars set the pattern for what was to follow in Boston. Prominent Lincoln clergy *could* be removed. Information was received in 1632 saying that some of the people of Boston refused to kneel while receiving communion. Despite the efforts of courtiers like the Earl of Dorset, who had been much moved by Cotton's preaching, this enabled Laud to press ahead and it was this that persuaded Cotton to at least leave for America. By November 1632 he was more or less in hiding and wrote his resignation from Boston in May 1633.

Looking Outwards:

This was also an era when Christians began to look at expanding the work of the Gospel overseas. Captain John Smith was aware of the need to bring the Gospel to American natives as discussed elsewhere, whilst British interests were also expanding in the east. One of the first chaplains to the East India Company was Henry Lord, vicar of Great Steeping until about 1614.[64] He was appointed as chaplain of the company in 1624 due to the influence of Francis White, who was Dean of Carlisle and later Bishop of Ely; Lord had reportedly been a curate to White, presumably at Broughton Astley, Leicestershire.[65] The interview process included preaching a sermon in London. His salary was fixed at a comfortable £60 a year, plus £20 for books. Lord seems to have been based in Surat (Gujarat), where the company had set up its first 'factory' in 1613. He did not enjoy his initial experience and wanted to go home by 1625, but was forbidden to do so by Thomas Kerridge, the President. Instead, Kerridge encouraged Lord to investigate local religions and in 1630 published a book about the religion of the 'Banians' or Hindus and Parsees or Zoroastrians, *A display of two forraigne sects in the East Indies.*

---

63 Holmes (1980), p.62
64 Hajzyk (1981) says 1624, CCED says 1614 when he was replaced by Nicholas Herring – a surname with radical connections across the Trent where John Herring was an associate of Smyth and Helwys at Basford and Marnham. The connection of these with the more famous Julines Herring, one of the Hildersham circle, is unlikely. A Francis Herring (c.1568-1628) of Notts went to Christ's College, became a physician and an author of anti-Catholic poetry.
65 A child names Henry Lord was christened at Gt Steeping in 1598, implying Lord senior was already there by this date.

He made a detailed study of these religions, for example of their creation stories and moralities, by learning the languages and holding talks with priests. His scholarly book was translated into several other languages; it is still highly regarded, though as a good puritan Lord was quick to comment on the 'forgeries' and 'vaine superstitions' he discovered.

The historian of the East India Company's religious work concludes that Lord's 'work….marks an exceptional moment, not only of venturing beyond his familiar Christian world, the world that the chaplains sought to replicate in the factories, but of communicating hid discoveries with integrity and skill'.[66] Nothing is known of Lord after he seems to have finished in Surat in 1629, although a man of the same name became vicar of Abingdon in 1632.

---

66   D O'Connor, *Chaplains of the East India Company*, London, 2011 p.69

CHAPTER FOURTEEN

The Great Migration: The Massachusetts Bay Company and the 'Second Wave'

1629-1635

The establishment of the Plymouth colony and the writings of Captain John Smith prompted growing interest in the coast of 'New England'. With the increased risk of prosecution for nonconformity that Laud's rise brought and despair at England's spiritual direction under Charles I, there was renewed impetus for moving to America. This interest was especially strong in areas of south and east Lincolnshire which had been influenced by Katherine Willoughby's planting of preaching ministers and the radical tradition of Boston; people from east Lincolnshire in particular played key roles in the spiritual struggles of Massachusetts.

Chronology:
1629: Massachusetts Bay Charter; meeting at Sempringham
1630: Winthrop fleet sails
1633: John Cotton sails to America
1634: Death of Samuel Skelton
1635: Sir Henry Vane arrives in Massachusetts
1636: Roger Williams banned from Massachusetts
1637: Vane returns to England
1638: Anne Hutchinson ejected from Massachusetts
1640: Vane marries Frances Wray (V)
1650: Anne Bradstreet's poems published
1652: John Cotton dies
1659: Persecution of Quakers
1660: Edward Whalley flees to New England

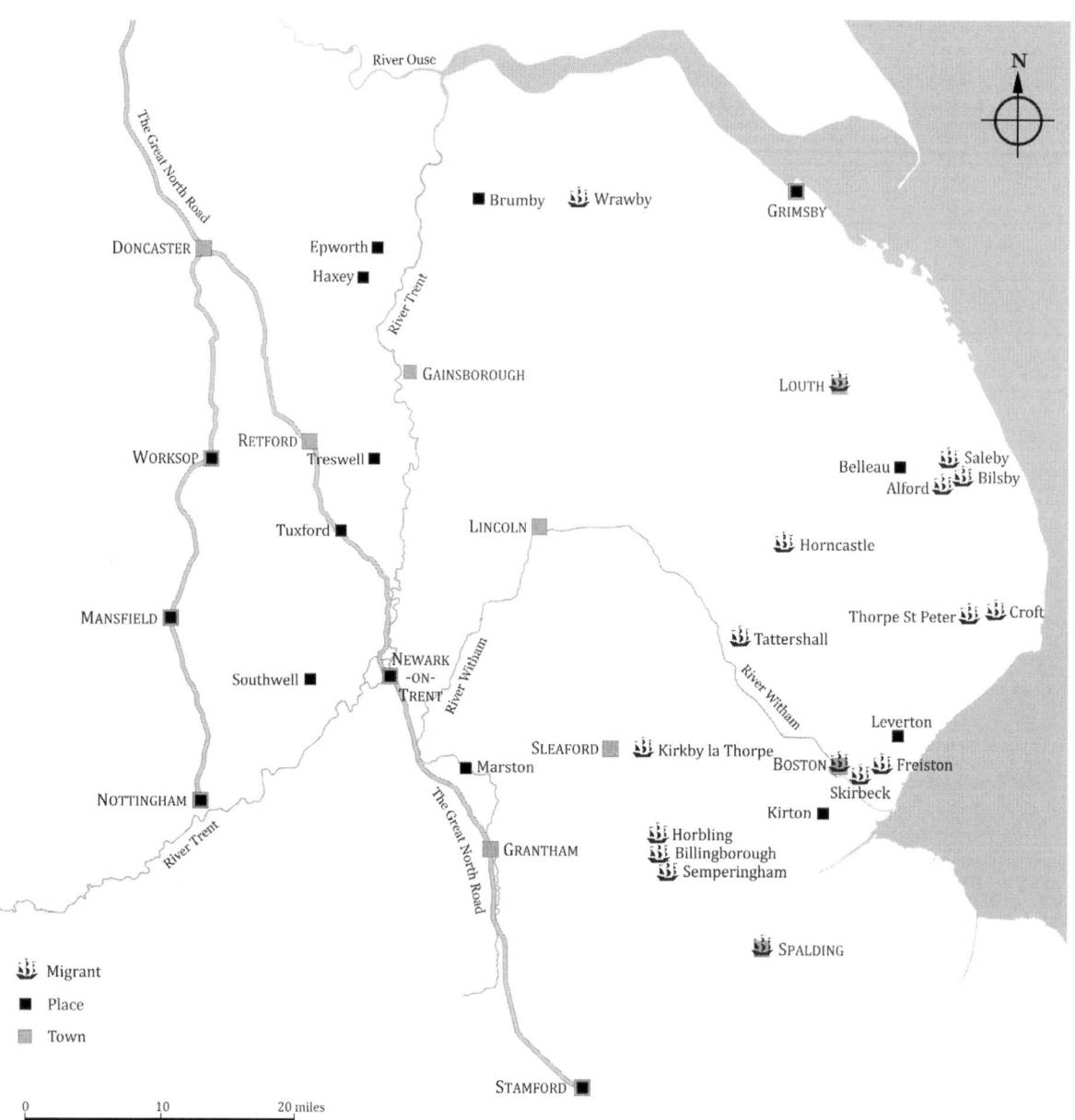

River Ouse

The Great North Road

N

Brumby Wrawby
GRIMSBY

DONCASTER

Epworth
Haxey

River Trent

Gainsborough

LOUTH

RETFORD
WORKSOP Treswell

Belleau Saleby
Alford Bilsby

Tuxford

LINCOLN

Horncastle

MANSFIELD

Thorpe St Peter Croft

River Witham

NEWARK
-ON-
TRENT

Southwell

River Witham

Tattershall

Leverton

SLEAFORD Kirkby la Thorpe
Marston

BOSTON Freiston
Skirbeck
Kirton

NOTTINGHAM

River Trent

The Great North Road

GRANTHAM

Horbling
Billingborough
Semperingham

SPALDING

Migrant
Place
Town

0   10   20 miles

STAMFORD

Planning for a New Life

In Thomas Dudley's view discussions over the Massachusetts Bay Company began in Lincolnshire in 1627. Theophilus Clinton, 4th Earl of Lincoln, with homes at Tattershall and Sempringham, sold his East India Company shares to finance this work, but also his high social position was a key in linking men like Lord Saye and Sele and the Earl of Dorset to the project. In 1628 the colonists obtained a land patent from the Council for New England with 'generous boundaries' possibly secured through the actions of the Earl of Warwick, Frances Wray's stepson.[1] This conflicted with some grants already made to the Gorges family in Maine, a conflict made worse by the charter of 1629; although also in correspondence with puritan leaders like Richard Bernard, the Gorges family lobbied Archbishop Laud against the Massachusetts puritans. In 1635 Sir Ferdinando Gorges, who had interests in Maine and Charles I's support, might have become governor-general in 1635 but for a shipwreck.

Mary Bernard and Roger Williams

Mary Bernard was born Worksop, 24 Sept 1609, probably in the old priory gatehouse that acted for a time as the vicarage and later as the school. By 1629 she was living with an Essex puritan family, the Mashams, to whom she had probably been introduced by the Whalleys of Screveton, their relatives, and who had first brought her father to the living of Worksop.

Williams was the chaplain to the family of Sir William Masham at Otes and nearby lived Lady Joan Barrington, whose nephew was Edward Whalley. Williams's first marriage proposal was to Jane Whalley his sister, who was living at the Barrington house at Hatfield Broad Oak; this caused a rift with Lady Joan who rejected Williams as an unsuitable match for social reasons. Also nearby at Leez Priory lived Frances Wray, the dowager Countess of Warwick, whose stepson – the second Earl – Whalley was a keen supporter of; Whalley was also a friend of Richard Baxter the famous puritan and in the same area for a time was Simon Bradstreet who worked for the dowager countess. Wray had financed Mary's father's education at Cambridge, and in return he praised her in the dedication of one of his later books.

Williams recovered from the setback to marry Mary Bernard at High Laver in December 1629. Despite the apparent hasty choice of a substitute, Mary and Roger stuck together through a life that involved very considerable challenges. Perhaps it was through her and her father's associations with Smyth, Helwys and Murton that Williams became focused on religious liberty – making extensive use of Murton's writings. The young couple left for America in 1630 via Bristol.

Jane Whalley soon married Rev William Hooke and they both went to New England in 1639, from where they returned in about 1656 when her husband became a chaplain to Cromwell – to whom she was connected as a cousin. Edward Whalley fled to New England in 1660 as a regicide.

---

1   M Winship, *The Times and Trials of Ann Hutchinson*, Kansas, 2005, p.27

As radical puritans, the merchant class of Boston had a reason for seeking a new life in America but as men with experience of trade and risk they also knew how to make such things possible.[2] The Forced Loan crisis of 1626 provided impetus. In March 1629 the first involvement of a Boston man in the Massachusetts Bay Company occurred and from that point interest accelerated, including substantial men from the region like Isaac Johnson, Thomas Leverett and Thomas Dudley. Men like Thomas Leverett and Richard Bellingham had experience of trade or business. The Massachusetts Bay Company Charter was issued on 4 March 1629.

Decisions had clearly been made already for Samuel Skelton, who had been the curate at Sempringham, was one of the first to go in early May 1629 – his family settled in Salem. He came from a family with a long association in Lincolnshire ministry – family members held the living of Coningsby for many years. After seven days, he was – significantly – chosen to be pastor of the church at Salem. Once there, though, letters between him and Cotton show the two had some disagreements with Cotton feeling he was going too far with 'separation', partly because Skelton almost immediately ceased using the *Prayer Book* in 1630. Skelton's church thus became an independent 'congregational' church.

In July 1629 a significant meeting was held at Sempringham, the home of the Earl of Lincoln. Early that month Isaac Johnson wrote out some invitations, one of which went to John Winthrop, an influential puritan from the Stour Valley in East Anglia who had family business connections to the Earls of Warwick. On 28 July Winthrop rode into Lincolnshire via Ely and fell into the bog on the way.[3] Several with connections to the Massachusetts Bay Company met there and were joined by prominent ministers John Cotton of Boston, Thomas Hooker of Chelmsford (who went into hiding to avoid prosecution in 1630), Emmanuel Downing (Winthrop's son in law), and Roger Williams, an indirect associate of the Nottinghamshire puritans through marriage to Richard Bernard's daughter Mary. Riding all the way from Chelmsford together, Williams disagreed with Thomas Hooker for using the *Book of Common Prayer* and also with Cotton when he joined them – Cotton indicating on this or another occasion that he picked the parts he liked.[4] Nonetheless, those at Sempringham decided to support an attempt to plant a community of the godly in the New World with the support of the Company. The Company, though, was firmly anti-separatist in its expectations and at this stage, all were within the Church of England still. John Winthrop attended this meeting, and perhaps others at Tattershall; he was chosen to be governor of the colony.

Another figure of this time was Isaac Johnson who was christened at Stamford and educated at Emmanuel College, before a move to the Clinton stronghold of Sempringham in 1623 ended with him literally in the arms of Lady Arbella Clinton, the sister of Theophilus Clinton, who he married against his father's wishes.[5] His authority, instead,

---

2   This thesis was outlined by Barry Cotton at the Boston History Symposium, Sept 2019.

3   *New England Historical and Genealogical Register*, 1899, p.68; Winthrop, *Experiencia*,

4   The discussion was recorded by Williams in *The Bloudy Tenent* (1652) and its sequel, *The Bloudy Tenent yet more Bloudy*. Winthrop probably knew Williams in Essex as he had acted on a law case for the Masham family, with whom Williams had been involved, and who had their own links to Notts/Lincs puritans.

5   Another sibling was Lady Frances Clinton, who married John Gorges. He was the son of Sir Ferdinando Gorges and brother of Sir Robert, who was briefly Governor of New England in 1623-4.

came from Archdeacon Johnson, who had shown his rebellious inclinations in the town fast at Stamford. Having inherited £20,000, Johnson linked up with the Massachusetts Bay Company and financed the *Arbella* expedition which landed there in 1630. Although he briefly led the settlement of Boston, both he and his wife died within a few months of their arrival.

Designated the future governor of Massachusetts, John Winthrop was the leader when the *Arbella* fleet (known thus as the 'Winthrop fleet') of four ships with almost seven hundred passengers set out in April 1630. John Cotton was invited to travel to Southampton (though Rosenmeier suggests it was Gravesend) to see them off and preached a famous sermon on 2 Samuel 7: 10 to a crowd of a thousand or more: 'Moreover I will appoint a place for my people Israel, and I will plant them, that they may dwell in a place of their own, and move no more'.[6] Winthrop, either then or soon thereafter, preached his own famous text of the 'city on a hill'.

But they were sailing into ongoing controversy for by this stage the character of Skelton's Salem church had changed – from 1 January 1630 it rejected the *Book of Common Prayer* and became an independent Congregational church.

On board were Anne and Simon Bradstreet, who were closely connected to the dowager countess of Warwick. Anne Dudley, as she had been born, moved to Horbling in Lincolnshire as a child in 1619 as her father Thomas[7] had become steward to Theophilus Clinton, Earl of Lincoln, on the recommendation of the puritan William Fiennes – who became his father in law the following year. The young Anne had free access to Clinton's library and also got to know Simon Bradstreet, son of the vicar of Horbling, who had gone up to Emmanuel College in 1617. In 1623 the Dudley family moved to Boston to be more involved in Cotton's congregation whilst the younger Bradstreet eventually became steward to Frances Wray (having helped with the Earl of Lincoln's estate), the dowager countess of Warwick, at Leez Priory in Essex, in autumn 1627; Simon and Anne married in 1628. The young couple sailed on the *Arbella* to Massachusetts in March 1630 along with the Dudley family. Thomas Dudley was deputy to Winthrop as governor. In America, Anne became celebrated as the first Anglo-American poet. Also arriving in 1630 from Lincolnshire was William Coddington,[8] who was influenced by Cotton (and had been a member of the congregation in Boston, Lincs) and Anne Hutchinson with her family from Alford; Coddington later left Massachusetts in support of Hutchinson and, knowing Roger Williams, moved to Newport, Rhode Island, although he did not always agree with Williams.

---

6   2 Samuel 7:10

7   Of Northamptonshire, and likely known to Rev John Dod a leading puritan. He had also been the steward at Tattershall according to P F M Zahl, p.90

8   His origin as Marston near Grantham has been suggested but is unproven.

The Bradstreets in America

Anne Bradstreet (1612-72) has become famous as the first poet of English-speaking America. With a father and a husband who were both prominent in the new colony, she had an influential position but at first struggled with the discipline of the new life. She also had to wait a while for her first child – it was after five years of marriage that Samuel arrived, the first of eight. Her children, depicted as birds in the nest, are beautifully celebrated in a window at Boston Stump, Lincolnshire.

Her first book of poems was published in London in 1650 although by this stage she had been writing for years; the first publication was probably arranged by her brother-in-law without her knowledge. Although celebrated as the first poet in America, Bradstreet was also the first English woman to publish a book of poems. Many of them reflected her love for her husband and children and also events like the English Civil War or the burning of their family home.

Simon survived his first wife for many years, having a lengthy career in New England politics that lasted into the era of Charles II and beyond – stepping down as governor in 1692. However, he is also an example of how a strand of puritanism became rigid and unyielding as even in the 1680s he was an opponent of freedoms for Baptists and Quakers. Indeed, when he came to England in 1662, he was challenged by George Fox, the Quaker leader, and accused of being complicit in the murder of Mary Dyer and other Quakers in 1659-60.

On 7 September 1630 it was decided to call the new settlement Boston; this was fitting, for in the two decades from 1620 migration from Lincolnshire was overwhelmingly from the Boston area and Fenland, with a minority from around Alford.[9] Other ships followed. Arrivals early in 1631 included the zealous cleric Roger Williams and his wife, Mary, the daughter of Richard Bernard of Worksop. They had left Bristol on the *Lyon* on 1 December 1630. Williams wanted total separation from the Church of England on the one hand, and the separation of civil and religious law on the other. Williams was to be the most famous in an evolving line of thinking that took in Smyth, Helwys and Murton. He settled at Salem where he assisted Samuel Skelton, who he presumably knew from the Sempringham meeting, and who had taken the route of separation from the Church of England that Williams favoured. From 1633 Williams began to be a serious problem for Massachusetts. He denied the power of the king to grant land to anyone, saying it should be bought from the Indians, and developed many other arguments that made him a threat to stability – yet was very popular in his base at Salem. We shall return to this issue shortly.

Arrivals in 1632 included Thomas James, son of the former Rector of Skirbeck, and his son also called Thomas who was probably born at Moulton. They settled first at Charlestown but became embroiled in the religious controversies of the era, relocating to Rhode Island by 1637 and then Connecticut.[10]

---

9 Barry Cotton indicates 65% from the Boston area (including places such as Billingborough and Spalding in this) and 25% from around Alford.

10 James returned to England in 1647-8 and gained the living of Needham Market, from which he was

In 1630 Cotton was not yet ready for America. He stayed behind although he was badly ill with ague in 1631 and convalesced at Sempringham and Tattershall. In April 1631 his first wife died. He consulted with the veteran John Dod, who had been at the Coventry meeting with Smyth years before.[11] Attempts by a broad puritan group at Ockley in Surrey in 1632 to persuade him to modify his preaching in order to stay within the Church had failed. Amidst gathering tensions in New England John Cotton finally left Boston, Lincolnshire, in 1633. Cotton and his friend Thomas Hooker decided on America and he resigned his living at Boston in May 1633. He sailed on the *Griffin* with Hooker and Samuel Stone, both ex-Emmanuel puritans from Essex. Hooker was an old friend of Cotton's from Emmanuel College and, living in Essex, had come under the protection of the Earl of Warwick. Another who left from Boston in 1633 was Thomas Leverett with his son John (1616-1678/9); John settled in what was to become Maine and over a long career in trade and politics favoured, in general, greater religious tolerance than others such as Winthrop, Increase Mather and Simon Bradstreet did. However, despite being tolerant of Baptists while Governor in the 1670s, he was still less kind to Quakers.

Cotton was succeeded as vicar by Anthony Tuckney, a popular puritan who won much support during the town's plague in 1637 and who also set up a library in the room above the church porch in 1635. Tuckney went on to play a key role in the Westminster Assembly and as master of two Cambridge colleges. He was friendly with Isaac Johnson, who had married the Earl of Lincoln's sister Arbella before going to Massachusetts, and Samuel Whiting of Skirbeck who later became minister at the New England town of Lynn. This perhaps accounts for Tuckney's reported great interest in the evangelising of the Indian population. Tuckney's daughter married the Presbyterian Whitlock of Nottingham in 1652.

Cotton's theology was quite progressive for the period. Unusually in puritan circles, he taught that Christians could receive revelation in addition to the Bible. He was especially involved with the issue of how a man or woman might know that they were saved in an age when the Calvinist view of predestination prevailed. If the only evidence of salvation ('election') was through lifestyle, then it might appear that 'works' was the evidence of salvation. Cotton had to work through this issue at the time of a significant crisis in New England and developed a more interactive awareness of the role of the Holy Spirit: 'the only satisfactory assurance of election lay in a noetic awareness of union with the Holy Ghost'. He was concerned for 'the witness of the Holy Spirit itself'. In *The Way of Life* (1641) he wrote that 'We receive the Spirit of the Sonne into our heart, whereby we are not only adopted but regenerated and made the sons of God, and thereby come to cry Abba, Father'.

Having considered and rejected a move to Holland,[12] Cotton left in July 1633. He became teacher at the church in Boston in America late in 1633, its pastor being John Wilson – who possibly knew Cotton from Emmanuel College. There he became embroiled in Roger Williams's dispute about the power of magistrates and took the view

---

ejected at the Restoration. He then led a congregation at West Creeting and died in about 1683. The clergyman at Needham who had replaced him would not permit his burial in any consecrated part of the churchyard.

11   Rosenmeier (2012), p.256
12   Coggins (1991), p.45

that magistrates could defend true godly worship.[13] Williams 'badly undercut his support in Salem when he tried to make the church choose between him and every other church in Massachusetts'.[14] The minister at Salem, Samuel Skelton, died in 1634. His library of books formed the nucleus of the Harvard library. Williams sought his position, using it to launch a series of attacks on established local policies. Cotton was heavily involved in the Massachusetts decision to banish Williams in 1636.

A Crisis in America

The crisis of theology and authority that swept Massachusetts in the mid-1630s was largely caused and managed by people from Lincolnshire who all knew each other well, with the additional involvement of Roger Williams with his Nottinghamshire wife. Apart from the question of survival, it was the first major challenge that had to be managed and had considerable impact on the colony's spiritual development.

In October 1634 some of Cotton's Lincolnshire adherents arrived, including Anne Hutchinson, neé Marbury, related to the controversial Lincolnshire cleric John Wheelwright by marriage, who had created some controversy on the voyage; nonetheless, she and her husband William joined Cotton's church. As the daughter of Francis Marbury, the radical Alford cleric who had spent time in prison for nonconformity, she had impeccable puritan credentials but also an unusual level of education for a woman.

The Hutchinsons were wealthy and of some status in east Lincolnshire, and Anne established herself in Massachusetts supporting women in childbirth. This was not enough for an educated, confident woman. She quickly moved to providing spiritual guidance, warning the women that they might still be under a 'covenant of works'. Initial impressions of her work were very positive for she was a woman of 'considerable intellectual powers and persuasive gifts'.[15] However, she quickly moved beyond Cotton's acceptance of revelation to the belief that a believer was 'taken over' by Christ and continually guided by the Holy Spirit – a belief that was tainted by its link with the murderous Anabaptists of Münster and the Familists who believed Christians became free from sin or any responsibility for it. Hutchinson believed in 'an immediate personal union with the Holy Ghost, so clear as to render the additional evidence of sanctification quite superfluous'.[16] This view was divisive as firstly, it appeared to say that someone need not fear involvement in sin, and secondly, 'only those who experienced this inward witness of the spirit enjoyed the sureties of the Covenant of Grace'.[17] In contrast, she thought the New Englanders were 'trusting to their works as evidence of salvation'.[18] And of course, that was their problem – you needed the outward evidence of works to show that you were certainly one of the chosen.

---

13 Winship (2005), p.29
14 Winship (2005), p.31
15 Winship (2005), p.36
16 Emery Battis, *Saints and Sinners: Anne Hutchinson and the Antinomian Controversy*, Williamsburg, 1962, p.39
17 Battis (1962), p.39
18 Battis (1962), p.85

Another arrival in 1634 was Christopher Marshall who, like Anne Hutchinson's husband, came from a family of mercers in Alford, Lincolnshire. He briefly attended Magdalene College in Cambridge and was one of Cotton's pupils as well as being married to a niece of Anne Hutchinson and John Wheelwright.

We have previously mentioned Richard Bellingham, who had been Recorder and MP for Boston. He had been born near Brumby, then became Recorder of Boston from 1625 to 1633. He immediately assumed a political status in his new homeland, consequent also upon having been a patentee of the Massachusetts Bay charter. During a long career in Massachusetts politics, he was often at odds with Winthrop. Another who came to Boston from Lincolnshire in 1634 was Ann Hibbins, née Bellingham, the sister of Governor Richard Bellingham. Perhaps she followed a different route, for she was excommunicated in 1641 and in 1656 sentenced to death for 'witchcraft'; more likely, she was a strong-minded woman who had enemies happy to denounce her.

Of more long-term significance, in October 1635 Sir Henry Vane, aged around 22, arrived. In his youth he had been 'startle[d]….into a view of the danger of his condition. On this, he and his former jolly Company came presently to a parting blow'.[19] His father was a privy councillor making him the nearest thing to aristocracy in New England, he had training and experience in diplomacy, but he had already experienced an intense conversion experience that motivated him for the rest of his life. He found himself at odds with the Laudian direction and sought a better life. Although his father served under Charles I, Vane went his own way in spiritual matters after having had 'an intense spiritual crisis' and experienced repentance as a young man. He literally refused to bow the knee to Laudian reforms by not kneeling to take the sacrament. Yet his status and fashionable long hair made him an object of suspicion on the voyage across. He immediately started using his skills to resolve disputes, including between Winthrop and Dudley.

Vane liked Cotton enough to build an extension to the minister's house and by May 1636 was governor, with Winthrop as deputy. He was such a success that he became Governor at the tender age of 23. Restless and searching in his theology, he was soon interested in the views of Anne Hutchinson. By early 1636 Boston was teetering into controversy as Thomas Shepard, one of the colony's ministers, challenged Cotton over a sermon which preached 'assurance by the immediate witness of the Spirit' which he felt encouraged people to abandon the Bible and seek their own revelations.

Meanwhile, Roger Williams was effectively put on trial in October 1635 with Thomas Hooker as his 'prosecutor'; the result was that he was forced out of the colony altogether in January 1636 for his 'diverse new and dangerous opinions'. Fleeing for his life, leaving behind Mary and his children for a time, he travelled through the bitter snows to seek refuge with native tribes who he had befriended and whose languages he had been learning. Once his family had joined him in the Spring, Williams built a new home at Narragansett Bay and named the new community Providence. Williams briefly became a Baptist in 1639 and is sometimes credited with starting the first Baptist church in America though this is also attributed to John Clarke. He maintained good relations with the native Americans and in 1643 published *A Key into the Language of America, the first guide to*

---

19   Cliffe (1984), p.16, from a contemporary source.

some of their languages. Most of all, though, Williams is famous for establishing a state with freedom of religion.

Arrivals into this turbulent atmosphere in New England in May 1636 included John Wheelwright and Samuel Whiting. The latter was the son of a mayor of Boston, a former curate to Cotton[20] and related to both John Cotton and Anthony Tuckney as well as another settler of 1633, Atherton Hough. Whiting was born near Boston in 1597 and after Cambridge – where he shared rooms with Tuckney – was a private chaplain and then held a living at King's Lynn, or Lynn Regis. He left this after complaints of nonconformity, despite some help from the Earl of Lincoln, but was able to take the rectory of Skirbeck, where there were again complaints. Whiting determined in 1635 to go to Massachusetts and leave nothing behind: 'I am going into the wilderness to sacrifice unto the Lord, and I will not leave a hoof behind me'.[21] Whiting travelled with Wheelwright and stayed for a time with Hough after his arrival in 1636, before enjoying a long career as minister at a new settlement that took the name of Lynn in some dubious way of honouring him. One of Whiting's sons, John, returned to England and was a minister at Leverton near Boston. However, many who sailed in the same year in the *Prosperous* were captured by French pirates.

These Lincolnshire settlers (including Vane, who was yet to become a Lincolnshire man) were involved in one of the biggest theological disputes to shake New England. In 1636 one of the ministers, Thomas Shepard, accused John Cotton of theological error. Cotton held the view that God saved sinners through grace, whereas most of the other ministers emphasised holy living was essential to demonstrate salvation which their critics saw as sanctification by works. John Wheelwright took the same side as Cotton and was dragged into dispute with Shepard. Meanwhile, Anne Hutchinson said that all of the Massachusetts ministers except Cotton and her brother-in-law Wheelwright taught a 'covenant of works', for 'they told their listeners to look to their own holiness rather than to Christ for assurance of salvation'.[22] This hardly helped either of them, opening them to attacks from the hard-line Thomas Shepard, but their theology of assurance of salvation coming first through the Holy Spirit *was* different.

How did these men come to hold a position tantamount to sanctification by works? As we have seen, the Protestants had rejected centuries of teaching that a person could earn their way to Heaven through good works or even by having prayers said for their soul. However, how you could know that you were saved then became a matter of great importance for them, especially in an era when Calvinism was so influential. They had no *direct* assurance but had to reflect indirectly on their own consciences. Effectively they were saying, 'I know I am saved because I have believed.[23]' Then came the next question: how do you *know* you have truly believed? The conclusion was that this would be evidenced by 'godly living' – and how could you be sure you had been godly enough? And so, through great complexity, they had ended up in a works-based position. As the Bible was held up to be the full and final work of God there was no prospect of any personal or further revelation to clarify the picture. But now some were speaking differently.

20 Hajzyk (1981), p.173
21 illiam Whiting, *Memoir of Rev. Samuel Whiting, D.D., and of His Wife, Elizabeth St. John*, Boston, 1873, p.58
22 Winship (2005), p.46
23 R T Kendall, *Holy Fire*, Florida, 2014, p.36-8

Of course, this in turn led to a hardening of their attitudes to those they perceived as not meeting their godly standards, including those with different views. When the test came of their tolerance, they largely failed it. The Pilgrims did not go to America *for religious freedom,* but for their *own* religious freedom.

Wheelwright had probably been born at Saleby in Lincolnshire in 1592. At Cambridge, he knew Oliver Cromwell and was a noted athlete, a legend at wrestling and, according to one tale, Cromwell had said he had been more afraid of Wheelwright on a football field than of any army.[24] He married Marie Storre, a daughter of the vicar of Bilsby,[25] in 1621 and then became vicar there himself in 1623. However, his first wife died in 1629 and he married again to Mary Hutchinson from the same Alford family – to be one of the great dynasties of the new America. This brought him into contact with the powerful Anne Hutchinson and the puritan minister, John Cotton. These influences helped turn Wheelwright into a different type of Christian – 'he encouraged (others) to seek a charismatic experience of the Holy Spirit'[26] and as he spread this, he was able to help others feel assured of their salvation. One of those he spread it to was Hanserd Knollys, who we shall study in more detail later.

Cotton was on his own journey which led the influential Christian writer R T Kendall to note that he was 'the first in his tradition to allow for the immediate witness of the Spirit'. Indeed, he taught the New Englanders 'not to be afraid of the word Revelation' – a challenge to those who staunchly believed there was no revelation outside the Bible. He offered the possibility that one could *feel* the call of God.[27] This opened him to charges that by 'advancing the Spirit, and revelation of the Spirit', he might 'destroy or weaken revelation of the Scriptures'; it is an argument that has continued ever since.[28]

Wheelwright had been convicted under a legal technicality for selling his Church living back to the patron in 1632 and left for Massachusetts in 1636. Here he met up with many others from Lincolnshire including other members of his wife's family, especially Anne Hutchinson who had arrived in 1634, and the governor, Sir Henry Vane. However, their teachings about the Holy Spirit and justification by faith not election led to controversy.

Meanwhile, Shepard then claimed that the problems originated with Anne Hutchinson, who he accused of teaching that 'the person of the Holy Ghost dwells in a justified person' and 'that no sanctification can help to evidence to us our justification'. Anne, the well-educated daughter of Francis Marbury, was not afraid of an argument.[29]
It is worth pausing to consider the Hutchinson family. They were descendants of Edward Hutchinson, a mercer who came from a prominent Lincoln family but who had settled in Alford in the east of the county. His grandson, Edward, was sent to New England in 1633 following which William, Edward's father, moved his whole family to Boston,

---

24 M P Winship, *John Wheelwright,* in *ODNB.*

25 Bilsby was held by the Wasteneys family, who also held puritan Headon in Notts. Arthur Collins, *The English Baronetage Vol. 1*, p535

26 Winship, ODNB

27 J M Barry, *Roger Williams and the Creation of the American Soul*, New York, 2012, p.245

28 Barry (2012), p.246

29 Marbury was thrown into gaol for preaching in Northampton without permission and condemned in 1578 as 'an overthwart proud puritan knave' by the Bishop of London. The Marburys held land at Biscathorpe, Burgh on Bain and at Girsby manor.

Massachusetts in 1634. William had married Anne Marbury in 1612, with whom he had fifteen children. William's brother Samuel arrived later in 1637 followed by Susanna Storre, a sister who had married Augustine the son of the vicar of Bilsby, in Lincolnshire. Another younger sister, Mary Hutchinson, in 1630 became the second wife of John Wheelwright who had succeeded Susanna's father in law as vicar of Bilsby in 1624; Susanna later remarried to another Lincolnshire emigrant, Atherton Hough, former mayor of Boston (Lincs). All this meant that Anne had significant connections on all sides.

Anne was also significant as she was a long-term member of Cotton's congregation but also as close to gentry as one might come in New England except for Vane. Her father was Lincolnshire gentry and the son of an MP, her mother a Dryden with impeccable gentry background and a puritan as well.[30] She was both well-educated and well-connected, but she stayed in Alford until the early 1630s. Perhaps influenced by both Cotton and Wheelwright, around 1630 she experienced her own profound 'assurance of salvation'.[31] Around 1633, increasingly convinced that she experienced direct revelation from God, she saw little hope of the Church of England. With Cotton the Hutchinsons fled to America in 1634, and Wheelwright followed later. Even on the voyage she upset other ministers by prophesying.

John Winthrop blamed the influence of Yorkshire minister Roger Brierley and the 'Grindletonians' on Hutchinson, but Cotton had been her chief influence and had taught that moral behaviour was no proof of salvation.[32] In New England, she preached about grace, inner light, revelation and joy – and began a large house group of women. Meanwhile, her brother-in-law, Wheelwright began preaching at outlying Mount Wollaston and by October 1636 was accused of being a 'familist' – an especially despised form of heresy.

Cotton tried to hold the church together by accepting that works could help to find grace from God although some of his congregation held more stringent free grace views and wanted Wheelwright as their assistant pastor. The dispute threatened to boil over, with Wheelwright denied a Boston church appointment through deputy governor Winthrop's actions and Vane, who sympathised with the Hutchinson faction, threatening to resign over it. That December, Vane announced he was going – annoyed by being blamed for the controversy; this did not save him from a savaging from the tongue of Hugh Peter.[33] Meanwhile, Anne Hutchinson continued to accuse some ministers of preaching a covenant of works with Cotton's position increasingly uncomfortable.

In January 1637 Wheelwright preached his famous 'fast day sermon' that inflamed tempers further by calling for spiritual warfare against magistrates and erroneous ministers; he was accused of heresy (though defended by Cotton on this) but found guilty of sedition, being banished in 1637. He moved to Exeter, New Hampshire, and set up a new congregation. Such comments as 'we must kill them with the Word of the Lord' hardly helped.[34] Perhaps exhausted by it all, and having fallen out with Winthrop, Vane left for England

30 M P Winship, *The Times and Trials of Anne Hutchinson*, Kansas, 2005, p.9
31 Winship (2005), p.17
32 Watts (1986), p.180
33 Winship (2005), p.60. Ironically both Peter and Vane would die on the orders of Charles II.
34 M P Winship, *Making Heretics: Militant Protestantism and the Grace in Massachusetts*, Princeton, 2014, p.112

in August 1637 amidst fears in some circles that he would return with Royal authority as Governor-General. His link to Roger Williams, though, continued.

Meanwhile, on 12 July 1637 another shipload of migrants arrived, including many from Lincolnshire such as another Hutchinson, Samuel, Anne's brother-in-law. Hanserd Knollys, another former cleric of a Lincolnshire parish also soon arrived.[35] Knollys had a bad voyage: 'my little child died with convulsion fits, our beer and water stank, our biscuit was green, yellow and blue, moulded and rotten….but God was gracious to us, and led us safe through those great deeps'. Probably also on this voyage were Augustine and Susannah Storre (nee Hutchinson) – the son and daughter in law of the previous vicar of Bilsby.

The new arrivals were asked immediately to disavow Wheelwright's teachings – which Knollys thought worse than Laud's High Commission – and, when they refused, were told to leave within four months. Altogether six members of the Hutchinson family were banished. The plan, possibly including Cotton himself, was to use Roger William's knowledge to buy land from the Narragansett Indians.[36] Knollys received an offer to preach at what became Dover, and decamped there, close to others in what became New Hampshire – Wheelwright and Christopher Marshall, all east Lincolnshire folk. However, he fell out with a rival minister, Thomas Larkham, and was accused of having attempted to seduce two maids in his household amidst riotous scenes. He returned to England in 1641, became a Baptist, and enjoyed a successful career; Larkham betrayed his congregation by also returning to England, accused of having sired a child on a 'handsome widow'.

For a time, the colony appeared on the brink of serious division, effectively between some of the Lincolnshire people and the rest.[37] Thomas Dudley, though, sided against Vane before he left and against Wheelwright. Hutchinson emphasised her position by getting her friends to leave whenever a preacher they did not like began to preach. Her 'conventicles' continued to be popular. But with Vane gone, Cotton tried to secure a compromise, whilst Dudley seems to have become prepared to tolerate Cotton. Wheelwright was unhelpful although eventually he was effectively pardoned.

At the synod in August 1637, it was effectively Cotton and his Boston church that were on trial. Cotton perhaps buckled under the pressure, abandoning Wheelwright and the others. In November the pressure shifted to Anne Hutchinson, with supporters like William Aspinwall[38] and William Coddington (from Lincolnshire[39]) marginalised, so that she could be charged with sedition in a trial where Winthrop was the dominant figure but which included many Lincolnshire interests such as Thomas Dudley and Simon Bradstreet.

Under great stress, Hutchinson finally gave her enemies what they wanted. She declared

---

35 The precise date of this is unclear; S Hardman Moore says 1638.

36 Winship (2014), p.89

37 Winship (2014), p.76, suggests ties with Lincolnshire and Cotton/Wheelwright were the main factors. The support of Lincs men like Coddington and Atherton Hough was certainly important. However, Thomas Dudley, who was also related to Bradstreet, was a harsh critic of 'heresy'.

38 After some time in Rhode Island he returned to England and became a Fifth Monarchist. A link to William Aspinwall of Mattersey is not known.

39 Coddington has been assumed to be from Marston near Grantham, though by the later 1620s he was living in Boston.

that when she had been fasting in England 'the Lord had sent her scriptures that showed her how to discern among the voices of Christ, Moses, John the Baptist, and Antichrist in ministers'. She confirmed she had 'immediate revelations' which she knew were from the Spirit.[40] Here she was stepping across a line on supernatural revelation that had been held firm by puritans for two generations – no revelation outside scripture. Cotton, invited to disavow her, said that 'revelations by the word of scripture and according to the word of scripture were possible,' quibbling only at her confidence that she might be delivered by a miracle.[41] But he could not save her and she, too, was sentenced to be banished.

Under house arrest and unable to leave because pregnant, Hutchinson's theology crumbled to become even more radical and closer to the familist heresies. In March 1638 she was brought back for a new church trial. First William Coddington and some of the Hutchinsons were given permission to go to join Williams at Narragansett Bay, including Anne's husband. At the end she was excommunicated for lying.

Williams acquired the island that was to become Rhode Island by 'love and favour', mentioning Vane as a factor in this. There it was decided that 'none be accounted a delinquent for doctrine' – an idea passed to Williams via the writings of Helwys and Murton.

Wheelwright was not banished until November 1637; he founded the town of Exeter, New Hampshire, and was joined by the Hutchinsons and a number of others with Lincolnshire origins including Christopher Marshall. In 1641 the expansion of Massachusetts forced him to relocate to Wells in Maine. His banishment was lifted in 1644, Wheelwright returned to England for a time in 1655 where he knew Sir Henry Vane who was living at Belleau in Lincolnshire and also Oliver Cromwell, with whom he had been at college. Wheelwright later returned to New England in 1662 and became minister at Salisbury, where he stayed until his death in 1679.

When he returned to England, Vane showed where he stood on Church matters by marrying in 1640 Frances Wray (V), the 16-year-old daughter of Sir Christopher Wray of Ashby cum Fenby – Lincolnshire's leading puritan family. She soon persuaded him to take a home in Lincolnshire, at Belleau, formerly held by the Earl of Lindsey. For a time, he held a Crown appointment as joint treasurer of the Navy but opposed ship money, Laudianism and the role of the bishops – dismissal in 1642 can hardly have been a surprise given that he had helped with the impeachment of Laud in 1641. Both he and his wife were host to Roger Williams when he returned to England in 1643, both in their London and Lincolnshire homes – and Williams was still considered too radical even by leading puritans although he had a 'great friendship' with Vane who introduced him to John Milton.[42] Williams stayed at Belleau with Vane and his wife, where Wheelwright also later visited and ministered during his English sojourn of 1655-62, a combination of radical forces boiling away in a remote Lincolnshire hamlet. Vane, Williams and later Milton pursued an interest in religious liberty and other spiritual topics in which they drew from Helwys and Murton; Vane's *A Healing Question* was an inspiration to Thomas Venner, the Fifth Monarchist, whose 1661 rebellion caused so much trouble for the

40   Winship (2014), p.110
41   Winship, p.111
42   J M Barry (2012), p.287

Baptists. Williams wrote *Experiments of Spiritual Life, and Health and their Preservation* whilst staying amidst the Native Americans – 'in the thickest of the naked Indians of America, in their very wild houses and by their barbarous fires'. This work he chose to dedicate to Lady Frances Vane when it was published in London in 1652, referring to her as 'truly honourable'.

Christopher Marshall was from Alford Lincolnshire and his wife Sarah was related to Anne Hutchinson and therefore also Wheelwright. Originally one of Cotton's pupils, he sided with Anne in the controversy and the Marshalls followed Wheelwright out of Massachusetts to found Exeter in New Hampshire, but his wife drowned soon afterwards. He returned to England in 1642 and, after being chaplain to Colonel Christopher Copley's troop, settled at Woodkirk (or West Ardsley) in Yorkshire by 1648 where there was an independent congregation dating back to the 1630s.[43] Two ministers from this parish had left for New England.[44] Intriguingly this was a place with a 'Grindletonian' reputation and James Nayler, who later achieved some infamy in his career as a Quaker, had been of the congregation until riding out to join Fairfax's forces in 1643.[45] Marshall's congregation seems to have met in the parish church but encountered problems when Nayler returned in 1651 and decided to expel him. The following year the Quaker leader George Fox himself sought out Marshall at the 'steeple house' but instead, the congregation turned against him, and Fox just about escaped a severe beating or a visit to the stocks. Marshall seems to have become the vicar during the free times of 1650, a time of some turbulence, but was inevitably ejected in 1662.

Hutchinson has received a bad press in the past, recently turning to a more favourable one. The main account of her trial was written by Winthrop, who was hardly a balanced witness, and who found Hutchinson a much safer scapegoat than Wheelwright, Cotton or Vane. The antagonistic Shepard later blamed the whole problem on Vane. Hutchinson left Massachusetts in March 1638 with her sister in law Mary Wheelwright and mother in law, planning to join Wheelwright's group in New Hampshire.

Instead, she went to Aquidneck Island with around 80 others, but others settled in Rhode Island and contributed to the success of this fledgling in the New England nest. Wheelwright, much more cautious, could not accept her latest beliefs, and by 1640 Anne had become a 'Seeker'. As Massachusetts expanded, Aquidneck started to come within its orbit and Williams went to England to get a charter for his colony – which became Rhode Island.

After the death of her husband, Hutchinson believed she had a new revelation and moved to an area being colonised by the Dutch – the future New York. She ignored Indian warnings not to settle and was later killed by Indians around September 1643. Almost her entire family was killed, save for one daughter who had been away from their home and instead, was taken captive for several years. Anne's sister Katherine married Richard Scott and, after a time in Rhode Island, was whipped at Boston for supporting her future son-in-law who had become a Quaker. Two of her closest supporters and also Coddington, in the 1660s, became Quakers.

43 Anne Whitrow, then Thomas Lawyer. After the English Restoration, Copley was one of
44 Susan Hardman Moore, *Pilgrims: New World Settlers and the Call of Home*, London, 2007, p.119
45 Susan Hardman Moore (2007), p.59

Cotton died in 1652 and his last work, *A Treatise of the Covenant of Grace*, was published posthumously in 1659. Cotton roundly denounced 'assurance by good works' as papist and emphasised assurance *in* faith alone.[46] Cotton went further by suggesting that the Bible was not the end of it – the Holy Spirit could witness 'immediately' to any individual. As one historian has put it, 'Although he denied the validity of prophetic or visual revelations 'without or besides Scripture', he accepted the worth of intuitional revelations 'such as breathed by the Spirit of God and are never dispersed but in a word of God'.[47]

For Wheelwright, this was a wound that never really healed. In 1643 he achieved some form of rapprochement with Massachusetts but was then upset by the 1644 publication of an 'official' account of the crisis which laboured his own faults. *Mercurious Americanus*, published the next year, put the counter arguments. In August 1654 he preached a sermon in Boston that reopened the issues and then left for seven years in England, where he spent time with Vane and also met Cromwell again. Back at Salisbury in New Hampshire he was intolerant of Quakers, dying in 1679.

In the midst of all this turbulence we should note another significant Lincolnshire impact on New England – the founding of Harvard in 1636 involved a committee that included seven men with Boston connections including Cotton, Bellingham and Dudley. The inception of a university was part of a plan to create a sustainable godly community in America.

Finally, we should note that the continued drift of people to New England also brought Richard Bernard's son Masakiell from Batcombe with the Joseph Hull party in 1636.

William Coddington (c1601-1678) was perhaps from Marston (Lincs) and was one of Cotton's Boston congregation in the 1620s; he sailed to America with the Winthrop fleet. He returned briefly in 1631, marrying a new wife at Terling in the Essex puritan heartland. At Boston he became a significant figure, building the first brick house and becoming a magistrate. However, as an associate of Cotton and Hutchinson, he became embroiled in the 'free grace' or antinomian controversy in 1637 in which he sided with Hutchinson and was opposed by many of the powerful voices in New England.

---

46   Kendall (2014), p.39
47   Emery Battis, *Saints and Sinners: Anne Hutchinson and the Antinomian Controversy*, Williamsburg, 1962, p.33

He was deeply unhappy about Hutchinson's trial and he retired to his house in March 1638 to discuss leaving to create a new colony in Rhode Island. The resulting 'Portsmouth Compact' was signed by many of similar mind, including John Clarke, a Suffolk man who later became a Baptist and William Dyer from Kirkby Laythorpe in Lincolnshire. The group settled in Rhode Island but Coddington had significant differences from Williams and the Hutchinsons as to how the colony should be run and wanted it to be separate from Providence; by 1640 he had, instead, founded Newport. The politics of Rhode Island remained fractious for years. Williams dismissed him as self-seeking and worldly, but his decision to become a Quaker in the 1660s is therefore somewhat surprising: he provided shelter for George Fox in 1672.

CHAPTER FIFTEEN

Crown and Parliament Collide the Growing Crisis
1634-1641

Under Charles and Laud, legal persecution of nonconformity increased at the same time as Laudian policies accelerated the prevalence of the practices that puritans found unacceptable. The re-issue of the Book of Sports *in 1633 provoked another crisis with ministers being forced to read it or be punished. New rules were set on the position of the altar, in 1637, and the need for a communion rail, which were a matter for controversy though not always enforced. However, puritans in Lincolnshire and around Nottingham showed a growing ability to organise themselves politically as well as in religion, having learnt from the 'forced loan' crisis; Laud's religious politics therefore increased the risk of a major political conflict.*

Chronology:

1633: William Laud becomes Archbishop of Canterbury; *Book of Sports* re-issued;

1633: A residential Catholic presence re-established in Lincoln

1634: Laud launches visitation of Lincoln diocese

1636: Knollys and Whiting leave for America

1637: Bishop Williams convicted and imprisoned; Ship Money crisis

1640: Parliament recalled, dismissed and recalled; Williams released; 'Root and Branch' petition; Laud arrested

1641: Williams appointed Archbishop of York; attacks on bishops begin

August 1642: Charles raises standard at Nottingham – war begins

---

Conflict Develops

The years 1633-4 brought some seismic changes in the Church of England. Laud finally became Archbishop of Canterbury in September 1633, giving him total control of Church disciplinary systems, and from 1634 he launched a programme of visitations to enforce conformity to the 1604 canon laws. The re-issuing in October 1633 of James I's *Book of Sports*, which set out what activities were permitted on a Sunday, was a threat to the puritan way of doing the Sabbath. It encouraged activities such as archery and maypole-dancing which puritans thought ought not to occur on a Sabbath. To make matters worse, Charles

N

River Ouse

Crowle

Great Limber

GRIMSBY

Belton

Ashby cum Fenby

Epworth

DONCASTER

South Kelsey

River Trent

Blyton

Scrooby

Saltfleetby All Saints

GAINSBOROUGH

LOUTH

Glentworth

Fenton

WORKSOP

EAST RETFORD

Goltho

Bilsby

Cherry Willingham

Fiskerton

LINCOLN

Edlington

Horncastle

Old Bolingbroke

Kneesall

Hucknall
Huthwaite

MANSFIELD

South Collingham

Timberland

Tattershall

River Witham

NEWARK
-ON-
TRENT

Averham

River Witham

Felley

SLEAFORD

Gedling

Silk Willoughby

BOSTON

Helpringham

NOTTINGHAM

Attenborough

River Trent

Owthorpe

GRANTHAM

Pickworth

Ingoldsby

Lavington/Lenton

Boothby
Pagnell

Osgodby

SPALDING

Whaplode

Stainby

Moulton

■ Place

▨ Town

Great Casterton

Deeping St James

STAMFORD

0   10   20 miles

insisted that all ministers read it publicly or face deprivation. Laud was widely blamed for all of this. A supporter of this was John Pocklington, who had been a chaplain to the Bishop of Lincoln and a prebendary of Lincoln, and in a sermon before John Williams in June 1635 denounced the puritan focus on the Sabbath, calling them 'the most gross, nay the most transparent hypocrites'; this sermon was published under the title *Sunday no Sabbath* and won Pocklington many enemies. On 25 January 1634, 14 youths died at Gainsborough when, playing Sunday football on the frozen river, the ice broke and they all fell through after 'meeting together in a shove'.[1] The incident was a staple warning in Sabbatarian books right through to the 1800s.

Richard Truman, father of the congregationalist Joseph Truman, had been one of the Nottinghamshire puritan gentry who had previously enforced the Sabbath but now he came across maypole-dancing on a Sunday and found that the dancers accosted him rudely and told him that they had the King's authority. The Trumans were minor gentry, with lands at Hucknall Howthwaite[2] and Gedling amongst other places; they were related by marriage to the Sylvesters of Mansfield, one of whom left Richard Rothwell his annual allowance, and the Hierons of Loscoe which was just inside Derbyshire. Richard lived at Gedling where his son Joseph was born. He told the dancers that their statement was true, the king's law allowed it, but they should also respect God's laws. The dancers complained to the justices about Truman's seditious words and a costly prosecution resulted, engineered by the Earl of Chesterfield – whose son, however, offered Truman his support and the prospect of meeting his costs in future. Altogether it cost Truman £1500, but in Calamy's account[3] one of the prosecutors suffered a fit of remorse as he faced death and begged Truman's forgiveness – which he provided. Calamy also reported that Truman's crops so grew that he was able to pay back all the costs.

The renewed pressures for conformity also once more ensnared Richard Bernard, for long fairly safe in Somerset, for his new bishop, William Piers, censured him for a long list of offences in October 1634 although he had been careful to avoid provoking trouble in his writing on the Sabbath.

In the Lincoln diocese, Bishop Williams's opposition to Laud's reforms of Church practice became increasingly a problem for him once Laud was finally confirmed as Archbishop. The Bishop of Lincoln seems to have taken a public view that the details of ritual were not that important – matters indifferent – and he would rather keep a good man in the Church than lose him to an argument over a surplice. In 1634 Laud quickly decided to make a metropolitan visitation – or inspection – of the Lincoln diocese and employed a commissioner, Sir Nathaniel Brent, known to be an enemy of Williams although a diocesan official; he and Dr Robert Sibthorpe supplied Laud with details of unchallenged puritanism. Dr John Farmery,[4] chancellor of the diocese, and later Brent reported on lapses at the cathedral including neglect and ill-disciplined clergy.

---

1   Richard Bernard mentioned this in his book, *Threefold Treatise*.
2   Richard's brother Henry lived here; he chose Gilbert Millington of Felley, the future regicide, as supervisor of his will. Joseph Hunter, *Gens Sylvestrina*, London, 1848, pps 32-40. Another of this family settled in Maryland. Another Henry Truman was vicar of Newark until 1655.
3   Edmund Calamy, *A Continuation of The Account of The Ministers, Lecturers, Masters ...*, Volume 2, p.693
4   Edward Farmerie was deputy registrar in the Archdeaconry of Nottingham from 1628.

Laud then started to use the Court of Ecclesiastical High Commission which had earlier been used by Whitgift. Laud did unearth other nonconformists; for example, Sidrach Edmonds at Edlington and William Chowne of Helpringham were deprived, the latter resurfacing at Clayton in Sussex in 1638.[5] Cotton and Whiting would have gone the same way. Unsurprisingly the High Commission was busy by 1635, with a number of Lincolnshire cases including Richard Knowles, the father of Hanserd Knollys, Hinchcliffe at Timberland and George Mason at Cherry Willingham. Edmund Lynold at Healing dragged his case on for several years but was deprived in 1637.[6] They also had to deal with Farmery Linley at Epworth, accused by his own curate of 'inconstancy' with his own wife's granddaughter. Suspensions possibly included Thomas Coleman in the Wray parish of Blyton cum Wharton, whilst several others have been suggested.[7]

In Boston, six were charged in issue relating to communion with Cotton, Richard Bellingham and Atherton Hough being fined – too late. All six were accused of being in conventicles and Edward Tilson (Tillson), a woollen-draper and alderman, was accused of entertaining the Scottish preacher Alexander Leighton – who was branded and had his ears cropped on Laud's orders in 1630; Tilson was one of eleven in Boston who had refused the forced loan. Lambe and his team had an array of deprivations, suspensions and fines which they could use to enforce discipline for practices such as 'gadding about' or not using the Prayer Book when visiting the sick.

Laud was actually a little slower than Neile in enforcing the new rituals and fabric, notably the position and furnishing of the altar. The 1634 visitation of Boston made no mention of imposing an altar rail – and one cannot imagine the church already had one![8]

Despite this, the pattern of protection still applied. Gentry like Sir William Armyne continued to protect clergy – two generations of Armynes protected two generations of Wood at Lenton, and other radicals in their livings at Silk Willoughby and Pickworth. Seth Wood, who was at Lenton from 1639, wrote that 'he was to such good men as lived under his wing and protection a shadow from the heat and a refuge from the storme of that persecution which scorched others very sore, for though the times he knew he was not too great to crush yet he was too wel beloved to provoke'. The relationship with Williams was a key factor here.[9] Wood clearly rode the tide of events well, for by 1657/8 he was preaching at St Margaret's Westminster every Sunday afternoon.

5   CCED does not have Edmonds.
6   Referred to as 'Edward Lynald' in earlier entries.
7   Daniel Neal, *History of the Puritans vol 5*, p.529 gives Edmund Small or Smith of Holme in Lincolnshire; I am not clear who this refers to. Neal also gives examples of other ministers outside the county such as Peter Bulkley, whose nonconformity Williams 'connived' at. Bulkley went to America.
8   Fincham, Kenneth. "The Restoration of Altars in the 1630s." *The Historical Journal*, vol. 44, no. 4, 2001, pp. 919–940. *JSTOR*, www.jstor.org/stable/3133545.
9   Cliffe, p.185

Bitter Foes: Laud and the Humbling of Williams

Williams remained uncooperative; whatever his theology, he had a personal dislike of Laud and the Lincoln diocese had remained a 'great loophole' for Laud[10] until he took direct action. However, Laud did have those who shared his Arminian theology in Lincolnshire such as Thomas Gibson at Horncastle. We might also note that quite separately the General Baptists, now established in Lincolnshire but discussed in another chapter, held some views that were Arminian, but they, of course, differed greatly from Laudian Arminianists who added sacramentalism and ceremonies.

His tolerance for puritans is shown in the great favour he showed to Hanserd Knollys in 1636, even after he had resigned his Church of England living, although Plumb thought that he 'detested sectaries, particularly the anabaptists'.[11] Following this Laud took direct control of Lincoln, but the case had damaged the Church. The 'accusations of fornication, intimidation, bribery and perjury against high ecclesiastics hardly enhanced the moral authority of the Church'[12] and he endured three years in the Tower but recovered to become an archbishop.

In 1628 a Star Chamber prosecution had begun against Williams on the rather thin grounds of having revealed a secret of the Privy Council (which he had in discussion with Lambe, Prigeon and the others at Buckden), and efforts to gather evidence were renewed in 1634 on Laud's behalf. Hence, in 1634 Laud imposed his own visitation on the Lincoln diocese, identifying many 'abuses' even in the Cathedral and unearthing 'anabaptists' in the city. Williams's main witness, Prigeon his diocesan registrar, was accused of being the father of an illegitimate child and Williams foolishly and without final success tried to bribe others to bury this information. Williams used Edward Ayscough as his agent – a name hardly likely to endear itself with Laud.[13] He was found out and charged with perjury.

In the midst of this Williams published his controversial book, *The Holy Table, Name and Thing* which the king wished him to recant; this was itself a response to *A Coale from the Altar*, published in 1637 as an attack on Williams' own anonymous *Letter to the Vicar of Grantham* – all triggered by the Titley case. A further response came from John Pocklington who later that year published *Altare Christianum or the Dead Vicar's Plea* which noted the destruction of Titley's stone altar after his death and mistakenly assumed John Cotton to have written the *Letter*; Pocklington briefly served Williams, but by this stage was a confidante of Lambe and as 'high church' as it was possible to be without joining Rome.[14] The pamphlet war was still going on in 1641 when Richard Day was stated to be the author of *Two Looks over Lincolne – or a View of his Holy Table, Name and Thing*. Williams' views on the position of the communion table were in line with the Elizabethan era and the canons of 1604 although he also believed in rails around it – something less common in a Calvinist; however, his views put him out of step with the official policy since late in 1633 and he directed the removal of a stone altar.[15] The

---

10   Holmes (1980), p.114
11   Plumb, p.81
12   Clive Holmes, *Why was Charles I Executed?* Hambledon, 2007, p.28
13   Hill, p.122
14   He was brought crashing down in 1641, deprived of all his benefices and his books burnt.
15   Hajzyk (1981), p.111

Grantham dispute over the altar continued long after Williams's downfall and in 1639-40 extended to another problem, the organs, which some citizens petitioned Laud to have removed. During the Short and Long Parliaments there were petitions to have the altar rail taken away, and counter-petitions in its favour.

In 1637 Williams was convicted on evidence from Lambe and Dr Sibthorpe, fined an enormous sum, and put into the Tower where he stayed until 1640. This has been described as a 'rather public and nasty conviction before the Star Chamber in 1637'.[16] Williams's use of John Pregion for his defence was easily undermined by accusations that he was an illegal peddler of tobacco, had defamed many church officials including Williams, and was the father of an illegitimate child – which he denied. This all contributed to Williams's problems when it seemed that he had interfered with witnesses. As well as perjury he was convicted of 'scandalous language on the King and his ministers' and refusing to pay ship money.[17] He was also fined eight thousand marks including for libellous correspondence with the Master of Westminster school in which Laud was called 'the little urchin'. Three of his staff were also fined and one briefly imprisoned, and one thousand marks had to be paid to Sir John Monson[18] alleging malpractice against him over the illegitimacy case for which Monson had been abused. Lambe assumed some of Williams's duties in Leicestershire but was himself to be brought down and humiliated in 1641. Late in 1635 Monson met the King at Belvoir and used this chance of blocking any form of deal with Williams.

It was quite an unprecedented outcome, but it depended in part on an organised faction within Williams's own diocesan officials who actively worked against him because they were committed to Laudianism.[19] Support for Williams came from the much less powerful puritan gentry – Hill gives an interesting list of gifts to Williams in 1633, headed by Edward Ayscough, the Countess of Warwick (Frances Wray, who died the next year), Sir John Wray and – not quite so godly – Robert Saunderson, Lord Castleton.[20] However, in the long term, these were better friends to have.

This left Laud free to control the diocese and visitations became more challenging in 1637, by which stage the King's imposition of the Ship Money had added to political stresses. A further visitation in 1638 attempted to sweep away any communion 'tables'. Disagreement at Grantham was such that Lady Packenham put in her will of 1639 precise instructions for her burial at St Wulfram's: *'lay mee not neare no not in sight of that place they call the alter'.*[21] By 1638 there were still 93 cases in Lincolnshire of breaching this rule.[22] Not until 1640 did Laud have the backing of new canon law to support his preferences for how altars should be.

---

16   Escrick, p.35
17   J P Lawson, *The Life and Times of William Laud*, volume 2, p.193
18   Monson's father Sir Thomas was a key witness against Williams; in 1615 he had been implicated in the Overbury poisoning case which led to the execution of Sir Gervase Helwys.
19   Hill, *Tudor and Stuart Lincoln*, p.122
20   Hill, ibid, p.123
21   Fincham and Tyacke, *Altars Restored: The Changing Face of English Religious Worship*, 1547-c.1700, p.180
22   Hajzyk (1981), p.290

Increasing Resistance

The Laud era caused an immediate increase in nonconformity – there was more to not conform with. At Belton in Axholme the numbers increased from 11 in 1631 to 13 in 1635 and then 36 in 1640. A significant proportion of these were more wealthy people who might be forced into forming a conventicle, and Lloyd has suggested there might also have been one at Epworth.[23] In Epworth the wardens were found to be slow, in 1635, in bringing in a new altar rail, a persistent few refused to stand up during designated parts of the service and in 1640 Nathaniel Brownlow disturbed the service when excommunicate to the extent that everyone left the church. Lloyd speculates that some of these offenders might have been Baptists. Events at Epworth culminated in the rector, Richard Massey, being 'plucked' out of the chancel and arrested in the churchyard in 1640, by two local men in the midst of a number of lawsuits and also antagonism amongst foreign settlers.[24] Matters got worse when the curate, Massey's own son, was accused of fathering a bastard. Clearly, trouble did not arrive with Samuel Wesley.

Neile had some problems. In 1634 William Clough, the generally more puritan vicar of Kneesall, was accused of slandering John Garnon from the pulpit by accusing him of attending nonconformist preachers rather than his own church; the case went to the Consistory Court with Garnon accused of holding conventicles of between ten and sixty people, taking it upon themselves to 'expound the holie scriptures and make prayers of their own', and for keeping the unbeneficed minister Luke Bacon as a 'pretended priest'. One of them complained of the Prayer Book that it was nothing but 'a company of shitten prayers' and in South Collingham in 1634 Thomas Ollivant was excommunicated for saying God's word was no longer preached – Brian Barton having died a few years before.[25] In other places parishioners made their own protests – at Attenborough Henry Ireton and his mother were presented for refusing to take communion at the altar rail in 1636.

Old problems with unlicensed preachers persisted. In 1634 the wardens at Scrooby typically claimed they were 'illiterate' and so unable to check a licence for Mr Willard. but in 1635 Thomas Cranage the curate was prevented from preaching at Nottingham St Mary's by the arrival of Mottershed himself and ordered to conform on a number of accounts.[26]

Neile acted in 1635 to improve enforcement by officials in the southern part of his diocese through appointing Edward Mottershed. The impact of Laudian reforms was 'rather later' in Nottinghamshire than many other areas. Nottinghamshire was brought into line by Mottershed over the next two years to at least ensure all ministers had a hood and the table was railed in at the east end of the chancel.[27] By Easter 1637 all the churches at least had the 'correct' furnishings, and by 1639 problems had declined, although this did not mean compliant behaviour – the two men at Farndon in 1635 who sat on the altar during communion were clearly stating their attitude. From 1635 St Peter's Nottingham was notably resistant to Laud's reforms. The wardens were excommunicated for refusing to put up an altar rail, and when one was eventually installed in 1636 the Holy Table was

23   Lloyd, p.197
24   Lloyd, p.200
25   Jennings (1999), p.99-100
26   Jennings (1999), p.88-91
27   Marchant (1969), p.201

not inside of it. George Coates was told not to administer communion to anyone who did not come to the rail. On Easter Day 1638 more than forty people refused to use the altar rail, including the Mayor.[28] Around thirteen parishes in the county had their wardens excommunicated for not providing rails – half of them in the old 'Pilgrim' area in the north.[29]

In 1636 in Lincolnshire Hanserd Knollys and Samuel Whiting, of Skirbeck, came within the sights of the Commission and they too left; both went to New England in 1636. John Wheelwright, a key figure in New England events, was deprived of his living at Bilsby after the Commission heard stories of him preaching God's judgement on England.[30] Edmund Lynold at Healing was condemned in 1634 but not ousted until 1637. At Tattershall, a puritan centre which had got away with no kneeling for years, they were expected to conform in 1636.[31] Yet it is plain that some still did as they wished – Sir William Armyne employed Thomas Cawton as his private chaplain (in part at his estate at Orton Hall) from 1633 to 1637. Cawton clearly took no account of his hosts – his son later wrote that 'he would neither smother faults nor smooth them over.[32]

Even though Parliament had been suspended whilst Charles tried to impose his personal rule from 1629 to 1640, the puritan gentry were bolstered for the battle. Sir Edward Ayscough of South Kelsey was, like the others, a second or third generation puritan with the noblest of heritages – one of his family had been the martyr Anne Askew. In 1634 John Clarke dedicated his book *Holy Incense for the Censers of the Saints* to Ayscough – 'God hath given you a mind to know him, a heart to love him' – and 'to his religious and noble lady'. But he also made the most of the heritage, naming Anne as 'the honour of this Country, the Praise of her own Sexe, and the Glory of your Noble family, Mistress Anne Ayscough, Martyr'. He also took space to name 'John Lacels' who was 'sacrificed with her in the same fire, for the Word of God and for the Testimony which they held'. Ayscough had sheltered Clarke for nearly two years after he was persecuted in his own city.[33]

John Clarke (c.1596-1658)

Clarke's origins are unknown, but he attended Magdalene College in Cambridge and was ordained in 1619. He became headmaster of Lincoln Free School at the age of 26 in 1622, until 1641. He was very progressive in his curriculum thinking, introducing lessons in English rather than Latin and even PE.

---

28   Marchant, p.195
29   Jennings lists the northern ones as Bawtry, Bole, Clarborough, Elkesley, Gringley and West Burton. Upton and Worksop were also slow to comply.
30   Holmes (1980), p.118-9
31   Hajzyk (1981), p.107
32   Cawton subsequently went to Wivenhoe in Essex, where he had many troubles with fishermen and was attacked on the road by 'sectaries' from Colchester. In 1641 he went to St Bartholomew's Royal Exchange, but a sermon against the execution of the King led to trouble and after a brief imprisonment in 1648-9 he lived until his death mainly in Rotterdam – having been too strong in his support for Charles II. His son wrote his biography and dedicated it to Sir Anthony Irby, for whom he was chaplain in the 1660s.
33   Cliffe (1984), p.134

He taught the future Colonel John Hutchinson, who considered him a 'supercilious pedant' and 'conceited of his own pedantique forms' though Lucy Hutchinson noted he was also 'very famous for learning and piety'. From 1634 he held the living of Fiskerton where he was buried in the chancel in 1658. The home city where he said he was persecuted is unknown.

He wrote a large number of books, the first of which was dedicated to the four sons of Robert Bertie, so it is assumed they were his pupils. In about 1630-1 he returned to Cambridge to study for a Divinity degree following which his writing became more about spiritual matters. *A Method of Prayer* was successful though a Latin book on preaching, *Oratoriae sacrae, Skia*graphia, was seen as plagiarism by some. From 1641 he ran his own school at Fiskerton.

John Ashburne (c1607-1661)

Sir John Wray was also using his authority to protect nonconformists and the classic example is that of Ashburne. It would seem that John Ashburne arrived at Glentworth with a significant history. Born in Crowle, he went to Emmanuel College in Cambridge as a sizar and had been in trouble at St Andrew's there for acting as curate 'not being licensed and seldom wering the surplesse'. He moved to Ipswich and married the daughter of the town's radical puritan preacher, Samuel Ward.

In the atmosphere of 1635 Ward was a high-profile target for the Laudians because of his preaching against the *Book of Sports* and other Laudian policies. He was banned from preaching and imprisoned. The bishop's commissioners were met with riotous scenes when they visited. Amidst all this Ashburne briefly held the living at his father in law's erstwhile church. Ward is very important for his high reputation and also his influence on the town, many of whose residents went to America around 1634.

He fled from Ipswich during the visitation of 1636. He then moved to Glentworth in September 1636, presented to the living by Wray, no doubt because of this reputation, before moving back to a Suffolk living in the safer days of 1646. Along the way he sired a batch of future clerics; a relative was probably Solomon whose gravestone at Crowle later attracted John Wesley's attention.[34] John Ashburne supplemented his income in Suffolk by taking in paying medical patients, one of whom was his own brother-in-law who suffered from mental illness and who murdered him with a pitchfork in 1661. Some see him as a father of the asylum system, though perhaps an unfortunate one. By that stage, Ashburne seems to have lost his radicalism and had joined in prosecuting the pastor of a Congregational church in Bury. Indeed, some pamphlets published after his death drew attention to the strange coincidence of him being murdered in the midst of his case against the pastor, Mr Taylor of Bury.

---

34   Cliffe (1984), p.184

The numbers cited for 'gadding' in Lincolnshire doubled between 1635 and 1637[35] partly as attempts at stamping it out increased; nonetheless, Hajzyk was able to list 16 Lincolnshire churches known for attracting 'gadders' which included puritan centres of Boston, Ingoldsby and Ashby-cum-Fenby. We can add Stainby near Colsterworth, where Francis Nabbs was Rector, which attracted puritans from Buckminster in Leicestershire where Sir Edward Hartopp was the lord of the manor – and another who supported Parliament in the struggle.[36]

Plainly, conventicles continued to survive, though perilously. Robert Stennet was holding one in his house at Bolingbroke in 1636 and another was discovered at Great Limber in 1638. Nonetheless, and despite those who left for America, most puritans stayed within the Church of England until 1640; indeed, they 'still hoped to colonize' it from within.[37]

Charles I was already unpopular in parts of Lincolnshire such as Axholme and Fenland due to his support for drainage schemes that adversely affected the poorer classes. We should note, though, that puritan gentry had often been enthusiastic supports of enclosure which was just as unpopular. However, in 1635 Charles, without the permission of Parliament, introduced an extra tax called 'Ship Money' which was demanded annually. This had the effect of consolidating political opposition among the gentry, and especially those who had puritan views. The seeming tolerance of Catholics increased tension and in 1634 there were even rumours that Sir Robert Tyrwhitt IV would invade Hull.[38]

Laudian forces were strengthened by the election of John Farmery, the diocesan chancellor, as a Lincoln MP in 1640 with the support of the Earl of Rutland – a Catholic sympathiser; however, the city also elected Thomas Grantham of Goltho, son of Sir Thomas, a solid Parliamentarian. But the county also elected Sir Edward Hussey, puritan gentry like Sir John Wray, Sir Edward Ayscough and others secured seats too. They were to bring godly religion very heavily into national politics.

Let us consider some of the key puritan gentry at this pivotal time. One ally of Bishop Williams was Sir John Wray (c1586-1655). His father was Sir William Wray and Isabel Wray was his aunt. Sir John, whose seat was at Wharton near Blyton, was described by Bernard as 'of more than ordinarie zeale for holiness and religion'. Although his family already had a strong Protestant element, the family history credits European travel for developing this in him; 'whither he travelled I know not, but he returned with a strong hatred of Papists and a love of hearing his own voice'. He supported more puritan clergy in the family tradition through patronage, including Thomas Coleman who held the living at Blyton from 1623 until 1646,[39] and was imprisoned for eight months for his opposition to the King over the 'forced loan' to Charles I in 1627 even though his father in law offered to pay it for him. He was released in 1628 and then re-elected as MP for Lincolnshire but continued to criticise the King and the influence of the Duke of Buckingham. In 1630 he

35 Hajzyk (1981), p.108
36 Cliffe (1984), p.161
37 Holmes (1980), p.44
38 Hajzyk (1981), p,409
39 Coleman was forced to leave in 1642 due to 'persecution' by royalists and moved to London where he was vocal in condemning idle cathedral staff and church prelates. 'A fretting gangrene, a spreading leprosy, an insupportable tyranny,' he called them. He died in 1647, leaving a number of puritan writings one of which was dedicated to Sir John Wray and Sir Edward Ayscough.

sided with the Axholme commoners against the King's drainage works. In Parliament, he was a known critic of Ship Money. When re-elected in 1640, he continued his opposition to the King in both the 'short' and 'long' Parliaments in 1640 with a record of denouncing Laud's reforms of the Church of England, demanding proper reformation and an end to idolatry, and opposition to the King's use of the Ship Money tax. Not only did he refuse to pay his share in 1636, he caused problems for the lieutenant of the county.[40] Wray wanted to restrict the power of the bishops but at times came close to supporting their abolition, as in 1641. He was active in organising Lincolnshire against the King but retired from politics in 1646, being buried at Glentworth in 1655. Holmes calls him the 'most interesting' and 'most vocal' of the followers of Pym's policies.[41]

A Note on the Ayscough family:

One of the challenges with reading an unfolding history such as this one is the overlapping of names. In the case of the Ayscough family, every generation had an 'Edward' and sometimes more than one…..Thus we have:
- Edward Ayscough, the Tudor courtier, who died in 1558. He had a son and a nephew also called Edward.
- Sir Edward Ayscough (1538-1612), son of Sir Francis and nephew to Edward
- Edward Ayscough (1589-1646), who was a lawyer, briefly MP for Stamford and associated with Bishop Williams
- Sir Edward Ayscough (1596-1654), knighted in 1613, the most famous puritan of the family
- Sir Edward Ayscough (1618-1668), who was an MP in 1659

But the Nuthall branch of the family also produced an Edward who was an MP in 1640-1.

Another of the sons of Sir William Wray was Sir Christopher (c1601-1646) who inherited the family estate at Ashby-cum-Fenby, near Grimsby, and also Barlings. He was the half-brother of Sir John by their father's second wife, Frances Wray II, and future father-in-law of Sir Henry Vane. He was prominent as MP for Grimsby from 1628 and gradually became an opponent of the King, for example helping defend the commoners of Axholme against the draining of the Carrs in 1630 – which would see the land handed over to Charles I. As a member of a family who could not be expected to side with the direction being taken by Archbishop Laud, Wray opposed Ship Money in 1636 and was re-elected at Great Grimsby in 1640 – alongside Sir Gervase Holles who was a Royalist. Sir Christopher's involvement in the Civil War was inglorious, being on the losing side at Ancaster Heath in April 1643. He had sided with Presbyterianism before his death in 1646. Wray's daughter Frances, who was 'very godly and virtuous….very desirable in all respects,'[42] married Sir Henry Vane in 1640.

As an aside, Sir Christopher's son William, Vane's brother-in-law, apparently led a tempestuous youth and 'little minded anything except drinking and folly'. His political

---

40 Holmes (1980), p.139
41 Holmes (1980), p.143
42 Ludlow, quoted in R E Myers, ODNB, *Sir Henry Vane*

career included being elected for Grimsby when actually still a legal minor. However, Gervase Holles identified him as a Presbyterian although by 1660 he had moved to the Royalist side and was knighted.

Sir William Armyne (1593-1651), MP for Boston, Grantham and Lincolnshire at various times from 1621 to 1651, was another opponent of the King who refused to pay the additional sums, opposed drainage and patronised puritan ministers.[43] He spent three months in the Fleet Prison in 1627-8 for refusing to pay the forced loan. Armyne was the son of Sir William Armyne of Osgodby, who had been the patron of Hugh Tuke, the puritan minister of Silk Willoughby, who acted as tutor to the Armyne boys including Eure before they were sent off to Oakham. Armyne's second wife was Mary (-1676), who was one of the Talbot family, and remained a significant patron of puritans unto the end of her life. She helped to equip her husband with the right environment, choosing servants for their 'holiness'.[44] Seth Wood wrote that Armyne kept his body 'as a Temple of the Holy Ghost' and 'he could not endure any vice should be master over him'.[45]

The next William Armyne seems to have been a more rebellious youth before repenting in advance of his death in 1658; Christopher Shute preached at the funeral and dedicated his sermon in print to another brother, Michael, who had also died.

Sir Anthony Irby, the MP for Boston in 1640, was another Lincolnshire leader trained at Emmanuel College – but he was also Sir John Wray's brother-in-law and led the local opposition to Ship Money despite becoming Sheriff in 1637. J T Cliffe considers his family likely to have been members of Cotton's covenanted inner congregation at Boston and notes that he employed a series of puritan household chaplains.[46]

To this group we can add Sir Edward Ayscough of South Kelsey, elected for Lincolnshire in 1640, and his brother-in-law Thomas Hatcher – another Emmanuel man – who sat for Grantham and Stamford in 1640. Sir Thomas Grantham of Goltho, Ayscough's friend, was also a noted puritan imprisoned and exiled over the forced loan but died in 1630. His son Thomas Grantham was elected for Lincoln in 1640 – described by Lucy Hutchinson as 'a fine gentleman bred beyond the seas according to the best education of those times'. The elder Grantham also forms a useful connection with Nottinghamshire as he provided a home in Lincoln in the 1620s for the young John Hutchinson who was attending school with the puritan cleric John Clarke in the city.

This underlines the lack of any similar puritan class guiding political policy and religious reality in Nottinghamshire. No figures of the status of Sir John Markham or Sir John Hercy existed, though there was a coming generation of Hutchinson, Whalley, Thornhagh and Ireton. There were also fewer Parliamentary seats in the county. In 1628 and 1640 Nottingham elected Sir Charles Cavendish, a Royalist, and only in the second election of 1640 did it bring in as second member a Parliamentarian, Gilbert Millington. The pocket borough of East Retford also elected Royalists until 1646, when Sir Francis Thornhagh

---

43   Holmes (1980), p.140

44   J T Cliffe, *The Puritan Gentry*, London, 1984, p.33

45   Cliffe (1984), p.45. Wood was vicar of Lenton (Lincs) having been presented by Armyne in 1639 and appointed vicar of Christ Church in London in 1654.

46   Cliffe (1984), p.94

of Fenton was chosen. Of the county MPs, Sir Thomas Hutchinson was the father of a Parliamentarian leader in the region but was not one himself.

Relations between gentry and clergy were not always secure. William Houlden at Whaplode, vicar until 1646 when he moved to Great Casterton, had a feud with his patron, William Welby, who complained that he did not say the *Book of Common Prayer* services distinctly or reverently. In 1638, Welby brought proceedings for Houlden not reading prayers on weekdays. Houlden's tactic was to interfere with the arrangement of pews and to sit his own wife in Welby's pew.[47] Welby had been deputy lieutenant of the county charged with arresting those who did not pay the forced loan, a task which he tried to avoid.[48]

In 1640 Bishop Williams was still in the Tower although he did consider, it would seem, withdrawing the troublesome *Holy Table*.[49] He was also in correspondence with a rebellious MP, John Hampden, which did nothing for his relations with Charles I. Williams' continued imprisonment became an issue with the House of Lords, of which he was a member, and Charles agreed to release him in November as the political climate changed. His first act was to move the table at St Margaret's Westminster.

Resentment against Charles I had increased in 1639 as he sought men and money to fight the Scots. As things went from bad to worse, he was forced to call Parliament in April 1640 and then, when it refused to play his game, tried to govern without it. New rules from Archbishop Laud made things worse and when Parliament was recalled in November 1640 Lincolnshire sent many opponents. Sir John Wray moved quickly from issues of money to ones of faith, demanding 'a thorough reformation'. However, Wray was not yet opposed to bishops per se; he saw men such as Cranmer and Ridley as 'rich jewels' but complained the office had been abused by 'evil men'.[50] The new committee on elections and privileges included two Wrays, Irby, Ayscough and Grantham – a good roll call of Lincolnshire puritan gentry. With Sir William Armyne was additionally elected for Grantham in 1641, Hill noted, 'Here were the puritan families who had appeared a generation earlier, only the St Pauls (whose line had died out) being missing'.[51] In the middle of this ferment, in May 1640, Sir Henry Vane married Frances Wray, daughter of Sir Christopher Wray aligning two of the most radical families. Vane, as we shall see, then settled in Lincolnshire and the release of Williams was one of the new Parliament's first demands.

Williams, in 1640-1, was again playing a prominent national role trying to resolve religious issues being appointed to a Lords committee with the support of Lord Saye and Sele. He included Robert Sanderson, more on the Laudian wing, in the discussions. With Laud sent to the Tower instead, Williams continued to support Charles in maintaining bishops – a sticking point with the Presbyterians. When he became Archbishop of York at the end of 1641, at Charles' decision, he found himself out of line with the times and the Commons

47   Judith Maltby, *Prayer Book and People in Elizabethan and Early Stuart England*, p.70
48   Thomas Welby was Mayor of Boston in 1643 so this dispute may not be a simple case of wings of the Church disagreeing.
49   ODNB, 14 June 2014
50   Holmes (1980), p.144
51   Hill (1956), p.146

men, under Pym, put him back in the Tower for a few months. Only in June 1642 did he make it to York before going to Wales where he fortified Conwy Castle. Thus, he passed out of our region's history and died in 1650. It would be easy to condemn such an openly political churchman, and one who courted favour, wealth and prestige; yet he was also 'notably steady in his Calvinist faith'[52] and tolerant of men who he saw as good Christian ministers.

Meanwhile, the Long Parliament continued. Sir John Wray presented the Lincolnshire petition against Ship Money and Sir Anthony Irby presented Boston's own. In late 1640 the 'Root and Branch' Petition was presented to Parliament, complaining of the abuses by bishops; it was largely the work of Sir Henry Vane.[53] Although it had far from universal support – Thomas Grantham was not a supporter for example – the position of the bishops was far from comfortable. The petition was supported by one from Lincolnshire drawn up by Sir Edward Ayscough and a Nottinghamshire petition of around 1500 signatures, but a counter-petition gathered 5,000. The Nottinghamshire petition, in which Henry Ireton was active, complained of restrictions being placed on preaching and added a detailed complaint about 'lofts' being pulled down in 'great congregations' to restrict access – perhaps a comment on one of the Nottingham churches. Lucy Hutchinson wrote that Ireton, 'a man of good learning, great understanding, and other abilities, he was the chief promoter of the parliament's interest in the county'.

In these debates Sir John Wray played a leading role with gradually hardening attitudes. In November 1640 he spoke against the 'exorbitant height' to which 'Popery is grown' and the need to 'lay the axe to the root' against 'the long and deep fangs of superstition'. Wray firmly believed at the start of the Long Parliament that it was called to fulfil God's purposes – 'And for what ends come wee hither if not to propagate and advance his Glory and Gospel?' 'God is angry with our national lukewarm temper,' he warned, but he hoped fortunes would be restored by 'pulling Dagon from the altar and whipping the buyers and sellers out of the temple,' but he was initially reluctant to join those who wished to do away with bishops altogether until later in 1641.[54] In December 1640 he joined several other puritan MPs on a committee for investigating the decay of preaching and 'scandalous' ministers. In April 1641 Sir Thomas Hutchinson of Owthorpe in Nottinghamshire sponsored a bill calling for the abolition of bishops and by May 1641 Sir John Wray was calling on the bishops to justify their existence on the basis of Scripture or be 'utterly abolished' and the same year Richard Bernard published his own attack on bishops. On 5 May 1641 he caused a panic in Parliament when he thought he smelt gunpowder; Wray was 'the most vocal of the Lincolnshire representatives'.[55] He presented a petition from his Lincolnshire constituents against bishops in November 1641 – 'this bill is as a vomit to them,' he declared[56]– supported by his protegé, Rev Thomas Coleman, rector of Blyton, who was soon to leave for London himself. Coleman was said to 'have viewed with equal repugnance both prelacy and Presbyterianism'.[57] With opinions both divided and plentiful complained of 'a world of base and unworthy pamphlets…that, like the frogs of

52   ODNB, 14 June 2014
53   Cliffe (1984), p.228
54   Holmes (1980), p.144, Cliffe p.222 – he 'desired rather their reformation than their ruin'.
55   Holmes (1980), p.143
56   BL Harley Ms, 477, fol. 108 (ODNB).
57   Cliffe (1984), p.184

Egypt, croak in every corner of the land'.[58] In December, though, Sir Robert Sutton of Averham tried to present a petition from Nottinghamshire in favour of them; this took the tactic of saying that ancient systems should not be abolished due to the 'errors and abuses' by individuals.

By the end of the month Laud had been arrested and put in the Tower – he was tried in 1644 and executed in 1645. Boston Stump has a famous window depicting Laud with an axe.

During 1641 John Pym's leadership of the House of Commons became increasingly radical and Gervase Holles made a speech critical of Pym's policy regarding the Scots although his fellow Grimsby MP, Sir Christopher Wray remained with Pym; Holles was expelled from the Commons. Sir Edward Ayscough, Sir Anthony Irby and Sir William Armyne remained on the side of the religious radicals.

During the second half of 1641 Laud's reforms were put in reverse by a Parliamentary order to sweep away idolatry and he was in custody (although not executed until 1645) but positive reforms to please the puritans were slow to come – even the idolatry order met with little support although in Nottinghamshire Sir Thomas Hutchinson tried to enforce it.[59] The hated *Book of Sports* was suppressed; its supporter John Pocklington was deprived of his living and had two of his own works burnt in retribution by the public hangman. An order for the return of altars or tables to a position in the chancel was issued. Diocesan court official Edward Lake, who had replaced Mottershed in Nottinghamshire was locked out of St Peter's Nottingham that year by its puritan parishioners;[60] Parliament had abolished the coercive powers of bishops, so they saw no reason to comply. At Worksop, the new altar rail was pulled out after only four years in place. There was a vacuum of spiritual power which Sanderson, the Boothby Pagnell clergyman, complained was filled up with pamphlets of new doctrines and heresy.[61] At Deeping St James Rev Christopher Smith was sent to gaol in 1641 for 'scandalous words' and a lecturer appointed in his place, who then also gained the revenues from Market Deeping during the civil war period.[62] A Parliamentary Committee was set up to unseat other ministers who they found to be on the wrong side, a process which accelerated in Lincolnshire from January 1644.

---

58 Holmes (1980), p152, from *Works of Sanderson*, vol II, p.155.
59 Cliffe (1988), p.3
60 S B Jennings, *When Women Preach and Cobblers Pray*,
61 Holmes (1980), p.194
62 Plumb (PhD), p.114

CHAPTER SIXTEEN

The Quakers

Several key Christian groups can claim to have had their origins in Nottinghamshire, but few can say that they actually began in the county. Though the founder of the Quakers, George Fox, is usually described as being from Leicestershire he began the new movement in Mansfield and his first followers were around that town. The Quakers were radical and demonstrative in their first decades, being quite prepared to shake up the religious orders.

Chronology:
1647: Conversion of George Fox at Mansfield
1649: Fox imprisoned in Nottingham
1651: Riots at Epworth
1655: Glentworth contest with Manifestarians
1656: Death of James Parnell at Colchester
1659-60: Executions of Quakers in Massachuetts
1660: Tolerance of Quakers in England under threat again
1661: Elizabeth Hooton travels to New England
1662: Simon Bradstreet confronted by Fox
1672: Death of Hooton

Fox was born at Drayton in the Clay in Leicestershire in July 1624, with a father who was a weaver and also known as 'Righteous Christer' due to his faithfulness[1] – 'there was a seed of God in him'. By 1643 Fox was desiring more from life, having been disappointed for example by drinking games in which people he had thought faithful encouraged him to take part. He went to London but was often downhearted until returning to Leicestershire where he spent much time with the priest of Drayton, Nathaniel Stephens, who later turned against him.

Fox travelled much, learning to turn away from 'established' ministers and to seek those with 'tender' souls. A word from the Lord told him that having been trained at Oxford or Cambridge was not enough to make a man a true priest, so he began to look to the 'dissenting people' from about 1646. In Nottinghamshire in 1647[2] he met Elizabeth Hooton: 'I met with a tender people, and a very tender woman whose name was Elizabeth Hooton…and with these I had some meetings and discourses'. Hooton, herself clearly on a journey, then seems to have become an important fellow traveller with Fox. By this stage he was living as a bootmaker and he had settled in Chesterfield Road, Mansfield, at a site that is now – ironically – a Catholic church. Great things happened at the meetings

1   George Fox, *Journal*, London, 1694, volume 1, p.49
2   *Journal*, vol. 1, p.54 – but we cannot be sure how precisely Fox has sequenced events.

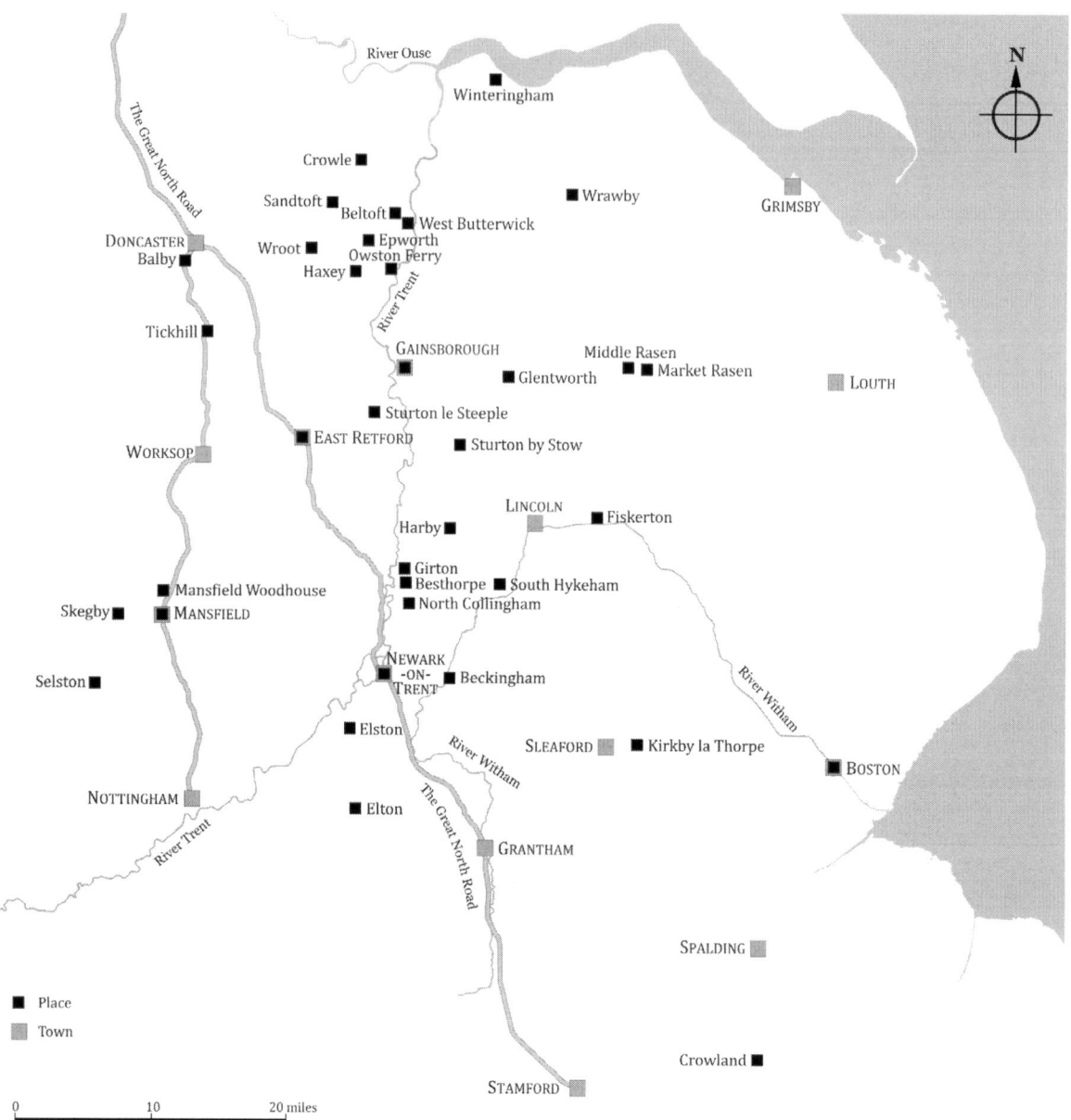

Place ■

Town ▨

0   10   20 miles

at Hooton's house:

> '…the Lord by his powers wrought many miracles to the astonishing of the world and confirming people of the truth which she there received about 1646'.[3]

The turning point in Fox's life, as he later recalled, came sometime in 1647 when he as he was 'walking by the steeple house side, in the town of Mansfield, the Lord said unto me, 'That which people trample upon must be thy food'. And as the Lord spoke He opened it to me, that people and professors trampled upon the life, even the life of Christ……There is one, even Jesus Christ, that can speak to thy Condition'.[4]

From then on Fox proclaimed the present accessibility of God who 'was now come to Teach his People himself'.[5] There was no need to rely on human teachers, Fox preached, for even the scriptures were less authoritative than one's inward guide, 'every man was enlightened by the divine light of Christ'. He relied on the Bible, which he knew well and whose words were prominent in his teaching and writing, but his stress on the primacy of the Spirit inevitably encouraged individualism that resulted in his diverse followers.[6] Fox offended puritan minds by suggesting that the Spirit might confer additional revelation over and above that contained in the Bible.

Fox rejected the concept of the Trinity as he could not find it in the Bible. He argued that God and the Holy Spirit dwelt in the hearts and minds of believers, all having the chance to accept or reject. He also attacked the organised Church on issues such as tithes, making himself very unpopular. His idea that the spirit of God was given to *every* man 'to profit withal' opened him to charges of antinomianism, of being incapable of sin.

At Broughton in Leicestershire great debates had sprung up among the Baptists and Fox went to take part. For the first time he began to experience great power, and his words opened up truths for many.[7] People began to flock to hear Fox preach and a dying man, Brown, prophesied great things of him from his deathbed. 'I was very much altered in countenance and person, as if my body had been new moulded or changed. While I was in that condition, I had a sense and discerning given me by the Lord through which I saw plainly, that when many people talked of God and Christ etc, the serpent spoke in them….'[8] The depression that he had felt began to lift, and be replaced by tears of joy.

Fox had friends in Nottinghamshire and while sitting in the home of one of these friends he had a powerful picture of the earth being shaken, which he took to mean men's hearts. At Mansfield in 1648 in a meeting of 'professors and people…..the Lord's power was so great that the house seemed to be shaken'. Yet when another man got up to pray, a 'deadness like a veil' came down on the meeting'. The first 'congregation' seems to have met at the house of Elizabeth Hooton in Skegby. This became the first Quaker meeting house and burials even took place there from 1673; in 1800 it was sold to fund a new

3   Manners, p.6, quoting from Oliver Hooton's account which seems to have brought the date forward a year or so.

4   Journal, 1694, p.8

5   Journal, vol 1, p.73

6   H L Ingle, *George Fox*, in *Oxford Dictionary of National Biography*, online edition, accessed 1/1/2014.

7   Journal, volume 1, p.60

8   Journal, volume 1, p.61

meeting house but survives to this day, presumably the oldest Quaker meeting place in the World.

In 1648 Fox was visiting the Vale of Belvoir where he met some people 'who had a notion that there was no God but that all things came by Nature'. Fox, of course, got into a debate with them, which ended when some of them 'confessed that there is a living God'.[9] Returning to central Nottinghamshire, he found some 'shattered Baptists' who joined him whilst the Lord's power was 'wonderfully manifest' in Mansfield and nearby towns; it tends to be assumed that this is the Hooton group. We don't always know who the 'shattered' were, but Thomas Wressle of Winteringham became a Baptist and then a Quaker by 1655, after which he settled at Butterwick.[10]

Fox describes several instances of taking direct action including when he went an addressed a powerful and wicked man, who was convicted of his sinfulness:

> At a certain time [in 1648], when I was at Mansfield, there was a sitting of the justices about the hiring of servants; and it was upon me from the Lord to go and speak to the justices, that they should not oppress the servants in their wages. So I walked towards the inn where they sat; but finding a company of fiddlers there, I did not go in, but thought to come in the morning, when I might have a more serious opportunity to discourse with them.

> But when I came in the morning, they were gone, and I was struck even blind, that I could not see. I inquired of the innkeeper where the justices were to sit that day; and he told me, at a town eight miles off. My sight began to come to me again; and I went and ran thitherward as fast as I could. When I was come to the house where they were, and many servants with them, I exhorted the justices not to oppress the servants in their wages, but to do that which was right and just to them; and I exhorted the servants to do their duties, and serve honestly. They all received my exhortation kindly; for I was moved of the Lord therein.

> Moreover, I was moved to go to several courts and steeple-houses at Mansfield, and other places, to warn them to leave off oppression and oaths, and to turn from deceit to the Lord, and to do justly. Particularly at Mansfield, after I had been at a court there, I was moved to go and speak to one of the most wicked men in the country, one who was a common drunkard, a noted whore-master, and a rhyme-maker; and I reproved him in the dread of the mighty God, for his evil courses.

> When I had done speaking, and left him, he came after me, and told me that he was so smitten when I spoke to him, that he had scarcely any strength left in him. So this man was convinced, and turned from his wickedness, and remained an honest, sober man, to the astonishment of the people who had known him before.[11]

---

9   George Fox, *Journal of George Fox*, London, 1852, p.84
10 Lloyd, p.228
11 George Fox, *Journal*, volume 1, chapter 2,

In 1649 Fox interrupted a church service in Nottingham, arguing for the power of the Holy Spirit rather than a reliance on Scripture alone.[12] He denounced the priest as 'a great lump of earth stood in his pulpit above'. He was put in 'a nasty stinking prison, the smell whereof got so into my nose and throat, that it very much annoyed me'.[13] Whilst he was there he was visited by a woman, with two friends, who had been possessed for 22 years and had resisted all efforts to exorcise the demons despite prayer and fasting. Fox was rescued from prison by none other than the sheriff, John Reckless, and taken to lodge at his house where his wife said, 'Salvation is come to our house'. For 29 years their house was used for Quaker meetings before the family emigrated to America; Recklesstown, New Jersey, was named after Joseph Reckless[14] though it is now called Chesterfield due to 'public scorn'.

At Mansfield Woodhouse in 1649 Fox encountered a woman with a tormenting spirit and was able to bring healing to her. This may have been the same woman he met at Nottingham, and she was brought to Hooton's house; the first effort to exorcise her seems to have been unsuccessful, but the second was, and Fox clearly saw that this would be a sign to the world that they were not 'false prophets, deceivers or witches.[15]' However, when he went to the church to admonish its priest and congregation he met with 'an unkind reception';[16] they beat him with sticks and Bibles. Then they put him into the stocks and eventually drove him out of town. At Derby he fared worse, being in prison for almost a year in 1650-1 on a charge of blasphemy, but even there he was visited by people such as the soldier who God had told to visit the gaol. It was about this time when the term 'Quaker' started to be used.

In 1651 he travelled into Derbyshire, back to Mansfield and then around Doncaster and at Balby where Richard Farnworth, who was to become an eminent preacher in his own right, was 'convinced'. One of the meeting places seems to have been at the house of Lieutenant Roper at Synderhill Green. Another who joined was Thomas Kilham of a family to become notable in the annals of Methodism as well as Quakerism. Wakefield, Selby and Beverley were also on the itinerary. Fox's words at the end of the service at Beverley created great impact – and it was told to him later that some had thought an angel had come to speak with them. His visit to Gainsborough that year 'caused an uproar in the town'.[17] Riots at Epworth in 1651 were blamed on the Quakers[18] although more closely linked to the Levellers.

---

12   Watts (1986), p.191

13   Journal, volume 1, pps 76-7

14   J Fox, 2002, p.24

15   Manners, p.6

16   Joseph Besse, *Collection of the Sufferings of the People called Quakers*, 1753, p.43

17   S Davies, *Quakerism in Lincolnshire*, Lincoln, 1989, p.1

18   Davies, p.6. There was much unhappiness in Axholme about the draining of the Carrs, which was seen as taking common land away from the people in order to give it to wealthy landowners and the King from about 1626. Many of the Dutch workmen are reputed to have 'disappeared'.

The Axholme Riots

When George Fox arrived in Axholme he entered an area that was a highly disturbed region at this time. The drainage schemes had produced a bitter feeling of resentment whilst Civil War had given opportunity for some of this to be expressed. Charles I had supported the drainage and effective takeover of common land, work which was led by 'Dutch' engineers and often manned by Dutch or French-speaking Huguenot refugees (sometimes called Walloons) from the low countries of northern Europe – some also settled at Crowland in the south. These gathered at Sandtoft where they built their own village and church, and also at Wroot, with others of similar origin who settled on the new lands.

Local opinion saw drainage scheme as a way of robbing commoners of their land for private profit. There had been a riot at Haxey in 1629. A court case against the drainage scheme had been lost in 1636 and trouble broke out in 1642-3 during the time of Civil War conflict. Problems were bad enough by November 1645 for the French minister at Sandtoft to petition the House of Lords on behalf of the settlers, complaining that ditches had been filled in and 'in spoyling of the Church, in breaking all the seats, and burning them; breaking all the glasse windows, pulling down the lead of the Church and steeple'.

Further riots at Haxey in 1647 led by Owston solicitor Daniel Noddel, a former officer in the Parliamentary army, led to him and two justices being summoned to the House of Lords. There was another court failure in 1650[19] prompting riots when fences were smashed and crops at Sandtoft destroyed. Michael Monckton, a Justice and future Quaker of Beltoft, was involved in this. Leaders included George Stovin, both a dissenter and a Leveller, supported for around a year from autumn 1650 by the famous Lt-Colonel John Lilburne[20] and Major John Wildman, a former Leveller and speculator in confiscated land.[21] Sandtoft itself was devastated in the rioting – 82 houses were destroyed with mills and barns burnt including over 3000 acres of crops. Lilburne probably took over the Huguenot minister's damaged house at this time, repairing it so his men could live there.

There was an infamous attack on the church at Sandtoft on 19 October 1651, when Noddel and Lilburne prevented the Huguenots from entering their own church;[22] Lilburne spoke to the minister in Latin saying 'this is our common. You shall come here noe more unless you be stronger than us'.[23] Lilburne went in with his own armed men and preached there. It was first defaced by burying carrion under the communion table, then stripped of lead and furniture, after which the rebels proceeded to destroy Sandtoft itself.

---

19 G S de Krey, *Following the Levellers vol* 2, London, 2018, p.29
20 W B Stonehouse, History and Topography of the Isle of Axholme, London, 1839, p.97
21 Lilburne and Wildman were both supporters of religious tolerance by the 1640s.
22 C Holmes in A Fletcher and J Stevenson, *Order and Disorder in Early Modern England*, p.160
23 Michael Braddick, *The Common Freedom of the People: John Lilburne and the English Revolution*, Oxford, 2018, p.213-4

Colonel Lilburne then used the church for stables and repaired the French minister's house sufficiently to keep his servants in it.[24] In 1652 the Dutch church at Sandtoft was burnt down and they left for Thorney, near Peterborough.[25] Stovin died in Lincoln Castle in 1652, imprisoned for opposition to the Church of England, and his son at least also became a Quaker. Lilburne wrote a petition to Parliament for the Axholme people but the vote went against it; it has often been assumed that Samuel Wesley's rectory was burnt down for his association with the appropriation of this land.

News of these riots was not well received in London, but they were defended by men with local knowledge like John Spittlehouse, another religious radical from Gainsborough. They were, he wrote in 1653, the result of 'bloody, barbarous, and inhumane massacres and tyrannies exercised upon us'.

Although Lilburne was not a Lincolnshire man, he had significant influence in the area. Born in 1614 he had been a radical puritan in his younger days but after imprisonment and beatings soon became a separatist and a soldier for Parliament. In 1644 he captured Tickhill Castle from the Royalists and was present at the siege of Newark which may explain his interest in Axholme. He soon fell out with Parliament and became famous as 'Freeborn John,' leader of the Levellers, though his involvement at Epworth may also have been speculative. One of the most turbulent characters of the period, he became a Quaker in 1656.

In Epworth, Fox tapped into an area that was already radical in politics and religion. After Fox's tour of Lincolnshire in 1652, Richard Farnworth led meetings at Axholme where 'much fier kindled' and he wrote to Fox about events at Haxey which 'shaketh kingdoms and turns the world upside down'.[26] Both Baptists and Quakers were to be strong here in the later 1600s and in North Axholme at Crowle. We should also note that there was a branch of the Parnel family at Haxey who became Quakers and who probably have some connection with the famous James Parnell of East Retford.

The infighting and disputing between different religious groups led some to want to reject all organised religion. These were sometimes called 'Seekers' who 'believed in an invisible church made up of scattered believers, as they waited for someone with apostolic authority who would restore the primitive church of apostolic times'.[27] The group of Seekers at Balby, near Doncaster, became one of the first significant groups of Quakers in 1652.[28] Margaret Kilham (Killam) from there became a well-known travelling Quaker

---

24   W B Monkhouse, *History and Topography of the Isle of Axholme*, p.98-9. The font from this church was collected by another Stovin and taken to his garden at Crowle, where Wesley later preached. Whilst writing this book, the author was able to locate this font in a hedge in the middle of a building project and ensure that the landowner recognised its significance.

25   Kershaw (1995), p.27. W B Stonehouse, *History and Topography of the Isle of Axholme*, p.239, says the 'Participants' Church' was destroyed by solicitor Daniel Noddell and 400 others.

26   Holmes (1980), p.205

27   Jane Shaw, *Miracles in Enlightenment England*, Yale, 2006, p.52

28   Shaw, p.52

preacher from about 1653.[29]

For details of Fox's ministry, we have to rely very much on his own written record. In 1652 Fox returned to Balby and north Lincolnshire, preaching at 'steeple houses' either side of the Trent. At Gainsborough one of the Friends had been preaching in the marketplace and the town was in 'uproar'; Fox went into a friend's house, but a crowd rushed in with him, including one man who accused Fox of preaching that he was himself the Messiah. Fox accused the man of being a Judas, but won over the hearts of the crowd, so his accuser went away cowed; soon after though the man hung himself and, after his burial, a stake was driven through his grave.[30] Fox was badly beaten again at Warmsworth in Yorkshire, then returned via Balby to Doncaster where he was again stoned and beaten – being rescued by an inn-keeper, who was also injured. On his way back to Balby he was waylaid and again stoned.

At Tickhill in 1652 Fox noted a 'mighty brokeness' amongst the people in his meeting, but then went to the parish church. There the clerk hit him with the Bible, so that his face bled. He was thrown over a hedge and dragged through the street. Fox got back to the meeting of his Friends, where the Tickhill priest soon arrived with his own supporters and denounced them as 'Quakers'. But when Fox began to preach, so too the priest began to shake and someone called out, 'Look how the priest trembles and shakes, he is turned a Quaker also'. Further trouble was averted at Balby as magistrates began to act to calm the attacks, but Fox refused to press charges. Fox then travelled widely throughout the north, gaining much support in Cumberland but enduring a further prison spell in Carlisle.

Tickhill was the home of Richard Farnworth who, at the age of 16, had experienced his own conversion and began a journey of rejection of infant baptism, a belief in attaining spiritual perfection in this life, and constant prayer – plus the loss of his job. Fox's arrival at Balby in 1651 had attracted Farnworth's attention and, barely into his twenties, he became a preacher of Quakerism. He became an advocate of the laying on of hands to heal the sick, which he reputedly did in 1651, later writing about this in *Antichrist's Man of War* (1655).[31]

The spread of the word became easier under the Protectorate from 1653, with some growth in numbers at Lincoln although disturbing church services still attracted official and unofficial abuse. Farnworth became a frequent preacher in Lincolnshire and Nottinghamshire, writing exhaustively about such issues as 'new songs of the Spirit'. He was especially noted for his impact at and around Haxey in 1652-3 when he engaged with the local Baptists. In 1653 he preached for half a week at Sturton-le-Steeple[32] and then for three nights at Mansfield before going on to Elizabeth Hooton's house. The Gospel, he said, should be taught by divine revelation not human wisdom. At Mansfield, he found the town's minister John Firth was boarded at the house of a family who had become Quakers – and the poor man promptly became sport for Farnworth and his associates. They had a three-hour debate at which 'all made bold to take a bout with him'. Despite Firth's apparent defeat in this unequal battle, others in the town petitioned Cromwell, in

29 Manners, p13
30 *Journals*, volume 1, p.115
31 In R L Greaves, *Richard Farnworth*, ODNB, online, accessed 3 July 2014
32 Perhaps this was the origin of the group that bought a site for a meeting house at South Leverton in 1730.

July 1654, to have his position as minister made permanent as the Quakers 'hath poisoned the spirits of very many with that erroneous spirit of Quaking, whereby the interests of Satan hath increased'.[33]

In 1654 Fox faced opposition from Rice (or Rhys) Davies/Jones of Nottingham, a Baptist turned Ranter who had formed a group at Castle Yard in 1650,[34] who circulated leaflets in Mansfield and around; when George Whitehead visited this group in 1657 he found them 'dead'. Fox came back to Balby and gathered some Friends there for a mission trip into Lincolnshire. There was some opposition from the Sheriff of Lincoln, Richard Craven; 'at length the Lord's power struck him….he was convinced of the truth, and received the word of life'. Craven became an adherent[35] and he later accompanied Fox into Derbyshire on several journeys. On the way they held a major meeting at Skegby, where 'the Lord's power went over them and all was quiet. The people were tuned to the Spirit of God, by which many came to receive his power'.[36] Such support was helpful, because some at least of the opposition to the Quakers was caused by the suspicion that they would attract those generally opposed to the form of government.[37] Craven's house in Lincoln was used for meetings. He died in 1670. On the same trip in 1654 Fox's Journal records that Sir Richard Wray, his brother (presumably Sir John), and his sister in law were all 'convinced' although it was only the latter who held fast to the belief.[38] Later comments report that both Sir John and his wife died 'in the faith'. Fox and James Nayler also had meetings with Lady Frances Vane, who was a Wray by birth, and her husband Sir Henry Vane who, as Chair of the Committee of Safety, was tolerant towards the Friends. Fox thought Vane 'vaine and high and proude and conceited' and 'there is a mountaine of earth and imaginations uppe in thee'. Fox visited Vane and his wife at Raby Castle for a long discussion, but disliked his theology which others concluded was influenced by Jacob Böhme.

Fox held a great meeting at Skegby near Mansfield, and 'the Lord's power went over them and all was quiet'. However, at Whetstone in Leicestershire Fox was taken into custody by Colonel Francis Hacker,[39] who sent him to London where he met Oliver Cromwell who set him free. The next year Fox again preached at Whetstone, where Hacker's wife came and was 'convinced'. Nonetheless, Fox endured several months in prison at Launceston in 1656 for preaching.

Fox tells a story of how the power of prayer averted an attack by Lincolnshire ruffians. Then he went in 1656 with Robert Craven and others to Crowland, where he found much heavy drinking which he suggested was the result of the poor practice of the town's priest and clerk; the two of them attacked Fox with the tongs and fire shovel. The reception in Boston was rather better.

In 1657 Fox was back in Nottingham, preaching at the Castle to members of Rice Jones' group. This was not an easy meeting, for Fox was of the view that Rice Jones had led his

33   *Extracts of State Papers Related to Quakers*, 1st series, 2-3. Quoted by T Llewellyn-Davies,
34   P J Cropper, *Sufferings of the Quakers in Nottinghamshire*, Nottingham, 1892, p.xiii
35   Journal, volume 1, p.178
36   Fox, quoted by Manners, p.15
37   Davies, 2002, p.6
38   Fox also records a similar meeting in 1656
39   Hacker was of East Bridgford and Colston Bassett, with a mother who was a Whalley.

group astray. In 1660 he was back travelling through the district for the annual meeting at Balby, held in an orchard and which he said 'thousands' attended. Troops were sent from York to stop the meeting, apparently riding overnight and arriving as Fox was standing on a stool to give his address. Fox managed to persuade the Captain to let them continue for an hour and to leave just a handful of troops, so the Captain went away, and the remaining soldiers allowed the Friends to do more or less as they wished.

Another early supporter was Martin Mason of Lincoln. Mason's house was used for the first Quaker marriage in Lincoln in 1658. He had gained a local reputation as a firebrand, attacking the City's puritan lecturer Edward Reyner during the era of Cromwell, for compromise and being 'a lyer and a blasphemer', and for running off to Norwich during the Civil War. Reyner's offence was to be paid and to address the mayor with titles such as 'right worshipful' which were 'Babylonian'. Yet he was also inspired by social justice, complaining that Reyner preached only 'patience and contentedness'.[40] He attacked the other lecturer George Scortwreth in *A Check to the Loftie Linguist*. He also criticised the Lincoln Baptist leader Jonathan Johnson against whom he published in 1659 *The Boasting Baptist Dismounted and the Beast Disarmed* with which Johnson responded as *The Quaker Quashed and His Quarrel Quelled*.

Soon there were Quaker meetings in Gainsborough, Glentworth, Sturton-by-Stow and Lincoln. John Whitehead (1630-96), a Yorkshire Quaker who had been inspired by the preaching of Farnworth,[41] went into Lincoln Cathedral in 1654 and challenged the preacher which caused a riot and nearly led to his death except soldiers intervened. Whitehead declared that 'it is the Light of the Glorious Gospel that shines in man's hearts and discovers Sin'. Whitehead spent four months in Lincoln Castle but settled near Lincoln, at Fiskerton,[42] to become a pillar of the Quaker community.

The meeting at Glentworth is interesting, due to its links with radical faith a few decades before. Sir John Wray invited various Christian leaders to a meeting at Glentworth, which the preacher Thomas Moore of the Manifestarians attended in May 1655.[43] The Quakers arrived late, so Moore started 'discoursing' first. James Nayler debated with Thomas Moore, but Moore broke it off to eat. Farnworth then challenged them to set out on a journey to preach and to fast for a fortnight on spring water alone, preaching without the use of books! Farnworth's precise challenge was this:

> First, that the chiefest of you grant to go abroad with me, where I shall be led to preach the word for two weeks together.
>
> Secondly, that you and I eat no food, as outward bread and flesh, nor any outward victualling, provided by any man, or creature for that time, nor drink either beer, ale, or wine, nor partake of any other outward thing, except a little spring water; and that neither you nor I look upon any book all that time seen with a visible eye.

---

40 Reyner himself died in 1660 but his son John shared many of his views and was friendly with another religious radical, Gervase Disney. He was ejected from Emmanuel College in 1662 for nonconformity and ended life as a schoolmaster in Nottingham.

41 Not to be confused with the more famous George Whitehead. John came from Holderness where he had had 'secret breathings and longings after God' and that the Spirit had opened 'treasures' to him.

42 Manners, p.13

43 Thomas Moore, *An Antidote against the Spreading Infections of the spirit of Antichrist, abounding in these last Days under many Visors*, 1655, available at: http://www.qhpress.org/texts/nayler/antidote.html

Thirdly, that for two weeks-time we have meetings every day (or every other day), one week for the first amongst those called Manifestarians (and others as the Lord shall please) and I be permitted amongst them to speak the word of the Lord, and each other day he that joins with me herein to speak also; and he shall permitted be, if he dare say and by the Spirit of truth affirm that he hath anything to speak immediately from the mouth of the Lord; he shall I say be then permitted to speak one day as I do another (or part of each) one week amongst those called Manifestarians and others, that the Lord shall lead unto (and no outward help, neither meat, drink nor book, as aforesaid) and another week amongst those that the world scornfully calleth by the nickname of Quakers.

And lastly, that for the two weeks' time he part not from me day nor night, that he receive no more outward help than I do.

Moore replied to the challenge from Bolingbroke in June, repudiating it all, and denying the name 'Manifestarian'. Moore's main accusation was that Nayler brought 'another Gospel' that denied the accepted view of Christ's divinity.

It would seem that the meeting broke up when Wray tried to send the Quakers away, but it is possible they resisted this, and were accused of burglary! Nayler wrote to Moore:

Also consider if thou dealt like a Christian in slandering us with burglary and breaking into the house, when we was sent for many miles to give you a meeting (as far as I know) at your desires, and I had free liberty to come into the house from the owner, with all other friends, nor did we resist his commands in departing (though we were unwilling to leave the work, so much desired by the people). And this can John Wray witness against thee, if he will, however, the thing is true in the sight of God, and we are free from burglary, or breaking his house, but out of envy wouldst thou cast this upon us, as that in thy conscience shall one day witness, though now through subtlety and disobedience thou be seared and blinded, and wouldst blind others also.

To this, Moore replied:

To the next, which at least you imply, that Mr. Wray commanded you to depart: it is like all the rest. You know he invited you all to dinner and told you should be all welcome, though I think you were most of you too scornful to accept it. And the reason he desired us to meet in the public after was only for conveniencey of room because of the multitude of the people, nor did you then say anything against meeting there, only when you perceived it was not like easily to be prevented you spake against breaking up a while for a dinner; but that also you did in such language as you might reasonably think would rather provoke not to listen to your proposal therein. And doubtless, whatever you pretend, you were glad of the occasion to be gone. I question not but you would have come freely enough to the other place (as we were all desired) had you looked for any advantage to your design of marring the visage of the Son of Man.

Moore wrote up an account of the debate from his home at Lynn in August 1655 and was still debating with the Quakers in 1658. Quakers were also embroiled in disputes with the Manifestarians of Thomas Moore and John Horne in southern Lincolnshire. George Whitehead had many arguments with them in 1659,[44] seeing them as natural converts to the cause as not Calvinist[45] but got involved in a 'pamphlet war' with them. John Whitehead was possibly involved as well since they seem to have worked together on *A Brief Discovery of the Dangerous Principles* (1659) which refuted Moore and Horne. That same year William Dewsberry, an itinerant preacher from the original Balby group, preached several times in Newark where meetings were attacked by a 'rude multitude' who assaulted the congregations. Many had their 'teeth beaten out and their faces bruised, women had their head clothes pulled off'.[46]

There is also known to have been a similar 'dispute' between Baptists and Quakers at Wrawby.

The Quakers took great care to record their own persecutions. One of the laws used against the Quakers was the requirement for Catholics to swear an oath denying the authority of the Pope. This could be used against the Quakers because they refused to swear oaths in general.[47] Mason, Craven and others were imprisoned for this. There was also the requirement, after the Restoration, to pay tithes.

In September 1654 Elizabeth Hooton was arrested for preaching at Beckingham, having been assaulted by a man at Barnby – presumably on the way home – and sent to Lincoln prison.[48] James Parnell of Retford became the first Quaker to die in prison in 1656, as described below. The Beckingham Quakers became noted refusers of tithes, for which they made periodic trips to the cells at the Castle. Between 1655 and 1660 at least 51 Quakers in Lincolnshire were imprisoned.[49] William Teff and his wife were stoned and driven out of Market Rasen after interrupting the service at Middle Rasen church and reproving the people of Market Rasen for bad language and other errors. Arnold Trueblood, a Quaker, died in the castle in 1658, and Thomas Bromby, James Wadeson and Edmund Woolsey also died.[50]

Thomas Bromby was a labouring man from Fillingham who was turned out of his house in 1657 on the actions of Ralph Hollingsworth, the priest of Fillingham. Bromby's gaoler declared that 'all in all her years at the prison she had never known a man use more spite than the priest did to this poor man'.[51] He died there in 1658. A number of the Quakers were released from prison when Charles II came to power in 1660, but Richard Frotheringham from South Hykeham lingered there for refusing to pay tithes until he died six years later.[52]

---

44   This meeting seems to have been at Lynn.
45   L Knoppers, *The Oxford Handbook of Literature and the English Revolution*, p.573
46   Joseph Besse, vol 1, p552
47   Davies, p.14
48   Manners, p.78
49   Davies, p.14. Besse, p.346
50   S M Brown, *Women, Gender and Radical Religion in Early Modern Europe*, Leiden, 2007, p.73
51   Davies, p.15, source not given
52   Davies, p.19

At the same time, Nottinghamshire Quakers also began to experience greater persecution. William Clayton of Elton spent over three years in Fleet prison in London from 1658, having been prosecuted by Rev Dove Williamson,[53] whilst two women from Mansfield Woodhouse were put in the stocks for using words 'displeasing' to a priest.[54]

Elizabeth Hooton (or Hooten)

Elizabeth Hooton (or Hooten) from Skegby in the Mansfield district first met Fox in 1647 and has often been described as his first convert; she came originally from Ollerton where she married a farmer and where a son was baptised in 1633. Hooten was, as was normal, married in the Church of England and her earliest children were christened of baptised there, but she later became a Baptist and may even have preached as one. Between 1633 and 1636 she moved with her husband to Skegby, west of Mansfield.[55]

At Skegby there seems to have been a group of Baptists who met in a converted building at the old hall but Hooton tired of them;[56] 'after some time finding them that they were not upright hearted to the Lord but did his work negligently' she left them and was thus interested in the message that George Fox brought in 1647, when she is seen to have become his first 'convert' although she was perhaps also influential on him – some recent historians have investigated the wider pre-existing influences in Fox's theology. She was clearly already a leader and in 1650 it was noted that 'from a true experience of the Lord's work in man, she felt herself moved publicly to speak the way of salvation to others'.[57] Her husband seems to have been reluctant to tread the same path, but seems to have also been converted later.[58] Her son wrote of Fox speaking at her group in 1648 where 'the mighty power of the Lord was manifest [and] startled [the members of] their former Separate meetings, and some came no more; but most that were convinced of the truth stood, of whom my mother was one and embraced it….'[59]

She opened her house at Skegby for Fox to hold meetings from about 1649, and incidents such as the healing of a demon-possessed woman attracted attention.[60] Those present were horrified by 'the stink that came out of her' as she writhed on the ground, but when she was healed, she sat down calmly and said 'Ten Thousand praise the Lord'. Fox later noted that 'she had many meetings at her house where the Lord by his power wrought many miracles to the astonishing of the world and the confirming people of the truth'.[61] She soon became a leading member of the Friends and their first woman leader, and was soon imprisoned in Derby as a result of 'reproving a minister' in 1651. Further spells of prison followed – York in 1652 following an offence in Rotherham, and Lincoln in 1654

53   Case described in pamphlet *The Ravenous Beast Discovered*, c. 1664
54   Joseph Besse, *A Collection of the Sufferings of the People called Quakers*, vol 1, 1753, p.552-3.
55   Elizabeth Manners, *Elizabeth Hooten, First Quaker Woman Preacher*, London, 1914, p.3
56   Manners, p.4
57   Fox, Journal, vol 1 p. 54
58   C L Leachman, *Elizabeth Hooten*, in *Oxford Dictionary of National Biography*, online edition, accessed 1 January 2014.
59   Davies, p.9, from Oliver Hooton's History…
60   P Mack, *Visionary Women: Ecstatic Prophecy in Seventeenth-Century England*, London, 1992, p.127-8
61   *George Fox's Book of Miracles*, p.60

(for interrupting services in the 'steeplehouse' at Beckingham, Lincs.) and 1655. She became a frequent writer of letters of complaint and also a contributor to pamphlets. Her husband died in 1657. It is not known at what time the Quaker burial ground at Skegby was first used or, for certain, that the house that became the Quaker meeting house was definitely Hooton's.[62]

In 1660 Hooten was back in Nottinghamshire where Charles Jackson, the puritan minister for Selston, violently assaulted her, allegedly without provocation, while she was walking along the road.

> On the 2d of the month called April (1660), Elizabeth Hooton, passing quietly on the Road, was met by one Jackson, Priest of Selston, who abused her, beat her with many Blows, knockt her down, and afterward put her into the Water.[63]

She made several journeys to New England and the West Indies. On the first trip in 1661 with Joan Brocksopp of Little Normanton she was immediately imprisoned in Boston by Governor Endicott; then she was abandoned in wolf-infested forests two days' travel out into the wilderness with just a few biscuits. She managed to return to Boston – via Rhode Island and Barbados! This time Endicott sent her to Virginia, from where she returned to England. Her son Samuel, who initially opposed his mother's venture, later crossed the Atlantic himself.

William and Mary Dyer

Hooton was persecuted in Massachusetts but survived – others did not. William Dyer was born at Kirkby Laythorpe in Lincolnshire in 1609 and became a member of John Cotton's Boston congregation. He went with his wife Mary, who was probably from London, to Massachusetts as part of the Winthrop fleet and there sided with Hutchinson and Wheelwright in 1638. Mary gave birth to a stillborn and deformed child, which Governor John Winthrop then had exhumed and declared it a monster sent as a judgement from God. Dyer moved with Coddington to Newport, Rhode Island, where greater tolerance was practiced, but after some time in England his wife returned as a Quaker and was arrested while passing through Boston – she narrowly escaped execution in 1659 but returned and was executed for her beliefs in 1660 under the authority of Governor Endecott. William survived to have an influential career at Rhode Island.

The executions of Mary Dyer and several others in 1659-60 for practicing their faith was a significant moment in American history, for it occurred more than four decades after the last such occasion in England and despite great tolerance being the practice in some colonies such as Rhode Island where magistrates generally tried to ignore them. Roger Williams, who firmly believed that Quakers were wrong and that their suffering was no sign of them being right, picked up his pen to fight them with words.

---

62 '…was believed by some..' is how Manners, p.16, describes this. In 1669 the house was used for the marriage of her daughter.

63 Besse's *Sufferings of the People called Quakers*

Relations between Rhode Island and the Boston authorities were also strained by the affair of William Coddington's books – an order for him from England was shipped via Boston, where Richard Bellingham impounded them and when Coddington wrote in protest Bellingham simply burnt his letter.

The executions did relations between Massachusetts and the Restoration Government no good, and the unlikely figure of Charles II ordered an end to the persecution of Quakers in New England; so it is interesting that Endecott did not practice a judicial execution on Hooton when she arrived the following year – he simply tried to kill her a more underhand way. John Endecott, on the other hand, assisted Edward Whalley and William Goffe in their escape from Royal retribution.

In 1662 Simon Bradstreet went with John Norton, Cotton's successor at Boston, to seek an agreement with the government of Charles II. The Quakers were waiting for them with two of their number who had lost ears in Massachusetts, and Fox accused Bradstreet of murdering Quakers, asking by what law of England they had been executed. In the Quaker version of events, Bradstreet made a lame excuse about a law for the execution of Jesuits and then got embroiled in the legality of persecuting Quakers for wearing hats in church. Fox, who normally showed scant interest in the laws of Man, had skilfully used Massachusetts' tricky legal position with the new Government to embarrass its leaders who could perhaps have been taken to court in England for the judicial murders of Quakers.

Later Quaker writers celebrated the demise of their New England persecutors. Besse wrote that 'Endecott was visited with a filthy and loathsome disease, so that he stunk alive, and died with rottenness'. Another persecutor from our region, Richard Bellingham of Brumby and associated with the Boston migrants, supported Endecott and died 'distracted' although not until 1672; in July 1656 he was in charge during Endecott's absence when the Quaker women arrived – he burnt their books and had them imprisoned. He had also written a pamphlet advocating the suppression of Quakers as more dangerous than 'the Popish Princes of Germany'. The Quakers wrote that 'the hand of the Lord cut him off, that other sons of Belial, of his persecuting spirit, might be warned not to put the evil day far from them'.[64]

Major-General Humphrey Atherton, was thrown from his horse and died instantly in 1661.[65] Joseph Besse wrote that 'being taken up and brought into the Courthouse, the place where he had been active in sentencing the innocent to death, his blood ran through the floor, exhibiting to the spectators a shocking instance of the Divine vengeance against a daring and hardened persecutor; that made a fearful example of that divine judgment, which, when forewarned of, he had openly despised, and treated with disdain'. John Norton, the minister of Boston, died suddenly of a stroke whilst preaching in April 1563, his last words being 'the hand' or 'judgments of God are upon me'.

---

64   George Bishop, *New England Judged*, 1703, p.319
65   Bishop (p.20) wrote that 'his eyes being started out of his head like saucers, his brain out of his nose, his tongue out of his mouth, and his blood out of his ears'.

In 1662 Hooton rented a farm in Leicestershire for her son, who was soon also arrested. Hooton showed no fear of authority. She criticised Cromwell to his face for employing corrupt judges and in London in 1662 she followed Charles II around St James's Park, haranguing him and causing a scandal by refusing to kneel before him; the following day she appeared in Whitehall dressed in sackcloth and ashes. However, she managed to obtain a licence from the King to settle in any of the American colonies, but still found the Boston authorities resistant. She was stripped and whipped through three towns, before again being abandoned in the wilderness with 'many bears, wolves and deep waters'. On another occasion she was left to walk through deep snow with a pregnant friend after her horse was seized by the King's Commissioners; she reported that she found her way by following the tracks of wolves. In March 1665 John Endecott, a governor of New England who had persecuted the Quakers, died; Hooton attended his funeral and, unsurprisingly, was arrested.[66]

Hooton returned to England for most of the rest of her life in about 1666, becoming a prominent author of letters and petitions. Elizabeth Hooton was recorded as one of the 'heads and teachers' at Harby, Lincolnshire, in 1669.[67] Her son Samuel took up the family tradition of going to New England and getting into trouble, for the first time in 1666. He married at Skegby in 1670 and returned to America, where the Hooton line has fascinated genealogists ever since; Oliver Hooton settled in Barbados and was still there in 1682, though thinking about Pennsylvania. In 1671 Elizabeth joined Fox and others in a further trip to the Barbados – her approach being evident from her letter to the islands' rulers which began 'To the rulers and magistrates of this island that ought to rule for God'. There she died in 1672.

By 1658 the Hootons had some issues with another new sect, the Muggletonians, whose views largely centred around the 'power' of two 'prophets' to discern those who would be saved and those who would be damned. Since they did not like damning anyone, they preferred to avoid discussion – unless the foe's destination was obvious. The Muggletonians thought the Quakers to be the greatest enemies of true religion. They were strong in Chesterfield hence Hooton came to the attention of Lodowicke Muggleton in the 1660s. He wrote that:

> It is supposed that you are the mother…to that Samuel Hooton of Nottingham, who was damned to eternity by me in 1662. It is no great marvel unto me that he proved such a desperate devil, seeing his mother was such an old she-serpent that brought forth him into the world….She hath shot forth her poisonous arrows at me in blasphemy, curses and words, thinking herself stronger than her brethren…. Therefore, I do pronounce Elizabeth Hooton, Quaker….cursed and damned, both in body and soul, from the presence of God, elect men and angels, to eternity.[68]

Samuel Hooton and William Smith, both Nottinghamshire Quakers, wrote to Muggleton in 1663 comparing him to Judas but even a discussion with the famous William Penn made no difference – he destined them all to damnation.

---

66   Manners, p.50
67   Manners, p.85
68   Quoted in Andrew Bradstock, *Radical religion in Cromwell's England*, London, 2011, p.151

James Parnell

Roger Williams may have thought that being persecuted did not mean you were necessarily right, but it was a young Nottinghamshire man who became the first 'martyr' of Quakerism. James Parnell was born in East Retford in 1636[69] and grew up in the town until, at the age of 15, he began searching for spiritual sustenance after finding little provided by the churches of his own town. The Parnells were a well-established family in Retford[70] and had been on the fringes of nonconformity in the recent past. He also probably attended the town's grammar school,[71] though in his own memoirs was sceptical of its impact:

> His wicked natural propensities were nourished by the education he received; so that, whilst at school, and also after leaving it, the same depravity of heart remained, and he grew in sin, and continued to follow the sinful vanities of the world.[72]

Despite his wayward lifestyle, Parnell had 'visitations of heavenly light' that led him to forsake his sinful but popular lifestyle and become some cause of amazement in the town so that he was sometimes mocked in the streets of Retford.

At Balby he found a group who 'waited together in silence to become instruments in the hand of the Lord' – an approach eventually central to the practice of the Society of Friends or 'Quakers' as they became known, although this congregation were not Quakers as such. When only 15 or 16, Parnell walked to Carlisle where George Fox, the leader of the Quakers, was in prison. Fox noted that Parnell was 'a little lad' but 'was convinced'.

In about 1654 Parnell left Retford for another local town – perhaps Newark – (although relatives seem to have moved to Epworth)[73] and then went to Cambridge where he was put in prison for criticising the clergy and the magistrates. Being young and small, he was referred to as 'the quaking boy'.[74] However, Parnell found that the power of God was in his speech and he could stop in their tracks those who came to condemn his message. Parnell became something of a travelling preacher of the message and found his way to Colchester, where, in 1655 he preached and discussed the new message at St Nicholas's Church. He was soon preaching to a crowd of a thousand from a window overlooking a yard. He also visited Chelmsford and started a Quaker congregation there by 1656.[75]

At some point around 1655-6 Parnell began publishing and we have the benefit of a 'review' of his work by Thomas Moore, the Manifestarian opponent:

> ....[His book] he calls *the Watcher, The Stone cut out of the Mountain without hands*. In that book speaking of that he calls corrupt reasoning or arguing, he saith, 'Before that was, I am'; with seeming allusion to that of our Saviour, 'Before Abraham was, I am'. What doth he less in this than equalize himself

---

69   His exact age has been debated. See Henry Callaway, *A Memoir of James Parnell*, London, 1846, p.1
70   At least one branch of the family was living in Moorgate in 1606.
71   The building was in Chapelgate and was demolished in about 1854.
72   Callaway, p.3
73   Richard Parnell of Epworth, a grocer, had his goods seized in 1659 as a Quaker and was noted by Lloyd (p.228) as having moved into the town quite recent to this.
74   Callaway, p.17
75   http://www.midessexquakers.org.uk/history-meeting-houses.php, accessed 5 August 2014

with God? which to that person only is no robbery who is the eternal and only begotten Son of God, it being the peculiar name and attribute of God, 'I am'; he is that which he is from everlasting to everlasting, and of himself, and he only is so that is the former of, and gives being to all things, and so the only begotten Son, by whom and for whom he made all things, is honoured with the same honour with the Father, the Father having given to him to have life in himself as the Father hath life in himself; yea he and the Father are one in nature, and being (though evidently distinct in manner of being) from everlasting to everlasting thou art God; not so James Parnell, he is not before all things, for by him they do not consist; but by him in whom it hath pleased the Father that all fullness should dwell, even the fullness of the Godhead bodily, that in all things he should have the pre-eminence (Col. 1:15-19 & 2:2,9; Heb. 1 total; John 5:20-23 & 1:1-14); in these things I say it appears that their bottom principles are one and also have secretly the same fruit, though gilded over with pretence of zeal, holiness, mortification, &c., in these, and I pray what stands that in, but in pretending themselves, and commanding others to abstain from meats created to be received, &c., in despising dominion, speaking evil of dignities, casting off all civil and natural respects where due, and like things?[76]

Parnell rarely shied away from a battle: when he heard that the clergy had organised a meeting in July 1655 at Coggeshall church to condemn those of his faith, he attended in person to make a contribution to discussion. After a lively debate, including an argument about taking his hat off, he left and was arrested outside for 'riotous entrance' into the parish church, obstructing the highway, and using menacing and threatening speeches.

During his trial at the Chelmsford Assizes the jury acquitted Parnell of the charges, but Justice Hills fined him £40 for contempt – a sum which he refused to pay.

He therefore had to stay in prison where the gaoler was known for his cruel, corrupt and vindictive ways. Conditions in Parnell's cell were terrible, and the efforts of local Quakers to help were barred. For a time, he lived in an enclosure within the walls, something like a baker's oven, twelve feet in the air and reached only by a ladder of about six feet so that he eventually fell and was injured. This, with the poor diet and constant damp, broke his health. Fox was able to visit Parnell and noted in his Journal that:

'Very cruel they were to him; the jailer's wife threatened to have his blood; and in that jail they destroyed him...'[77]

By the Spring of 1656 he had become weak and for ten days he could take no food. By the morning of 10 April, he had died. He was buried in an unmarked grave in the grounds of Colchester Castle. A plaque commemorating his life has been placed in the cell where he died.

Others were less convinced he was a martyr than had brought about his own death. Christopher Wade accused him of killing himself by 'inordinate fasting....to show himself to be a Prophet of the Lord'. Parnell had, in 1655, published *The Fruits of a Fast*,

76 Thomas Moore, *Postscript to The Answer to the foresaid Queries*, London, 1655
77 George Fox, *Journal*, volume 1, p.202

appointed by the Churches gathered against Christ and His Kingdom. Ralph Josselin, the vicar of a nearby parish, wrote in his diary on 11 April 1656:

> Heard this morning that James Parnel the father of the Quakers in these parts, having undertaken to fast 40 days and nights, was die. In the morning found dead, he was by Jury found guilty of his own death, and buried in the castle yard, the lord awaken those thereby, that give heed to the light of their own spirits, and will not put themselves under direction of word and spirit; thus god chooses the delusions of sinners, and wherein men deal proudly god is above them[,] I tremble at his folly, the lord recover poor worms out of the snare.

William Smith of Besthorpe, who had been a local constable and independent preacher, was converted to the Quakers in 1658 and soon became a prominent Quaker leader. He was imprisoned for non-payment of tithes in 1658 and 1662-5 following prosecution by William Pocklington of North Collingham.[1] Near neighbours, Edward Langford of North Collingham and Thomas Elsham of Girton were also imprisoned. He was a prolific author, engaging in a pamphlet war with Baptists Henoch Howet and Jonathan Johnson of Lincoln with titles such as *The Lying Spirit in the Mouth of the False Prophet*. Smith later wrote an attack on the persecutors under the title, *The Ravenous Beast Discovered and the Devourer Pursued;* this dealt with the Elston case of Rev Dove Williamson against William Claytor. In 1672-3 he battled it out against Ralph James at Willingham, again with the Baptists.

Smith's work has been described as 'an outstanding example of early Quaker writing…skilled in verse as well as prose'.[2] His amazing literary output seems to owe much to his time spent in gaol, often at Nottingham.

He suffered many of the typical abuses. As well as the tithes issue, he was arrested at Worcester in 1661 for refusing to take the oath of allegiance. George Fox's journal reported a visit to Lincoln at Christmas 1667 when Smith was lying sick. Fox reported that all his property had been seized for debt, including the bed he had been in.

He died in 1673 at Besthorpe, of fever, and was buried in his own garden. Presumably he is still there. Muggleton had an argument with William Penn over his death, caused by Penn having incorrectly thought Smith was already dead – only for him to die a few days later!

Overall the Quakers had perhaps benefited more than most from the relative toleration of the 1650s but, it would transpire, were to become once again the most persecuted sect in the 1660s.

---

1   Jennings
2   R C Allen and Rosemary Moore, *The Quakers, 1656–1723: The Evolution of an Alternative Community*, Pennsylvania, 2018

CHAPTER SEVENTEEN

The Triumph & Demise of the 'Godly'
1642-1660

It is certainly the case that Lincolnshire played a much greater role in the campaign to challenge Charles I than did Nottinghamshire, where the 'godly' were 'few in number and ineffective'.[1] However, during the two decades that followed Nottinghamshire produced significant figures like Ireton, Whalley and Colonel Hutchinson which redressed the balance of influence. Control of the Church had been a cause of the fighting, but the impact of the Civil War itself was to let radical religion off the leash – and an array of groups proliferated. Yet, by the end of the war, Lincolnshire's radical tradition had been largely exhausted.

Chronology:
1642: Charles raises standard in Nottingham
1643: Period of Royalist success ends at Winceby; Westminster Assembly begins
1645: Archbishop Laud executed for treason
1646: Ireton marries Cromwell's sister; Lucy Hutchinson influenced by Baptists
1648: Second Civil War breaks out
1649: Execution of Charles I; 'Rump' Parliament
1650: Blasphemy Act
1653: Cromwell's Protectorate begins
1655: Wheelwright joins Vane at Belleau
1658: Cromwell dies
1660: Restoration of Monarchy; Whalley flees to America

Early in 1642, Charles fled London and the court settled in York. This precipitated a struggle for control of the magazine at Hull in which Lincolnshire forces, including the core of puritan gentry, were soon prominent with the county generally siding with Parliament. Hull's governor was Sir John Hotham, whose son John married to Frances, daughter of Sir John Wray.[2] Lincolnshire's parliamentary committee for the militia also included the usual names such as Irby, Wray and Armyne whilst the Earl of Lindsey was appointed by the King as his lieutenant – he died at the battle of Edgehill.

In July Charles rode to Newark and then to Lincoln which showed some support for

---

1   P Seddon, *Major Edward Whalley*, in *TTS vol 103* (1999), p.137
2   Both Hothams were executed on 1 and 2 January 1645

River Ouse

■ Burton upon Stather

The Great North Road

🏠 Greetwell
🏠 Somerby by Bigby

GRIMSBY

DONCASTER ■

Ashby cum Fenby 🏠   ■ Tetney

🏠 South Kelsey

River Trent

🏠 Blyton

GAINSBOROUGH
Saltfleetby ■

■ Mattersey
✗ Gainsborough (1643)

LOUTH

Fenton 🏠
🏠 Knaith

WORKSOP ■
EAST RETFORD

Belleau 🏠

🏠 Welbeck

LINCOLN
🏠 Barlings

🏠 Thoresby

Winceby (1643) ✗
■ Partney

🏠 Rufford

MANSFIELD
🏠 Coleby

Sutton in Ashfield ■

River Witham

Kelham ■
NEWARK-ON-TRENT
Averham 🏠
✗ Newark (1643, 1644, 1645-6)
Southwell ■

Greasley ■
SLEAFORD

Nuthall 🏠
Gedling ■
🏠 Screveton
✗ Ancaster Heath (1643)

NOTTINGHAM ■
BOSTON 🏠

🏠 Holme Pierrepont
Wyberton ■

Attenborough 🏠
Kirton in Holland ■

River Trent
Owthorpe 🏠
Belvoir 🏠
GRANTHAM
■ Folkingham

■ Gotham

The Great North Road

■ West Leake
🏠 Osgodby

✗ Willoughby on the Wolds (1648)

🏠 Grimsthorpe
SPALDING
■ Gedney

🏠 Parliamentarian
🏠 Royalist
✗ Battle
■ Place
▦ Town

■ Crowland

STAMFORD ▦ ■ Uffington

0   10   20 miles

N

the Royal cause in the area. In Lincoln Charles Dallison of Greetwell, widely held to be a 'papist', was spokesman, and Charles knighted him.[3] In 1648 Dallison wrote a famous book, *The Royalist Defence*, whilst in exile in France; this argued for the balance of Parliament, judiciary and Monarchy as the 'supreme governor'.

Boston, though, remained fully committed to Parliament, whilst Stamford remained resolute for the King. Life for some radical puritans became uncomfortable, and Thomas Coleman the puritan parson at Blyton left Lincolnshire for St Peter's Cornhill in London (replacing an ejected minister by order of the Commons) where he became a vocal critic of bishops and cathedral staff, under the patronage of Sir John Wray and Sir Edward Ayscough. He preached to the House of Commons in 1645 but was also known for his Hebrew scholarship and 'Erastian' views on the disciplining of non-believers during the Westminster Assembly of Divines in 1643 which discussed the future of the Church of England. He published a number of works in the 1640s including the sermon delivered at St Margaret's, Westminster.

Charles arrived at Nottingham on 19 August 1642, having identified it as a key strategic location. Local supporters of Parliament, like the Hutchinsons, kept away in Leicestershire. Charles raised the royal standard at Nottingham on 22 August, one of his first acts being to arrest Captain Thomas Lister of Coleby Hall, who was married to Armyne's daughter and had caused an offence as an MP in the Long Parliament. However, Charles then marched west, allowing his opponents to reclaim Nottingham.

Nottinghamshire remained largely Royalist. Lucy Hutchinson, the diarist wife of John Hutchinson the son of Sir Thomas of Owthorpe, thought it 'so wholly for the king that the godly…were forc'd to forsake their habitations and seeke other shelters'. Sir John Digby, the high sheriff, was active in the early months in taking control of Newark but he was unable to prise Nottingham itself from John and George Hutchinson; John, though, found that the puritan soldiers were unconvinced that anyone could be a gentleman and still on the side of the godly.[4] The great landowners like William Cavendish, the Earl of Newcastle, Kingston (Robert Pierrepont) and Chesterfield stayed with the King as did a large proportion of the gentry – the three Earls had all been given their new titles by Charles in 1628. In January 1643 Lord Fairfax complained to the Commons that William Cavendish, the Earl of Newcastle, was raising an army of 'Papists for the most part'. Sir John Byron was another notable Royalist commander although he died in exile in France in 1656; his second wife went on to be a mistress of Charles II. The most significant Nottinghamshire gentry to side with Parliament were Sir Thomas Hutchinson and Sir Francis Thornhagh of Fenton, with his eponymous son; two of the Pierreponts, sons of the Earl of Kingston, also went with Parliament. Edward Ayscough of Nuthall sided with his Lincolnshire kin, Henry Ireton of Attenborough, of course, followed his puritan conscience, while Edward Whalley – destined to be one of the great figures – was not even in the area at the time. As a second son of Richard Whalley, Edward had left to try his fortune elsewhere, but being a cousin to Cromwell through his mother was to stand him in good stead. Lucy Hutchinson noted that support in the county was strongest amongst the 'middle sort' and this may be where decades of puritanism had taken root. However, in John Hutchinson, Whalley, Ireton and Francis Thornhagh the county produced four of

---

3   Hill, p.150
4   Cliffe (1988), p.52

the seminal figures of the era who saw themselves as fighting for God: Hutchinson 'found the Lord's protection and glorious presence not only in all he did but in all he suffer'd for him and from him,' his wife wrote.

Lincolnshire largely sided with Parliament from the outset. There was a series of skirmishes in Lincolnshire in autumn 1642 involving Ayscough and Irby, but in December the Royalists seized control of Newark and Gainsborough in January 1643. Grantham followed in March, then Stamford. Captain John Hotham played an equivocal role in secret correspondence with Royalists despite holding a general's command in the Parliamentary army;[5] in a few months he and his father were arrested and sent to London. They had aroused the suspicions of Oliver Cromwell and John Hutchinson at Nottingham. The younger Hotham fled to Lincoln but was captured as he then tried to get to Hull. Both Hothams were beheaded in 1645, but the younger Hotham at least had the chance to leave a legacy of sorts due to his spirited third wife Isabel:

> 'The night preceding the execution of the young officer, his wife Isabel, from whom he had been separated during his imprisonment, was allowed to visit him in the Tower. She quitted him only in the morning when he was led out to die. And in the dawning of that year, which to the one was to bring death and the other bereavement, the sorrowful couple bid each other a last fare well. Nine months later Isabel gave birth to a son, Henry, but who, the child of tears and grief, sank to an early grave.'[6]

J T Cliffe's analysis of puritan families at the outbreak of war makes this division clear.[7] He identifies ten such families in Lincolnshire and only two in Nottinghamshire – Hutchinson and the much less important Ireton family.

In 1642 Sir Henry Vane was a leading figure in setting up the Scottish alliance which led to the Solemn League and Covenant; but by 1646 he was less involved having been wearied by factionalism. However, he played a key role as a friend of both Roger Williams and the poet John Milton, who by 1644 had also become an advocate of freedom of religion.[8] Vane was condemned as a 'covetous earthworm' in one Civil War pamphlet but defended by a historian as 'an exalted mystic and one of the few politicians who did not rob the Commonwealth'.[9] Vane often showed great humanitarian concerns, protesting forcefully in 1655 against the sending of Royalist captives as slaves to the Caribbean.[10]

More extraordinarily, in March 1642 the vicar of Crowland himself led a Royalist raid on Spalding, where he captured and carried off a puritan minister. John Williamson of Saltfleetby All Saints was his equal, who left his parish in November 1642 to ride with the Cavaliers 'with his sword and pistols' leaving nobody to care for the parish so that they had to make their own arrangements. Laurence Palmer, the rector of Gedling, became a captain of horse for Parliament whilst Samuel Coates, who Col Hutchinson said was a

5 Hill, p.153
6 A W M Stirling, *The Merry Wives of Battersea and Gossip from Three Centuries*, London, 1955. Quote from Hullwebs.co.uk. Hotham's first wife, Frances Wray IV, had died in 1635.
7 Cliffe (1998). p.197
8 Barry (2012), p.288
9 Brailsford, quoting also from the pamphlet *Jonah's Cry*.
10 Brailsford, p.334

minister, was a captain of troop. The period of royal ascendancy forced Ayscough and Thomas Grantham, deputy lieutenants for Lincolnshire, to write to the Speaker of the House of Commons expressing their fears. It culminated in the battle of Ancaster Heath in April 1643, with Cavendish's cavalry routing those of Lord Francis Willoughby.[11] One effect was the disruption of normal Church life, a void which was to be filled by a proliferation of sects; when the puritan minister at Keelby fled, he was replaced by an absent royalist who hired a former kennel-boy, who was illiterate, to be the curate.[12]

This era was cut short when in late April 1643 Crowland was captured for Parliament by Oliver Cromwell who then had a skirmish at Belton before going on to Nottingham. Gainsborough was captured for Parliament in July but endured a difficult siege as Royalists regrouped and was retaken. Fighting on the side of Parliament was Lord Willoughby of Parham, whose house was at Knaith, whereas the Willoughby line at Grimsthorpe took the side of the King and included the Earl of Lindsey. Within days Royalists flooded Lincolnshire, plundering Sir William Armyne's house in June 1643, so that even Boston feared it would be taken. Armyne lost all his sheep, cattle and deer but 'patiently and cheerfully he bore it for the common good'.[13] Things were to get worse though, for Armyne later lost his younger son Theophilus at Pontefract in March 1645. Throughout this period John Hutchinson held Nottingham Castle for Parliament, surrounded by Royalist centres like Welbeck and Shelford. After the death of his father in August 1643, Royalists plundered his house at Owthorpe so that when he got it back in 1647 he thought it as cheap to build a new one as rebuild the old – he never received any compensation.[14] However, we should note that such suffering was at least an equal opportunity activity at this stage – Royalist Sir Robert Sutton at nearby Averham had his house burnt to the ground. At Christmas 1643 the position looked very bleak with Newcastle nearby in his own house at Welbeck, but Hutchinson was saved by the intervention of the Scots.

Not surprisingly, some clergy could not take the risks. Two of Armyne's men, John Weld of Pickworth and Robert Lawrence at Silk Willoughby, took off to the safety of Suffolk. Armyne appointed Michael Drake at Pickworth and Laurence Sarson to replace them. Weld, Laurence and Drake all eventually became Presbyterians whilst a former chaplain, Thomas Cawton, persuaded the English in Rotterdam to do the same.[15]

Although it is clear that the radical puritans joined Parliament, the Catholics did not rush to support Charles. Holmes found that less than a quarter of the Lincolnshire Catholic gentry fought for Charles whilst their leader, Sir John Thimbleby, did his best to avoid any involvement and found it better to leave the country.[16]

In autumn 1643 Parliament regained ground and the Royalists suffered a serious defeat at Winceby that October when Cromwell was again prominent. In December, the royalist strongholds of Gainsborough and Burton Stather were taken leaving Lincolnshire free of Royalists except in Axholme although they still held Newark and Belvoir. This was

11   Willoughby became gradually estranged from the Parliamentary cause and by 1648 had sided with the Royalists.
12   Holmes (1980), p.195
13   Seth Wood, from Armyne's funeral sermon.
14   Cliffe (1988), p.87
15   J T Cliffe, *Puritans in Conflict*, London, 1988, p.143
16   Holmes (1980), p.40

seen as vindication of the Lincolnshire puritans: 'Lincolnshire is at liberty. The Lord Willoughby, Sir John Wray, Sir Edward Ayscough, Sir Christopher Wray and Sir Anthony Irby, are now by orbicular providence, by an admirable revolution, reinstated, re-entered, relincolnshired again'.[17] However, Cromwell seems to have been unimpressed by some of the Wrays, whose military role declined thereafter.[18] Sons of Ayscough and Sir John Wray were taken prisoner.[19] Irby showed a radical streak that shocked many by suggesting that MPs who opposed the proposed Solemn League and Covenant with the Scots in December 1643 should be sent to prison and deprived of their estates.

A siege of Newark failed when Prince Rupert arrived with royal reinforcements in March 1644; within days he also took control of Lincoln and, briefly, Crowland. According to one account, the Lincoln puritan Edward Reyner narrowly escaped being shot by escaping through a window – the first of two escapes, or three if we include his escape from the High Commission in 1640;[20] his house, though, was plundered but he escaped to East Anglia. Once again Hutchinson felt in immediate danger in Nottingham, but Rupert passed down to Oxford.

This situation was reversed by Manchester,[21] who retook Lincoln for Parliament in May but could not take Newark or Belvoir; instead, he spent some time removing 'scandalous' ministers in Lincoln. In September and October Royalists had a brief recovery and Crowland changed hands again. Throughout that autumn and winter, the counties were plagued by raiding parties from Newark, plundering the countryside. But in November 1645 the Scottish army arrived outside Newark, finally capturing Belvoir and then Newark itself on 8 May 1646. The famous story of the siege of Newark is of Alderman Hercules Clay, trapped in Newark with his family; three nights in a row he dreamt that his house had caught fire, and he took this as a divine warning and moved out. Soon after the house was struck by a missile and burnt down, so in his 1694 will he left money for an annual sermon on 11 March to commemorate his family's deliverance. As a side effect of this campaign, some houses of the Royalist gentry were taken and destroyed.

King Charles's attempt to reach an agreement with the Scots or join his own forces in Newark failed with his arrival at what was then the *King's Head* in Southwell on 5 May 1646, after which he was taken – effectively in custody – to Kelham by the Scots. The Scots and the English then held a meeting in a field between Kelham and Farndon to discuss what to do with him.

The fighting gradually depleted some of the puritan families. Perhaps slightly redressing the balance, some returned from America to fight including Thomas Leverett who had left Boston in 1633 at the age of seventeen and came back in 1644. He spent around four years with Parliamentary forces, developed a relationship with Cromwell, and imbibed a great awareness of ideas of religious liberty.

---

17   *Mercurius Britannicus*, 28 December 1643.
18   Hill (1956), p.156
19   Cliffe (1988), p.92. Perhaps this was Theophilus Wray, who drowned at Winteringham on 21 Nov 1664.
20   Plumb, vol II, p.324
21   Manchester was a cousin of the Wrays. Lucy Montagu of that family had married Sir William Wray and was mother of Sir John and Edward Wray.

As Parliament took control, discussions continued about what sort of Church was wanted. The Westminster Assembly, or 'Assembly of Divines', convened in 1643 – it continued for ten years. As well as Thomas Coleman, formerly of Blyton, those attending included John Foxcroft of Gotham and even Robert Sanderson who might have had an interesting time chatting with Anthony Tuckney, a puritan theologian from Kirton-in-Holland who was Cotton's successor as vicar of Boston, except he never attended; Tuckney was chairman of a committee. Sir Henry Vane also attended as a 'commoner'. It was a time of gathering reaction – King Charles' *Book of Sports* was ordered to be burnt, and maypoles to be taken down. Foxcroft, like Coleman, seems have found a safer and perhaps more prosperous place in London[22] but still found time to lament his home county: 'Give me leave only to shed a few tears on the neck of the bleeding county of Nottingham, now as much beloved as that which gave me breath; having been the place of my ministry for the longer half of my life,' he wrote in the dedication to a published sermon in 1646.

When the Earl of Manchester took control of Lincolnshire, he began a process of ejecting clergy who did not meet his expectations. Between 1644 and 1645 around two dozen 'Royalist' clergy were ejected in Lincolnshire, perhaps another fifty later; in Nottinghamshire, the total in the Civil War was around 28, around 15% of the total.[23] Some of the victims were obvious for moral reasons, such as the 'lecherous' serial fornicator[24] John Leake at Frodingham, but the effect on parish spiritual life was destabilising. In 1646 Thomas Gibson of Horncastle was accused of Laudianism, Hugh Barcroft at Wyberton (who upset his Calvinist parishioners on his first Sunday and petitioned in favour of bishops) and Thomas Hurst, of Leadenham and Barrowby which were sequestrated in 1647. Gibson so detested the lecturers that he had locked the church and ridden off with the key in 1641.

Some livings like Morton were simply too poor to get a decent replacement.[25] At Uffington, Michael Hudson was off serving the King, so he was ejected – with evidence he only preached once a quarter anyway. In other cases, the ejected minister hung around and caused problems for his successor. In Nottinghamshire, the vicars of St Mary's Nottingham, West Leake, Cromwell, Ordsall, Laxton and Worksop were removed for their Royalists views. Hugh Bancroft at Welbourn in Lincolnshire was ejected by Manchester for being an Arminian. Thomas Holt at Stamford All Saints, a Laudian who had petitioned in favour of bishops, was another easy target, though he may have retained another living. John Chappell at Irnham was another. John Tireman clung onto Swayfield until 1658 (which he then reclaimed) although apparently losing another living at St Mary Woolnoth in London.[26]

Although there was certainly a cull of Laudians, several clergy lost their livings for moral reasons. In Royalists areas, there were clearances of the more puritan. In Parliamentary areas there was an expectation that clergy lived a moral life and performed their duties but William Underwood of Hareby had to borrow a Bible, lacking one of his own, and

---

22 Various sources differ on the nature of his stay in London – for Wood (1947) and others show him as a member of the Nottingham classis in the 1650s and then rector of Goathland in N Yorkshire after the Restoration.

23 Jennings (1999): p.157

24 Holmes (1980), p.55

25 Holmes (1980), p. 197

26 *Lincolnshire History and Archaeology*, 1984, p.92. There are too many in both counties to list them all.

drank heavily. The Rector of Ordsall, Marmaduke Moor, was ejected in 1652 for playing cards with his wife.[27] In contrast Edward Bigland, Rector of West Leake in south Nottinghamshire from 1621-46, lost his living, had his personal estate plundered, and then was bundled in the back of a cart for taking to Nottingham under arrest; he caught cold and died. However, according to other sources, he was in the Cavalier garrison at Ashby-de-la-Zouch and because of this was imprisoned at Nottingham, where he died in 1651. Paul Prestland, the rector of Market Deeping in Lincolnshire, lived for six months in a barn with his wife and five children.[28] In January 1643 Edward Laycock, vicar of Nottingham St Mary's, and Franck Withington of West Bridgford, were imprisoned for being Royalists[29] whilst Thomas Savage of Sutton Bonington was another plundered. Robert Morris of Trowell was also imprisoned by Hutchinson. More than a dozen Nottinghamshire clergy were removed by 1650 including John Hill of Nuthall for supplying arms to the Royalists and the unpopular George Groome at North Collingham for being a drunkard and a 'scoundrel'. John Featley of Langar was reported to have gone off to join the Royalists in Newark leaving a curate in charge – he was back in charge in 1663. One result was that there were too few clergy to go around and Mansfield had to complain to Cromwell in 1654 that it had none.

Ministers also made themselves unpopular for being too puritanical. In the late 1650s, several Lincolnshire parishes brought actions against their ministers for 'not administering the Lord's Supper to all their parishioners, according to the statute of Edward VI'.[30] At the assizes Justice Windham sided with the parishioners, condemning 'tyranny' and noting that parishioners could lawfully refuse their tithes.

The ejections also created space for the ambitious. Obadiah Howe, son of William Howe, vicar of Tattershall, secured the living of Stickney in this way in 1647 and showed his new conventionality by publishing a booklet against 'free grace' believers in 1648. By 1651 he had secured the living of Horncastle instead, where, in 1655 he wrote *The Pagan Preacher Silenced* against John Goodwin, a radical independent who had rejected predestination. Then he moved to the next vacancy – Gedney – staying only a few months before landing the plum – Boston. This coincided with the return of the Monarchy, which Howe embraced with enthusiasm including the use of the magistracy to enforce matters of belief; in 1663 he wrote in *God and the Magistrate* that 'when the magistrate commands, it is not man in the magistrate, but God in the magistrate that obligeth'. This was the total opposite to the words of Smyth, Helwys, Murton and Vane. Howe managed the journey from puritan to Presbyterian and back to Anglican under the Monarchy.

Henry Ireton

The principal figure from the region to emerge in the fighting was Henry Ireton (1611-1651) of Attenborough, whose family had been persistent nonconformists there for years. The family had originally been from Derbyshire, had lived for some

27   Cox, Hall, Morden, *Nottinghamshire – Somersetshire*, p.300
28   Fiona McCall, *Baal's Priests: Loyalist Clergy and the English Revolution,* Farnham, 2014, p.163
29   Wood (1947), p.193
30   Watts (1986), p.155

time at Norton Cuckney in Nottinghamshire and then settled at Attenborough from 1595 through the influence of Isabel Foljambe née Wray. He was brought up with 'an education in the strictest way of Godliness' according to Lucy Hutchinson, whose husband was his cousin. The Iretons at Attenborough were in constant legal battles over the impropriation of the rectory income and the maintenance of the church there. His father was often in trouble for nonconformity and children were baptised without the sign of the cross, possibly including Henry who was born in 1611. His mother had refused twice to be 'churched' after childbirth and in 1620 permitted a 'strange minister' to hold a service with the church doors locked.

As he grew, Henry maintained the same opposition to Church rules. He was presented for not kneeling in communion and not attending some services, and in 1636 refused the Laudian practice of leaving the pew for communion.

At the outbreak of war, he immediately joined the Parliamentary army and fought at Edgehill in 1642. Ireton attracted great attention for his role in the battle at Gainsborough in 1643 and became closely linked with Oliver Cromwell thereafter – indeed he married Cromwell's daughter Bridget in 1646. Cromwell sent him to govern the Isle of Ely where he put his 'advanced' religious views into practice – locals were shocked when Ireton's soldiers began preaching from their pulpits. All his career he combined a rigorous puritan faith with commanding soldiers – he was 'best prayer-maker and preacher in the army'.

He played a pivotal role in removing the Earl of Manchester from command of the Parliamentary army and turning it into the New Model Army. He is credited with being a significant influence on the New Model Army. After Gainsborough he was rapidly promoted, though narrowly escaped disaster and death at Naseby in 1645. From 1647 he was the dominant figure in the complex matters of Army politics dealing both with the treatment of the king and John Lilburne and the levellers. In matters of religion he favoured a 'godly commonwealth' and was at odds with the free for all that seemed to be developing by 1649. Late in 1648, for example, he opposed Baptist views and insisted that magistrates should be able 'to punish things which were sin, sin against god'.[31]

Initially cautious in politics, he came to believe in the execution of Charles I. By 1650 he was in command in the brutal campaign in Ireland, where he became ill and died. His behaviour there has attracted much critical comment after executions at Limerick and he could certainly be harsh, yet he also had a sense of justice; he was especially incensed by others who executed soldiers who had surrendered whilst he disliked the Royalist officers at Colchester for needlessly wasting life.

Ireton's death did not entirely save him from a vengeful King Charles II, for he was numbered amongst the regicides. His body was dug up, hanged and beheaded, then the head put on a spike so it could look towards the scene of Charles I's execution.

---

31   Wright (2006), p.210

The capture of Newark brought a temporary cessation of hostilities in the region until Royalists began a new campaign based from Pontefract. Sir Edward Rossiter, another of the Lincolnshire Parliamentary gentry, from Somerby by Bigby and at times MP for Grimsby or Lincolnshire, was sent to subdue this rising leading to a decisive fight at Willoughby-on-the-Wolds in July 1648. Meanwhile, Colonel Francis Thornhagh, Hutchinson's school friend, went north with Cromwell but was killed in skirmishes after the Battle of Preston.

The execution of Charles I took place in January 1649. Those who signed the warrant included four from Nottinghamshire, of which three were leading puritans: Edward Whalley, John Hutchinson, Henry Ireton and Gilbert Millington of Felley, the latter a lawyer of questionable lifestyle. In contrast, prominent Lincolnshire families had no involvement although Sir Peregrine Pelham of Hull came from a family with Lincolnshire connections.

Sir Francis Thornhagh (1617-48) was another of the Nottinghamshire puritan gentry who rose to fame on the Parliamentary side. He was born of the Thornhaghs of Fenton and educated at Lincoln and Cambridge – Lincoln seems to have been the place of choice at that time.

Having gained experience in the Netherlands, Thornhagh joined the Parliamentary army to fight in his father's regiment. He was wounded at Gainsborough in 1643 and Newark in 1644 and distinguished himself at Rowton Heath in Cheshire. Lucy Hutchinson was certainly an admirer of his godly qualities: 'a man of most upright faithfull heart to God and God's people….a man of greater valour or more noble daring fought not for them'.

After East Retford was freed from Royalist control, he was elected one of its MP – as his father and grandfather had been.

In the renewed fighting of 1648, he was again active in Wales but then went North against the Scots. Following the Battle of Preston, he was killed near Chorley. Mrs Hutchinson reported his last words as being, 'I now rejoice to die, since God hath let me see the overthrow of this perfidious enemy; I could not lose my life in a better cause, and I have the favour from God to see my blood avenged'. Perhaps it was the tawny hair and flowing 'yellow' beard he was said to possess that also impressed her.

Elsewhere we discuss how the turbulence of the period brought out many strange groups and even prophecies. Thornhagh's father was mentioned as 'Sir Francis Thorny' in the published story of the Carlton-in-Lindrick prophetess of 1641. In this a servant of Sir Francis's was married and two young women came to visit his sister at the Thornhagh's house nearby – they had lands at Osberton. Soon after both died – except the young lady at the centre of the story came back to life and declared she had been told she would live another week in order to convey the Lord's message. She described a heavenly scene and then being sent back to deliver a warning. This was essentially about a judgement on England for its sin of pride, and after delivering the messages she stayed alive precisely one week and died – just as she had predicted.[32]

---

32 *The Wonderful Works of God as Declared by a Strange Prophecie of a Maid*, 1641 – printed in London but otherwise anonymous.

An Expansion of Sects

At the same time, the presence of the Parliamentary Army and the breakdown of religious order allowed many new approaches to flourish. Certainly, the Army itself was often a melting pot of religious ideas. Private meetings, of conventicles, became common if not commonplace.

The classic example of how war led to change in ideas is that of the conversion of Hutchinson and his wife to a Baptist viewpoint, even though it may be incorrect to say they 'became Baptists'.[33] Colonel Hutchinson and his wife in Nottingham were able to track the developments, the radicalism of his soldiers in Nottingham not always being liked by the people of the town and its dominant Presbyterian clergy. By 1644 soldiers were holding their own conventicles and some were Baptists, for the town confiscated some Baptist tracts. A visiting minister, Garland, attracted some of the townspeople and led to further tension which Hutchinson resolved by transferring to Cromwell the apparent leader, Captain Hooper. Lucy Hutchinson though noted that her husband was 'reviled' by the town's Presbyterians and he could not accept their 'mallitious zeale and imposing spirit'. She thought him impartial, but this was not a position that made friends.

Hutchinson's wife, Lucy, became pregnant in 1646 and after reading some notes left by Baptist soldiers she had doubts about child baptism. Her husband summoned some local ministers to discuss the scriptural basis for child baptism and became Lucy convinced that her child should not be christened as Foxcroft of Gotham had assured her it was a sin to do something not directed in the Word itself.[34] Nottingham became something of a meeting place of the new groups such as when George Fox of the Quakers debated with Rice (or Rhys) Jones in 1650 while he was in the House of Correction; Jones had been a soldier and a Baptist but by the time he met Fox he was prepared to dismiss the very existence of Jesus. Fox we have discussed in detail already.

Popular in Boston was Thomas Moore,[35] a weaver from Lynn who led a 'Manifestarian' sect who claimed to have seen both Christ and the Devil. They were waiting for the 'sons of God' to again manifest. He refused to celebrate festivals at times of war and meet with anyone in any type of building.[36] In 1644 Moore was arrested by Colonel Edward King (himself of Ashby-de-la-Launde) at Boston and put into gaol for refusing to mark public fast days but his group, who allowed women to preach, multiplied in Holland. Manifestarians opposed Calvinists in that they taught that anyone *might* be saved, and Moore's sect persisted for at least a decade. Baptists also gained in strength – at least until the Quakers began to abstract their members – and more extreme views multiplied such as those of Lawrence Clarkson of the Ranters, who preached that 'the elect' were incapable of sinning.[37] In some cases, this ended in disillusionment but it also profoundly shook the religious status quo:

> '.....the attack on the legitimacy of tithes and oaths, and on the need for an educated, professional ministry; the allowing of women preachers; the emphasis

---

33 M C Bingham, *Orthodox Radicals*, Oxford, 2019, p.147

34 Jennings (1999), p.136

35 There is another Thomas Moor (born c 1648), who was for as time a barber in Cambridge, but was not active in England until at least 1680. He had some similar, though not identical views.

36 Benjamin Brook, *Lives of the Puritans*, vol 3, p.31

37 Holmes (1980), p.198

on the individual conscience as the touchstone of religious truth…'[38]

Moore may have been described as 'obscure' but he was important enough for Calvinist theologian John Owen to publish, in 1648, *Salus electorum, sanguis Jesu* (1648) and *The Death of Death in the Death of Christ*, (1647) to refute Moore's Arminian claim that Christ died for all men.[39] This was prompted by Moore's *The Universality of God's free-grace*, which he had published two years earlier. Moore had an important debate with the Quakers at Glentworth in 1655, discussed in the Quaker chapter above.

Moore's son Thomas engaged in several public debates, including in 1659 at Gedney with John Whitehead and at Lynn with several others and with Quakers. By this stage Moore senior had perhaps died, his son taking the leadership with John Horne who was also from Lynn. Moore's career reflects the general open debate on religious matters by this time, but it was not always 'open house' on debate. In 1648 the Blasphemy Ordinance was passed and in 1650 the Blasphemy Act – there were constraints to the new freedom. The law on compulsory attendance was abolished but preachers still required a licence.

Fighting Parsons

It seems strange to us, in the 21st century, that members of the clergy might actually lead military groups, yet in summer 1648 conflict returned when Thomas Styles,[40] the combative Royalist vicar of Crowland and Michael Hudson, a former rector of Uffington and King's Cliffe, gathered a small royalist force in Stamford with the intent to retake Crowland.

Hudson had profited well from his links with the King, and had been his scoutmaster-general, having enjoyed the fruits of several wealthy benefices including Greetham and Uffington in Lincolnshire, to which he had been presented by the Duke of Buckingham, and from which he was ejected in 1642. He became a chaplain with King Charles I in Oxford and went to meet the Scots commissioners who were staying in the archbishop's palace at Southwell in 1642. He went to Newark with Charles in 1646. Hudson had twice previously escaped from the Tower, once with a bucket of apples on his head as a 'disguise'[41] and had written about divine principles of government. Charles travelled in disguise as a tutor with Hudson, and Hudson was with Charles when he surrendered to the Scots at Southwell on 5 May 1646. The Scots took Charles to Kelham.

Styles and Hudson staged their attack in 1648. It ended in defeat and Styles 'escaped being cut to pieces when Dr Hudson was so cruelly murdered at Woodford House' in Northamptonshire in June 1648. The Royalists had been chased to Woodford, at Helpston, by Colonel Thomas Waite and Hudson had been trapped on the roof.

---

38 Holmes (1980), p.199
39 D Wallace, *Puritans and Predestination: Grace in English Protestant Theology*, New York, 2004, p.110
40 Referred to as 'William' in *A History of Crowland Abbey*, 1839
41 F Peck, *Desiderata Curiosa*, London, 1779, p.378

> His head cut open, he had been thrown or jumped off, then he clung to a pipe or stone until his fingers were cut away and he fell into the moat; a man from Stamford killed him and cut out his tongue, carrying it about as a trophy.[42]

The Second Civil War of 1648 broke out in 1648 which ultimately sealed the fate of King Charles, who was lodged in prison on the Isle of Wight. At first Royalists did well. There was a Royalist assault on Axholme in June 1648, and then a crossing of the Trent to Lincoln where they plundered the city and abused the puritan lecturer, Edward Reyner, who had returned after two years. He was seized by soldiers in the cathedral library.[43] Only the timely arrival of a former pupil of his at Market Rasen, the Royalist Captain Gibbon, saved his life. This force was later chased south and defeated at Willoughby-on-the-Wolds in Nottinghamshire.

However, there was also increasing tension within the Parliamentary faction, which had split over the issue of church government between Presbyterians and Independents. By 1644 distinct factions were emerging: leaders of the Independents included Lord Saye and Sele, Vane and the influential Oliver Cromwell. This had caused a significant strain in 1645 when Presbyterians supported a 'Directory of Worship' with a new liturgy to be supported by draconian legal enforcement – the Helwys and Murton view of religious liberty was as yet far from common. Some of those associated with our region became notable Independents including John Hutchinson, Sir Henry Vane, Ireton and William Pierrepont but Sir Anthony Irby opposed them. This came to a head during the Newport discussions with Charles in late 1648 when it seemed a compromise might be reached between the King and the Presbyterians. Some elements within the Army were so angered by Parliament's majority support for the talks with Charles on 5 December that on 6 December 1648 they 'purged' Parliament leaving what is called the 'Rump' Parliament comprising those of more Independent views. In Lincolnshire the two Wrays, Armyne and Grantham survived as did men like Hutchinson, Millington and Francis Pierrepont in Nottinghamshire, the latter being MP for East Retford in 1640. Vane and Ireton were influential in bringing Charles back to a safer place on the mainland – both Independents. Hutchinson, however, was deeply unhappy about the Army's action although it perhaps prevented a new religious dictatorship emerging. Sir Anthony Irby, an MP on the Presbyterian wing, was arrested and briefly kept at an inn on the Strand although he was re-elected for Boston in 1656; in 1659 a Royalist agent still thought him Presbyterian and only apparently tolerant of Royalists out of hatred for the current regime.

---

42 Peck gives various versions of this event, including one in which Hudson jumped off the roof to hide (used by Scott in *Woodstock*), and several versions as to what happened to his body – burial at Denton seeming most likely. It is Stukeley's account that talks of him being thrown off, clinging to the spout until his hands were cut off, then being caught again in the moat when his tongue was cut out.

43 Reyner was appointed as a lecturer in the dioceses of Winchester, Chichester and Lincoln in 1621.

Robert Sanderson (1587-1663)

The conflict had a severe impact on the career of Robert Sanderson, a controversial figure who has been tarnished by his reputation as Cotton's 'enemy'.

Sanderson was far from a Laudian as his theology was largely that of a conventional Calvinist, though he thought the puritans stirred unnecessary trouble ion the issue of ceremonies when the real enemy should be Rome. Though from Sheffield, his career was centred on Lincoln from the time he became a chaplain to Bishop Montaigne and married the daughter of a Lincolnshire clergyman. He was briefly rector of Wyberton, close to Cotton, then Heckington and Boothby Pagnell where he stayed from 1619 until 1660. For a time, he was a preacher to Charles I: 'I carry my ears to hear other Preachers', said the king, 'but I carry my Conscience to hear Mr. Sanderson, and to act accordingly'. He was briefly involved in London affairs but never took his place at the Westminster Assembly.

He had been appointed professor of divinity at Oxford in 1642, only to be removed from the post in 1648 having had little chance of doing anything. He was forced to amend the Prayer Book he used at Boothby Pagnell, sequestered from that living in 1644 and in 1648 taken as a hostage to Lincoln, where he was probably imprisoned in the Bishop's Palace,[44] for the puritan minister Robert Clark, who was being held at Newark. He survived all this to become Bishop of Lincoln 1660-3.

Charles was put on trial for treason before a much-reduced House of Commons. When Charles I was executed in 1649, one of those who signed the death warrant was Colonel John Hutchinson of Owthorpe, Notts, who had been governor of Nottingham castle from 1643. Hutchinson was later arrested for apparent involvement in the 'Yorkshire Plot' – in 1663 – and died in prison in 1664. Hutchinson's father, Sir Thomas, had been 'obsessed with theology' but was probably a 'conforming puritan' rather than a great radical. John himself grew up with a puritan love of activity – 'he never was at any time idle and hated to see anyone else soe'. Perhaps he had read Richard Bernard's words of 1629, when he advised that heads of households should 'keep all from idlenesse, the nurse or rather mother of all wickednesse'.[45] The execution of Charles produced a new list – that of the regicides, people who had signed their support. As well as Hutchinson, this list (including some who did not actually sign) included Edward Whalley, Henry Ireton, Gilbert Millington and Francis Hacker of East Bridgford and Colston Bassett– all Nottinghamshire men. Charles II, for reasons of his own, later added Sir Henry Vane to the list even though he was not a participant. Sir William Armyne was appointed a judge but took little part. Thomas Lister, of Coleby Hall in Lincolnshire, was nominated as a judge but mainly avoided the trial.

44   Plumb (PhD), p.118
45   Cliffe (1984), p.105

Edward Whalley

One of the great figures to emerge was Edward Whalley (c.1599-1674/5), who was the son of Richard Whalley of Kirketon Hall, Screveton, the former High Sheriff of Nottinghamshire.

The Whalley family had had some evangelical connections from the time of the dissolution; Edward had a Hercy great grandmother and his father had presented Richard Bernard at Worksop in 1601. His mother was the sister of Oliver Cromwell. His sister, Jane, was the woman that Roger Williams had proposed marriage to whilst in Essex and when he had been rejected – she had, instead, married William Hooke and emigrated with him to America in 1640; she returned to England two years before her husband, in 1654. After the Restoration, Hooke lived a somewhat furtive existence in London. Ironically Williams had then married the daughter of a man who owed his first substantial living to her father's patronage.

In 1614 he went, perhaps inevitably, to Emmanuel College.

After a somewhat unsuccessful career in farming, the Civil War provided Whalley with an opportunity and his efforts for Parliament at Gainsborough in 1643 won Cromwell's attention. After 1643 he fought alongside his cousin in most conflicts. He was trusted with a key command in the New Model Army in 1645. His soldiers were famously radical in their religious thinking, indeed too radical for Whalley's friend Richard Baxter who was briefly their chaplain. Although Charles I praised him for his courtesy when in Whalley's custody, he was the fourth signatory on the king's death warrant. He sat as MP for Nottinghamshire in 1654 and 1656, then was appointed by Cromwell as the administrative Major-General covering the East Midlands including Lincolnshire and Nottinghamshire in 1655. With his rise in influence he was able to buy the manor of Sibthorpe in his home county.

As Major-General, he took to his task enthusiastically, chasing out ungodly ministers, closing down illegal alehouses and reducing the level of vagrancy. He was also an opponent of enclosure as he understood its effects and acted to prevent cheating at markets. Despite his own views on religion, he was more tolerant than many and advocated the return of the Jews to England.

Not obviously radical in religion himself, he did take part in the prosecution of Quakers such as James Nayler and ejected some Royalist clergy who had survived in his region – Keyworth and Edwinstowe for example. Although a 'godly' man he was not always censorious, allowing horse racing to take place at Lincoln in 1656 but ejecting 'scandalous' ministers.

In 1660 he fled to America to escape likely execution as a regicide and landed in Boston. King Charles's attitude to him becoming more evident, Whalley and Goffe escaped to New Haven, where he clearly used contacts from his sister's time in America: he hid with Rev John Davenport, who had been the minister when William Hooke (Jane Whalley's husband) had been teacher in the 1640s and early 1650s. He eventually went into hiding under a false name deep into Massachusetts, dying in about 1674. Stories are still told about the cave in which he supposedly sheltered. His last known words, reported by his companion and son-in-law William Goffe, were 'I desire nothing but to acquaint myselfe with Je: Chr: & that fullnesse that is in him for those that Beleeve and have interest in him'.

Sir Henry Vane: A Man of Integrity?

Vane has already played a major part in our story through his short but turbulent time in Massachusetts. Back in England, Sir Henry Vane was a very significant Parliamentary leader in the years 1643-6 and returned again to front line politics in 1649, helping the survival of the Commonwealth, and playing a leading role until 1653. His position of influence in Lincolnshire is due to his marriage in 1640 to Lady Frances Wray, the daughter of Sir Christopher, which was certainly a marriage based on shared faith and progressive spiritual views. In works like the *Healing Question* he explored ideas about the legitimacy of revolution. His skills included managing the supplies for Cromwell's campaigns in Scotland and Ireland. However, his staunch support for religious freedom, even for the 'Ranters', alienated him from Cromwell. He became more settled in Lincolnshire after about 1650-1, buying the Belleau estate for his wife the 'virtuous' Frances, by whom he had 15 children.[46] He also became friendly with Richard Cust, the county's MP. For a few years he saw himself as 'retired', holding household prayers every evening and reading scripture at home – preferring this to public worship. He even wrote a book called *The Retired Man's Meditation*.

Despite his significant political duties in the military, Vane was presumably at home at Belleau for at least some of the time when Roger Williams, the great American cleric, stayed during his visit to England in 1651-4; during this he published *Experiments of Spiritual Life and Health and their Preservation* which he dedicated to 'the truly honourable the Lady Vane'. On one of these occasions Williams journeyed up from London with the pregnant Lady Vane while her husband was involved in Navy business, staying ten weeks; on 1 April 1653, he wrote a letter to his friends at Providence from Belleau. On 21 May, Lady Vane gave birth to a boy, Christopher – at least three of their many children were born there.

Vane and Williams had a close relationship, cemented by his help in getting Rhode Island a charter in 1644 and then confirming it a few years later – that was in 1653, when Williams visited Belleau. He wrote to Providence to say that 'Under God, the sheet anchor of our ship is Sir Henry, who will do as the ye of God leads him'.[47] Both men shared a

46 Holmes (1980), p.204 says 1651.
47 Letter of Roger Williams, 1 April. 1654, in J D Knowles, *Memoir of Roger Williams*, RI, 1834.

commitment to religious liberty with friends like the poet John Milton and Vane disliked the blasphemy legislation. In 1651 he wrote the highly regarded *Zeal Examined, or, A Discourse for Liberty of Conscience*. *Zeal Examined* and *Healing Question* (1656) both argued for toleration – in the first case of Catholics or other idolaters and in the second as a major reason why the Civil War had been fought, a hopeful interpretation with which most historians disagree. Vane himself was on a radical journey, coming to detest clergy in most forms and this contributed to the reports of him holding his own ceremonies at Belleau. In the end he broke with Cromwell, in 1653, and retired to Belleau although he spent more time at his Durham estates after 1656. At home he practiced true family religion, holding his own services and happy to preach to his own household – a daughter kept some records of this. Vane was, indeed, a theologian amongst his many other capabilities. A product of this reflective period was *The Retired Man's Meditations* of 1655, a work of theology which was variously seen as brilliant or impenetrable and which also discussed the nature of godly government, magistracy and many other issues. David Hume later described it as 'absolutely unintelligible' and 'cloudily formed'.

But he followed this with the *Healing Question*, a more political work in which he pondered the future of the Protectorate. He clearly indicated that Parliament should be sovereign over the Army and not the reverse. Vane was defeated in the elections and his book labelled 'seditious'; Vane was imprisoned in Carisbrooke Castle, seeing his erstwhile friend Cromwell developing the absolutist tendencies of Charles I. His influence was yet such a threat that Richard Baxter tried to use the worst of all insults – he was a 'masked Papist'. The Protectorate's collapse gave him a brief Indian Summer of influence in 1659, but it was not to last.

In Lincolnshire, Vane arranged the rebuilding of the church at Belleau after 1656 when he also decided to demolish the decrepit churches at Aby and Swaby to use the materials – though there are some apocryphal claims he rebuilt the manor house from the remains. To help manage his estates, he brought John Browne from Massachusetts in 1655-6 who lived at Belleau for four years.[48] This Browne was reputedly a relative of Robert Browne, the separatist, and returned to Providence at the time of the Restoration where he was a noted tolerationist and was kindly towards Quakers.

Of great interest is that John Wheelwright, who came from east Lindsey and had known Vane in America during the crisis over Anne Hutchinson in 1637, applied for permission in 1655 to be preacher at Belleau at the time when Vane was living there. Of course, he would also have been known in the district from his time at Bilsby. Wheelwright's application was supported by London merchants with New England connections, and by Richard Hutchinson – one of Anne's relatives. Whether Williams, Wheelwright and Vane were ever at Belleau together is unknown – but it would have made a fascinating meeting! At the end of the 1650s Wheelwright referred to himself as 'late of Belleau in the County of Lincolnshire' and is also listed in the Calendar of State Papers as minister at Belleau 1659-60.

---

48   G Clapp, *Ancestors and Descendants of Harvey Towner and Caroline (Waterman) Cole of Williamstown, MA, 1810-1881*, 2002, p.86. He was most likely the 'New England magistrate' that George Fox met at Raby Castle with Lady Vane in 1657. Browne returned to New England in about 1660 and died a wealthy man at Rehoboth. There has been much dispute about his origins and family connections.

Even some of his fellow puritans were critical of Vane's spiritual direction in the latter years, including Martin Finch(er) of Tetney, who was himself ejected in 1662.[49] Finch published *Animadversions upon Sir Henry Vane's Book* to comment on his deviations. Vane's reputation has grown with the years, partly because he was so strongly endorsed by Milton. 'Vane, young in years, but in sage counsel old,' Milton wrote in the early days, concluding that 'Therefore on thy firm hand Religion leans/In peace, and reckons thee her eldest son'. Perhaps less successful was the defence of Vane mounted by Henry Stubbe (1631-1676), an intellectual prodigy of the time who Vane had supported through school and university, who published *A Vindication* in his defence in 1659. But Vane also had many enemies, gathered from his work in the Civil War era including on the Committee for Compounding and Sequestration.

Henry Stubbe or Stubbes was born at Partney in 1631 where his father was Rector though there is some evidence his parents were not married at the time of his conception. Ejected from the living, probably for being 'anabaptistically inclined', the family moved to Ireland but the mother fled back to England during the revolt of 1641 taking Henry with her. At school in Westminster, his impressed schoolmaster pointed him out to Vane, who fed and clothed him and arranged a scholarship to Oxford where he became a keeper at the Bodleian Library – until ejected at the Restoration having used his library time for several publications. He turned to medicine, though abandoning a post in Jamaica, and disputes with members of the Royal Society. His notorious temper was blamed on being 'carrot topped'. His religious views were less clear – one of his fellow doctors commenting that he was 'a person of no fixed principles, and whether he believed those things which every good Christian doth, is not for me to resolve'. He drowned in a river near Bath in 1676.

His father Henry (1605/6-1678) also returned to England and resumed a career in the mainstream church around Bristol and Wells. He left at the Restoration and found another job, from which he was ejected in 1662. After this he took up independent preaching in Wiltshire and London, becoming a licensed Presbyterian preacher in London in 1672-5, until a sympathetic bishop gave him another living at Horsley in Gloucestershire. His status is reflected in the two funeral sermons that were delivered by the very eminent Richard Baxter and Thomas Watson.

From 1649 to 1653 England was governed by the 'Rump' Parliament from which many Lincolnshire members were excluded. This was followed by the brief 'Parliament of Saints' then the Protectorate under Cromwell. To start with there was a degree of tolerance and a Lincolnshire JP was dismissed after arresting some Baptists at Gedney[50] with even Quakers enjoying some freedom to preach. But in 1651 Williams, Vane and John Milton the poet had to join in protests against new proposals to prosecute 'heretics,' eventually dropped in 1653. In 1654 the government set up committees in each county to purge any remaining 'scandalous ministers' but in Lincolnshire at least it had limited impact this

---

49 Finch moved to Norwich, where the Old Meeting House was built for him. From 1672 he also briefly kept a meeting in his own house at Grimsby.

50 Holmes (1980), p.213

time. In 1650 a survey in Nottinghamshire had found four ministers too old and frail, and at Collingham George Greene was a 'drunkard and swearer'. Fifteen livings had no minister at all, including Mansfield, but in other places men like Henry Ireton and Edward Whalley appointed their chosen man. From 1649 the Baptists certainly prospered, although they had a tendency to become involved in wrangling with the Quakers after 1653.

During an era of seemingly perpetual arguments between Protestant groups, the Catholics were not forgotten. In the Lincoln diocese, John Hudd SJ died in prison in 1649. In April 1655 a proclamation required that an Oath of Abjuration against Papal authority should be sworn by Roman Catholics.

In 1651 Henry Ireton died in Ireland and was brought back to England for a funeral in London at which John Owen preached. He was, according to a contemporary, Heath, 'absolutely the best prayer maker, and preacher, in the Army'.[51] In 1661 he was dug up again as a regicide on the orders of Charles II and 'executed'; his memorials were destroyed.

Cromwell's Protectorate began in 1653 and showed notable tolerance at first, for example to Baptists in the incident at Gedney when many were arrested. Even Quakers enjoyed a degree of freedom, though the law was still used against them when they disrupted church services. Nonetheless, in 1654 each county was told to appoint a committee on 'scandalous ministers'.

Church Organisation

Under the Church of England, churches were governed by a diocesan structure of archdeacons and bishops. In the 1640s this structure was dismantled, leaving a debate about what should replace it. One option was Presbyterianism, whereby each minister belonged to a local group sometimes called a 'classis' and to a national assembly. This is what was developed in Nottingham and at Folkingham. A 'classis' could ordain new ministers in the place of a bishop.

An alternative was the congregational model which had been taken to New England, whereby each congregation made its own decisions and determined its policy independent of any others. A system of checks and balances is meant to restrain the undue authority of minister over people, or people over minister. These were sometimes considered as 'independents', especially if more openly separatist from the national structure. Vane and Ireton supported this approach, but Presbyterianism was stronger in other areas, including London.

Nottingham became a radical centre, with activity from Baptists and Quakers amongst others, but it is best known for its Presbyterianism which Lucy Hutchinson so reviled. St Mary's was in the hands of John Whitlock and William Reynolds from 1651, who more or less ran it as a Presbyterian centre. In Nottingham, by 1656, sixteen of the ministers

---

51   William Orme, *The Life of the Rev. John Owen, D.D., abridged from Orme's Life of Owen*, p.64

organised a Presbyterian 'classis' (later expanding to 23)[52] which held a monthly assembly and the Corporation provided funding for its chosen men, John Whitlock and John Barrett; two-thirds of these were ejected at the Restoration. In choosing a schoolmaster, they consulted Anthony Tuckney, the Boston man, then at Cambridge, who was Whitlock's father-in-law.[53] As late as May 1660 they were able to hold Presbyterian ordinations at St Mary's which ordained Callis of Lambley, William Frith of Fledborough, William Parker of Lenton and William Aspinwall of Mattersey – 'a plain, practical, edifying preacher of an unblameable life'.[54] Meetings seem to have finished in June 1660.[55]

No other Presbyterian 'classis' was as important. There was for a time one at Folkingham but this did not have the benefit of a large urban community supporting it. Its members included Michael Drake, an Armyne nominee at Pickworth who was ejected in 1662, James Morton of Horbling and George Becke of Allington.

A few miles away at Selston, Charles Jackson ran a covenanted congregation within a parish which he had become minister of in 1654 – having previously been active there in a less clear capacity. He recorded in the registers that 'the church of Christ, ye officers, members thereof that continue breaking of bread and walking in ye apostles doctrine associated and retained into church fellowship within ye prescints of Selston which are the persons hereafter written…' and went on to list 29 others. This is the same man who assaulted Elizabeth Hooton, the Quaker; sources vary about whether he retained his living at the Restoration with one suggestion that he was licensed as a preacher at 'Halsam' (Notts) in 1672.

The 'Independents' favoured local control of congregations and rejected wider church hierarchies or presbyteries. One of the national leaders of this group in the 1650s was John Owen, who had been military chaplain for Edward Whalley. The greater freedoms of that era allowed such independent congregations to flourish from 1650 and supporters of this included Henry Ireton, Edward Whalley at Screveton, Hutchinson at Owthorpe and Gervase Pygott of Thrumpton. It is possible that such a congregation existed at Sutton-in-Ashfield from 1651, and in Nottingham from 1655 under Major Thomas Palmer, although he left for Ireland after the Restoration in about 1663.[56] Certainly, Palmer described himself as 'Pastor of a church of Christ in Nottingham' in 1659 but he also had a church just inside Derbyshire for a time, and he had links to a radical Fifth Monarchist group at Skegby. The Nottingham church was most likely the origins of the Castle Gate congregation and was scattered in the persecution after the Restoration, several joining John James at Sutton-in-Ashfield, although it returned to Nottingham in the late 1600s. It was quite separate from the continuing Presbyterian group whose church was later established at High Pavement.

The existence of such freedoms made England an alternative to those who wished to leave New England. The wheel had turned significantly and people like Baptists and Quakers were less severely persecuted in England than Massachusetts – for a time;

---

52 These included Boyer of Rempstone, who was later a Baptist, and Fisher of Blyth.
53 Jennings (1999), p.149
54 Of these, only Callis appears to have conformed and he stayed at Lambley until his death in 1712.
55 Wood (1947), p.195
56 Jennings (1999), p.152

several Quakers were executed in Massachusetts in 1659-60 whereas the last person to be executed for their beliefs in England was in 1612. Wheelwright we have mentioned as one who returned, but also of interest is Edward Bendall who was a merchant in New England, but nonetheless, came back to became Rector of Cotgrave in Notts – for which he had support from Edward Winslow (an original *Mayflower* passenger) and Edward Whalley, then the presiding major-general for the region.[57] His puritan credentials were clear from the names of his children including Freegrace, Hoptfor and More Mercy. John Whiting, the son of Samuel, returned to Lincolnshire and was rector first at Butterwick and then at Leverton as a 'conformist'. He and his wife were both buried on the same day.

William Pierrepont (1607/8-1678/9)

Pierrepont's father, whose seat was at Thoresby, was a Royalist but William had attended Emmanuel College and this was the route he followed in life. Through family connections, his early political career was representing Shropshire seats and during the Long Parliament he gained the reputation of being 'Wise William'. He was a strong opponent of Ship Money in 1640 and then played a leading role in preparing Parliament for war. In the fruitless negotiations with Charles at Oxford in 1643 he again showed wisdom and skill.

Pierrepont then emerged as one of the Nottinghamshire puritans who opposed Presbyterianism along with Ireton by 1644; Lucy Hutchinson recognised him as a leading Independent. By 1647 he was aligned with Cromwell in an influential group including also Ireton and Sir Henry Vane. His role in the Newport discussions with Charles might have caused a problem, for he was seen as so opposed to Presbyterianism that he might consider some moderate version of bishops, but nonetheless, he survived Pride's Purge. Although he dropped out of front-line politics for a while, he was an influential adviser to Oliver Cromwell and his son Richard, but ultimately unable to establish a stable regime.

George Becke had been a chaplain to the Earl of Lincoln but during the war became a chaplain to the Earl of Manchester. He was present at the Battle of Winceby, which many commentators took to be the reason for Bishop Sanderson's later hatred of him. He was appointed to the living of Rippingale after the incumbent, Cranwell, was sequestrated, and from 1655-6 the living of Allington; this was convenient for him to also deliver the Tuesday lecture in Grantham. Calamy reported that 'his preaching was much applauded and his life unblameable'.[58] He was of course ejected in 1662 and died of Plague in London in 1666.[59] Becke replaced as lecturer John Angell who had been nonconformist teacher and lecturer in Leicester until 1650, after which the Mercers' Company appointed him to Grantham.

Elections in 1656 produced defeat for those who are a familiar part of this story – Vane, two of the Wrays and their associate Richard Cust all lost. They were perhaps seen as

---

57   Susan Hardman Moore, *Pilgrims – New World Settlers and the Way Home*, New Haven, 2007, p.120
58   Calamy, volume 2, p.606
59   *Transactions of the Unitarian Historical Society*, 1919, p.13

too radical.[60] This perhaps marks the start of the decline of the radical generation in Lincolnshire, soon to be followed by Nottinghamshire. Sir Christopher Wray had died in 1646, but Sir William Armyne, Grantham and Ayscough all died in the early to mid-1650s. Armyne's funeral cost a reported £1000 (over £100,000 today), but his annual income was £4000.[61] His son died in 1657, lamented by the preacher as a sinner who had repented at the last. Whilst Irby survived until 1682 in Lincolnshire, the Nottinghamshire trio of Hutchinson, Whalley and Ireton were all off the scene from 1660. The gentry impetus behind the ongoing puritan revolution was at an end – for the next hundred years, the vanguard of radical religion lay with more humble people.

The final generation was perhaps William Wray who was elected several times for Grimsby until 1660; he was described by John Evelyn as 'a good drinking gentleman' and his being made a knight and a baronet in June 1660 underlines his drift to the Royalist side. His son Christopher, seduced into marriage by a Scottish 'adventuress' in Paris, was even less made of the rock that had formed the basis for this influential family.

Lemuel or Samule Tuke

The early life of Lemuel, or Samuel, Tuke is obscure but he is mentioned at a separatist church in Colchester in 1620 and then with Henry Jacob's separatist congregation in Southwark, though he left within a year to become a preacher at 'Dry'. Perhaps he was the 'Mr Tuke' who was a lecturer at St Antholin's in Budge Row, London. We next hear of Lemuel Tuke when he was ordained in 1623 and then appointed as vicar of Greasley in 1628. A later critical account alleged that he was a weaver with no university education and 'had intruded into a cure of souls in Nottinghamshire, for which ever since the Parliament began he has been a non-resident'. He must have been there sometimes as he was cited for Prayer Book issues repeatedly from 1633 and suspended in 1638 and 1639. One offence was administering communion to 'strangers' while they were sitting – two puritan offences at once! The same account alleges that his parishioners accused him of 'battery, drunkenness and 'whoredom'. We do not know how long he was at Greasley after that, but by 1642 he was down in Essex and preaching at Bocking whilst also delivering lectures at Rayne; he was again cited for being 'derogatory' about the Prayer Book. He was indicted before Essex quarter sessions when his origins as a weaver were mentioned and that he had left Greasley after complaints about his conduct.[62]

Then the Civil War broke out and Tuke was in the right place. He preached against the King – he 'laboured to poison his people with sedition and rebellion, affirming openly that in some cases it was lawful not only to resist but (which I tremble to relate) to *kill the King*'.[63]

---

60 Holmes (1980), p.215
61 Cliffe (1988), p.188
62 J Walter, Confessional Politics in Pre-Civil War Essex: Prayer Books, Profanations, and Petitions, in *The Historical Journal,* 44(3), 2001, p677-701. Retrieved from http://www.jstor.org/stable/3133579
63 Bruno Ryves, *Mercurius Rusticus*, London, 1642, p.20. This is a strongly pro-Royalist booklet.

Tuke secured the living at Rayne as the previous vicar, Edward Simmons, had been ejected in 1642 for his Royalist views somehow having ousted Thomas Atkins who was intended for the living. Again, at this time Tuke was mentioned as having been a 'weaver'.[64] The next time he is mentioned is at Steeple in Essex, one of the livings where the patron had been the Warwicks. Tuke moved North; perhaps he was the Lemuel Tuke 'chosen minister of Typpon (Tipton) by ye inhabitants'[65] in August 1648 then listed as curate until 1651-2 when he was ejected; more certainly he was at Sutton-in-Ashfield by 1658,[66] where he seemingly ran the parish and also a 'gathered congregation' at the tail end of a long puritan career.[67] Inevitably he was ejected in 1662 when said to have been 'old and blind', cited for going to conventicles in 1663 and dying in 1670.

John Spittlehouse

Many interesting individuals flourished during this period. Spittlehouse (c1612-c1657) was from Gainsborough and may have been taught by Hanserd Knollys at the town's school. He had an extensive military career from 1643 to 1651 when he seems to have been dismissed, probably for writing critical pamphlets.

He was living as a Baptist in London in the early 1650s, and was an enthusiastic supporter of the practice of 'laying on of hands'; Baptist influence may explain his views on religious tolerance – he denied that magistrates had any right to meddle in religious affairs and wanted even the Qu'ran to circulate unhindered (placing him in the tradition of Murton etc). He was an ardent believer in the imminent return of Christ, known as 'Fifth Monarchists', and was arrested for his opposition to drainage in Axholme. He joined a radical church at Lothbury Square in London in about 1652. This church perhaps influenced Spittlehouse's Sabbatarianism, for by 1657 he was calling for the Sabbath to be moved to Saturday. He was in custody for a time in London from December 1653 but released in April 1654. With John More (a fellow member of the Lothbury church), he published *A Vindication of the Continued Succession of the Primitive Church* in 1652 which is generally seen as the first attempt by a Baptist to prove themselves the 'original' church and all others since (Catholic, Church of England and Presbyterian) a deception of the Antichrist, arguing that the absence of records did not necessarily disprove the continuing existence of Baptists:

> 'The not-appearance of a visible body or Society of Saints to public view of Antichrist, etc. does no more prove, that the true Church had no visible estate in itself, then the Sun ceases to be a Sun, during the absence of the light thereof; neither is it more to be imagined, that the true Church, during its hidden, or wilderness condition, did desist from practicing according to

64 Philanglus, *The Protestants Remonstrance Against Pope and Presbyter*, London, 1684, p.3
65 *Records of the Deanery of Wednesbury*, p.62. It is tempting to grasp at this straw as the name is so unusual; this Tuke was married at Tipton in 1616 and still there in 1625.
66 *Transactions of the Unitarian History Society*, vol 9, p.256
67 Jennings

the Apostle's Rules, and precepts, (so far as the well-being of such small societies did require) then it is to imagine, that there was not two or three saints left living upon the face of the earth, which I suppose you will not affirm.'

This debate about Baptist continuation remains a topic of strong debate in the United States.

He was active in producing pamphlets at the time of the 'Rump' Parliament, arguing against the Church having political control but gradually changing to accept Cromwell. For a time indeed, he ardently supported Cromwell as God's lieutenant on earth. Later he was arrested several times during the 1650s as he criticised the Army, Cromwell and almost everyone else...

Millenarianism

The disruption of war prompted a wave of more extreme climactic religious thinking, including **millenarianism**. By the early 1640s millenarian beliefs were common in the region's gentry with Sir John Wray owning millenarian manuscripts whilst Sir Henry Vane wrote that 'the time of the End....in which Christ is to judge the World in Righteousness...is at the very doors, and ready to open itself upon us'. Richard Bernard also embraced these views.[68] Such beliefs were also labelled 'Fifth Monarchy'.

In 1651, Sir John Wray arranged the publication of the millenarian writings of Robert Parker, *The Mystery of the Vialls Opened*, who had died in exile in 1614.

Another Fifth Monarchy man was Christopher Feake, an Emmanuel College graduate who was vicar of Elsham (Lincs) from 1637 to 1646. By 1650 he was in London and had joined a Baptist church, becoming absorbed by the prophecies of Daniel and in Revelation, and effectively launching the Fifth Monarchists in 1651. He was fiercely critical of Cromwell, calling him a 'perjured villain', leading to his arrest in 1654. He spent a brief time in prison with Vane in the Isle of Wight. By 1659 he was effectively the leader of the movement, though some also thought Sir Henry Vane to be involved in its leadership. William Aspinwall, a noted advocate of this after his return to England, had associated with Wheelwright and Anne Hutchinson in New England. Another millenarian, Rev John Stoughton of London, was linked to the Earl of Warwick.

Yet others succeeded in riding the tide of events still to emerge wealthy if not always as influential. Sir William Ellis was one of these – born in Lincoln of a Grantham family, his political career began as MP for Boston. As an apparent Presbyterian, he came under suspicion in 1648 but emerged to manage the Cromwell era with confidence; he built an

---

68   Cliffe (1984), p.230-1

influential legal career, which sustained him on a high income even after Charles II took the throne – he even managed to be re-elected for Boston in 1679.

Catholicism After 1633

Catholicism in Lincolnshire was led by the Residence of St Dominic at Lincoln founded by Richard Blount in about 1633, renamed the College of St Hugh from about 1675, which suffered a setback when its library was stolen or destroyed in 1644. Several of the fathers in residence were men with local connections including Richard Ashby or Thimbleby, Francis Berry and Robert Neale. By 1678 the College included seven priests, though over the next century it declined to only three.

A key Catholic from the region was Guy Holland, born in Gainsborough in 1585. In about 1606 he became a Catholic and went to the English College in Valladolid by 1608. From 1613 he was back in England as a missioner, becoming a Jesuit. From 1631 to 1642 he was in London, largely escaping persecution, although he was arrested in 1627 when the Jesuit College was discovered in Clerkenwell. He was the author of a noted defence of the belief that the soul survives the death of the body, *The Grand Prerogative of Humane Nature*.

The Thorold family maintained their links with Catholicism. Clifton Thorold entered the English College at Douai in 1638 and took the alias of Father Francis Benson. Anthony Thorold, son of Sir Robert, left for Flanders in 1646 and joined the English College in Rome in 1651 – declaring that he had always been a Catholic though his father not. His career was cut short by illness and he died in Flanders. Eugenia Thorold of Hough near Grantham became a nun at Ghent in 1639 and eventually Abbess of Pontoise in 1661, dying in 1667; Mary Thorold became a nun in 1642, Elizabeth in 1648, Christina in 1657 at Boulogne and Catherina in 1671.

Another family of interest are the Kents, alias Neale. Robert Kent the elder entered the Jesuit order in 1631 and returned to Lincolnshire, where he visited Catholics often at night and dressed as a labourer. He became father in residence at the College of St Hugh. Another Robert, probably a nephew, was born in Lincoln in 1643 with a Protestant father but he explained 'I was converted from heresy about four years ago by means of my good mother' – about 1658. Also a Jesuit, he returned to England in 1668.

There were also several Catholics in the Tyrwhitt family, including John (1600-71) who took the surname of Spenser. He became a Catholic at Cambridge, then a Jesuit in 1626. He was at the residence of St Dominic in Lincolnshire from about 1637, then returned to Europe until a lengthier stay in Worcestershire from 1659.

Another key Catholic family since the time of King Edward were the Thimblebys of Irnham where Robert Thimbleby was 'always a harbourer of priests'. By this stage Irnham was certainly the main Catholic centre in Lincolnshire as Catholics 'coagulated into groups' around gentry households.[69] In the early 1600s, three Thimbleby brothers went to the English College at St Omer or to Rome whilst a sister became an Augustinian nun at Louvain. Richard became a Jesuit in 1632 and was for a time attached to the residence of St Dominic in Lincolnshire, and was placed with the Earl of Lincoln, then returned to Europe.

Hough, Little Pinton, Blankney, Canwick, Nocton and Scopwick had similar pockets. These families reinforced their traditions by marrying Catholics from further afield, much as puritan families had done 100 years before.

The 1640s was an especially dangerous era for the Catholic clergy and many were liable to be arrested, with prison often proving fatally damaging to health. For example, John Grosse died shortly after release from Lincoln gaol in 1645, John Forster died in the prison in 1648 and John Hudd also died just after release in 1649. It was also dangerous for the Catholic gentry, who Holmes sees as choosing to maintain a low profile – barely a quarter of the Lincolnshire Catholic gentry turned out for Charles I whilst Sir John Thimbleby chose a safer life abroad.

Sir Edward Golding of Colston Bassett maintained Catholic sympathies until, late in life and having had a family, he retired to be a Capuchin friar in Rouen, dying in the 1660s. His son also followed the same route.

The Declaration of Indulgence in 1672 revealed eight centres of Catholicism in Nottinghamshire with about 320 people.[70] By 1676 there were reported to be 176 Catholics in Kesteven, of whom a third lived around the Thimbleby family at Irnham. There were other 'pockets' associated with Catholic gentry at Blankney and some neighbouring villages towards Lincoln. These figures at least give us an idea of the relative strength of Catholicism during the Civil War era and suggest that precious little had been won by the huge investment in fugitive priests.

Conclusion

Oliver Cromwell died in 1658 and attempts to continue his regime using his son as its leader were doomed to failure despite the efforts of Vane and others. With Cromwell disappeared some shadowy figures of interest, including one of his chaplains Conyers Rutters who was from Luddington, a graduate of the school at Kirton-in-Lindsey and of Magdalene College; he had been made Rector of St Mary Magdalene in London 1658 but was quickly ejected in 1660.

Vane managed to get elected in 1659 and argued for a government with foundations 'as firm and deep as in the Word of God'. From May to October that year he was influential in the restored republic, showing tolerance to imprisoned Quakers. He was made chair of a

---

69   Holmes (1980), p.39
70   Jennings in *TTS*, 1995

Parliamentary committee to review the imprisonment of prisoners of conscience.[71] But by January 1660 he was out of favour again and returned to Belleau. An old guidebook refers to the local belief that 'eccentric' Vane 'amused himself here on Sundays in assembling and preaching to his country neighbours'.

Puritan dreams of a godly England had come close to fruition but had ultimately been lost – now there was only the prospect of the return of an ungodly king. Lucy Hutchinson lamented the failures for even without the advent of Charles II 'true religion was now almost lost, even among the religious party, and Hipocrisie became an epidemicall disease'.

Charles II returned to England in May 1660 and set about restoring the Church of England to its full power. In a future volume, we shall see how he systematically ejected from the Church those who refused to follow his own brand of religion. He also, controversially, insisted on executing Vane, whilst Whalley fled to New England. The era of puritanism seemed finished. The main evangelical families of the counties had exhausted themselves or lost their passion – no longer were names like Wray, Ireton, Ayscough, Whalley or Armyne to form the vanguard of religious radicalism.

We end the story, for the time being, in 1660. With the Restoration of the monarchy and an established, governing Church of England, the stage seemed set for a new era of frustration.

Although the settlement of America is most often discussed as the greatest legacy of puritanism in our region, the establishment of the Baptists matters just as much whilst these same Baptists gave us a yet greater gift by developing the idea of tolerance. The execution of the Quakers in New England in 1659-60 was quite a shocking event, shocking especially as nothing like it had been seen in England for decades. Although true liberty was as yet two centuries or more away, the persecutions of the restored monarchy were mainly modest in comparison.

Migration to America continued, but Britain was eventually to turn to 'new' continents and a focus on evangelical mission would transfer how British Christianity saw its place in the World. This would see people from our region travelling to Africa, India and Pacific islands to take the Gospel to new peoples. To come there was also the evangelical revival, the birth in 1703 of one of the most transforming preachers of all time.

More than a century of being at the cutting edge of religious change had, for our two counties, come to an end, although the Baptists had established a foothold and the Quakers a sparky presence which was soon to lose its fire; it was to be another century before a new man arose from Lincolnshire to become, arguably, England's greatest ever preacher – John Wesley; and a century more before a Nottingham man of humbler origins, William Booth, was to create a worldwide Christian movement with a very distinctive social force. Radical Christianity was not dead, but sleeping.

---

71   Watts (1986), p.213

Index

Browne, John (of Belleau) 379

Browne, Robert 143, 155, 172, 173, 205, 276, 379

Brownists 160, 172, 173, 191, 205, 220, 227, 228, 232, 262, 283, 286

Brownlow, Nathaniel 333

Brown, Richard 283

Broxtowe 281

Broxtowe Hall 211, 212

Brumby 67, 317, 357

Brumhedde, Thomas 119, 212

Bucer, Martin 81, 113, 116, 124, 125, 157

Buckden 40, 43, 49, 50, 82, 116, 124, 180, 259, 296, 298, 331

Buckingham, John (Bishop) 61, 65, 66

Buddle, George 182, 265, 269

Bullinger, Heinrich 117

Bullingham, Nicholas (Bishop) 118, 121, 133, 136, 137, 139, 140, 163, 166

Bullington 59, 60, 124

Bulwell 185, 186

Bunyan, John 235

Burgh le Marsh 61

Burghley 152. *See* Cecil, Sir William (Lord Burghley)

Burgh, Lord Thomas 94

Burnett, Henry 72

Burnham (Axholme) 14

Burton, Brian 203

Burton, Ezekias 261

Burton, Ezekiel 193, 204

Burton on Trent 55

Burton-upon-Stather 367

Burton-upon-Trent 186

Burton, West 191, 204, 207, 215, 216, 334

Bury St Edmunds 140, 173, 214

Busher, Leonard 277

Butterwick 209, 261, 346, 383

Butterwick, West 208, 210, 248, 255, 283, 284

Butts, Sir William 92, 110

Buxton 166, 179

Byrd, William 154

Byron, Sir John 91, 92, 365

Bytham, Castle 30, 53, 285

Bywater, Ursula 246

C

Cadney 91, 119

Caistor 7, 9, 25, 30, 38, 94, 95, 96, 233

Calceby 202

Caldwell, Richard 265

Calke Abbey 187

Calvert, George, Lord Baltimore 241

Calvinism 157, 169, 245, 248, 250, 261, 291, 293, 302, 318, 354, 373

Calvin, John 169, 183

Cambridge 134, 359

Cambridge, Christ's College 135, 174, 205, 209, 210, 215, 227, 243, 247, 260, 303, 306, 431

Cambridge, Corpus Christi College 215, 269

Cambridge, Emmanuel College 159, 164, 195, 255, 270, 300, 301, 304, 312, 313-316, 335, 338, 352, 377, 383, 386

Cambridge, Jesus College 80, 81, 120, 164

Cambridge, King's College 52, 139, 207

Cambridge, Magdalene College 123, 138, 140, 147, 158, 164, 190, 224, 317, 334, 388

Cambridge, Queens' College 183

Cambridge, St John's College 101, 145, 147, 157, 203, 242

Cambridge, Trinity College 134, 135

Camock, William 305

Campion, Edmund 163, 177, 178

Cantley 227

Canwick 388

Cape Cod 254

Car Colston 134

Careby 295

Carey, John (Lord Hunsdon) 247

Carleton, George 166

Carlile, Christopher 262

Carlisle 146, 224, 227, 269, 306, 350, 359

Carlton-in-Lindrick 25, 135, 183, 228, 231, 372

Carlton-le-Moorland 52, 137

Carlton, Little 304

Carlton, near Lincoln 237

Carlton, South 241

Carte, William 262

Carthusians 85, 86, 90

Cartwright, Francis 181

Cartwright, Thomas 136, 142, 144, 157, 160, 169, 172

Carver, John 7, 12, 87, 216, 253, 254

Casterton, Great 339

Casterton, Little 173

Catesby, Robert 239

Catholicism 3, 33, 62, 75, 99, 101, 103, 113, 118-120, 131, 132, 136, 144, 148, 151, 153, 154, 157, 177-179, 186-190, 197, 218, 237-242, 268, 296, 387, 388

Catley 59

Catterton, Richard 144, 145

Oxford, Lincoln College 66, 297

Y

Z